IRENAEUS AND PAUL

PAULINE AND PATRISTIC SCHOLARS IN DEBATE

SERIES EDITORS

Todd D. Still
George W. Truett Theological Seminary, Baylor University
and
David E. Wilhite
George W. Truett Theological Seminary, Baylor University

PREVIOUS BOOKS IN THIS SERIES:

The Apostolic Fathers and Paul
and
Tertullian and Paul

IRENAEUS AND PAUL

edited by
Todd D. Still
and
David E. Wilhite

LONDON • NEW YORK • OXFORD • NEW DELHI • SYDNEY

T&T CLARK
Bloomsbury Publishing Plc
50 Bedford Square, London, WC1B 3DP, UK
1385 Broadway, New York, NY 10018, USA
29 Earlsfort Terrace, Dublin 2, Ireland

BLOOMSBURY, T&T CLARK and the T&T Clark logo are trademarks of
Bloomsbury Publishing Plc

First published in Great Britain 2020
This paperback edition published in 2021

Copyright © Todd D. Still, David E. Wilhite and contributors, 2020

Todd D. Still and David E. Wilhite have asserted their right under the Copyright, Designs
and Patents Act, 1988, to be identified as Editors of this work.

Cover design: Charlotte James
Cover image © Saint Paul, and a Subsidiary Study of his Head. Giuseppe Porta,
Il Salviati (1520-After 1570) © Christie's Images Ltd / SuperStock

All rights reserved. No part of this publication may be reproduced or
transmitted in any form or by any means, electronic or mechanical,
including photocopying, recording, or any information storage or retrieval
system, without prior permission in writing from the publishers.

Bloomsbury Publishing Plc does not have any control over, or responsibility for, any
third-party websites referred to or in this book. All internet addresses given in this
book were correct at the time of going to press. The author and publisher regret any
inconvenience caused if addresses have changed or sites have ceased to exist, but can
accept no responsibility for any such changes.

A catalogue record for this book is available from the British Library.

A catalog record for this book is available from the Library of Congress.

ISBN: HB: 978-0-5676-7287-2
PB: 978-0-5677-0232-6
ePDF: 978-0-5676-7288-9
ePUB: 978-0-5676-9330-3

Series: Pauline and Patristic Scholars in Debate

Typeset by Newgen KnowledgeWorks Pvt. Ltd., Chennai, India

To find out more about our authors and books visit www.bloomsbury.com
and sign up for our newsletters.

CONTENTS

List of Contributors	viii
Chapter 1 IRENAEUS AND PAUL: AN INTRODUCTION David E. Wilhite	1
Chapter 2 IRENAEUS AND HIS OPPONENTS ON CREATOR, CREATION, AND THE APOSTLE Michael A. Williams	15
Response PAUL, IRENAEUS, AND THE CREATION IN DIALOGUE WITH MICHAEL A. WILLIAMS Jason Maston	55
Chapter 3 THE USE OF PAUL IN IRENAEUS'S CHRISTOLOGY Stephen O. Presley	65
Response MESSIAH CHRISTOLOGY IN PAUL AND IRENAEUS Joshua W. Jipp	81
Chapter 4 THE PERSONAL/SUBSTANTIAL SPIRIT OF PROPHECY: IRENAEUS'S USE OF PAUL AGAINST THE HERESIES David E. Wilhite	89
Response IRENAEUS'S USE OF PAUL ON THE SPIRIT: A RESPONSE TO DAVID E. WILHITE Craig S. Keener	113

Chapter 5
ON SIN: IRENAEUS'S APPROPRIATION OF PAUL
Thomas J. Holsinger-Friesen   123

Response
ON SIN IN IRENAEUS'S APPROPRIATION OF PAUL: A RESPONSE TO
THOMAS J. HOLSINGER-FRIESEN
Jutta Leonhardt-Balzer   139

Chapter 6
THE COVENANT OF PROMISE: ABRAHAM IN IRENAEUS
Ben C. Blackwell   147

Response
IRENAEUS, ABRAHAM, COVENANTS, AND THE ONE THING
NEEDFUL: THE SECOND ADAM
Mark W. Elliott   169

Chapter 7
TEACHING THE RULE OF FAITH IN LOVE: IRENAEUS ON
1 CORINTHIANS 8:1
Scott D. Moringiello   177

Response
BEING KNOWN BY GOD: A RESPONSE TO SCOTT D. MORINGIELLO
Carla Swafford Works   195

Chapter 8
IRENAEUS AND PAUL: SEXUALITY, VIRGINITY, AND WOMEN
Helen Rhee   203

Response
IRENAEUS'S RECEPTION OF PAULINE TEACHING ON SEXUALITY,
VIRGINITY, AND WOMEN: A RESPONSE TO HELEN RHEE
Judith Gundry   219

Chapter 9
PAUL AND THE JERUSALEM CHURCH IN IRENAEUS'S *AGAINST
HERESIES*
Benjamin White   225

Response
IRENAEUS, JERUSALEM, AND REMEMBERING THE POOR: A RESPONSE
TO BENJAMIN WHITE
Bruce W. Longenecker   245

Chapter 10
PAUL IN IRENAEUS ON THE LAST THINGS
  Adela Yarbro Collins   253

Response
APPROPRIATING PAUL: IRENAEUS'S USE OF THE APOSTLE IN
FORMING AND EXPRESSING HIS ESCHATOLOGICAL THOUGHT
  Todd D. Still   271

Bibliography   275
Index of Ancient Sources   293
Scripture Index   306
Subject Index   315

CONTRIBUTORS

Ben C. Blackwell is associate professor of theology at Houston Baptist University, USA.

Adela Yarbro Collins is Buckingham Professor Emerita of New Testament Criticism and Interpretation at Yale Divinity School, USA.

Mark W. Elliott is professor of divinity and biblical criticism at the University of Glasgow, UK.

Judith Gundry is research scholar and associate professor (adjunct) of New Testament at Yale Divinity School, USA.

Thomas J. Holsinger-Friesen is associate professor of theology at Spring Arbor University, USA.

Joshua W. Jipp is assistant professor of New Testament at Trinity Evangelical Divinity School, USA.

Craig S. Keener is professor of New Testament at Asbury Theological Seminary, USA.

Jutta Leonhardt-Balzer is honorary senior lecturer at the University of Aberdeen, UK.

Bruce W. Longenecker is professor of Christian origins and W.W. Melton Chair of Religion at Baylor University, USA.

Jason Maston is assistant professor of theology at Houston Baptist University, USA.

Scott D. Moringiello is assistant professor at DePaul University, USA.

Stephen O. Presley is associate professor of church history and director of the Center for Early Christian Studies at Southwestern Baptist Theological Seminary, USA.

Helen Rhee is professor of history of Christianity and religious studies at Westmont University, USA.

Todd D. Still is the Charles J. and Eleanor McLerran DeLancey Dean and the William M. Hinson Professor of Christian Scriptures in the George W. Truett Theological Seminary at Baylor University, USA.

Benjamin White is associate professor of religion at Clemson University, USA.

David E. Wilhite is professor of Christian theology at Baylor University, USA.

Michael A. Williams is adjunct professor at the University of Washington, USA.

Carla Swafford Works is associate professor in New Testament at Wesley Theological Seminary, USA.

Chapter 1

IRENAEUS AND PAUL: AN INTRODUCTION

David E. Wilhite

Irenaeus of Lyons had to debate his opponents about the true legacy and the correct understanding of Paul. The present collection of chapters sets out to explore the second-century bishop's understanding of the apostle, and so it will prove helpful to begin with a brief introduction to Irenaeus himself. In what follows, Irenaeus's life, writings, and influence will be surveyed, followed by a review of the current state of scholarship and a preview of the chapters in this volume.

Although he is one of the most influential writers from early Christianity, relatively little is known about Irenaeus's life and background. He was from Smyrna, where he learned from Polycarp's teaching,[1] and he spent time in Rome before moving to the ancient Gallic city of Lugdunum (= Lyon, France),[2] to serve as a presbyter under Bishop Pothinus. He returned to Rome in 177 as an emissary sent to appeal to the Roman bishop Eleutherius, who had rejected the "Montanists" in Phrygia.[3] There, Irenaeus successfully pleaded for tolerance. In 190 Irenaeus visited Rome once again, this time to address the Quartodeciman controversy. Some in Rome had claimed that the church's use of the Roman calendar for celebrating Easter should be normative, in opposition to those in Asia Minor who used the Jewish calendar to mark this holy day. Irenaeus appealed—again, successfully—to the Roman bishop to allow for diversity on this issue. His name, which means "Irenic" or even "Peacemaker," may even be a nickname, or at least it was noted to be apt, given his work to reconcile the bishops of Rome and other

---

1. Just how extensive this influence is is unclear from the sources. See Irenaeus, *Haer.* 3.3.4; and Eusebius, *Hist. eccl.* 5.3.8; 5.20.5–8.

2. He claimed (*Haer.* 1.Preface.3) that living among "the Celts," he had to speak in a "barbaric" language. This may, however, be an exaggeration for rhetorical effect, since it is part of his claim that his work be judged on content, not literary skill.

3. On the New Prophecy, or "Montanism" as it was later called, see William Tabbernee, *Fake Prophecy and Polluted Sacraments: Ecclesiastical and Imperial Reactions to Montanism* (Leiden: Brill, 2007); and Antti Marjanen, "Montanism: Egalitarian Ecstatic 'New Prophecy,'" in *A Companion to Second-Century Christian "Heretics,"* ed. Antti Marjanen and Petri Luomanen (Leiden: Brill, 2008), 185–212.

parties.⁴ Between these two controversies, Pothinus died during a local outbreak of persecution.⁵ Following this, Irenaeus was appointed as the bishop of Lugdunum. Little else is known of his life or even how he died. Jerome knows of a tradition claiming Irenaeus became a martyr, but with other writers like Eusebius remaining silent on this subject the validity of Jerome's claim is highly problematic.⁶

Irenaeus's Works and Teachings

Irenaeus's known oeuvre is relatively small, and its extant form is problematic. Because he wrote against specific opponents, his works became unnecessary and unused in their entirety. However, even though these works fell into disuse, Irenaeus's influence can still be seen in the innumerable quotations found in works by later writers.

Only two of Irenaeus's works survive.⁷ The first is entitled *A Refutation and Overthrow of the Knowledge Falsely So-Called* (Ἔλεγχος καὶ ἀνατροπὴ τῆς ψευδωνύμου γνώσεως). The importance of this title as paradigmatic for the work should be noted for this present study, given its explicit indebtedness to the Pauline statement from 1 Tim 5:20.⁸ In modern studies, this work is more commonly and concisely called *Against Heresies* (*Adversus haereses*). A critical edition of this work is available,⁹ but since the surviving manuscripts of the work are all in Latin and derive from a translation likely made around the end of the fourth century, all citations of Irenaeus remain somewhat tenuous in their reliability. Fortunately, the large number of Greek fragments have enabled scholars to reconstruct the original Greek to a considerable degree. This likely explains why until recently the only English translation available was from the *Ante-Nicene Fathers* series. The new English edition¹⁰ will possibly enhance Irenaean studies in that this text will be more accessible to students earlier in their careers, and it will help nonspecialists have an easier entrée to reading Irenaeus.

---

4. Eusebius, *Hist. eccl.* 5.24.18.

5. Eusebius, *Hist. eccl.* 5.3.8.

6. Jerome, *Comm. Isa.* 17.34.

7. For his nonextant works and some fragments, see Eusebius, *Hist. eccl.* 5.20.1-8; 5.24.1-17; 5.26.1.

8. Similarly, Irenaeus's opening lines of the *Haer.* explicitly name "the apostle" and quote 1 Tim 1:4.

9. A. Rousseau et al. (eds.), *Irénée de Lyon: Contre les hérésies* (SC 100.1, 100.2, 152, 153, 210, 211, 263, 264, 293, 294; Paris: Cerf, 1965–82).

10. Dominic J. Unger and J. J. Dillon, *Irenaeus, Against the Heresies, Book 1* (Ancient Christian Writers 55; New York: Paulist Press, 1992); Dominic J. Unger, *St. Irenaeus of Lyons: Against the Heresies (Book 2)* (Ancient Christian Writers 65; New York: The Newman Press, 2012); and Matthew C. Steenberg and Dominic J. Unger, *St. Irenaeus of Lyons: Against the Heresies (Book 3)* (Ancient Christian Writers 64; New York: Paulist Press, 2012).

Irenaeus's only other extant work is his *Demonstration of Apostolic Teaching* (Εἰς ἐπίδειξιν τὸν Ἀποστολικὸν Κηρύγματος), which survives only in an Armenian translation rediscovered in 1904.[11] This text counters the "Gnostics," but without the detailed review of their positions found in *Against Heresies*. Instead, it is a summary of essential Christian teaching, which attempts to support those key doctrines by reading what later Christians would call the Old Testament and the New Testament in harmony with one another.

Despite the problematic reception and survival of his writings, Irenaeus significantly impacted later Christian writers. In terms of his teachings, Irenaeus is arguably one of the most influential thinkers in all of Christian history. Because he wrote against the "Gnostics" (a problematic category, to be sure), he established several guiding principles for what became "Orthodoxy" (no less problematic, in historical terms).[12] Irenaeus demonstrated that what one teaches about a certain doctrine, such as protology, inevitably affects other doctrines, such as Christology and thereby soteriology. While not offering his own systematic theology per se, Irenaeus does operate with the assumption that theology is systematic—a coherent, consistent, and comprehensive faith.

Along these same lines, and of clear import for our present volume, Irenaeus attempted to read scripture in what could be called a systematic fashion as well. He aimed for consistency of meaning and plot when it came to all the works of the "prophets and the apostles" taken together. He thus gives the first clear instance of what could be called a canonical approach (although his notion of "canon" has more to do with the Canon of Truth, or Rule of Faith, that guides one's readings of inspired texts than with a fixed set of texts deemed to be inspired).

Through his commitment to doctrinal consistency and intertextual coherence, Irenaeus offers posterity a few axioms for proper Christianity. For example, Irenaeus operates with a clear Creator/creature distinction: God creates; everything else is created.[13] This comes to the forefront in the debate with certain groups who think in terms of a chain of being spanning from God through various emanations of God, such as the numerous "aeons" in the pleroma and even below them some human spirits who have been trapped in material bodies within the cosmos. This view of certain spirits as droplets of God or sparks of divinity, according to Irenaeus, conflates the Creator/creature distinction. Whether or not any of this is a fair description of what Irenaeus's opponents actually taught is another matter altogether, and one that is addressed at multiple points in the present volume and in virtually any modern discussion of Irenaeus. Here, it should be noted

---

11. See further discussion (and an English translation) in John Behr, *Irenaeus: On the Apostolic Preaching* (Crestwood, NY: St Vladimir's Seminary Press, 1997).

12. For the problems with "Gnosticism," see Wilhite, *The Gospel According to Heretics: Discovering Orthodoxy through Early Christological Conflicts* (Grand Rapids: Baker, 2015), 61–86. For problems with "Orthodoxy," see the introductory and concluding chapters of that same work.

13. E.g., *Haer.* 4.11.1-2.

that Irenaeus's opponents would not even concede to these categories: they (at least, many of them) view the "Creator" or "Demiurge" as a lower being made to bring order out of the chaos of the material realm, a necessary evil as it were. Furthermore, Irenaeus's opponents by and large readily accepted that divinity and humanity were not distinct categories but were instead in continuity with one another, only at different levels of participating in pure Being (in Platonic terms) or in proximity to the highest Being (in mythic terms). Even so, Irenaeus's Creator/creature distinction is one that will become a litmus test for later teachers in terms of what is accepted as orthodoxy or unorthodoxy.

In addition to the distinction between the Creator and the creation, another Irenaean teaching that becomes axiomatic for later Christians is the relationship between the Creator and creation. While Irenaeus insists on keeping a clear *distinction* between the two, he does not *divide* the two or place any gap between them. He depicts his interlocutors as opposing divinity to materiality, and with this opposition God could not (and would not) be contaminated by participating in the material order. Even the aeons who allegedly emanated from and still participate in the highest/Father God would not (or could not?) interact and intermingle with the material world. Such action would constitute a fall, as famously was the case with Sophia in certain "Gnostic" cosmogonies. In other words, only those emanations that were so low down in the chain of being and thus distant from God could (or would) intermingle with and be contaminated by matter. Within this framework, human spirits, as droplets of God but merely so, have been trapped in material bodies and need to be liberated so they can return to the divine state. In sum, creation is divided from the divine and the two should not mix. For Irenaeus, the Creator/creature distinction in no way requires a gap. Instead, the creature can participate in the divine, even materially, as he thinks is proven with the sacraments and as occurred in the incarnation of the Word. While the Creator and the creation always remain distinct, they nevertheless can (and should) remain in an ontologically participatory relationship. For later Christians, this Irenaean axiom proves crucial in determining proper teaching, as can be seen in the Manichaean and Priscillianist controversies, and of course the implication for Christology is clearly evident in the debates leading up to and following Chalcedon. More importantly for the current volume, Irenaeus believes that this doctrinal orthodoxy is based on the clear meaning of the scriptures. Where things really get interesting is in evaluating Irenaeus's reading of Paul in particular, for before the clear dividing lines between "Orthodoxy" and "heresy" were established in Irenaean terms, all parties were reading Paul to find support for their views.

One other axiomatic teaching from Irenaeus pertains to Christology. The various genealogies of aeons in his opponents' schemes prompted Irenaeus to attack their claim of belief in "one Christ," since they in fact spoke of many. For example, Irenaeus's opponents, allegedly, can distinguish the Only-Begotten from the Savior, who in turn is distinct from Christ, who is still different from Jesus (e.g., *Haer.* 3.16). For Irenaeus, the oneness of Christ is a shibboleth for true, orthodox Christianity. Even though the bishop of Lyon explicitly speaks of Christ's two natures, he emphatically avoids any form of adoptionism wherein a heavenly being possesses or speaks through the earthly Jesus. Instead, Irenaeus insists that Jesus is "one and the same" as the Word of God. This phrase will be paradigmatic at key points in later doctrinal debates, as when Nestorius—who has no apparent indebtedness to "Gnosticism" of any kind—will be heard as dividing the human Jesus from the divine Word. This Irenaean axiom is paradigmatic for many later Christians, and the oneness of Christ is even paradigmatic for Irenaeus for much of his own ideas, as can be seen in his view of scripture.

Irenaeus's emphasis on the unity of Christ guides or at least correlates with his understanding of the unity of the scriptures. His understanding of the scriptures' nature is complex, as is his hermeneutic.[14] In short, the various scriptures form a mystical unity, which allows for various forms of interpretation, but all of these are clearly set within the bounds of the church's teaching. Although certain passages and books may seem idiosyncratic when compared to others, Irenaeus sees the scriptures as a whole and interprets them in light of the Rule of Faith. That having been said, Irenaeus would not see his hermeneutical parameters as somehow imposed on the scriptures. Instead, he believes the Rule of Faith is derived from the scriptures themselves. Even so, since the scriptures can be misinterpreted, the Rule and the guidance of the church's elders are the best guidelines to follow. Ultimately, for Irenaeus, Christ is the center of the scriptures, for he is the one who speaks through them individually and all of them collectively, and this is true both for the "prophets" who spoke before the incarnation and for the "apostles" who wrote thereafter. As mentioned above, this will become poignant in many of the essays in this collection, which attempt to single out Irenaeus's reading of Paul, something that Irenaeus's writings do not readily lend themselves to since Paul is read in light of the whole canon. Paul, "the apostle," features prominently in Irenaeus's extant works, and yet he appears as one authoritative voice among many, and for Irenaeus, all of these voices speak harmoniously—another axiom for later Christians until the rise of historical-critical studies.

As for Irenaeus's scriptures more generally, we can briefly summarize what constituted his canon and his view of the scriptures. He accepted the Old Testament in the form of the Septuagint, repeating the legend of its miraculous and inspired translation.[15] In terms of what later became the New Testament, Irenaeus insists upon a fourfold Gospel collection and accepts the collection of Paul's letters, including the Pastoral epistles (but not Philemon or Hebrews, which he knows and seems to agree with but does not cite as scripture), as well as John's epistles, the book of Revelation, and one letter from Peter (= 1 Peter). It is commonly accepted that Irenaeus included the *Shepherd of Hermas* as an authoritative text (cf. *Haer.* 4.20.2), but this is debatable and the question helps illustrate how complex the issue was for Irenaeus.[16]

---

14. See Norbert Brox, "Irenaeus and the Bible," in *Handbook of Patristic Exegesis: The Bible in Ancient Christianity*, ed. Charles Kannengiesser (Leiden: Brill, 2006), 483–506.

15. *Haer.* 3.1.1; 3.11.8-9.

16. Dan Batovici, "Hermas' Authority in Irenaeus' Works: A Reassessment," *Augustinianum* 55.1 (2015), 5–31.

In the current volume, Irenaeus's reading of Paul is addressed topically, in what Irenaeus would happily accept as a proper order of subjects, and these topics are arranged roughly in systematic order, beginning with creation and ending with eschatology (although many topics are not normally the headings of a systematic outline). This approach admittedly is less than perfect for a number of reasons, and yet we believe that it is a helpful heuristic approach in that it neatly segments Irenaeus's thought so that a direct assessment can be made regarding his reading of Paul for the given subject. In response to each chapter, we have asked scholars who specialize in New Testament studies to situate the findings in comparison with contemporary readings of Paul on the given subject. Before further introducing these subjects and findings, more needs to be said to situate our volume within the current climate of Irenaean studies.

Irenaeus: A Brief Review of the (Very) Recent Literature

At this point we need to say a word about the timing of this volume and where it belongs in relation to recent scholarship on Irenaeus. This is the third in our series on the reception of Paul, but it is one that we began planning immediately after our first (and what was originally thought to be our only volume) on this subject, *Tertullian and Paul* (2013). However, "the best laid plans" and so forth occurred, and the timeline changed significantly. The details need not be recited here, since they would constitute little more than excuses, but suffice it to say that this volume is woefully late, which means that many of the chapters collected here were written years before their final publication, and for that we as the editors take responsibility. Even so, we remain confident that these chapters are still a timely contribution to the field, and the only real detriment is that they have not been able to engage the most recent publications on Irenaeus and Paul—and said recent publications have not had the benefit of seeing these findings. Therefore, we offer in what follows a very brief review of the *status quaestionis* for the past few years of Irenaeus studies in particular.

Fortunately for most of our authors, John Behr's recent work, *Irenaeus of Lyons: Identifying Christianity*,[17] had just been published. Behr offers a fresh assessment of Irenaeus's life, background, and works. In addition, he argues against the current scholarly narrative of Irenaeus as a domineering agent of the Great Church enforcing an exclusionary agenda. Instead, he claims the church was decentralized and could not enforce such a view, and that Irenaeus himself was known to advocate for tolerance of diversity.

Similar to Behr, the work of Giuliano Chiapparini has defended Irenaeus's depiction of the Valentinians against those who would dismiss it as biased and

---

17. John Behr, *Irenaeus of Lyons: Identifying Christianity* (Oxford: Oxford University Press, 2013).

unreliable.¹⁸ Chiapparini even contends that the material in Irenaeus's first book of *Against Heresies* is indebted to historically valuable sources from the mid-second century (much closer to Valentinus himself), and thereby Chiapparini offers a very early dating of Books 1 and 2 of Irenaeus's work, placing them in the 160s while Irenaeus was still in Rome.¹⁹ Even so, this initial draft is thought to be revised around 180.²⁰

Several recent works have also contributed to our understanding of Irenaeus's theology. For example, in his 2014 monograph, Jackson Lashier argues for an immanent understanding of the divine persons in Irenaeus (not just an economic Trinity, as most modern scholars have claimed).²¹ Another reassessment of Irenaeus's thought has been offered by Anthony Briggman, who examines a key passage in *Against Heresies* to claim that Irenaeus did in fact affirm natural knowledge of God and thereby viewed certain philosophical understandings of God as positive.²² Briggman has elsewhere reviewed Irenaeus's description of the "mixture" of the body and soul, and the correlation for Christ's divine and human natures,²³ and he has more recently supplemented our understanding of Irenaeus's own theological approach, arguing that Irenaeus did allow for "theological speculation," only with certain important caveats in place about what is unknowable.²⁴ Along the lines of salvation and recapitulation, Maria del Fiat Miola contextualizes Irenaeus's metaphor in the material culture of ancient Greco-Roman practice.²⁵

In terms of Irenaeus's approach to interpreting scripture, a number of recent studies have provided fruitful findings. In this area Briggman has contributed two articles in which he argues that rhetoric played a more central role in Irenaeus's works,²⁶ and finds three hermeneutical principles that guide Irenaeus's use of

---

18. Giuliano Chiapparini, "Irenaeus and the Gnostic Valentinus: Orthodoxy and Heresy in the Church of Rome around the Middle of the Second Century," *Zeitschrift für antikes Christentum* 18.1 (2013), 95–119; summarizing his *Valentino gnostico e platonico: Il Valentinianiesimo della "Grande Notizia" di Ireneo di Lione: fra esegesi gnostica e filosofia medioplatonica* (Milan: Vita e Pensiero, 2012).

19. Chiapparini, "Irenaeus and the Gnostic Valentinus," 97–9.

20. Chiapparini's chronology needs to be placed in conversation with that of Behr, *Irenaeus*, 66–71.

21. Jackson Lashier, *Irenaeus on the Trinity* (Supplements to Vigiliae Christianae 127; Leiden: Brill, 2014).

22. Anthony Briggman, "Irenaeus on Natural Knowledge," *CH* 95.2 (2015), 133–54.

23. Anthony Briggman, "Irenaeus' Christology of Mixture," *JTS* 64.2 (2013), 516–55.

24. Anthony Briggman, "Theological Speculation in Irenaeus: Perils and Possibilities," *VC* 71.2 (2017), 175–98.

25. Maria del Fiat Miola, "Mary as Un-tier and Tier of Knots: Irenaeus Reinterpreted," *JECS* 24.3 (2016), 337–61.

26. Anthony Briggman, "Literary and Rhetorical Theory in Irenaeus, Part 1," *VC* 69.5 (2015), 500–27. Further discussion on Irenaeus's use of "reason" has also enhanced our understanding of Irenaeus's use of classical philosophy and education; see Agnès Bastit,

scripture[27] (contra Manlio Simonetti, who said Irenaeus had no principles of interpretation).[28] Briggman's findings have been supplemented by Lewis Ayres, who demonstrates that classical rhetorical and hermeneutical methods found in Irenaeus were likely first used by the Valentinians themselves.[29] In terms of how Irenaeus viewed and classified scripture, Jeffrey Bingham has recently shown that Irenaeus used "scripture" (*graphē*) for numerous texts in the Christian tradition (e.g., *Hermas*, Papias, Polycarp), but he nevertheless prioritized the writings of "the prophets and apostles."[30] Two essays by Behr and Stephen O. Presley have also further enhanced our understanding of Irenaeus's use of scriptures by examining how he places different scriptures in relation to one another,[31] and to these can be added the papers given in 2014 in Lyon, now published as essays.[32]

As for Irenaeus's use of Paul in particular, it will be evident from the current collection of chapters that certain studies still remain indispensible,[33] and these studies continue to influence the recent literature. To these works must now be added the study by Benjamin L. White, *Remembering Paul*, since he has a chapter

---

"Quelques appels à la rationalité chez Irénée de Lyon," *Revue de Théologie et de Philosophie* 149.1–2 (2017), 105–24.

27. Anthony Briggman, "Literary and Rhetorical Theory in Irenaeus, Part 2," *VC* 70.1 (2016), 31–50.

28. Manlio Simonetti, *Biblical Interpretation in the Early Church: An Historical Introduction to Patristic Exegesis* (Edinburgh: T&T Clark, 1994).

29. Lewis Ayres, "Irenaeus vs. the Valentinians: Toward a Rethinking of Patristic Exegetical Origins," *JECS* 23.2 (2015), 153–87.

30. Jeffrey Bingham, "Senses of Scripture in the Second Century: Irenaeus, Scripture, and Noncanonical Christian Texts," *Journal of Religion* 97.1 (2017), 26–55.

31. Behr, "Scripture and Gospel: Intertextuality in Irenaeus," and Stephen O. Presley, "The *Demonstration* of Intertextuality in Irenaeus of Lyons," in *Intertextuality in the Second Century*, ed. D. Jeffrey Bingham and Clayton N. Jefford (Leiden: Brill, 2016), 179–94 and 195–214.

32. Agnès Bastit and Joseph Verheyden, *Irénée de Lyon et les débuts de la Bible chrétienne. Actes de la Journée du 1. VII. 2014 à Lyon* (Turnhout: Brepols, 2017).

33. William Sanday, Alexander Souter, and Cuthbert H. Turner, *Novum Testamentum Sancti Irenaei episcopi Lugdunensis: being the New Testament quotations in the Old-Latin version of the Elenchos kai paratrope pseudonymou gnoseos* (Oxford: Clarendon Press, 1923); Rolf Noormann, *Irenäus als Paulusinterpret: Zur Rezeption und Wirkung der paulinischen und deuteropaulinischen Briefe im Werk des Irenäus von Lyon* (WUNT 2.66; Tübingen: Mohr Siebeck, 1994); Eric Osborn, *Irenaeus of Lyon* (Cambridge: Cambridge University Press, 2001), 189–92; Ben C. Blackwell, "Paul and Irenaeus," in *Paul and the Second Century: The Legacy of Paul's Life, Letters, and Teaching*, ed. Michael F. Bird and Joseph R. Dodson (London: T&T Clark, 2011), 190–206. Also, for the use of Paul by Irenaeus's opponents, see Elaine Pagels, *The Gnostic Paul: Gnostic Exegesis of the Pauline Letters* (Philadelphia: Trinity Press International, 1975); while Irenaeus's opponents themselves do not necessarily become the focus in the current volume, his response to them is clearly shaped by them.

devoted to Irenaeus.[34] There is also an interesting study that has drawn parallels between Paul's use of "Gospel" with Irenaeus's use of "Tradition."[35] In addition to these recent works on Irenaeus we can now introduce the chapters collected in the present volume, which will certainly supplement and enhance the current work being done in this field.

Irenaeus and Paul: Topical Analyses

The following chapters examine Irenaeus's use of Paul on a range of subjects. It should be noted that the topical arrangement is merely a heuristic device which allows us the convenience of setting the parameters for any given chapter and then analyzing Irenaeus's use of Paul on that topic in depth. The obvious downside to such an approach is the way in which so much of Irenaeus's thinking is intertwined, and so isolating any given doctrine risks reifying his thinking. However, in the chapters that follow careful attention has been given to this problem, and so there is multiple cross-referencing of subjects between chapters. Furthermore, the subject addressed by each chapter is meant to be an entry point into Irenaeus's thought. No chapter claims to be completely exhaustive on the given topic, and some chapters needed to be narrowed down in scope more than others due to the sources and scholarly debates. Nevertheless, each chapter does provide the necessary bibliography that should assist any who wish to go beyond the scope of what is offered here.

Our first contributor, Michael Williams, revisits the subject of God as Creator. Whereas Irenaeus famously refutes his opponents for their complex cosmogonies as foreign to Paul's Jewish monotheism, Williams finds that Irenaeus and his opponents in fact share their fundamental commitment to the oneness of God; they differ only in how much speculative philosophy can inform this God's relation to creation and in how (not whether) the one God related to creation. This is a question, Williams observes, on which Paul remained largely silent; this allowed both parties to assume Paul shared their views. Many of the so-called Gnostics (which of course is a category that Williams himself has rejected[36]) can now be seen to share in Paul's concern for God's will and providence in relation to creation.

In response to Williams's study, Jason Maston offers a reflection on how Paul understands the Creator along three lines. First, when speaking of God as the

---

34. Benjamin L. White, *Remembering Paul: Ancient and Modern Contests over the Image of the Apostle* (Oxford: Oxford University Press, 2014), 135–69.

35. Andrés Sáez, "La Tradition d'Irénée et l'Évangile de Paul: La naissance de la conscience canonique néotestamentaire et quelques conséquences sur la nature de la Révélation chrétienne," *Revue des sciences religieuses* 90.3 (2016), 357–83.

36. Michael A. Williams, *Rethinking "Gnosticism": An Argument for Dismantling a Dubious Category* (Princeton, NJ: Princeton University, 1996).

actor or agent who creates, Paul speaks of Jesus as part of this agency. Second, Paul thinks of the whole creation story, or the ages of creation (cf. Ireaneus's concept of *oikonomia*), in light of Jesus who brings about a discontinuity with the present cosmos, but in order to redeem it—a recapitulation of discontinuity into continuity as it were. Third, Maston finds Paul to think of Christ's resurrection as the "telos of Creation," and so contemporary scholarly debates about Paul's view of the resurrection of a "spiritual body" should understand this in light of Jesus' resurrected body. Maston notes how the comparison between contested readings of Paul in Irenaeus's time and contemporary scholarship often brings to light some illuminating insights.

In Chapter 3, Stephen Presley revisits Irenaeus's well-known use of Paul's Adam-Christ typology for the purposes of recapitulation. As opposed to some prior studies which sought to judge how correctly Irenaeus approximated (their understanding of) Paul's original aims or how far the bishop of Lyon developed the apostle's ideas, Presley attempts to assess how Irenaeus accommodated and developed Paul in light of other biblical texts. By tracing the various ways that other texts are paired with Pauline passages, Presley demonstrates how much these other texts serve as commentary for Irenaeus in that Irenaeus finds Pauline words and phrases to point to, or at least overlap with, concepts found in other scripture passages. Taken as a whole, one can better appreciate the development of Pauline ideas that resulted from interweaving other biblical passages, and still acknowledge the centrality of Pauline texts within this tapestry.

Joshua W. Jipp responds to Presley by agreeing with his notion that Irenaeus both draws upon and expands Paul's Adam-Christ typology, and Jipp applies Presley's model to Paul's adaptation of Jewish messianism as attested in Irenaeus. He even shows that Irenaeus draws on more Jewish messianic sources than Paul, albeit at least in part because he is following Paul's example in doing so. Jipp's treatment of Irenaeus, therefore, furthers his project of demonstrating the Jewish messianic influence on Christianity, even the Christianity of the late second century.

In my own chapter, I offer an overview of Irenaeus's definition and use of "Spirit." This concept has proven difficult to assess, because Irenaeus sometimes speaks of the "spirit" in terms of a nonmaterial substance, while at other times he speaks of the/a S/spirit as a distinct and active person. The difficulty lies largely in the fact that Irenaeus never offers any explanation or shows even an awareness of these two distinct meanings. Therefore, I borrow Derrida's understanding of language in order to revisit Irenaeus's pneumatology (broadly defined), all the while showing how much he cites Paul to support his views. Beyond the substance/person distinction in modern interpretations, Irenaeus himself privileges the role of the Spirit, which is that of divine communication, or "prophecy."

In response to this analysis of Irenaeus's use of the Spirit, Craig Keener provides a broader array of sources with which Irenaeus's thought can be compared. Paul is still seen to be informing Irenaeus's understanding of *pneuma*, but Irenaeus and Paul are set within the wider philosophical and cultural framework.

Tom Holsinger-Friesen surveys Irenaeus's use of Paul under the broad category of sin, but he does so by examining four "clusters" of images. These are false knowledge, arrogance, separation, and unfruitfulness. For each concept Holsinger-Friesen shows how much Paul's language set the precedent for Irenaeus, but also how the latter developed the former's imagery. Pauline images take on new life when Irenaeus applies them to his contemporary opponents. Even so, these four images do cohere within a larger theological framework of sin and salvation for Irenaeus, and Holsinger-Friesen shows how this larger understanding of sin and God's remedy for it also echoes Paul's language of the divine economy of salvation.

In response to Holsinger-Friesen, Jutta Leonhardt-Balzer uses the passages collected on sin to reevaluate Irenaeus's attention to the original Pauline context. She finds that Irenaeus is often aware of Paul's original usage, even when adapting certain statements for his own aims. Leonhardt-Balzer goes beyond Holsinger-Friesen's focus on Pauline statements about sin in order to assess more broadly Irenaeus's appropriation of Paul when using combined quotations, borrowed metaphors, the original context of the quotation, and general concepts. This broader assessment is then brought to specific conclusions on how faithful Irenaeus was to Paul on this subject.

Next, Ben C. Blackwell looks to Irenaeus's use of the Old "Testament" in general, but by way of focusing God's covenant with Abraham in particular, a topic that is often neglected because of the amount of attention given to Irenaeus's view of creation. Irenaeus's use of Abraham, which does feature as a recurring motif in his work, is often influenced by Paul's treatment of the patriarch.

Mark W. Elliott takes up Blackwell's particular point about better understanding Paul's own theology in regard to the "New Perspective," and he attempts to do the same with Irenaeus's own theology. The understanding of the concept of covenant and of the roles Adam and Abraham play in relation to salvation is still debatable.

In Chapter 7, Scott D. Moringiello finds Irenaeus to have 1 Cor 8:6 in mind throughout much of *Against Heresies*, a point rarely noted by scholars. Paul speaks of a kind of knowledge that "puffs up" and therefore is inferior to love that "builds up." While Irenaeus does not often cite this distinction explicitly, it can be traced through many parts of his argument against his opponents. Therefore, not only is the Pauline warning against "*gnosis* falsely so-called" (1 Tim 6:20) a guiding maxim for Irenaeus, but Paul's definition of improper knowledge and edifying love (from 1 Cor 8:6) can also be seen as a key guiding principle for the bishop of Lyon.

In response to Moringiello's findings, Carla Swafford Works reviews where Irenaeus's context and Paul's differ. While appreciating the similarities in their arguments about love and knowledge, the difference between Paul's correction of "parishioners" in 1 Corinthians 8 and Irenaeus's attack against "heretics" results in different aims and accomplishments for each writer. Furthermore, even though Works does see the influence of 1 Cor 8:6 in Irenaeus, she thinks it is important to note how "the law of love" for Irenaeus is explicitly drawing on an array of texts from throughout the canon. Even with these differences, Works finds that both Paul and Irenaeus are each promoting the love of God and love of neighbor.

Next, Helen Rhee explores what would be deemed the classical doctrine of "anthropology," by looking at how Irenaeus treats sexual difference and practice. She finds him to follow Paul's cue of recapitulation of Adam by Christ, and yet

Irenaeus's extension of this framework to Eve and Mary results in his additional comments on virginity, marriage, and procreation. The latter two, Rhee argues, were part of God's original plan for humanity, and not a result of the fall. Furthermore, this "Pauline paradigm" shapes how he reads other passages about humanity's creation, but in a way that highlights "female fertility"; therefore, instead of deeming female sexual identity as inferior (here he omits some Pauline passages), Irenaeus describes it as potent enough to shape history for all humanity, both from the earliest days of creation in Eve, to the ultimate eschatological end ushered in through Mary. This positive view of women, Rhee avers, helps us better understand Irenaeus's defense of women's prophetic voices.

Judith Gundry responds by expanding the focus from recapitulation to Paul's comments on women more generally. She finds therein more significant differences between Paul and Irenaeus, with the latter often oversimplifying the former. While there are certainly some differences and some similarities, in light of her own Christian feminist perspective Gundry sees Irenaeus to have lost some of the "more amenable" aspects of Pauline teaching on sexuality.

In Chapter 9, Benjamin White returns to the long-debated question of Paul's relationship to Peter and the other Jerusalem disciples, exploring how Irenaeus had to insist that *the* apostle belonged with all the apostle*s*. To be sure, Irenaeus conveniently omits passages from Galatians in making the case that Paul and Peter cooperated harmoniously. Even so, White shows that even if Irenaeus conceded these passages (since he certainly knows them), the doctrinal harmony between Peter, Paul, James, and the rest of the apostles is still widely testified in the sources—especially if one follows Irenaeus's chronology of Paul's encounters with Jerusalem. The main conclusion White draws from this pertains to how scholars understand the various attempts, including manuscripts and witnesses, to retrieve Paul.

In response to White, Bruce Longenecker inquires as to why two classes of evidence are omitted in Irenaeus's treatment. There are numerous passages from the Pauline corpus that further ties Paul, and more specifically, Paul's collection for those in need in Judaea, with the Jerusalem church and her apostles. Furthermore, there is the specific statement in Gal 2:10 where James, Cephas, and John request that Paul "remember the poor." Longenecker finds Irenaeus's silence on this statement to be deafening, and thereby Irenaeus's treatment of the topic more generally in fact adds insights to a debate over how to interpret this passage.

In the final chapter, Adela Yarbro Collins reviews Irenaeus's statements on the culmination of history and the predictions about the final judgment. She does so while noting his biblical sources, especially how much Paul informs his understanding. There are significant differences between the two, as would be expected since Irenaeus fits Paul's statements together with other scriptural teachings about the end times, such as the Johannine descriptions of the Antichrist and the Beast. Irenaeus also views the resurrection to come and the millennial reign in terms of resurrected flesh, something that Pauline scholars debate in terms of the apostles' understanding of a "spiritual body."

The final respondent is Todd D. Still, who acknowledges Irenaeus's conflation of Pauline and Johannine eschatology, and then briefly explores what kind of discontinuity this sets up for Irenaeus's own expectations in relation to Paul. Pauline scholars may debate what kind of development took place in the apostles' anticipation of an imminent return of Christ, but the obvious shift from Paul to Irenaeus in terms of a delayed parousia does not negate other elements of continuity and indebtedness when it comes to the ultimate basis for their shared hope.

One final word that needs to be said in this "Introduction" to our volume is a word of thanks. We have been supported in this project by many people, and although a passing mention does not adequately convey our gratitude to them, we would nonetheless like to name them as a token of our appreciation. First of all, thanks go to our colleagues and administrators at Baylor University's George W. Truett Theological Seminary. Their support, encouragement, and collegiality is a major part in making our work together so enjoyable and rewarding. Next, we would like to thank the team at T&T Clark and Bloomsbury. Many people had a hand in bringing this project to completion, and we very much appreciate their professionalism and their patience. We would especially like to thank Dominic Mattos: turning this project into a series was his idea, and his ongoing support for the project has been invaluable. We also would like to mention the graduate assistants who played various parts with this volume at various points in its production: thank you Jeremy Crews, Bobby Martinez, and Joshua Sharp. Finally, we, the editors, would like to thank our wives, Carolyn and Amber, for what Irenaeus describes in very Pauline language as, *praecipuum dilectionis munus, quod est pretiosius quam agnitio*—"the eminent gift of love, that which is more precious than knowledge" (Haer. 4.33.8; cf. 1 Cor 13:8, 13).

Chapter 2

IRENAEUS AND HIS OPPONENTS ON CREATOR, CREATION, AND THE APOSTLE

Michael A. Williams

Since certain people, throwing aside the Truth, are introducing lying discourses and "endless genealogies that produce debates rather than," as the Apostle says, "God's foundation in Truth" (1 Tim 1:4); misguiding the minds of the inexperienced by means of craftily fabricated persuasiveness and taking them captive; treating recklessly the sayings of the Lord, becoming bad interpreters of things said well; destroying many, leading them through a pretense of knowledge away from the one who established and adorned the universe, on the grounds that they are able to demonstrate something higher and better than the God who created heaven and earth and all things in them.

—Irenaeus, *Haer.* 1.Preface.1

In these opening lines of his "Exposure and Refutation of Falsely-Named 'Gnosis'" Irenaeus famously introduces a quotation from 1 Tim 1:4. He refers to his opponents' faulty interpretation of *logia* of the Lord, and over the five volumes of this work he points out passages from the gospels that he believes they have "treated recklessly" through wild misinterpretation. However, he begins with an appeal to "the Apostle." This chapter will examine debates between Irenaeus and certain contemporaries over teachings about creator and creation, and special attention throughout will be given to the use of Pauline tradition.

Without the slightest hint of irony, Irenaeus opens this project by citing a voice that scholars today usually consider that of a second-century-CE admirer of Paul rather than Paul himself. Irenaeus displays no indication that he is aware of the dispute about, or that he feels a need to defend, the Pauline authorship of the Pastorals, 2 Thessalonians, Colossians, or Ephesians.[1] Some of his adversaries may

---

1. For this reason, in this chapter terms such as "Pauline corpus" or "Pauline" will refer, unless otherwise qualified, to all writings under Paul's name now in the New Testament. Thus I assume the persona of Irenaeus on this point, even though I myself accept as the best hypothesis that the Pastorals, 2 Thessalonians, Colossians, and Ephesians are all

either have rejected or not yet even known of the Pastorals.² However, many or possibly most of them will have considered at least Colossians and Ephesians to be words from "the Apostle."³ This is important for our purposes because these two letters are among the decisive factors shaping notions of creator and creation on the part of both Irenaeus and at least his principal opponents.

The actual quantity of material in the Pauline corpus that refers directly to creator and creation is in fact limited. By the time Irenaeus writes, a central issue had become whether one could distinguish the creator God of Genesis from a higher deity. But that question is never posed anywhere in the Pauline corpus. There are simply a handful of passages that refer to God as creator and sometimes Christ as instrument or agent of creation.⁴ We can state at the outset that Irenaeus

---

pseudo-Pauline. Cf. the similar approach in the important article by the late Richard A. Norris, Jr., "Irenaeus' Use of Paul in his Polemic against the Gnostics," in *Paul and the Legacies of Paul*, ed. William S. Babcock (Dallas: Southern Methodist University Press, 1990), 80.

2. E.g., see Tertullian, *Marc.* 5.21 (who refers specifically to Marcion's rejection of 1 and 2 Timothy and Titus); Clement of Alexandria, *Strom.* 2.52.6 (after quoting the reference to "falsely-named knowledge" in 1 Tim 6:20f): "Those from the sects (ἀπὸ τῶν αἱρέσεων) who are convicted by this utterance reject the letters to Timothy."

3. Of course, at least in Marcion's case, these were edited versions of Pauline letters, even though details about the editing remain uncertain; see now Jason David BeDuhn, *The First New Testament: Marcion's Scriptural Canon* (Salem, OR: Polebridge Press, 2013). Irenaeus does mention this (*Haer.* 1.27.2), so that is as close as he comes to revealing any knowledge about debate over the Pauline authenticity of any of the letters mentioned. It is conceivable that Irenaeus's general language about Marcion "excising" the letters of Paul, "removing" portions pertaining to "the God who made the world," might have included by implication Marcionite rejection of the Pastorals altogether. But Irenaeus does not say that. And it is interesting that he never includes the rejection of the authenticity of the Pastorals, in spite of their thematic role in his polemic, as a part of his argument against Valentinians or any of his other opponents. (Of course, he accuses the "Ebionites" of rejecting Paul altogether; *Haer.* 1.26.2.) Nicholas Perrin, "Paul and Valentinian Interpretation," in *Paul and the Second Century*, ed. Michael F. Bird and Joseph R. Dodson (LNTS 412; London: T&T Clark, 2011), 130-32, argues that the *Gospel of Truth* 25,10-35 may be paraphrasing 2 Tim 2.20-21, but I do not find his case very convincing. (That Valentinus himself was in fact the author of *Gospel of Truth*, a conclusion Perrin accepts, is also quite uncertain, though an issue separate from the intertextuality just mentioned.)

4. The nouns ποιητής and δημιουργός are never used for God as "Creator" in writings that came to be included in the New Testament. The one occurrence of the noun (or any cognate) δημιουργός is in Heb 11.10, but there it is of God as "craftsman" of the eschatologically promised "city," not the cosmos. But the verb ποιεῖν is frequently used of God's creating (e.g., in the Pauline corpus: Rom 1:25; 1 Cor 11:9; Col 1:16; Col 3:10; 1 Tim 4:3). For a recent brief survey of the topic of creation in the Pauline corpus, particularly with respect to Genesis 1-3, see Peter Bouteneff, *Beginnings: Ancient Christian Readings of the Biblical Creation Narratives* (Grand Rapids: Baker, 2008), 33-54.

was unquestionably correct that Paul himself (including New Testament authors we might classify as "pseudo-Paul") certainly was not proposing that the creator God of Genesis was different from some more transcendent deity. Yet that is only part of the story, and in important respects it is beside the point if we are to understand how Pauline writings were being read by Irenaeus and his adversaries. For none of those involved in the controversies behind Irenaeus's attack were simply pursuing a thorough and dispassionate analysis of the Pauline corpus in order to discover what Paul's position on this issue might be. All came to these writings with differing fundamental questions arising from differing presuppositions.[5] In actuality, precisely the *absence* of elaborate discussion of creator and creation per se in the Pauline corpus would mean that several passages within it could be susceptible to multiple interpretations on this topic.

Irenaeus began with the presupposition that the Old Testament and New Testament constituted the single story of one God with a single purpose activated through multiple covenants. Though modern scholarship on Irenaeus has rightly underscored his original contributions, he had also inherited a rule of faith/truth that established the basic structure as well as important boundaries for his argument. He began with the one God as the one creator and Christ and the Spirit as God's hands in the actions of creation. As far as he was concerned, there was no revelation about what preceded the event of creation, and therefore it was pointless for humans to fret about it, and speculation on it led only to the cliff of blasphemy. Instead, the task was to elucidate how the same God would have been responsible for such different demands in different ages, and how the whole story converged in a single goal. Among other scriptures, Pauline writings could be read in this way.

Valentinians,[6] who constituted a major target of Irenaeus's criticism, were also convinced of a single big picture, a unified story, but they held different

---

5. Cf. Joseph R. Dodson, "Introduction," in *Paul and the Second Century*, ed. Michael F. Bird and Joseph R. Dodson (LNTS 412; London: T&T Clark, 2011), 5, who remarks, citing similar observations by other scholars, that writers in the second century "hardly ever used Paul's letters to achieve the same ends for which Paul penned them."

6. I will use the label "Valentinians" in this chapter for a collective pattern of teachings assembled and treated by Irenaeus as belonging to a Valentinian "sect" (αἵρεσις), and for certain other primary sources manifesting some features in those teachings. However, I am quite aware of and in agreement with scholarship contending that the notion of an organized Valentinian "sect" is largely a construct for which Irenaeus himself is responsible, since the devotees involved clearly considered themselves Christian and since the sources are rather diverse. See, e.g., Einar Thomassen, "Notes pour la délimination d'un corpus valentinien à Nag Hammadi," in *Les textes de Nag Hammadi et le problème de leur classification: Actes du colloque tenu à Québec du 15 au 19 septembre 1993*, ed. Louis Painchaud and Anne Pasquier (BCNH:E 3; Québec: Les presses de l'Université Laval and Éditions Peeters, 1995), 243–59; Ismo Dunderberg, "The School of Valentinus," in *A Companion to Second-Century "Heretics,"* ed. Antti Marjanen and Petri Luomanen (VCSup 76; Leiden: Brill, 2005), 64–99, among many excellent studies.

convictions about the boundaries of the discussion as far as creator and creation were concerned. Like Irenaeus they were Christian monotheists, interested in the story of salvation from one God through Christ. But unlike Irenaeus they felt that understanding an *overall* unity in the testimony of scriptures old and new required beginning with the frank admission of some apparent *disunity* among the parts. And thus, what was required was the application and adaptation of presuppositions and insights from the best of "modern" philosophy. To get at the single big picture meant informed Christian reflection on some basic questions about existence, about the origin of the world, about "how we got here." More to the point, it required more than only reading about Adam and Eve, important as that was. One had to search deeper, think deeper, about the relation of the one perfect God to a created realm that contained imperfection and therefore evil. Among other scriptures, Pauline writings could be read in this way.

Creation and creator are central themes in Irenaeus's work, as so many scholars have demonstrated in learned studies.[7] And, of course, in modern scholarship these themes are usually treated as trademark preoccupations of Valentinian, "Gnostic," and Marcionite Christians like those criticized by Irenaeus.[8] My attention here will return with frequency to the role of the Pauline corpus in the dispute between Irenaeus and his antagonists.

But even more specifically, in this study I want to turn the spotlight on aspects of the dispute that have not received much attention but that can significantly

---

7. E.g., in addition to pertinent sections in general studies on Irenaeus, see Thomas Holsinger-Friesen, *Irenaeus and Genesis: A Study of Competition in Early Christian Hermeneutics* (Winona Lake: Eisenbrauns, 2009); Matthew Craig Steenberg, *Irenaeus on Creation: The Cosmic Christ and the Saga of Redemption* (VCSup 91; Leiden: Brill, 2008).

8. The literature is vast on creation and creator in such movements and texts, since cosmogonic myth has so often been a profiling marker by which they have been rounded up as suspects in the first place. For only a few recent examples of general treatments, see Nicola Denzey Lewis, *Introduction to "Gnosticism": Ancient Voices, Christian Worlds* (Oxford: Oxford University Press, 2013); David Brakke, *The Gnostics: Myth, Ritual, and Diversity in Early Christianity* (Cambridge, MA: Harvard University Press, 2010); Birger A. Pearson, *Ancient Gnosticism: Traditions and Literature* (Minneapolis: Fortress Press, 2007); Christoph Markschies, *Gnosis: An Introduction*, trans. John Bowden (London: T&T Clark, 2003). For critical reflection on problems with the category "Gnosticism" itself, see further: Michael Allen Williams, *Rethinking "Gnosticism": An Argument for Dismantling a Dubious Category* (Princeton: Princeton University Press, 1996); Karen L. King, *What Is Gnosticism?* (Cambridge, MA: The Belknap Press of Harvard University Press, 2003); and the diverse perspectives in Antti Marjanen (ed.), *Was There a Gnostic Religion?* (Göttingen: Vandenhoeck & Ruprecht, 2005). In this chapter I will normally use the term "Gnostic" only when it is employed in a cited source. When I use the term "demiurgical" in this study, I am referring to a general type of cosmology portraying one or more creators as lower than the true God.

alter how one understands the historical situation. From time to time others have articulated versions of a fundamental observation that is at the core of my argument—namely, that, diverse as they were, at least most of Irenaeus's opponents were actually in agreement with him on some basic issues, and above all, on the premise that there is only one true God.[9] But even when that point has been granted a degree of legitimacy, important implications have been underappreciated. As we will see, central among these is the question of ultimate *responsibility* for creation. In short, was "God" responsible or was it some other entity? Closely related are implications for how the *purpose* of creation was imagined. Finally, what are the implications for *perceptions of the material world*, the physical environment of everyday life, on the part of Irenaeus and his principal antagonists?

I do not mean that such questions never come up in research on Irenaeus, for at least the first two (responsibility for and purpose of creation) are well-established as essential dimensions in general analyses of Irenaeus's own thought. And of course, the principal reason we know so much about Irenaeus's thoughts on these matters is that he feels called upon to spell them out in response to the views of opponents. We can thank the collective efforts of numerous modern scholars for providing an excellent picture of Irenaeus's notions about God as creator and the purpose of creation.[10] However, characterizations in these works of the positions of Irenaeus's adversaries are generally far less satisfactory, so much so that there are obstacles to a true grasp on what was at stake in these conflicts. The more recent scholarship on Irenaeus has begun to benefit from what is being learned in Nag Hammadi research, but far more progress in this direction is possible, and in what follows I suggest specific examples related to the topic at hand. But in addition, certain evidence in Irenaeus's own work deserves more careful examination, for it makes a difference in how we understand him and his opponents on creator, creation, and the Apostle.

---

9. To mention only one example, see the excellent discussion in Richard A. Norris, "Who Is the Demiurge? Irenaeus' Picture of God in *Adversus haereses* 2," in *God in Early Christian Thought: Essays in Memory of Lloyd G. Patterson*, ed. Andrew B. McGowan et al. (VCSup 94; Leiden: Brill, 2009), 9–11, about how Irenaeus and Valentinians of his acquaintance were in some respects speaking past one another, covering "different territories," as far as the nature of God is concerned.

10. Space allows the mention of only a few of the more recent examples. In addition to the studies by Steenberg and Holsinger-Friesen (see above), cf. relevant sections in: Jacques Fantino, *La théologie d'Irénée: Lecture des Ecritures en réponse à l'exégèse gnostique: une approche trinitaire* (Cogitatio fidei 180; Paris: Editions du Cerf, 1994); Eric Osborn, *Irenaeus of Lyons* (Cambridge: Cambridge University Press, 2001); Denis Minns, *Irenaeus: An Introduction* (London: T&T Clark, 2010); John Behr, *Irenaeus of Lyons: Identifying Christianity* (Oxford: Oxford University Press, 2013).

Creator and Responsibility for Creation

To Irenaeus nothing could be clearer than that the God proclaimed by Paul was the creator of heaven and earth, the one God who had been proclaimed by the prophets, the Father of the one Jesus Christ, and that in all this Paul was in complete agreement with the other apostles (e.g., *Haer.* 3.12.1-10). He includes this insistence on one God in his articulations of the canon or "rule" of "faith"/"truth" confessed by churches everywhere.[11] Though Irenaeus is certainly original in his adaptation of the "rule," he is drawing on tradition and explicitly refers to earlier Christian authorities such as Justin Martyr[12] and the teaching of "Presbyters"[13] in support of his doctrine of one God and one Jesus Christ. It would appear from Irenaeus's remarks that passages from Pauline writings had already been invoked as proof-texts for "one God" in that earlier tradition, to show, for example, that Pauline texts attest to divine justice and divine punishment just as in Jewish scriptures.[14] Irenaeus insisted that the one true God is attested throughout Jewish and Christian scriptures, revealing a single divine will throughout three covenantal generations: "natural laws" from Adam to Moses; more elaborate laws in the Mosaic covenant; and freedom in the gospel of Jesus Christ.[15] Irenaeus

---

11. E.g., *Haer.* 1.10.1-2; among the many discussions of Irenaeus's appeal to the "rule," cf. Fantino, *La théologie d'Irénée*, 15–28; Osborn, *Irenaeus*, 145–50; Thomas C. K. Ferguson, "The Rule of Truth and Irenaean Rhetoric in Book 1 of 'Against Heresies,'" *VC* 55 (2001), 356–75; Behr, *Irenaeus of Lyons*, 111–12.

12. E.g., *Haer.* 4.6.2: "Justin has put it well in his book against Marcion: 'I would not have believed the Lord himself if he had announced a God other than our Creator and Maker and Nourisher'" (the first part preserved in Eusebius, *Hist. eccl.* 4.18.9).

13. See *Haer.* 4.27-32. The debate over the precise delineation of traditions that Irenaeus ascribes to "the Presbyter," or "the Presbyters" is an old one; e.g., Adolf von Harnack, "Der Presbyter-Prediger des Irenäus (IV,27,1-32,1): Bruchstücke und Nachklänge der ältesten exegetisch-polemischen Homilieen," in *Philotesia: Paul Kleinert zum LXX Geburtstag* (Berlin: Trowitzsch & Sohn, 1907), 1–37; Andreas Lindemann, *Paulus in ältesten Christentum: Das Bild des Apostels und die Rezeption der paulinischen Theologie in der frühchristlichen Literatur bis Marcion* (BHT 58; Tübingen: Mohr Siebeck, 1979), 390–92.

14. E.g., 1 Cor 6:9-10; 10:1-12; 2 Thess 1:9 (see *Haer.* 4.27.3-28.1). Rolf Noormann, *Irenäus als Paulusinterpret: Zur Rezeption und Wirkung der paulinischen und deuteropaulinischen Briefe im Werk des Irenäus von Lyon* (WUNT 2 Reihe 66; Tübingen: Mohr Siebeck, 1994), 387, rightly notes that proof-texts from other New Testament writings also appear in traditional material from the "Presbyter" in this section, but he suggests that there is a concentration of Pauline references that is likely due to Marcionite opponents as targets. He could be right, though Marcionites are not specified and other opponents could have been included.

15. *Haer.* 4.16.1-5; cf. Osborn, *Irenaeus*, 235–36; Noormann, *Irenäus als Paulusinterpret*, 387–426. Noormann provides extensive evidence of how texts from the Pauline corpus were used by Irenaeus in mapping out these three stages. For instance (395–96), Irenaeus calls

cites numerous Old Testament and New Testament passages to prove that there is only one true God and that this God is creator of heaven and earth, including several from the Pauline corpus.[16] Ephesians 4:6 is one of the more frequent of these, perhaps in part due to its succinct formulation: "One God and Father of all, who is over all, through all and in all."[17] But other reasons may be inferred from evidence that I discuss later. For Ephesians also contained testimony to two motifs that were central to Irenaeus's theological program: "recapitulation" (1:10) and divine "economy" (3:9). Furthermore, Ephesians was among pieces of hotly contested territory in Irenaeus's battle with his adversaries.

Irenaeus was adamant about the one God as creator, but he was also heir to Christian speculation, developed from Hellenistic Jewish traditions, about the instrumentality of divine Reason/Word and Wisdom, whom he identifies with preexistent Son and Holy Spirit, respectively.[18] Now he would probably object to the use of the term "instrumentality" in this connection, since he insists that, contrary to the teachings of some opponents, the Father was not in need of any assistance (*ministerio*) in the fashioning of created things and the economy pertaining to human affairs.[19] To be sure, God "commanded and they were created; he spoke and they came into being,"[20] but then Irenaeus asks, "*Whom* did he command? It was the Word," since Ps 32 also proclaims, "By the Word of the Lord the heavens were established, and by the Spirit (breath) of his mouth is all their power."[21] Though surely not intending to step outside the authority of Pauline tradition and its articulations of Wisdom Christology, Irenaeus does nevertheless go beyond the latter when he imagines Word and Wisdom, or Son/Christ and

---

the laws instituted by Moses after the people turned to worship a golden calf the "yoke of slavery" (Gal 5:1; *Haer.* 4.15.1). Here I am focusing on creator and creation; there is neither space nor need to expand on all dimensions of Irenaeus's argument for monotheism.

16. E.g., *Haer.* 3.6.5 (Gal 4:8-9; 2 Thess 2:4; and 1 Cor 8:4-6, against false gods); *Haer.* 4.33.3; 4.33.7 (1 Cor 8:6); see Noormann, *Irenäus als Paulusinterpret*, 118–21; and Norris, "Irenaeus' Use of Paul," 84–85, who also notes Irenaeus's "primary appeal … to texts in which Paul deprecates pagan polytheism."

17. See *Haer.* 2.2.6; 4.20.2; 4.32.1; 5.17.4; 5.18.2. On Eph 4:6 as a favorite Irenaean prooftext for monotheism, cf. Noormann, *Irenäus als Paulusinterpret*, 385; Ben C. Blackwell, "Paul and Irenaeus," in *Paul and the Second Century*, ed. Michael F. Bird and Joseph R. Dodson (LNTS 412; London: T&T Clark, 2011), 199.

18. E.g., *Haer.* 2.30.9; 4.7.4; 4.20.1-4.

19. *Haer.* 4.7.4; I use the technical term "economy" here to translate *dispositio*, which probably renders οἰκονομία from the Greek original; cf. the translation and suggested retroversion in Adelin Rousseau and Louis Doutreleau (eds.), *Irénée de Lyon, Contre les hérésies* (SC; Paris: Éditions du Cerf, 1952–82), vol. 100, 465. And see my discussion below of the significance of οἰκονομία for the analysis in this study.

20. *Haer.* 3.8.3; see Pss 32:9 and 148:5.

21. Ps 32:6; *Haer.* 3.8.3.

Spirit, as God's "hands" fashioning the cosmos and the human being.[22] For him this was presumably an image capable of linking to the language of agency used of Wisdom and Word in scriptures (and specifically of Christ in Pauline scripture!), while at the same time underscoring God's own direct and intimate responsibility for creation and avoiding the slightest whiff of polytheistic heresy. Since to refer to the Word/Son/Christ as one of God's hands was for Irenaeus to refer to nothing less than God himself, he can sometimes speak simply of the Word as Creator.[23] It is important to keep all this in mind amid the dust of Irenaeus's battle against opponents like Valentinians, because it may help avoid a misleadingly stark dichotomizing of positions.

For though their speculations may genuinely have seemed to Irenaeus little more than disguised polytheism, Valentinians also insisted on the oneness of God. Irenaeus knows very well that they *say* this; he just cannot believe them: "For as numerous as the sects (*haereses*) are, nearly all of them say God is one, but then they change him through bad doctrine, being ungrateful to the one who made them, just like the Gentiles do through idolatry" (*Haer.* 1.22.1). In the case of certain Valentinians, at least, Irenaeus had had opportunity to hear in person their claims to monotheism. He recalls a "lengthy discussion/debate" (*multam quaestionem*) with certain of the opponents on matters pertaining to their teaching (*Haer.* 2.17.9). He says that they preach to throngs of church members to win over the less sophisticated (*simpliciores*),

> imitating our approach (*nostrum tractatum*) so that (the crowds) might listen more often. They complain that, even though they hold views like ours we keep ourselves away from fellowship with them, and that though they say the same things and hold the same teaching (*doctrinam*), we call them "sectarians" (*haereticos*).[24]

---

22. *Haer.* 4.Preface.4; 4.20.1; 5.1.3; 5.6.1; 5.28.4; *Epid.* 33. The image is probably borrowed from Theophilus of Antioch (*Autol.* 2.18); on this language in Irenaeus, cf. Osborn, *Irenaeus*, 91–93; Minns, *Irenaeus*, 64–66.

23. E.g., *Haer.* 1.15.5: "the Word of God, the Founder (Κτίστης), and Framer (Δημιουργός), and Maker (Ποιητής) of all things"; 3.22.3: "This is also why Adam himself is termed by Paul 'the figure of Him that was to come' (Rom 5.14). Because the Word, the Maker (*fabricator*) of all things, had formed in him in advance the future economy (*dispositio*) of the humanity of the Son of God"; 5.12.6: "the Fashioner (*fabricator*) of all things, the Word of God, who also from the beginning formed the human"; 5.18.3: "For the Maker (*factor*) of the world is truly the Word of God; and this is our Lord, who in the last times was made a human … The Word of God governs and arranges all things. Because of this he came <visibly> to his own (John 1.14), and was made flesh and hung on a tree (Acts 5.30, etc.), so that all things might be summed up (*recapituletur*) in himself (Eph 1.10)"; 5.24.4: "The Word of God, the Maker (*artifex*) of all things "

24. *Haer* 3.15.2; cf. 2.28.4: "You seem to state with solemnity that you believe in God."

Such people outwardly look like sheep, since "their speech externally seems to be like us because they are saying the same things we say, but inwardly they are really wolves" (*Haer.* 3.16.8). These statements from Irenaeus are well known in scholarship, but in my view some implications of these opponents' claims to shared discourse and even common presuppositions have not been adequately appreciated.

First of all, there is the issue of responsibility for creation. It is true that several of the mythic accounts that Irenaeus summarizes in Book 1 refer to lower entities as creators. But generalizing references to this fact have frequently led to unfortunate exaggerations and mischaracterizations that do not stray much further than simply echoing *Irenaeus's* perspective. For example, in a book that provides genuinely helpful insights on almost every page, Denis Minns notes that Irenaeus had his hands full organizing an attack on a diverse assortment of opponents that reminded him of slithering snakes (*Haer.* 3.2.3). "Irenaeus overcame this difficulty," says Minns, "by choosing one doctrine that most of the major heresies he opposed did have in common: the complete disjunction between the creator God of the Old Testament and the God revealed by Jesus."[25] Now Minns perhaps means only to say that Irenaeus wished his readers to see it this way,[26] but this is not correct. To put it more radically: for most of Irenaeus's opponents, the interpretations they offered made sense precisely because what they proposed was *not* a complete disjunction between the creator God of the Old Testament and the God revealed by Jesus. What do I mean?

I begin with Valentinians,[27] since apparently for Irenaeus they constituted an obvious threat within the gates and were evidently his primary target.[28] We may

---

25. Minns, *Irenaeus*, 29.

26. Later Minns (*Irenaeus*, 34) observes that Irenaeus actually knew that at least Marcion and Valentinians differed on this point, with only Marcion insisting that there was absolutely no relation between the two Gods while Valentinians held that the supreme deity and the creator, "although vastly separated from one another, belong in the same chain of being." But then Minns's earlier general statement seems unnecessarily confusing.

27. Here I underscore my earlier acknowledgment that "Valentinian" has become a somewhat contested label, since they evidently did not constitute a tightly organized sect. They understood themselves to be "Christians," and there was obvious diversity in details and structures of their mythic speculations and interpretations of Christian tradition.

28. E.g., in *Haer.* 4.Preface.2, Irenaeus says that writers prior to him had not been able to refute the followers of Valentinus because they had not known about the Valentinians' system of teachings (*regula*). He says he has now supplied that in Book 1 and has shown that "their doctrine is a recapitulation of all the sects (*haereticorum*)." The *regula* of the Valentinians, he says, is "more blasphemous than all, since they claim that the Maker and Creator (*factorem et fabricatorem*), whom we have shown to be the one God, was emitted due to failing or defect" (4.Preface.3). For an important analysis of some of Irenaeus's aims in this work, and particularly on the foregrounding of Valentinians, see Geoffrey S. Smith, *Guilt by Association: Heresy Catalogues in Early Christianity* (Oxford: Oxford University Press, 2014).

stipulate at the outset what has long been common knowledge in research on Valentinian tradition: Graeco-Roman philosophy, and especially Platonism, played a decisive role in shaping Valentinian reflection on the teachings of Jesus and the apostles and the relation of Christian revelation to Jewish scriptures. Irenaeus is not uninformed or uninterested in some of the philosophical currents of his day,[29] but in reading and listening to Valentinian Christians develop expanded maps of the invisible realm of divine perfection (Pleroma) he could not help hearing something that had already slid the slope into polytheistic culture.[30]

However, for Valentinians their mythic portrait of eternal divine attributes, the "Aeons," was an adaptation of truths from Platonic-Pythagorean ontology to the truths in the heritage of biblical Wisdom tradition. Irenaeus tells us that his Valentinian opponents interpreted various passages from scripture as references to the realm of the Aeons. Paul had very clearly mentioned the Aeons, they pointed out,[31] and was speaking of the Totality of Aeons when he called the Savior "All/Everything" (πάντα; Col 3:11), and when he said that "All are unto him and from him are All" (Rom 11:36), or that "in him dwells the whole (πᾶν) Pleroma of divinity" (Col 2:9), or that "All (τὰ πάντα) are summed up in Christ" (Eph 1:10).[32] To follow the connections here, one has to recall that earlier Irenaeus had said that an important moment in their story of the Aeons was the unified action that resulted in the preexistent Jesus, who was the distillation of the most beautiful and most splendid qualities contributed by each of the Aeons—in other words, the perfect representation of the divine. This "most perfect beauty and star (ἄστρον)

---

29. E.g., *Haer.* 3.25.5, in a context referring to both Marcionites and Valentinians: "Plato is shown to be more pious (*religiosior*) than these people, since he confessed the same God to be both just and good, possessing power over all things, carrying out judgment himself" (which Irenaeus supports then with a quotation from *Leg.* 4.715e), "showing that the Maker and Creator is good" (then quoting *Tim.* 29e). Irenaeus insists that therefore Plato was saying that "the beginning and cause of the creation of the world was the goodness (*bonitatem*) of God, but not ignorance nor Aeons who go astray, nor the fruit of a failing, nor a Mother wailing and weeping, nor another God or Father." Osborn (*Irenaeus*, 15) describes Irenaeus himself as displaying "a form of horizontal Platonism" that was likely a pattern of thought of which he was not even conscious (16–17). Osborn (as have other scholars) discusses Irenaeus's indebtedness also to such influences as Xenophanes, Xenocrates, and Stoicism (e.g., 32–38).

30. Irenaeus says that because they do not join step with the authority of the church, all the sectarians are outside the realm of the Spirit (*Haer.* 3.24.1); therefore they are full of instability since "they are not founded upon the Rock, but on sand that contains within itself many stones. And because of this they invent many gods" (*Haer.* 3.24.2).

31. *Haer.* 1.3.1: "Paul often quite openly named these Aeons, they say, and even preserved their order (τὴν τάξιν αὐτῶν) when he said: 'unto all the generations of the Aeon of the Aeons' (Eph 3.21); but (they say that) we also, when we say at the Eucharist, 'unto the Aeons of the Aeons,' are signifying those Aeons."

32. Irenaeus recounts this list in *Haer.* 1.3.4.

of the Pleroma," its "perfect fruit," was called by various names: Jesus, Savior, Christ, Logos, and τὰ Πάντα, "All/Everything" (*Haer.* 1.2.6).

Now a little later in Irenaeus's report we learn that Valentinians ascribed to this Savior responsibility for the creation of the world. In modern summaries of Valentinian myth, the more conventional claim is that these people completely distinguished the creator from the true God, assigning responsibility for creation not to God, but to a lower Demiurge. However, the reality is far more nuanced according to the surviving evidence for various forms of Valentinian tradition, including from Irenaeus's own accounts. It is of course correct that most of these sources do include a lower figure called Δημιουργός, "Fashioner, Demiurge."[33] But ultimate responsibility for the creation of the world is actually not invested in this lower figure, who typically is only a puppet whose strings are being pulled by divine powers above. Even the specific label "Demiurge" is sometimes also applied to higher levels of divinity. Clement of Alexandria's *Excerpts of Theodotus* is a compilation containing quotations not only from the Valentinian teacher Theodotus but also from other sources,[34] including one section (*Exc.* 43.2-65.2) with teaching closely resembling doctrines reported in Irenaeus (*Haer.* 1.4.5-1.7.1). Though both accounts are a bit opaque at points, the elements relevant to our current inquiry are clear. We find essentially the same "Savior/Jesus/Christ" figure whom I mentioned above, and again identified with the Pauline Christ: "For by/ in him all things were created, visible and invisible, thrones, lordships, kingdoms, divinities, services."[35] This creative agency is explained as the Savior working through Wisdom to bring forms of solid matter into being. The *Excerpts* passage then states:

> The Savior therefore became the first universal Demiurge, while "Wisdom," the second (Demiurge), "builds a house for herself and has set up seven pillars" (Prov 9:1 LXX). And first of all she put forth a God who was an image of the

---

33. E.g., Irenaeus, *Haer.* 1.5.1.

34. Otto Stählin, Ludwig Früchtel, and Ursula Treu (eds.), *Clemens Alexandrinus: Dritter Band*, 2nd ed. (GCS 17; Berlin: Akademie-Verlag, 1970), 105–33; Robert Pierce Casey, *The Excerpta ex Theodoto of Clement of Alexandria* (SD 1; London: Christophers, 1934); and see, e.g., Einar Thomassen, *The Spiritual Seed: The Church of the "Valentinians"* (NHMS 60; Leiden: Brill, 2006), 29–38; Elaine Pagels, "Conflicting Versions of Valentinian Eschatology: Irenaeus' Treatise vs. The Excerpts of Theodotus," *HTR* 67 (1974), 35–53.

35. *Exc.* 43.3: πάντα γὰρ ἐν αὐτῷ ἐκτίσθη τὰ ὁρατὰ καὶ τὰ ἀόρατα, θρόνοι, κυριότητες, βασιλεῖαι, θεότητες, λειτουργίαι. Almost the same adaptation and application of Col 1:16 by Valentinians to the Savior is cited in Irenaeus, *Haer.* 1.4.5: "the Paraclete, i.e., the Savior, to whom the Father has granted all power (cf. Matt 11:27; Luke 10:22) and placed all things under his authority, and the Aeons likewise (i.e., granted these to the Savior), so that 'by/ in him all things were created, visible and invisible, thrones, divinities, lordships.'" Cf. Fantino, *La théologie d'Irénée*, 174–75, who rightly observes that *Exc.* 43.2-3 confirms the creation is effected by Christ in conformity with the design of the Father.

Father, through whom she made the heaven and the earth, that is, "heavenly things and earthly things" (Phil 2:10), things on the right and things on the left.³⁶

In the parallel passage in Irenaeus, the noun δημιουργός is not used of the Savior here, but the verb δημιουργεῖν is: "And therefore (the Valentinians) say that the Savior had virtually performed the creating (δυνάμει ... δεδημιουργηκέναι)" (*Haer.* 1.4.5).³⁷

With some variation in details, Valentinian sources most definitely trace the actual responsibility for creation to divine realms higher than the lowest demiurgical actor.³⁸ In commenting on John 1:3, the Valentinian Heracleon understood the words "All things were made through Him" to mean that "the one who supplied the Demiurge with the cause (τὴν αἰτίαν) for the origin of the world, the Word, was not the one 'from whom' (ἀφ οὗ) nor 'by whom' (ὑφ' οὗ), but rather the one '*through* whom' (δι' οὗ)."³⁹ In commenting on Jesus's words about true worship in John 4:23, Heracleon says that those who had previously worshipped in the flesh the one who is not the Father (i.e., the Jewish god) "worshipped the

---

36. *Exc.* 46.2-47.1: Πρῶτος μὲν οὖν δημιουργὸς ὁ Σωτὴρ γίνεται καθολικός, "ἡ δὲ Σοφία" δευτέρα "οἰκοδομεῖ οἶκον ἑαυτῇ καὶ ὑπήρεισεν στύλους ἑπτά." καὶ πρῶτον πάντων προβάλλεται εἰκόνα τοῦ Πατρὸς θεόν, δι' οὗ ἐποίησεν τὸν οὐρανὸν καὶ τὴν γῆν, τουτέστι "τὰ οὐράνια καὶ τὰ ἐπίγεια," τὰ δεξιὰ καὶ τὰ ἀριστερά.

37. The same thought is evidently expressed in the Nag Hammadi text to which modern scholars have given the title *A Valentinian Exposition* (NHC XI,3). In spite of lacunae in the section 35,10-36,38, one can see that Jesus is described as producing "a creation" (κτίσις) giving form to the "seeds of Wisdom," while Wisdom worked with him in this (35,12-17). The result is a "fullness"/"perfection" (πλήρωμα) of aeons, which is modeled after the uncreated "pattern" (τύπος) of the Perfection of the Father. The verb δημιουργεῖν is used for Jesus's creative activity (35,31). Behind this process is Providence (πρόνοια), helping to produce "shadows and images" of supernal realities that first existed, that exist, and that shall be (36,10-15). "This," the text says, "is the arrangement (οἰκονομία) pertaining to trusting (πιστεύειν) in Jesus" (36,15-17).

38. See Einar Thomassen, "The Platonic and Gnostic 'Demiurge,'" in *Apocryphon Severini: Studies in Ancient Manichaeism and Gnosticism Presented to Soren Giversen*, ed. Per Bilde et al. (Aarhus: Aarhus University Press, 1993), 226–44, for a discussion of the application of demiurgical responsibility to figures such as the Savior and Wisdom; Fantino, *La théologie d'Irénée*, 172–73; see already the several levels outlined in the index under Δημιουργός in François-M.-M. Sagnard, *La gnose valentinienne et le témoignage de Saint Irénée* (Études de philosophie médiévale 36; Paris: Libraire philosophique J. Vrin, 1947), 636; and cf. the analysis by Antonio Orbe, "San Ireneo y la creacion de la materia," *Gregorianum* 59 (1978), 103–8, regarding the role of the Savior as Demiurge, and the tracing of ultimate responsibility: the leap from the ideal existence to realization in the creation comes, in the final instance, from the power and will of the Father (106).

39. Heracleon, Frag. 1 (*apud* Origen, *Comm. in Jo.* 2.14).

creation and not the true Creator (τῷ κατ' ἀλήθειαν κτίστῃ; Cf. Rom 1.25), who is Christ."[40]

The untitled writing in Nag Hammadi Codex I conventionally called the *Tripartite Tractate*[41] is the largest original Valentinian text known to us, and an important further illustration of points I am making here. The author is aware of some Pauline themes and incorporates them in places,[42] though Paul is never mentioned by name in the writing and there are (as is the case with all the Valentinian sources) other influences represented as well. However, the principal feature I wish to underscore is that in spite of the fact that the text does have an important role for a lower Demiurge,[43] this Demiurge is, as in the other sources discussed above, only an instrument of a higher creative actor, the Logos. In the *Tripartite Tractate* the Logos has much the same role that Sophia, "Wisdom," has in other Valentinian sources. There is not space here to summarize fully the tractate's myth or everything about the role of this Logos. In brief, in this story the Logos is the last of the aeons to appear, but out of intense love this aeon tries to grasp what cannot by grasped by reason or speech (Logos), namely, the incomprehensible Father (*Tri. Trac.* 76,5-77,36). Indeed, no single eternal aspect of the divine could comprehend the ineffable Father. The Logos's departure from simple participation in unified praise is the initiative that transitions from eternal, unchanging stability

---

40. Heracleon, Frag. 22 (*apud* Origen, *Comm. in Jo.* 4.23).

41. See the relevant sections in: Harold W. Attridge (ed.), *Nag Hammadi Codex I (The Jung Codex)*, 2 vols (NHS 22–23; Leiden: Brill, 1985); and in Einar Thomassen and Louis Painchaud (eds.), *Le traité tripartite (NH I, 5)* (BCNH:T 19; Québec: Les presses de l'Université Laval, 1989); for a brief introduction by Thomassen and English translation by Marvin Meyer, see Marvin Meyer and James M. Robinson (eds.), *The Nag Hammadi Scriptures: The Revised and Updated Translation of Sacred Gnostic Texts* (New York: HarperOne, 2008), 57–101.

42. E.g., the reference in *Tri. Trac.* 58,30-33 to the "Ekklesia of many people that existed before the Aeons, which is properly called the 'Aeons of the Aeons,'" is reminiscent of the passage in Irenaeus, *Haer.* 1.3.1, that I mentioned earlier where this language interprets Eph 3:21; the Savior as head of the body (the spiritual race) in *Tri. Trac.* 118,32-35 (cf. Col 1:18; Eph 1:22-23); the reference in *Tri. Trac.* 108,5-12 to "death reigning" after Adam's transgression bears the influence of Rom 5:12-14; 6:9 and so on; in *Tri. Trac.* 132,23-28 we find a formula combining and adapting Gal 3:28 and Col 3:11: "The place where there is not male and female, nor is there slave and free, nor is there circumcision or uncircumcision, nor is there angel, nor is there human, but rather All is in All, Christ."

43. The demiurgical figure is an Archon placed over the material realm *Tri. Trac.* 100,19-21, who is "also called 'father' and 'god' and 'maker' (ⲣⲉϥⲧⲁⲙⲓⲟ) and 'king' and 'judge' and 'place' and 'dwelling' and 'law'" (*Tri. Trac.* 100,28-29). The Coptic ⲣⲉϥⲧⲁⲙⲓⲟ here might not translate δημιουργός, but rather, e.g., ποιητής; so Thomassen and Painchaud, *Le traité tripartite*, 394. But the actual Greek term ⲇⲏⲙⲓⲟⲩⲣⲅⲟⲥ (δημιουργός) is used of this creator later in 104,35-105,1 (though here with the orthographic variant ⲧⲙⲓⲟⲩⲣⲅⲟⲥ) and 105,18.

to movement and change, and eventually the material realm of the cosmos.⁴⁴ The Logos eventually uses the Demiurge "like a hand" (100,31-32) in the beautifying and fashioning of things in the cosmos, and uses him "like a mouth" (100,34-35) to speak what will appear as prophecies in scripture. So although there is a lower Demiurge in this text, the ultimate responsibility for creation does not reside in that figure but rather in the divine Logos who employs him as instrument.

But I suggest we go even further: the true responsibility actually transcends even the Logos and is located in the Father's will. The author of this tractate is adamant that the actions of the Logos are not to be criticized:

> It was not without the will of the Father that the Logos was begotten, which is to say that it was not without it that (the Logos) would go forth … Therefore it is inappropriate to blame (κατηγορεῖν) the movement that is the Logos; rather, it is appropriate that we say about the movement of the Logos that it is a cause of an economy (οἰκονομία) destined to come into being.⁴⁵

Thus, *Tripartite Tractate* stresses that everything, including creation, happened in accordance with the will of the one true God, the ineffable Father.

There is a paradoxical tension in Valentinian myth, and in some related traditions, which was seemingly at the core of their general theological vision, and specifically their theodicy. The myth in the *Tripartite Tractate* and Valentinian myths known to Irenaeus convey the message that precisely the very highest values, love for and knowledge of God (i.e., represented in the aspirations of Sophia or Logos), somehow eventuate in imperfection and therefore evil.⁴⁶

In this section I have been arguing that the targets of Irenaeus's criticism, who were evidently the largest burr under his saddle, the Valentinians, assigned ultimate responsibility for creation to the one true God. For them there was not at all a "complete disjunction between the creator God of the Old Testament and the God revealed by Jesus," to recall the formulation from Denis Minns. They did *distinguish* between the Old Testament creator God and the highest divinity, but they imagined everything in control of the most transcendent deity. For certain Valentinians this chain of responsibility even meant that the term "Demiurge" itself could be applied to divine figures higher than the Old Testament creator God.⁴⁷

---

44. The Platonic elements in this are clear; e.g., see Williams, *The Immovable Race: A Gnostic Designation and the Theme of Stability in Late Antiquity* (NHS 29; Leiden: Brill, 1985), 115–21.

45. *Tri. Trac.* 76,24-27 and 77,6-11. I will return below to the significant term οἰκονομία in this writing and in others.

46. I have elaborated on this dynamic in Williams, "Negative Theologies and Demiurgical Myths in Late Antiquity," in *Gnosticism and Later Platonism*, ed. John D. Turner and Ruth Majercik (SBLSymS 12; Atlanta: Society of Biblical Literature, 2000), 287–90.

47. Scholarship on Irenaeus has very often remained content with reporting only his viewpoint or rhetoric in the conflict with his opponents; e.g., Michael Slusser, "The Heart of Irenaeus's Theology," in *Irenaeus: Life, Scripture, Legacy*, ed. Paul Foster and Sara Parvis

A similar situation applies to certain other traditions that Irenaeus characterizes in Book 1 of *Against Heresies*. He summarizes material (in *Haer.* 1.29-30) that has attracted special attention from scholars for the past century and that in the past few decades has occasioned particularly lively debate. A copy of the *Apocryphon (or Secret Book) of John* was discovered toward the end of the nineteenth century, and three other copies turned up among the Nag Hammadi manuscripts found in 1945.[48] The theogonic myth in the first portion of this writing bears resemblance to the myth Irenaeus records (in *Haer.* 1.29). There are also certain similarities between the *Apocryphon of John* and part of the content in *Against Heresies* 1.30, yet there are also very significant differences. It has been argued by Tuomas Rasimus that the tradition in 1.30 represents a distinct and actually older strand to which *Apocryphon of John* was only secondarily related.[49] According to Rasimus, original works more closely related to the myth in *Against Heresies* 1.30 would include the *Hypostasis of the Archons* (NHC II,4), *On the Origin of the World* (NHC II,5),

---

(Minneapolis: Fortress, 2012), 137, characterizing Irenaeus's polemic: "The only way that his opponents can conceive of a transcendent god is by isolating him so completely from the created world that he is barred from creating it, caring for it, or communicating with rational creatures." From my discussion above one can see that this obscures actual positions of Irenaeus's opponents. Moreover, I would argue that the result is also an inadequate appreciation for Irenaeus's own position and what shapes his rhetoric. Who can understand the significance of the conflict if the opposition remains a caricatured cutout?

48. A copy of *Ap. John* constitutes the second tractate in Berlin Codex 8502 (abbreviated BG for *Berolinensis gnosticus*), whose discovery was first announced in 1896, though various factors prevented publication until after the Second World War. The other three copies are the first tractates in Nag Hammadi Codices (NHC) II, III, and IV. These four manuscripts fall into two major groups consisting of a shorter version (BG and NHC III) and a longer version (NHC II and IV) of *Ap. John*. For a synopsis of the Coptic texts with English translation, see Michael Waldstein and Frederik Wisse (eds.), *The Apocryphon of John: Synopsis of Nag Hammadi Codices II,1; III,1; and IV,1 with BG 8502,2* (NHS 33; Leiden: Brill, 1995).

49. See Tuomas Rasimus, *Paradise Reconsidered in Gnostic Mythmaking: Rethinking Sethianism in Light of the Ophite Evidence* (NHMS 68; Leiden: Brill, 2009). It has long been recognized that the mythology reported in *Haer.* 1.30 is different in detail from that in 1.29, and that it matches elements in materials that other heresiologists also described and called "Ophite." Rasimus contributes a new systematic analysis that charts correlations of this mythology with several of the Nag Hammadi tractates. The "Ophite" evidence overlaps with the evidence for what many scholars today call "Sethians" or "Gnostics" (in the particular sense of a specific sect). Rasimus contends that a proper analysis of the "Ophite" material is essential to understanding "Sethianism," and he proposes that these overlapping sets of evidence should be treated as a single "Classic Gnostic" corpus, but one that manifests distinct stages of development. He suggests that the "Ophite" type of mythology seems to be older than the other layers, and that it "seems to have developed out of a Platonic reading of Genesis through Christian lenses" (284).

Eugnostos the Blessed (NHC III,3; V,1), and the *Sophia of Jesus Christ* (NHC III,4; BG 8502,3).[50] Rasimus has justifiably called for revisiting the distinctive content in *Against Heresies* 1.30 with renewed and more systematic attention to its potential significance, especially for understanding some related sources that have suffered relative neglect in the shadow of research more concentrated on texts classified according to a typological model for "Sethian Gnosticism." Rasimus's project is of interest for this current chapter not only because it is focused on a significant section in Irenaeus's first volume against opposing views on creator and creation. Rasimus also entertains the possibility that this "Ophite" mythologizing may have interacted very early with Pauline tradition, and especially themes found in 1 Corinthians.[51]

Whatever one's judgment about specifics in Rasimus's thesis, his arguments do shine a new spotlight on *Against Heresies* 1.30 and invite us to consider its significance within the context of Irenaeus's debate with opponents over creation and the responsibility for it. Although in this myth there is a lower and negatively portrayed creator figure (given the name Ialdabaoth), the actual dynamic that leads to the created world begins from above, not from this lower creator. The most transcendent entities are the Father or First Human, his Son (Second Human) produced from the Father's thought, and a Holy Spirit, and beneath the Spirit the separated elements: water, darkness, abyss, and chaos (1.30.1). This last is obviously an interpretation of Gen 1:2, and what follows can be understood as a philosophical-mythological account of divine Wisdom's creative activity. In this myth, the Father and Son have intercourse with the Mother, the Holy Spirit (called here also "Mother of the Living"),[52] and a third male, Christ, is begotten. But the divine Mother cannot contain all the light received from this union, so some of the light or power "boiled over (*superebullientem*) on the left" (1.30.2). This light or power is Wisdom (1.30.3), and her descent into the realm of matter is portrayed

---

50. Rasimus, *Paradise Reconsidered*, 3. I have mentioned above only the principal manuscripts for each, and have not listed the other evidence that Rasimus analyzes (other patristic texts; amulet).

51. E.g., see Rasimus, *Paradise Reconsidered*, chapters 2 and 3 et passim. Rasimus is not at all dogmatic on the nature of the relationships, which he considers at different stages. He hypothesizes that Ophite myth might have come to Corinth within Paul's lifetime, and might have represented a version of Adam-Christ speculation different from Paul's own in 1 Corinthians 15. "The Ophite Sophia speculations greatly resemble Jewish Wisdom traditions as found, for example, in *1 Enoch*, Wisd, Prov, and Philo … Clearly the Ophite authors were very familiar with such Wisdom speculations, as probably were Paul's Corinthian opponents" (157). Though the Ophite writers held views that Paul opposed, some of Paul's modifications to Jewish Wisdom speculations were accepted with additional modifications in Ophite texts: the enlargement of the concept of gnosis and the very concept of Wisdom Christology (157). Rasimus knows that some connections with Pauline tradition must belong to later stages, such as the comments in the prologue of *Hyp. Arch.* (see below).

52. Of course, this alludes to Gen 3:20 and the name "Eve."

more as a kind of gravitational inevitability than as a mistake.[53] Yet what Wisdom does is to introduce motion into the previously motionless material elements, an apparent interpretation of the moving Spirit of God in Gen 1:2 and also of the Platonic motif of the "vitalizing world soul in the cosmos."[54] The material elements rush toward the light in Wisdom, forming around her a body that could have entirely absorbed her were she not in possession of the power in light. Enabled by that light, Wisdom ascends on high and spreads herself out, forming the visible heavens. At first Wisdom remains beneath the heavens, but then desiring the light above she casts off her body, the latter left behind as her offspring, the lower creator Ialdabaoth (1.30.3). These elements of the myth clearly constitute an interpretation of the first statements of Genesis, incorporating into a Platonizing frame Wisdom's role in the creation of heaven and earth, as well as the disposition of light.

Thus the creation of the visible cosmos really begins from the effort of divine Wisdom, the superabundant and overflowing light from the most transcendent realm. Wisdom comes to reside in the Eighth heaven, and her son Ialdabaoth and his own six offspring occupy the set of seven heavens below the Eighth. Irenaeus says that these people called the seven heavens "the Holy Hebdomad," identifying them as "the seven stars that they call the planets" (1.30.9). But then Ialdabaoth produces yet another offspring, Mind (Nous), who is serpentine in form (1.30.5). While Ialdabaoth is the Jewish God, this serpentine figure is the Devil who opposes him, since he produces his own (lower) Hebdomad of seven demons of the world (1.30.8). Though we do not find in *Against Heresies* an *explicit* reference to the control of the entire creation process by the highest deity, we have seen divine responsibility conveyed in the overflowing of light and then Wisdom's creation of the visible heaven, and the rest of the story overall certainly conveys the working of providence at crucial points. It is Wisdom who secretly provides the model for the creation of the first human by the powers of the upper Hebdomad (1.30.6). The snake is used as a tool by Wisdom to instruct Adam and Eve about the true God (1.30.7). It is by Wisdom's providence (*providentia*)[55] that Seth and Norea are born (1.30.9). Though Ialdabaoth and his sons speak through the prophets in Jewish

---

53. I borrow the gravity metaphor from the apt summary by John D. Turner, *Sethian Gnosticism and the Platonic Tradition* (BCNH:E 6; Québec: Les presses de l'Université Laval, 2001), 203: "The Spirit emits (by overflow 'on the left') the androgynous Sophia-Prunicos, who by gravity and without any trace of moral culpability descends and agitates the waters below, taking on a material body. When she is empowered from above to escape this body and ascend to the height, her abandoned body fathers the Archon Yaldabaoth."

54. Rasimus, *Paradise Reconsidered*, 133.

55. Origen says that Sophia's providence (σοφίας πρόνοια) was a feature depicted in the famously obscure Ophite diagram (*Cels.* 6.38). Rasimus, *Paradise Reconsidered*, 18, thinks that aspects of the diagram might have corresponded to the notion in *Haer.* 1.30 of the Holy Spirit giving birth to Sophia and her providence. In *Orig. World.* 113,5-10, Wisdom's providence (πρόνοια) is responsible for the creation of Adam; cf. Rasimus, *Paradise Reconsidered*, 140.

scripture, Wisdom herself also inspires some of those prophecies in order to reveal truth to humanity about the First Human and the Christ (1.30.11).[56]

The only explicit quotation of a Pauline text in Irenaeus's account of this tradition occurs in *Against Heresies* 1.30.13, but it is a very important one. Just before, in 1.30.12, we are told that these opponents teach that the transcendent Christ united with Wisdom and then descended into Jesus. The latter was "purer, wiser, and more righteous" than other men, because though he had been begotten "by the action of God (*per operationem Dei*; i.e., Ialdabaoth)," this begetting was through the Virgin. After this union of Christ/Wisdom with Jesus he began to work miracles, proclaim the unknown Father,[57] and identify himself as "Son of Man." Ialdabaoth and his powers are angered by this and bring about Jesus's crucifixion, though not before Christ/Sophia departs from him and ascends to the incorruptible Aeon. Yet Christ provides Jesus with "a certain power" that enables Jesus to rise from the dead with a psychic and pneumatic body, not a fleshly one. Seeing him risen from the dead, his disciples "did not recognize him"—that is, his actual nature—and thought he had a worldly body, not knowing that "flesh and blood do not obtain (*apprehendunt*) the kingdom of God."[58] This appeal to 1 Cor 15:50 to prove the error of testimony by disciples about a "worldly" (i.e., presumably fleshly) resurrection body reveals the high esteem in which these "Ophites" must have held Pauline authority in general. It might be a powerful hint that they made broader claims to Paul's authority for other aspects of their mythology.[59]

Just such evidence of more encompassing appeal to Paul is found in the *Hypostasis of the Archons*,[60] one of the texts that Rasimus groups with *Against*

---

56. Cf. Rasimus, *Paradise Reconsidered*, 133–34.

57. Irenaeus does not specify here that these particular people cited Matt 11:27/Luke 10:22 in this regard. But he does say in *Haer*. 1.20.3 that this passage is invoked by some opponents as a most important proof-text (cf. also 2.6.1; 4.6.1).

58. *Haer*. 1.30.13. In 5.9.1 Irenaeus quotes the passage from 1 Cor 15:50 and says that it is "brought forward by all the sectarians (*ab omnibus haereticis*) in their madness, and they try by means of it to prove that the thing molded (*plasmationem*) by God is not saved." This whole section of Book 5 (*Haer*. 5.9-13) is essentially an extended refutation of that interpretation. However, in spite of Irenaeus's observation that this passage was cited by "all the sectarians," it is interesting that the passage in *Haer*. 1.30.13 is the only place in the entire catalog of "sects" in Book 1, or anywhere else in the five volumes so far as I can see, where 1 Cor 15:50 is cited in recounting the teaching of a specific group.

59. Cf. Rasimus, *Paradise Reconsidered*, 163. In n.18, Rasimus cites *Haer*. 1.30.13 and its reference to the use of 1 Cor 15:50, though he remains cautious about how much we may infer about dependence on 1 Corinthians 15 in their language about Adam in Ophite myth.

60. See especially Elaine Pagels, "Exegesis and Exposition of the Genesis Creation Accounts in Selected Texts from Nag Hammadi," in *Nag Hammadi, Gnosticism, and Early Christianity*, ed. Charles W. Hedrick and Robert Hodgson, Jr. (Peabody, MA: Hendrickson, 1986), 257–85.

Heresies 1.30 as "Ophite" material. The author announces at the outset that the writing will be an exposition on some Pauline references:

> Because of the real existence (ὑπόστασις) of the authorities, the great Apostle spoke to us by the Spirit of the Father of truth about the "authorities of darkness" (Col 1:13): "Our fight is not against flesh and blood, but against the authorities of the cosmos and the spiritual entities of wickedness" (Eph 6:12). I have sent these things because you asked about the real existence of the authorities.[61]

Elaine Pagels has argued that 1 Corinthians 15 lies behind several features of the creation account in *Hypostasis of the Archons*. Though not all of her suggested

---

61. *Hyp. Arch*. 86,20-27. It has sometimes been argued that this prologue is an entirely superficial element in a "non-Christian" text; e.g., Klaus Koschorke, "Paulus in den Nag-Hammadi-Texten: Ein Beitrag zur Geschichte der Paulusrezeption in frühen Christentum," *ZTK* 78 (1981), 200. Koschorke makes too neat a division between actual "Christian gnosis" and texts manifesting a merely secondary or peripheral Christianizing. One might find Pauline allusions in the latter, he avers, but it is only "trimming" (*Zutat*), and the example he gives is *Hyp. Arch*. and its opening quotation from "the Apostle." Koschorke argues that this is a document with a gnosis exclusively based on Jewish tradition. He is justified in finding Jewish tradition in *Hyp. Arch.*, but to call the Pauline framework mere "trimming" is too facile and ignores other elements within the text. Similarly, and with broader relevance for this study, Lindemann, *Paulus in ältesten Christentum*, 328–29, approaches *Hyp. Arch*. as a "non-Christian gnostic text" to which only a few secondary Christian allusions have been attached. The author of *Hyp. Arch*. does seem to have drawn on sources, but that is true of all sorts of early Christian writings, and judging whether the final product as a whole should be counted as "Christian" or not easily falls under the control of theological bias and hindsight determined by who eventually "won." In the second century much was still up in the air. Throughout Lindemann's learned and richly documented book, he tends too quickly to dismiss the influence of Pauline tradition in truly *shaping* aspects of "Gnostic" thought, as opposed to merely being a handy tool to support existing doctrine. For example, he asserts that "the Valentinians basically 'discovered' their doctrines in all the texts available to them," so that "there can be no question of a substantive 'Paulinism'" (302). The hermeneutical high-handedness that Lindemann implies is definitely to be found among Valentinian sources, but it is not absent from Irenaeus and many other writers. It becomes a matter of calculating "degrees" of what we judge to be arbitrariness versus impact of "genuine" Pauline themes. There are certainly such differences in degree, but Pauline themes may have been more of a formative element in the thought of some of Irenaeus's opponents than Lindemann's analysis admits. The unnecessary acrobatics into which Lindemann must often throw himself as a result of his approach are visible in his treatment of Marcion, where he wrestles with whether Marcion was more a "Paulinist" or a "gnostic" (esp. 387–90). It might be better simply to examine ways in which Marcion (and Valentinians and others, including Irenaeus) *understood and made use* of Pauline materials, without having always to decide whether a given "use" qualifies as "Paulinism."

instances of intertextuality are so convincing, the cumulative argument for Pauline language (among other scriptural allusions) is quite plausible.[62] The author not only frames the treatise as an explanation of Pauline terminology about "the authorities of the cosmos and the spiritual entities of wickedness," he/she also presents a creation account that involves lower creators while specifically asserting that the true God ultimately controls the creative process. The author assures the readers that "it was by the will of the Father of the All that they [i.e., Ialdabaoth and his offspring] came into being, after the pattern of all the things above" (96,11-13).

This announcement may come as a shock to some modern readers who know only generalizations about "a complete disjunction" in such sources between true God and Jewish creator, a complete absence of responsibility for creation on the part of the highest deity. This model and what we saw in Valentinian sources are unquestionably different in structure from Irenaeus's vision of Word/Christ and Wisdom/Spirit simply being God's extended "hands" fashioning world and humanity. Yet they all were imagining one true God, and creation in accordance with divine will.[63]

The case of Marcion is different. As far as one can discern given the limitations of the sources,[64] Marcion's myth did not involve a chain of emanations such as found in traditions discussed above. Certainly Irenaeus knows of no such feature but instead simply says that Marcion taught two Gods: the Father of Jesus "who is above the creator God" (*qui est super mundi fabricatorem Deum*; Haer. 1.27.2),

---

62. See her summary of potential instances in Pagels, "Exegesis and Exposition," 279–85; cf. Rasimus, *Paradise Reconsidered*, 166; and Bentley Layton (ed.), *Nag Hammadi Codex II,2-7*, 2 vols (NHS 20–21; Leiden: Brill, 1989), 222, on the Christian character of the text and that, among other scriptures, its author and users "accept the authority of Paul."

63. Divine providential control is also found in the *Apocryphon of John* as well as other texts with lower creators, as I have argued elsewhere; e.g., most recently, Williams, "A Life Full of Meaning and Purpose: Demiurgical Myths and Social Implications," in *Beyond the Gnostic Gospels: Studies Building on the Work of Elaine Pagels*, ed. Eduard Iricinschi et al. (STAC 82; Tübingen: Mohr Siebeck, 2014), 28–33. In this essay I have chosen to focus mainly on the "Ophite" tradition because I find plausible Rasimus's argument that the tradition in *Haer.* 1.30 represents an earlier stage than the versions of *Ap. John* known to us. It also provides a more extensive story than the brief, seemingly truncated myth in *Haer.* 1.29, and reveals a clearer example of engagement with Pauline tradition.

64. None of his own work has survived, and information about his views must be reconstructed largely from what is said by those who attacked him. Among various interpretations and general treatments, see Adolf von Harnack, *Marcion: The Gospel of the Alien God*, trans. John E. Steely and Lyle D. Bierma (Durham, NC: Labyrinth Press, 1990); Gerhard May, "Marcion in Contemporary Views: Results and Open Questions," *SecCent* 6 (1987–88), 129–51; Barbara Aland, "Marcion: Versuch einer neuen Interpretation," *ZTK* 70 (1973), 420–47; Heikki Räisänen, "Marcion," in *A Companion to Second-Century "Heretics*," ed. Antti Marjanen and Petri Luomanen (VCSup 76; Leiden: Brill, 2005); Sebastian Moll, *The Arch-heretic Marcion* (WUNT 250; Tübingen: Mohr Siebeck, 2010).

the creator being the God of Jewish scripture.⁶⁵ There appears to be no sign that Marcion had ever sought to explain the *origin* of this creator, and it is possible that he simply did not address the issue. Some scholars have suggested that his postulation of the good God who is "*above* the creator" and corruptible matter might allow for "the assumption that Marcion knows a comprehensive classification of being" comparable in basic structure of worldviews in some philosophy of the day or Valentinian myth, and so on.⁶⁶ It seems very plausible that Marcion did imagine something like a "spatial stacking"⁶⁷ of the invisible realm of the good God above the visible realm of the "God of this age/world."⁶⁸ But in any event, nothing

---

65. E.g., *Haer.* 2.1.4; 3.25.3; 4.33.2.

66. May, "Marcion in Contemporary Views," 145–46. Tertullian says Marcionites assert that "the creator is ignorant of any god above him (*creator quidem ignorans esse alium super se deum*)," and that the creator "used to declare with an oath that he was the only (God)" (*Marc.* 1.11.9; cf. 2.26.1). This sounds much like the parodies of passages such as Isa 45:5-6 found in the "vain claim" of Ialdabaoth in several sources (e.g., Irenaeus, *Haer.* 1.29.4; 1.30.6; *Ap. John* NHC II 13,8-9 par; and several other Nag Hammadi texts); see Nils A. Dahl, "The Arrogant Archon and the Lewd Sophia," in *The Rediscovery of Gnosticism: Proceedings of the International Conference on Gnosticism at Yale, New Haven, Connecticut, March 28–31, 1978; Vol. 2: Sethian Gnosticism*, ed. Bentley Layton (SHR 41; Leiden: Brill, 1981), 689–712; Rasimus, *Paradise Reconsidered*, 171–72. So it is tempting to imagine Marcion's general cosmological *structure*, at least, to have been similar to those underlying these other sources. Part of the problem is that we know that Marcionite theologies evolved significantly over time, the figure Apelles being a notable example; e.g., Eusebius, *Hist. eccl.* 5.13.2-7; Harnack, *Marcion*, 99–121. Therefore, it is not always possible to distinguish with certainty Marcion's own thinking from later adaptations.

67. May, "Marcion in Contemporary Views," 145. Barbara Aland, "Sünde und Erlösung bei Marcion und die Konsequenz für die sog. beiden Götter Marcions," in *Marcion und seine kirchengeschichtliche Wirkung/Marcion and his Impact on Church History: Vorträge der Internationalen Fachkonferenz zu Marcion, gehalten vom 15.-18. August 2001 in Mainz*, ed. Gerhard May et al. (TUGAL 150; Berlin: De Gruyter, 2002), 156, contends that "at no point does a fundamental enmity exist between the two Gods, but instead a relationship of one overtowering the other (*das Verhältnis der Übergipfelung*)."

68. 2 Cor 4:4. Tertullian explicitly says that Marcion appealed to 2 Cor 4:4 to prove there was a "god of this age" (*deus aevi huius*) distinct from the Father of Christ (*Marc.* 5.11.9-12; cf. 5.17.7-9). Already Irenaeus mentioned such a claim, and he also may have been referring to a uniquely Marcionite interpretation and use of the verse, though he does not make that clear:

> However, they say that Paul stated plainly (*aperte*) in the second (letter) to the Corinthians, "In whom *the god of this age* (*deus saeculi huius*) has blinded the minds of unbelievers," and they say that there is the "god of this age," and another (God) who truly is above every principality and beginning and power (cf. Eph 1:21; Col 1:16). It is not our fault if these people, who say that they know "mysteries" that are above God, don't know how to read Paul! (*Haer.* 3.7.1)

suggests that Marcion assigned to the good God some ultimate responsibility for the material creation, or spoke of creation having come into being "in accordance with the will" of the good God.

The Purpose of Creation

Beyond the question of ultimate responsibility for creation, what about its purpose? Paul undoubtedly must have held fundamental convictions about the purposefulness of creation, though he was less interested in exploring God's original intentions than in proclaiming imminent eschatological outcomes. But he does of course stitch the significance of that eschatology to Genesis, most notably in his discussions of first Adam–last Adam in 1 Corinthians 15 and Romans 5, and for Irenaeus this Adam/Christ theme is developed into one of the pillars undergirding his understanding of creation's purpose.

Irenaeus's convictions about the purpose of creation have been examined so extensively by others that I need not expand on the topic here.[69] As others have discussed at length, for Irenaeus creation and salvation essentially form a single package.[70] He insists that everything that has happened from creation to the present has happened "for the sake of the human who is being saved, causing his free choice to ripen toward immortality and preparing him for the eternal submission to God. For this reason the creation is put at the disposal of the human (*conditio insumitur homini*); since the human was not created for (creation), but creation for

---

Irenaeus responds that "of this age" grammatically goes with "unbelievers": "God has blinded the minds of unbelievers *of this age*." See Noormann, *Irenäus als Paulusinterpret*, 121–23; Norris, "Irenaeus' Use of Paul," 82–83. Presumably Irenaeus understands the syntax the same way when he quotes 2 Cor 4:4 again in *Haer.* 4.29.1, though there he does not mention it; cf. David K. Rensberger, "As the Apostle Teaches: The Development of the Use of Paul's Letters in Second Century Christianity" (PhD dissertation, Yale University, 1981), 212, n. 343. Given how Irenaeus must stretch to counter the interpretation of 2 Cor 4:4 as referring to a lower creator, and that this verse evidently was popularized as a proof-text among Marcionites, it is actually very interesting how little evidence we find that others used the reference to this end. Perhaps there is an echo of its use by the "Peratae," who allegedly referred to "the god of this world" (ὁ θεὸς τοῦδε τοῦ κόσμου) and "the master of this world" (ὁ τοῦδε τοῦ κόσμου δεσπότης), but the Greek is rather different from 2 Cor 4:4; Hippolytus, *Haer.* 5.16.9.

69. E.g., beyond the relevant sections in general works on Irenaeus, see the recent studies of Steenberg, *Irenaeus on Creation*; and Holsinger-Friesen, *Irenaeus and Genesis*.

70. E.g., several general treatments return to this often: Minns, *Irenaeus*; Osborn, *Irenaeus*; see also Fantino, *La théologie d'Irénée*, 126; Steenberg, *Irenaeus on Creation*, 1, comments, "Irenaeus presents no 'chapter on creation' no concise reduction of his protological and cosmological thought to a neat, autonomous unit. To the contrary, Irenaeus' investigation of creation lies everywhere throughout his works as a scattered but consistent story."

the sake of the human."⁷¹ Matthew Steenberg has put it succinctly: "When Irenaeus speaks of creation, he does so through the lens of human growth and salvation that he sees as its aim."⁷²

The interpretive devices by which Irenaeus inseparably fuses creation to salvation (along with Old Covenant to New Covenant) into a single grand-scale vision entail what turned out to be among his most historically influential contributions. One of the most celebrated of these interpretive devices is what Irenaeus does with the term οἰκονομία ("economy," "arrangement," "management," "administration").⁷³ This word came to play a storied role in Christian theology as a technical term for the divine "plan" of salvation as well as related applications in Trinitarian theories, and the noun and its cognates have been analyzed almost exhaustively.⁷⁴

I devote attention to it here not only because of its centrality in Irenaeus's theorizing about the purpose of creation, but also because of its comparable importance among some of Irenaeus's opponents. Moreover, applications of οἰκονομία in some passages in the Pauline corpus arguably constitute an important, though probably not the only, inspiration behind deployments of this terminology by both Irenaeus and some of his adversaries. Evidence that "economy"-language was not only important to Irenaeus but also played a role in the thinking of at least

---

71. *Haer.* 5.29.1. The Greek for the first part of this significant passage illustrating Irenaeus's theme of "maturing" or "ripening" toward immortality has survived in a later scolion (see SC 153, 362): ὑπὲρ τοῦ σῳζομένου ἀνθρώπου γέγονεν, τὸ αὐτεξούσιον αὐτοῦ πεπαίνοντα πρὸς τὴν ἀθανασίαν καὶ ἐπιτηδειότερον αὐτὸν πρὸς τὴν εἰς ἀεὶ ὑποταγὴν τοῦ θεοῦ καταρτίζοντα.

72. Steenberg, *Irenaeus on Creation*, 6. Cf. the chapter on "Human Growth from Creation to Resurrection" in Osborn, *Irenaeus*, 211–31; and literature cited by both scholars.

73. Norris, "Who Is the Demiurge?," 10: "The subject matter of the Rule of Truth, as Irenaeus sees it, is coincident with that of the Scriptures. What it embraces is phrased summarily—the way, the οἰκονομία of the Creator with regard to human creatures. This οἰκονομία is therefore the sole legitimate object of theological inquiry and discourse. Whatever goes beyond it is unsure, and therefore unsafe, speculation."

74. E.g., among only the more specialized studies, see Adhémar d'Alès, "Le mot οἰκονομία dans la langue théologique de Saint Irénée," *Revue des Études Grecques* 32 (1919), 1–9; Otto Lillge, "Das patristische Wort οἰκονομία, seine Geschichte und seine Bedeutung bis auf Origines" (PhD dissertation, Friedrich-Alexander Universität Erlangen, 1955); Martin Widmann, "Der Begriff οἰκονομία im Werk des Irenäus und seine Vorgeschichte" (PhD dissertation, University of Tübingen, 1956); John Henry Paul Reumann, "The Use of *Oikonomia* and Related Terms in Greek Sources to about A.D. 100, as a Background for Patristic Applications" (PhD dissertation, University of Pennsylvania, 1957); John Reumann, "Oikonomia = 'Covenant'; Terms for Heilsgeschichte in Early Christian Usage," *NovT* 3 (1959), 282–92; Gerhard Richter, *Oikonomia: Der Gebrauch des Wortes Oikonomia im Neuen Testament, bei den Kirchenvätern und in der theologischen Literatur bis ins 20. Jahrhundert* (AKG 90; Berlin: De Gruyter, 2005).

his Valentinian opponents has been known for generations, so it is not surprising that comparisons and relationships have been examined before.[75] However, in my view, some significant things have been missed. This is partly due to lack of awareness of the relevance of certain Nag Hammadi evidence,[76] but closer inspection is warranted even for what is found in Irenaeus's account and in other sources available since long before the Nag Hammadi find.[77]

"Economy" as a special theological term appears several times in Book 1 of *Against Heresies*, mostly recounting Valentinian usage.[78] What has too often been missed in previous research is the degree to which the employment of "economy" language reflects fundamentally similar concerns shared by Irenaeus and opponents. Without a doubt there are differences in specific applications and nuances, and it is these that past philological analyses have seized upon so readily. But in the process the "big picture" is easily lost sight of. For example, it is immediately apparent that one of the specific uses of οἰκονομία by Irenaeus's Valentinian opponents is with reference to the psychical realm of the Demiurge.[79] Valentinian doctrines about Jesus or the Savior and his role in salvation display

---

75. In addition to works cited in the previous note, cf. especially the article by Norris, "Irenaeus' Use of Paul," which is important not only for its quality but also its specific relevance to the topic of this chapter.

76. And, of course, for the earlier-twentieth-century studies, since the Nag Hammadi evidence was not yet fully accessible.

77. Previous studies of οἰκονομία often include some attention to "Gnostic" evidence, but usually have been too content with fine-tuning distinctions in specific applications, underscoring differences from Irenaeus's use and so on. While such philological exercises are important, they have usually missed more fundamental concerns that I will discuss below. And frankly, such treatments of this specific theme have too often been hampered by other generalizations about "Gnostics" that have not encouraged closer reading. An adequate treatment of this topic has not yet been produced, nor can I really offer one here given the limitations of space; I can only attempt to hint at what might be a more helpful approach.

78. Fantino, *La théologie d'Irénée*, 85–106, and appendix 3, catalogues 125 or so probable occurrences of the term οἰκονομία in *Haer.* (17 in Book 1) and seven instances in *Epid.* In some two dozen instances throughout *Haer.* the Greek οἰκονομία is attested by a Greek fragment, but in other passages one must infer the underlying Greek. Based on the data, it appears that the Latin *dispositio* (or *dispensatio*, in a handful of cases) is usually translating οἰκονομία in *Haer.* Fantino's general analysis of the theme of "economy" in Irenaeus is one of the most systematic and extensive.

79. On the well-known Valentinian division of experienced life here into the material, psychical, and spiritual, see, e.g., *Haer.* 1.5.1–1.6.1. The Demiurge is Lord of everything outside the entirely spiritual realm of Perfection (Pleroma) and Maker of all that is material and psychical (1.5.2) though he is used as a puppet by higher entities, as I have already discussed earlier. The Valentinian Theodotus spoke of the "Archon of the οἰκονομία" (*Exc.* 33.3).

some variety, including across sources used by Irenaeus, and sorting out details is notoriously tricky.[80] But what is clear is that Valentinians were attempting to account for the significance of the appearance of the Savior on earth, in spite of the fact that (as all sides agreed) the divine is spiritual, not material. Why was such an appearance even necessary? In this regard, Valentinians could speak of the Jesus of the οἰκονομία, the "economy," meaning by this the body or aspect that the spiritual Savior necessarily took on from the realm of the Demiurge in order to appear among humans during his ministry.[81] This application of οἰκονομία to things pertaining to the realm of the Demiurge can obviously be distinguished from specific usages in Irenaeus. However, for Irenaeus, too, divine "economy/arrangement" serves to explain the appearance of the invisible God in visible form and the meaning of his suffering.[82]

Though the term οἰκονομία and its cognates were common in the day, and could refer to a variety of instances of "management, administration, arrangement, etc.," for Irenaeus it was particularly apt for referring not only to divine purpose in general, but also to specific instances in which divine purpose manifested itself.[83] But this was also the case for some of his opponents. A Valentinian leader named Marcus, active in Asia Minor, had evidently also attracted many followers in

---

80. E.g., see relevant sections in Thomassen, *The Spiritual Seed*.

81. E.g., *Haer.* 1.6.1; 1.7.2; 1.15.3; at later points Irenaeus refers several other times to this Jesus of the "economy": *Haer.* 3.10.4; 3.11.3; 3.16.6; 3.17.1. A Valentinian source used by Clement of Alexandria (though evidently a source other than Theodotus) contains a similar reference to this psychical element of the incarnate Jesus Christ that was from the "economy" (*Exc.* 58.1-2).

82. E.g., *Haer.* 4.5.5—Because Abraham was a prophet, he foretold "the day of the Lord's coming, and the arrangement (*dispositionem*) involving his suffering"; 5.17.4: Irenaeus refers to the cross as "the arrangement involving the tree (τῆς τοῦ ξύλου οἰκονομίας)." For the plentitude of similar passages, see Fantino, *La théologie d'Irénée*, 94–95. Widmann, "Der Begriff οἰκονομία," 99: "The oikonomia relates to the Demiurge as the creation to the creator, as the fashioned realm relates to the fashioner. Oikonomia is the world fashioned by the Demiurge, 'this world' in terms of its psychical being" (cf. 106). That is accurate as the description of a specific usage, and it is often as far as analysts have pursued the question. Yet this narrow parsing of specific connotations or applications of the term οἰκονομία can obscure the whole picture of which it is a part. It seems to me that overall Valentinians were attempting to comprehend much the same issue as Irenaeus: How do you explain the intersection of divine activity with the material world? That there is an "economy" regarding the created realm is a part of that larger divine plan. Illustrating a lack of adequate attention to this dimension is Richter, *Oikonomia*, 121, who says that "Gnostic dualism tears apart the oikonomia of God, that is, the unity of his creation." Richter evidently has his ear tuned only to Irenaeus's evaluation of Valentinian thought.

83. In addition to the extensive treatment in Fantino, *La théologie d'Irénée*, cf. also Osborn, *Irenaeus*; Minns, *Irenaeus*, 69–95; and the specific studies of the term οἰκονομία I have cited above.

Irenaeus's own Rhône valley neighborhood (*Haer.* 1.13.7), which may explain why there is a lengthy section in Book 1 (13.1–21.5) devoted primarily to teachings from or related to Marcus.[84] Modern research has usually focused on Marcosian ritual practice or on what Irenaeus reports about their number symbolism. But Marcosians also display a remarkable interest in the theme of divine "economy." They referred to the human born to Mary as an event "by design" or "in accordance with arrangement" (κατ᾽ οἰκονομίαν; 1.15.3). The secret significance of numerical groups of divine Aeons in the Pleromatic realm, such as the primordial Ogdoad and the Decad, are embedded in scriptural narrative. That "the saving Ogdoad" (τὴν σωτήριον Ὀγδοάδα) signified by the eight persons saved by Noah's ark is called "the *arrangement* involving the ark" (τὴν τῆς κιβωτοῦ δὲ οἰκονομίαν; 1.18.3).[85] That after ten years Sarah sends her female slave Hagar to Abraham to have him sire a son from her is called "the *arrangement* involving Sarah (τὴν <κατὰ> Σάρραν δὲ οἰκονομίαν; 1.18.3). These instances are similar to the ways in which Irenaeus referred to the "arrangements" of God throughout the period of the patriarchs and prophets.[86] Irenaeus was not appealing to the number symbolism as were Valentinians, and that is a distinction that scholars normally record. However, the similarity in the fundamental dynamic ought not to be ignored. In both cases, what was previously "secret" is now made plain in Christ.

One instance in which Irenaeus finds divine significance in a number is interesting not only because it involves the creation account in Genesis, but also because he might even have borrowed from Marcosian interpretation, and because

---

84. Niclas Förster, *Marcus Magus: Kult, Lehre und Gemeindeleben einer valentinianischen Gnostikergruppe; Sammlung der Quellen und Kommentar* (WUNT 114; Tübingen: Mohr Siebeck, 1999); see also more recently Joel Kalvesmaki, "Formation of the Early Christian Theology of Arithmetic: Number Symbolism in the Late Second and Early Third Century" (PhD dissertation, The Catholic University of America, 2006), 79–104. Kalvesmaki's dissertation offers a superb analysis of number symbolism in several early Christian sources, including the evidence for Marcus. *Haer.* 1.13.1-1.21.5 evidently also includes tradition from other Valentinian sources; see Förster, *Marcus Magus*, 8–13; cf. Kalvesmaki, "Theology of Arithmetic," 132–39. Sorting out definitively which teaching Irenaeus is assigning to Marcosians is problematic, but fortunately this particular issue does not make a significant difference for the argument in this chapter.

85. "In short, they say that whatever is found in the scriptures that can be brought under the number eight fulfills the secret (τὸ μυστήριον) of the Ogdoad" (*Haer.* 1.83.3).

86. E.g., *Haer.* 4.31.1: Since Lot was unaware that it was his own daughters with whom he was having sex (Gen 19:33-35), and was "not a slave to lust" (as Irenaeus presumably infers from Lot's drunken state!), then this all happened only that "an arrangement" (οἰκονομία) might be achieved; cf. 4.21.3; 4.33.10; 4.26.1: "Every prophecy, before it is accomplished, is an enigma and contradiction to humans," but after the fulfillment in Christ, then "the most precise interpretation presents itself"; this is why the Law is like a mere story (μύθῳ) to Jews, but to Christians like "a treasure hidden in a field" (Matt 13:44), revealed and explained by the Cross of Christ, which illuminates God's "arrangements" regarding humans.

for the Marcosians a Pauline framework is suggested. In *Against Heresies* 5.23.2, Irenaeus says that Jesus' crucifixion on the day of preparation for the Sabbath, the sixth day, recapitulated the creation of the human on the sixth day. In 1.14.6, he had reported that Marcosians made the same connection:

> For this reason Moses said that the human came into being "on the sixth day" (Gen 1.31), and the arrangement (οἰκονομία) happened on the sixth day, which is the day of preparation, by which the Last Human appeared for the regeneration of the First Human (cf. 1 Cor 15.47). Of this arrangement (οἰκονομία), both the beginning and the end were at that sixth hour, at which he was nailed to the tree.

Irenaeus may have adapted a Marcosian interpretation, or both could be dependent on a motif conceived by others.[87] Some scholars since at least the early twentieth century have entertained the possibility that Irenaeus's general theological vision, different though it is from those of Valentinians and other opponents, nevertheless not only took some shape through the struggle against them but also adapted some of their language and even concepts.[88] Whatever one's view on this debate, some of Irenaeus's opponents also were using the language of divine "arrangement" or "economy" to refer to an overall divine plan as well as its component events.[89]

87. Kalvesmaki, "Theology of Arithmetic," 218, points out how Clement of Alexandria (*Strom.* 6.141.3-4) must be adapting the Marcosian version (*Haer.* 1.14.6) of this tradition. Like the latter, Clement identifies Christ with the Greek numeral letter six, the *episemon*. Christopher R. Smith, "Chiliasm and Recapitulation in the Theology of Ireneus," VC 48 (1994), 323–24, contrasts Irenaeus's use of the numerology with Marcus's:

> For the Gnostics, at least as Ireneus describes their teaching, the point is the talismanic power of the number six ... For Irenaeus, on the contrary, the point is the coincidence; and not to establish the coincidence, but rather something else by appeal to it, that is, that the serpent lied, based on what the end says about what the beginning must have been like. In this particular case, however, when we consider the larger context, we discover that recapitulation is actually flowing in both directions. The minor point is that Adam died "on the same day" he ate the fruit; the major point is that the devil was therefore a liar in claiming that he would not.

Smith's argument seems loaded with a certain conventional dismissiveness of "Gnostic" exegesis, since surely more is going on in *Haer.* 1.14.6 than merely "talismanic" speculation! He could be quite justified in contending that for Irenaeus the more important point is the lie of the Devil. However, might that indicate that Irenaeus has picked up the sixth day argument from the Marcosians as a target of opportunity?

88. For a brief critical overview of aspects of this dimension of scholarship on Irenaeus since Harnack, see Holsinger-Friesen, *Irenaeus and Genesis*, 1–41.

89. In *Haer.* 1.24.4, Irenaeus mentions the concept of a divine "economy" also as a part of the tradition connected to Basilides: everything in the world was fashioned by angels who now dwell in the heaven that is lowest and visible to humans. With the God of the Jews as

Mythological traditions from Nag Hammadi offer further evidence. I have called attention earlier to the way in which the Valentinian *Tripartite Tractate* stresses that the action of the Logos was not to be criticized, even though it was the moment in that myth that transitioned from a state of complete divine perfection to, eventually, the material cosmos. Because this action by the Logos was quite in accordance with the Father's will and the "cause of an economy (οἰκονομία) destined to coming into being" (*Tri. Trac.* 77,9-11). The presupposition of divine will is illustrated by the prolific use of the term οἰκονομία to describe the "arrangement," the "economy" involving the realm that comes into being as a result of the action of the Logos,[90] an "arrangement/economy" that can simply be called "the οἰκονομία of the Father's will."[91]

The *Wisdom of Jesus Christ* is a redaction of the writing *Eugnostos the Blessed*, and while there has been some debate about whether or not the latter already is a Christian text, there is no question about the former, since it has adapted material from *Eugnostos the Blessed* into a revelation dialogue between Christ and disciples after his resurrection. The opening scene finds the disciples

> perplexed about the real nature (ὑπόστασις) of the All (i.e., universe), and the arrangement (οἰκονομία), and the holy Providence (πρόνοια), and the strength (ἀρετή) of the powers, about everything that the Savior did with them as a mystery (μυστήριον) of the holy arrangement (οἰκονομία).

When the Savior appears and asks them, "What are you seeking?" Philip responds: "For the real nature (ὑπόστασις) of the All and the arrangement (οἰκονομία)."[92] In the *Wisdom of Jesus Christ* this exchange introduces the Savior's revelation regarding issues that in *Eugnostos* are addressed in the form of instruction from a teacher rather than as revelation during an epiphany. These issues involve the nature of God and the ordering (διοίκησις) of the cosmos, and then both texts list several inadequate theories to demonstrate prevailing disagreement among philosophical currents of the day.[93] For our purposes, it is

---

their leader, they divided up control of the earth and its nations. Mind/Christ, son of the Father, came to liberate those who believe in him, from the power of the angelic creators. When the powers attempted to kill Christ, they mistakenly crucified Simon of Cyrene. This mission of Christ is referred to as the "arrangement/plan" by which "he might destroy the works of the makers of the world (*uti per dispositionem hanc opera mundi fabricatorum dissolveret*)." It is conceivable that Irenaeus has merely used his own terminology here, but this kind of application of "economy/arrangement" to refer to soteriological strategy is attested widely enough among demiurgical sources that the possibility that Basilideans also employed it cannot be dismissed out of hand.

90. *Tri. Trac.* 77,3; 77,10; 88,4; 89,35; 91,15; 94,8; 95,8.21; 96,14; 99,19; 100,7; 101,11; 108,10.17; 115,29; 116,8.25; 118,11; 122,32; 127,32; 133,9.

91. *Tri. Trac.* 108,10-11; cf. 127,22-23.

92. *Wis.Jes.Chr.* BG 78,2-11/NHC III 91,3-9, and BG 80,1-3/NHC III 92,4-6.

93. *Eug.* NHC III 70,3-71,1/V 1,3-24; *Wis.Jes.Chr.* BG 80,4-81,17/NHC III 92,7-93,8

noteworthy that a similar trope about conflicting and inadequate philosophical theories about the nature of things is found in *The Tripartite Tractate* 109,5-23.[94] Thus, both the *Wisdom of Jesus Christ* and the *Tripartite Tractate* provide superior answers regarding the ordering and meaning of the cosmos, and both invoke the language of οἰκονομία and πρόνοια to trump other explanations.[95] While several studies have underscored that οἰκονομία was widely used in this period,[96] it is interesting that its introduction in the opening frame of *Wisdom of Jesus Christ* is in an explicitly Christian expansion of *Eugnostos*. Furthermore, that the scene refers to "everything that the Savior did with them as a mystery (μυστήριον) of the holy arrangement (οἰκονομία)" is tantalizingly reminiscent of the combinations of μυστήριον and οἰκονομία in Eph 1:8-10, 3:1-4, 9 and Col 1:25-27. In these Pauline texts, in Valentinian sources I have discussed, in Irenaeus's own theology, and in *Wisdom of Jesus Christ*, there is the claim that a secret divine "economy" has now been revealed in Christ.[97]

---

94. Cf. Ismo Dunderberg, *Beyond Gnosticism: Myth, Lifestyle, and Society in the School of Valentinus* (New York: Columbia University Press, 2008), 178–82.

95. In both *Tri. Trac.* 109,8 and *Wis.Jes.Chr.* BG 81,9/NHC III 93,2 (and *Eug.* III 70,20 par), one of the rejected, inadequate opinions listed is that Providence (πρόνοια) is the cause of the cosmos or the source of its order. This is almost certainly a criticism of Stoic philosophy, yet just as Middle Platonic philosophers often made Providence an integral part of their model while redefining it in criticism of Stoicism, so also did Jewish and Christian thinkers. Thus, *Wis.Jes.Chr.* can speak of "holy Providence" while rejecting an unenlightened, limited understanding of πρόνοια. Cf. *Tri. Trac.* 107,19-108,12: In spite of the rejection in 109,8 of a certain theory of πρόνοια, here the author says that the expulsion of the first humans from Paradise after their transgression was "a work of Providence (πρόνοια)," so that the humans might experience the greatest evil, death, so that eventually they should receive the greatest good, eternal life. Death reigned because of the transgression of the first human (cf. Rom 5:12-14), but all of this was due to "the οἰκονομία of the Father's will" (108,10).

96. E.g., Richter, *Oikonomia*; Reumann, "The Use of Oikonomia"; Widmann, "Der Begriff οἰκονομία"; and Lillge, "Das patristische Wort οἰκονομία."

97. Only a couple of other examples can be briefly noted: in *Orig. World* 117,24-28 we read that "an arrangement (οἰκονομία) took place regarding Eve, in order that the creations (πλάσματα) [i.e., the material bodies of humans] of the authorities might become containers of the light; then, (the light) will condemn (the authorities) by means of their creations (πλάσματα)." This reminds one of the way in which other sources discussed above (including Irenaeus) refer to specific events or scriptural references as individual divine "arrangements" that are manifestations of divine strategy. Though Providence plays a quite prominent role in all of the manuscripts of *Ap. John*, the longer recension expands this role even further by, among other ways, adding a lengthy first-person recitation by Providence of her threefold descent to bring salvation (NHC II 30,11-31,25). In the second descent Providence enters the "midst of the darkness and the interior of Hades, turning toward my

My argument is that these various appeals to "economy" are evidence, in addition to the theme of the "will" of the divine discussed earlier, for the assumption that material creation itself is actually part of an overall "arrangement."[98] Creation has a purpose. In my view this is one of the more misunderstood aspects of mythologies like those represented among Irenaeus's opponents. Rather ubiquitous in modern works is the proposition that Valentinians and some other demiurgical traditions held that creation was an "accident," or "mistake," meaning that these religionists viewed creation as a development contrary to the divine plan, contrary to the intention of the true God.[99] But what I hope to have shown is that such an assertion ignores the recurrent insistence in such traditions on divine providence, on things having happened in accordance with divine will, on the role of divine "economy." The notion of creation as "mistake" or "accident" of course draws its inspiration from the various versions of the story of Wisdom's "fall" from the Pleroma, and it is true that Wisdom's action sometimes appears to be a mistake *to characters within the story*. But ancient devotees were producers and readers/hearers of the story, not characters within it. They could see the whole message.[100] To hold analytic

---

arrangement (οἰκονομία)," thus referring to the work of salvation as providential, divine "economy."

98. Fantino, *La théologie d'Irénée*, 101, avers that by contrast with the usage in Irenaeus, in "Gnostic" sources there does not appear explicitly a universal οἰκονομία of the creation and the salvation of humans. Though there are indeed differences is specific formulation, Fantino's characterization obscures important aspects of the thought of Irenaeus's opponents, among whom we do find instances of intent to present an encompassing plan, as I am attempting to demonstrate here.

99. I have discussed this misleading cliché at some length in Williams, "A Life Full of Meaning and Purpose," 28–33. Minns, *Irenaeus*, 23, illustrates the resort to this cliché, though with an immediate caveat that does point in the right direction: "Matter, evil, suffering belong to the world beyond the Pleroma, which came into being by accident, as it were, but still by the agency of divine Aeons." In other words, we readers of the myth know very well that there is a divine plan.

100. I can illustrate my point by citing an analogous one made about Irenaeus by Behr, *Irenaeus of Lyons*, 147:

> We are also far removed from any attempt to think of creation and salvation as being respectively, in rather crude terms, "Plan A," followed by the "Fall," which is then rectified by "Plan B." Starting with Christ, Irenaeus would rather see creation and salvation, with carefully defined nuances considered below, as being not two moments within one economy, but rather as coextensive, as the one economy: God's continuously creative work throughout the economy, resulting in the end in the one who is in the image and likeness of God, is salvation.

> What happened in Adam's disobedience
>
>> must be placed within the scope of the larger arc that moves from the original formation of Adam to its completion in Christ … The unfolding of the economy

attention riveted exclusively to that moment within the story is to miss the larger point of such myths, which is assurance that the overall outcome is entirely under the control of the divine.[101] Irenaeus would insist on the same, and thus needed his own explanation for why the almighty God did not produce a perfect creation from the start, why evil had to get so out of hand, why figures like the Devil were even allowed.

Both Irenaeus and his opponents found help of a special kind in the Pauline corpus, where "the Apostle" had referred to "the mystery/secret" now revealed in Christ (Eph 3:1-4), the "arrangement of the mystery hidden for (or 'from') the Aeons in God who created all things" (Eph 3:9; cf. Col 1:25-27).[102] In a response apparently directed at Marcionites, Irenaeus rejects the notion that "Paul alone knew the truth, since it was to him that the mystery was disclosed by revelation"

> cannot, therefore, be told by beginning with Adam, considered in himself, proceeding to the "Fall," then the "history of salvation," and finally to Christ, but must be told in such a manner that the end and the beginning mutually inform each other in one arc, both synchronously, in that the arrangement of the whole is revealed together in its recapitulation, and diachronously, as it is unfolded throughout time. (148)

Cf. 208: "Christ, for Irenaeus, is emphatically not 'plan B'!" Behr's aptly articulated characterization of Irenaeus's use of Paul's Adam/Christ concept also matches remarkably well what is going on in Valentinian (and certain other) myths! What happens with the Savior/Jesus/Christ in Valentinian myth is not "plan B," to mop up after a near-catastrophic "mistake" has interrupted "plan A."

101. This is a point on which the thorough and insightful study by Steenberg, *Irenaeus on Creation*, falls short, in my opinion. He quite appropriately stresses the importance of "intentionality" in Irenaeus's teaching on creation, and he finds the roots of this in Jewish sources: "Creation is commenced intentionally by God, with the express purpose of its progression toward the eventual salvation of Israel and, through Israel, all humankind. There is a glimmer of an 'economy' of the sort that will be of such importance to Irenaeus" (30). But Steenberg sees a distinct contrast between Irenaeus and his opponents on this point: "Irenaeus expressly rejects the entire notion of ignorance as causative for creation. While he is not always entirely at odds with the theories and systems of the other groups around him, on this question Irenaeus and the followers of Valentinus are entirely in opposition" (32-33). This is true only in one sense, in that the Demiurge is ignorant—and that assertion was more than enough to make Irenaeus apoplectic. However, that Valentinians taught that creation came into being entirely without any true divine contribution misses the big picture and is incorrect.

102. On οἰκονομία and other terms serving in Ephesians in a "revelation-schema," and implications for later usage by movements such as the Valentinians and others, cf. Widmann, "Der Begriff οἰκονομία," 169-71. Some of his assumptions about what count as "Gnostic motifs" are rather dated by the standards of more recent scholarship, but his study in general remains quite valuable.

(Eph 3:3; *Haer.* 3.13.1). In the continuation of the passage it is not clear whether Irenaeus is referring to Marcionite use of οἰκονομία or is simply applying his own terminology when he says, "For neither did our Lord come to save Paul alone, nor is God so poor that he would have only one apostle who knew the arrangement (*dispositionem*) regarding his Son." But other evidence suggests that Marcionite versions of Pauline letters still retained at least some of the references to the divine οἰκονομία.[103] They would hardly have applied it to intentionality for creation in the manner of some of the sources discussed above, but it is conceivable that they might have used it for the "arrangement" involving Jesus. For Marcionites, one assumes that while creation was indeed intentional, that intention would have been restricted to the purposes of the creator god.

Perceptions of the Material Creation, and Everyday Life

Finally, what are the implications for *perceptions of the material creation*, the physical environment of everyday life? I would argue that this dimension of the larger subject of creator and creation is probably the most misunderstood and therefore most misrepresented as far as what was at stake between Irenaeus and his opponents is concerned.

I begin with the simplest of observations but also the one that is, so far as I can tell, never made: Irenaeus and his opponents in reality spend very little time discoursing about the material creation per se! In spite of repeated assertions in modern scholarship that the debate was about hatred of a detestable material cosmos versus appreciation for a beautiful one, this was not really among the major talking points. Eric Osborn includes a section on aesthetics in his general study,[104] and there is no doubt that one can find references to beauty or the glory of nature in Irenaeus. For example, Osborn cites *Against Heresies* 2.30.2-3, where Valentinians are challenged to name what works *they* have produced by themselves through the "Savior" or their "Mother" (Wisdom) that would prove their alleged superiority to the Demiurge: "What heavens have they made? What earth, stars, other lights in the heavens, rains, frosts, snows, heat or dryness, rivers or fountains, flowers, trees, or animals?" Though Osborn cites only a few other passages along this line,[105] there is no reason to question his justification in asserting Irenaeus's appreciation for such things.

---

103. E.g., in discussing Eph 1:9-10, Tertullian gives no indication that Marcionites avoided the language of the οἰκονομία of the fullness of time (*Marc.* 5.17.1). Marcionites also evidently cited Eph 3:8-9, so that they may have had this significant reference to οἰκονομία. Though Tertullian (*Marc.* 5.18.1) complains that their text lacked the Greek preposition ἐν before "God," and they understood the verse to mean "the mystery hidden for the Aeons *from* the God who created all things." It should be noted that some manuscripts actually lack the ἐν; see the discussion in BeDuhn, *The First New Testament*, 312.

104. Osborn, *Irenaeus*, 193–210.

105. There are in fact few to cite. Osborn himself does not want Irenaeus's aesthetics confused with the Romantic movement; Osborn, *Irenaeus*, 209–10. But quite apart from

However, the blind spot in most modern research on this topic involves Irenaeus's opponents. I illustrate this by referring again to the fine general introduction by Denis Minns:

> [Irenaeus's] religious awe and love for the Creator God went hand in hand with a religious awe and love for the world he believed that God to have created. The whole force of his argument is turned toward proving that the Creator God whom the heretics deride is the only God there is: that he alone is all-powerful, all-good, all-knowing, all-loving. Irenaeus' own piety is so intimately caught up in this battle that his argument is sometimes weakened in consequence. He often expresses his amazement that anyone should suppose that a weak, foolish, jealous God, or anything less than God, could have brought into being so rich and manifold a world.[106] In this he seems oblivious of the fact that *disgust at the phenomenal world lies close to the heart of the heretics' thesis that it cannot have been created by the best and highest God*. He argues, for example, that to say that angels created our world independently of God is to imply that angels are more powerful than God, since they would have achieved a great thing, while God would not have. (*Haer.* II.2.1)[107]

What I find interesting about Minns's comment is both his acute clear-sightedness in spotting what he must, given his presupposition, consider an oddly missed opportunity in Irenaeus's argument, and at the same time the blind spot that this very presupposition constitutes. The blind spot is the assumption that Irenaeus would even have been *aware* of some "disgust at the phenomenal world" lying "close to the heart of the heretics' thesis that it cannot have been created by the best and highest God." I would suggest that Irenaeus had no such awareness, because his opponents had displayed no such disgust.

On this point modern scholarship should be alert not only to what Irenaeus says, but also to what he does *not* say. In a passage cited by both Osborn and Minns as an example (*Haer.* 2.30.2-3; see above), Irenaeus never says that his opponents dismiss the impressiveness of, or complain about, the natural phenomena that he lists. In fact, if they had, Irenaeus would need to have altered his rhetoric (just

---

aesthetics, Irenaeus simply does not mention specific elements of the natural cosmos all that often; among the handful of examples: *Haer.* 4.27.1 (Solomon expounded the wisdom of God in creation, "the nature of every tree, every herb, and of all fowls, quadrupeds, and fish"); *Haer.* 4.6.6 (the Word reveals God as creator by means of the creation itself; cf. 4.6.7; 2.9.1—though he feels no need to elaborate with specifics). Another kind of context in which Irenaeus touches on things in nature is in connection with the Eucharist: God nourishes the body of Christ through vine and grain, in the cup and the bread (*Haer.* 5.2.2-3; cf. 4.17.5; 4.18.1; 4.18.4-5). For a few other instances, see 2.28.1-2; 3.11.5.

106. In a footnote here, Minns cites: *Haer.* 2.2.1; 4.3; 10.3; 25.2; 26.3; 29.2; 30.3; 3.Preface.
107. Minns, *Irenaeus*, 33 (emphasis added).

as Minns remarks).[108] But Irenaeus never accuses opponents of speaking of the ugliness of nature, or enumerating problems in the natural world, and so on. That is not the shape of the controversy.

Modern analysis has too conventionally assumed that if persons imagined the material cosmos to have been the work of a lower creator, then as a consequence some exceptional angst about life here and now must have weighed very heavily on their shoulders, a special "attitude" toward the visible cosmos, namely, one of disgust, hatred, or profound alienation.[109] Yet none of this is evident in Irenaeus's

---

108. In spite of the genuine importance and strengths of the books by Minns and Osborn, they illustrate two different kinds of problems in understanding the issue at hand. As I argue above, Minns's perceptiveness in noticing what Irenaeus has *not* said proceeds no further, because of a conventional assumption. Osborn, in my view, has not broken through even that far on this point, since throughout most of his study he is content to present portraits of the opponents offered by Irenaeus. He even resorts to citing Plotinus: "The objections which Plotinus raises against the Gnostics are the same as those which Irenaeus has raised: proliferation of first principles and denigration of the physical world" (Osborn, *Irenaeus*, 44); and cf. in another section on Plotinus: "For the end of Gnostic fantasy is the despising of the world and moral values" (63). Yet denigration of the physical world is not really the argument actually raised by Irenaeus! His argument is not about how opponents speak about the physical world, but rather that they distinguish (in different ways) between the true God and the creator(s). Moreover, the evidence so commonly cited from Plotinus on this topic needs serious reexamination, as I have argued elsewhere; Williams, "Life and Happiness in the 'Platonic Underworld,'" in *Gnosticism, Platonism and the Late Ancient World: Essays in Honour of John D. Turner*, ed. Kevin Corrigan et al. (NHMS 82; Leiden: Brill, 2013), 497–523. Unfortunately, in Osborn's book on Irenaeus, fundamentally important though it is, the portrayal we are provided of opponents is not much more than a repetition or paraphrase of Irenaeus's own depiction; this is true also in his appendix devoted to "Gnosticism" (265–73).

109. Because of dependence on conventional characterizations in works by specialists on "Gnosticism," such perceptions have been inherited in even the most insightful and indispensable studies of Irenaeus; e.g., Fantino, *La théologie d'Irénée*, 150–51:

> Gnosticism is based on a characteristic attitude in relation to the world and to that which constitutes human existence. This attitude is based on an anti-cosmic dualism that is more or less strong among the different systems … What is it then that separates gnosticism from the Church? It is the attitude toward the world and the corresponding doctrine … We have seen that the gnostic considers himself a stranger to the world and even as a stranger to that which he is, a fleshly and psychical being.

Blackwell, "Paul and Irenaeus," 203, comments that Irenaeus's insistence on resurrection of the flesh "stands in direct opposition to *gnostic disparagement of physical existence* and is a thread that relates to various topics" (emphasis added). This sort of formulation is all too often left as a handy but unexamined distillation of "Gnostic" thought about the natural world. True, at least many of Irenaeus's opponents did indeed consider it contrary to reason

description of his opponents or in most other sources we have for discerning how such persons went about life in society. I have explored this topic at some length elsewhere,[110] so only a few examples will be given here.

First of all, what is seldom mentioned in more conventional treatments is that even Irenaeus describes most of his opponents as engaged in society, and, in fact, oftentimes if he has a criticism, it is that they are *too* "normal" in this regard, *too* accommodated to the social world. In a couple of instances he does mention ascetic practices such as the rejection of sexuality or eating of meat,[111] but more often his complaint is the opposite. He accuses opponents (Valentinians, apparently) of eating even meat from animals offered to "idols," of attending gladiatorial contests, of being the first to show up at public festivals in honor of gentile gods, and so on (*Haer.* 1.6.3).[112] In another context, Irenaeus is responding to criticisms by opponents of unethical behavior depicted in scripture, including God's command that the Israelites abscond with valuable property (vessels, clothing, etc.) when they flee Egypt (Exod 3:21-22). Irenaeus quotes the rejoinder by "the Elder" to such an objection, to the effect that members of the Christian community often possessed much property acquired prior to conversion; or inherited; or given by non-Christian parents or relatives who had gain from some "unrighteous" source; or even from ordinary involvement in trade or some other occupation *after* becoming a believer; or property used by believers (slaves?) who belong to the imperial household (*Haer.* 4.30.1). Now what is interesting is that in this argument Irenaeus apparently takes for granted that his own opponents enjoyed the same sorts of benefits from ordinary economic activity that the Elder had enumerated. The opponents accuse the Israelites of dishonesty, yet "they themselves, carrying in their belts gold, silver and copper coins with the inscription and image of Caesar, (gained) from the work of others, say that they act justifiably" (*Haer.* 4.30.2). Irenaeus says that followers of the teachings of Marcus included wealthy women (*Haer.* 1.13.3). Of course, his point is to defame Marcus as a con artist, but the characterization tells us something important about the socioeconomic position of devotees to this form of Christianity.

Given the scarce attention to the natural world in the debates between Irenaeus and his opponents, we should not be surprised at such evidence for continuing engagement in social and economic life *within* the physical cosmos. Moreover,

---

that "flesh and blood" could inherit immortality, but in this they could feel that they had Paul definitely on their side. That their handling of 1 Cor 15:50 is the instance of exegesis that Irenaeus "takes the greatest pains to refute" (Norris, "Irenaeus' Use of Paul," 83) indicates how convincing it must have been for many (e.g., *Haer.* 5.9-13, passim). But my point is that that presupposition, shared by many in their society, about matter's natural limits ought to be distinguished from a groaning "disparagement of physical existence" tout court.

110. E.g., see Williams, *Rethinking "Gnosticism,"* 96–115; Williams, "A Life Full of Meaning and Purpose"; Williams, "Life and Happiness."

111. E.g., in the case of followers of Satornil (Saturninus): *Haer.* 1.24.2.

112. The accusation about idol meat is directed against others beyond Valentinian circles: *Haer.* 1.24.5; 1.28.2.

there are even indications of an appreciation by Valentinians and others of beauty in the natural world. After all, the visible creation is an image of the invisible.[113] Of course, the material cosmos is not perfect, but neither is it depicted as something hideous or detestable. For instance, one famous Valentinian mytheme mentioned by Irenaeus is the formation of the material realm from the passions of Wisdom. Often modern scholars interpret this as an exclusively negative, world-rejecting sentiment, but the reality is far more nuanced. The passions of Wisdom

> became the substance of the matter from which this cosmos was formed. From her conversion the entire soul of the cosmos and the Demiurge received its beginning and from her fear and grief the rest originated. For from her tears all liquid substance came into being; from her smile (or "laughter"; γέλως) came what is luminous; and from her grief and perplexity all the corporeal elements of the world. For sometimes she would cry and lament, as they say, because of being left alone in the midst of darkness and emptiness, and at other times, thinking of the light which had left her she would relax and laugh; then, again, she would be afraid; or, at other times, would be undecided and beside herself. (*Haer.* 1.4.2)

Mentioning that they do not convey these mysteries publicly, Irenaeus sarcastically remarks:

> For who would not spend all one's resources, in order to learn that from the tears of the pondering (ἐνθύμησις) of the Aeon involved in passion there originated seas, and fountains, and rivers, and all liquid substance, and that light came from her smile, and that from her perplexity and embarrassment the corporeal elements of the cosmos had their formation? (*Haer.* 1.4.3)[114]

---

113. E.g., *Haer.* 1.17.1; 2.7.5–6; 2.8.1. It is notable that a distinctive motif about the visible cosmos pointing the way to its invisible model occurs within texts that Rasimus groups as "Ophite" and aligned with the mythology attested in Irenaeus, *Haer.* 1.30. Thus, *Eugnostos* III 74.12–19: one should "go from what is hidden to the limit of what is visible" (i.e., one should follow the descending steps in the description of the supernal realms described in *Eugnostos*), "and this mental reflection will teach one how confidence in the invisible was found in what is visible"; this instruction is then incorporated also in *Wis.Jes.Chr.* BG 90.4–12/III 98.13–19; cf. *Orig. World* 123.28–31: "Then it will be manifest how confidence in the hidden things has been discovered <in> the visible things, from the foundation down to the consummation of the age"; and *Hyp. Arch.* 87.8–11: "by starting from the hidden (i.e., invisible) things the visible things were discovered." See Williams, "A Life Full of Meaning and Purpose," 24–25. There is no reason to conclude a dependence on Rom 1:19-20 in particular. But I do want to point out that, like Paul (and Irenaeus), such writers were capable of a kind of "natural theology," or "cosmological argument" for knowing about God.

114. Cf. *Haer.* 2.10.3. Pheme Perkins, "Irenaeus and the Gnostics: Rhetoric and Composition in Adversus haereses Book One," *VC* 30 (1976): 196–97, discusses the parody in these passages, but focuses only on the ridicule.

What is never noticed is that there is no indication here that the Valentinians' etiologies for elements in the material world involve some special *complaint* about the cosmos, much less a hatred of it. They are simply offering an explanation for the world in all its complexity—including the happiness that a sunny day can sometimes evoke! There is no sign that Valentinians were somehow depressed at the sight of rivers, fountains, or seas just because of the etiological connection with Wisdom's tears. Why would this mythopoeic notion not have been more comforting than off-putting? The world is what it is—and it had its origin in divine Wisdom.

Marcion is usually brought on stage as someone who truly did despise the material world and hated life within it. Yet if so, it is remarkable how little Irenaeus seems to know of that! What is clear to Irenaeus is that Marcion taught that the world was not created by the true God, but there is precious little information, even from later critics, about what Marcion said regarding the natural world as such. Sebastian Moll has stated that Marcion "had nothing but disgust and hatred for the world and for life itself, hatred so huge that he even refused to promote the continuation of mankind ... the world is a terrible place."[115] However, Moll here is doing much of the Marcionites' emoting for them, as far as I can tell, and perhaps rather more than they themselves felt any need of, as they went about their business day to day.[116] To be sure, Marcionites saw evil in their world; so did

---

115. Moll, *Marcion*, 22.6.

116. This assumption that the Marcionite redeemed must have dragged themselves in heavy cheerlessness day by day through life is expressed already in the classic study by Adolf von Harnack, *Marcion: Das Evangelium vom fremden Gott* (TUGAL 45; Leipzig: Hinrichs, 1924), 137: Because of persecution by Jews, heathen, and other Christians, the redeemed

> are the community of "the wretched and despised" in the world, and all their comfort lies in their faith and in the future. Not a single ray of light falls upon their outward situation in the present. Only in *one* respect are they strengthened by this situation, namely, in the conviction that they are no longer children of the creator of the world but they belong to "the alien one," for the creator would not let his children suffer and bleed so (Adamantius, Dial. I 21). (Emphasis in the original and in the English translation: Harnack, *Marcion*, 89–90)

But how do we know that Marcionites felt "not a single ray of light" in their everyday situation? Harnack adds the caveat that "only in *one* respect" was life different: they had a divine patron! Are we really to imagine that conviction of redemption and future salvation by this patron, the true God, would not have markedly changed perceptions about life *here and now*? Gloomy portraits of Marcionite feelings about the material world and everyday life within it turn out to be based on a surprisingly small handful of evidence. See further, Williams, "A Life Full of Meaning and Purpose," 41–43; Andrew McGowan, "Marcion's Love of Creation," *JECS* 9 (2001), 304: "Marcion's world denial is not first and foremost utter rejection and condemnation of the material, but refusal to acknowledge the dominion expressed in the ethos of the world"; cf. Aland, "Sünde und Erlösung," 156:

Irenaeus; so did everyone. But the focus was on *moral* evil. There is some evidence that Marcion did identify sex and procreation as a poster issue, but this was surely not the only front in the battle against evil. And for his part, Irenaeus says remarkably little about Marcion's view on marriage or procreation.[117] Meanwhile, Marcionites celebrated the good news of redemption due to the grace of the divine Father of Jesus.

What was at stake in Irenaeus's engagement with most of his opponents was not cheeriness about life and appreciation of the physical world versus daily angst, dark pessimism, and disgust at the natural environment. All sides accepted a difference between creation as we know it and something more perfect, more eternal, more divine. For Irenaeus, that more perfect creation will be known only in the future Kingdom, and meanwhile the creation that we know is the context for maturing toward immortality. True, most of the groups he attacks would have had no interest in the millennial kingdom Irenaeus anticipated on a renewed material earth. Valentinians' Platonizing values, for example, entailed a decidedly contrasting viewpoint on whether immortality would accommodate a material earth or material bodies. Still, many people of the day looked toward eventual transcendence of the body, without being riddled with some unusual anxiety or depression about life in the world that marked them off from their neighbors or prevented ordinary social activity.[118]

> The concern of Marcion—this is my thesis—is not about the cosmos, and it is not even about demonstrating the redemption of the human "from the nature that had been foisted upon him" [quoting Harnack, *Marcion*, 19–20], but rather it is about the power of evil, the depth of which can be measured only in light of salvation, and it is about this salvation that can only be comprehended, as he describes it, in light of Christ.

117. It is notable that in his summary of Marcion's teaching in *Haer.* 1.27.2-3 no prohibition of marriage or procreation is mentioned at all! Yet the next section (1.28.1) introduces the "Encratites" who "preached not to marry (ἀγαμίαν ἐκήρυξαν)" and says they are "from Saturninus and Marcion"; also Tatian, "in a manner similar to Marcion and Saturninus, proclaimed marriage to be corruption and fornication." The sudden introduction of this information about Marcion in 1.28.1 may be the result of revisions in the source adapted by Irenaeus; see the new study by Smith, *Guilt by Association*. However, so far as I can tell, Irenaeus never shows any further interest in a Marcionite prohibition or even depreciation of marriage.

118. Minns, *Irenaeus*, 154, offers an eloquent contrast between Irenaeus as "empiricist" and his opponents as "escapist"—eloquent in rhetorical terms, but in my view, leading quite in the wrong direction for any adequate understanding of real people in the circles Irenaeus is opposing. Minns says Irenaeus could not understand how

> people who need to eat and drink every day, who know the pleasure of sexual arousal and the pain of physical separation from those they love, who suffer in their bodies when ill or diseased, who know they are going to die, quite possibly

Conclusions

Some elements in the above analysis have been noted by other scholars—for example, that most of Irenaeus's opponents would have thought of themselves as monotheists, or that the lower Demiurge was really only a puppet creator in Valentinian myth. However, other aspects have essentially gone unnoticed—for example, that neither Irenaeus nor his opponents devote much discussion to the natural world per se. And an examination of the *totality* of interrelated factors discussed in this study has never been undertaken, as far as I am aware. Yet how we understand what differentiated Irenaeus and the primary opponents he criticizes in his famous heresiological opus makes an important difference in how we understand both those adversaries and Irenaeus himself.

Irenaeus knows very well that most of his opponents would claim to believe in only one true God, but he is convinced that some do not recognize how little their position differs from the polytheism of the day. From his own description of their teachings it is obvious that he is aware that Valentinians wish to shift responsibility for creation above the head of the Demiurge and even that of his mother Wisdom, still higher to the very Savior himself. But Irenaeus considers this not only pointless speculation pretending to provide a peek behind Gen 1:1, but a blasphemous denial of creation by God's very "hands." Irenaeus also realizes that some of his opponents speak a divine "economy" involved in creation, but this has inspired him to expostulate at great length on what the "*whole* economy of God" truly entails. Neither Irenaeus nor his opponents indicate that the real issue was what so many modern studies depict as world-rejection or anticosmism. From both sides, where evil is the subject the focus is on *moral* evil, not imperfections in the natural world.

> in the same agony of body they have seen others endure—how could anyone who shares this common lot of all humanity *suppose that the body is incidental to the business of being human being*? (Emphasis added)

Just so. Minns says that it is

> easy enough to see the attraction of the belief that the real and essential element of a human being is something spiritual, temporarily and distressingly associated with the body, but destined to be freed from it and to return to the purely spiritual realm that is its real home. *This is attractive because it is escapist, but escapism is not a real option for an intelligent adult.* (Emphasis added)

Of course, snide critics of Irenaeus (or Paul) himself might dispute where empiricism has left off and escapism has begun. But my point here is rather that Minns's characterization presupposes that Irenaeus's opponents did indeed "suppose that the body is incidental to the business of being human being." It presupposes that they had no interest in the everyday business of life; they wanted only "escape." This is an old, ubiquitous, and seriously misleading cliché; cf. Williams, "A Life Full of Meaning and Purpose," 21–22 et passim.

This was true of the Pauline corpus on which both Irenaeus and opponents drew in support, along with other scriptures. Todd Still is of course correct that "far from disdaining the created order, the apostle concurred with the psalmist who declared 'the earth and its fullness are the Lord's' (1 Cor 10.26 citing Ps. 24.1; cf. Pss. 50.12; 89.11)."[119] And yet it is also true that little interest is apparent anywhere in the Pauline (including pseudo-Pauline) corpus in much expostulation on specific features of the material cosmos. These writings do not gush about flora and fauna, and indeed they hardly mention them or much else about what we would call the natural world.[120] I am not at all contending that the general absence of extensive references to specific elements in the natural world is somehow proof that Paul or pseudo-Pauline authors were, unlike most people in their societies, incapable of any enjoyment of features of the physical cosmos—in fact, the opposite is my point: that such was not a central topic in these letters is because the focus of the letters is elsewhere. Generations of scholars have recognized that the interest in these sources is on theological implications pertaining to humans, the anthropological situation. The preoccupation is not with beauty or terror related to plants and animals, mountains, valleys, streams, or lakes, but with implications now and eschatologically of human and divine goodness and evil, justice and injustice.

So it was with Irenaeus as well as with many of his opponents, all appealing to the Apostle and claiming to understand what he had meant by the divine "mystery" hidden from/for Aeons, finally revealed in Christ.

---

119. Todd D. Still, "Shadow and Light: Marcion's (Mis)Construal of the Apostle Paul," in *Paul and the Second Century*, ed. Michael F. Bird and Joseph R. Dodson (LNTS 412; London: T&T Clark, 2011), 105.

120. It is no particular surprise to find an isolated metaphor from the everyday life of oxen at work (1 Cor 9:9, though there Paul comments that the scripture, from Deut 25:4, surely cannot mean that God cares about oxen!). And that Paul happens to mention "wild beasts" only upon recalling what was likely a terrifying event in the arena in Ephesus (1 Cor 15:31-32) will not in itself seem odd even to most who have not had the experience. However, it is simply worth registering the fact that one would not have gone to Pauline letters for extensive discussions of the created world and its wonders. Paul's one streak of zoological prose about "birds, quadrupeds and reptiles" (Rom 1:23) is in reference to cult images in his day.

RESPONSE
PAUL, IRENAEUS, AND THE CREATION IN DIALOGUE WITH MICHAEL A. WILLIAMS

Jason Maston

"Irenaeus of Lyons has earned the reputation of a theologian of creation."[1] Such a claim would not normally be applied to Paul, since according to many Pauline scholars he had little interest in the topic of creation. When Pauline scholars have discussed creation, the focus has tended to be on a handful of texts, most prominent among these being Rom 4:17 and 8:19-22. According to many scholars, when Paul did write about creation, he did so in a thoroughly pessimistic manner for he viewed the present world as corrupt and passing away (cf. 1 Cor 7:31; Gal 1:4). Recent Pauline scholarship, in line with a broader movement in biblical scholarship, however, has seen an uptake in studies of Paul's view of creation. These studies have been diverse in that they focus on different issues (e.g., word usage, scriptural engagement) and have different starting assumptions.[2] My aim in this brief study is to survey three questions that are of relevance for understanding Paul's view of creation: (1) the identity of the creator; (2) Paul's two-age eschatology; and (3) his view of the resurrection. The first two questions overlap with the first two sections of Williams's study of Irenaeus. In the conclusion to the chapter, I will

---

1. Matthew Craig Steenberg, *Irenaeus on Creation: The Cosmic Christ and the Saga of Redemption* (VCSup 91; Leiden: Brill, 2008), 1.

2. In addition to numerous articles on individual texts, the follow monograph-length studies highlight the range of work currently being done: Edward Adams, *Constructing the World: A Study in Paul's Cosmological Language* (SNTW; Edinburgh: T&T Clark, 2000); David G. Horrell, Cherryl Hunt, and Christopher Southgate, *Greening Paul: Rereading the Apostle in a Time of Ecological Crisis* (Waco: Baylor University Press, 2010); J. J. Johnson Leese, *Christ, Creation and the Cosmic Goal of Redemption: A Study of Pauline Creation Theology as Read by Irenaeus and Applied to Ecotheology* (LNTS 580; London: Bloomsbury T&T Clark, 2018); Jonathan D. Worthington, *Creation in Paul and Philo: The Beginning and Before* (WUNT 2.317; Tübingen: Mohr Siebeck, 2011).

The Actor of Creation: Paul's View of the Creator God

Pointing to the first main argument in Romans, James D. G. Dunn writes, "God's role as creator is another fundamental taken-for-granted of Paul's theology."[3] In Rom 1:25 Paul identifies God as "the creator" (τὸν κτίσαντα). Interestingly, this is the only instance in the Pauline letters where God is called "creator." Paul maintains that God created humanity (1 Cor 11:9), citing at one point Gen 2:7 (1 Cor 15:45). The letter to the Ephesians identifies believers as God's "creation, created in Christ Jesus for good works, which God prepared beforehand" (Eph 2:10). The statement highlights that God not only created believers, but that he has in some way designed the path of obedience they will walk. Paul describes God as "potter," which is a scriptural image used to stress God's sovereign control as creator (Rom 9:19-22; cf. Jer 18:1-10). This assertion of divine sovereignty aligns with Paul's occasional use of prepositions to make theological points. For example, in his reflections on the wisdom of God in Rom 11:33-36, Paul concludes with the claim that "all things are from him and through him and to him" (cf. 1 Cor 8:6; Eph 4:6).

While it may be true that Paul took for granted that God is creator, we should not assume that his understanding was identical to that of other ancient Jews.[4] In particular, Paul's thought is sharply distinguished from other Jews by his claims that Jesus Christ was involved in the act of creation.[5] This reformulation of Paul's understanding of God is evident in Paul's bold interpretation of the Shema in 1 Cor 8:4-6. The Shema (Deut 6:4) functions as the most concise statement of Jewish theology. It singles out the being YHWH as the unique, personal God of Israel and demarcates him from all other divine beings. In 1 Cor 8:4-6 Paul interprets the Shema Christologically as a monotheistic claim about the divine identity revealed as the Father and Jesus Christ: "we know ... that there is no God except one ... but for us there is one God, the Father from whom are all things and we are unto him, and one Lord, Jesus Christ, through whom are all things and we are through him."

In this statement, Paul coordinates the mutual relationship between the Father and Jesus as externally focused on creation. Similar to some philosophers, Paul

---

3. James D. G. Dunn, *The Theology of Paul the Apostle* (Grand Rapids: Eerdmans, 1998), 38.

4. Francis Watson makes this point strongly in his "The Triune Divine Identity: Reflections on Pauline God-Language, in Disagreement with J.D.G. Dunn," *JSNT* 23.80 (2001), 99–124.

5. Richard Bauckham, *Jesus and the God of Israel: God Crucified and Other Essays on the New Testament's Christology of Divine Identity* (Milton Keynes: Paternoster, 2008), 27–29, 213.

engages in prepositional theology to indicate how the Father (ἐξ οὗ τὰ πάντα καὶ ἡμεῖς εἰς αὐτόν) acts. Notably, Paul's statement incorporates all of creation (τὰ πάντα) and specifically believers (ἡμεῖς). The statement is, therefore, both cosmological and anthropological. Creation originates from God the Father and came into existence through Jesus. Believers likewise came into existence through Jesus and are oriented to the Father. The phrase "unto him" (i.e., God) likely indicates purpose, and together the two prepositional statements about the Father encompass the beginning and end of creation. Paul's interpretation of the Shema indicates that for him the two figures are united as one while performing different tasks. Their unity in creation reveals their oneness, while their different tasks evidence their distinctiveness.

Paul's lengthy reflection on Christ's relation to creation is found in Col 1:15-20. The Son is "the firstborn over all creation," which indicates his supremacy over creation. Verse 16 states that "all things in heaven and upon the earth were created by/in him." The "all things" includes things seen and unseen and every type of ruler. Again, Paul employs several prepositional phrases to make his points about Jesus's role in the creation process. Jesus's role in bringing creation into existence is supplemented here with a statement about his role as the one who sustains creation (v.17). Notably, in the latter part the passage turns from creation to redemption indicating a strong correlation between the two.

In another text Paul indicates that the God who is active in the gospel is the same God who brought light into existence. Over against the activity of "the god of this age" who "blinds the minds of unbelievers," the God who spoke light into existence at the beginning is now shining the gospel into the lives of believers (2 Cor 4:4-6).[6] To make his point, Paul quotes Gen 1:3. For Paul God's creative activity at the beginning of creation is analogous to his present activity of shining the gospel's penetrating light. Genesis 1:3 provides Paul with a vocabulary and a pattern of divine action to explain God's act in Jesus.

The texts explored so far indicate clearly that Paul's understanding of God as creator was Christologically grounded. To this should be added a couple of texts that also describe the Spirit as involved in the act of creation. In 2 Cor 3:6 Paul remarks "the Spirit makes alive." This simple statement points to the most basic function for Paul that the divine Spirit performs. To speak of the Spirit is to speak of him in relation to God's resurrecting activity (Rom 8:11), or more simply as "the Spirit of life" (Rom 8:2; cf. v.10).

Dunn is certainly correct that a basic presupposition of Paul's theology is that his God is the creator. Yet, Paul develops this idea in a manner that moves in a different direction than his Jewish contemporaries. Paul envisions creation as brought into existence by the Lord Jesus and sustained through him. Moreover, Paul incorporates the Spirit into this creational activity when he writes of resurrection life. Paul's view has a trinitarian pattern to it.

---

6. Irenaeus's exegesis of this verse is creative but wrong (*Haer.* 3.7.1).

The (Dis)Unity of Creation: Paul's Two-Age Eschatology

When scholars discuss Paul's view of creation, reference is often made to 1 Cor 7:31: "the form of this world is passing away." The statement indicates a pessimistic view of the world, but what exactly Paul meant remains a matter of dispute. Does the phrase indicate something that is happening now or will happen (a future use of the present)? Does "the form" indicate the external properties but not the essence of the world? Does "this world" refer to humanity (an anthropological interpretation) or the created order (a cosmological interpretation)?[7]

To explain Paul's pessimistic remarks about the world in 1 Cor 7:31 and elsewhere, scholars appeal to Paul's two-age eschatology. In this two-age eschatology, the present age is run by evil powers and death reigns over humanity. The future age is when God will return to establish justice and inaugurate his kingdom. The two-age eschatology is considered, by most Pauline scholars, typical of Jewish thought, especially apocalyptic.[8] Paul, while adopting the basic structure, modifies it because he believes that the future has been brought into the present by God's activity in Jesus.[9] The Christ-event creates an overlap in time, a "now-not yet" in which the characteristics of the future are seen already in the present, but evil still impacts lives.

This conception of time as divided into two ages is particularly crucial for the apocalyptic reading of Paul associated with the work of Ernst Käsemann and J. Louis Martyn and extended by others.[10] This view pushes beyond the mere idea of

---

7. For a discussion of this verse, see Adams, *Constructing the World*, 130–36, who argues that Paul is referring to the structures of the present world which "is already on its course toward final destruction" (quote from 134).

8. I leave to the side here the question of whether the two-age scheme is in fact typical of Judaism as well as the question of Jewish eschatology generally and the implications for Pauline interpretation. One should consult on these matters the vital works by Loren T. Stuckenbruck, for example, "Posturing 'Apocalyptic' in Pauline Theology: How Much Contrast to Jewish Tradition?," in *The Myth of Rebellious Angels: Studies in Second Temple Judaism and New Testament Texts* (WUNT 335; Tübingen: Mohr Siebeck, 2014), 240–56; idem, "Some Reflections on Apocalyptic Thought and Time in Literature from the Second Temple Period," in *Paul and the Apocalyptic Imagination*, ed. Ben C. Blackwell, John K. Goodrich, and Jason Maston (Minneapolis: Fortress Press, 2016), 137–55.

9. For example, Paul identifies Jesus' resurrection as "the first fruits" (1 Cor 15:20, 23; cf. Rom 8:29; Col 1:18).

10. For example, Ernst Käsemann, "On the Subject of Primitive Christian Apocalpytic," in *New Testament Questions of Today*, trans. W. J. Montague (London: SCM Press, 1969), 108–37; J. Louis Martyn, "Apocalyptic Antinomies in Paul's Letter to the Galatians," *NTS* 31.03 (1985): 410–24; idem. *Galatians: A New Translation with Introduction and Commentary* (AB 33A; New York: Doubleday, 1997). For a review of the debate over the apocalyptic reading of Paul, see chapters 1 and 2 in Ben C. Blackwell, John K. Goodrich, and Jason Maston (eds.), *Paul and the Apocalyptic Imagination* (Minneapolis: Fortress Press, 2016), 3–41.

an overlap in the ages when it is claimed that the future age inaugurated by Christ completely replaces the present age. Martyn de Boer writes, "The new age does not merely succeed the old age as on a timeline; it *replaces* this age with another age. For the two ages are not merely temporal epochs; they are also, perhaps even primarily, orbs of spheres (spaces) in which certain activities take place."[11] In other words, Paul's eschatology is fundamentally about one world replacing another. Importantly, this reading of Paul does not claim that the physical cosmos is destroyed and the future age is a disembodied, immaterial existence. Rather, this reading envisions a physical cosmos, but it nevertheless presses the point of discontinuity between the present and the future. The "new creation" is not a renewed creation.

Other Pauline scholars also insist that Paul holds a two-age eschatology but they do not envision a complete replacement of the present world/age with a new one. N. T. Wright, for example, contends that in Jewish thought the two-ages eschatology "was a way of affirming the goodness of the created world and the belief that its creator would eventually liberate it from its present condition."[12] Although there is some discontinuity, Wright stresses the continuity between the present and the future. God's new activity does not bring a collapse of the present created order or replace it, but rather is the culmination of God's plan for creation.

A two-age eschatology raises the question of the continuity between the present age and the future one. For the apocalyptic Paul reading, the present age is passing away in the sense that it is coming to a complete end and there is no significant continuity between the two ages. For others the two-ages scheme highlights the serious problems of the present age and how in the future age the problems are made right as the plan of God is brought to its culmination. The difficulty is that Paul's statements point in both directions.

It is not just that the end of the ages has arrived (1 Cor 10:11), but that the arrival of the future age spells the end to the present world order (1 Cor 7:31). Paul considers himself crucified to the present cosmos (Gal 6:15), suggesting a fundamental break with "the present evil age" (Gal 1:4). Yet, he contends in Rom 8:19-23 that the present age, which is currently groaning because of its enslavement, will be redeemed when believers are resurrected. Paul's movement between continuity and discontinuity creates the tensions that exist between these two scholarly perspectives.[13] The divide, though, is not merely about eschatology.

---

11. Martinus C. de Boer, "Apocalyptic as God's Eschatological Activity in Paul's Theology," in *Paul and the Apocalyptic Imagination*, ed. Ben C. Blackwell, John K. Goodrich, and Jason Maston (Minneapolis: Fortress Press, 2016), 50n.26 (emphasis original).

12. N. T. Wright, *Paul and the Faithfulness of God*, 2 vols (London: SPCK, 2013), 2:1059. Wright discusses the two-ages eschatology in several places in *Paul and the Faithfulness of God*; see 1:163-75, 476-78. This scheme underlies his entire analysis of Paul's eschatology (2:1043-1265).

13. Tied up in this debate is also the question of whether the language of cosmic destruction is literal or metaphorical. See Edward Adams, *The Stars Will Fall From*

Rather what distinguishes these perspectives is Christology. Is the Christ-event the climax of a growing story or a plot twist that requires a radical rereading of the first part? In summary, then, Paul's two-age eschatology raises the issue of the relationship of the present creation to the future, new creation. Is it one of continuity or discontinuity?

The Telos of Creation: Paul on the Resurrection

The final issue that I will address is Paul's view of the resurrection. This topic is, to some extent, a narrower take on the question of continuity between the present and future ages discussed in the previous section. Whereas the earlier question focused on the creation as a whole, discussing the resurrection brings the focus to anthropology. Scholars have strongly rejected the idea that Paul viewed the future body as a nonmaterial (often referred to as "spiritual") existence. This view is difficult to square with the Pauline texts as well as ancient views of the afterlife. Yet, the commonality in scholarship ends here as scholars divide over the material substance of which the resurrection body will be made. The differences come out clearly in interpretations of 1 Corinthians 15.[14]

According to one interpretation, Paul argues that the resurrection body will be made of heavenly material, specifically pneuma. He describes a hierarchy in which heavenly bodies are superior to, that is, more glorious than, earthly bodies (vv. 40-42). He proceeds to place the resurrected body on the side of heavenly bodies when he identifies it as "glorious" and as a "pneumatic body" (vv. 42-44). He contends further that the body inherited from Adam was made of dusty material, that is, the substance of earth, whereas the body associated with the resurrected Jesus is made of heavenly substance, that is, pneuma (vv. 45-49). The argument comes to a climax in v. 50 when Paul asserts that "flesh and blood cannot inherit the kingdom of God," which means that the substance of the present body, which is composed of flesh and blood, must be changed. Dale Martin summarizes this view clearly when he writes,

> The resurrected human body will partake of a nature similar to that of heavenly bodies and will be as much higher than the current earthly body in the physiological hierarchy as the heavenly bodies are in comparison to earthly bodies ... What human beings have in common with heavenly bodies is, in Paul's system, incorporation as a "pneumatic body"—that is, a body composed only of pneuma with sarx and psyche having been sloughed off along the way.[15]

Heaven: "Cosmic Catastrophe" in the New Testament and Its World (LNTS 347; London: T&T Clark, 2007); Wright, *Paul and the Faithfulness of God*, 1:163-75.

14. Cf. also Rom 8:10-11, 23-24; 2 Cor 5:1-10; Phil 3:20-21; 1 Thess 4:13-5:11.

15. Dale B. Martin, *The Corinthian Body* (New Haven: Yale University Press, 1999), 126.

How exactly this change will take place is debated. Martin suggests a discarding of the lower elements that currently form the human body. Troels Engberg-Pedersen argues for a complete transformation.[16] Nevertheless, this perspective on the resurrection holds that the present body is changed in some manner into a new substance, a heavenly material, a material spiritual body.

The opposing view contends, however, that Paul is not contrasting material substances but characteristics of the human body. The purpose of the contrast between earthly and heavenly bodies (vv. 39-41) is not to establish a hierarchy of superiority, but to support the claim that God creates different bodies according to his will (v. 38). When Paul describes the present and resurrected bodies in vv. 42-43, he highlights qualities or, as Thiselton puts it, *"modes of existence or of life."*[17] The descriptions of the body as "natural" or "spiritual" indicate, then, the characteristics of the body in its present and future states. The resurrected body is a spiritual body in that it is enlivened by the Spirit of God.

This brief discussion of how some scholars understand 1 Corinthians 15 highlights the main issue at stake: how much continuity exists between the present body and the resurrected one? And, what does this level of continuity indicate about God's plan for humanity?[18] These questions become more urgent because Paul borrows language from Genesis 1 (and likely Psalm 8) and quotes explicitly Gen 2:7 (1 Cor 15:45). The relationship between the present body and the resurrected body brings to the forefront God's intention for humanity and his goals for the created order. It is worth highlighting as well the Christological element of Paul's argument. Christ is the first one raised (1 Cor 15:23) and believers will bear a body like his in the next age.

Conclusion

I conclude by drawing some connections with Irenaeus on Paul and creation. The theological discussion, Williams notes, has shifted between Paul's time and that of Irenaeus, so that in the case of the latter, the identity of the creator and the nature

---

16. Troels Engberg-Pedersen, *Cosmology and Self in the Apostle Paul: The Material Spirit* (Oxford: Oxford University Press, 2010), 32; see also the thorough study of Jeffrey R. Asher, *Polarity and Change in 1 Corinthians 15: A Study of Metaphysics, Rhetoric, and Resurrection* (HUT 42; Tübingen: Mohr Siebeck, 2000).

17. Anthony Thiselton, *The First Epistle to the Corinthians: A Commentary on the Greek Text* (NIGTC; Grand Rapids: Eerdmans, 2000), 1276 (emphasis original).

18. This point arises quite sharply in Rom 8:20-23 when Paul claims that the freedom of creation from its enslavement will come only when believers' bodies are redeemed. Irenaeus saw a link between Romans 8 and 1 Corinthians 15, indicating in fact that 1 Cor 15:50 should be interpreted in light of Romans 8 (*Haer.* 5.7-13). See D. Jeffrey Bingham, "Irenaeus Reads Romans 8: Resurrection and Renovation," in *Early Patristic Readings of Romans*, ed. Kathy L. Gaca and L. L. Welborn (New York: T&T Clark, 2005), 114-32.

and purpose of creation are debated topics. Such is simply not the case for Paul. He assumes throughout his letters that the God and Father of Jesus is the same God who elected Israel and made promises to Abraham. Even Paul's arguments about Jesus as the agent of creation are presented in non-polemical ways. For example, in 1 Cor 8:4-6 it is not the inclusion of Jesus into the divine identity that is disputed by the Corinthians, but rather what the "oneness" of God means for daily life.[19] For Irenaeus, though, the relationship between the Father as creator and Jesus is precisely the point of debate. Williams contends that Irenaeus and his opponents agreed that there was only one creator God and that creation happened according to the divine will. Yet, this agreed monotheism seems to overlook the sharp distinction that exists between Irenaeus and his opponents regarding the identity of the creator God: the issue is not simply whether there is one God and whether he is the creator; rather the issue is precisely the identity of the one creator God and whether he has brought creation into existence through Jesus (and the Spirit), who are, in fact, part of the identity of the one God.

As Williams notes, Irenaeus had a grand vision that moved from creation to salvation, which is captured by Irenaeus's use of the word οἰκονομία. The language occurs in Paul, but takes on a special role in Irenaeus that it does not have in Paul's writing. Yet, the point that Irenaeus is after (namely, the single plan of God) compares interestingly to Paul's two-age eschatology. As noted above, Pauline scholarship is divided over the implications of Paul's two-age eschatological scheme: does it suggest a strong discontinuity between what is happening in the present age or does it indicate that the age to come is the culmination of God's plan? Irenaeus aligns closely to the latter view in his understanding of God's purpose for creation and the relationship between the two ages.

Finally, although not a topic directly addressed by Williams, several references are made to the resurrection. In particular, he notes the ancient debate over the meaning of 1 Cor 15:50. Irenaeus mentions this text as widely quoted by his opponents to defend their views (*Haer.* 5.9.1; cf. 1.30.13), and he offers a lengthy discussion of it (*Haer.* 5.9-13). This text, one might think, stands as the great counter to Irenaeus's vision of God's coherent and consist redemptive plan.[20] Just as its meaning was widely debated in the ancient world, so also in current Pauline studies this verse remains problematic. While modern Pauline scholarship has largely rejected the idea that the resurrected body is a nonmaterial existence, it is interesting that the lines of the contemporary debate are comparable to the ancient debate as scholars divided over the nature of the resurrected body.

In conclusion, Pauline scholars would find Irenaeus's interpretations misguided at key points (e.g. his interpretation of 2 Cor 4:4), but it is interesting how debates

---

19. Cf. Larry W. Hurtado, *Lord Jesus Christ: Devotion to Jesus in Earliest Christianity* (Grand Rapids: Eerdmans, 2003), 123-24.

20. On Irenaeus's treatment of this text, see Benjamin L. White, *Remembering Paul: Ancient and Modern Contests over the Image of the Apostle* (Oxford: Oxford University Press, 2017), 158-66.

currently alive in Pauline studies align with the disputes in which Irenaeus was involved. To be sure, the precise issues have shifted significantly, but nevertheless the big picture issues remain quite similar. Irenaeus offers to current scholars a witness to not only how Paul was read, but also in some instances perspectives that may help Pauline scholars avoid certain pitfalls and move beyond our current impasses.

Chapter 3

THE USE OF PAUL IN IRENAEUS'S CHRISTOLOGY

Stephen O. Presley

Within the contours of his analysis of early Christian theology, J. N. D. Kelly begins his summary of Irenaeus's Christology saying:

> Although influenced by the Apologists, Irenaeus owed much more to the direct impact of St. Paul and St. John. In Christology his approach was conditioned negatively by his opposition to Gnosticism and Docetism, positively by his tremendous vision of Christ as the second Adam, Who summed up in Himself the whole sequence of mankind, including the first Adam, thereby sanctifying it and inaugurating a new, redeemed race of men.[1]

According to Kelly, Irenaeus organizes his Christology around an economic vision of salvation history that is, in part, directed by a Pauline theology attentive to the connections between Adam and Christ. The general synthesis between Irenaeus's economic vision, his Christology, and references to the Pauline Adam-Christ are mentioned by others as well. Aloys Grillmeier, for example, writes that "creation, the incarnation of Christ, redemption and resurrection belong together as different parts of the one all-embracing saving work of God."[2] This unified vision of God, he continues, culminates in Christ's incarnation that is a "recapitulation of creation and above all of fallen Adam."[3] John Behr draws similar associations between Paul and Irenaeus's use of the Adam-Christ typology, saying that Irenaeus's discussion of the person and work of Christ follows "Paul's correlation and contrast between Adam and Christ."[4] Finally, even Rolf Noormann, who authored the most detailed treatment of Irenaeus's use of Paul to date, concludes that Paul's

---

1. J. N. D. Kelly, *Early Christian Doctrines* (New York: Harper San Francisco, 1978), 147.
2. Aloys Grillmeier, *Christ in Christian Tradition: From the Apostolic Age to Chalcedon*, trans. John Bowden (Atlanta: John Knox, 1964), 101. See also Robert Grant, *Jesus after the Gospels: The Christ of the Second Century* (Louisville: Westminster/John Knox, 1990), 106.
3. Grillmeier, *Christ in Christian Tradition*, 102.
4. John Behr, *Irenaeus of Lyons: Identifying Christianity* (Oxford: Oxford University, 2013), 122.

major contribution to Irenaeus's thought may be summarized under three key themes, including salvation history, Christology, and anthropology.[5] Noormann's discussion of Christology, moreover, begins with a summary of Irenaeus's Adam-Christ typology as the organizing feature.[6] This is not to say that the relationship between the first and second Adam is the only issue in Irenaeus's Christology, but, as Kelly, Grillmeier, Behr, and Noormann attest, it is the most prominent feature.

Continuity, Discontinuity, and Development

The narrow study of Irenaeus's use of Paul's Adam-Christ typology within his Christological arguments has also been a point of discussion with a spectrum of views. While there are older studies that consider their relationship, the standard has been set by Jan Tjeerd Nielsen's work, *Adam and Christ in the Theology of Irenaeus of Lyons*.[7] Nielsen recognizes that the "Adam-Christ typology is one of the threads leading to the centre of the theology of Irenaeus in *Adversus Haereses*" and observes his attentiveness to the "complete similitude" between Adam and Christ.[8] Nielsen's careful analysis works systematically through Irenaeus's text and concludes that Paul was more concerned with the place of Adam in salvation history, while Irenaeus was more concerned with Adam's corporeality. The contrast between Nielsen's interpretations of Paul and Irenaeus is most explicit when he characterizes their interpretations of Christ, saying, "Paul was concerned with the *second* Adam, while Irenaeus was concerned with the second *Adam*."[9] This contrast between Paul's intention and Irenaeus's interpretation is not unique. Benjamin White traces this hermeneutical bifurcation between Paul and Irenaeus back to Werner, who was very critical of Irenaeus's use of Paul and ultimately concluded that he distorts Paul.[10] White shows how Werner and others read Irenaeus within

---

5. Rolf Noormann, *Irenäus als Paulusinterpret: Zur Rezeption und Wirkung der paulinischen und deuteropaulinischen Briefe im Werk des Irenäus von Lyon* (Tübingen: J.C.B. Mohr, 1994), 523–29.

6. Noormann, *Irenäus als Paulusinterpret*, 427–66.

7. Jan Tjeerd Nielsen, *Adam and Christ in the Theology of Irenaeus of Lyons: An Examination of the Function of the Adam-Christ Typology in the Adversus haereses of Irenaeus, against the Background of the Gnosticism of His Time* (Assen: Van Gorcum, 1968), 6.

8. Nielsen, *Adam and Christ*, 13. Among his collection of texts on early Christian Christology, Richard Norris includes several sections from *Haer.* that discuss the theological correspondence between Adam and Christ, including *Haer.* 3.18.1-7; 3.19.1-3; and 5.1.1-3. The allusions to Paul's use of Adam-Christ typology is prominently on display in each of these sections. Richard A. Norris Jr., *The Christological Controversy* (Philadelphia: Fortress, 1980), 49–60.

9. Nielsen, *Adam and Christ*, 82 (emphasis original).

10. J. Werner, *Der Paulinismus des Irenaeus* (TU 6,2; Leipzig, 1889), 212–13.

a developing Lutheranism and focused on Paul's theology of the cross, which they found lacking in Irenaeus's work.[11]

John Lawson's study of Irenaeus's use of Paul, however, does not find the same sharp contrast. He concludes that Irenaeus "was a fairly sound expositor of S. Paul."[12] When he interprets Paul's Adam-Christ typology, Lawson believes Irenaeus is "most nearly adequate to the thought of S. Paul" and "quite in accord with Pauline thought."[13] Irenaeus, in Lawson's reading, is much closer to Paul's meaning. After his extensive treatment, Noormann sides with Lawson and acknowledges the greater continuity between Irenaeus and Paul.[14]

These contrasting perspectives, however, share similar assumptions. They both question the degree to which Irenaeus's interpretation approximates Paul's isolated intention.[15] Though they offer different conclusions, they begin with the same question, "does Irenaeus interpret Paul correctly?" This analysis of his "approximation" of Paul's intention continues to be the way many studies speak about Irenaeus's use of Pauline texts.

Within Irenaean scholarship, though, Irenaeus's use of the Adam-Christ typology is most often articulated in terms of *development* rather than approximation.[16] For example, in his work on biblical typology, Jean Daniélou argues that the

---

11. Benjamin White, *Remembering Paul: Ancient and Modern Contests over the Image of the Apostle* (Oxford: Oxford University, 2014), 137.

12. John Lawson, *Biblical Theology of Irenaeus* (Eugene, OR: Wipf & Stock, 2008 [reprint of 1948 orig.]), 82.

13. Lawson, *Biblical Theology of Irenaeus*, 76. Wingren contrasts Paul and Irenaeus's Adam-Christ typology in a similar way; see Gustaf Wingren, *Man and the Incarnation: A Study of the Biblical Theology of Irenaeus*, trans. Ross Mackenzie (Eugene, OR: Wipf & Stock, 2004 [reprint of 1947 orig.]), 16–17.

14. Noormann, *Paul and Irenaeus*, 518–19.

15. Another study that approaches Irenaeus and Paul in a similar fashion is Benjamin Blackwell, "Paul and Irenaeus," in *Paul and the Second Century: The Legacy of Paul's Life, Letters, and Teaching*, eds. Michael F. Bird and Joseph R. Dodson (London: T&T Clark, 2011), 190–206 (see esp. 197–98).

16. Some conceive of the relationship between Paul and Irenaeus in different terms. Richard Norris argues that Irenaeus uses Paul more constructively, while David Balas simply states that Pauline language saturates his arguments even when he is not citing Paul. For further discussion, see John S. Coolidge, "The Pauline Basis of the Concept of Scriptural Form in Irenaeus's Scriptural Form," in *Protocol of the Colloquy of the Center for Hermeneutical Studies in Hellenistic and Modern Culture*, ed. Wilhelm Whellner (Berkeley, CA: Center for Hermeneutical Studies, 1975), 1–16; R. A. Norris, "Irenaeus' Use of Paul in His Polemic Against the Gnostics," in *Paul and the Legacies of Paul*, ed. W. S. Babcock (Dallas: SMU, 1990), 79–98; David L. Balas, "The Use and Interpretation of Paul in Irenaeus' Five Books *Adversus Haereses*," *Second Century* 9 (1992), 27–39; J. McHugh, "A Reconsideration of Ephesians 1,10b in Light of Irenaeus," in *Paul and Paulinism: Essays in Honour of C.K. Barrett*, eds. M. D. Hooker and S. G. Wilson (London: S.P.C.K., 1982), 302–9.

"Adamic typology, broadly enunciated by St. Paul, finds its fullest *development* in St. Irenaeus" and later adds that "Irenaeus integrates into a theological scheme the scattered remarks of St. Paul, attempting further *precision* and *systematization*."[17] Irenaeus's reading of the Adam-Christ typology, for Daniélou, exercises even greater theological development, precision, and systematization. Irenaeus does not construe Paul's meaning, but gathers Pauline texts into an organized theological system. Similarly, Behr argues that "what Paul posits as a typological correlation between Adam and Christ, Irenaeus *expands* into an all-embracing account of the economy of God, understanding the end in terms of the beginning, with the end in turn shedding light on the beginning."[18] For Behr, Irenaeus receives Paul's texts and explores new horizons as he reads the apostle within the context of his received apostolic testimony. Irenaeus's *expansion* of Paul develops an appreciation for the overarching divine economy represented in the anchor points of the figures of Adam and Christ. More recently, John VanMaaren finds in Irenaeus "a substantial expansion" of the Pauline Adam-Christ typology, especially in terms of a more detailed correspondence between Adam and Christ.[19]

Of course Irenaeus would not affirm that he misrepresents Paul's intent, but his hermeneutical vision is concerned with an apostolic kerygma which includes, but is not limited to, the Pauline testimony. Whatever Paul means, Irenaeus assumes that it coheres with the nature of the person and work of Christ expressed in the apostolic faith. Thus, Irenaeus finds in Paul's testimony some of the most important Christological conceptions that thread together the testimonies from other apostolic texts. Paul's Adam-Christ texts serve as the theological borders of his Christological framework. Once these Pauline borders are established, he fills in the particular aspects of Christ's person and work by drawing upon other apostolic texts.[20]

Paul, Agreement, and Truth

On several occasions in *Against Heresies*, Irenaeus explains how he reads Paul in light of the church's faith. For example, (in *Haer.* 3.12.9) Irenaeus summarizes the doctrine of God taught by the apostles throughout the book of Acts and, after

---

17. Jean Daniélou, *From Shadows to Reality: Studies in the Biblical Typology of the Fathers* (London: Burns & Oates, 1960), 30–31 (emphasis added).

18. Behr, *Irenaeus of Lyons*, 122 (emphasis added).

19. John VanMaaren, "The Adam-Christ Typology in Paul and Its Development in the Early Church Fathers," *Tyndale Bulletin* 64.2 (2013), 284–85. See also Mary Ann Donovan, *One Right Reading? A Guide to Irenaeus* (Collegeville, MN: Liturgical, 1997), 87. For similar discussions, see Blackwell, "Paul and Irenaeus," 200–201. Peter C. Bouteneff, *Beginnings: Ancient Christian Readings of the Biblical Creation Narratives* (Grand Rapids: Baker, 2008), 77–85.

20. *Haer.* 1.8.1.

mentioning a few quotations from Paul's sermons, he remarks, "That all his [Paul's] letters agree with these sermons [in Acts], we shall demonstrate, in the proper place, from the letters themselves; namely, when we come to explain the apostle ... For you ought to know that scriptural proofs cannot be illustrated except from Scripture."[21] In Irenaeus's words, Paul's letters "agree" (*consonant*), or are theologically harmonious, with his sermons in Acts.[22] But Irenaeus does not stop there; he extends this logic to the whole of scripture and offers a succinct summary of his approach to scripture in general: "scriptural proofs cannot be illustrated except from scripture."[23] The Irenaean interpretation of Paul in particular, and of scripture in general, requires an attentiveness to the coherence of Paul with other Pauline texts, as well as the rest of apostolic testimony.

Elsewhere, Irenaeus is even more specific about the hermeneutical relationship of Paul to the apostolic testimony when he writes (in *Haer.* 4.41.4), "the apostle was a preacher of the truth, and ... he taught all things agreeable (*consonantia*) to the preaching of the truth: it was one God the Father who spoke with Abraham, who gave the law, who sent the prophets beforehand, who in the last times sent His Son, and conferred salvation upon His own handiwork, that is, the substance of flesh."[24] The Apostle is, in Irenaeus's rendering, a "preacher of the truth" and what he taught was "agreeable" (*consonantia*) to the truth.[25] Irenaeus receives and accepts Paul's testimony, but interprets it in harmony and concord with the rest of the scriptural witness.

Taking these studies into account, any discussion of Irenaeus's use of Paul must consider his hermeneutics and recognize the way he integrates Paul's Christological statements within his conception of the apostolic faith. At the same time, the studies mentioned above have not explained precisely *how* Irenaeus develops his reading of Paul with the theological network of texts. In other words,

---

21. *Haer.* 3.12.9. English translations of *Haer. 1-3* are from Dominic J. Unger and John J. Dillon, *St. Irenaeus of Lyons: Against the Heresies (Book 1)* (ACW 55; New York: Newman Press, 1992); Dominic J. Unger, John J. Dillon, and Michael Slusser, *St. Irenaeus of Lyons: Against the Heresies (Book 2)* (ACW 65; New York: Newman, 2012); Dominic J. Unger, John J. Dillon, and Matthew Steenberg, *St. Irenaeus of Lyons: Against the Heresies (Book 3)* (ACW 64; New York: Newman Press, 2012). English translations of *Haer.* 4-5 are from A. Roberts and J. Donaldson, *Ante-Nicene Fathers. Vol. 1* (Peabody, MA: Hendrickson, 1994). Discussions and citations of the Latin or Greek retroversion are from A. Rousseau et al., *Contre les hérésies, Livre I-V.* 10 vols. *Sources Chrétiennes*, nos. 100.1-2, 152-3, 210, 211, 263-64, 293-4 (Paris: Éditions du Cerf, 1965–82).

22. For a discussion of Irenaeus's theology of coherence and the way it applies to his hermeneutics, see Stephen Presley, *The Intertextual Reception of Genesis 1–3 in Irenaeus of Lyons* (Leiden: Brill, 2015), 12–27. See also Presley, "The Demonstration of Intertextuality in Irenaeus of Lyons," in *Intertextuality in the Second Century* (Leiden: Brill, 2016), 195–213.

23. *Haer.* 3.12.9.

24. *Haer.* 4.41.4.

25. *Haer.* 4.41.4. White, *Remembering Paul*, 137.

how did he use Paul and the Pauline association between Adam and Christ to fashion the theological coherence of his Christological argumentation? The rest of this chapter will trace Irenaeus's expansion of the Pauline Adam-Christ typology through his discussion of Rom 5:12-21 and 1 Cor 15:21-22. In his discussion of Adam and Christ, which are pivotal to his discussions of Christology, the bishop of Lyons develops Paul's exegesis through the integration of other Pauline concepts and allusions to other Old Testament and New Testament texts. Throughout his scriptural reasoning, the Pauline Adam-Christ typology maintains an organizing scheme around which he arranges textual building blocks to construct the edifice of his Christological vision.

Irenaeus, Christology, and Rom 5:12-19

Turning to Irenaeus's work, a discussion of Christology and the use of Rom 5:12-19 intersect in *Against Heresies* 3. The whole of 3.18-23 contains a series of chiasms organized around particular issues related to Christology, and Rom 5:12-19 appears in three important instances.[26] An appeal for a unified vision of the divine economy pervades the chapters, though in each context he situates Paul within a different network of texts.

The first prominent allusion to Rom 5:12-19 surfaces in *Against Heresies* 3.18.7, which is the conclusion of a larger chiasm organized around his view of the incarnation and its soteriological implications. In this discussion of Christology, Paul plays a formative role that helps situate Christ's work within a general economic portrait of redemption. Romans 5:14 summarizes the key soteriological functions of the incarnation through a vision of the history of salvation. According to Irenaeus, the Gnostics "who assert that He was manifested putatively and was not born in the flesh was not made man [John 1:14], are still under the old condemnation; they extend patronage to sin, since according to them death has not been overcome, which reigned from Adam to Moses, even over those whose sins were not like the transgression of Adam [Rom 5:14]."[27] Although framed by his polemical theology, his argument situates the Christology of Paul and John in a logical relationship. He assumes that the incarnation, as expressed in John 1:14, is the logical conclusion to Paul's summary of sin and death reigning from

---

26. Donovan, *One Right Reading?*, 82–90. According to *Biblia Patristica*, Irenaeus alludes to Rom 5:12-19 in *Haer.* 3.16.9, *Haer.* 3.18.6-7, Haer. 3.21.1,10, *Haer.* 3.22.3-4, *Haer.* 3.23.7, and *Haer.* 4.4.1. Three of these instances (*Haer.* 3.18.6-7, Haer. 3.21.10, *Haer.* 3.22.3-4) offer the most explicit and helpful allusions to this passage for the purposes of this chapter. See J. Allenbach et al., *Biblia Patristica: Index des citations et allusions bibliques dans la littérature patristique*, vol. 1 (Paris: Éditions du centre national de la recherché scientifique, 1975), 432–33.

27. *Haer.* 3.18.7. It may be that Irenaeus conflates his allusions to John 1:14, "the Word became flesh (*sarx*)," with the *anthropos* language in Phil 2:7-8.

Adam onward in Rom 5:14. Paul's economic vision anticipates the Johannine emphasis on the incarnation. He asserts that death had gained power over Adam and it reigned from Adam to Moses and even over all people (Rom 5:14); *therefore* Christ became incarnate and was "made man" (John 1:14). Of course Irenaeus assumes that his Gnostic interlocutors reject the theological continuity between these claims, but his interpretation of the incarnation remains the conclusion to the predicament of sin and death.

A few lines later (in *Haer.* 3.18.7), Irenaeus reinforces this point when he reframes the argument in light of the Adam-Christ typology of Rom 5:19, saying:

> For, just as through the disobedience of one man who was fashioned first from untilled earth [Gen 2:1] many were made sinners and lost life, so it was fitting also through the obedience of the one man, who was born first of the Virgin [Isa 7:14], that many be made just and receive salvation [Rom 5:19]. Thus, then, the Word of God was made Man [John 1:14].[28]

Once again, the Adam-Christ typology of Rom 5:19 (like Rom 5:14 above) possesses the controlling economic idea of a theological history linking Adam and Christ. But Irenaeus *extends* this Pauline imagery by weaving key theological statements derived from other passages including: Gen 2:1, Isa 7:14, and John 1:14. The allusions to other scripture passages and the general reference to Christ as conceived from a virgin are *infused* into the Irenaeus quotation of Rom 5:19. His Christological vision extends Paul by means of scriptural threading through an inter-scriptural conversation where Paul's statement about the disobedience of the one man (Adam) in Rom 5:19a is blended with the qualification that he was also the one "who was fashioned from untilled soil."[29] The intensive reading of the soil imagery in Gen 2:1 presses the typology in a way that might seem unconvincing, but Irenaeus wants to be certain that this one through whom sin and death came is not identified as anyone other than the one whom God created from the earth in Gen 2:6-7. His theology of the incarnation and the language of Paul encourage him to think economically. The symmetrical parallels between their respective births heighten the asymmetrical contrast between their relations toward sin made explicit in Paul's text (Rom 5:12 and 19). This is also why he clarifies the identity of Christ as the one "who was born first of the Virgin," to solidify the economic continuity expressed in Paul.[30]

Finally, the last sentence in the quotation above is the theological conclusion of the economic predicament expressed in Rom 5:19.[31] Through the one born of the virgin many would be made righteous, "thus, then, was the Word of God made Man [John 1:14]."[32] The language of John 1:14 is the logical conclusion to

---

28. *Haer.* 3.18.7.
29. *Haer.* 3.18.7.
30. *Haer.* 3.18.7.
31. A similar use is found in *Epid.* 31.
32. *Haer.* 3.18.7.

the reference to the fact that many will be "made just and receive salvation."[33] The Pauline language and imagery contain the controlling idea that necessitates the incarnation.

In a second reference several chapters later, Irenaeus again reads Paul and extends the nature of the typological relationships through personal and material associations.[34] In this context, he freely integrates the correlation between sin and death in Rom 5:12 with the emphasis on obedience, disobedience, and righteousness in Rom 5:19. He also conflates these Pauline texts with other passages including: Eph 1:10, Gen 2:5, Gen 2:7, Ps 118(119):73, Matt 1:23-25, and John 1:3. He enlarges Paul's asymmetrical parallelism between Adam and Christ with more symmetrical aspects of these figures. From the beginning, Pauline texts and imagery frame the incarnation:

> He has recapitulated in Himself even the ancient first-fashioned man [Eph 1:10]. To explain, just as by one man's disobedience ... sin came ... and death through sin ... reigned, so by one man's obedience [Rom 5:12, 19], justice was brought [Rom 5:19] and produces the fruit of life for those who in times past were dead. First, just as the first-fashioned Adam got his substance from untilled and as yet virgin soil, for God has not yet caused it to rain [Gen 2:5] ... and man had not yet tilled the ground—and was formed by God's hand [Ps 118(119):73[35]]—that is, the Word of God—for all things were made through Him [John 1:3]—and the Lord took mud from the earth and fashioned man [Gen 2:7]. In like manner, since He is the Word recapitulating Adam in Himself [Eph 1:10], He rightly took from Mary, who was yet a virgin [Matt 1:23-25[36]], His birth that would be a recapitulation of Adam.[37]

To begin, the opening allusion to the concept of recapitulation in Eph 1:10 sets the framework for Irenaeus's reading of Rom 5:12 and 19.[38] Irenaeus interprets the language of "recapitulation" (*recapitulare*) in an economic fashion while simultaneously attending to the personal aspects that firm up the whole structure between Christ's human nature and the "ancient first-formed man." He broadens Paul's language through more explanation of the theological continuity between Adam and Christ. Whereas Paul merely states "through one man" (Rom 5:12 and 19), Irenaeus extends his reading by explaining the continuity between the

---

33. Donovan, *One Right Reading?*, 84.
34. Donovan, *One Right Reading?*, 87.
35. Cf. Job 10:8.
36. Cf. Isa 7:14 and Luke 1:27-34. In this instance, I believe that the language of the Matthean citation of Isa 7:14 in Matt 1:23-25 is in view. The argument of *Haer.* 3.21.1-10 focuses on Irenaeus's interpretation of the fulfillment of Isa 7:14 and his defense of the virgin birth.
37. *Haer.* 3.21.10.
38. Grant, *Jesus after the Gospels*, 106–7.

human natures of Adam and Christ. In this case, Irenaeus defines the "one man" in terms of his formation in Gen 2:5 and 2:7. The substance of Adam's formation, in Gen 2:5, (i.e., the substance of the earth) is characterized as undisturbed, or "untilled," until the Word of God (John 1:3), or the Hand of God (Ps 118[119]:73), fashions the original formation.

In the same quotation above, he alludes to the preexistence of the Word as the One through whom all things are made, which adds another Christological aspect not explicit in Paul. The active presence of the Word of God in the creation of Adam is the theological connection between the formation of Adam and the incarnation. This same Word of God that fashioned Adam recapitulated Adam in himself (Eph 1:10) in the incarnation. He articulates this through association with the formation of Adam from the "untilled soil," which is why Christ received the same formation from Mary, who was also a virgin (Matt 1:23-25). He extends the substantive continuity between Adam and Christ through theological correspondence in relationship to Paul. For Irenaeus, this reading is not opposed to Paul; rather it is an extension of the Pauline analogy resident in the passage that frames Irenaeus's Christology.

Finally, Irenaeus builds upon the preceding discussion and the nature of the incarnation (in *Haer.* 3.22.3). In this section he points to Rom 5:14, where Paul argues that Adam was "a type of him who was to come (*typus futuri*)." The larger context of the section is the same extended reference to the humanity of Christ that Irenaeus has been marshaling against the various Gnostic dualisms for the past few chapters. His discussion (in *Haer.* 3.22.2) is an intricate reflection on Christ's incarnate flesh that draws together a tissue of texts, mostly from the Gospels, portraying Christ's human nature, including how he required food, grew tired, was wounded, grieved, sweat blood, and was pierced.[39] Together, all these conditions illustrate, in Irenaeus's words, "signs of the flesh" which was formed from the earth, weak and corruptible. Attention to the substance of Christ's flesh introduces the discussion of Adam-Christ typology, which draws together an intricate exposition of Pauline thought, saying:

> Wherefore Luke points out that the pedigree which traces the generation of our Lord back to Adam contains seventy-two generations, connecting the end with the beginning [Luke 3:23-38], and implying that it is He who has summed up in Himself [Eph 1:10] all nations dispersed from Adam downwards, and all languages and generations of men, together with Adam himself. Hence also was Adam himself termed by Paul "the figure of Him that was to come," [Rom 5:14] because the Word, the Maker of all things, had formed beforehand for Himself the future dispensation of the human race, connected with the Son of God; God having predestined that the first man should be of an animal nature, with this view, that he might be saved by the spiritual One [1 Cor 15:46].[40]

---

39. See Matt 4:2, 26:38; John 4:6, 11:35, 19:34; Ps 68:27(69:26), and Luke 22:44.
40. *Haer.* 3.22.3.

In this passage, he interprets Paul in the same way that he has the previous references, only in this case it is a highly intensive intra-Pauline reading. For Irenaeus the associations between Adam and Christ are expressed most clearly in historical terms in Luke's genealogical account in Luke 3:23-38.[41] Unlike Matthew's Gospel, which only traces his genealogy to Abraham, the Gospel of Luke connects the "end" in Christ with the "beginning" in Adam. This historical record of the lineage of Christ "signifies" (*significans*) that Christ has "recapitulated in himself" (*in semetipso recapitulatus est*; Eph 1:10) all the generations from Adam downward. At the same time these two passages, Luke 3:23-38 and Eph 1:10, are read in theological continuity with the reference to Adam as "a type of him who was to come" in Rom 5:14. Irenaeus sees an economic structure to Paul's reference; Adam is not merely a "type," but a specific type of Christ who was *to come*. The temporal reference anticipates the incarnation, which is expressed in the Lukan genealogy. Following the reference to Rom 5:14, Irenaeus writes: "Word, the Maker of all things, had formed beforehand for Himself the future dispensation of the human race, connected with the Son of God."[42] In his reading of Rom 5:14, then, Luke's genealogy in Luke 3:23-38 and Paul's reference to recapitulation in Eph 1:10 are the historical and theological expansion of the Pauline thought implicit in Rom 5:14. After this, Irenaeus again finds in Paul's discussion of recapitulation in Eph 1:10 the anticipation of the typology expressed in Rom 5:14. In other words, the first Adam "was the type of him who was to come" (Rom 5:14), so therefore the second Adam has indeed come and "recapitulated all things in himself" (Eph 1:10). These two interconnected Christology statements, supported by Luke's genealogy, express the way Irenaeus develops Pauline thought in his defense of the humanity of Christ.

One other final allusion to 1 Cor 15:46 in the quotation above concludes Irenaeus's Christological argument and defines the effect of the incarnation. In the formation of Adam from the dust, God predestined that this one "might be saved by the spiritual One" (1 Cor 15:46). Reading this text in continuity with Luke 3:23-38, Eph 1:10, and Rom 5:14 brings the temporal and salvific effects of the incarnation to the forefront. The formation from the dust in the first Adam is bound to an economic trajectory leading to the incarnation, where Christ sums up in his person the formation of Adam and effects salvation. This final quotation of the Adam-Christ typology reinforces the premise that Irenaeus reads Pauline epistles as an interconnected commentary within themselves.[43] The central passage for Irenaeus's Christology is Eph 1:10, which he develops theologically in conversation with the economic trajectory of other Pauline passages.

Irenaeus's reading of Rom 5:12-19 begins to develop the way this Pauline pericope frames his Christology and the interplay of texts within the economic vision of Christ's work. The Pauline imagery offers Irenaeus the language and

---

41. Behr, *Irenaeus of Lyons*, 145.
42. *Haer.* 3.22.3.
43. *Haer.* 3.12.9.

imagery to articulate the economic framework for the incarnation. Paul sets the theological borders of Irenaeus's Christological portrait, which blend together with the other elements of the apostolic witness. The incarnation is at the forefront of his interpretive logic as he presses the economic aspects of Paul's thought and integrates other passages into this structure described in Rom 5:12-19.

Irenaeus, Christology, and 1 Cor 15:21-22

Alongside his use of Rom 5:12-19, 1 Cor 15:21-22 is another Pauline passage crucial to Irenaeus's Christology. Like Rom 5:12-19, this passage continues to participate in Irenaeus's Christological framework through his Adam-Christ typology. At the same time, it transitions Irenaeus's focus from a protological orientation and the continuity between the first and second Adam toward an eschatological orientation focused on the resurrection of Christ and its effect upon the first Adam. Whereas Rom 5:12-19 helps Irenaeus describe the history and nature of the incarnation and typological connections between the first Adam and Christ, 1 Cor 15:21-22 provides a framework to continue the narrative toward the future resurrection. Together Rom 5:12-19 and 1 Cor 15:21-22 envision a unified divine economy moving from creation to incarnation to resurrection. Once again, the key sections of *Against Heresies* 3.18-23 are important for their discussion of the person of Christ, but the reflection on this passage resurfaces in the course of Book 5 as well.[44]

First, (in *Haer.* 3.18.3) Irenaeus turns to 1 Cor 15:21-22 in the midst of his polemical response to the function of the redeemer figure within the Valentinian myth. In this context, Irenaeus filters the Pauline language of 1 Corinthians 15 into his polemical theology and emphasis on Christ's humanity. He connects the work of Christ in 1 Cor 15:3-4 with the reference to the resurrected Christ in 1 Cor 15:12 and his identity as a human person in 1 Cor 15:21. The Adam-Christ typology of 1 Cor 15:21 in particular seals the argument by linking the economic poles of the history of salvation.

Against his Gnostic interlocutors, Irenaeus finds in 1 Cor 15:3-4 a unified, summary statement of the work of Christ. According to Irenaeus, the Christ that Paul knew was one who was born, suffered, died, and rose again. But Irenaeus also notes that Paul argues Christ performed these acts as a "man" (*hominem*). Irenaeus writes that "Paul did not know another Christ besides Him alone who suffered and was buried and rose again, who was also born, who he also called man."[45] Irenaeus wants to be sure that Paul is not read in a way that would deny Christ's

---

44. According to *Biblia Patristica*, Irenaeus alludes to 1 Cor 15:12-22 in *Haer.* 3.18.3; 3.22.4; 3.23.7-8; 5.1.3; 5.12.3; and 5.14.1. Four of these instances (*Haer.* 3.18.3; 3.22.4; 5.1.3; and 5.12.3) offer the most explicit and helpful allusions to this passage for the purposes of this chapter. See J. Allenbach et al., *Biblia Patristica*, 468.

45. *Haer.* 3.18.3.

human nature nor the unity of the acts he performed in his human nature. For this reason he continues with the close connection between 1 Cor 15:12 and 1 Cor 15:21 saying, "For, when he [Paul] has said, 'Now if Christ is preached as raised from the dead [1 Cor 15:12],' he continued giving the reason for his incarnation, for as by man came death, by a man has come also resurrection from the dead [1 Cor 15:21]."[46] In 1 Cor 15:12 Christ is preached as "raised from the dead," but this passage is not explicit enough. Irenaeus notes that he was raised as a "man" (*hominem*) so that by this man also comes the resurrection of the dead (1 Cor 15:21). Like the other recapitulation passages, Irenaeus finds within the language of 1 Cor 15:21 the general structure of the divine economy progressing toward the incarnation and ultimately the resurrection of the dead. In Irenaeus's logic the incarnation is necessarily tied theologically to Christ's resurrection as its objective and goal.

Second, a few chapters later in *Haer.* 3.22.4, a section closely related to the discussion of Rom 5:12-19 above, Irenaeus laces together a succession of passages that epitomize the salvific effect of the incarnation through the logic of the Adam-Christ typology. The broader context includes a discussion of both the Adam-Christ typology and the Eve-Mary typology. The Pauline text of 1 Cor 15:20-22 is essential to this discussion, but it also participates in conversation with several other passages, including: Matt 19:30,[47] Ps 44(45):17, Col 1:18, 1 Cor 15:22, and Luke 3:23-38. Each of these texts is framed by the logic of recapitulation:

> With this in view the Lord said, "the first will be last, and the last first [Matt 19:30]." The prophet, too, pointed out the same thing: "in place of your fathers," sons were born to you [Ps 44(45):17]," he said. For the Lord, who was born "the Firstborn of the dead," [Col 1:18] receiving the ancient fathers into His bosom, regenerated them to the life of God, having become the beginning of living beings, since Adam had become the beginning of the dying [1 Cor 15:22]. For this reason Luke, when he began the genealogy of the Lord, carried it back to Adam [Luke 3:23-38], pointing out that they did not regenerate Him for the Gospel of life, but He them.[48]

Here he begins with the dominical saying that articulates the logic of recapitulation which Irenaeus finds elsewhere in scripture. His point is that the culmination of the economic trajectory of salvation is the person of Christ, who will effect salvation and become the first-born from the dead. This is clear in his three allusions to Matt 19:30, Ps 44(45):17, and Col 1:18. He interprets the reversal of the "last" being "first" in the Matthew passage within an economic framework that marks the superiority of Christ over the line of Adam. In a similar way, Irenaeus interprets the Psalm imagery of sons born in place of their fathers economically,

---

46. *Haer.* 3.18.3.
47. Matt 20:16.
48. *Haer.* 3.22.4.

as the "sons" coming after, but becoming superior to, the "fathers." The ultimate "son" in Irenaeus's reading is, to borrow the imagery of Col 1:18, the "First-born from the dead," while the "fathers" reflect the line from Adam downward. This first-born son, moreover, receives back the fathers and grants them life and resurrection. Irenaeus seals this intertextual logic with an appeal to Pauline Adam-Christ typology in 1 Cor 15:22, where, just as Adam became the beginning of death, Christ also became the beginning of life. Together, Matt 19:30, Ps 44(45):17, 1 Cor 15:22, and Col 1:18 provide Irenaeus the scriptural language and concepts to frame his theology of recapitulation.

Furthermore, in the context, the language of "all" dying in Adam and "all" made alive in Christ (1 Cor 15:22) becomes clearer when put in conversation with the recapitulation logic of Matt 19:30, Ps 44:17, and Col 1:18. The logic of the "last" being "first" in the Matthean dominical saying, the inversion of the imagery of "fathers" and "sons" in the Psalmist, and the emphasis on Christ as the "first-born" (Col 1:18) extend the Pauline argument with an economic emphasis directed toward the incarnation and subsequent effect of the resurrection. The "all" are those who inherited sin and death from Adam, and, conversely, those who inherit life and resurrection from Christ. To support the economic structure of this theological reading, he appeals again to Luke's genealogy account (Luke 3:23-38). In this case he notes that the structure is written backwards beginning with Christ and concluding with Adam; only in this context he points out that it is Christ who is now the author of life and resurrection, not Adam or those after him. Amid these texts, 1 Cor 15:21-22 is decisive in his Christological claims that exemplify the logic of recapitulation that culminates in the incarnation and resurrection.

Third, the discussion of 1 Cor 15:22 and the effect of the incarnation returns again (in *Haer.* 5.1.3) where Irenaeus applies his Adam-Christ typology comparing Adam's formation in the "beginning" and Christ's formation in the "end."[49] The immediate context is a refutation of the Christology of the Ebionites, who according to Irenaeus reject Christ's deity, and specifically the virgin birth. According to Irenaeus, the Ebionites' denial of the incarnation amounts to a denial of the potentiality for union, or "mingling" (*commixtionem*), between God and the human person. In Irenaeus's words, the Ebionites "do not receive by faith into their soul the union of God and man."[50] As mentioned above, for Irenaeus the incarnation is a logical conclusion of salvation history.[51] Irenaeus's polemical response draws together the imagery and theology of Gen 1:26, 2:7; Luke 1:35; and 1 Cor 15:22 and 44:

> Therefore do these men reject the commixture of the heavenly wine ... not considering that as, at the beginning of our formation in Adam, that breath of life which proceeded from God, having been united to what had been fashioned,

---

49. *Haer.* 5.1.3.
50. *Haer.* 5.1.3.
51. Donovan, *One Right Reading?*, 143.

animated the man [Gen 2:7], and manifested him as a being endowed with reason; so also, in the end, the Word of the Father and the Spirit of God, having become united with the ancient substance of Adam's formation [cf. Luke 1:35], rendered man living and perfect, receptive of the perfect Father, in order that as in the natural *Adam* we all were dead, so in the spiritual *Adam* we may all be made alive [1 Cor 15:22, cf. 1 Cor 15:44]. For never at any time did Adam escape the hands of God, to whom the Father speaking, said, "Let Us make man in Our image, after Our likeness [Gen 1:26]." (Emphases added)

In this context, Irenaeus frames his theology of the incarnation with the Adam-Christ typology as he correlates the nature of Adam's formation "in the beginning" (cf. Gen 2:7), and Christ's formation "in the end" (cf. Luke 1:35). As in other sections, Irenaeus's economic logic draws on the entire textual atmosphere of the narrative of Adam's formation in Genesis. He reads these key terms and concepts in correspondence with that of the presentation of the incarnation in Luke 1:35, with the effect of the incarnation being that it "rendered the human person living and perfect." While the body in Gen 2:7 is formed from the dust, Adam becomes a "living human" (Gen 2:7) through the infusion of the "breath of life." The child born of Mary was united with the "ancient substance of Adam's formation," becoming, once again, "living and perfect" and created in the image and likeness of God.

The theological thread knitting together these connections between Gen 1:26, Gen 2:7, and Luke 1:35 is the Pauline imagery of 1 Cor 15:22 (and 1 Cor 15:44). Whereas Irenaeus reasons theologically through these economic connections between Adam and Christ, the Pauline language offers him a succinct summary of the typological connections in one passage. Even the phrase that follows his allusion to 1 Cor 15:22, when he remarks that the formation of Adam never escaped the "hands of God," implies that God continually formed and created all things throughout the history of salvation from the creation of Adam to the incarnation of Christ.

At the same time, the allusion to 1 Cor 15:22 also has an anthropological orientation that gives close attention to the very substance of Adam's formation and its relationship to the corresponding modes of life or death. For Irenaeus, Paul's words are the theological summary of the purpose and anticipation of the incarnation. Irenaeus's allusion to 1 Cor 15:22 is much closer to the wording of the text in this instance, though it is infused with the imagery of "natural" and "spiritual" from 1 Cor 15:44, and Irenaeus's use of parallel texts extends Paul's emphasis on sin and death that has passed to all people. At the same time, 1 Cor 15:22 is also attentive to the resurrection and the future resurrection of the faithful, but Irenaeus extends the Pauline analogy to connect the incarnation and resurrection as one continuous salvific event in the person of Christ, even if he gives still more attention to the anthropological aspects of both Adam and Christ. For Irenaeus, the modality of life that is lost in Adam is initially overturned in the incarnation and eventually conquered through resurrection. Thus, the "spiritual" man (1 Cor 15:44) is Christ, the Son of God, who became incarnate by means of the Spirit (Luke 1:35) and later rose from the dead (1 Cor 15:22).

Finally, (in *Haer.* 5.12.3) Irenaeus solidifies his Christological and anthropological argument by establishing the economic continuity and discontinuity between the breath of life in Gen 2:7 and the vivifying Spirit in 1 Cor 15:45. This section is part of an extended commentary on the Gnostic reading of 1 Cor 15:50, "flesh and blood cannot inherit the kingdom of God." For Irenaeus, death and life are ontologically contrasting conditions that cannot mutually coexist within the same person. The flesh is a bystander that may be drawn in the direction of corruption or incorruption, but Irenaeus must address the reality that, in the present, even those who experience life are still subject to death and corruption. In this context, Irenaeus stresses the dissimilarity between the experiences of life and death, saying:

> For it is not one thing which dies and another which is quickened, as neither is it one thing which is lost and another which is found, but the Lord came seeking for that same sheep which had been lost [Luke 15:4-6[52]]. What was it, then, which was dead? Undoubtedly it was the substance of the flesh; the same, too, which had lost the breath of life, and had become breathless and dead [Gen 3:19]. This same, therefore, was what the Lord came to quicken, that as in Adam we do all die, as being of an animal nature, in Christ we may all live, as being spiritual [1 Cor 15:22, cf. 1 Cor 15:44], not laying aside God's handiwork, but the lusts of the flesh, and receiving the Holy Spirit.[53]

Here again Irenaeus reflects on the correspondence between Adam's formation and Christ's incarnation. In his economic vision, the same substance that was formed in Adam dies and dissolves back into the earth (Gen 3:19). In this instance he appeals to the imagery of the lost sheep in Luke 15:4-6 to stress the importance of the humanity lost in Adam, which he also reads in continuity with the Pauline summary of 1 Cor 15:22. In his incarnation, Christ came seeking after that "lost" humanity, which he recovered in his person. The substantive focus of his reading of the parable alongside his economic vision of Gen 3:19 is solidified in the imagery of 1 Cor 15:22 so that "in Adam we do all die, as being of an animal nature, in Christ we may all live, as being spiritual" (1 Cor 15:22, 44). Thus, the same Christ who experiences corruption is also raised from the dead in the Spirit. Here again, Irenaeus focuses on the substance of the flesh that is implicit in the corresponding modes of death and life in Adam and Christ in 1 Cor 15:22 (and more explicit in 1 Cor 15:44). He extends Paul's correlation with various other passages that serve as commentary on the natures of Adam and Christ. The Pauline imagery, once again, is the summary of the Adam-Christ connections that are developed and expanded through other passages.[54]

---

52. Cf. Matt 18:11.
53. *Haer.* 5.12.3.
54. This soteriological tension between solidarity with Adam in death and solidarity with Christ in life (1 Cor 15:22) is explained in the immediate context by a series of Pauline texts (Col 3:5, 9-10, and Phil 1:22) and a final allusion to Gen 1:26.

Conclusion

Many treatments of Irenaeus's Christology recognize how he organizes the work of Christ around an economic vision of salvation history that is, in part, oriented by the Pauline Adam-Christ typology. In every major section of *Against Heresies* that contemplates the nature of the person and work of Christ, Paul's Adam-Christ typology is prominently on display. Previous studies of Irenaeus's use of Paul have fallen along two lines. First, there are many works that approximate the degree to which Irenaeus interpreted Paul rightly. These works contrast their distinctive exegetical perspectives and label Irenaeus a better or worse interpreter of Paul. Second, there are other studies that frame Irenaeus as an expander or developer of Pauline thought. These works argue that Irenaeus received Paul's testimony and developed it through further theological reasoning and exegesis. As these studies suggest, Irenaeus never conceived of the exegetical task as isolating Paul's meaning. Instead Irenaeus receives Paul's texts and reads them in continuity with other passages that also express the apostolic faith. As Irenaeus himself attests, his reading of Paul aims to situate the apostle within the other apostolic witnesses (*Haer.* 3.12.9; 4.41.4).

Throughout the analysis of Irenaeus's use of Paul in his Christology, it is evident that Paul's Adam-Christ typology is pivotal. In several key sections of *Against Heresies*, the Bishop of Lyons appeals to Adam-Christ typology from Rom 5:12-19 and 1 Cor 15:21-22 in order to frame a broad economic vision of his Christology. Whereas Rom 5:12-19 helps him capture the nature of the incarnation and typological connections between the first Adam and Christ, 1 Cor 15:21-22 provides a framework to continue the narrative toward the future resurrection. Together Rom 5:12-19 and 1 Cor 15:21-22 envision a unified divine economy moving from creation to incarnation to resurrection. Within the borders of this economic vision of Christology, however, Irenaeus fills in the rest of his Christology with a variety of other scriptures including: Gen 1:26, 2:1, 2:5, 2:7, 3:19; Ps 118(119):73, 44(45):17; Isa 7:14; Matt 1:23-25, 19:30; Luke 1:35, 3:23-38, 15:4-6; John 1:3, 1:14; Eph 1:10; and Col 1:18. Each of these texts stands in various theological relationships with the economic framework established through Rom 5:12-19 and 1 Cor 15:21-22. For example, within the context of an economic vision fashioned by the Adam-Christ typology, these texts help explain the reason for the incarnation, thread together the theological narrative of salvation history between Adam and Christ, reflect on Christ's human nature in correspondence to Adam's formation, and connect the formation in Adam with the resurrection in Christ. From beginning to end, creation to resurrection, Rom 5:12-19 and 1 Cor 15:21-22 fashion the economic boundaries upon which his understanding of Christ's work is built. In this way, Irenaeus envisions himself receiving the Pauline Christology, and he thereby integrates Paul into his own theological vision. Paul is pivotal for Irenaeus's Christology, but only when Paul is read in continuity with his perspective of the apostolic faith.

RESPONSE
MESSIAH CHRISTOLOGY IN PAUL AND IRENAEUS

Joshua W. Jipp

It is no surprise that Stephen Presley's helpful and clearly articulated chapter focuses on Paul's Adam-Christ typology given its preeminence and programmatic character in Irenaeus's Christology. Paul's Adam-Christ texts (Rom 5:12-21; 1 Cor 15:21-22) are shaped by Irenaeus in such a way that they express the apostolic economy of God's salvation history, focused upon creation, incarnation, and resurrection.[1] Presley argues that Irenaeus uses Paul's Adam-Christ typology to "serve as the theological borders of his Christological framework" and then draws upon a variety of other apostolic texts to provide further detail about Christ's work and person. Presley emphasizes throughout his chapter the way in which Irenaeus develops his exegesis of Paul and his Adam–Christ typology *by means of* a scriptural interpretation which includes a variety of "other Pauline concepts and allusions to other Old Testament and New Testament texts."

I would like to offer a brief contribution to one of these additional Pauline concepts, occurring within the "theological borders" of Irenaeus's Adam-Christ typology, which Irenaeus draws upon in some detail in Book 3 of *Against Heresies* in order to articulate his divine economy of salvation. In brief, my argument is that Irenaeus is a witness to Jewish messianism in his reading of scripture, articulation of the identity of Jesus as the Son of God, and the accomplishment of humanity's salvation in their becoming sons of God.[2] Irenaeus's Messiah Christology, furthermore, draws upon *and expands* the Messiah Christology of the Apostle Paul. Jewish messianic language, texts, and concepts have, I suggest, deeply influenced Irenaeus's saving divine economy, mediated in part through Paul's own Messiah Christology. More broadly, I suggest that Irenaeus provides evidence that Jewish

---

1. In my understanding of this aspect of Irenaeus, I have been greatly aided by Behr, *Irenaeus of Lyons*, esp. 144–62.

2. For a strong argument that Jewish Messianism made a profound impact on early Christianity, see William Horbury, *Jewish Messianism and the Cult of Christ* (London: SCM Press, 1998).

messianism continued in a significant way into second-century Christianity, but here I will simply seek to make this case briefly with respect to Irenaeus.[3]

As Presley has argued, Irenaeus is more concerned with the "apostolic kerygma" and so Irenaeus's Messiah Christology is articulated through a variety of biblical texts, concepts, and metaphors that go beyond the Pauline corpus. But there are significant points of overlap in Irenaeus's and Paul's interpretation of Old Testament "Messiah-texts," and Irenaeus draws upon one important aspect of Paul's messianic discourse in order to articulate his own Christology.[4] I offer here a brief sketch of Paul's and Irenaeus's messianism as focused upon their common use and interpretation of Jesus as the anointed one, their shared witness to a messianic reading of Israel's scriptures, and Irenaeus's use of Paul's articulation of humanity's salvation as consisting in their adoption to sonship. I should note here that I am not interested so much in whether Irenaeus rightly understands Paul, as much as I am in continuities between Irenaeus and Paul and which texts and traditions have been called forth to provide a particular remembrance or interpretation of Paul.[5]

The Anointed One

One of the defining features of Israel's messianic figures is that they were anointed by oil in a ritual which effectively marked them out as sacred and elected by God as his holy ruler. Within Israel's scriptures, the honorific "Messiah" is most often used as shorthand for "the Lord's Messiah" (e.g., 1 Sam 2:10, 35; 24:7-11; 26:9-16; 2 Sam 1:14, 16; 19:22; Lam 4:20). And in the act of anointing, Israel's ruler was set forth as the Lord's anointed, thereby effecting a special relationship between the king and God.[6] The act of anointing the king thereby marks him out as holy, sacred, powerful, and associated deeply with God's presence, often by means of bearing the Holy Spirit (e.g., 1 Sam 24:6; Isa 11:1-4).

---

3. More broadly, however, see Matthew V. Novenson, *The Grammar of Messianism: An Ancient Jewish Political Idiom and Its Users* (Oxford: Oxford University Press, 2017), 217–62; David Flusser, "Jewish Messianism Reflected in the Early Church," in *Judaism of the Second Temple Period*, trans. Azzan Yadin, vol. 2 (Grand Rapids: Eerdmans, 2007–2009), 258–88; William Horbury, *Messianism among Jews and Christians* (London: T&T Clark, 2003), 275–88.

4. Messiah texts and messianic discourse are labeled as such due to their ability to be "deployed in the context of a linguistic community whose members shared a stock of common linguistic resources." See throughout Matthew V. Novenson, *Christ among the Messiahs: Christ Language in Paul and Messiah Language in Ancient Judaism* (Oxford: Oxford University Press, 2012), here, 47.

5. See here especially, Benjamin L. White, *Remembering Paul: Ancient and Modern Contests over the Image of the Apostle* (Oxford: Oxford University Press, 2014), 174.

6. Roland de Vaux, "The King of Israel, Vassal of Yahweh," in *The Bible and the Ancient Near East* (London: Darton, Longman & Todd, 1971), 152–66, here, 152.

I have argued that Paul's Christology makes good sense as a particular version of a Messiah Christology, and I will not try to summarize that argument here.[7] Paul does refer to Jesus as "Messiah" (*Christos*) 269 times alone within his seven undisputed epistles.[8] In 2 Cor 1:21-22 Paul plays with the language of anointing as he declares that it is "God who establishes us with you into the anointed one and has anointed us. He has also sealed us and given to us the down-payment of the Spirit in our hearts." Without invoking later Trinitarian language, one can see that Paul speaks of God as the subject whose agency works to establish a relationship between Christ the anointed one, the Holy Spirit, and "us" who are established "in the anointed."[9]

Irenaeus too uses the language of anointing to draw together God the Father, Jesus, and the Holy Spirit into a unified economy of salvation for humanity. Thus, Irenaeus invokes Ps. 45:6-7: "Thy throne, O God, is forever and ever; the scepter of thy kingdom is a right scepter. Thou hast loved righteousness, and hated iniquity; therefore God, thy God, hath anointed Thee." He suggests that it is the Spirit who refers to both characters as God—"both him who is anointed as Son, and him who does anoint, that is, the Father" (*Haer.* 3.6.1). Irenaeus is concerned here to establish that the Spirit truly names both the Father and his Son as truly God. In his *Demonstration of Apostolic Preaching*, Irenaeus quotes the same Psalm and suggests that the Son receives "the oil of anointing" from the Father, which he defines as "the Spirit by whom he is the anointed" (*Epid.* 47).

Irenaeus later reflects upon the potentially problematic baptismal scene where the Spirit of God descends upon Jesus. But Irenaeus here argues that what is depicted is "the Word of God, who is the Savior of all, and the ruler of heaven and earth, who is Jesus … [and] was anointed by the Spirit from the Father was made Jesus Christ" (*Haer.* 3.9.3).[10] The Son is anointed here not with oil, but with the Holy Spirit which comes from the Father. Irenaeus invokes Isa 11:1-4 which foretells of a ruler from the line of David whose rule will be empowered by the Spirit of God, which rests upon him. Irenaeus further draws upon Isa 61:1, quoted by Jesus in Luke 4:18-19, to speak of "the reason why [Jesus] was anointed," namely, God's Spirit anointed Jesus to proclaim the gospel and provide salvation for the poor and brokenhearted. Irenaeus's economy of salvation is evident in his use of anointing language, for the Spirit of God has anointed Jesus the Word of God *and* true human from the line of David and has "anointed him to preach the Gospel to the lowly." This anointing was for no other purpose than the accomplishing of humanity's salvation: "the Spirit of God did descend upon him, the Spirit of him who had promised by the prophets that he would anoint him, so that we, receiving

---

7. Joshua W. Jipp, *Christ Is King: Paul's Royal Ideology* (Minneapolis: Fortress Press, 2015).

8. A strong case for the messianic significance of Paul's Christ has also now been set forth by Paula Fredriksen, *Paul: The Pagans' Apostle* (New Haven, CT: Yale University Press, 2017).

9. See here Novenson, *Christ among the Messiahs*, 146–49.

10. All of the following quotations from Irenaeus in this paragraph are from *Haer.* 3.9.3.

from the abundance of his unction, might be saved." Irenaeus reflects upon the naming of Jesus as the Anointed and gives a twofold reason which corresponds to Christ as both divine and human: first, he is Christ because it is "through him that the Father anointed and adorned all things" (*Epid.* 53); second, he is Christ "because in his coming as man, he was anointed by the Spirit of God his Father, as he himself says of himself, by Isaiah, 'The Spirit of the Lord is upon me, because he has anointed me, to bring good news to the poor'" (Isa 61:1; Luke 4:18). Thus, Irenaeus's language is constrained by the language of the scriptures and by Paul's (and indeed the rest of the apostolic testimony's) understanding of Jesus as the anointed Messiah, but for Irenaeus this anointing of Jesus further establishes Jesus' identity as both truly God and truly human.

The Davidic Messiah in the Scriptures of Israel

Paul and Irenaeus provide testimony for the early Christian practice of reading Davidic texts, particularly the Davidic Psalms, as clear and obvious sources for understanding Jesus as the Messiah. For both Paul and Irenaeus, Jesus' Davidic Messiahship is the foundational hermeneutical assumption for their reading of Israel's scriptures.[11] Paul, for example, appeals to Psalms 2, 8, and 110 in 1 Cor 15:20-28 in order to portray the resurrected and enthroned Messiah as God's agent of final victory (see further citations and echoes of these Psalms in Rom 8:34-38; Eph 1:20-23; Phil 3:20-21; Col 3:1-4).[12] In Rom 15:1-3, Paul invokes the royal psalm of David in order to call the Roman believers to love their neighbors when he portrays the enthroned Messiah speaking as follows: "even the Messiah did not please himself, but as it has been written, 'the insults of those insulting you have fallen upon me'" (Rom 15:3; cf. Ps 68:10 LXX).[13] And as many have noted, Paul's discursive argument in his letter to the Romans both begins and ends with a Davidic inclusio whereby the resurrected and enthroned Messiah is portrayed as ruling over the nations (Rom 1:3-4; 15:9-12). The final words of the exalted Messiah come from Isa 11:10 (Rom 15:12): "The root of Jesse will come, the one who rises to rule the nations, the nations will hope in him."[14] Much more could be said here, but I suggest that for Paul, the Davidic Messiahship of Jesus was a crucial

---

11. This is not to say this is the *only* hermeneutical assumption for Paul and Irenaeus in their reading of the Old Testament.

12. See further Jipp, *Christ Is King*, 139–210; Novenson, *Christ among the Messiahs*, 143–46.

13. Matthew W. Bates, *The Hermeneutics of the Apostolic Proclamation: The Center of Paul's Method of Scripture Interpretation* (Waco, TX: Baylor University Press, 2012), 240–55; Richard B. Hays, "Christ Prays the Psalms: Paul's Use of an Early Christian Convention," in *The Future of Christology: Essays in Honor of Leander E. Keck*, ed. Abraham Malherbe and Wayne A. Meeks (Minneapolis: Fortress, 1993), 122–36.

14. See further Jipp, *Christ Is King*, 177–79.

and non-negotiable feature of Jesus' identity and that Paul's citation of a variety of Davidic Messianic texts enabled Paul to articulate his own economy of salvation which centered upon Jesus' incarnation, suffering and death, and resurrection and heavenly enthronement.

So too, and in an even more explicit manner than Paul, does Irenaeus read Israel's scriptures through a messianic paradigm. In fact, Irenaeus draws upon a variety of messianic texts to explain the identity and work of the Messiah that are not found within Paul's writings. For example, Irenaeus invokes Judah's prediction of a coming ruler who will rule the nations from Gen 49:8-12 (*Epid.* 57) as well as Balaam's prophesy from Num 24:17 ("a star shall come out of Jacob, a ruler shall arise in Israel"; *Haer.* 3.9.2; *Epid.* 58).

As we have seen already, like Paul, he quotes Isa 11:1-4 to proclaim a messianic ruler who, coming from the seed of Jesse, will rule righteously because he is endowed with the Father's Holy Spirit (*Haer.* 3.9.3; *Epid.* 30, 59-60). Irenaeus invokes the Psalms of David as a means of explaining the preexistence of the Messiah (Pss 71:17; 109.3 LXX; *Epid.* 43).[15] Irenaeus continues the early Christian tradition of drawing upon Ps 110:1 (and Ps 2:7), but his emphasis is primarily upon the way in which the Father's address to his son *as Lord* demonstrates that both the Father and Son are truly God (*Haer.* 3.6.1; 3.10.5). Jesus' Davidic ancestry is significant for Irenaeus because it ensures that Jesus' flesh is truly human flesh. The Prophets announced that "his flesh would blossom from the seed of David, that he would be, according to the flesh, son of David, who was the son of Abraham, through a long succession" (*Epid.* 30).[16] But Jesus' Davidic sonship is interpreted by Irenaeus also as a fulfillment of God's promises to David, namely, that God would give David a son who would rule Israel forever (2 Sam 7:12-13; Ps 132:11). "And this King is Christ, the Son of God become the Son of man, that is, become the fruit from the Virgin, who was of the seed of David" (*Epid.* 36; cf. *Haer.* 3.9.2 and 3.16.2 both quoting Ps 132:11). Thus, Ps 110:1 is used both to affirm Jesus' human Davidic ancestry *and* that he is truly God; again, Irenaeus in quoting Ps 110:1 comments: "He who is the son of the Highest, the same is himself also the Son of David. And David, knowing by the Spirit the dispensation of the advent of this Person, by which he is supreme over all the living and dead, confessed him as Lord, sitting on the right hand of the Most High Father" (*Haer.* 3.16.3).[17]

---

15. See here also Horbury, *Jewish Messianism and the Cult of Christ*, 94–96; Adela Yarbro Collins and John J. Collins, *King and Messiah as Son of God: Divine, Human, and Angelic Messianic Figures in Biblical and Related Literature* (Grand Rapids: Eerdmans, 2008), 55–58.

16. On Irenaeus's reading of Israel's Scriptures in this section of *The Demonstration of the Apostolic Preaching*, see Nathan MacDonald, "Israel and the Old Testament Story in Irenaeus's Presentation of the Rule of Faith," *JTI* 3 (2009), 281–98, here, 290–94.

17. On Irenaeus's (and other early Christian authors') practice of reading Psalm 110 as David reporting the speech of God the Father as addressing the Son, see Matthew W. Bates, *The Birth of the Trinity: Jesus, God, and Spirit in New Testament and Early Christian Interpretation of the Old Testament* (Oxford: Oxford University Press, 2015), 67–71.

Adopted into the Messiah's Sonship

One of the ways Paul articulates God's salvation of humanity is through the image of adoption unto sonship. But this is a specific divine sonship that is a participation in the *Messiah's sonship*. This metaphor is stated clearly in Rom 8:14-16 wherein Paul declares to the believers in Rome: "you have received a Spirit of adoption by which we cry out, 'Abba Father'" (Rom 8:15b). And again, in Gal 4:4-6: "When the fullness of time had come, God sent forth his son, born from a woman, born under the Torah, so that he might buy back those who were under the law, so that we might receive adoption. And since you are sons, God sent forth the Spirit of his Son into our hearts crying out 'Abba Father.'" Humanity's adoption unto sonship is predicated upon the sonship of Jesus.[18] In other words, Paul articulates humanity's adoption unto sonship as a participation in the Messiah's sonship. In Rom 1:3-4 Paul declares that his gospel is "about [God's] son who was born from the seed of David according to the flesh, who was installed as God's Son in power according to the Spirit of holiness by means of the resurrection of the dead, Jesus Messiah our Lord." The themes of gospel, Davidic messiahship, seed, resurrection, the Spirit of holiness, power, and lordship set forth a compact description of Jesus as God's Messiah and royal ruler. The intertextual echoes and allusions to 2 Sam 7:12-14; Ps 2:7-8; and Ps 110:1 have been noted by many. Paul depicts the Messiah as identifying with fleshly human existence as he is "born from the seed of David according to the flesh" (Rom 1:3b), and this statement about the Son's fleshly human existence is further affirmed in Rom 8:3, Phil 2:7, and Gal 4:4. But the incarnate Messiah not only shares in the sufferings of fleshly existence, he is enthroned as the Son of God in power by means of his resurrection from the dead (Rom 1:4). In brief, this is the foundation for Paul's claim in Romans 8 that those who belong to Christ are now "God's sons" (Rom 8:14, 19, 21, 23, 29-30). That is to say, their divine sonship is rooted in their sharing in the messianic sonship of the one that was "installed as God's Son in power" (Rom 1:4). The resonances here with Israel's royal ideology whereby Israel's Davidic king was a son to his father Yahweh are evident (e.g., 2 Sam 7:14; Ps 2:6-8).[19] In fact, this divine sonship results in believers crying "Abba Father" (Rom 8:15; Gal 4:6) may be rooted in Ps 88:27-28 (LXX) where the king cries out to Yahweh: "you are my father, my God, and the Rock of my salvation" (cf. also Mark 14:36). The relationship between the Messiah's sonship and humanity's adoptive sonship is explicit in Gal 4:6, where it is "the Spirit of *his Son*" that inspires the cry of Abba Father.

Irenaeus expands upon Paul's concept of adoption as an image of humanity's salvation by appealing to Jesus' Davidic descent. He quotes both Rom 1:3 and Rom

---

18. I have argued this at more length in Jipp, *Christ Is King*, 167–79, 186–92.

19. The royal aspects of the narrative of the Messiah in Romans 8 are persuasively argued for by Douglas A. Campbell, "The Story of Jesus in Romans and Galatians," in *Narrative Dynamics in Paul: A Critical Assessment*, ed. Bruce W. Longenecker (Louisville: Westminster John Knox, 2002), 97–124.

9:5 to establish that the Son of God was born "of the seed of David according to the flesh" and is descended from Israel's forefathers as "the Christ according to the flesh" (*Haer.* 3.16.3).[20] Irenaeus draws upon Gal 4:4-5 to further indicate that in this way God has fulfilled the promises made to David, namely, through sending the Messiah "who was of the seed of David according to his birth from Mary" and was the very same "Son of God made the Son of Man."[21] The Son of God's incarnation whereby he takes human flesh from the line of David is absolutely necessary for Irenaeus, since it is "through him that we may receive the adoption," that is, "humanity sustaining and receiving and embracing the Son of God" (*Haer.* 3.16.3). Irenaeus repeatedly draws these Pauline texts together with statements from Luke's Gospel which proclaim that the Messiah comes from the house of David *and* that this Messiah will rule over the house of Jacob forever (Luke 1:31-35; 1:68-69; 2:1-11; *Haer.* 3.9.2; 3.10.1-3; 3.16.3; *Epid.* 36-37). Again, invoking Rom 1:3-4 and Gal 4:4, Irenaeus affirms why the Son of God's Davidic ancestry is so crucial to humanity's salvation as adopted sons: "For if he did not receive the substance of flesh from a human being, he neither was made man nor the Son of man; and if he was not made what we were, he did no great thing in what he suffered and endured" (*Haer.* 3.22.1).[22] Or again: "It was for this end that the Word of God was made man, and he who was the Son of God became the Son of man, that man, having been taken into the Word, and receiving the adoption, might become the son of God" (*Haer.* 3.19.1). It would take my argument too far afield to engage in any detail Irenaeus's frequent quotation of Psalm 82 to show how the Father and Son work to accomplish adoption for the church, but this Psalm is often combined with Pauline notions of adoption to sonship.[23] For example, Irenaeus quotes from Rom 8:15 to prove that believers in Christ "have received the grace of the 'adoption by which we cry, Abba Father'" (*Haer.* 3.6.1). And again, in *Haer.* 4.4.1, Irenaeus refers to believers in God and Jesus as the Messiah the true Son of God with Pauline resonances as "those who have received the Spirit of adoption." As I have argued above, Irenaeus's reading practices whereby Rom 1:3-4, 8:14-16; Gal 4:4-6 (among other texts) are brought together as a means of articulating the necessity of the incarnation for humanity's adoption as sons of God. This same reading practice, which assumes the Davidic ancestry of Jesus as Israel's Messiah, is

---

20. See further Rolf Noormann, *Irenäus als Paulusinterpret: Zur Rezeption und Wirkung der paulinischen und deuteropaulinischen Briefe im Werk des Irenaus von Lyon* (WUNT 2.66; Tübingen: Mohr Siebeck, 1994), 128–32.

21. Helpful here is Ben C. Blackwell, *Christosis: Pauline Soteriology in Light of Deification in Irenaeus and Cyril of Alexandria* (WUNT 2.314; Tübingen: Mohr Siebeck, 2011), 48–50.

22. See here further Matthew W. Bates, "A Christology of Incarnation and Enthronement: Romans 1.3-4 as Unified, Nonadoptionist, and Nonconciliatory," *CBQ* 77 (2015), 107–27, here, 118–20.

23. On Psalm 82 in Irenaeus, see Julie Canlis, *Calvin's Ladder: A Spiritual Theology of Ascent and Ascension* (Grand Rapids: Eerdmans, 2010), 205–9.

witnessed by Ignatius, Tertullian, Origen, John Chrysostom, Theodoret of Cyrus, Athanasius, Cyril of Alexandria, and Apollinaris of Laodicea.[24]

Paul's Adam-Christ deserves the focus of attention when it comes to Irenaeus's use of Paul's Christology, and Presley seems to me to be exactly right to suggest that this typology forms the theological borders for his Christological framework. But I have argued in this brief section that Paul's messianic interpretation of Jesus as Israel's Messiah also has important ramifications for Irenaeus's Christology, interpretation of Israel's scriptures, and articulation of humanity's adoption to divine sonship. If I am correct, then this would also further suggest that Jewish messianism did not fade away but rather had continuing significance for early Christianity.

---

24. For references, see Jipp, "Ancient, Modern, and Future Interpretations of Romans 1.3-4: Reception History and Biblical Interpretation," *JTI* 3 (2009), 241–59, here, 248–54.

Chapter 4

THE PERSONAL/SUBSTANTIAL SPIRIT OF PROPHECY: IRENAEUS'S USE OF PAUL AGAINST THE HERESIES

David E. Wilhite

In treating Irenaeus's view of "the Spirit" Anthony Briggman summarizes a twofold understanding: "the peculiar ambiguity of the terms *spiritus* and πνεῦμα is that they can refer to either who God is (the Holy Spirit, distinct from the Father and the Son) or what God is (Spirit, that—the immaterial divine stuff—which is common to the Father, Son, and Holy Spirit)."[1] In what follows, these two sides of the "ambiguity" about "Spirit" in Irenaeus will be described as personal and substantial respectively. In light of this duality of meaning Briggman explains how "we must evaluate each use of the terms *spiritus* or πνεῦμα to determine their referent."[2] While I concur and will carry out this approach in what follows, I will differ slightly from Briggman's assumption in this statement.[3]

The two definitions of πνεῦμα/*spiritus* differ only in the modern reader's mind. Irenaeus betrays no awareness of the potential confusion that might arise from using the same term for two different meanings.[4] However, the distinction is a necessary evil in that a modern reader brings competing categories to Irenaeus's texts, and so not to acknowledge them would be to risk obfuscation. Nevertheless, we must always hold to our categories loosely and allow them to be deconstructed by Irenaeus's usage.

To help ballast this semiotic analysis, I will use Jacques Derrida's notion of différance.[5] For Derrida, the act of reading allows words to shift between various

---

1. Anthony Briggman, *Irenaeus of Lyons and the Theology of the Holy Spirit* (Oxford: Oxford University Press, 2012), 41. In what follows, I do not attempt to trace development in Irenaeus's writings as Briggman does (i.e., between *Haer.* 1-2, and *Haer.* 3–5/*Epid*).

2. Briggman, *Irenaeus*, 41.

3. Briggman, it should be noted, represents the general scholarly view.

4. For later writers forced to clarify, see Andrew Radde-Gallwitz, "The Holy Spirit as Agent, Not Activity: Origen's Argument with Modalism and Its Afterlife in Didymus, Eunomius, and Gregory of Nazianzus," *VC* 65 (2011), 227–48.

5. See especially Jacques Derrida, "Différance," in *Margins of Philosophy*, trans. Alan Bass (Chicago: University of Chicago, 1986), 1–28.

meanings, a phenomenon which reflects his understanding of words themselves as being in something like an in-between-ness, or a both-and-ness. That is to say, one must allow that words involve a "playing movement" or slippage between the two poles of meaning wherein one never suffices and one never excludes the other ("defer")—and yet the one is not equivalent with the other ("differ"). Whereas Hegel's dialectics entailed progress past the thesis/antithesis, Derrida reinterprets Hegel preferring Kierkegaard's inverted dialectic, the aporia, wherein the both/and (and/or the neither/nor) remains inescapable.[6]

I find such an understanding of language to be helpful for exploring Irenaeus's use of πνεῦμα/*spiritus*.[7] His "peculiar ambiguity" of this term, mentioned above, entails two meanings (the substantial and the personal) that are never far removed from each other, so that traces of each meaning always remain. In other words, the term itself remains for Irenaeus ever in a state of différance wherein *Spiritus* is a *substantia* and/as a *persona* (or vice versa). Such an approach allows Irenaeus's usage to be analyzed without artificial or anachronistic partitions.

In what follows, Irenaeus's use of "s/Spirit" will be discussed roughly along the order found in his *Against Heresies*: the opponents' views are faulted, and then contrasted in terms of cosmogony (and theology), anthropology (and Christology), and finally the Spirit's primary role, which is that of prophecy. Throughout the analysis, Irenaeus's explicit citation of Paul will be brought to the forefront, and Paul's influence will be shown to be pertinent at several important junctures in Irenaeus's teaching.[8] One finding in particular from this study is that Irenaeus so links prophecy to the Spirit of God that any reference to or about God (the Father and/or the Son) is implicitly a reference inspired by God's s/Spirit. Therefore, the placement of the Spirit into the primary role of knowing God (the Father and/or the Son) will be both our point of departure and conclusion.

---

6. See especially Derrida's discussion of the Latin *differre* ("Différance," 7–8). My understanding of this aspect of Derrida relies heavily on John D. Caputo, *Radical Hermeneutics: Repetition, Deconstruction, and the Hermeneutic Project* (Bloomington: Indiana University Press, 1987); idem, *More Radical Hermeneutics: On Not Knowing Who We Are* (Bloomington: Indiana University, 2000); idem, *The Prayers and Tears of Jacques Derrida: Religion without Religion* (Bloomington: Indiana University, 1997); idem, *On Religion* (London: Routledge, 2001); and idem, *The Weakness of God: A Theology of the Event* (Bloomington: Indiana University, 2006).

7. Although Irenaeus would object to the term given its abuse by his opponents (e.g., ἔκπληξις/*aporia* in *Haer.* 1.5.4), I think the humility and patience required by such an epistemology fits Irenaeus's own explicit commitments (e.g., *Haer.* 2.28.7).

8. For a more comprehensive study, see Rolf Noormann, *Irenäus als Paulusinterpret: Zur Rezeption und Wirkung der paulinischen und deuteropaulinischen Briefe im Werk des Irenäus von Lyon* (WUNT 2.66; Tübingen: Mohr Siebeck, 1994), 70–375, whose detailed study of every citation is indispensible. It should be noted, however, that despite sections devoted to "Heilsgeschichte," "Christologie," and "Anthropologie," Noormann does not treat Irenaeus's relation to Paul along the lines of pneumatology.

The Opponents' Spiritual Mistake, According to Paul

Irenaeus prefaces his work *Against Heresies* by quoting 1 Tim 1:4: "Some have repressed the truth and introduced false words and 'unending genealogies which present more questions rather than,' as the apostle says, 'the edification of God which is in faith.'"[9] This preface helpfully establishes Irenaeus's pattern of using Paul in counterattacking his opponents.[10] Another pattern is also detectable: Irenaeus finds that all heretics fall guilty of at least one of three mistakes: (1) They falsely "interpret the scriptures [τὰ λόγια/*verba*]"; (2) they claim a gnosis of one higher than he who "established and ordered the universe"; and (3) they blaspheme the one who is the "Maker [*Fabricatorem*/Δημιουργὸν]" of all things.[11] Although it is admittedly cryptic in this paragraph, I detect in this threefold error an inversion of Irenaeus's Canon of Truth. For Irenaeus, the Father is the ultimate Creator (contra mistake #3), the Son is the one who establishes the world (contra mistake #2), and then the scriptures, both in their original inspiration and their proper interpretation (contra mistake #1), are always the work of the Spirit—a point which will be illustrated in this chapter.

Corroboration for this reading can be found in Irenaeus's other extant work, *Demonstration of the Apostolic Preaching*, which ends with the following summary statement. After referencing his earlier work (i.e., *Against Heresies*), Irenaeus declares, "So, error, concerning the three heads of our seal, has caused much straying from the truth, for either they despise the Father, or do not accept the Son—they speak against the economy of His incarnation—or they do not accept the Holy Spirit, that is, they despise prophecy."[12] In this instance, Irenaeus's ordering more obviously corresponds to the threefold pattern of the Canon of Truth, and once again prophecy is linked to the work of the Spirit.

Since Irenaeus's opponents "do not accept" the Holy Spirit, they are led by "a spirit of error."[13] Irenaeus clearly thinks of "evil spirits," or "demons," as personal

---

9. *Haer.* 1.praef.1; with ref. to 1 Tim 1:4 (and cf. 1 Tim 1:3). It should also be noted that 1 Tim 6:20, "knowledge falsely so-called," is the basis of Irenaeus's title for this work. The text of Irenaeus, *Haer.*, is from A. Rousseau et al. (eds.), *Irénée de Lyon: Contre les hérésies* (SC 100.1, 100.2, 152, 153, 210, 211, 263, 264, 293, 294; Paris: Cerf, 1965–82); all translations of *Haer.* are my own unless otherwise noted.

10. By opponents I here mean the so called Gnostics, which is now a problematized category. See Michael A. Williams, *Rethinking "Gnosticism": An Argument for Dismantling a Dubious Category* (Princeton, NJ: Princeton University Press, 1996); Karen King, *What Is Gnosticism?* (Cambridge, MA: Belknap Press of Harvard University, 2003); and Ismo Dunderberg, *Beyond Gnosticism: Myth, Lifestyle, and Society in the School of Valentinus* (New York: Columbia University Press, 2008).

11. *Haer.* 1.praef.1.

12. *Epid.* 100. All translations of *Epid.* are from John Behr (trans.), *St. Irenaeus of Lyons: On the Apostolic Preaching* (Crestwood, NY: St. Vladimir's Seminary, 1997).

13. E.g., *Haer.* 1.9.5; 1.16.3; 2.31.3.

entities.[14] However, the same term is used with a sense of a substance that can "fill" another, the nuances of which will become clear as we explore his metaphors for spirit in the next section.[15] Regardless of which meaning we take to be salient, the role of inspiring prophesying is still prevalent, even though the spirits are evil.[16] The concept of filling brings us to Irenaeus's metaphors that inform his usage.

Irenaean (and Pauline?) Metaphors for Spirit

Irenaeus's metaphors for the Spirit do more than simply compare; the metaphors to some extent govern Irenaeus's usage of the concept of Spirit.[17] Therefore, these metaphors will merely be introduced at this juncture with minimal examples. They will reappear below in the analysis of Irenaeus's use of πνεῦμα/*spiritus*.

The most basic analogy for the Spirit is the concept of wind or breath, which is obviously due to the term's etymology.[18] The concept of breath for Irenaeus seems to entail moisture as well, not simply dry air. The Spirit for Irenaeus nourishes like streams of water.[19] This moisture imagery explains how the Spirit converts dry flour into the bread of life in the Eucharist.[20] The metaphor lends itself to additional sacramental thinking, such as "drinking" in the Spirit and even being baptized in the Spirit.[21] The latter instance should be coupled with the

---

14. E.g., *Epid.* 2.3.96; *Haer.* 1.10.1; 3.8.2; and 5.26.2.

15. E.g., *Epid.* 1.2.17.

16. *Haer.* 4.33.6, where even "an evil spirit" is characterized by its attempt "to prophecy." Elsewhere, Irenaeus believes that Marcus had a demon because he could prophecy (*Haer.* 1.13.3; cf. Paul's actions in Acts 16:16-18). Marcus summons "Charis" upon his followers, and they too prophesy. Irenaeus, however, thinks that Marcus's followers prophesied simply because they became frenzied in their soul from "a heated spirit [τεθερμαμμένη πνεύματος/*calefacta spiritu*]," that is "empty air [κενῷ ἀέρι/*vacuo aere*]."

17. The extent to which these metaphors govern his thinking is debatable. See Hugo Koch, "Zur Lehre vom Urstand und von der Erlösung bei Irenaeus," *Theologische Studien und Kritiken* 96-97 (1925), 183-214; and more recently Eric Osborn, *Irenaus of Lyons* (Cambridge: Cambridge University Press, 2001), esp. 22-24 and 253-56. For a further study of Irenaeus's view of participation, see Ben Blackwell, "Two Early Perspectives on Participation in Paul: Irenaeus and Clement of Alexandria," in *"In Christ" in Paul: Explorations in Paul's Theological Vision of Union and Participation*, ed. Kevin J. Vanhoozer, Constantine R. Campbell, and Michael J. Thate (WUNT II; Tübingen: Mohr Siebeck, 2015), 331-55.

18. E.g., *Haer.* 3.11.8; 4.20.10. Also, cf. *Haer.* 5.24.4; and 5.28.2; 5.15.1.

19. E.g., *Haer.* 3.17.3; 4.33.14; *Epid.* 2.3.89.

20. See *Haer.* 3.17.1-2; 4.18.5; and 4.19.1. For commentary and bibliography, see Briggman, *Irenaeus*, 78-85.

21. On drinking, see *Epid.* 2.2.57; ref. to Gen. 49:10-11; cf. Justin Martyr, *1 Apol.* 32.5-11. On baptism, see the thorough treatment of A. Housiau, "Le baptême selon Irénée de Lyon," *Ephemerides theologicae lovanienses* 60.1 (1984), 45-59.

anointing received in the initiation ritual; for Irenaeus, one is anointed with/by the Spirit.[22]

With baptism and anointing, the analogy is such that a person or thing is covered by and saturated with the Spirit. Likewise, the baptismal robes function as a metaphor since Adam was originally clothed with holiness while the angels, like the Demiurge, are clothed with light—holiness and light both being synonymous with the Spirit for Irenaeus.[23] In sum, the Spirit is like wind, water, oil, and clothing, in that it rests upon, covers, and infuses the Spirit's object. In other words, believers can participate—materially, as it were—in the Spirit.

One last point to be made about these metaphors is in regards to Paul's influence. On the whole, Irenaeus draws imagery from across the scriptures. While I suspect that he is highly indebted to a Platonic thought-world that assumes a schema where lower substances can participate in higher substances,[24] there are noteworthy instances where Irenaeus finds Paul to support his understanding of the Spirit in terms of material analogies. For example, the "Spirit of God" rests on the faithful like a "wedding gown," which Irenaeus credits to Paul.[25] The image of being clothed in "immortality" from Paul is given a different metaphor later when Irenaeus refers to "the bread of immortality," which is "the Father's Spirit," and this "feeding" is also credited to Paul.[26]

It is very likely that Irenaeus shares his understanding of substantial (or at least materially analogous) participation with his opponents and that both parties read Paul for support.[27] We should, then, turn to Irenaeus's opponents to see how they define the concept of Spirit and how Irenaeus differs.[28] These opponents'

---

22. Esp. *Epid.* 2.1.47; *Haer.* 3.18.3.

23. *Haer.* 3.23.5, on Adam; *Haer.* 2.30.1, on Angels and the Creator.

24. As is convincingly argued yet carefully nuanced in Osborn, *Irenaus*, 15–17. For review of scholarly opinions about Irenaeus's knowledge of philosophical sources, see Briggman, *Irenaeus*, 89–95, who finds that Irenaeus accommodated Middle Platonism. More generally, see Robert M. Grant, "Irenaeus and Hellenistic Culture," *HTR* 42.1 (1949), 41–51; and William R. Schoedel, "Philosophy and Rhetoric in the *Adversus haereses* of Irenaeus," *VC* 13.1 (1959), 22–32.

25. *Haer.* 4.36.6, with ref. to 2 Cor. 5:4; cf. Noormann, *Irenäus als Paulusinterpret*, 249–50.

26. *Haer.* 4.38.1-2, with ref. to 1 Cor 3:2; cf. Noormann, *Irenäus als Paulusinterpret*, 260–62. Also see Ignatius, *Eph.* 20.2.

27. For detailed analysis of Irenaeus's view of participation, see Osborn, *Irenaus*, chapters 7–11, and a summary on 257–62.

28. Whether Irenaeus accurately portrays his opponents is tangential to this study. For bibliography of earlier scholars, see Mary Ann Donovan, *One Right Reading? A Guide to Irenaeus* (Collegeville, MN: Liturgical, 1997), 175–77. More recently, Marvin W. Meyer, *The Gnostic Discoveries: The Impact of the Nag Hammadi Library* (San Francisco: HarperSanFrancisco, 2005), 41, finds Irenaeus to be relatively fair in his presentation.

understanding especially becomes clear in their articulation of how various substances, including spiritual ones, came into existence.

Cosmogonical (and Theological) Substances

Irenaeus's opponents affirm the Pleroma to be a purely spiritual realm.[29] This implies that all divine emanations (or "aeons," such as Christ and the Holy Spirit) are spiritual, not material.[30] Leaving aside the extensive narratives where Sophia fell from the Pleroma and produced material substances,[31] suffice it to say that her rescue[32] itself produced animal/soul-ish substance.[33] The resulting taxonomy is the material (ὕλη/*materia*), the animal (τὸ ψυχικόν/*animale*), and the spiritual (τὸ πνευματικόν/*spiritale*).[34] Irenaeus largely agrees with his opponents when it comes to their categories (except perhaps in terms of anthropology—see below). The point of departure for Irenaeus is not ontology, but theology.

The notion of πνεῦμα/*spiritus* as substance is especially important for Irenaeus's view of God.[35] The gnostic view of divine emanations is in fact correct, except Irenaeus finds "the only-begotten Word of God [*Unigenitum Dei Verbum*]" alone to emanate from the Father.[36] Perhaps more surprising is when Irenaeus next concedes that "God produced material substance [*substantia materiae ... Deus eam protulit*]."[37] In the case of the material world, however, Irenaeus immediately guards

---

29. *Haer.* 1.1.3, a "spiritual Pleroma [πνεθματικὸν ... Πλήρωμα/*spiritale ... Pleroma*]"; cf. 2.18.1; 2.19.2; 2.3.1.

30. Cf. *Haer.* 1.11.1; 1.2.5; 2.12.7; and 2.19.9.

31. See esp. *Haer.* 1.2.3-4; 1.4.1-2.

32. For earlier bibliography of the secondary literature, see M. C. Steenberg, *Irenaeus on Creation: The Cosmic Christ and the Saga of Redemption* (VCSup; Leiden: Brill, 2008), 23.

33. *Haer.* 1.4.5. Similarly, the devil/Cosmocrator is spiritual (namely, "the spirit of wickedness" of Eph 6:12), according to some groups, and so he knows of things above (see *Haer.* 1.5.4).

34. *Haer.* 1.5.1. On the three kinds of humans corresponding to these substances, see 1.7.5 and 1.8.3. Also, cf. 1.30.5.

35. Briggman avers, "The identification of what God is, that God is Spirit, is fundamental to Irenaeus' theological construct" (*Irenaeus*, 42).

36. *Haer.* 2.28.6. As to the aeons, Irenaeus inquires about their ontology: are they uniform in "substance [*substantiae*]," like "wind and light [*spiritus et lumina*]," or are they somehow composite (*Haer.* 2.17.2). Also, are the qualities of the aeons that of shape, size, and so on, which would belong to "a body, and not to a spirit [*corporis, et non spiritus*]" (*Haer.* 2.17.3)? Irenaeus then proceeds to list numerous descriptions of the aeons that could not be true "of spiritual beings [*in spiritalibus*]" (*Haer.* 2.17.9). He later rejects any interpretation of Paul as referring to "spiritual aeons [πνευματικῶν Αἰώνων/*spiritalibus Aeonibus*]" (*Haer.* 3.20.2; with ref. to Rom 11:32).

37. *Haer.* 2.28.7; for the Pauline references in this section (cited below), see Noormann, *Irenäus als Paulusinterpret*, 104–6.

against this being explained as an emanation from God's own substance: "From where or in what manner he emitted it [*Unde autem vel quemadmodum emisit eam*]" is unknown.[38] This partial knowledge of creation is not to deny the perfect knowledge the "Savior's Spirit [*Spiritus Salvatoris*]" has of God the Father, for Paul teaches how the Spirit searches the "depths of God."[39] To protect this mystery, Irenaeus invokes "Paul" who taught about a diversity of gifts, which is to say, "We know in part, and we prophecy in part."[40] In short, the heretics contradict "the apostle," whose teaching of partial knowledge is repeated, and so they cannot be trusted on matters earthly, much less with "spiritual and heavenly" things.[41]

Alternatively, Irenaeus views God as simple—that is, God is simply greater than all things, which places a limit on human epistemology.[42] This radical view of simplicity entails a rejection of a chain of being from ultimate reality to the lower matter, but an apparent problem remains for Irenaeus's own theology.[43]

How does Irenaeus believe the divine to be both simple and differentiated? He attempts to explain by contrasting God with human thought, which is "spiritual," and human speech, which is "fleshly," for the two acts occur sequentially.[44] However, for God, these aspects are all simultaneous: "For God exists completely as Mind, and completely as Word; that which he thinks, the same also he speaks, and vice versa."[45]

---

38. *Haer.* 2.28.7.

39. *Haer.* 2.28.7; with ref. to 1 Cor 2:10.

40. *Haer.* 2.28.7; with ref. to 1 Cor 12:4-6.

41. *Haer.* 2.28.9; with ref. to 1 Cor 13:9.

42. *Haer.* 4.20.1. It is worth noting that Derrida's description of *différance* is explicitly a "negative theology" (Derrida, "Différance," 6).

43. Irenaeus rejects the possibility of a chain of being wherein each being is of a lower substance than the prior: the whole Pleroma would have to be "of the same substance [*eiusdem substantiae*]" (*Haer.* 2.18.5). When it comes to substances, Irenaeus assumes like begets like, as in the case of "fire in fire, wind in wind, and water in water [*ignis in igne, et spiritus in spiritu, et aqua in aqua*]" (*Haer.* 2.18.5; cf. Doutreleau, SC 294:181; and Dominic J. Unger, *St. Irenaeus of Lyons: Against the Heresies (Book 2)* [ACW 65; New York: Newman, 2012], 62). I suspect that Irenaeus thinks in terms of the creation account where things produce "according to [their] kind [κατὰ γένος]" (e.g., Gen. 1:11LXX). He elsewhere refutes certain interpretations of scripture on the basis that the gnostic aeons allegedly were of "the same kind and spirit [*eiusdem generis et spiritus*]" (*Haer.* 2.21.2). For the gnostic ontology, see William R. Schoedel, "'Topological' Theology and Some Monistic Tendencies in Gnosticism," in *Essays on the Nag Hammadi Texts in Honour of Alexander Böhlig*, ed. Martin Krause (Leiden: Brill, 1972), 90–91, 102–3. Also, cf. Michel René Barnes, "Irenaeus's Trinitarian Theology," *NV* 7 (2009), 67–106.

44. *Haer.* 2.28.4.

45. *Haer.* 2.28.5. The lack of an explicit reference to the Spirit in this passage will be revisited at the end of the chapter. Cf. *Haer.* 4.20.1; and Justin Martyr, *1 Apol.* 46. The Spirit is explicitly the Wisdom who speaks in Proverbs (*Haer.* 4.20.3), and therefore the Son and the Spirit existed "before all things were made" (*Haer.* 4.20.3; cf. *Epid.* 1.1.10 and 2.3.97).

Irenaeus explains divine simplicity as scriptural since God has no parts (arms, legs, etc.), and so God is understood as "completely spirit [*totus spiritus*]."[46] To be clear, the highest God is not "emptiness [*vacuum*]," for that would be to say that God is nothing, a denial of "that which is his spiritual substance [*substantiam ... quod est spiritalis eius*]."[47] God, being real but spiritual, "can fill" other beings, and so this understanding of participation—recalling the material analogies mentioned above—turns us to Irenaeus's description of the God/world relationship.[48]

More than a philosophical first principle, Irenaeus's primary commitment is articulated in the opening line of his Canon of Truth: God is the creator of all things. God creates "from nothing" by calling into being "that material of his manufacturing when beforehand it did not exist [*cum ante non esset*]."[49] It is important to remember even here how creation is prophetic, or vocative.[50] The communicative aspect of God's Spirit(-ual substance) characterizes much of what Irenaeus has to say about the God/world relationship.

Once all things are said to be created ex nihilo, Irenaeus further explains how all things relate to their Creator, and in so doing Irenaeus once again follows the threefold pattern of the Canon: "For the Father carries the world and his Word, and the Word carries the Spirit from the Father to all as the Father wills."[51] He then supports this statement with a Pauline teaching, "And so one God the Father is made known, the one who is above all and through all and in all. For the Father is above all, and the same is the head of Christ. The Word is through all, and the same is the head of the church. The Spirit is in all, and the same in all, the water of life."[52] In effect, Irenaeus replaces the gnostic commitment to a *scala naturae* with a *scala relationis*, and in so doing he displays the Spirit as a personal subject on par with the Father and Son in terms of subjective/personal activity. This can be seen when Irenaeus insists on "the uniting of man with the Spirit, and the inhabiting of the Spirit in man; [Christ] becomes the head of the Spirit and gives the Spirit as head to man. For through [the Spirit], we see and hear and speak."[53]

---

46. *Haer.* 2.13.3; cf. 2.18.5-6 and 2.28.4.

47. *Haer.* 2.13.7.

48. *Haer.* 2.13.7; cf. Eph 1:23. His opponents view the earthly and spiritual as incompatible (2.19.4).

49. *Haer.* 2.10.4.

50. Cf. Rom 4:17: καλοῦντος τὰ μὴ ὄντα ὡς ὄντα, which Irenaeus curiously never cites according to Noormann, *Irenäus als Paulusinterpret*, 566.

51. *Haer.* 5.18.2. That Irenaeus has the Canon of Truth in mind is verified by the corresponding passage *Epid.* 1.1.5-6 (cited below).

52. *Haer.* 5.18.2, with ref. to Eph 4:6. Irenaeus's concern in this passage is to link Christ with creation, and so he does not elaborate on the three persons' roles (and he does not attempt to correlate them with Eph 4:4-5); instead, he proceeds to cite the prologue of John (1:1-3). Also, cf. *Epid.* 1.1.5, with ref. to Ps 32:6, Eph 4:6, and Gal 4:6/Rom 8:15.

53. *Haer.* 5.20.2 (note the uncanny parallel to Paul's statement in Acts 17:28, only with a shift from ontology to epistemology; earlier in the paragraph Paul's call for humility has

This order is reversed in human experience,⁵⁴ for the righteous "ascend through the Spirit to the Son, and through the Son to the Father," and to support this claim Irenaeus cites Paul on how the Son subdues all enemies and delivers the kingdom to the Father.⁵⁵

For Irenaeus, then, the Spirit plays the primary role in the God/human interaction. In fact, Irenaeus can say, "without the Spirit it is not [possible] to see the Word of God, and without the Son one is not able to approach the Father; for the knowledge of the Father is the Son, and knowledge of the Son of God is through the Holy Spirit."⁵⁶ This capacity to know God (the Father and the Son) only by the Spirit corresponds to the capacity to speak of God (the Father and the Son) only by the Spirit. The Spirit's role itself is almost exclusively described with reference to prophecy.⁵⁷ The human experience of God via prophecy raises the wider question of human nature.

---

already been cited [with ref. to Rom 12:3]). This personal aspect of *Spiritus* does not exclude a substantial meaning since the "spiritual" and "heavenly" is still explicitly contrasted with the "human" and "earthly" (*Haer.* 5.20.2).

54. On this order in human experience, Bruce D. Marshall, "The Deep Things of God: Trinitarian Pneumatology," in *The Oxford Handbook of the Trinity*, ed. Gilles Emery and Matthew Levering (Oxford: Oxford University, 2011), 411, credits Irenaeus for observing this "pattern" (in *Epid.* 7), which Marshall finds in Pauline texts (Rom 8:9-17, 26-30; 1 Cor 12:3-6, 12-13; Gal 4:4-7; Eph 1:13-14).

55. *Haer.* 5.36.2, with ref. to 1 Cor 15:24-28; cf. Noormann, *Irenäus als Paulusinterpret*, 374–75. It is worth noting that Irenaeus shifts from Pauline to Johannine sources in 5.36.3, and thereby he ceases to speak of the Spirit. This turn includes the subsequent section only found in the Armenian text. When the Latin text continues (5.36.3 line 56), the "Apostle Paul" immediately retakes center stage.

56. *Epid.* 1.1.7.

57. *Epid.* 1.1.6, "And the third article: the Holy Spirit, through whom the prophets prophesied." In contrast to the heretics who do not understand "what prophecy is," the true message is inspired by "the prophetic Spirit [τοῦ Πνεύματος προφητικῶς/*per Spiritum prophetice*]" (*Haer.* 4.20.5), and the Spirit is God per se because no one can see God, except God for whom "all things are possible" (*Haer.* 4.20.5, with ref. to Luke 18:27). All of the forms of Old Testament prophecy (predictive, exhortative, visionary, etc.) are then outlined according to "the apostle" who taught diversities of gifts from one Spirit (*Haer.* 4.20.6, with ref. to 1 Cor 12:4-7; cf. 4.20.8). Additionally, the patriarchs could live for centuries because of the Spirit, as evidenced by the fact that they were "taken up by spiritual prophesying [τὴν ἀνάληψιν τῶν πνευματικῶν προφητευῶν]" (*Haer.* 5.5.1 [following the Greek fragm. and Armen.; cf. Rousseau, SC 153 (1969), 62–63]). Paul again is invoked, since he was "caught up [μετατεθέντας ἐκεῖσε/*translati sunt*]" in a prophetic moment, and all those who "have the Spirit [πνευματοφόροις/*Spiritum habentibus*]" are destined to do the same in Paradise (*Haer.* 5.5.1, with ref. to 2 Cor 12:4).

Anthropology (and Christology), or the First Man (and the Second)

Corresponding to the three kinds of substances, Irenaeus's opponents delineate a tripartite anthropology.[58] Most humans consist of body and soul, while the elect also have spirit. The special status of the elect means that the "spiritual ones [πνευματικοὺς/*spiritales*]" are not bound by earthly morals.[59] Just how accurately Irenaeus represents his opponents on this point is obviously debatable: they may in fact be teaching a Pauline ethic in regard to the Law.[60]

Regardless of what is implied for those having πνεῦμα/*spiritus*, the question arises for this study regarding the distinction between soul and spirit. Some of his opponents say the soul is a defect, which resides in the body, just as the spirit, which is completely incorruptible, resides in the soul.[61] Correcting this view, Irenaeus asserts a resurrection where the elect will "have their bodies, their souls, and their spirits."[62]

When using such a tripartite description, Irenaeus seems to differentiate the human soul from the human spirit by defining the former as the mind, the mental capacity. Like many ancients, Irenaeus probably has to acknowledge the materiality of such a mind/soul, or at least an intermingling of soul/body.[63] After all, if someone is struck on their material head, the "mind" is affected. The opponents say the animal is a "middle" substance that can be governed by either the material or the spiritual, and Irenaeus never denies this assumption since the soul can be led by the flesh or by the s/Spirit.[64] Therefore, Irenaeus refers to the human spirit as distinct from the soul in that the former is the wholly nonmaterial aspect of

---

58. See Steenberg, *Irenaeus*, 101–52, for the creation of humankind in particular.

59. *Haer.* 3.15.2.

60. See *Haer.* 1.6.2, where they contrast the works of the carnally minded and the faith of the spiritual ones (cf. Rom 8:6). The explanation is that the spirit(-ual) is incorruptible, and so apart from material works the spiritual ones will be saved. Irenaeus, however, hears this to allow libertinism, against which he quotes Paul (*Haer.* 1.6.3, with ref. to Gal 5:21). On the Pauline ethic, Noormann, *Irenäus als Paulusinterpret*, 500, places this passage in comparison with Bultmann's explication of the Spirit in Paul (cf. Rudolf Bultmann, *Theology of the New Testament*, trans. Kendrick Grobel [London: SCM, 1965], 1:337–38).

61. *Haer.* 1.21.4; and cf. 2.19.3-4, where this "small emission [*parvum emissum*]" is mocked. For the Ophite view, see *Haer.* 1.30.4-13.

62. *Haer.* 2.33.5. For the relative emphasis on the body in particular, see Sophie Cartwright, "The Image of God in Ireaneus, Marcellus, and Eustathius," in *Irenaeus: Life, Scripture, Legacy*, ed. Sara Parvis and Paul Foster (Minneapolis: Fortress, 2012), 173–82.

63. See full discussion in Paul S. MacDonald, *History of the Concept of Mind: Speculations about Soul, Mind and Spirit from Homer to Hume* (Aldershot: Ashgate, 2003), esp. 52.

64. *Haer.* 1.6.1. The difference lies in that while his opponents fault a cosmogonic defect, Irenaeus can speak of humans as created rational but choosing to become irrational (cf. Rom 1:22-25), and thereby "handing themselves over to every earthly spirit [*terreno spiritui*]" (*Haer.* 5.4.3; cf. Jam 3:15 and Eph 4:19).

the human.⁶⁵ This definition of the soul, however, is complicated by the fact that his opponents' definitions are often in view and Irenaeus is not consistent in his usage. When speaking in bipartite terms, the human soul is nonmaterial because it is contrasted with the body.⁶⁶ This definition makes the body/soul distinction (at times) synonymous with the flesh/spirit distinction.⁶⁷

A growing scholarly consensus finds Irenaeus to prefer the bipartite anthropology, even if he must speak in tripartite terms to dialogue with his opponents and be faithful to Paul's usage (e.g., 1 Thess 5:23).⁶⁸ This can be seen in Irenaeus's explanation of the creation of humans. The Father, by his "two hands"⁶⁹—the Son and the Holy Spirit—made man as body, soul, and spirit.⁷⁰ Here, Irenaeus seems to be countering his opponents' anthropology, and so he must accommodate their tripartite structure of the human nature in order to correct it. The tripartite constitution implies for Irenaeus that the body of a human is not a human, but only a body. Nor is the soul of a human a human, but only a soul. Likewise, the spirit of a human (as his opponents claim) would not be a human, but only the spirit of a human. All three substances anticipate full redemption, according to Paul whose prayer is quoted.⁷¹ After this citation of Paul, however, Irenaeus seems to shift to his own bipartite view, for from this point he clearly identifies the "Spirit" as the

---

65. E.g., *Haer.* 4.17.1 and *Epid.* 1.2.24.

66. E.g., *Haer.* 5.7.1.

67. See the spirit/flesh contrast, with no mention of soul in *Haer.* 5.9.2, with ref. to Matt 26:41. Also, see where humans receive a body from the earth and "a soul ... from the Spirit of God" (*Haer.* 3.22.1).

68. See Behr, *Irenaeus*, 152–58; and for more detail, see Behr, *Behr, Asceticism and Anthropology in Irenaeus and Clement* (Oxford: Oxford University Press, 2000), 99–115. For additional bibliography, see Briggman, *Irenaeus*, 149–50, who also holds to this view. Steenberg, *Of God and Man: Theology as Anthropology from Irenaeus to Athanasius* (London: T&T Clark, 2009), 40, problematizes the bipartite/tripartite distinction, but still affirms that the Spirit in humans is God's, bestowed on the human body and soul. It is also noteworthy for this chapter how Bernhard Mutschler, *Irenäus als johanneischer Theologe: Studien zur Schriftauslegung bei Irenäus von Lyon* (Studien und Texte zu Antike und Christentum 21; Tübingen: Mohr Siebeck, 2004), 269, concludes, "für die irenäische Anthropologie und die damit verbundene Soteriologie ist es weithin die paulinische Theologie." For more details on this point, see François Altermath, *Du corps psychique au corps spiritual: Interpretation de 1 Cor 15,35-49 par les auteurs chrétiens des quatre premiers siècles* (Tübingen: Mohr Siebeck, 1977), 78–92. For Paul, George H. van Kooten, *Paul's Anthropology in Context: The Image of God, Assimilation to God, and Tripartite Man in Ancient Judaism, Ancient Philosophy, and Early Christianity* (WUNT 232; Tübingen: Mohr Siebeck, 2008), offers a helpful study because Paul's sources can be compared to Irenaeus's.

69. See *Haer.* 4.praef.4; cf. 5.28.4. For Irenaeus's two hands motif as dependent on Jewish sources and from Theophilus, see Briggman, *Irenaeus*, 107–19.

70. *Haer.* 5.6.1.

71. *Haer.* 5.6.1, with ref. to 1 Thess 5:23.

"Spirit of God" who perfects man's body and soul. This becomes clear in the next sentence where Irenaeus again cites Paul, but this time to speak of humans as the "temple" in which "the Spirit or God" dwells.[72] Furthermore, Christ's resurrection seems to indicate a bipartite structure to human nature, for Christ's death in the fleshly "substance" is matched by his resurrection in the flesh; both require the animation of Christ's Spirit, as seen when Paul only refers to the latter but indicates the former.[73] It is worth noting here that the future resurrection, wherein our animal bodies become spiritual bodies "by the Spirit," implies for Irenaeus a prophetic element: as Paul says, now we know and "prophecy in part" but in the resurrection will do so "face to face."[74]

When speaking in this bipartite approach, Irenaeus affirms two aspects of humanity, for "we are body which is taken from the earth and soul which partakes in the Spirit of God," and therefore, the Word of God also had to have accepted a material body from the virgin, a tenet supported by citing "the apostle Paul" who taught that Christ was "made from woman" and "made from the seed of David according to the flesh [σάρκα/*carnem*]."[75] The bipartite anthropology is still assumed when Irenaeus describes Adam as originally clothed in "holiness from the Spirit," but he later had to clothe himself with fig leaves.[76] In other words, the human soul is not on its own "spiritual," but it can participate in God's Spirit.[77] This participation brings up the role of God's Spirit in human salvation, which further illustrates Irenaeus's preferred bipartite anthropology.[78]

The heretics' understanding of the fruits of the Spirit must be corrected, for they assume it is man's own spirit while Irenaeus insists that it is the Spirit of God at work in the believer.[79] The soul and the flesh are later given further explanation

---

72. *Haer.* 5.6.2, with ref. to 1 Cor 3:16-17 and 1 Cor 6:15; this is elaborated further in 5.8.1, where Paul is cited extensively—Eph 1:13-14, 2 Cor 5:4, Rom 8:9, 8:15, 1 Cor 13:12; in these passages it is clear that God does not quicken a human spirit, but instead imparts the divine Spirit, by which we cry Abba, Father; cf. *Haer.* 5.9.1, where the Spirit of God quickens man, not the spirit of man; and cf. 5.9.3, where fallen humans receive the Spirit—the Spirit is not their own.

73. *Haer.* 5.7.1, with ref. to Rom 8:11.

74. *Haer.* 5.7.2, with ref. to 1 Cor 13:9, 12.

75. *Haer.* 3.22.1, with ref. to Gal 4:4 and Rom 1:3-4.

76. *Haer.* 3.23.5.

77. Cf. *Haer.* 5.9.4, where this is clarified so that the flesh passively participates, while God's Spirit actively pervades the flesh. The analogy then given is the wild olive branch grafted into a domesticated olive tree (*Haer.* 5.10.1, with ref. to Rom 11:17, 24). The tree for Irenaeus is implicitly the body, while the sap from the tree is explicitly "the Spirit of God" (*Haer.* 5.10.1-2, with ref. to Rom 8:9-11).

78. For detailed discussion of Irenaeus's view of salvation in relation to Paul, see Blackwell, *Christosis: Pauline Soteriology in Light of Deification in Irenaeus and Cyril of Alexandria* (WUNT II/314; Tübingen: Mohr Siebeck, 2011).

79. *Haer.* 5.11.1, with ref. to Gal 5:19-20 and esp. 1 Cor 6:9-11. Cf. *Epid.* 2.3.99, where "the gifts of the Holy Spirit" are a "prophetic grace."

in terms of salvation because the soul should be led by "God's Spirit," but in sin it follows the flesh; it is only when the Spirit of God is again given to the human that the body can be called a "spiritual body."[80] In other words, "the fleshly substance" can "participate [κοινωνίαν/*communionem*]" in the Spirit.[81]

The primary passage invoked by the opponents which negates a salvation of the flesh is the verse from Paul that denies "flesh and blood [σὰρξ καὶ αἷμα/*caro et sanguis*]" entrance into the kingdom of God.[82] They, however, fail to see what Paul truly teaches about the Spirit's work: those who have "the Spirit of God," that is, "the Spirit who enlivens man," are still in the flesh, but their soul and flesh now rightly live by the Spirit and so belong to the kingdom of God.[83] In correcting this eschatology, Irenaeus shifts to protology in order to correlate human creation and resurrection.[84]

Irenaeus distinguishes "the enlivening Spirit [Πνεῦμα ζωοποιοῦν/*Spiritus vivificans*]" from "the breath of life [πνοὴ ζωῆς/*afflatus vitae*]."[85] The latter is an explicit reference to Genesis (2:7LXX: πνοὴν ζωῆς; and then also Is 42:5).[86] Paul contrasts the first man, who was "animal [τὸ ψυχικόν]," with the second man, Christ, who was "spiritual [τὸ πνευματικὸν]" (1 Cor 15:46). For Irenaeus, the Spirit appears to be the substance which is uniquely divine (τὸ μὲν Πνεῦμα ἰδίως ἐπὶ τοῦ Θεοῦ/*Spiritum quidem proprie in Deo*), contrasted with the "breath [πνοὴν/*afflatum*]" which is the common condition and is created ... breath is temporal; the Spirit is eternal."[87] Irenaeus immediately cites Paul, but shifts from temporal to qualitative language about what is primal and what is teleological: since "that which is first is animal, and the spiritual comes after" (with ref. to 1 Cor 15:46), then "the Spirit embraces the inner and outer man, so as always to abide, never abandoning him."[88] Irenaeus also believes the "substance of the flesh which loses the breath of life [τὴν πνοὴν τῆς ζωῆς/*afflatum vitae*] and breathing itself is made to die."[89] He then clarifies Paul's exhortation to "mortify the flesh," which actually entails ending the fleshly/sinful acts; it is not a denial of the body's inherent goodness.[90] For proof, Irenaeus turns again to Paul who

---

80. *Haer.* 5.9.1, explaining 1 Cor 15:50.
81. *Haer.* 5.9.2.
82. *Haer.* 5.9.1, with ref. to 1 Cor 15:50.
83. *Haer.* 5.9.1.
84. Steenberg, *Irenaeus*, 213: "Protology and eschatology combine."
85. *Haer.* 5.12.2. However, Irenaeus can cite Is 42:5, with no further comment on the parallel between πνοὴν/*afflatum* and Πνεῦμα/*Spiritum* (*Huer.* 4.2.1).
86. Is the former equal to Paul's phrase? (cf. 1 Cor 15:45: πνεῦμα ζωοποιοῦν). Behr, *Irenaeus*, 155, concludes, "That he uses the term 'soul' here, rather than 'breath,' is due to the fact that he is commenting on 1 Cor 15.45–6, and the use it makes of Gen 2.7, rather than the Genesis text itself." See Noormann, *Irenäus als Paulusinterpret*, 310–15.
87. *Haer.* 5.12.2.
88. *Haer.* 5.12.2.
89. *Haer.* 5.12.3.
90. *Haer.* 5.12.3, with ref. to Col 3:5.

elsewhere affirms "living in the flesh."[91] Irenaeus, contra his opponents, hears Paul to differentiate the flesh per se from the works of the flesh.[92] Irenaeus then cites Paul's statement that "mortality will be swallowed up in life" and this, still citing Paul, occurs by the "Spirit [Πνεύματος/*Spiritus*]."[93] Irenaeus also hears Paul to say "God's Spirit writes ... on the tablets of the fleshly heart"—the polemical import here being that Paul affirms the Spirit's work on the flesh(ly heart).[94] This view of human nature becomes important when reading Irenaeus's understanding of Christ's humanity, and so we can now turn there where we will find the "Spirit" to play an important role.

Irenaeus's opponents in various ways disassociate Jesus from Christ.[95] Against this docetic commitment, Irenaeus teaches that in the incarnation, one and the same Christ participates in two substances: "the spiritual and invisible" as well as "the visible and the bodily."[96] Within this apparently bipartite framework Christ's Spirit is never carefully differentiated from Christ's human soul, except that Christ exchanged his "soul for our soul, and his flesh for our flesh."[97] Irenaeus employs material analogies for the participation of the flesh in the Spirit: the Word-incarnate is like the mixture of water and wine, and it is comparable to "the breath of life [πνοὴ τῆς ζωῆς/*aspiratio vitae*]" given to Adam at creation.[98] The first Adam, therefore, prefigures the second: "the Word of the Father and the Spirit of God united with the ancient substance of Adam's shaping."[99]

Christ's two substances then, the (hu)man and the Spirit(ual), both function to save the descendants of Adam fully, that is, both their flesh and spirit. Irenaeus proves Christ had a material body by citing Paul: "we are members of Christ's body, of his flesh and of his bones."[100] The Spirit is still spoken of as a personal

---

91. *Haer.* 5.12.4, with ref. to Phil 1:22.

92. *Haer.* 5.13.3.

93. *Haer.* 5.13.3, with ref. to 2 Cor 5:4-5.

94. *Haer.* 5.13.4, with ref. to 2 Cor 3:3. It is worth noting that the Spirit's role of communication is also salient here, although Irenaeus does not underscore it in this paragraph.

95. See *Haer.* 3.9.3, for an aeon's possession of Jesus at his baptism; see 1.7.2 and 1.8.2 for four "substances" (i.e., material, animal, spiritual, and Christ) in Jesus; and Cerinthus's version in 1.26.1.

96. *Haer.* 3.16.6.

97. *Haer.* 5.1.1; Rousseau, SC 153:117, entitles this section, "La résurrection de la chair prouvée par les Épîtres de Paul."

98. *Haer.* 5.1.3.

99. *Haer.* 5.1.3. Thus it is, using Pauline phraseology, "in the animal one we all died, so also in the spiritual one we all may live" (*Haer.* 5.1.3, with ref. to 1 Cor 15:22). Earlier, Irenaeus had stipulated how the first "animal man" is to be saved by "the Spiritual Man," a reading of Adam credited to Paul (*Haer.* 3.22.3, with ref. to Rom 5:14).

100. *Haer.* 5.2.3, with ref. to Eph 5:30 (cf. the variant readings). Cf. Noormann, *Irenäus als Paulusinterpret*, 271–74.

4. The Personal/Substantial Spirit of Prophecy

subject who acts in the life of Christ.[101] This especially relates to when the Spirit of God descends on Christ during his earthly ministry, which requires additional explanation.[102]

Irenaeus must give some rationale for why the omnipotent Word needed the Spirit.[103] His explanation is that Christ received "the anointing" by the Spirit for the purpose of prophecy.[104] Christ's name "anointed" implies a threefold event: the Father anoints, the Son is anointed, the Spirit is the anointing.[105] This rationale is also given for the Mount of Transfiguration, in which the Father states that his Spirit has been placed upon the Son: the Son will not be "heard" until he speaks the final judgment.[106] The Spirit's primary role then, that of prophecy, is revealed even in Christ's ministry. This role will now be shown to be mirrored in Christ's people.

The Prophetic Spirit: The Old and New Witnesses

Irenaeus frequently refers to what "the Spirit" said in certain passages of scripture. For the Old Testament, he can speak in general terms, such as when he mentions the Spirit's speaking through all the prophets.[107] One significant way in which the

---

101. The Spirit of God is as personal as the demons rebuked by Christ: e.g., *Haer.* 4.20.4, where Christ eschewed "every sinful spirit" and instead clung to "God's Spirit." For more examples where this différant meaning can be seen clearly, cf. *Epid.* 1.3.40-41; 2.1.51; and 2.3.71.

102. Cf. Justin Martyr, *Dial.* 87–88.

103. For scholarly debate, see D. A. Smith, "Irenaeus and the Baptism of Jesus," *TS* 58 (1997), 618–42; and K. McDonnell, "*Questio disputata*: Irenaeus on the Baptism of Jesus," *TS* 59 (1998), 317–19.

104. A fact which itself was foretold by the Old Testament prophets: see *Haer.* 3.9.3; with ref. to Is 11:1–4; 61:1–2; cf. *Haer.* 3.12.5; 3.17.1. The Spirit's role in proclamation is also evident in *Epid.* 2.2.59 and 3.2.53. This prophetic function is overshadowed in the scholarly debates by the focus on the soteriological principle (see previous note; exceptionally, see Smith, "Irenaeus," 626).

105. *Haer.* 3.18.3. For the bibliography of scholars who contest whether this is an impersonal power or the person of the Spirit, see Briggman, *Irenaeus*, 67. My employment of différance to understand Irenaeus's usage circumvents this discussion precisely the same way Derrida handled the translation of Hegel ("Différance," 13–14).

106. *Haer.* 3.11.6, with ref. to Matt 12:18-21/Is 42:1-4; cf. 3.12.7 with ref. to Acts 10:38. Similarly, Irenaeus reads Luke 1:9 where Zachariah claims his son John will prepare the people for the Lord "in the s/Spirit and power of Elijah" (*Haer.* 3.10.1; citing Luke 1:17; cf. 3.10.2; 3.10.6, with ref. to Mark 1:1-3; and 3.11.4, with ref. to John 1:6-7), which corroborates the centrality of prophecy as the Spirit's role in Irenaeus's thinking.

107. Examples include *Haer.* 2.33.3, 2.34.3, 3.19.2, 4.2.4, 4.14.2, 4.5.5, 4.7.1, 4.36.8, 5.20.2; *Epid.* 1.1.8, 1.2.30, 2.pref.42, 2.3.67, 2.3.93. The term "prophets" can even be synonymous with the Old Testament (e.g., *Haer.* 1.8.1). Also see where the Spirit of Christ spoke through

Spirit speaks in these saints of old is by prophesying about Christ.[108] On this point in particular, Irenaeus cites Paul for his "spiritual" reading of the Law, and for the notion that to confess—even prophetically—Jesus as Lord is a work of the Spirit.[109]

The Spirit's role in prophecy is not limited to the old covenant, but continues in witnesses of the new. Irenaeus can speak of individuals, like Mary and John, but his primary concern is to insist that the same Spirit who spoke through the Old Testament prophets also speaks through the New Testament voices.[110] True believers call on the "name of our Lord," the same one whom "the prophets foretold [*prophetae praedixerunt*]."[111] At one point, Irenaeus uncharacteristically prays directly to God, asking "through our Lord Jesus Christ the gift of the Holy Spirit would be given" so that readers may know God rightly.[112] He then quotes

the prophets (*Epid.* 2.3.73; ref. Ps 3:6). Even Irenaeus's opponents teach that "the prophetic Spirit" spoke through the Jewish scriptures, only the Demiurge despised them and knew not whence their origin, since he was unspiritual (*Haer.* 1.7.4). For a detailed analysis of Irenaeus's use of Old Testament prophets, see Philippe Bacq, *De l'ancienne à la nouvelle Alliance selon S. Irénée: Unité du livre IV de l'Adversus Haereses* (Paris: Editions Lethielleux, 1978), 322–41.

108. See esp. *Haer.* 3.16.3 (discussed below); cf. *Epid.* 2.2.56.

109. On a Spiritual reading of the Law, see *Haer.* 3.18.7, with ref. to Rom 7:14, where the Law is "spiritual"; 4.27.3, with ref. to 1 Cor 10:1-12; and *Epid.* 2.3.90, with ref. to Jer 38 (31):31-34, Heb 8:8-12, but also informed by Rom 7:6. Regarding the ability to confess Jesus as Lord, Irenaeus refers to the "Spirit of holiness" that rested on Christ and insists that such was "the promise given through the prophets" in the Old Testament, including David himself who could "know by the Spirit" and thus "confess him as Lord [Κύριοω αὐτὸν ὡμολόγησεν/*Dominum eum confessus*]" (*Haer.* 3.16.3). This last phrase is clearly indebted to Pauline thinking (cf. 1 Cor 12:3: καὶ οὐδεὶς δύναται εἰπεῖν, κύριος ἰησοῦς, εἰ μὴ ἐν πνεύματι ἁγίω). Also, see where the Spirit corroborates Abraham through Paul's witness (*Haer.* 4.8.1, with ref. to Rom 4:3/Gal 3:6). The Spirit, therefore, even enabled the Old Testament prophets to see the pre-incarnate Word as "I AM" (e.g., *Epid.* pref.2; ref. Ps 1:1; Exod 3:14; cf. *Haer.* 4.20.9 and 4.31.2).

110. Cf. *Haer.* 3.10.2; ref. to Luke 1:46, where Mary's "spirit has rejoiced [ἠγαλλίσεν τὸ πνεῦμά/*exsultavit spiritus*]," for she "prophesies about the church." The "Holy Spirit" speaks in Revelation, only he refuses to utter the name of the Antichrist (*Haer.* 5.30.4). More generally, the scriptures are always spiritual (*Haer.* 2.28.3). In *Haer.* 3.12.5, Irenaeus explains how those who are perfected, be they Old Testament heroes, the apostles, or current disciples, are "perfected by the Spirit and can invoke God (ἐπικαλουμένων τὸν Θεὸν/*invocaverunt Deum*)."

111. *Haer.* 2.32.5. Also, cf. *Haer.* 3.11.8-9 (which older commenters think addresses Montanism: see discussion of the potential textual issues to blame here in Rousseau and Louis Doutreleau, SC 210:289; for bibliography on this passage, see Unger and Steenberg, *St. Irenaeus of Lyons: Against the Heresies (Book 3)* [ACW 64; New York: Newman, 2012], 150–51).

112. *Haer.* 3.6.4. Although I follow the corrected Latin text (see Rousseau and Louis Doutreleau, SC 210:257), it is worth reconsidering the original *dominationem* in light of the

Paul on the proper gnosis.[113] Iterating the claim that it is the same Spirit who spoke through the Old Testament writers and still speaks today, Paul's statement about "prophesying in part" is cited, as well as his teaching that the Spirit enables believers to cry "Abba, Father."[114]

The gift and reception of the Holy Spirit seems to refer to—or at least include—one's baptism, and in this imagery the material analogies once again govern his explanation.[115] In baptism the water washes the body while the Spirit washes our soul.[116] Christ himself received the Spirit from his Father, and he in turn "sends the Holy Spirit" on believers.[117] In contrast to baptism, the act of dying completes the Christian journey: the true church has a "crowd of martyrs," martyrdom being a concept which still carries the sense of witness, for just as the prophets were persecuted for testifying to Christ, so are the martyrs of the church who bear the "same Spirit" as the prophets.[118]

The primary manifestation of the Spirit is Pentecost.[119] In this sense, the Spirit of God is an outpouring or a grace.[120] An interesting description of Spirit-inspired prophecy occurs when debating Paul's meaning (in 2 Cor 4:4): Irenaeus first explains how the apostle's language is overexuberant due to "the Spirit in him."[121] This phenomenon is further described as Paul asking a question, with "the Spirit responding."[122]

---

citation of Gal 4:8-9 (which Rousseau and Doutreleau do not acknowledge). Cf. Briggman, *Irenaeus*, 47–48, who argues for *dominationem* on the basis of "Lukan influence" (i.e., Luke 10:16 and Acts 1:8).

113. *Haer.* 3.6.5, with ref. to 1 Cor 13:9-10 and Gal 4:8-9.

114. *Haer.* 4.9.2, with ref. to Gal 4:6; cf. Noormann, *Irenäus als Paulusinterpret*, 187.

115. Cf. *Epid.* 1.3.42.

116. *Haer.* 3.17.2.

117. *Haer.* 3.17.2. Cf. *Haer.* 4.4.3, with ref. to Matt 3:11-12/Luke 3:16-17, where John is quoted to say Jesus will baptize with the Holy Spirit and fire. Elsewhere, it is said Christ "cleanses their souls and bodies by the baptism of water and the Holy Spirit, distributing and dispensing the Holy Spirit, which they received from the Lord to the faithful" (*Epid.* 1.3.41).

118. *Haer.* 4.33.9; cf. 4.33.10.

119. On the Spirit poured out on all flesh, see *Haer.* 3.12.1, with ref. to Acts 2:15-17/Joel 2.

120. Irenaeus lists the innumerable "gifts," including "foreknowledge …, visions, and prophetic sayings" (*Haer.* 2.32.4). Moreover, "the Apostle Paul … in his letter to the Corinthians" endorses the "prophetic gift [τῶν προφητικῶν χαρισμάτων/*de propheticis charismatibus*]" (*Haer.* 3.11.9). For Marcus's false "Charis," see *Haer.* 1.13.4.

121. *Haer.* 3.7.2; cf. Noormann, *Irenäus als Paulusinterpret*, 121–22.

122. It should also be noted that in the same paragraph another citation of Paul is given (from 2 Thess 2:8-9) which foretells how Christ will slay Satan "with the breath of his mouth [τῷ πνεύματι τοῦ στόματος αὐτοῦ/*spiritu oris sui*]" (*Haer.* 3.7.2; cf. 5.25.3).

The Grace of Pentecost extends to all who come to the faith in succeeding generations, as illustrated by the conversion of "the nations" who prophesy.[123] The letter from the Jerusalem Council in Irenaeus's citation includes an added sentence, exhorting the audience to "walk in the Holy Spirit [πορευόμενοι ἐν τῷ ἁγίῳ Πνεύματι/*ambulantes in Spiritu sancto*]."[124] While the last sentence in Irenaeus partially corresponds to the so-called western text of Acts,[125] Irenaeus's final phrase is likely indebted to Paul.[126] Gentiles are only able to participate in the kingdom because "the Holy Spirit rested on them, causing them to prophesy."[127] Later, Irenaeus explicitly cites Paul, who spoke of "the Spirit" at work among the Galatians, who had also worked with Abraham to instill faith.[128]

In addition to general comments about the Spirit's inspiration of prophecy among believers, Irenaeus frequently explains how the Spirit inspires correct interpretation of the Old Testament.[129] Similarly, the Spirit enables the correct interpretation of Christ, "for one and the same Spirit of God who proclaimed the Lord's advent by the prophets, also enables elders to rightly interpret the right prophets" of the church; the content of both is found when "the Holy Spirit" teaches about Christ's two natures, for he is both "God and man."[130] This same theme is taken up a little later where the "Spirit foreknew" that the Son of David would be born of woman apart from a man, meaning that Christ would have the "substance [σύστασιν/*substantiam*]" both of a human and of God.[131] Irenaeus adds further proof for this from Paul, for just as Christ recapitulated the actions of the first man, so Eve was recapitulated in Mary.[132] Thus, Christ took a body from the virgin, and this too relies on Paul who taught about the "Spirit of holiness" forming Christ's flesh from Mary (citing Gal 4:4 and Rom 1:3–4).[133] In sum, Christ is truly

---

123. The Spirit enables all nations and tongues to "sing hymns to God [συμπνοῦντες ὕμνουν τὸν Θεόν/*hymnum dicebant Deo*]" (*Haer.* 3.17.2). See *Haer.* 4.14.2, where the Spirit's role is so tied to speech that "the voice of God" (in Rev. 1:15) is assumed by Irenaeus to be the Spirit.

124. *Haer.* 3.12.14, with ref. to Acts 15:29.

125. For the manuscript tradition with which this aligns, see Rousseau and Doutreleau, SC 210:303; and Denis Minns, "The Parable of the Two Sons (Matt. 21:28-32) in Irenaeus and Codex Bezae," in *Irenaeus: Life, Scripture, Legacy*, ed. Sara Parvis and Paul Foster (Minneapolis: Fortress, 2012), 55–63.

126. See Gal 5:16, πνεύματι περιπατεῖτε.

127. *Haer.* 3.12.15, with ref. to Acts 10:28-29.

128. *Haer.* 4.21.1, with ref. to Gal 3:5–9; cf. Noormann, *Irenäus als Paulusinterpret*, 211–12.

129. E.g., *Haer.* 2.28.2; 4.27.1; 4.33.15; cf. 5.34.3.

130. *Haer.* 3.21.4; repeated 4.11.1. Also, cf. *Haer.* 3.16.8, with ref. to 1 John 4:1-3.

131. *Haer.* 3.21.9, with ref. to Jer 22:28-31.

132. *Haer.* 3.21.10; with ref. to Romans 5.

133. *Haer.* 3.21.10; cf. 3.22.3, with ref. to Rom 5:14.

human and truly divine, yet "one and the same," which requires and received a "witness" from the Holy Spirit.[134]

Since heretics do not have the Spirit of God, they hold to incorrect interpretations of the scriptures and of Christ.[135] Against the heretics who differ among themselves, the church universal shares one proclamation of the Father, Son incarnate, and "gift of the Spirit."[136] The "church's preaching" has always been preserved and inspired by God's Spirit, with the former likened to a jar and the latter to the substance which fills the jar, constantly offering refreshment.[137] Similarly, "God's Gift" in the church is analogous to the "breath [ἡ πνοή/*aspiratio*]" given to Adam.[138] Once again, Paul is cited as support, for God has gifted the members of the church, and the specific spiritual gifts invoked are those to do with speaking (apostles, prophets, and teachers).[139] Thereby, correct proclamation becomes a boundary marker between the true church and the schismatics: the unpardonable sin is schism, which is to be "against the Spirit of God."[140] Irenaeus's famous pneumatological ecclesiology comes to the forefront, because where the "Spirit of God" is there is the church, and vice versa.[141]

---

134. *Haer.* 4.6.7.

135. *Haer.* 3.16.1; cf. 3.16.9; 3.21.8; 4.praef.3. Irenaeus's opponents completely misunderstand the "divine substance, God's goodness, and spiritual virtue [*virtute spiritali*]," since they have a "wicked spirit [*nequitiae spiritum*]" (*Haer.* 2.31.3; cf. 1.5.4 with ref. to Eph 6:12).

136. *Haer.* 5.20.1.

137. According to Rousseau and Doutreleau, SC 210:389-90, this image is indebted to 2 Tim 1:14. Also, the refreshment bestowed by the church's confession echoes the description of Blandina's martyrdom (cf. Eusebius, *Hist. Eccl.* 5.1.19). For this study, it is noteworthy that the churches of Vienne and Lyons offer a bipartite blessing (5.1.3), but one of the "witnesses" (5.1.4 and passim) who is "fervent in Spirit" (5.1.9) and who "confesses" because he has "the Advocate in him, the Spirit" (5.1.10) speaks on behalf of the Christians. Similarly, a commentary on the Father and the Son is inserted into one Christian's torture scene (5.1.23), but it is later said that "the Father's Spirit" supported all the martyrs in their act of confession (5.1.34). While in prison, the confessors even have visions and alter their teaching because of the guidance of "the Holy Spirit" (5.2.3).

138. *Haer.* 3.24.1.

139. *Haer.* 3.24.1, with ref. to 1 Cor 12:28. The importance of this passage will be revisited in the conclusion below.

140. *Haer.* 3.11.9; cf. Matt 1:31-32.

141. *Haer.* 3.11.9 (repeated at 4.36.2). This, moreover, is "the Spirit of Truth [τὸ ... Πνεθμα ἀλήθεια/*vero Spiritum*]" (cf. John 14:17, 16:13, 1 John 5:6), and therefore no heretic can separate from the church and claim the Truth.

Talk of God and/or God's Talk

As mentioned in an earlier section of this chapter, in his triune formula or Canon, Irenaeus aligns the Spirit's work to prophecy: "and in the Holy Spirit, who proclaimed through the prophets."[142] Once this is appreciated, the Spirit's place in Irenaeus's theology can be better understood.[143] Whereas modern scholars often read Irenaeus as omitting the person of the Holy Spirit in some of his references to the Rule of Faith,[144] the Spirit can now be understood as explicitly referenced vis-à-vis the Spirit's role in prophetic utterances.[145]

One such example is the allegedly truncated rule of faith given in 3.1.2 which does not mention the Holy Spirit as the content of the apostolic preaching. However, the Holy Spirit is explicitly named as the inspirer of that preaching, including its written and traditioned forms: the apostles had perfect gnosis when "the Holy Spirit" descended upon them; the response was to preach "the good

---

142. *Haer.* 1.10.1; cf. 4.praef.4-4.1.1.

143. Richard A. Norris, Jr., "Irenaeus' Use of Paul in his Polemic against the Gnostics," in *Paul and the Legacies of Paul*, ed. William S. Babcock (Dallas: Southern Methodist University, 1990), 84, failed to account for this when he identified (1) the Marcionite view of the demiurge, and (2) the Valentinian view of the incarnation, as "the two broad sets of issues" which constitute "all of the exegeses" opposed by Irenaeus. Rather than mentioning the role of the "spiritual man" as an excursus (96; cf. 97 which returns to the treatment of 95), I would contend that the use of the Spirit's scriptures was also an explicit issue for Irenaeus.

144. Which is always perplexing to those same scholars since Irenaeus is clearly committed to a baptism under the triune formula (e.g. *Epid.* 1.1.13; cf. *Haer.* 1.1.7); see Briggman, *Irenaeus*, 3–5, for earlier bibliography). This negative assessment has been reversed: e.g., Hans-Jochen Jaschke, *Der Heilige Geist im Bekenntnis der Kirche: eine Studie zur Pneumatologie des Irenäus von Lyon im Ausgang vom altchristlichen Glaubensbekenntnis* (Münster: Aschedorff, 1976), esp. 222–33; and Bacq, *De l'ancienne*, whose analysis of *Haer.* 4 can be applied to Irenaeus's work in general. See discussion in Jacques Fantino, *La theologie d'Irené. Lecture des Écritures en reponse à l'exégèse gnostique: Une approche trinitaire* (Paris: Éditions du Cerf, 1994), esp. 343–56 and 364–81, who argues for full trinitarianism in Irenaeus (albeit without "langage philosophique" of the fourth century—p. 389). For a recent survey and discussion, see Alistair Stewart, "'The Rule of Truth ...which He Received through Baptism' (*Haer.* I.9.4): Catechesis, Ritual, and Exegesis in Irenaeus's Gaul," in *Irenaeus: Life, Scripture, Legacy*, ed. Sara Parvis and Paul Foster (Minneapolis: Fortress, 2012), 151–58.

145. Brendan Leahy, "'Hiding behind the Works': The Holy Spirit in the Trinitarian Rhythm of Human Fulfillment in the Theology of Irenaeus," in *The Holy Spirit in the Fathers of the Church: The Proceedings of the Seventh International Patristic Conference, Maynooth, 2008*, ed. D. Vincent Twomey and Janet E. Rutherford (Dublin: Four Courts, 2010), 11–31, claims the Spirit remains "hidden" because the Spirit points beyond himself to the Son and Father.

4. The Personal/Substantial Spirit of Prophecy

news of God."[146] Irenaeus, of course, thinks the scriptures and the tradition should both be kept, but he knows that heretics have the scriptures but wrongly read them, whereas the "barbarians" do not have scripture but have "the salvific message and the ancient tradition written on their hearts by the Spirit."[147] The content of this message is once again the Canon of Truth, except given in a truncated form only naming the one God and his Son. The omission of the Holy Spirit requires no comment from Irenaeus because the belief in the Father and the Son has been placed in their hearts by the Spirit, and so the formula is explicitly triune when seen in context.

Another example is in Irenaeus's *partitio* in Book 4. All heretics, as we mentioned above, make the same set of errors, which correspond to the Canon of Truth:

> For whatsoever all the heretics may have advanced with the utmost solemnity, they come to this at last, that they blaspheme the Creator, and disallow the salvation of God's workmanship, which the flesh truly is; on behalf of which I have proved, in a variety of ways, that the Son of God accomplished the whole dispensation of mercy, and have shown that there is none other called God by the Scriptures except the Father of all, and the Son, and those who possess the adoption.[148]

Whereas the Father and the Son are the only ones named, Irenaeus assumes the role of the Holy Spirit, as evidenced by the next sentence where this adoption is clarified as the "Spirit of adoption."[149] Here again it is Paul who supplements Irenaeus's thinking in terms of pneumatology.

This tendency to leave the Spirit unreferenced but still present via prophecy has an interesting affinity with a Pauline passage referenced by Irenaeus. True believers confess the Father, the Son, and "the Spirit of God," and it is the Spirit who "gives the knowledge of truth" (a clear echo of 1 Tim 2:4).[150] The first two chapters of 1 Timothy make no mention of the Spirit (not until 1 Tim 3.16-4.1, where the Spirit "speaks"). Only the Father and the Son have been named (in 1 Tim 1:2 and 2:5),

---

146. *Haer.* 3.1.1. The examples of such preaching is Matthew, Mark, Luke—"the companion of Paul," and John, whose preaching were "handed down to us through writings [ἐγγράφως ἡμῖν παραδέδωκεν/*per scripta nobis tradidit*]" (*Haer.* 3.1.1).

147. *Haer.* 3.4.2. The notion of Lyons as "barbarian" must be nuanced: see Jared Secord, "The Cultural Geography of a Greek Christian: Irenaeus from Smyrna to Lyons," in *Irenaeus: Life, Scripture, Legacy*, ed. Sara Parvis and Paul Foster (Minneapolis: Fortress, 2012), 25-33, who concludes by noting that Irenaeus's mission to the Celts was itself in "*imitatio Pauli*."

148. *Haer.* 4.praef.4 (ANF1 trans.).

149. *Haer.* 4.1.1; cf. Rom 8:15.

150. *Haer.* 4.33.7, with ref. to 1 Tim 2:4; cf. Noormann, *Irenäus als Paulusinterpret*, 76-77, who curiously neglects this Pauline reference in this passage of Irenaeus, but does acknowledge Irenaeus's use of this verse in 1.10.2.

but Irenaeus intuitively places the Spirit in the role of "knowing" God (cf. 1 Cor 2:10-11).[151]

Given Irenaeus's pattern of placing the Spirit in the role of enacting divine communication, we should not be surprised to find Irenaeus also teaching about a role for the Spirit in God's speech-act of creation.[152] The Spirit's role in creation is always assumed by Irenaeus even when not explicitly stated, for God creates by speaking forth the Word, which cannot be uttered without God's Breath. Explicitly invoking the "Canon of Truth," which in the statement itself only mentions the "one omnipotent God" and the "Word," Irenaeus offers the correct view of creation by citing Ps 32:6, wherein the Word established creation by "the Spirit of his mouth [τῷ πνεύματι τοῦ στόματος αὐτοῦ/*Spiritu oris eius*]."[153] Furthermore, instead of the Pleroma full of aeons, "God through his Word and Spirit creates all things."[154] Therefore, even when Irenaeus's formulaic statement omits the Spirit's role, he can clearly proceed to explain how the Spirit cooperates in the divine act of creation.

Another aspect of his opponents' teaching must be corrected in regard to creation, and Irenaeus's response once again illustrates the Spirit's role.[155] When Paul experienced the third heaven, wherein he heard "unspeakable words" which are thus "spiritual," Irenaeus sees proof that the Creator is Spirit, and therefore not carnal: "And he truly is the Spirit of God, not a psychic Demiurge, or else he could not have made spiritual things."[156] After dismissing the false interpretation of Christ as poly-prosoponic, Irenaeus counters by insisting that Christ, the Savior, the Son, the Word, are all one and the same. Christ is even "a s/Spirit," given the statement from Lamentations: "The Spirit of our face [Πνεῦμα ... προσώπου ἡμῶν/*Spiritus ... faciei*], Christ the Lord."[157] In other words, one and the same Word who had a preincarnate spiritual nature took on real flesh, contra the docetic understanding. Such a reading, however, risks reducing Irenaeus's understanding of the term, for as Briggman demonstrates, the role of the Holy Spirit as the one who is Christ's anointing is also present in this passage.[158] The passage, therefore, retains both meanings, even if substantial imagery of "breath" appears the most salient.

151. 1 Cor 2:10 is cited at *Haer.* 2.28.7.

152. Cf. the Spirit hovering over the waters (*Haer.* 1.18.1, with ref. to Gen 1:2) and to "the prophetic Spirit" who in scripture told of God's creative speech (*Haer.* 2.34.3; with ref. to Ps. 148:5-6). For God's "two hands," see above.

153. *Haer.* 1.22.1.

154. *Haer.* 1.22.1.

155. For the wider development of this theme, see Michel René Barnes, "The Beginning and End of Early Christian Pneumatology," *Augustinian Studies* 39.2 (2008), 169–86, who concludes that Irenaeus is the last to affirm the Spirit's role in creation for several generation.

156. *Haer.* 2.30.8. Cf. Briggman's translation (*Irenaeus*, 44), whose interpretation (that *Spiritus Dei* = the Spirit who is God) illustrates the slippage between these terms. Briggman also observes that Irenaeus reads the spiritual substances into Paul's passage.

157. *Haer.* 3.10.3, with ref. to Lam 4:20.

158. Briggman, *Irenaeus*, 70, arguing against translating this passage with "breath" or "power." Also, cf. *Epid.* 2.3.71, with ref. to Lam 4:20. Behr, *Irenaeus*, 115 n.188, comments,

Recognizing, on the one hand, how Irenaeus's ability to see the Spirit implicitly at work in all divine speech and, on the other, how even Christ and the Father are Spirit(-ual) draws attention to another question about the place of the Spirit in Irenaeus's theology. The few passages in his work that suggest binitarian thinking can now be understood in light of the differánce inherent in the term "s/Spirit." For example, is Christ's divine nature "spiritual"? Or is he God's Spirit incarnate? Or, is he anointed by the Holy Spirit? The answer—to put it simply—is complex.

Irenaeus can speak of how the "Spirit of God" is to the church what the soul is to the body; this certainly echoes Paul (cf. 1 Cor 3:16, 6:19), and Paul's statement on the many members with many gifts is cited, namely, those who are "apostles, prophets, and doctors" are all said to be "animated by the Spirit."[159] The "Spirit is truth [Πνεῦμα ἀλήθεια/*Spiritum ... Veritas*]," which sounds dangerously close to encroaching upon Christ's title, and yet Irenaeus betrays no reluctance to share said title.[160]

It seems that to Irenaeus the Spirit animating Christ's human body is the same who animates Christ's ecclesial body, and this is God the Father's Spirit. This certainly does not say God is less than three persons—Irenaeus constantly looks for opportunities to remind the reader that God is three.[161] Likewise, he clearly does not hold to a Spirit-Christology in the usual sense of that category.[162] Instead, the Father's Spirit, be it in Christ or in the Church, (is the One who) inspires talk of God (subjective and/or objective). Paul's influence, while not necessarily predominant in Irenaeus's pneumatology, supplements the bishop of Lyons's thinking at various times, especially in regard to the Spirit's role in confessing Jesus as Lord to the glory of God the Father.

"While the Spirit is sometimes identified with the pre-Incarnate Christ in some early writers (e.g. Justin, *1 Apology* 33:6; *Herm. Sim.* 5:6); the word "Spirit" is clearly used here in a more general sense, as it can also be applied to the Father."

159. *Haer.* 3.24.1, with ref. to 1 Cor 12:28; cf. Noorman, *Irenäus als Paulusinterpret*, 282, curiously only mentions this passage in relation to *Haer.* 5.6.1, and not in relation to this passage in Book 4.

160. *Haer.* 3.24.1.

161. E.g., *Haer.* 4.20.12.

162. As demonstrated by Briggman, *Irenaeus*, 182.

RESPONSE
IRENAEUS'S USE OF PAUL ON THE SPIRIT: A RESPONSE TO DAVID E. WILHITE

Craig S. Keener

I have learned much from David Wilhite's chapter. Because I am not an expert of any sort on Irenaeus (though I have read Irenaeus with pleasure), I will focus my response on Irenaeus's New Testament basis and the broader ancient context in which both Irenaeus and his earliest Christian predecessors wrote.

Some of Irenaeus's arguments and illustrations go beyond Paul and extant first-century Christian sources in general, but many do reflect themes present in the works of Paul and his colleagues. In general, however, I can confirm Wilhite's observation that while Irenaeus's pneumatology does draw on Paul, Paul was by no means Irenaeus's only source. To this end I shall note several themes on which Wilhite touches.

Clearly the Holy Spirit is the agent through whom Christians know God, in Paul as in Irenaeus (1 Cor 2:10-16; Rom 8:15; Gal 4:6). This connection is not unique to Paul (consider, e.g., John 16:13-15), but Irenaeus's citation of Paul here is apropos.[1]

The author would like to thank Ben Blackwell, Benjamin White, and Michael Williams for reading a draft of this chapter and offering helpful suggestions.

1. Wilhite notes the use of 1 Cor 2:10 in *Haer.* 2.28.7. On the Pauline function of this passage, see fuller discussion in Craig S. Keener, *The Mind of the Spirit: Paul's Approach to Transformed Thinking* (Grand Rapids: Baker Academic, 2016), 173–206; briefly, Keener, *1 and 2 Corinthians* (New Cambridge Bible Commentary; Cambridge: Cambridge University Press, 2005), 38–40; on the role of John 16:13-15 and John's larger theme of knowing God, see Keener, *The Gospel of John: A Commentary*, 2 vols (Grand Rapids: Baker Academic, 2003), 1:234–47; 2:1035–43.

The Spirit as Substance?

I wonder if the emphasis on spiritual substance engages with some philosophic notions of the day.[2] For Stoics, whatever genuinely exists consists of substance[3]; only material things truly exist.[4] Some others concurred with the physicalist approach.[5] "Spirit" in Stoicism was an impersonal cosmic substance, "the finest form of matter,"[6] a mixture of fire and air[7] that interpenetrated all other matter and was like the soul of the universe.[8] This conception fits Stoic monism.[9]

Stoic metaphysics differed from Paul's more Jewish conception: the Stoics knew πνεῦμα ἱερόν (sacred spirit) but not πνεῦμα ἅγιον.[10] Some seek to read this Stoic concept into Paul's usage,[11] but Paul usually refers to God's Spirit, which would be no more material than is God.[12]

---

2. I borrow most of this paragraph from Craig S. Keener, *Acts: An Exegetical Commentary*, 4 vols (Grand Rapids: Baker Academic, 2012–15), 1:530–31.

3. See Daniel Nolan, "Stoic Gunk," *Phronesis* 51.2 (2006), 162–83; Katja Maria Vogt, "Sons of the Earth: Are the Stoics Metaphysical Brutes?" *Phronesis* 54.2 (2009), 136–54.

4. Arius Didymus *Epitome of Stoic Ethics* 2.7.5a, lines 5-6; 2.7.5b7, p. 20, line 28—p. 22, line 1; Hierocles, *Elements of Ethics* 1.14-15.

5. See, e.g., Christopher Gill, "Galen and the Stoics: Mortal Enemies or Blood Brothers?" *Phronesis* 52.1 (2007), 88–120. Joshua Abelson, *The Immanence of God in Rabbinical Literature*, 2nd ed. (New York: Hermon, 1969), 212–23, contends that the Spirit could also be portrayed in somewhat materialistic language in rabbinic sources.

6. So Kirsopp Lake, "The Holy Spirit," 5:96–111 in *The Beginnings of Christianity: The Acts of the Apostles*, 5 vols, ed. F. J. Foakes-Jackson and Kirsopp Lake (London: Macmillan, 1926), 103; see Hans-Josef Klauck, *The Religious Context of Early Christianity: A Guide to Graeco-Roman Religions*, trans. Brian McNeil (Minneapolis: Fortress, 2003), 353–54; Ernest F. Scott, *The Spirit in the New Testament* (London: Hodder & Stoughton; New York: George H. Doran, 1923), 52–53.

7. A. A. Long, *Hellenistic Philosophy: Stoics, Epicureans, Sceptics* (New York: Scribner's, 1974), 155–58; cf. Max-Alain Chevallier, *Ancien Testament, hellénisme et judaïsme, la tradition synoptique, l'oeuvre de Luc* (vol. 1 of *Souffle de Dieu: Le Saint-Esprit dans le Nouveau Testament*; Point théologique 26; Paris: Beauchesne, 1978), 41–42.

8. Long, *Philosophy*, 171; cf. Eduard Schweizer, *The Holy Spirit*, trans. Reginald H. Fuller and Ilse Fuller (Philadelphia: Fortress, 1980), 29; Sextus Empiricus *Pyr.* 3.218.

9. D. Friedrich Büchsel, *Der Geist Gottes im Neuen Testament* (Gütersloh: Bertelsmann, 1926), 45–49, especially 47; Klauck, *Context*, 353–54.

10. Arthur Darby Nock, *Early Gentile Christianity and Its Hellenistic Background* (New York: Harper & Row, 1964), 51; also Büchsel, *Geist*, 52–53.

11. Troels Engberg-Pedersen, "The Material Spirit: Cosmology and Ethics in Paul," *NTS* 55.2 (2009), 179–97; idem, *Cosmology and Self in the Apostle Paul: The Material Spirit* (Oxford: Oxford University Press, 2010).

12. For some responses to Engberg-Pedersen on this point, see, e.g., John R. Levison, "Paul in the Stoa Poecile: A Response to Troels Engberg-Pedersen, Cosmology and Self in the Apostle Paul: The Material Spirit (Oxford, 2010)," *JSNT* 33.4 (2011), 415–32; John

Wilhite may be correct that Irenaeus did not need to distinguish Briggman's two definitions of πνεῦμα/*spiritus* the way that post-Sabellians did. The New Testament claim that God is a spirit appears in John's Gospel (4:24), which elsewhere distinguishes the Spirit from the Father as well as the Son (14:16, 26; 15:26). For Philo, God as "spirit" makes him devoid of human passions,[13] but John merely communicates that God is not physical/material. God is not one among many spirits, nor a pervasive spiritual force, but God's nature is spirit rather than flesh (cf. 3:6; 6:63).[14]

John probably expands his teaching from 3:6: Spirit can relate to spirit, so those who relate to and worship God must do so through the gift of his Spirit (cf. Paul's teaching in 1 Cor 2:11-12; Phil 3:3). Although Paul is sometimes thought to confuse the Son with the Spirit in 2 Cor 3:17, context supplies better explanations.[15]

Some Images of the Spirit

Below I compare some images of the Spirit that appear in Irenaeus, as noted in Wilhite's chapter, and among Irenaeus's predecessors.

The Spirit as Moisture

Although some streams of ancient Jewish thought associated water imagery with Wisdom[16] or the Torah,[17] early Christians developed the Old Testament

---

M. G. Barclay, "Stoic Physics and the Christ-Event: A Review of Troels Engberg-Pedersen, Cosmology and Self in the Apostle Paul: The Material Spirit (Oxford: Oxford University Press, 2010)," *JSNT* 33.4 (2011), 406–14.

13. E.g., *Sac.* 95. For Philo's heavy stripping of anthropomorphism, cf., e.g., A. Marmorstein, *Essays in Anthropomorphism* (London: Oxford University Press, 1937), 4–6.

14. Cf., e.g., George B. Stevens, *The Johannine Theology: A Study of the Doctrinal Contents of the Gospel and Epistles of the Apostle John* (New York: Scribner's, 1894), 46; Raymond E. Brown, *The Gospel according to John*, 2 vols (AB 29, 29A; Garden City, NY: Doubleday, 1966-70), 1:172; Keener, *John*, 1:615–19.

15. See, e.g., F. F. Bruce, *Paul: Apostle of the Heart Set Free* (Grand Rapids: Eerdmans, 1977), 120–21; Richard B. Hays, *Echoes of Scripture in the Letters of Paul* (New Haven: Yale University Press, 1989), 143; Linda L. Belleville, *Reflections of Glory: Paul's Polemical Use of the Moses-Doxa Tradition in 2 Corinthians 3.1 18* (JSNTSup 52; Sheffield, UK: Sheffield Academic, 1991), 256–72; Margaret E. Thrall, *A Critical and Exegetical Commentary on the Second Epistle to the Corinthians*, 2 vols (Edinburgh: T&T Clark, 1994–2000), 278–81; Frank J. Matera, *II Corinthians: A Commentary* (NTL; Louisville: Westminster John Knox, 2003), 96; Keener, *Corinthians*, 169–70; cf. also Theodoret of Cyr *Comm. 2 Cor.* 305–6.

16. E.g., Prov 16:22; 18:4; Bar 3:12; Sir 15:3; 51:23-24; 1 En 48:1; 49:1; Philo *Worse* 117; *Alleg.* 2.86-87; *Cain* 138; *Drunk* 112; *Laws* 4.140; *Virt.* 79; 4 Ezra 8:4; 14.47; 2 Bar 59:7; Sib. Or. 1.33-34.

17. E.g., M. Ab. 1.4; 2.8; Mek. *Vay.* 1.74ff; *Bah.* 5.99; Sifre Deut. 48.2.7; 306.19.1; 306.22-25.

stream that used it for God's Spirit (Isa 44:3; Ezek 36:25-27),[18] which was also associated with "pouring" (Isa 32:15; 44:3; Ezek 39:29; Joel 3:1-2 [ET 2:28-29]; Zech 12:10),[19] like other invisible entities (e.g., 1 Sam 1:15; Ps 42:5 [LXX 41:5; ET 42:4]; Lam 2:11).[20] Some early Jewish circles, especially the Essenes, also associated the Spirit with purification.[21] The image of "filling" probably envisions the Spirit similarly, again already in the Old Testament (Exod 31:3; 35:31; Deut 34:9; Mic 3:8).[22] Even drinking the Spirit (1 Cor 12:13) is not exclusively Pauline (John 7:37-39). Paul's baptism in or by the Spirit (1 Cor 12:13) likewise echoes early Christian tradition more generally (Mark 1:8; Matt 3:11; Luke 3:16; John 1:33; Acts 1:5; 11:16).

The Spirit as Breath

The Spirit-breath in John 20:22 evokes Gen 2:7, and perhaps also Ezekiel 37 by way of John 3:8.[23] If Luke identified the Spirit with wind or fire in Acts 2:2-3, he might have envisioned the Spirit as a "substance," as in Hellenistic sources.[24] But Luke's pneumatology is more Jewish and biblical,[25] and fits theophanic storm images of wind and fire,[26] which would be intelligible even to recent pagan

---

18. Cf. the use of Ezekiel 36 in Jub 1.21, 23; John 3:5-6; 2 Cor 3:3.

19. Cf. also 1 En 62:2; 91; 4Q504 f1-2Rv.15.

20. Cf. also 1QHa 16.33; Ps. Sol. 16.2; 4 Ezra 14 :40.

21. Cf. 1QS 3.7; 4.21; 4Q255 f2.1; J. Coppens, "Le don de l'Esprit d'après les textes de Qumrân et le quatrième évangile," in *L'Évangile de Jean: Études et problèmes* (RechBib 3; Leuven: Desclée de Brouwer, 1958), 209–23, also 211–12, 222; Émile Puech, "L'Esprit saint à Qumrân," *SBFLA* 49 (1999), 283–97; Ju Hur, *A Dynamic Reading of the Holy Spirit in Luke-Acts* (JSNTSup 211; Sheffield, UK: Sheffield Academic, 2001), 230.

22. Cf. 4Q365 f10.4 and Philo *Giants* 23, both following Exodus 31; Philo *Decal.* 175; for evil, cf. T. Asher 1:9.

23. See Max Turner, *The Holy Spirit and Spiritual Gifts in the New Testament Church and Today*, rev ed. (Peabody, MA: Hendrickson, 1998), 90–92; Keener, *John*, 1:555-58; 2:1204-5; cf. Philo *Creat.* 135; *Virt.* 217. Later Targums interpreted God's breath into Adam as endowment with speech (*Tg. Ps.-Jon.* on Gen 2:7; *Tg. Neof.* on Gen 2:7; probably analogous to the Spirit of prophecy's frequent effects).

24. J. H. E. Hull, *The Holy Spirit in the Acts of the Apostles* (London: Lutterworth, 1967; Cleveland: World, 1968), 58–59.

25. See, e.g., Craig S. Keener, *The Spirit in the Gospels and Acts: Divine Purity and Power* (Peabody, MA: Hendrickson, 1997), 7–8, 10–13.

26. Exod. 3:2; 19:18; 40:34-38; 2 Sam 5:24; 2 Kgs 2:11; 2 Chron 7:1-3; Job 38:1; Ps 29:3-10; 97:2-5; 104:3; Isa 6:4; 29:6; 30:27-28; 66:15; Ezek 1:4; Jub. 1.3; *L.A.E.* 25.3; 4 Ezra 3:19; cf. 4 Ezra 13:27; at the law-giving at Sinai, Exod 19:16, 19; Deut 4:11; *L.A.B.* 11.5; 23.10; 32.7. Cf. discussion in, e.g., Angelo P. O'Hagan, "The First Christian Pentecost (Acts 2.1–13)," *SBFLA* 23 (1973), 50–66; C. K. Barrett, *A Critical and Exegetical Commentary on the Acts of the Apostles*, 2 vols (Edinburgh: T&T Clark, 1994–98), 113.

converts.[27] Luke's rare term for "wind" probably evokes Gen 2:7 and its LXX echoes,[28] and his usage in context especially evokes Ezek 37:9-10.[29] At some point Jewish tradition connected the divine breath of Gen 2:7 with the reviving, eschatological wind of the Spirit in Ezekiel 37.[30] Ezekiel's "dry bones" prophecy figured prominently in Jewish end-time thought, especially among eschatologically oriented sects.[31]

The verbal association of spirit and breath was frequent in Hebrew; early Israelite writers may have distinguished spirit, breath, and wind more as various nuances of a connected concept.[32] John the Baptist's "Spirit and fire" (Luke 3:16// Matt 3:11) may have originally included a wordplay on the wind and fire of the threshing floor (Luke 3:17//Matt 3:12).[33]

Being Clothed with the Spirit

Irenaeus's *Haer*. 4.36.6 links 2 Cor 5:4 with Matt 22:11-13; his association of 2 Cor 5:4 with the Spirit implicitly assumes the context (5:5), and probably also evokes Paul's image of being clothed with or having put on Christ (Rom 13:14; Gal 3:27; Col 3:10; cf. Rom 13:12; Col 3:12-14; Eph 4:24; 6:11; 1 Thess 5:8).[34]

But like Paul himself in using this image, Irenaeus might also take for granted other precedents. Scripture already used such imagery figuratively (Isa 52:1; 61:10; Zech 3:3-4), and other Jewish sources also spoke of being "clothed" with righteous qualities[35] or the Spirit.[36] The apostolic fathers also speak of figuratively clothing

---

27. Pieter W. Van der Horst, "Hellenistic Parallels to the Acts of the Apostles," *JSNT* 8.25 (1985), 49–60, here 49–50; cf. Homer *Il*. 19.159; Maximus of Tyre 4.8.

28. Keener, *Acts*, 1:800.

29. Cf. Joseph A. Grassi, "Ezekiel xxxvii.1–14 and the New Testament," *NTS* 11.2 (1965), 162–64, here 164; Jacques Dupont, *The Salvation of the Gentiles: Essays on the Acts of the Apostles*, trans. John R. Keating (New York: Paulist, 1979), 40.

30. *Gen. Rab.* 14:8; Grassi, "Ezekiel xxxvii.1–14," 164; a midrashic link on "breathe" in Gen 2:7 and Ezek 37:9 is logical.

31. See 4Q386; 4Q388; 4Q385 frg. 2 (for wind, see lines 7-8); also see Diaspora frescoes at Dura Europos (Marc Philonenko, "De Qoumrân à Doura-Europos: La vision des ossements desséchés (*Ézéchiel* 37,1–4)," *RHPR* 74.1 [1994], 1–12); for Ezekiel 37 and the hope of the Spirit raising the dead, e.g., *Sipre Deut.* 306.28.3; *y. Sheq.* 3:3; *Gen. Rab.* 96:5; *Exod. Rab.* 48:4.

32. See Craig S. Keener, "Spirit, Holy Spirit, Advocate, Breath, Wind," in *The Westminster Theological Wordbook of the Bible*, ed. Donald E. Gowan (Louisville: Westminster John Knox, 2003), 484–96, also 484–87.

33. Cf. Harold J. Flowers, "En pneumati hagiō kai puri," *ExpT* 64.5 (1953), 155–56; Isa 4:4; Mal 3:2.

34. Later developed spiritually by Chrysostom *Homily* on Rom 13:14; Gal 3:27.

35. E.g., 4 Macc 6:2; *Apoc. Mos.* 20.1; perhaps *Ab.* 6.1, bar.; *Pesiq. Rab.* 1.2; clothed with evil in 4 Ezra 3:26. Cf. Philostratus *Vit. soph.* 2.10.590.

36. *L.A.B.* 27.9-10; *b. Meg.* 14b; cf. Philo *Virt.* 217.

oneself with virtues, and apparently not in a baptismal context.³⁷ Perhaps most important here, being clothed with the divine Spirit appears in LXX Judg 6:34; 1 Chron 12:18; 2 Chron 24:20.³⁸

The Prophetic Spirit

Irenaeus does often speak of the prophetic Spirit.³⁹ While this conception of the Spirit was common in early Judaism, however (see discussion below), Irenaeus's conception is distinctly Christian, since he treats the Spirit alongside Father and Word as a divine Person.⁴⁰

Pagan associations of πνεῦμα with prophetic inspiration were rare in this period.⁴¹ Even most of the sources associating "spirit" with the Pythoness's inspiration⁴² are late enough to betray Christian influence. Plutarch's association of inspiration with πνεῦμα⁴³ has more to do with Stoic-like conceptions of a pervasive substance, or with exhalations from the earth such as those affecting the Pythia, than with a spirit associated *particularly* with inspiration.⁴⁴

---

37. *1 Clem.* 30.3; Polycarp *Phil.* 1.2; *Hermas* 20.2; 22.8; 26.2; 27.4; 34.8; 39.7, 10; 42.1, 4; 43.4; 44.1; 45.4; 61.2, 4; cf. 65.3; 75.1; 90.2.

38. I borrow much of this paragraph from Craig S. Keener, *Galatians* (Cambridge New Testament Commentary; Cambridge: Cambridge University Press, 2018), 166–67.

39. See, e.g., *Haer.* 1.7.4; 1.13.4; 2.34.3; 3.11.9; 4.7.1; 4.20.6; 4.36.2, 8.

40. Irenaeus *Haer.* 1.22.1; 1.23.1; 4.7.4; 4.20.3; 5.18.2. Justin links the prophetic Spirit with the Father and the Son as an object of worship (Justin *Apol.* 1.6, 13); earlier, see Matt 28:19; 2 Cor 13:13; cf. 1 Cor 12:4-6; Gal 4:6; Eph 4:4-6; probably Rev 1:4-6. Irenaeus seems so eager to find the triune God that he inadvertently adds a third spy to Joshua's two (Josh 2:1; *Haer.* 40.20.12). There may be overlap with the Word in 3.10.2.

41. Marie E. Isaacs, *The Concept of Spirit: A Study of Pneuma in Hellenistic Judaism and Its Bearing on the New Testament* (Heythrop Monographs 1; London: Heythrop College Press, 1976), 15; David E. Aune, *Prophecy in Early Christianity and the Ancient Mediterranean World* (Grand Rapids: Eerdmans, 1983), 34 (contrast Chevallier, *Ancien Testament*, 39–40).

42. Hans Leisegang, *Pneuma hagion: Der Ursprung des Geistbegriffs der synoptischen Evangelien aus der griechischen Mystik* (Leipzig: J. C. Hinrichs, 1922), 32.

43. *Obsolescence of Oracles* 41, *Mor.* 432F-433A. On the spirit in Plutarch, cf. Büchsel, *Geist*, 49–52.

44. H. W. Parke, *A History of the Delphic Oracle* (Oxford: Blackwell, 1939), 22–24; Isaacs, *Spirit*, 15, 50; Schweizer, *Spirit*, 30; Aune, *Prophecy*, 34. Cf. Dio Chrys. *Or.* 72.12; Cic. *Div.* 1.36.79; 2.57.117.

Early Jewish sources regularly associate the Spirit with prophetic inspiration,[45] often of the scriptures.[46] This association with prophetic inspiration already appears in many Old Testament passages (e.g., Num 11:25-26; 1 Sam 10:6, 10; 19:20, 23; Joel 3:1-2 [ET 2:28-29])[47] and is clearly developed in the New Testament (e.g., Mark 13:11; Luke 1:67; Acts 2:17-18; 19:6; 21:11; 2 Pet 1:21; Rev 2:7; 19:10), including in Paul (Rom 8:15-16; 1 Cor 12:3, 10; 14:1).[48]

Irenaeus rightly emphasizes significance of the outpouring of the prophetic Spirit; this experience both marks the eschatological people of God and demonstrates gentile believers' inclusion in this body, for both Luke (Acts 2:17-18; 10:44-48; 11:15-18) and Paul (Rom 14:17; Gal 3:2, 5, 14; 4:29).

The true Spirit's role in proclaiming truth as opposed to error clearly has earlier Christian warrant as well (1 Cor 12:2-3, 10; 1 John 4:1-6). Irenaeus's mention of spirits of error (*Haer.* 1.9.5) presumably evokes 1 John 4:6, though the language also has a wider history in early Jewish usage.[49]

---

45. E.g., Sir 48:24; Jub. 25.14; 31.12; 1 En. 91:1; *L.A.B.* 28.6; 4 Ezra 14:22; 1QS 8.16; Josephus *Ant.* 6.166; Philo *Flight* 186; *Heir* 265; *Moses* 1.175, 277; 2.265; *Decal.* 175; *Laws* 4.49; *Sipre Deut.* 22.1.2; *t. Pisha* 2.15; 4.14; *Mek. Pisha* 1.150ff; *Mek. Shir.* 7.17-18; see further, e.g., Ernest Best, "The Use and Non-use of Pneuma by Josephus," *NovT* 3.3 (1959), 218-25, here 222-25; Robert P. Menzies, *The Development of Early Christian Pneumatology with Special Reference to Luke-Acts* (JSNTSup 54; Sheffield, UK: Sheffield Academic, 1991), 53-112; idem, *Empowered for Witness: The Spirit in Luke-Acts* (London: T&T Clark, 2004), 49-101; Max Turner, *Power from on High: The Spirit in Israel's Restoration and Witness in Luke-Acts* (Sheffield, UK: Sheffield Academic, 1996), 86-104; Keener, *Spirit*, 10-13, 31-33.

46. 1QS 8.16; Josephus *Ag. Ap.* 1.37; *4 Ezra* 14.22; *Sipra VDDen.* par. 1.1.3.3; 5.10.1.1; *Shemini Mekhilta deMiluim* 94.5.12; *Behuq.* pq. 6.267.2.1; *Sipre Deut.* 355.17.1-3; 356.4.1; cf. Büchsel, *Geist*, 57-58. In early Christian texts, see *1 Clem.* 47.3; *Barn.* 9.2; 14.2, 9; *Herm.* 43.9; Justin *Dial.* 25.

47. See further Chevallier, *Ancien Testament*, 27-29; Wonsuk Ma, *Until the Spirit Comes: The Spirit of God in the Book of Isaiah* (JSOTSup 271; Sheffield, UK: Sheffield Academic, 1999), 30-32, 202-3, 206-7; Christopher J. H. Wright, *Knowing the Holy Spirit through the Old Testament* (Downers Grove, IL: IVP Academic, 2006), 63-86; Keener, "Spirit," 486-87.

48. For the Spirit and scripture, see also Mark 12:36; Acts 1:16; 4:25; 28:25; Heb 3:7; cf. 2 Tim 3:16.

49. Note Jub. 25.14; 1QS 3.18-19; 4.9, 21-25; 4Q257 5.7; 6.2-4; T. Jud. 14.8; 20.1, 5; T. Sim. 3.1.

Pauline and Other Ancient Anthropology

Valentinians believed that the truly enlightened are spirit in contrast to other, merely binary people such as ordinary Christians.[50] Although Irenaeus combats such gnostic anthropology,[51] he can still use tripartite language,[52] as Wilhite notes.

Similarly, for functional purposes, Paul distinguishes the human νοῦς and πνεῦμα (1 Cor 14:2, 14-15).[53] He mentions together πνεῦμα, ψυχή, and σῶμα, but to emphasize the whole person (1 Thess 5:23).[54] Another early Christian writer also distinguishes πνεῦμα and ψυχή,[55] although in a context that suggests that they are closely connected, like joints and marrow (Heb 4:12).

Usually, however, Paul does not use potentially tripartite language. Although he echoes Platonic language such as "inner person," he rarely if ever uses ψυχή in a Platonic sense; his usage resembles the Septuagint.[56]

More generally, ancient anthropology was considerably diverse; Pharaonic Egypt envisioned numerous components or aspects.[57] Most Stoics normally divided the soul into eight parts,[58] although Marcus Aurelius envisioned three

---

50. Irenaeus *Haer.* 1.6.2; for the πνεῦμα there as the true, preembodied self, see Robert M. Grant, *Gnosticism and Early Christianity*, 2nd ed. (New York: Columbia University Press, 1966), 7–8 (cf. Irenaeus's rebuttal in 5.6.1). This conception may have been limited to Valentinians; see R. McL. Wilson, "The Spirit in Gnostic Literature," in *Christ and Spirit in the New Testament: Studies in Honour of C.F.D. Moule*, ed. Barnabas Lindars and Stephen S. Smalley (Cambridge: Cambridge University Press, 1973), 345–55, also 348–49. Cf. Philo *Alleg.* 2.4.

51. See esp. Irenaeus's argument in *Haer.* 5.3-7.

52. As in Irenaeus *Haer.* 5.9.1; cf. Tatian 12. For early Christian trichotomy compared with Peripatetic and Stoic thought, cf. also Marie Simon, "Entstehung und Inhalt der spätantiken trichotomischen Anthropologie," *Kairos* 23.1–2 (1981), 43–50.

53. Cf. Keener, *Corinthians*, 114; Anaxagoras in Arist. *Soul* 1.2, 405a.

54. Hans Conzelmann, *An Outline of the Theology of the New Testament* (New York: Harper & Row, 1969), 174; Isaacs, *Spirit*, 73; Ernest Best, *A Commentary on the First and Second Epistles to the Thessalonians* (London: Adam & Charles Black, 1977), 244; Henrik Tronier, "The Corinthian Correspondence between Philosophical Idealism and Apocalypticism," in *Paul Beyond the Judaism/Hellenism Divide*, ed. Troels Engberg-Pedersen (Louisville, KY: Westminster John Knox, 2001), 165–96, also 195.

55. Cf. also, e.g., Josephus *Ant.* 1.34.

56. See Keener, *Mind*, 267–78, esp. 275–78; contrast, e.g., Wis 9.15; Josephus *Ant.* 17.353; *War* 1.650; 3.372. See discussion in Harry Austryn Wolfson, *Philo: Foundations of Religious Philosophy in Judaism, Christianity, and Islam*, 2 vols; 4th rev. ed. (Cambridge, MA: Harvard University Press, 1968), 1:395–413.

57. Ludwig D. Morenz, "Ka," 7:1–2 in *Brill's New Pauly*, 1; John H. Walton, *Ancient Near Eastern Thought and the Old Testament: Introducing the Conceptual World of the Hebrew Bible* (Grand Rapids: Baker Academic, 2006), 211.

58. Diogenes Laertius 7.1.110, 157; Iamblichus *Soul* 2.12, §369.

parts of a person.[59] Platonists subdivided the soul into three parts,[60] although Plato envisioned further division in one struggling with passion.[61] Cicero divides the spirit into reason and impulse.[62] The Neoplatonist Plotinus envisions a perfect higher self, of which the lower soul is merely an emanation and image.[63]

The Jewish Middle Platonist Philo divides the soul into three parts, each of which is further divided into two.[64] His initial division presumably follows Plato's tripartite soul, but Philo is not consistent in this regard, elsewhere thinking of two parts[65]; but he divides further than Plato.[66] From the fourth century through the nineteenth, Samaritans generally held a tripartite view of humans.[67] Thirteenth-century Kabbalists divided the soul into ten parts, with a trinity of triads.[68]

---

59. Marcus Aurelius 3.16; 12.3. Posidonius apparently envisioned a tripartite soul; John M. Cooper, "Posidonius on Emotions," in *The Emotions in Hellenistic Philosophy*, ed. Juha Sihvola and Troels Engberg-Pedersen (TSHP 46; Dordrecht, Netherlands.: Kluwer Academic, 1998), 71–111, also 71.

60. See, e.g., Plato *Rep.* 6.504; 9.580D; *Timaeus* 89E; Diogenes Laertius 3.67, 90; Lucian *Dance* 70; Iamblichus *Soul* 2.11, §369 (cf. discussion in Philip Merlan, *From Platonism to Neoplatonism* [The Hague: Martinus Nijhoff, 1953], 25–27); for that of Pythagoras, see Diogenes Laertius 8.1.30; for Middle Platonists (also drawing on Aristotelians and Posidonius), see Paul A. Vander Waerdt, "Peripatetic Soul-Division, Posidonius, and Middle Platonic Moral Psychology," *Greek, Roman & Byzantine Studies* 26.4 (1985), 373–94. For intellect, soul, and body, see, e.g., Porphyry *Marc.* 13.234–35; but the soul is the mind's body in 26.412.

61. Stanley K. Stowers, "Paul and Self-Mastery," in *Paul in the Greco-Roman World: A Handbook*, ed. J. Paul Sampley (Harrisburg, PA: Trinity Press International, 2003), 524–50, also 529, 538; Richard Sorabji, *Emotion and Peace of Mind: From Stoic Agitation to Christian Temptation* (New York: Oxford University Press, 2000), 303–5 (esp. on Plato's divided soul; more generally, 303–15). Cf. Philo *Alleg. Int.* 2.91; Donald A. Stoike, "De genio Socratis (Moralia 575A-598F)," in *Plutarch's Theological Writings and Early Christian Literature*, ed. Hans Dieter Betz (SCHNT 3; Leiden: E. J. Brill, 1975), 236–85, also 278 (on Plutarch *Mor.* 592B); Iamblichus *Soul* 2.11, §369.

62. Cicero *De Officiis* 1.28.101; *Tusc. Disp.* 2.21.47; 4.4.9.

63. Plotinus *Ennead* 1.1.

64. *Heir* 225; *Alleg. Int.* 1.70, 72; 3.115; *Conf.* 21.

65. *Studies* 26; John M. Dillon, *The Middle Platonists: 80 B.C. to A.D. 220* (Ithaca, NY: Cornell University Press, 1977), 174.

66. David Konstan, "Of Two Minds: Philo on Cultivation," *Studia Philonica Annual* 22 (2010), 131–38.

67. John MacDonald, *The Theology of the Samaritans* (Philadelphia: Westminster, 1964), 227.

68. Christian D. Ginsburg, *The Essenes: Their History and Doctrines; The Kabbalah: Its Doctrines, Development, and Literature* (London: Routledge & Kegan Paul, 1955), 114.

Of course, as Wilhite points out, many viewed the soul as material. Most thinkers,[69] especially Platonists,[70] distinguished the soul from the body. Yet Aristotle envisioned the incorporeal soul as merely providing "form" or structure to the matter of the body.[71] Both Stoics and Epicureans were materialists[72]; the soul was a fine substance.[73] For many Stoics, the soul in the body was a particular case of universal divine reason permeating and structuring matter[74]; the soul intermingled throughout the body.[75] Even Middle Platonists were not always full Cartesian dualists. Sometimes they associated the rational soul with fire, so that the soul was a substance, merely lighter and purer than the body.[76]

As for Irenaeus, reference to the πνεῦμα in Paul is usually to the divine Spirit except where specified otherwise.[77] Reference to the Spirit being to the church what the soul is to the body may echo Paul (1 Cor 3:16; 6:19), as Wilhite suggests, though I wonder if this image had developed further in early Christianity,[78] perhaps under philosophic influence of Stoic cosmology (in which the universe was compared to a body).[79]

---

69. Cicero *Tusc.* 3.3.5; 3.10.22; 4.13.28; *Fin.* 3.22.75; Musonius Rufus 6, p. 54.4–6; Arius Didymus 2.7.7b, p. 46.11-18; Sextus Empiricus *Pyr.* 1.79; cf. Aristotle *Eth. nic.* 1.12.6, 1102a.

70. E.g., Plato *Phaedrus* 250C; Plutarch *Plat. Q.* 3.1, *Mor.* 1002B; *Table Talk* 5.intro, *Mor.* 672F-673A; *Pleas. L.* 14, *Mor.* 1096E (protesting detractors); *Affections of the Soul*, *Mor.* 500B-502A, passim; Maximus of Tyre 33.7–8; Diogenes Laertius 3.63 (on Plato); Porphyry *Marc.* 9.154–58.

71. Iamblichus *Soul* 1.3, §363; Dale B. Martin, *The Corinthian Body* (New Haven: Yale University Press, 1995), 7–8. I borrow much of this paragraph from Keener, *Mind*, 268–69.

72. Ilaria Ramelli, *Hierocles the Stoic: Elements of Ethics, Fragments, and Excerpts*, trans. David Konstan (SBLWGRW 28; Atlanta: SBL, 2009), 44n24; see, e.g., Lucretius *Nat.* 3.417-977 (esp. 417–829); Iamblichus *Soul* 2.10, §367. An Epicurean could expect the soul at death to leave easily through the body's many pores; Philodemus *Death* 7.6-20; see W. Benjamin Henry, "Introduction," in Philodemus. *On Death* (SBLWGRW 29; Atlanta: Society of Biblical Literature, 2009), xiii–xxxiv, also xix.

73. Lucretius *Nat.* 3.370-95; Iamblichus *Soul* 1.2, §363; 1.9, §366.

74. A. A. Long, "Soul and Body in Stoicism," *Center for Hermeneutical Studies Protocol* 36 (1980), 1–17; idem, *Philosophy*, 171 (citing Diogenes Laertius 7.156); cf. Martin, *Body*, 21; Stowers, "Self-Mastery," 527–28.

75. Hierocles *Elements of Ethics* 4.4-6, 44–46. They therefore necessarily affected each other (Hierocles *Elements of Ethics* 4.11-14).

76. Martin, *Body*, 13; Stowers, "Self-Mastery," 527.

77. See fully and extensively, Gordon D. Fee, *God's Empowering Presence: The Holy Spirit in the Letters of Paul* (Peabody, MA: Hendrickson, 1994).

78. Cf. the church in the world as the soul in the body in Diogn. 6.1-7.

79. Epictetus *Disc.* 1.12.26; Marcus Aurelius 7.13; cf. Plato *Timaeus* 30–38; Diodorus Siculus 1.11.6; Long, "Soul and Body."

Chapter 5

ON SIN: IRENAEUS'S APPROPRIATION OF PAUL

Thomas J. Holsinger-Friesen

Even though Irenaeus's characterization of sin expresses the nuances of his own distinctive theological vision, "Paul"[1] is clearly an indispensable authority and source of inspiration. Before we embark on a closer look at Irenaeus's writings, it is helpful to keep in mind Cyril O'Regan's broad observation that "Irenaeus's position on sin is relatively undeveloped."[2] Irenaeus "does not attempt to correlate disobedience with all the biblical namings for sin" nor does he "probe in the way Augustine does the motivational structure of sin, in which the categories of self-love and pride loom large."[3] Despite the less-than-systematic form of his doctrine of sin, Irenaeus employs themes and patterns that clearly express coherence and a certain logic. He writes the five volumes of *Against Heresies*[4] because he believes that the teachings of his opponents constitute a threat to the operation of God's economy in the lives of Christians entrusted to his pastoral care. To the extent that their doctrines inform their lifestyles, his opponents are—for Irenaeus—instantiations of sin. Using unrestrained, quite vehement language, Irenaeus imagines the opposition to be a "wild beast," fit to be stalked, exposed, and "wound[ed] from all sides."[5] Our study of sin, then, will encompass both

---

1. Since our interests lie in discerning how *Irenaeus* read and used biblical texts in the Pauline tradition, we will adopt a similarly pre-critical view of Pauline authorship. In so doing, "Paul" will also include texts that most scholars today would categorize as pseudo-Pauline.

2. Cyril O'Regan, *Gnostic Return in Modernity* (Albany: State University of New York Press, 2001), 165.

3. O'Regan, *Gnostic Return in Modernity*, 165.

4. These writings, abbreviated as *Haer.*, constitute his primary work and are our focus in this chapter.

5. *Haer.* 1.31.4. Unless otherwise indicated, quotations from *Haer.* Books 1, 2, 3 are from the more recent translations in the Ancient Christian Writers series (D. J. Unger, *St Irenaeus of Lyons Against the Heresies, Book 1*, rev. J. J. Dillon [ACW 55; New York: Paulist Press, 1992]; D. J. Unger, *St Irenaeus of Lyons Against the Heresies, Book 2*, rev. J. J. Dillon [ACW 65; New York: Paulist Press, 2012]; and D. J. Unger, *St Irenaeus of Lyons against the Heresies,*

Irenaeus's theological cogitations and his personal attacks on opponents. The broadened scope of our inquiry will not be limited to explicit uses of a term (e.g., "sin"), but will consider patterns of thought and behavior that Irenaeus stringently challenges.[6] In *Against Heresies*, Irenaeus's portrait of sin emerges more clearly when viewed as a confluence of four motifs: (1) false knowledge and ignorance, (2) arrogance, (3) separation and fragmentation, and (4) unfruitfulness. While each motif contributes a distinctive emphasis, they are interrelated.

False Knowledge and Ignorance

It should not be entirely surprising that Irenaeus has more in common with his Gnostic opponents than he is willing to admit. Significantly, for example, he identifies "ignorance" (*ignorantia*) as the "mother" of sins and "sickness."[7] Michel R. Desjardins, in his assessment of the concept of sin in Valentinianism, observes that the connection of "sin with ignorance and righteousness with knowledge is ... part of the Greek philosophical tradition."[8] Indeed, in *Timaeus* 86B, folly (ἄνοια) is termed a "disease (νόσος) of the soul," and one type of folly is "ignorance" (ἀμαθία).[9] In *Against Heresies* (2.20.3) Irenaeus asserts a sharp contrast. The Valentinians depict the passion of the twelfth divine aeon (Wisdom) as resulting in—perhaps ironically, in his view—ignorance and weakness. However, states Irenaeus, the "Lord" by his passion "destroyed death, dispelled error, put an end to corruption, and destroyed ignorance." Irenaeus submits Paul's words (in Eph 4:8) as substantiation: "When he ascended on high he made captivity itself a captive; he gave gifts to his people." Thus we see that for Irenaeus, not unlike his opponents, the overcoming of ignorance and error is an essential characteristic of the divine economy of salvation.[10]

Book 3, rev. M. C. Steenberg [ACW 64; New York: Newman Press, 2012]). Quotations from Books 4 and 5 (yet to be translated in the ACW series) are taken from the older *Ante-Nicene Christian Library* version (Alexander Roberts and James Donaldson [eds.], *The Ante-Nicene Fathers*, 10 vols [Grand Rapids: Eerdmans, 1986–90], 1:315–567).

6. Though vital, Pauline texts were not his only source of ammunition. For example, in the latter half of *Haer.* Book 5, Irenaeus particularly looks to Johannine texts when accusing his opponents of being "blind."

7. *Haer.* 3.5.2. To cite another example of similarity between Irenaeus and his opponents, both envision a cosmos which includes seven heavens (cf. *Epid.* 9 with *Haer.* 1.5.2).

8. Michel R. Desjardins, *Sin in Valentinianism* (Atlanta, GA: Scholars, 1990), 119.

9. Plato, *Timaeus* in *Plato in Twelve Volumes*, vol. 9, trans. W. R. M. Lamb (Cambridge, MA: Harvard University Press, 1925).

10. Riemer Roukema succinctly relates the primary theme of the Valentinian text *Gospel of Truth*: it is "a meditative, mystical address about redemption from ignorance and about the riches of the knowledge of the truth" (*Gnosis and Faith in Early Christianity* [London: SCM, 1999], 143).

Where Paul leads, by looking to Genesis 1–3 for language to describe sin and salvation, Irenaeus follows. Adam's sin of disobedience had resulted in his "com[ing] to the knowledge of evil things."[11] In the church, "planted," as it were, "as a garden (*paradisus*) in this world," some people offer a forbidden fruit they claim to possess: the "knowledge of good and evil." Drawing on 2 Tim 3:7 and Rom 12:3, Irenaeus warns believers not to repeat Adam and Eve's mistake. The "heretics" who question the "knowledge of the holy presbyters" are "as blind men … led by the blind," and will "fall into the ditch of ignorance lying in their path, ever seeking and never finding out the truth." Instead of being wise "beyond what it is fitting to be wise," we are to "be wise prudently, that we not be cast forth by eating of the 'knowledge' of these men from the paradise of life."[12] On other occasions, Pauline texts help Irenaeus clearly define a litmus test for distinguishing friend from foe. Precisely because of their boasts of hidden knowledge, the followers of Marcus should be "avoided."[13] In fact, the title Irenaeus gives his five-volume work uses a phrase from 1 Tim 6:20: "Avoid the profane chatter and contradictions of *what is falsely called knowledge.*"[14]

Along with false knowledge and ignorance, Irenaeus's conception of sin also includes the lack or rejection of the knowledge of God, his ways, and his word. He begins *Against Heresies*, Book 1, by appropriating words from 1 Tim 1:4: "Certain people are discarding the Truth and introducing deceitful myths and endless genealogies, which, as the Apostle says, promote speculations rather than the divine training that is in faith."[15] Perhaps "by quoting Paul, Irenaeus seems to indicate that Paul, by anticipation, condemned full-blown Gnosticism, the seeds of which were beginning to sprout already in Paul's day."[16] On occasion, Irenaeus charges them with ignorance and blindness without clearly implying an act of volition on their part. But in the preponderance of cases, "heretics" are culpable because of their willful decisions. Humanity has received the "mental

---

11. *Haer.* 3.23.5. For a recent study that frames Genesis 2–3 as a wisdom rather than a Fall narrative, see Ziony Zevit's *What Really Happened in the Garden of Eden* (New Haven: Yale University Press, 2013), 261: "In its own historical time it was not a story about sin … death or redemption. It was a story about the origins of humanity and human nature, about proper comportment, dignity, the acquisition of knowledge, and, ultimately, ethical self-awareness." Whereas Zevit speaks from a Jewish context, Peter Enns comes to some similar conclusions about the wisdom character of Genesis 3 (which he finds to be consonant with the interpretations of Irenaeus and Theophilus) from an evangelical one (*The Evolution of Adam* [Grand Rapids: Brazos, 2012], especially chapters 5 and 7).

12. *Haer.* 5.20.2.

13. *Haer.* 1.16.3; cf. 3.3.4; Titus 3:10.

14. *Haer.* 1.23.4; 2.preface; cf. 2.14.7 (emphasis added). Though commonly called *Against Heresies*, Irenaeus's work bears a longer title: *Exposé and Overthrow of What Is Falsely Called Knowledge* (Unger and rev. Dillon, *Against the Heresies, Book 1*, 1).

15. *Haer.* 1.Preface.1.

16. Unger and rev. Dillon, *Against the Heresies, Book 1*, 125.

power" (*magnanimitas*) to know good and evil,[17] but they "despise the handiwork of God" by "not admitting the salvation of their flesh."[18] Insofar as they presume superiority over the Demiurge-creator, and reject the *bodily* resurrection of Christ, they "do not choose to understand."[19] So "having alienated themselves from the truth, they deservedly wallow (*voluto*) in every error … because they wish rather to be sophists of words than disciples of the truth."[20] Addressing the Marconians specifically, Irenaeus quotes 2 Cor 4:4, 2 Thess 2:12, and Rom 1:28 to assert that their willful rejection of the knowledge of God constitutes a "consent to iniquity," which evokes God's judgment of blindness.[21] The knowledge they reject is the knowledge of God that is legitimate and fitting: that the Father, Creator of all, has effected redemption for his physical handiwork through the salvific work of his Son.[22] Ignorance of the Father results in ignorance of his "arrangements" (*dispensatio*),[23] and of his "Word."[24] Ephesians 1:10 would seem to be *the* focal text in Irenaeus's counterattack on both fronts: "There is, therefore … one God the Father and one Christ Jesus our Lord, who comes through every economy and recapitulates in himself all things."[25] Knowledge of God's greatness (which Irenaeus's opponents claimed to have) is beyond human reach; knowledge of God made accessible by his *love* is fully sufficient.[26] Indeed, notes Irenaeus, Paul highlights the uselessness of knowledge when isolated from love.[27] In Irenaeus's view, his opponents are those who "refuse to love the truth and so be saved."[28] Given that Irenaeus and the Valentinians appeal to many of the same sacred texts as materials for theological construction, differentiation is due to hermeneutical factors. "Ignorance of the Scriptures and of the dispensation of God" has yielded a harvest of blasphemy

---

17. *Haer.* 4.39.1.
18. *Haer.* 5.31.1; cf. 5.2.2.
19. *Haer.* 5.31.1. Irenaeus uses Eph 4:9 in this context as he challenges Valentinian Christology.
20. *Haer.* 3.24.2; cf. 2.11.1.
21. *Haer.* 4.29.1.
22. Cf. *Haer.* 3.16.3; Rom 1:1-4; 9:5; Gal 4:4-5; and Col 1:14-15.
23. *Haer.* 5.19.2.
24. *Haer.* 3.16.6; cf. 4.Preface.3.
25. *Haer.* 3.16.6; cf. 1.3.4; 1.10.1; 5.20.2. Eric Osborn's detailed examination of the theme of recapitulation (including the role of Eph 1:10) is a valuable resource (*Irenaeus of Lyons* [Cambridge: Cambridge University Press, 2001], especially 97–140).
26. *Haer.* 4.20.1. Michael Slusser argues that "*magnitudo* and *dilectio*" are the central themes in Irenaeus's work ("The Heart of Irenaeus's Theology," in *Irenaeus: Life, Scripture, Legacy*, ed. Paul Foster and Sara Parvis [Minneapolis: Fortress, 2012], 133). "The vision of God which is metaphysically impossible *secundum magnitudinem* … is granted *secundum dilectionem*; and *dilectio* here refers not just to God's benevolent love for people but the love with which people love God back, a relationship of love" (138).
27. *Haer.* 4.12.2; 1 Cor 13:2.
28. *Haer.* 5.25.3; 2 Thess 2:10.

and error.[29] Whereas—in Irenaeus's mind—individual biblical texts are pieces that, when fitted together, comprise a beautiful mosaic depicting a king, his opponents use the same pieces to produce a highly distorted and unrecognizable image of God.[30] Perhaps Irenaeus's audacious claim that ignorance is the "mother" of sin is better appreciated then, once we see this theme embedded throughout the span of his argument.

Arrogance

Ignorance and error, as a constituent and expression of sin, quite logically relates to another primary motif found in *Against Heresies*: arrogance. Among other things, Irenaeus accuses his opponents of "preferring their own zeal to God himself,"[31] "sin[ning] against their Father, rather subjecting him to insult than giving him thanks,"[32] despising God the Creator,[33] and being "impudent and presumptuous."[34] In the middle of outlining Ptolemy's tripartite anthropological system, Irenaeus, quite characteristically, pauses for an aside: "Because of this doctrine, the most perfect among them *shamelessly* do all the forbidden things, about which the Scriptures give guarantee that those who do such things shall not inherit the kingdom of God."[35] Teachings that engender arrogance among the self-described *pneumatikoi* justify their licentious behavior.[36] In particular, Irenaeus accuses the followers of Marcus—perhaps the main target of his treatise[37]—of "deceiving" and

---

29. *Haer.* 3.12.12; cf. 5.2.3-5.3.2; 2.11.1 et al.

30. *Haer.* 1.8.1. The longest-running hermeneutical dispute attested in *Haer.* concerns the interpretation of 1 Cor 15:50 ("flesh and blood cannot inherit the kingdom of God") in *Haer.* 5.1-19. Cf. also the discussion in 5.14.4 on Rom 6:12 and Col 2:19.

31. *Haer.* 4.11.4.

32. *Haer.* 4.18.4.

33. *Haer.* 2.10.2.

34. *Haer.* 3.21.3. This is a representative, though not exhaustive list of references on the topic of pride.

35. *Haer.* 1.6.3 (emphasis added); cf. Gal 5:21.

36. Since primary source Valentinian texts in the Nag Hammadi Library evidence no justification for licentious behavior, Irenaeus's claims are generally viewed as "greatly exaggerated and polemic in nature" (Ismo Dunderberg, "The School of Valentinus," in *A Companion to Second-Century Christian "Heretics,"* ed. Antti Marjanen and Petri Luomanen [Leiden: Brill, 2005], 70). On this subject, see also Giovanni Filioramo, *A History of Gnosticism* (Cambridge, MA: Blackwell, 1992), especially 186-89. In the end, though, assessing Irenaeus's texts in light of non-heresiological evidence is not directly relevant for our purposes.

37. Desjardins notes that Adelin Rousseau's compositional analysis of *Haer.* Book 1 places the section on Marcus and his school (chapters 13-20) in the center of a chiastic structure (*Sin in Valentinianism*, 28-29). This would support the notion that this group has especially attracted Irenaeus's attention.

"defiling" women who subsequently have "seared" consciences.[38] Those who are "evil-minded," insofar as they reject a biblical understanding of the covenants, "have been deserted by the Father's love and puffed up by Satan."[39] Irenaeus traces the root cause of their apostasy to arch-heretic, Simon Magus, insofar as he was the "first to assert that he himself is the God above all things."[40] Simon and his successors are deemed to exemplify those who "served the creature rather than the Creator."[41] The "pretense" of knowledge causes one to "puff up," as the apostle observes, whereas love "builds up."[42] Those that exalt themselves will "fall away from love, which gives life to man."[43] In this same context, Irenaeus accuses his opponents of "extolling" their own minds through their detailed theological speculations.[44] By contrast, only God knows the degree and extent to which each individual element of creation fits into a larger harmonious whole. Three times in one short section, Irenaeus invokes 1 Corinthians in order to emphasize the provisional and partial scope of human knowledge.[45] As will be examined below, Irenaeus eschews Valentinian teaching that portrays humanity as heterogeneous, whether distinguished by race or historical epoch.[46] Instead, humankind is a homogeneous group: "all men come short of the glory of God."[47] Those whom God has "grafted into the tree" ought never to presume upon their newfound status, and the one who "thinks he stands" must "take heed, lest he fall."[48] Christ's response of trust in the midst of his wilderness temptation reminds Irenaeus of Paul's teaching: "Minding not high things, but consenting to things of low estate."[49]

Perhaps in line with his pastoral calling as bishop, Irenaeus not only draws attention to Paul's *teaching* that warns against pride, he also looks to the apostle's *praxis*, as depicted in scripture. There, it seems, he finds a foil to the Valentinians' lifestyle.[50] Paul, he notes, describes the experience of being "caught up into the third heaven."[51] According to Valentinian cosmology, he would have been yet four

---

38. *Haer.* 1.13.6; cf. 2 Tim 3:6.
39. *Haer.* 3.12.12.
40. Justin Martyr had previously singled out Simon for blame (1 *Apol* 26; cf. Acts 8:5-25).
41. *Haer.* 2.9.2; Rom 1:25.
42. *Haer.* 2.26.1; 1 Cor 8:1.
43. *Haer.* 2.26.1.
44. *Haer.* 2.26.3.
45. *Haer.* 2.28.7; 1 Cor 2:10; 12:4, 5, 6; 13:9.
46. See, e.g., the argument over whether people like Adam living under the old covenant could—or even must—be saved (*Haer.* 3.23.8).
47. *Haer.* 4.27.2; Rom 3:23.
48. *Haer.* 4.27.2-3; Rom 11:21, 17; 1 Cor 10:1.
49. *Haer.* 5.22.2; Rom 12:16.
50. Ben C. Blackwell offers a very informative summary and analysis of Irenaeus's references to Paul's life and ministry ("Paul and Irenaeus," in *Paul and the Second Century*, ed. Michael F. Bird and Joseph R. Dodson [New York: T&T Clark, 2011], 194–96).
51. 1 Cor 12:2.

heavens below the place to which the *pneumatikoi* are said to rise. Would *they* presume to be better than the apostle?[52] Irenaeus takes up this biblical text again in Book 5 as evidence that God's power can be manifest in the frailty of the human body. Given a "thorn in the flesh," Paul's response is exemplary. He "glories" in his infirmities.[53] Although Paul is addressing the Corinthian church in his letter, one might envisage a hint of autobiography when he writes, "Consider your own call, brothers and sisters; not many of you were wise by human standards … God chose what is low and despised in the world."[54] With this citation, Irenaeus attempts to undermine Valentinian doctrine and ethos which stands in such stark contrast. Finally, when challenging his opponents' charge that human bodies cannot and will not be redeemed in God's economy, Irenaeus employs athletic imagery. They are blind to the "light of the truth," just like a wrestler who imagines himself winning, all the while falling down.[55] Although Irenaeus does not quote Paul in this regard, he, no doubt, would have been influenced by Paul's references comparing life as a follower of Christ with that of an athlete in training. Humility, discipline, and endurance are the qualities of those who will ultimately receive the "prize."[56]

Separation and Fragmentation

Arguably, Irenaeus's most evocative and pervasive articulation of human sinfulness employs the language of separation, fragmentation, and even dismemberment. We will examine this recurrent motif as it concerns people, scripture and apostolic tradition, God (with his two "hands" of Son and Spirit), and the divine economy of salvation. Titus 3:10, as noted above, provides the rationale for avoiding those who "apostatize" themselves from the church.[57] Out of pride, they desire to be teachers.[58] Their proclivity to divide and separate is evidenced by the multiplicity of their doctrines of redemption.[59] Indeed, just as leaven impacts the whole loaf,[60] the schism introduced into the church threatens to "cut into pieces" and "destroy" the whole body of Christ.[61] The heretics are themselves "liable to death" because they have "not yet been united (*commisceō*) with the Word of God the Father."[62] Phrased differently (using a metaphor evoked by Eph 1:10 and, thus, Irenaeus's

---

52. *Haer.* 2.30.7.
53. *Haer.* 5.3.1; 1 Cor 12:7-10.
54. *Haer.* 2.19.7; 1 Cor 1:26, 28; cf. 1 Cor 15:8-9.
55. *Haer.* 5.13.2.
56. Cf. 1 Cor 9:24-27; Phil 3:13-14; Eph 6:13; 1 Tim 4:8; 2 Tim 2:5.
57. *Haer.* 1.16.3; cf. 3.15.2; 4.preface.3, citing 2 Tim 2:23.
58. *Haer.* 1.28.1; cf. 1.10.3; 1.11.3; 1.21.1.
59. *Haer.* 1.21.1.
60. *Haer.* 4.27.4; cf. 1 Cor 5:6.
61. *Haer.* 4.33.7.
62. *Haer.* 3.19.1.

concept of recapitulation), they are cut off from the head.[63] This condition is both cause and effect, as far as sin is concerned.[64] Irenaeus notes that God has, indeed, established a certain diversity in the church—apostles, prophets, teachers[65]—but Valentinians presume a differentiation among people that is ontological (*pneumatikoi, psychikoi, hylikoi*).[66] In Irenaeus's mind, Paul emphatically asserts the contrary. Humanity is united in that all have "come short of the glory of God."[67] If anything, any division in humankind derives from the exercise of free will, that is, the kind of fruit produced through action.[68]

From Irenaeus's perspective, the unity of the church and the unity of the church's interpretation and teaching of scripture are interrelated. The Gospel, as handed down by and inextricably linked to the apostles, constitutes the "foundation and pillar of our faith."[69] He accuses his opponents of "disjointing" the truth[70] by improperly "adapting" scripture to their "fabrication."[71] When it suits them, they even make their own separate translations of scripture.[72] Through their hermeneutical efforts, the Valentinians fragment the scriptures.[73] It is not the case, asserts Irenaeus, that scripture lacks diversity, but rather that the Valentinians do not discern the underlying unity, for example, between the Mosaic covenant and the New Covenant. Their interpretations do not take into account the "entire doctrine" of the apostles.[74] "In words they profess one Christ Jesus, but in doctrine they reveal a division."[75] The four Gospels are "four pillars, blowing imperishability from all sides and giving life to men."[76] The writings of Paul and Luke are different, yet consonant.[77] Paul and Peter are entrusted with two different missions, observes

---

63. Cf. *Haer.* 5.14.4; 4.34.4; Eph 4:15-16.

64. Perhaps a slight distinction can be seen on this topic between Irenaeus and the Valentinians. From the *Gospel of Truth*, Desjardins infers a Valentinian view that people's "sins do not alienate them from the Father; rather, they seem to reflect this alienation" (*Sin in Valentinianism*, 82).

65. *Haer.* 3.24.1; 1 Cor 12:28.

66. *Haer.* 1.8.3. It does seem likely, though, that Valentinians drew upon Pauline texts such as 1 Cor 15:48 and 1 Cor 2:14-15 to justify (formulate?) their anthropology.

67. *Haer.* 4.27.2; Rom 3:23.

68. *Haer.* 4.27.2.

69. *Haer.* 3.1.1; 1 Tim 3:15. Even though in the context of 1 Tim 3:15, the pillar refers to the church itself, the church's foundational "mystery" (i.e., teaching) is summarized in verse 16.

70. *Haer.* 1.8.1.

71. *Haer.* 2.preface.1.

72. *Haer.* 3.21.3.

73. Cf. Irenaeus's discussion of the Mosaic law in *Haer.* 4.2.1-3.

74. *Haer.* 3.16.1.

75. *Haer.* 3.16.1.

76. *Haer.* 3.11.8.

77. *Haer.* 3.14.1-4.

Irenaeus, but have the same Sender.[78] By "deviating from the way" and "walking in various roads,"[79] the Valentinians "pervert" the sense of scripture.[80]

Having erroneously discerned fragmentation and division in scripture, the Valentinians propound erroneous divisions within God (concerning both the Father and Jesus Christ). Those with proper knowledge "know" only one God.[81]

> All things were present in a new manner when the Word arranged his coming in the flesh, so that he might make into God's possession that human nature which had gone astray from God. For this reason [man] was likewise taught to worship God in a new manner, but not another God, since there is one God who justifies the circumcised on the ground of their faith, and the uncircumcised because of their faith.[82]

Unity in the arrangement of creation is predicated upon the unity of God.[83] The claims that "every economy" comes through Christ and that he "recapitulates in himself all things" depend upon the unity of God's Word.[84] Physical substance is not excluded from such comprehensive unity. Instead of positing a fragmented economy, Irenaeus envisions one in which nothing is "unplanned," "untimed," or "out of harmony."[85] After recounting his understanding of Marcus's intricate theological system, Irenaeus is exasperated: "Who will put up with you who confine the Creator of all things, the Framer and Maker, the Word of God, to figures and numbers… and then divide him into four combinations and thirty characters?"[86] Similarly, Marcion, with his division of God into two beings—one good, another having judicial power—might as well be guilty of deicide.[87]

Twentieth-century Swedish theologian Gustaf Wingren boldly suggests that "it is *recapitulatio* which creates unity in the theology of Irenaeus." Furthermore, Wingren goes on to say, when Irenaeus uses the term "recapitulation," he simply refers to "everything that Christ has done or is doing."[88] God's activity

---

78. *Haer.* 3.13.1; Gal 2:8.

79. *Haer.* 5.20.1.

80. *Haer.* 5.26.2. Jouette M. Bassler suspects that Irenaeus's enforcement of a unifying "pattern," as regards the interpretation of Pauline texts, stems from the deeper level issue of "the one and the many." Truth, for Irenaeus, "is singular by definition" ("A Response to Jeffrey Bingham and Susan Graham: Networks and Noah's Sons," in *Early Patristic Readings of Romans*, ed. Kathy L. Gaca and L. L. Welborn [New York: T&T Clark, 2005], 139).

81. *Haer.* 3.6.5; 1 Cor 8:4-6; Gal 4:8-9; 2 Thess 2:4.

82. *Haer.* 3.10.2; Rom 3:30.

83. *Haer.* 2.25.1-2; cf. 2.11.1.

84. *Haer.* 3.16.6; Eph 1:10.

85. *Haer.* 3.16.7.

86. *Haer.* 1.15.5.

87. *Haer.* 3.25.3.

88. Gustaf Wingren, *Man and the Incarnation: A Study in the Biblical Theology of Irenaeus*, trans. Ross MacKenzie (London: Oliver and Boyd, 1959), 81–82.

in human history is cohesive and is directed toward accomplishing the goal of comprehensive unity. To the extent that the Valentinians introduce fragmentation (or the fabrication of a different unified system[89]) into their teachings on humanity, scripture, and God, they thwart the divine purpose. Whether or not Irenaeus specifically labels it as "sin," the implication is clear enough. Pauline texts enable Irenaeus to sketch the outlines of God's economy wherein one God reconciles human beings to one other, and to himself, through the "gathering up" of all things in Christ.[90] In one beautiful passage, Irenaeus finds inspiration in 1 Cor 15:20-22 (and Gen 2:7) when he insists that "Adam" (i.e., we, as humanity) has never "escaped" from the caring hands of God, which are forming us to be living images and likenesses of God.[91] Creation is the very medium through which our comprehensive salvation comes.[92] The incarnate Word causes humanity to "adhere to and be united with God."[93] However, by positing that the Creator God and the Father of Jesus Christ are distinct beings with distinct economies, the Valentinians aim to "separate our creation from the Father."[94] Paul's characterization of the human predicament highlights our state of alienation from one another and our separation from the Source of life. Since it was the "original handiwork" of flesh and blood that was estranged from God, redemption is effected through that same flesh and blood: "Now you have been reconciled in the body of [Christ's] flesh, through his death."[95] The Valentinians err by insisting that 1 Cor 15:50 implies that physical human bodies cannot be transformed and saved. In the first half of his fifth book, Irenaeus attacks this claim as presumptively putting limits on the power (and will) of the Father. The "flesh and blood" which, according to Paul, cannot enter the kingdom of God actually refers to those who indulge in sinful actions.[96] God's economy brings reconciliation and union both *within* the human individual and *between* individuals. When the Spirit of God "rests" on us, our "mortality is swallowed up by immortality."[97] Whereas Valentinian teaching has yielded schismatic effects, God's work in Christ has "gathered into one and united those who were afar off with those who were near, that is, the uncircumcised with the circumcised."[98] By the Spirit, God has grafted the branches of the "wild olive" tree into the "good" olive tree[99] so that Jews and Gentiles alike can partake of God's life. In the divine economy, those who "shun the light and separate themselves from

---

89. Cf. *Haer.* 4.preface.3-4.
90. E.g., *Haer.* 5.20.2; cf. Eph 1:10.
91. *Haer.* 5.1.3.
92. Cf. *Haer.* 5.1.1 et al.
93. *Haer.* 3.18.7.
94. *Haer.* 2.31.1.
95. *Haer.* 5.14.2; Col 1:21.
96. *Haer.* 5.11.1.
97. *Haer.* 4.36.6; 2 Cor 5:4; cf. 1 Cor 15:53, cited in *Haer.* 5.13.5.
98. *Haer.* 3.5.3; Eph 2:17.
99. *Haer.* 5.10.1; Rom 11:17.

God" will be judged.[100] These are those who have "received not the love of God, that they might be saved."[101] The Word of God "reveals" the Father "through many dispensations, lest man, falling away from God altogether, might cease to exist."[102] In other words, this fate is one of being "cut off from life."[103] When envisioning the divine economy and its antithesis, Irenaeus bluntly highlights dichotomies of connection versus separation, and of unity versus fragmentation. Again, Paul's organic metaphor of the human body helps Irenaeus to sustain his point:

> The Apostle Paul [says] in like manner, "There is one Lord, one faith, one baptism, one God and Father, who is above all, and through all, and in us all"—this man will first of all "hold the head, from which the whole body is compacted and bound together, and, through means of every joint according to the measure of the ministration of each several part, makes increase of the body to the edification of itself in love."[104]

At the end of God's work, all things will be subject to him so that "God may be all in all."[105]

Unfruitfulness

The fourth and final cluster of imagery for sin we will examine is that of unfruitfulness. A modest example of the types of connections between the sin motifs may be found in 1.13. Irenaeus frequently condemns his opponents for spurning God's action of uniting his own creation under the headship of Christ. Now we are told that Marcus's disciples are promoting sexual promiscuity as a way of effecting a different type of union.[106] As noted above in the section on arrogance, their boasts of "perfect" knowledge are used instrumentally to seduce and "defile" women.[107] Throughout *Against Heresies* Irenaeus points to the Valentinians' behavior to argue that their teachings must be rejected because the results of such are either barrenness or the bearing of bad fruit. As to the former, their inability to heal, cast out demons, or raise the dead (in contrast with the ability of some within the church) constitutes the bearing of no fruit.[108] By refusing to receive

---

100. *Haer.* 5.28.1.
101. *Haer.* 5.28.1; 2 Thess 2:10. Cf. Irenaeus's quotations in 4.12.2 about the indispensable role of the love of God in Rom 13:10; 1 Cor 13:2, 13.
102. *Haer.* 4.20.7.
103. *Haer.* 4.11.4.
104. *Haer.* 4.32.1; Eph 4:5, 6, 16; Col 2:19.
105. *Haer.* 5.36.3; 1 Cor 15:27-28.
106. *Haer.* 1.13.3.
107. *Haer.* 1.13.6.
108. Cf. *Haer.* 2.31.2.

the life-giving moisture of the Holy Spirit, they remain "dry earth" that doesn't "produce the fruit that is life."[109] In 4.36.4, Irenaeus observes that the desiccation of the unfruitful fig tree and the deluge of water in Noah's day both express the "Son of God['s]" work to "check the sin" of those who do unrighteous deeds. Concerning the "bad fruit" which Irenaeus associates with his opponents, he asserts that they "offer up" to the Father "the fruits of ignorance, passion, and apostasy"—the very same characteristics they systematically ascribe to the creator deity.[110] In so doing, they "sin against their Father rather subjecting him to insult than giving him thanks."[111] In the previous context, Irenaeus cites Phil 4:18 to identify the offering that pleases God as *gratitude* "to God our Maker." Through the Eucharist, the church gives thanks to God as it offers to him elements of creation.[112] Irenaeus often describes the giving of thanks (or the withholding of thanks) to the Creator as a sign of proper or improper fruit-bearing. Even where he doesn't quote a Pauline text directly, Irenaeus's language of "giving thanks" seems to be drawn from the Pauline "well" (so to speak).[113] Since "life is not from ourselves or from our nature, but is given according to God's grace," the one who "rejects it" is guilty of ingratitude and will not live forever.[114] In his "long-suffering," God has been merciful to all human beings.[115] Therefore, we ought to "continue to be grateful to God," return to him love, know our own mortality and weakness, and acknowledge God's greatness.[116] As expected, Irenaeus doesn't simply attack his opponents for their general attitude of ingratitude, but specifically for their refusal to give thanks to their Creator for their creaturely identity.[117] Furthermore, Irenaeus (following Paul) maintains that "giving thanks" is associated with the rejection of carnal behavior.[118] Irenaeus (in *Haer.* 4.37-39) articulates an eschatological destiny for humankind that demonstrates a continual progression into the image and likeness of God. Milk-drinking "infants" displaying carnal behavior need to grow up.[119] "God has given that which is good," and our response should be "work" (fruit) that is, likewise, good.[120] In Luke 6:43-49, Jesus compares a tree bearing bad fruit

---

109. *Haer.* 3.17.2. Irenaeus doesn't quote Titus 3:5, but in that passage, the author makes a similar connection between the reception of the Holy Spirit as water which enables the bearing of good deeds (fruit).

110. *Haer.* 4.18.4.

111. Ibid.

112. *Haer.* 4.18.4. Other references to thanksgiving in the context of the Eucharistic ritual include 3.11.5, 4.17.5, and 4.18.4-5.

113. See, e.g., Rom 1:21; 14:6; 1 Cor 1:4; 15:57; Eph 5:20; Col 1:12; 3:17; 1 Thess 1:2; 2:13; 5:18; 2 Thess 1:3; 2:13.

114. *Haer.* 2.34.3.

115. *Haer.* 3.20.2; Rom 11:32.

116. *Haer.* 3.20.2.

117. *Haer.* 4.11.2.; *Haer.* 4.38.4 et al.

118. *Haer.* 4.37.4; Eph 4:25, 29; 1 Cor 6:11.

119. *Haer.* 4.28.2; 1 Cor 3:2-3.

120. *Haer.* 4.37.1; Rom 2:4, 5, 7.

with those who "call me 'Lord, Lord,' and do not do what I tell you." Irenaeus links this reference to 1 Cor 2:14 and 3:1 as he accuses the Valentinians of "adopt[ing] the lives of swine and of dogs, giving themselves over to filthiness, to gluttony, and recklessness of all sorts. Justly therefore, did the apostle call such 'carnal' and 'animal.'"[121] They are "not adorned with works of righteousness," which is the fruit of those who receive God's Spirit.[122] God is a cultivator who grafts wild olive branches into a good tree so that they would bear good fruit in his garden.[123] In God's economy, this ripening fruit is immortality.[124] Paul's assertion that "flesh and blood cannot inherit the kingdom of God"[125] is, for Irenaeus, simply another way to say that non-fruit bearing trees will be "cast into the fire."[126] Those that "live after the flesh" will die.[127] Whereas the Valentinians appeal to Paul to support a tripartite, Gnostic-informed anthropology, Irenaeus thinks their interpretation of 1 Cor 15:50 is not in line with Paul's intention. "Flesh" does not refer to human bodies, but to the sinful works of the "old" human nature which should be put to death: "fornication, uncleanness, inordinate affection, evil concupiscence, and covetousness, which is idolatry."[128] Instead of allowing sin to "reign" in our bodies,[129] we are to "bear fruit unto life" through our righteous deeds.[130]

The Divine Economy of Life

Given Irenaeus's explication of sin as it concerns these four categories—false knowledge, arrogance, separation, and unfruitfulness—it is now time to "connect the dots" by addressing a question that gets to the heart of the matter: How does Paul influence Irenaeus's judgment that sin disrupts the divine economy of life? A few key texts in *Against Heresies* enable a more comprehensive understanding of *humanity's* condition, marked by sin, and of *God's* activity through his two "hands" (Son and Spirit)[131] to overcome sin and thus fashion a "*homo vivens*."[132]

On "Irenaeus's depiction of the overcoming of sin by Christ," O'Regan's observation is pertinent: "The emphasis falls more nearly on overcoming the major

---

121. *Haer.* 5.8.4.
122. *Haer.* 5.8.4.
123. *Haer.* 5.10.1; Rom 11:17.
124. *Haer.* 5.29.1.
125. 1 Cor 15:50.
126. *Haer.* 5.10.2.
127. Rom 8:13, cf. 8:8.
128. *Haer.* 5.12.3-4; Col 3:5, 9, 10. Cf. Irenaeus's citation of Rom 6:12 in *Haer.* 5.14.4.
129. Rom 6:12.
130. *Haer.* 5.14.4
131. *Haer.* 4.20.1.
132. *Haer.* 4.20.7: "For the glory of God is a living man." Cf. 5.16.1: God "from the beginning even to the end, forms us and prepares us for life"; 5.15.4; 4.38.3.

consequence of the loss of perfection, that is, *mortality*, than on the healing of the dispositional dynamics, which is the emphasis of Augustine and a significant part of the Western tradition."[133] In *Against Heresies* 4.33.15 Irenaeus offers a clear echo of Rom 2:5 when he describes his opponents: "Those, on the other hand, who depart from Him, and despise His precepts, and by their deeds bring dishonor on Him who made them, and by their opinions blaspheme Him who nourishes (*alo*) them, heap up against themselves most righteous judgment."[134] This section should be read in light of the themes in the context preceding Rom 2:5 in which Paul makes implicit reference to the Adam narratives (1:19-25),[135] and claims that creation mediates divine revelation (1:20). The Giver of life intends to feed and support (i.e., "nourish") his creation, but instead—to highlight the aforementioned four sin motifs here—sinful persons *separate* ("depart") from him, are willfully *ignorant* of his knowledge ("precepts"), *bear fruit* ("deeds") that dishonors God, and, indeed *arrogantly* "blaspheme" him by their teachings. If we might reasonably deem God's "feeding" of his creation as his activity to communicate and sustain life, Irenaeus elsewhere elaborates upon this metaphor. By "wallowing in falsehood," the Valentinians have "lost the bread of true life."[136] Furthermore, by refusing to "accept the love of the truth,"[137] they follow Satan's lead and "draw [others] away from life."[138] To separate from God and from God's love is to separate oneself from the source of life,[139] and thus engender death. Life and death cannot both be present in a person.[140] "To keep [God's] commandments ... is the life of man; as not to obey God is evil, and this is his death."[141] People are "deprived of life" when they indulge in "carnal deeds" that "pervert" them to sin.[142]

Two relevant sections of *Against Heresies* in which Irenaeus adopts and adapts Pauline texts to articulate God's economy of life, as enabled by God's two hands, are 3.18.7–3.19.1 and 5.20.2. In the former, Irenaeus asserts that Christ's "pass[ing] through every stage of life" restored "to all communion with God."[143] Irenaeus cites Rom 5:19 and 6:23 (among others) to describe Christ as offering the "antidote of

133. O'Regan, *Gnostic Return in Modernity*, 166 (emphasis added).

134. In Rom 2:5, Paul states: "But by your hard and impenitent heart you are storing up wrath for yourself on the day of wrath, when God's righteous judgment will be revealed."

135. James D. G. Dunn, *Romans 1–8* (Word Biblical Commentary 38A; Dallas: Word, 1998), 53.

136. *Haer.* 2.11.1. It would seem that Irenaeus here envisions his opponents as repeating the original sin of Adam and Eve in Genesis 3.

137. *Haer.* 5.25.3; cf. 2 Thess 2:8.

138. *Haer.* 3.16.1.

139. *Haer.* 2.26.1; 5.27.2; 5.8.4.

140. *Haer.* 5.12.1.

141. *Haer.* 4.39.1.

142. *Haer.* 5.14.4; Rom 6:12.

143. *Haer.* 3.18.7. Adolf von Harnack's interpretation of Irenaeus wherein Christ's soteriological significance is located in the incarnation more than in the crucifixion has been much debated. (See, e.g., Emil Brunner's *The Mediator* [London: Lutterworth, 1934]).

life" for a post-Adamic humanity that is in a state of death.[144] Christ, the "prince of the life of God,"[145] by his own flesh and blood, "joins" us to the Father. Elsewhere, Irenaeus describes the "gifts" Christ gives to his people through his passion (cf. Eph 4:8) by relating two pairs of concepts: death and ignorance on the one hand, and life and truth on the other. Christ "destroyed death, dispelled error, put an end to corruption, and destroyed ignorance; on the other hand, he manifested life, displayed the truth, and bestowed incorruption."[146] Paul's contrast of law and promise in Gal 3:15–4:7 gives Irenaeus occasion to identify Christ as the one who reversed Adam's defeat and obtained for us the "palm" of victory against death.[147] In *Against Heresies* 5.20.2, he describes the two hands of God working together. Christ has "introduced" those who obey God into the "paradise of life" insofar as he "sum[s] up in himself all things which are in heaven and which are on earth."[148] In this "recapitulation," Christ is "uniting man to the Spirit and causing the Spirit to dwell in man."[149] The Spirit is "the food of life,"[150] who enlivens (*vivifico*) human beings.[151]

Irenaeus's drive to overturn Valentinian teaching doesn't merely express a struggle over theological ideas. He seeks to define and defend the church's boundaries against invaders precisely because he ascribes a key role to the church in God's economy of life. In *Against Heresies* 3.24.1, Irenaeus boldly insists that "where the church is, there is the Spirit of God." The church has been entrusted with a "gift": a proper understanding of God's ways. Just as Adam was vivified by the gift of God's breath, so also are the members of the church "vivified" by receiving this gift from the church. Those who "do not join themselves to the church … defraud themselves of life through their perverse opinions and infamous behavior."[152] Instead of being "nourished into life from the mother's breasts," they "dig for themselves broken cisterns" and "drink putrid water out of the mire."[153] The church is the repository of "truth," holding the "water of life" from which people may draw.[154] Affirming its divinely prescribed role, Irenaeus terms the church the "entrance to life."[155]

It is quite clear, though, that Irenaeus's vision of salvation as recapitulation accords relatively greater significance to Christ's incarnation and life than do dominant Western soteriologies.

144. *Haer.* 3.19.1.
145. *Haer.* 4.24.1; 2.22.4.
146. *Haer.* 2.20.3.
147. *Haer.* 5.21.1.
148. *Haer.* 5.20.2; Eph 1:10.
149. *Haer.* 5.20.2; Eph 1:10.
150. *Haer.* 4.38.2. Irenaeus describes this nourishment as he comments on Paul's "milk and meat" metaphor regarding spiritual sustenance (1 Cor 3:2, 3).
151. *Haer.* 5.9.1; cf. 5.12.2.
152. *Haer.* 3.24.1.
153. *Haer.* 3.24.1.
154. *Haer.* 3.4.1.
155. *Haer.* 3.4.1.

Irenaeus's close attention to practical ministry issues in local churches helps to explain his enduring appeal across the spectrum of Christian tradition. Certainly, when exploring Irenaeus's portrayals of sin, one encounters his vibrant imagery and his rich theological speculation grounded in Pauline texts. However, it is his pastoral concern about concrete situations that motivates and guides his thinking. Fittingly, then, Irenaeus may be described as "*par excellence* the theologian of the flesh."[156]

---

156. John Behr, *Irenaeus of Lyons: Identifying Christianity* (Oxford: Oxford University Press, 2013), 209.

Response
On Sin in Irenaeus's Appropriation of Paul: A Response to Thomas J. Holsinger-Friesen

Jutta Leonhardt-Balzer

This contribution does not aim to reproduce the previous chapter, but in the selection of Pauline passages it will largely follow the parallels identified by Holsinger-Friesen. The aim is to study the manner of Irenaeus's use of Paul and compare the texts used by Irenaeus with their original context.

Irenaeus does not distinguish between disputed and undisputed letters.[1] He can also link the letters with the Gospels.[2] Sometimes a text permeates the argument of a large part of a book,[3] and even where it is not a single text, frequently there are clusters of different texts combined to make a certain point.[4] There also are instances where a single Pauline passage is slotted in among other biblical texts as a subtext to add further information.[5] Occasionally, a single text provides the

---

1. This can be seen in *Haer.* 3.18.7–3.19.1, 5.20.2: Rom 5:19, 6:23 in *Haer.* 3.19.1; Eph 4:8 in *Haer.* 2.20.3; Gal 3:15–4:7 in *Haer.* 5.21.1.

2. Such as the tree with the bad fruit in Luke 6:43-39 with the carnal animals in 1 Cor 2:14 and 3:1 in *Haer.* 5.8.4.

3. E.g., 1 Cor 15:50 in the whole of the first part of *Haer.* 5 (1-15).

4. E.g., 2 Tim 3:7, Gen 2:16, Rom 12:3, Eph 1:10 in *Haer.* 5.20.2; Exod 9:35, Matt 13:11-16, 2 Cor 4:4, Rom 1:28, and 2 Thess 2:12 in *Haer.* 4.29.1; Rom 1:1-4; 9:5, Gal 4:4-5, and Col 1:14-15 in Haer. 3.16.3; 1 Pet 3:19, Rom 3:23 and 11:21 and 1 Cor 10:1 in *Haer.* 4.27.2-3; Rev 2:17, 1 Cor 15:50, 53 and Rom 8:8-10, 13 in *Haer.* 5.10.2; 1 Cor 8:4-6, Gal 4:8-9, 2 Thess 2:4, 1 Cor 8:4 in *Haer.* 3.6.5; Rom 13:10, 1 Cor 13:2, 13 in *Haer.* 4.12.2; Eph 4:25, 29; 1 Cor 6:11 in *Haer.* 4.37.4.

5. E.g., the ethical admonition of Titus 3:10 in *Haer.* 1.16.3; the falsely called "gnosis" in 1 Tim 6:20 in *Haer.* 1.23.4 and 2.14.7; the divine gifts of 1 Cor 2:10; 12:4, 5, 6; 13:9 in *Haer.* 2.28.7; minding not the high but the low things of Rom 12:16 in *Haer.* 5.22.2; those not wise by human standards as chosen of 1 Cor 1:26, 28; cf. also 1 Cor 15:8-9 in *Haer.* 2.19.7; the offices in the church of 1 Cor 12:28 in *Haer.* 3.24.1; the church as a pillar of faith of 1 Tim 3:15 in *Haer.* 3.1.1; Christ's gathering those near and far of Eph 2:17 in *Haer.* 3.5.3; the

basis for the argument of a whole paragraph.[6] Yet Irenaeus is aware of the different origins of the biblical texts; thus he uses texts attributed to Paul to substantiate an account of Paul's life in Acts.[7] At times there is merely a hint at the language or use of the same metaphors.[8]

These different ways of engaging with Pauline texts show that Irenaeus's use of Paul is not systematic. In this he follows the exegetical conventions of his time. The question remains whether Irenaeus is aware of or interested in the Pauline context of the metaphors, language, and the passages he quotes and alludes to. In addition to these details, there is the fundamental question as to whether he develops his theories on sin from Paul or whether the Pauline allusions are secondary. In the present context it is impossible to comment on all these Pauline quotations; thus only a few examples for each aspect—cluster quotations, metaphors, context, and overall motifs—will be studied.

Combined Quotations

A biblical passage can provide the theme of a whole section of Irenaeus's work. Thus 1 Corinthians 15, especially 15:50, and the rebuttal of the opponents' reading of flesh and blood as bodily life is the theme of *Against Heresies*, Book 5, at least of 5.1-15. Other Pauline and non-Pauline passages are used in the exposition of the correct reading of this passage.[9] In *Against Heresies* 5.9 Irenaeus

universality of sin leading to the universality of grace of Rom 11:32 in *Haer.* 3.20.2; and the revelation of the lawless one of 2 Thess 2:8 in *Haer.* 5.25.3.

6. E.g., the concept of the knowledge that puffs up of 1 Cor 8:1 in *Haer.* 2.26.1; the person carried up into the third heaven of 1 Cor 12:2 as proof against the Demiurge in *Haer.* 2.30.7; Satan's thorn in Paul's flesh of 1 Cor 12:7-10 in *Haer.* 5.3.1; all men are sinful before God of Rom 3:23 in *Haer.* 4.27.2; salvation through Christ's flesh of Col 1:21 in *Haer.* 5.14.2; and God's inevitable judgment of Rom 2:4, 5, 7 in *Haer.* 4.37.1.

7. 2 Tim 4:10-11 and Col 4:14 in *Haer.* 3.14.

8. E.g., the athletic metaphors of 1 Cor 9:24-27, Phil 3:13-14, Eph 6:13, 1 Tim 4:8, 2 Tim 2:5 in *Haer.* 5.13.2; one God in Eph 4:5, 6 and Col 2:19 in *Haer.* 4.32.1; the olive tree of Rom 11:17 in *Haer.* 5.10.1; the milk and meat metaphor of 1 Cor 3:2-3 in *Haer.* 4.38.2; flesh as sinful life of Col 3:5, 9, 10 in *Haer.* 5.12.3-4; the Adam motif of Rom 1:19-25 in *Haer.* 4.33.15. Occasionally, the identification of Pauline links by Holsinger-Friesen is somewhat optimistic, and thus he identifies the language of thanksgiving of Rom 1:21; 14:6; 1 Cor 1:4; 15:57; Eph 5:20; Col 1:12; 3:17; 1 Thess 1:2; 2:13; 5:18; 2 Thess 1:3; 2:13 in *Haer.* 4.18.4 and 2.34.3, but the parallels do not go beyond the general theme of gratitude.

9. Rom 11:34 on the necessity of the incarnation in order to understand God together with Jas 1:18 on Christians as first-fruits of creation (5.1.1); 1 Cor 15:22 on being dead with Adam but alive in Christ together with John 1:13 on salvation by the will of God (5.1.3); 1 Cor 10:16 on the salvation through the body and blood of the Eucharist; and Col 1:14 on the salvation through the blood of Christ with a subordinate addition of Matt 5:45 (5.2.2); Eph 5:30 on Christians as body of Christ with the subordinate quotation of Luke 24:39 on

explicitly addresses 1 Cor 15:50 with the help of Matt 26:41 (in 5.9.1) and the context of 15:50: 1 Cor 15:48-49 in 5.9.2. Likewise, in 9.10.2, when he discusses the implications of Rom 11:17 on 1 Cor 15:50 he adds 1 Cor 15:53 (as well as Rom 8:9-10, 13; cf. *Haer.* 5.13.3). Here he clearly moves against the separation of a passage from the context. Yet this is only the context of the main quotation, which is the theme of the argument in 5.1-15. Altogether the whole argument may not interpret 1 Corinthians 15 in context, but the main gist is comparable, as Irenaeus, like Paul, argues against opponents who deny the bodily resurrection. The interest in the context does not extend at all to the sub-quotations. Thus, in *Against Heresies* 5.12.3-4, Irenaeus interprets Col 3:5, 9, 10 with the addition of Phil 1:22. While the Colossians text indeed describes the sinful pre-Christian life, in Philippians Paul refers to his earthly life in suffering and affliction (the same difference occurs in the quotation of Phil 3:21 in 5.13.3). Here the text which takes precedence is clearly Colossians and the Philippians passage is merely added on account of the key word "flesh."

As has been shown, frequently Irenaeus combines several biblical passages to make a specific point, which is not sufficiently made in the main quotation. Thus, in *Against Heresies* 4.37.4 there is a whole series of quotations. In the context of the argument that it is not advisable to disobey God he quotes 1 Cor 6:12: "All things are lawful to me, but all things are not expedient." Paul accuses misbehavior within the congregation, indicating that he will not be governed by the body. In the immediate context he addresses food—probably thinking of idol meat, which he would be willing to eat, but not in the presence of those within the congregation who would be scandalized by it. Paul himself does not specify this, for immediately after he turns to fornication, which interferes with the holiness of the body, which is a temple of Christ. Irenaeus expands on Paul's hint in 1 Cor 6:12 by adding a quotation of 1 Pet 2:16, which warns against using the Christian freedom as excuse to do evil. As positive examples of good behavior Irenaeus then adds quotations

---

the general belief that spirits do not have flesh progressing to 1 Cor 15:53 on changing the mortal body to an incorruptible body (5.2.3); 2 Cor 12:7-9 on the sting of Satan in Paul's flesh and God's reassurance of the continuing presence of his grace (5.3.1), then Gen 2:8 on Adam planted in paradise leading to 2 Cor 12:4 on Paul's being lifted up to paradise, another instance of a link by key word (5.5.1), the perfect human from 1 Cor 2:6 is taken as consisting of those who have the spirit—which is not contained in the Pauline text—and the blessing of 2 Thess 5:23 is quoted to prove it (5.6.1); 1 Cor 3:16-17, combined with John 2:19-21, serves to prove that Christians are the temple of God (5.6.2). The next chapters demonstrate that flesh and blood represent the pre-Christian sinful life without the Spirit using ample quotations (John 20:23, 1 Cor 6:14, Rom 8:11, LXX Ps 22:31, 1 Cor 15:42, 36 in 5.7.1; 1 Cor 15:43-44 and 13:9,12, 1 Pet 1:8 in 5.7.2; Eph 1:13, 2 Cor 5:4, Rom 8:9, 15 in 5.8.1; Matt 5:5 in 5.9.4; Rom 11:17 together with Matt 7:19 in 5.10.1; Gal 5:19, 22 and 1 Cor 6:9-11 in 5.11.1; Gal 1:15 in 5.12.5; Luke 7:12, John 9:30, 1 Cor 15:52, John 5:28 in 5.13.1; 1 Cor 5:4, 6:20 in 5.13.3; 2 Cor 4:10, 2 Cor 3:3 and 4:10, Phil 3:11, 1 Cor 15:13 in 5.13.4; Rom 6:12, Col 2:19 in 5.14.4).

of Eph 4:25 on speaking only truth and Eph 4:29 on speaking no evil but only things that build up. Then Irenaeus returns to a quotation of 1 Cor 6:11, which describes the previous wicked state of the Christians before coming to believe, which he uses to argue for the free decision of humans for good. Thus 1 Cor 6:11-12 frame the whole passage, and all the other quotations are subordinate. Just like his exegetical predecessors, Irenaeus chooses a main text, which he then interprets by adding quotations from other texts, before returning to the main passage, and then proceeding in the overall argument of the book.[10]

When Irenaeus combines different biblical passages, sometimes he starts with a gospel quotation.[11] Sometimes the Pauline quotation comes first. Thus, in *Against Heresies* 4.18.4 Irenaeus quotes Phil 4:18 and combines it with Mark 4:28 to argue for the proper thanksgiving to the creator as the giver of all good things, which the opponents deny (neither is addressed by Holsinger-Friesen). Philippians 4:18 describes the gifts of the Philippians to Paul as a pleasing offering to God, and Irenaeus sees the gifts of the church as parallel to this. So Paul's text serves as a precedent to the later practice. The Markan text is an illustration of the value of the material world, serving the Pauline text.

Altogether, Irenaeus is well aware of the difference of the scriptural books, Old Testament as well as gospels and Pauline letters, but the combinations of the different Pauline texts with each other and with other biblical texts shows that Irenaeus regards them not as the same text, but as witnessing to the same truth.

Metaphors

Not every metaphor comes from scripture. Thus, Irenaeus uses a metaphor taken from wrestling, describing a very specific technique in *Against Heresies* 5.13.2. While Paul uses athletic metaphors, in 1 Cor 9:24-27 it is a race, in Phil 3:13-14 and in 2 Tim 2:5 it is the goal, the victory prize, in Eph 6:13 the background is not even in competition, but the wearing of armor in warfare. Therefore, Irenaeus's metaphor is not taken from reading Paul but from the general background of the games of his time, and, at any rate, the main focus of the passage is on the opponents' reading of 1 Cor 15:50 (5.13.2-5).

Even where a metaphor comes from Paul, it is not always used in the same way. In *Against Heresies* 5.14.4 Irenaeus quotes Eph 4:15-16, but while in Ephesians the metaphor of the head and the body is used to call the believer to emulate Christ the head, Irenaeus uses the metaphor to describe the salvation that comes to the body through the salvation of the head.

An example of a very important metaphor is that of the branches grafted into the olive tree which permeates the whole of *Against Heresies* 5.10. In 5.10.1

---

10. An example of this is the exegesis of Philo of Alexandria; see J. Leonhardt, *Jewish Worship in Philo of Alexandria* (TSAJ 84; Tübingen: Mohr Siebeck, 2001), 152–56.

11. E.g., Luke 6:43-39 together with 1 Cor 2:14 and 3:1 in *Haer.* 5.8.4.

Irenaeus quotes Rom 11:17 to describe the contrast between the previous life in the flesh and the life which produces the fruit of the Spirit. The passage in Rom 11:17-24 serves to remind the Gentile Christians that they have been grafted into the promise of Israel. Again, Irenaeus uses the metaphor, but applies it to a different context.

In *Against Heresies* 4.38.2 Irenaeus uses the milk and meat metaphor of 1 Cor 3:2-3 in the context of a discussion of the effect of the Spirit as the progression from the word of God as milk to the Eucharist as bread in *Against Heresies* 4.38.1. For Paul, the milk and the meat likewise describes the progress of understanding in a Christian, even if in 1 Corinthians he argues against the divisions within the Corinthian church.

Thus Irenaeus uses Pauline metaphors, but he is free to adapt them in their function to whichever point he intends to make.

Context of the Quotations

The survey so far has shown that Irenaeus's argument provides the structure for his quotations. He mainly uses key words to select his Pauline quotations, either given by his main text or by his opponents. There is no need to go into detail; just one example of his use of the Pauline context suffices. In an argument for the existence of only one God, Irenaeus draws on a barrage of Pauline texts in *Against Heresies* 3.6.5: In 1 Cor 8:4-6 Paul emphasizes that there is only one God; the context here is eating idol meat. In Gal 4:8-9 Paul also rejects idols, but does not explicitly say that there is only one God, and in 2 Thess 2:4 there is the theme of the lawless one who seeks to be worshipped instead of God. All these texts deny the worship of beings alongside the one God, which is the context of Irenaeus's argument against the opponents' division of a transcendent God and the Demiurge. To make exactly this point Irenaeus quotes the emphasis on one God in Eph 4:5-6 in *Against Heresies* 4.32.1. In Ephesians the context, however, is not a rebuttal of idolatry, but a call for union within the Christian congregation. This, once again, indicates that Irenaeus follows the Pauline context where it suits him, but is not tied down by it.

Concepts

There is not sufficient space to look into every motif or concept raised by Holsinger-Friesen; just a few examples should suffice. Sometimes Irenaeus combines texts to develop a Pauline concept. Thus, the love which fulfills all the commandments of Rom 13:10 and the love as the highest gift in 1 Cor 13:2, 13, are quoted and combined in *Against Heresies* 4.12.2 to demonstrate the need for love.

The knowledge, which puffs up of 1 Cor 8:1, is used as argument against the Gnostics in *Against Heresies* 2.26.1. Paul argues against the Corinthians' preference of worldly wisdom for his inverted view of God's wisdom in Christ. Both speak against opponents, but their argument is different. While Paul's opponents favor a common knowledge, those of Irenaeus advocate a hidden wisdom. The common theme is that of false knowledge. All these are good examples of Irenaeus's use of Pauline texts, which follows terms and general ideas, but not the context.

Even where Irenaeus used the same content, the overall intention does not need to be the same. Thus, the different offices in the congregation, mentioned in 1 Cor 12:28, are not meant to be taken as a comprehensive system, as they clearly are in *Against Heresies* 3.24.1. In *Against Heresies* 5.14.2 Irenaeus argues that Christ's incarnation brings salvation of the flesh, while the quoted text in Col 1:21 talks about the salvation through Christ's death, which then enables the Christians to be holy.

The situation is more complex in *Against Heresies* 5.10.2. Irenaeus's point is that the human body must be transformed through the Spirit in order to be saved, and somewhat similarly, Paul argues in 1 Cor 15:53 that the fleshly body will be transformed into a spiritual body, although in Paul this is clearly a future eschatological event. Likewise, the people in the flesh of Rom 8:8, who cannot be saved, do not refer to the pre-Christian existence only, but to all those who think they can expect to be saved through works of the Law. Therefore, Irenaeus develops what he thinks is Paul's message to his own situation of conflict with Gnostic opponents.

This cumulative picture has implications regarding the fundamental issue of Irenaeus's concept of sin. In *Against Heresies* 2.20.3 Irenaeus uses a range of biblical texts on Christ's victory (e.g., Eph 4:8 to prove that sin is ignorance). However, for Paul sin is not lack of knowledge but the human incapability to do the will of God; it is not ignorance, but disobedience, which must not be allowed to rule in the Christian (Rom 6:12). Sin is not only the previous life, but also a present temptation, that of building one's worth on one's own merits. Therefore, it must be said that the whole of Irenaeus's concept of sin as ignorance, arrogance, fragmentation, and unfruitfulness, as reconstructed by Holsinger-Friesen, does not correspond to Paul's view of sin, but is derived from the common philosophical description of sin that Irenaeus shared with his opponents. For Paul, Adam's mistake is not ignorance of what is good or evil or following the false advisers, as described in *Against Heresies* 5.20.2, but a refusal to do what God commanded. Likewise, in Titus 3:10 the author merely gives some practical advice on how to deal with misbehavior; it does not suffice to produce a whole category of fragmentation within the concept of sin, as Holsinger-Friesen derives from *Against Heresies* 1.16.3.

Yet even if Irenaeus's use of Paul is merely as secondary substantiation of his argument, Paul as individual is clearly important for Irenaeus. Paul's emphasis on his—as well as Jesus' own—Jewish descent (Rom 1:1-4; 9:5; Gal 4:4-5; Col 1:14-15) is used to rebut the opponents' rejection of the Old Testament in *Against Heresies* 3.16.3. Paul's experiences also serve to prove Irenaeus's argument, thus the "thorn in the flesh" of 1 Cor 12:7-10 proves that God's grace is effective in the weak flesh. Paul's worldview is also accepted, thus the cosmology expressed by Paul in 1 Cor 12:2 is used to refute the cosmology of the Valentinians in *Against Heresies* 2.30.7. Irenaeus therefore clearly takes Paul's testimony as expression of truth. The same function is given to Paul's letters when proving the accuracy of the Acts account of the Pauline mission in *Against Heresies* 3.14.1-4.

Altogether Irenaeus's use of Paul is twofold. First, he uses the texts attributed to the apostle as part of scripture, one of many different streams of testimony flowing from the one source of truth and to be mixed without further hermeneutical hesitation. Second, the apostle himself is a witness to the truth revealed by God. Both aspects do not have any function in the context of the life of the apostle, but are applied to Irenaeus's own situation of his debate with the opponents of his time.

Comparison to Other Pauline Interpreters (Ancient and Modern)

This use of Paul was the customary approach to scripture in Jewish (and Christian) sources ever since Second Temple times. The immediate reading into the present, the mix of quotations from different texts to make an exegetical point, and the use of sub-quotations in the interpretation of main texts, linked by key words, these all were standard exegetical methods in the Jewish and the early Christian context. Irenaeus stands in this tradition, and after him the same approach was used throughout the history of the church: by Augustine in his arguments against Pelagius or the Manicheans, by Thomas Aquinas in the highly theoretical questions in his *Summa Theologica*, by Luther in his writings on the freedom of a Christian, on the grace of God, and it remained the standard approach to scripture well into the Enlightenment and the Pietistic movement. It was not until the critical approach of the nineteenth century that the actual historical context of the Pauline texts began to take precedence over the context of the reader.

Chapter 6

THE COVENANT OF PROMISE: ABRAHAM IN IRENAEUS

Ben C. Blackwell

Those who are of faith are the children of Abraham, and they shall be blessed with faithful Abraham. Now God made promise of the earth to Abraham and his seed. However, neither Abraham nor his seed, that is, those who are justified by faith, receive any inheritance in it now, but they shall receive it at the resurrection of the just.

—*Against Heresies* 5.32.2

In Pauline studies the prevailing paradigm related to the role of Abraham in Paul's theology has recently been challenged by N. T. Wright. Abraham, he argues, is not merely a model of faith chosen because Paul found an Old Testament passage speaking of him (Gen 15:6) that combines two key terms in his theology—"faith" and "righteousness" (Gal 3:6; Rom 4:3).[1] Rather, Paul uses Abraham particularly because he sees Christianity as a fulfillment of the promises from the Abrahamic covenant.[2] One could say that Wright serves as a modern-day Irenaeus,[3] so his reevaluation of Abraham in Paul could serve as an impetus for reconsidering the

---

1. Throughout this chapter I will refer to the Old and New Testaments and "the Bible." I am, of course, speaking of a functional canon since the canon was still being formed at the time of Irenaeus. See Ben C. Blackwell, "Paul and Irenaeus," in *Paul and the Second Century: The Legacy of Paul's Life, Letters, and Teaching*, ed. Michael F. Bird and Joseph R. Dodson (London: T&T Clark, 2011), 190–206, at 191–93. However, it is important to note that Irenaeus, with his focus on the covenants, helped spur the church's use of *testamentum* as a designation for the different parts.

2. N. T. Wright, *Romans* (NIB 10; Nashville: Abingdon, 2002), 487–507; idem, *Justification: God's Plan and Paul's Vision* (Downer's Grove: InterVarsity, 2009), 131–36, 216–24; idem, "Paul and the Patriarch: The Role of Abraham in Romans 4," *JSNT* 35 (2013), 207–41.

3. Both Irenaeus and Wright use Pauline texts to battle (real and perceived) "Gnostics" by emphasizing salvation-historical continuity between the Old Testament and New Testament, the renewal of creation, and the resurrection of the body.

role Abraham plays in the theology of Irenaeus himself, a second-century patristic writer whose theological vision is highly shaped by his interaction with "the apostle."[4] This revised interest in Abraham arises from Pauline studies, but what about Abraham within Irenaean studies?

Those familiar with Irenaeus might not immediately think of instances where Abraham plays a role in his work, perhaps only how he is used in the context of Jesus being about fifty years old when he died (*Haer.* 2.22.6). Besides this episode, one is hard pressed to find a focus upon Abraham in previous Irenaean scholarship, except in a few non-English studies.[5] The discussion of specifically Jewish issues (Abraham, Abraham's children the Jews, or the Mosaic law)[6] pales in comparison to the treatments of creation and Genesis 1–3 in modern scholarship.[7] In light of Irenaeus's emphasis upon salvation as a fulfillment of creation, the relative scholarly emphasis on the Adam-Christ connection is expected, but the salvation-historical continuity of God's work through the rest of the Old Testament and its fulfillment in Christ are no less relevant to Irenaeus's argument. This fact has been demonstrated particularly by contemporary scholarship on the topic of the

---

4. See especially Blackwell, "Paul and Irenaeus," 190–206; David L. Balás, "The Use and Interpretation of Paul in Irenaeus' Five Books Adversus Haereses," *SecCent* 9 (1992), 27–39; R. A. Norris, "Irenaeus' Use of Paul in His Polemic Against the Gnostics," in *Paul and the Legacies of Paul*, ed. W. S. Babcock (Dallas: Southern Methodist University, 1990), 79–98.

5. See Emmanuel Lanne, "La 'xeniteia' d'Abraham dans l'œuvre d'Irénée: Aux origines du thème monastique de la 'peregrinatio,'" *Irénikon* 47 (1974), 163–87; J. Roldanus, "L'héritage d'Abraham d'après Irénée," in *Text and Testimony: Essays on New Testament and Apocryphal Literature in Honour of A.F.J. Klijn*, ed. T. Baarda et al. (Kampen: J.H. Kok, 1988), 212–24; Real Tremblay, *Irénée de Lyon: L'empreinte des doigts de Dieu* (Rome: Editions Academiae Alfonsianae, 1979), 63–88; Manuel Aróztegui Esnaola, *La Amistad del Verbo con Abraham según San Ireneo de Lyon* (Rome: Editrice Pontificia Università Gregoriana, 2005). Minns has brief discussions of Abraham: Denis Minns, *Irenaeus: An Introduction* (London: T&T Clark, 2010), 97–98, 119–22, 145.

6. With their discussions of Jewish issues, exceptions include John Lawson, *The Biblical Theology of Saint Irenaeus* (London: Epworth, 1948), 234–41; Gustaf Wingren, *Man and the Incarnation: A Study in the Biblical Theology of Irenaeus* (Edinburgh: Oliver & Boyd, 1959), 62–75; Philippe Bacq, *De l'ancienne à la nouvelle Alliance selon S. Irénée: Unité du Livre IV de l'Adversus Haereses* (Paris: Éditions Lethielleux, Presses Universitaires de Namur, 1978); Rolf Noormann, *Irenäus als Paulusinterpret. Zur Rezeption und Wirkung der paulinischen und deuteropaulinischen Briefe im Werk des Irenäus von Lyon* (WUNT II/66; Tübingen: Mohr Siebeck, 1994); Ronald E. Heine, *Reading the Old Testament with the Ancient Church* (Grand Rapids: Baker, 2007), 62–70.

7. Recent work on creation in Irenaeus include: M. C. Steenberg, *Irenaeus on Creation: The Cosmic Christ and the Saga of Redemption* (Leiden: Brill, 2008); Thomas Holsinger-Friesen, *Irenaeus and Genesis: A Study of Competition in Early Christian Hermeneutics* (Winona Lake, IN: 2009); Stephen O. Presley, *The Intertextual Reception of Genesis 1-3 in Irenaeus of Lyons* (Leiden: Brill, 2015).

covenants in Irenaeus.⁸ However, while it is universally noted that the *oikonomia* (divine economy) is important to Irenaeus, few have explored the role of covenants in Irenaeus's explanation of the *oikonomiai* (economies, dispensations),⁹ and fewer have focused just on Abraham. Accordingly, our task will be to determine how Irenaeus's use of Abraham contributes to his theological purposes, focusing mostly on *Against Heresies* with its more extensive treatment.¹⁰ The *Demonstration of Apostolic Preaching* (particularly *Epid.* 24 and 35) presents a very similar interpretation of Abraham and will receive less attention.¹¹

This focus on Abraham will illuminate not only our understanding of Irenaeus but also that of Paul. Both Irenaeus and Paul want to maintain continuity with Judaism and with God's Old Testament promises, but they also see a new direction on account of the advent of Christ and the Spirit. While Irenaeus's emphasis on salvation-historical continuity is undisputed,¹² the role of salvation history in Paul

---

8. J. Ligon Duncan, "The Covenant Idea in Irenaeus of Lyons: An Introduction and Survey," in *Confessing our Hope: Essays in Honor of Morton Howison Smith on His Eightieth Birthday*, ed. J. A. Pipa, Jr. and C. N. Willborn (Taylors: Southern Presbyterian, 2004), 31–55; Susan L. Graham, "Irenaeus and the Covenants: 'Immortal Diamond,'" in *Studia Patristica* XL (Leuven: Peeters, 2006), 393–98. See also these unpublished dissertations: J. Ligon Duncan, "The Covenant Idea in Ante-Nicene Theology" (PhD dissertation, University of Edinburgh, 1995), 132–56; Susan L. Graham, "'Zealous for the Covenant': Irenaeus and the Covenants of Israel" (PhD dissertation, University of Notre Dame, 2001).

9. Graham ("Irenaeus and Covenants," 393–94) notes how the covenants to Noah, Abraham, Moses, and Christ are central to the structure of *Dem*. Even more enlightening is the direct correlation between οἰκονομία and διαθήκη in Irenaeus. John Reumann ("Oikonomia = 'Covenant': Terms for *Heilsgeschichte* in Early Christian Usage," *NovT* 3 [1959]: 282–92, at 289) writes: "It is certain *oikonomia* was being used for *diathēkē* in everyday Greek at precisely the time Irenaeus was employing *oikonomia* to refer to covenants (διαθῆκαι)."

10. The primary translations I use for *Haer*. 1-3 are St. Irenaeus of Lyons, *Against the Heresies*, Books 1–3, trans. Dominic J. Unger et al. (ACW 55, 64, 65; New York: Newman, 1992–2012). I then used sections of Books 4–5 translated by Grant, where available: Irenaeus of Lyons, *Against Heresies: On the Detection and Refutation of the Knowledge Falsely So Called*, trans. Robert M. Grant (New York: Routledge, 1997). Otherwise, the English translation in the ANF collection is used: Irenaeus, *Against Heresies: Books 1-5 and Fragments* in *The Ante-Nicene Fathers. Vol. 1, The Apostolic Fathers with Justin Martyr and Irenaeus* (Edinburgh: T&T Clark, 1885–87). For critical editions, I consulted Irénée, *Contre les hérésies*, ed. A. Rousseau et al. (Sources Chrétiennes 100.1, 100.2, 152, 153, 210, 211, 263, 264, 293, 294; Paris: Cerf, 1965–82).

11. For the *Demonstration*, I use St Irenaeus of Lyons, *On the Apostolic Preaching*, trans. John Behr (Crestwood, NY: St. Vladimir's Seminary, 1997).

12. For example, see Robert L. Wilken, *Judaism and the Early Christian Mind: A Study of Cyril of Alexandria's Exegesis and Theology* (Eugene: Wipf and Stock, 2004 [1971]), 98.

is highly disputed.[13] Irenaeus's discussion of Abraham could add fodder to the current debate among Pauline scholars about whether the Abrahamic covenant plays much, if any, role in Paul's own theological construction.

Though underexplored in Irenaeus's theology, we will see that Abraham and the Abrahamic promises help unite God's *oikonomia*, linking together some of Irenaeus's central doctrines—namely, the unity of God's work in the Old and New Testament, the formation of the church, and the restoration of all creation. In order to explore the role of Abraham in Irenaeus, we will first briefly note how Abraham fits in Paul's letters and in Irenaeus's second-century context. We will then discuss how Irenaeus utilizes Abraham's story and the particular themes he associates with Abraham. So, first, we turn to Irenaeus's context.

Establishing the Context

As we think about Irenaeus's use of Abraham, it will help to consider the context out of which Irenaeus engaged this topic. As Irenaeus presents his theological vision, his construction is derived from a reading and interpretation of biblical texts, often for the purpose of responding to positions he considered weak and even heretical. As we establish his context, we will first note where Abraham appears in the biblical traditions, especially the Pauline letters, and then explore how Irenaeus's second-century context influences his reading.

Abraham in Paul

Abraham is the central character of Genesis 12–22, and he, along with Isaac and Jacob, is mentioned regularly in the Old Testament as the first of the Jewish patriarchs. In the New Testament Abraham is again recognized as a patriarch and is therefore received as the father of the Jews (Matt 1:1; 3:9; John 8:33-58), as well as father of those in the church, both Jews and Gentiles (Galatians 3 and Romans 4). In these Pauline texts and others (i.e., Heb 11:8-17; Jas 2:21-23), Abraham is commended primarily for his faith.

Paul mentions Abraham more often than Moses,[14] but Mosaic themes appear more important to his discussion: the topic of the Mosaic law is a central issue that Paul treats regularly, whereas Paul's explicit discussion of Abraham is limited to Romans 4 and 9 and Galatians 3-4. In each of these passages, the topics of Abraham's children and the promise of God are central. In particular, Paul explains the *promise* of many children (Gal 3:17-18; Rom 4:16-17), and he argues that both Jews *and Gentiles* are to be considered the descendants of Abraham (Gal 3:7, 29; Rom 4:11-12). In two passages (Gal 3:6; Rom 4:3) Paul's quotation of Gen

---

13. See, for instance, a whole issue devoted to this debate with regard to the interpretation of Galatians in the *Journal for the Study of Paul and His Letters* 2.2 (2012), 65–170.

14. Moses is mentioned ten times, and Abraham sixteen times.

15:6 serves as an important foundation of his argument about faith, justification, and works of the law. In particular, Paul emphasizes that Gentiles do not need to continue practicing circumcision, the sign of the Abrahamic covenant (Gen 17:9-14), to be a part of Abraham's family. Thus, Paul wants the church to maintain continuity with Abraham, as part of his family, yet he also distances Gentile Christians from the covenantal sign of circumcision (yet cf. Rom 2:25-29). Though Paul struggled against those wanting Gentiles to adhere to Jewish practices, such as circumcision, the nature of the discussion shifted in the second century since some at that time wanted to distance themselves from the Old Testament.

Abraham in Irenaeus's Second-Century Context

Paul helped establish the church as distinct within Judaism, though still in continuity with it, whereas Irenaeus was much more concerned with those who separated Christ from the Old Testament.[15] His concern, therefore, is to demonstrate that the one and the same God serves as both the Creator and the Savior in both the Old Testament and the New. To achieve this goal Irenaeus emphasizes the continuity and coherence in God's work through these different economic dispensations. Rather than documenting how Irenaeus's chosen opponents use Abraham in their own texts, we will focus on how Irenaeus describes his opponents' use of Abraham because this will give us a better perspective of what Irenaeus finds most important.

Unlike Adam (and Eve), Abraham and the Abrahamic covenant play little role in Irenaeus's direct engagement with his chosen opponents. For instance, in *Against Heresies* 1.30 Irenaeus traces out a history of the Bible in light of one of the Gnostic systems, in which Ialdabaoth is the creator God, who is confused, thinking he is the only God. He is thwarted at key points by his mother Sophia because she knows his true identity. In this retelling the core elements of Abraham's story are nonpolemically summarized: "Ialdabaoth himself chose a certain man named Abraham and made a covenant with him, promising to give him the earth for an inheritance if his seed would continue to serve him" (*Haer.* 1.30.10). In fact, this aptly summarizes Irenaeus's own perspective on Abraham, excepting the role of Ialdabaoth, which is why Irenaeus does not respond negatively to this view.[16]

---

15. Irenaeus does address the Ebionites, those who were likely messianic Jews, but his main concern by far is Marcion and the Gnostics.

16. Elaine Pagels (*The Gnostic Paul: Gnostic Exegesis of the Pauline Letters* [Philadelphia: Trinity Press International, 1975], 24–26, 37–38, 106–8) documents other Gnostic interpretations of Abraham that are not mentioned by Irenaeus. Regarding Gal 3:6-11 she writes, "Why does Paul refer to Abraham …? The initiated reader would recognize that Paul's reference to Abraham is no more to be taken literally than his previous references to the Jews. Hippolytus explains that 'Abraham' signifies the demiurge, as the 'children of Abraham' are the psychics [*Ref* 6.34]. Characterized as Abraham, the demiurge exemplifies faith in God (3:6), as Heracleon says; 'the demiurge believes well'" (106).

While Irenaeus usually reserves his refutation of his opponents to Books 2–5 of *Against Heresies*, Marcion's position on the Old Testament saints is met with a direct riposte in Book 1. Irenaeus marks as blasphemy that Cain and the like turn to Jesus when Jesus descended to Hades but the other main Old Testament characters (Abel, Abraham, etc.) did not and so remain there (*Haer.* 1.27.3). Later, Irenaeus responds to Marcion's exclusion of "Abraham from the inheritance" (*Haer.* 4.8.1) and argues that Abraham is fundamental to the *Gentiles*' experience of salvation (not just the Jews') because Abraham and his seed, the church, will receive "the adoption and the inheritance promised to Abraham" through Jesus Christ (*Haer.* 4.8.1).[17] Though Irenaeus will use Abraham to respond to Marcion's overall position, ultimately Marcion does not appear to focus on Abraham or make him any more (or less) important than other Old Testament characters. However, Irenaeus does find Abraham an especially helpful character for rebutting Marcion.

Second-century Jews, in contrast to Marcion, are not addressed as opponents, though Irenaeus does refute their scriptural interpretations. In the face of those who reject or diminish the Jewish scriptures like Marcion, Irenaeus elevates the Jewish scriptures and argues for their validity and continuity with the Christian Gospel. Accordingly, the Jews do not receive the polemical force of his rhetoric;[18] however, he does not hold them blameless in light of their rejection of the revelation of the Word in their own scriptures and in the life of Christ.[19] Irenaeus makes much of John the Baptist's retort to the Pharisees and Sadducees in Matt 3:9 that they should not presume upon their relationship to Abraham because God can raise up children for Abraham from stones.[20] While not excluding (believing) Jews from the church—excluding the Jews would only give ground to his opponents—Irenaeus's emphasis is on the inclusion of Gentiles as a fulfillment of promises to Abraham.[21] Minns rightly notes that Irenaeus's "understanding of the relationship between Church and Synagogue was not worked out in that polemical context [of Christians against Jews], but in the context of his own debate with other Christians who denied any continuity between the Old Covenant and the New."[22]

Since Abraham did not play a central role in Irenaeus's engagement with his interlocutors, Irenaeus does not seem to have developed his perspective about Abraham in contrast to them. However, as we now turn to Irenaeus's use and portrayal of Abraham, we will see how Abraham helps reinforce Irenaeus's

---

17. For a discussion of adoption in Irenaeus, see Blackwell, "Partakers of Adoption: Irenaeus and His Use of Paul," *Letter & Spirit* 11 (2016), 35–64.

18. Only offhandedly does he mention that the church suffers persecution from the Jews (*Haer.* 4.21.3).

19. Cf. *Haer.* 4.7.4. See also *Haer.* 4.2.3; 4.10.1.

20. Cf. *Haer.* 3.9.1; 4.7.2; 4.8.1; 4.25.1; 4.39.3; 5.32.2; 5.34.1.

21. For a (perhaps overstated) critique of Irenaeus, see Clark M. Williamson, "The 'Adversus Judaeos' Tradition in Christian Theology," *Encounter* 39 (1978), 273–96, at 283.

22. Minns, *Irenaeus*, 121.

salvation-historical argument in disagreement with his opponents, particularly Marcion.

Abraham and Abrahamic Themes: Key Passages

In order to see how Irenaeus presents Abraham for his own purposes, we will take several soundings by exploring key passages where Irenaeus employs Abraham in his argument. These are not the only passages where Irenaeus uses Abraham, but they represent the primary ones. Rather than organizing our initial discussion according to a taxonomy, I will address the passages in their order, and then we will explore the key themes that arise from the passages. As we explore these primary passages, we will see that the Pauline letters serve as his primary interpretive lens as Irenaeus emphasizes the unity of God's work, the inclusion of the Gentiles in the church, and the restoration of the created world. We will begin with *Haer.* 3.11.8, which is one of the key passages where Abraham plays a factor in Book 3.

One God and Four Covenants (Haer. 3.11.8)

In *Against Heresies* 3.9-12 Irenaeus explains how the four Gospels demonstrate that Jesus represents the one God, and he links the faith of the New Testament writers to Abraham and other key characters of the Old Testament. In that way, Irenaeus desires to show that it is the "one and the same God who had given the promise to Abraham ... and who through his Son Christ Jesus called us from the worship of stones to the knowledge of himself" (*Haer.* 3.9.1). To establish this connection between Jesus and the covenanting God, he defends the witness of the four Gospels that later became canonical. In the midst of his argument, he associates the four Gospels with the progression of four covenants in the Bible.[23]

The four covenants (*testamenta*) progress from Noah (with the rainbow), to Abraham (with sign of circumcision), to Moses (with the law), and climax with Jesus. Though there is a textual difficulty with regard to Abraham's position in this list,[24] the evidence overwhelmingly points to including

---

23. *Haer.* 3.11.8. Abraham remains important in the argument through *Haer.* 3.12. Cf. Graham, "Zealous," 166-74.

24. Almost universally, scholars (including the Sources Chrétiennes critical edition) follow the Latin of the passage, which lists these as the four primary covenants—Adam, Noah, Moses, and the Gospel—substituting Adam for Abraham. The Greek fragment surviving at this point includes Abraham and does not mention Adam. See SC 211: 169-70; SC 210: 95-124, esp. 122-23. The ANF translators mention the textual difficulty and note that they follow the "old Latin, which seems to represent the original with greater exactness," though no substantiation is given (1:429.3). No mention of the textual difficulty is made in the ACW translation. Perhaps Adam is often given preference because the importance of the Jewish covenants is generally minimized in Irenaean scholarship. Admittedly, Adam would be the harder reading because Irenaeus nowhere mentions a covenant with Adam,

Abraham.²⁵ The Jesus revealed through the fourfold Gospel is the same Word who was at work through the fourfold unity and progression of the covenants.²⁶ The majority of passages treating Abraham are in Book 4,²⁷ and Irenaeus's focus is on how Christ is the climax of the divine economy that begins in the Old Testament. Of course, Irenaeus is not unaware of the discontinuities between the covenants, particularly between Christ and Moses, and we will see how he sets Abraham as a point of unity between these covenants.

Children of the Same Faith (Haer. 4.5.3-5)

In the heart of Book 4 (*Haer.* 4.1-36) Irenaeus explains the continuities and discontinuities between the Old Testament and the New.²⁸ He attempts to demonstrate how God "is one and the same" (*unus et idem*) in the Old Testament, where he is "announced by the law and the prophets," and in the New Testament, where he is "confessed by Christ as his Father" (*Haer.* 4.5.1). As part of this argument, Irenaeus highlights two encounters Jesus had with the Jews (Matt 22:29-32 and John 8:56-57), in which Jesus' response is based on an appeal to Abraham (*Haer.* 4.5.2-5). After discussing the hope of resurrection with regard to Matthew 22 (*Haer.* 4.5.2), he explains how in John 8:56 Abraham "rejoiced that he should see [Christ's] day, and he saw it and was glad" (*Haer.* 4.5.3). The link between Abraham and Christ is Abraham's faith: through a quotation of Gen 15:6 (cf. Rom 4:3; Gal 3:6), Irenaeus explains how Abraham believed in God's promise to give him many descendants. This faith is demonstrated in his sacrifice of his beloved and only-begotten son Isaac, which meant that "God also might be pleased to offer up for all his seed his own beloved and only-begotten Son as a sacrifice for our redemption" (*Haer.* 4.5.4). Thus, Abraham (in terms of John 8:56) was able to see the Word's advent and suffering by pre-enacting the event himself.²⁹ Abraham's faith in the promise of his having children and his resulting joy is directly linked

---

though he repeatedly notes the covenant with Abraham (e.g., *Haer.* 1.30.10; 3.10.2; 3.12.3; 3.12.10-11; 4.25.1-3). However, given the extant Greek text and the weight of Irenaeus's wider argument, it seems likely that the Greek best captures the original. Rousseau, one of the editors of the SC critical edition, later shifted his weight to Abraham over against Adam. See Adelin Rousseau (ed.), *Irenee de Lyon, Demonstration de la predication apostolique* (SC 406; Paris: Cerf, 1995), 386–88. Cf. Graham, "Zealous," 40–41.

25. E.g., Graham ("Irenaeus and Covenants," 393–94) has argued convincingly that the covenants represented by the Greek text—that is, the list which includes Abraham but not Adam—form the structure for the *Demonstration*.

26. Elsewhere, Irenaeus highlights the fact that the Abrahamic covenant is the fulfillment of the promises of the Noahic covenant (cf. *Epid.* 24).

27. See Graham, "Zealous," 180–98.

28. For a discussion of the coherence of the argument of *Haer.* 4, see Bacq, *De l'ancienne à la nouvelle Alliance*; and Balás, "The Use and Interpretation of Paul," 35–36.

29. In distinction to interpretations of Genesis 22 as obedient faith (e.g., Jas 2:23), Noormann (*Irenäus*, 178) argues that Irenaeus "interpretiert diese Tat Abrahams jedoch

to the later Christ event but also equally to God's work in creation. For the Word also reveals "the most high God, who made the heaven and the earth" (*Haer*.4.5.5, quoting Gen 14:22).[30] Accordingly, Abraham serves as evidence for how the whole economy from creation to Christ, through the Old Testament, holds together. After discussing the revealing work of the Word (in *Haer*. 4.6), Irenaeus describes (in *Haer*. 4.7.1) how this relates to Abraham's rejoicing in John 8:56.

Children from Stones (Haer. 4.7.1-4.8.1)

Abraham, Irenaeus tells us, is able to rejoice through his descendants because his rejoicing is passed to them, particularly to Simeon (Luke 2:22), the shepherds (Luke 2:8), and Mary (Luke 1:46). At the same time, their rejoicing also "passed backwards from the children to Abraham" (*Haer*. 4.7.1). This reciprocal enactment parallels that of the Isaac-Christ sacrifice; the two events mutually embody the reality of the other.[31] Moving beyond Abraham's physical descendants, Irenaeus explains several Gospels texts (via Pauline passages)[32] to affirm that Christian believers, in particular Gentile believers, are really the children of Abraham. However, since these are not physical descendants, Irenaeus draws on God's act to make descendants from stones (cf. Matt 3:9):[33]

> Now, Jesus did this by drawing us off from the religion of stones, bringing us over from hard and fruitless contemplations, and establishing in us a faith like Abraham's. Thus, Paul also testifies, saying that we are children of Abraham (*filios Abrahae*) because of the similarity of our faith (*secundum similitudinem fidei*) and the promise of inheritance (*et repromissionem hereditatis*).[34]

This trope of the children of Abraham being made from stones also allows him to refute Marcion since believers will celebrate with Abraham eschatologically when he and his children inherit his promise of incorruption and also the land (*Haer*. 4.8.1).[35]

---

weniger als eine besondere Gehorsamsleistung denn als Ausdruck seiner prophetischen Begabung."

30. Cf. Tremblay, *Irénée de Lyon*, 69–70.

31. I found the discussion by Taylor on higher and ordinary time helpful for conceptualizing connections like these; Charles Taylor, *A Secular Age* (Cambridge: Belknap, 2007), 55.

32. Noormann (*Irenäus*, 179.56) highlights this: "Das Verständnis des synoptischen Textes, der fast immer im Kontext von Paulus-Zitaten angeführt wird, ist durch paulinische Abraham-Aussagen bestimmt."

33. Later, in *Haer*. 4.25.1, Irenaeus associates the stones motif with Eph 2:20-21, with Christ as the cornerstone and the church as the building of God.

34. *Haer*. 4.7.2. Cf. Rom 4:12; Gal 4:28.

35. He cites Luke 13:29//Matt 8:11.

With his focus on the continuity between the Old and New Testaments—"All things therefore are of one and the same substance, that is, from one and the same God" (*Haer.* 4.9.1)—Irenaeus has the task of making sense of the discontinuity between the Mosaic and Gospel covenants in response to Marcion's challenge (cf. *Haer.* 4.11-13). As part of this reconciliation of the differences in the divine economies, Irenaeus includes a discussion of Abraham (in *Haer.* 4.16.1-3).

Faith, Signs, and Righteousness (Haer. 4.16.1-3)

With Marcion's critique of the Old Testament still in mind, Irenaeus argues that the law is not in opposition to God's saving work in Christ. Ultimately, the salvation (even stylized as "justification") with regard to the law is the same as that of Christ (*Haer.* 4.13.1). Irenaeus follows Paul's logic that Abraham was righteous before having the law (Rom 4:10-12), but at the same time he also argues with James that obedience is fundamental to the nature of faith (Jas 2:21-26). Coming to *Haer.* 4.16 Irenaeus explains how circumcision and keeping Sabbath, the respective "signs" of the Abrahamic and Mosaic covenants (*testamenta*), are to be interpreted in light of Christ. Neither of the signs, or types, complete righteousness in themselves, but they point to the fulfillment found in Christ (*Haer.* 4.16.1). Circumcision points to the circumcision of the Spirit not made with hands (Col 2:11), which circumcises the hardness of your hearts (Deut 10:16). Likewise, Sabbath is a sign of the future Sabbath of rest in the kingdom of God.

Irenaeus is concerned to show that the higher purpose of God's intention for humans is that they have righteousness in their hearts, as the "circumcision of the heart" makes clear:

> A person was not justified by these things, but … they were given as a sign to the people. This fact shows that Abraham himself, without circumcision and without observance of Sabbaths, "believed God, and it was reckoned unto him as righteousness; and he was called the friend of God" (Jas 2.23) … Moreover, all the rest of the multitude of those righteous men who lived before Abraham, and of those patriarchs who preceded Moses, were justified independently of the things above mentioned, without the law of Moses.[36]

Making use of Paul's argument (as in Rom 4:10-12) that Abraham was justified before practicing circumcision or keeping Sabbath, Irenaeus cites Jas 2:23 in which Abraham's faith is shown through obedience. (Irenaeus does not appear to share post-Reformation concerns about the discontinuity between Paul and James.) Why then was the law given if people could be righteous without it? The patriarchs "had the meaning of the Decalogue written in their hearts and souls, that is, they loved the God who made them … But when this righteousness and love to God had passed into oblivion, and became extinct in Egypt," God revealed

---

36. *Haer.* 4.16.2.

himself through the law that they might follow him (*Haer.* 4.16.3). Though the law became written, this does not nullify the divine intention that it be internalized, for the signs included in the covenants were to lead those of faith to this inner heart transformation. Accordingly, obedience to Christ, who fulfills the law, is necessary for the Christian. This argument extends into *Against Heresies* 4.17.1, where Irenaeus continues to focus on the typological role of the Mosaic covenant which points to righteousness in their hearts. As Irenaeus moves from Moses to the prophets (*Haer.* 4.20-35),[37] he furthers his case about the continuity between the old and new.

Faith, Fatherhood, and Inheritance (Haer. 4.21-25)

Against Heresies 4.20, a central part of his discussion about prophecy, is one of the climactic chapters in Irenaeus's work. It explores the revelation of God through Christ and the Spirit in both testaments and the resulting union with God for those that attend to this revelation. Those in the Old Testament have encounters with God that are typologically united with God's later work, "in order that through them he might prefigure and show forth future events beforehand" (*Haer.* 4.20.12). Giving examples of this union, Irenaeus describes how the unrighteous and Gentiles are included in the people of God using examples of Hosea and his wife and children, Moses and his Ethiopian wife, and Rahab. Moving from these shorter examples, Irenaeus chooses the patriarchs—Abraham (*Haer.* 4.21.1), Isaac (*Haer.* 4.21.2), and Jacob (*Haer.* 4.21.3)—to explain this typological relationship more fully.

As with the more brief examples, when Irenaeus comes to the covenant (*testamentum*) made with Abraham, he emphasizes the inclusion of the Gentiles in the church as the fulfillment of the Old Testament prefiguration. He identifies this with Abraham's faith through an extended quotation of Gal 3:5-9:

> But that our faith was also prefigured (*praefigurabatur fides nostra*) in Abraham, and that he was the patriarch of our faith, and, as it were, the prophet of it, the apostle has very fully taught, when he says in the letter to the Galatians: "Does God supply you with the Spirit and work miracles among you by your doing the works of the law, or by your believing what you heard? Just as Abraham 'believed God, and it was reckoned to him as righteousness,' so, you see, those who believe are the descendants of Abraham. And the scripture, foreseeing that God would justify the Gentiles by faith, declared the gospel beforehand to Abraham, saying, 'All the Gentiles shall be blessed in you.' For this reason, those who believe are blessed with Abraham who believed" (Gal 3.5-9). For which (reasons the apostle) declared that this man was not only the prophet of faith, but also the father of those who from among the Gentiles believe in Jesus Christ, because his faith and ours are one and the same (*una et eadem*): for he believed in things

---

37. Bacq, *De l'ancienne à la nouvelle Alliance*, 153–61.

future, as if they were already accomplished because of the promise of God, and in like manner do we also, because of the promise of God, behold through faith that inheritance in the kingdom (*in regno hereditatem*).[38]

The Gentiles, Irenaeus argues, have the same faith as Abraham, and it is through this common faith that they become his descendants. Just as Irenaeus has argued for the unified work of the "one and the same God" in other passages (e.g., *Haer.* 3.9.1; 4.9.1), he now emphasizes "one and the same faith."[39] Importantly, this reconstituted family, now including Gentiles, will experience a reconstituted inheritance represented as "the kingdom."[40]

Reiterating that Old Testament saints and Christians did not have a distinct faith, he describes how those who "desired to see Christ" will be received in the kingdom:

> For there is one God who led the patriarchs in his economies (*dispositiones*), and "who justified the circumcised by faith and the uncircumcised through faith" (Rom 3.30). Just as we were prefigured (*nos praefigurabamur*) and foretold in the first men, they again are shaped in us (*in nobis illi deformantur*), that is, in the church, and receive the wage of their labors.[41]

This typology is not merely a similar repetition or an image, but an organic link of sorts. In the Old Testament "we [the church] were prefigured," and the Old Testament saints are "represented in us, the church." In the Old Testament and in the New, believers experience God directly but they both must still look toward the future for fulfillment of his promised kingdom. It is this combination of present experience with an orientation to the future that allows Irenaeus to call Abraham (and many others in the Old Testament) prophets. With his faith established before the giving of circumcision and the law, Abraham is thus able to join together Jews and Gentiles into the one people of God: "But this faith which is in uncircumcision, as connecting the end with the beginning,

---

38. *Haer.* 4.21.1.

39. Cf. Wingren, *Man and the Incarnation*, 74.

40. Ernst Dassmann (*Der Stachel im Fleisch: Paulus in der frühchristlichen Literatur bis Irenäus* [Münster: Aschendorff, 1979], 311) critiques Irenaeus at this point because he does not contrast justification by works with justification by faith as Paul did (according to his reading of Galatians), but rather highlights how Abraham's faith consists of believing God's promises of a large family: "Glaube ist nicht mehr nur im Sinne paulinischer Mystik Gemeinschaft mit dem erhöhten Christus, sondern Bindung an die kirchliche Tradition, die bei Paulus noch keine Rolle spielte, für die Gemeinden zur Zeit des Irenäus dagegen lebensnotwendig wird." That is, Irenaeus emphasizes the church over the individual's standing before God. This critique of Irenaeus is similar to those critiques leveled at N. T. Wright's understanding of justification.

41. *Haer.* 4.22.2.

has been made (both) the first and the last."⁴² At the same time, the covenant of "bondage" is prefigured in Abraham, as well as the Gospel covenant of "freedom." Therefore, Abraham is the father of all, but the culmination of the Abrahamic faith is found in the Lord who returned the sons of Abraham to uncircumcision.

The argument attempts to show the continuity between the economies of God, moving from Abraham to the law and then to Christ, while also capturing the discontinuity of the latter pair. However, seeing a greater affinity between Abraham and Christ, Irenaeus describes those who have faith in Christ as children of Abraham, just as Paul does. Though the majority of passages discussing Abraham are found in Book 4, as he shows the continuities between the old and new, the culmination of Irenaeus's teaching about Abraham is found in the climax of Book 5 when he describes the universal restoration of the world.

The Children's Inheritance (Haer. 5.32)

The last major section of Book 5 (*Haer.* 5.16-36) treats the establishment of God's kingdom within creation.⁴³ After reiterating the reality of Christ's incarnation and his salvific recapitulation of humanity, Irenaeus recounts an eschatological scheme that culminates in the restoration of the whole created order, including the flesh. As he describes this "inheritance of the kingdom" (*Haer.* 5.32), Irenaeus argues that believers should reign in the same creation in which they previously suffered (*Haer.* 5.32.1). As evidence he quotes Rom 8:19-21, which ends with a statement about the glory of the "sons of God."⁴⁴ Irenaeus then immediately turns to a discussion of the promise of land given to Abraham,⁴⁵ quoting Gen 13:14-15, 17 and later Gen 15:18:

> Though [Abraham] did not receive the inheritance of the land (*hereditatem terrae*) during all the time of his sojourn there, if God promised it to him, it must be that he shall receive it at the resurrection of the just together with his seed, that is, those who fear God and believe in Him.⁴⁶

---

42. *Haer.* 4.25.1. When discussing protology and eschatology, or the end and beginning, Irenaeus most often associates Adam with the beginning (cf. *Haer.* 4.20.4; 4.34.4; 5.14.1; 5.16.1; 5.23.2). In this unique circumstance, Abraham is cited as the "beginning."

43. Cf. Balás, "The Use and Interpretation of Paul," 37–38.

44. On the wider topics related to Romans 8 in this passage, see D. Jeffrey Bingham, "Irenaeus Reads Romans 8: Resurrection and Renovation," in *Early Patristic Readings of Romans*, ed. Kathy L. Gaca and L. L. Welborn (New York: T&T Clark, 2005), 114–32, at 127–28.

45. He is likely associating the "son's" language (Rom 8:14-17, 23) with the promise of being children of Abraham (Rom 4:11-12), thus reading Romans 8 in light of Romans 4.

46. *Haer.* 5.32.2 (ANF modified).

Though God promised the land of Canaan and its environs to Abraham, Irenaeus interprets this as a promise of the land of all creation. He juxtaposes this expansion of the inheritance with the expansion of Abraham's progeny: Abraham's "seed is the church, which receives the adoption to God through the Lord" (*Haer.* 5.32.2). This extension of the filial promise to all the nations thus serves as the basis of an extension of the land promise to all the earth.

Returning to his favorite verse on Gentile inclusion (Matt 3:9), which speaks of God raising up stones, Irenaeus immediately explains what this means by citing Gal 4:28—Gentile believers are "children of the promise." Through a quotation of Gal 3:16, he argues that those "who have believed in Christ receive Christ, the promise to Abraham" (*Haer.* 5.32.2). His following quotation of Gal 3:6-9 helps show that those who believe as Abraham did are children of Abraham, even the Gentile nations, and they will all be blessed with his blessing.[47] He thus concludes, "Now God made promise of the earth to Abraham and his seed. However, neither Abraham nor his seed, that is, those who are justified by faith, receive any inheritance in it now, but they shall receive it at the resurrection of the just" (*Haer.* 5.32.2). As we noted earlier, the commonality between the faith of Abraham and his descendants is that both had to wait for a future consummation of the promise. This promised restoration of all creation is at the heart of Irenaeus's theological vision: the God who created the world will restore creation, and yet here this is framed as a fulfillment of his covenantal promise to Abraham to give his descendants land. Just as the promise to Abraham was to a specific land and to his physical descendants, when God expanded the promise to include Gentiles from all nations, he also expanded the promised restoration of the land for those resurrected Gentiles to experience in the eschaton.

Now that we have explored these various passages which discuss Abraham, we can draw together a larger picture of Irenaeus's use of Abraham in his theological construction.

Abraham in Irenaeus

With Irenaeus's focus on the continuity in God's salvation-historical economy, Abraham provides him with a direct connection between the old and the new. Since *Against Heresies* 4 is centered on the question of how the old and new relate together, it is no surprise that the most references to Abraham are found there. Graham rightly notes that promise and fulfillment are central to Irenaeus's discussion of all the covenants,[48] and this is no less true with the two broad emphases related to Abraham: Abraham's children and Abraham's faith.

---

47. Cf. *Haer.* 5.34.1, where Irenaeus describes the Old Testament promises of restoration from exile to pertain to the church who will be "saved from all the nations."

48. Graham, "Zealous," 42–48, 114–18.

Abraham and His Progeny

A central focus of the biblical testimony about Abraham is the idea of election: Abraham's children are marked out as the people of God. We will discuss Christ as a son of Abraham and then the church as his children.

The connection between Abraham and Christ is utilized in various ways. In some instances the focus is not so much on Abraham himself, but on the reality of Jesus' *humanity* (vis-à-vis his divinity). For example (in *Haer.* 3.11.8), Irenaeus highlights how Matthew's Gospel portrays Jesus as a *man*: "Matthew narrates his generation inasmuch as he is man, saying, 'The book of the generation of Jesus Christ, the son of David, the son of Abraham'" (quoting Matt 1:1).[49] In a later passage, Irenaeus quotes the same Matthew text but now highlights the *covenantal* continuity between the promises to David and to Abraham through Christ (*Haer.* 3.16.2; cf. *Haer.* 3.12.3). This connection between Abraham and Christ stands in the background of several passages in *Haer.*, but drawing specifically on Gal 3:16 Irenaeus follows Paul in arguing that Christ is "the" seed of Abraham (*Haer.* 5.32.2). These passages show not only that Christ is human but also that he stands in direct continuity with the divine economy beginning in the Old Testament and finding its fulfillment in the New Testament.

One of the most repeated topics from all the texts we have considered is that of the children of Abraham, as he draws on the repeated promise in Genesis that Abraham would have many descendants (e.g., Gen 12:2; 15:5). Though believing Gentiles capture much of his discussion, Irenaeus does not ignore the fact that believing Jews are also still descendants of Abraham. For instance (in *Haer.* 4.7.1), he describes how Abraham's rejoicing was fulfilled through Simeon, the shepherds, and Mary. At the same time, Irenaeus notes that the Jews on the whole rejected Christ. Thus, believing Gentiles will celebrate the kingdom with Abraham and the other patriarchs in lieu of unbelieving Jews.[50]

Accordingly, the focus of the majority of Irenaeus's discussion about the children of Abraham in *Against Heresies* is about believing Gentiles who participate (along with believing Jews) in the promises given to Abraham.[51] Irenaeus's favorite verse to describe this is Matt 3:9 (para. Luke 3:8), where John the Baptist promises that "God is able to raise up children for Abraham from stones." However, Irenaeus derives the basis for this interpretation from his reading of Paul that these stones (i.e., believing Gentiles) are the descendants of Abraham, and they build up the church with Christ as the cornerstone (*Haer.* 4.25.1). In particular, we noted how Irenaeus describes Christ as "the" seed of Abraham (cf. Gal 3:6-18), and it is then through Christ that Gentiles also become the children of Abraham: "for

---

49. The divine-human juxtaposition is also evident in *Haer.* 3.9.3.

50. Cf. *Haer.* 4.8.1; 4.36.8.

51. Though Paul associates the "administration of the mystery" (οἰκονομία τοῦ μυστηρίου) in Eph 3:9 with the unity of one people of God that contains Jews and Gentiles, Irenaeus almost universally rejects the use of mystery language, noting throughout *Haer.* 1 and *Haer.* 2 how his opponents make use of hidden and unspeakable mysteries.

his seed is the Church, who receives the adoption (*adoptionem*) to God through the Lord."[52] That is, they share in the same faith of Abraham, a faith in Christ, and therefore become Abraham's children because he was justified in his faith before becoming circumcised (cf. Rom 4:1-12).[53] Though not central to his discussion of being children of Abraham, Irenaeus does associate justification with "adoption," a (Pauline) metaphor central to Irenaeus's soteriological construct.[54]

In addition to the promise that Abraham would have many descendants, God also promised the land (of Canaan) as an inheritance, a topic intimately tied to being children. Paul, in Romans 4 (and 8?) and Galatians 3–4 directly correlates being a child of Abraham and gaining an inheritance. Irenaeus is well known for his dogged defense for the resurrection of *the body*, which serves as the inheritance (*hereditas*),[55] but the primary focus for Irenaeus in the context of Abraham is the restoration of *the world* as a fulfillment of the promise to Abraham (cf. *Haer.* 5.32.2). Just as the promise of descendants was expanded beyond the people of Israel, the promise for inheritance (and restoration) of the land is also expanded beyond the land of Israel to include the whole world. In other words, he appears to be reading Romans 8 in light of Romans 4, yet Galatians 3 is a passage that he regularly returns to in this context. Irenaeus repeatedly reminds us of the faith Abraham had, a faith in the promises that he would have numerous children and that they would inherit the land, which leads us to our next topic.

Abraham and His Faith

Abraham's faith is most clearly associated with his role as a prophet, but Irenaeus, like Paul, sets Abraham's faith in the context of justification and the law. Though not often considered a prophet by most (Christian interpreters) today, Irenaeus describes Abraham as a "prophet" several times (e.g., *Haer.* 4.5.5; 4.21.1; *Epid.* 44).

---

52. *Haer.* 5.32.2. Interestingly, Irenaeus regularly correlates the promise that they will be as the stars in the heavens (Gen 15:5; 22:17; 26:4) with being "lights of the world" (Phil 2:15) or "the light of the world" (Matt 5:14). See *Haer.* 3.9.1; 4.5.3; 4.7.3; *Epid.* 24, 35. Tremblay (*Irénée de Lyon*, 75) states, "L'évêque de Lyon n'interprète pas la comparaison 'pareille aux étoiles du ciel' dans la sens biblique de la quantité ou de la multiplication numérique, mais dans le sens de la qualité ou de la luminosité." Cf. Roldanus, "L'héritage d'Abraham," 214. For a similar argument about Paul, see David A. Burnett, "'So Shall Your Seed Be': Paul's Use of Genesis 15:5 in Romans 4:18 in Light of Early Jewish Deification Traditions," *JSPL* 5 (2015), 211–36.

53. Cf. *Haer.* 4.16; 4.21-25; *Epid.* 24.

54. In particular, Irenaeus identifies adoption with participation in immorality and deification. Cf. Blackwell, *Christosis: Engaging Paul's Soteriology with His Patristic Interpreters*, rev. ed. (Grand Rapids: Eerdmans, 2016), 44–50, 59–60; idem, "Partakers of Adoption."

55. In addition to the resurrection body as the inheritance of believers, Irenaeus also describes the body as the inheritance (i.e., possession) of the Spirit in *Haer.* 5.9.1-4.

With Irenaeus's intention to show the unity in God's work in the Old Testament and the New, this prophetic role serves to refute those who would divide God's work or posit a distinction between the Creator and the Savior. Irenaeus does not merely present Abraham as foretelling the future by the Spirit; rather, Abraham also experiences the Word firsthand, and his actions proclaim, even enact and prefigure, God's future work in later dispensations.[56] For example, Irenaeus is able to parallel the sacrifice of Abraham's only son Isaac and the sacrifice of Christ: Abraham "delivered up, as a sacrifice to God, his only-begotten and beloved son, in order that God also might be pleased to offer up for all his seed His own beloved and only-begotten Son, as a sacrifice for our redemption" (*Haer.* 4.5.4).[57] In addition to this connection, note the organic link between other Abrahamic events and the later Christological fulfillment: the rejoicing at Christ's advent (*Haer.* 4.7.1), circumcision (*Haer.* 4.16.1), and the expectation of judgment (*Epid.* 44). Accordingly, Abraham's own narrative prophetically proclaims the work of the Lord.

Abraham's faithful response in his interaction with God serves as the connection with his descendants and their experience of these promises. They are mutually reciprocal. Of all the things that pass from Abraham to his progeny, his faith is central since believers share one and the same faith in Christ, and his faith like his rejoicing is enacted in them—both Jewish and Gentile believers.

Like Paul, Irenaeus often emphasizes Abraham's faith in God when he speaks of his reception of these promises of progeny and land. Abraham believed not only in the Word that he received, but his faith is acted out as he "follows the Word" (*Haer.* 4.5.3-4).[58] By means of Gen 15:6, as communicated by Paul and James (cf. Gal 3:6-18; Rom 4:1-21; Jas 2:21-26), Irenaeus often associates Abraham's faith with his being reckoned as righteous.[59] Though Irenaeus followed Paul in making a distinction between Abraham being justified before the institution of circumcision, he does not always emphasize a contrast between faith and works of the law, but he does note the discontinuities between the old and the new covenants, describing them in Pauline terms as the covenants of "bondage" and "freedom."[60] He underscores how Abraham's justification by faith precedes the

---

56. See, e.g., Brian E. Daley, "Christ, the Church, and the Shape of Scripture: What We Can Learn from Patristic Exegesis," in *From Judaism to Christianity: Tradition and Transition*, ed. Patricia Walters (Leiden: Brill, 2010), 267–88, at 272–75.

57. Cf. Rom 8:32.

58. Roldanus, "L'héritage d'Abraham," 217–18.

59. Cf. *Haer.* 4.5.3-5; 4.7.1-2; 4.8.1; 4.13.4; *Epid.* 24, 35. Though Hebrews 11 also commends Abraham for his faith, that passage only plays a small role in Irenaeus's exegesis: D. Jeffrey Bingham, "Irenaeus and Hebrews," in *Irenaeus: Life, Scripture, Legacy*, ed. Paul Foster and Sara Parvis (Minneapolis: Fortress, 2012), 77. Cf. Roldanus, "L'héritage d'Abraham," 218, 224.

60. Cf. Everett Ferguson, "The Covenant Idea in the Second Century," in *Texts and Testaments: Critical Essays on the Bible and Early Church Fathers*, ed. W. Eugene March

mandate of circumcision, but his emphasis in this context often relates to how Jews and Gentiles form one people of God.

While not promoting an argument identical to those in the New Perspective, Irenaeus does highlight similar issues when discussing Abraham, a fact that has led modern (particularly German) interpreters to critique his position.[61] While the German critique is not baseless, this other perspective on Abraham which Irenaeus has drawn primarily from Paul does highlight other emphases that Paul presents. Owing to the underdetermined nature of biblical texts, Irenaeus has highlighted an aspect in Paul that fits his rhetorical purpose. Of course, this is a larger debate in Pauline studies itself, and without having adequately studied the role of the law in Irenaeus, this is a knot we cannot untie here.

Conclusion

Even though Abraham is not the focus of Irenaeus's theological construction in the way that Adam is,[62] Abraham does play an important role within his salvation-historical perspective on the divine economies. The Son did not become incarnate as just any man in his work to recapitulate humanity. Rather, the Word arranged a number of covenants, proceeding particularly from Noah, to Abraham, and to Moses, before climaxing in his work of the Gospel. Accordingly, the Jewish context of the incarnation is not irrelevant to Irenaeus's theological construction: Jesus is the seed of Abraham, a fact that does not receive enough scholarly attention. In line with Wright's assessment of Paul, Irenaeus does not merely choose Abraham as an example, as just one who has "faith" and is declared "righteous."[63] Rather, through the economies of God, Abraham prefigures, even enacts in his own life, the faith of his children who will follow him. Tremblay captures his pivotal position in the divine economy well: "Abraham est présenté … comme une figure qui joue, par rapport aux membres de l'Alliance nouvelle, un rôle de source, d'origine, en un mot, de père."[64] Thus, Abraham and the Abrahamic covenant play an important

---

(San Antonio: Trinity University, 1980), 135–62, at 144–48; Wingren, *Man and the Incarnation*, 72.

61. E.g., Noormann, *Irenäus*, 416–20; Dassmann, *Der Stachel im Fleisch*, 311. Lawson argues that "Werner goes too far in maintaining that Irenaeus had little conception of the faith of Abraham." Lawson, *The Biblical Theology of Saint Irenaeus*, 77, citing Johannes Werner, *Der Paulinismus des Irenaeus* (TU 6.2; Leipzig: J.C. Hinrichs, 1889), 102.

62. Note how Irenaeus in *Demonstration*, for example, spends much more time on Adam (*Epid.* 11-18), Noah (*Epid.* 19-23), and Moses (*Epid.* 25-29), each with multiple chapters, than he does on Abraham (*Epid.* 24).

63. Of course, a more complete comparison and contrast with Wright's reading is impossible here.

64. Tremblay, *Irénée de Lyon*, 74.

role in the progression of the economies which find their fulfillment in the advent of Christ (cf. *Haer.* 3.11.8).

In contrast to Moses and the Old Covenant whose discontinuities with the Gospel must be explained, Abraham (as considered through a Pauline lens) presents Irenaeus with an Old Testament character in direct continuity with the New Testament. Thus, Abraham serves as a basis to refute those who would separate the work of the God between these two testaments. In particular, the Abraham narrative enables Irenaeus to show how it is the one and the same God who both makes the Old Testament promise and brings it to fulfillment through Christ. It is for this reason that Irenaeus repeatedly returns to the description of God as the "God of Abraham, Isaac, and Jacob."[65] Moringiello rightly notes the important place of Abraham in the salvation-historical progression:

> Of all the prophetic authorities, Abraham warrants special attention. We could say that Abraham represents Irenaeus's strongest *refutatio* because it is his faith that begins the economy of salvation. Although Adam and Eve play an important role in Irenaeus's thinking, Abraham is the first Scriptural figure of faith.[66]

Thus, while we cannot overestimate the importance of the creation to new creation arc (or the Adam-Christ typology) in Irenaeus's theology, that does not mean we should ignore the fundamental role of the covenants for Irenaeus.[67] In many ways Irenaeus's use of Adam more directly refutes his (Valentinian) Gnostic opponents who disparage physical creation and the resurrection of the flesh, whereas his use of Abraham serves to refute Marcion and his disparagement of the Jewish aspects of Christianity.

With the continuity between the Jewish covenants and Jesus as the emphasis of *Against Heresies* 4 and the *Demonstration*, Abraham plays a regular role in those pieces. However, the conceptuality runs throughout the whole corpus, even finding its climax in the promised restoration of the world at the end of *Against Heresies* 5. Though Irenaeus would not refer to the Abrahamic as an "abandonment" of the Adamic, Levenson's comments about Paul could apply to Irenaeus:

> One cannot adequately grasp Paul's theology without reckoning with this simple but momentous fact: for Paul, *the Gentile Christian has abandoned the Adamic identity for the Abrahamic*. He has left the universal identity associated with the sin-infected human essence and been recreated as one who attains righteousness

---

65. Cf. *Haer.* 1.221; 2.30.9; 3.6.3-4; 3.12.3; 4.5.2; 4.8.1; 4.36.8; *Epid.* 8, 21, 24-25.

66. Scott D. Moringiello, "Irenaeus Rhetor" (PhD dissertation, University of Notre Dame, 2008), 142.

67. Tremblay (*Irénée de Lyon*, 65.10) writes: "Il est indéniable qu'Irénée voit en Abraham le commencement d'un nouvel âge du monde, idée qu'il trouve dans l'Ecriture et qui s'impose."

in the sight of God on the basis of his faith, just as Abraham did in the Pauline reading of Genesis 15:6.[68]

The children of Abraham who share in his faith in the saving, re-creative work of God in Christ, are part of a new family uniting Jews and Gentiles who will enjoy the inheritance of a renewed creation. Irenaeus draws this message from Paul, but, of course, this does not mean that Irenaeus merely parrots Paul, or has the same overall theological construction.[69]

One significant area of overlap between Irenaeus and Paul is the focus on Christological exegesis: Abraham is important, but not in and of himself. We have seen throughout that Abraham is cast vis-à-vis the Word who directly engages Abraham and whose advent fulfills the promises to Abraham. Thus, we should properly say that Abraham is an important step in God's economy which finds its climax in Christ.[70] However, just as we understand Abraham in light of Christ, we also understand Christ in light of Abraham. Because even as Christ is the fulfillment of the economy, we could not arrive at Christ without the preparation that God had set out through the covenants.

Paul and Irenaeus both present a picture of continuity and discontinuity between the Old Testament and the Gospel, but due to Irenaeus's emphasis on continuity, most see a distinction between these two writers at this point. At the same time, the diversity of opinions about Paul and Abraham (as the debates between Wright and his detractors show) make it difficult to pronounce Irenaeus as simply "Pauline" or "unpauline."[71] Irenaeus's different rhetorical and polemical setting means that Irenaeus is addressing different questions and opponents. Had he just repeated Paul, his arguments would be flat and uninteresting since ideas have to be (re)contextualized to have meaning for a new audience. As a representative of a tired approach to the Paulinism of Irenaeus, Lawson is an example of one

---

68. Jon D. Levenson, *Inheriting Abraham: The Legacy of the Patriarch in Judaism, Christianity, and Islam* (Princeton: Princeton University Press, 2012), 157 (emphasis original).

69. On the reception of Paul in Irenaeus with regard to Abraham, see Roldanus, "L'héritage d'Abraham," 224.

70. See especially, John J. O'Keefe and R. R. Reno, *Sanctified Vision: An Introduction to Early Christian Interpretation of the Bible* (Baltimore: Johns Hopkins University Press, 2005), 38; Daley, "Christ, the Church, and the Shape of Scripture," 272–75.

71. This distinction between Irenaeus and Paul is sometimes framed as the distinction between a salvation-historical and apocalyptic lens. However, even Pauline interpreters debate the meaning of "apocalyptic" in Paul with some having a more prospective (reading forward from Judaism to Christ) and others more retrospective (reading backward from Christ to Judaism) view. See the introduction and the essays in Blackwell, John K. Goodrich, and Jason Maston (eds.), *Paul and the Apocalyptic Imagination* (Minneapolis: Fortress, 2016). What makes Irenaeus an interesting reader is that he reads retrospectively but with a bias toward continuity.

who is concerned with how well Irenaeus *repeats* Paul's own theology. In reality, this assessment reflects the question of whether Irenaeus is more "Catholic or evangelical" (i.e., Catholic or Protestant) in his theology.[72] Of course, this depends not only on how one interprets Irenaeus, but on how one interprets Paul, a matter which is not by any means settled. With the underdetermined nature of texts, the seed of Paul's letters will produce fruit in various orchards.[73] The actual picture, therefore, will be much more complicated than simple binary options. Certainly, there are differences, but the differences are what make the conversation between two thinkers interesting.

---

72. Lawson, *The Biblical Theology of Saint Irenaeus*, passim, esp. 231–51.

73. E.g., see Blackwell, "Two Early Perspectives on Participation in Paul: Irenaeus and Clement of Alexandria," in *"In Christ" in Paul: Explorations in Paul's Theology of Union and Participation*, ed. Michael J. Thate et al. (WUNT II; Tübingen: Mohr Siebeck, 2015), 331–55; idem, "Second Century Perspectives on the Apocalyptic Paul: Reading the *Apocalypse of Paul* and the *Acts of Paul*," in *Paul and the Apocalyptic Imagination*, 177–97.

Response
Irenaeus, Abraham, Covenants, and the One Thing Needful: The Second Adam

Mark W. Elliott

Ben Blackwell has done us a great service in appealing to the significance of the covenant with Abraham for Irenaeus in his version of a salvation-history scheme that permeates and structures *Against Heresies*. Blackwell agrees concerning with the continuity of Pauline Christianity with the very faith of the great patriarch of Genesis that has been noted by N. T. Wright. Gentiles in particular inherit this very type of "religion," which is not a *novum* (even if the list of contents might be supplemented, hence fuller). For according to Hebrews 11, Abraham even had a faith in a resurrection, albeit of a slightly different type. One slight problem emerges with the key text of *Haer* 3.11.8, in that the Latin version does not have "Abraham" but "Adam."

One issue with Irenaeus is that one has to tread carefully in establishing his meaning in that much of what he wrote in Greek is only preserved in Latin or Armenian. If "the underdetermined nature of texts" can be said about Paul, as Blackwell puts it at the end of his chapter, with some canonical warrant (2 Pet 3:16, in the context of a discussion of Eschatology), something similar can be said a fortiori about Irenaeus.[1] Much care has to be taken, even tentativeness in drawing conclusions from texts which come to us at second and third remove. However, as Blackwell usefully observes, the Greek (fragments) do read "Abraham" as the second of four Old Testament covenanters, and this is likely to be truer to the original, since elsewhere Irenaeus speaks of a covenant with Abraham, but not of one with Adam.

Incidentally, Noah, Moses, and Jesus are the other three covenanters. In Matthew 22 ("God is of the living not of the dead") and John 8:56 ("Abraham rejoiced to see my day") Jesus himself points to Abraham and thereby asserts a common faith with him. The importance of a "flesh" tie to Abraham as a condition of being an inheritor

---

1. See Sven Lundström, *Die Überlieferung der lateinischen Irenaeus-übersetzung* (Studia Latina Upsaliensia 18; Uppsala: S. Academiae Ubsaliensis, 1985). One of his concerns is to value the Latin more and the Armenian less in terms of "reliability" of witness.

of Abraham, and the promises made to him are undermined by the mention of God's making descendants out of stone (Matt 3:9 in *Haer.* 4.7.2):

> As John the Baptist says: For God is able from these stones to raise up children unto Abraham. Matthew 3.9. Now, this Jesus did by drawing us off from the religion of stones, and bringing us over from hard and fruitless cogitations, and establishing in us a faith like to Abraham. As Paul does also testify, saying that we are children of Abraham because of the similarity of our faith, and the promise of inheritance.

Indeed, there is a nice allusion here to the "heart of flesh"/"heart of stone" opposition as found in Ezek 36:26, while also connoting the futility of idol worship with the phrase "religion of stones." For Irenaeus, the Law provided signs that would encourage an internal, personal faith like that of Abraham (*Haer.* 4.21.1), who nevertheless did not eschew physical signs, even while guarding against an overreliance on these (as with "Moses") that might result in "bondage." Abraham's faith and that of the Christian believer are similar, not least in their future-orientation toward eventual inheritance. At *Haer.* 4.21.1 Abraham is called a prophet by Irenaeus (unusually for early Christian writers):

> He is not merely a prophet of the faith but the father of those who believe in Jesus—who believed in future events as though already taken place on account of God's promise, just as we too look ahead through faith to that inheritance in the kingdom on account of God's promise.
> (*Ob quae non solum prophetam eum dixit fidei, sed et patrem eorum qui ex gentibus credunt in Christum Jesum, eo quod una et eadem illius et nostra sit fides: illo quidem credente futuris quasi jam factis propter repromissionem Dei; nobis quoque similiter per fidem speculantibus eam quae est in regno haereditatem, propter repromissionem Dei.*)

Blackwell emphasizes that in the Irenaean scheme there is not just a typology of repetition between the two testaments but indeed something that ties them even more tightly together, an organic connection. The eschatology of Book 5 of *Against Heresies* in turn relates the inheritance of the righteous to the promise of the land to Abraham, of a special part of material creation, on the way to "the restoration of the whole creation." Blackwell, with reference to *Haer* 5.32.2 and 5.34.1, claims Irenaeus uses this or a variation—"restoration of the created order/whole world/creation"—on four occasions. Yet "restoration of the creation" is not the term that gets used by Irenaeus here and might mislead. The phrase that *does* get used—*restituens in patrum haereditatem*—means something different, viz., restoring people into the inheritance of the fathers.[2] The interest of the section that follows

---

2. *Haer.* 5.32.2: *Itaque qui ex fide sunt, benedicentur cum fideli Abraham. Sic ergo qui sunt ex fide, benedicentur cum fideli Abraham, et hi sunt filii Abraham. Repromisit autem Deus haereditatem terrae Abrahae et semini ejus: et neque Abraham neque semen ejus, hoc est qui ex fide justificantur, nunc sumunt in ea haereditatem: accipient autem eam in resurrectione justorum.* It seems they get a better reward than land.

(*Haer.* 5.35) admittedly and certainly lies in a physical new Jerusalem coming down to earth to reinforce the belief that those resurrected will be embodied, *but* if anything it is more about the restitution of 3-D *people* (or 4-D), who require not less than 3-D (or 4-D) props, and it does not concern the whole creation, or even "land," at least not explicitly.

In *Haer.* 5.36.1 Abraham is represented as one who engaged with God repeatedly ("*semper nova confabulans Deo*"); the Greek fragment has καὶ προσμιλῶν τῷ Θεῷ ("associating closely with God"), so that he the patriarch-prophet could communicate the mind of God to others. One finds the same language of *confabulans* in his paraphrase of Gen 18:1-3 in *Demonstration of Apostolic Preaching* 44: "And again Moses tells us about the Son of God coming close to the engagement of association to Abraham (*Et iterum Moyses prope-venientem ad commercium-confabulationis Filium Deo ad Abraham*)." This offers another way of connecting the Old Testament and the New Testament, as when Abraham offers up Isaac to "parallel" the sacrifice of Christ (*Haer.* 4.5.4). One might also mention here *Haer.* 4.21.1—"Abraham followed the logos," leaving "ship and homeland (τὸ πλοῖον καὶ τὸν πατέρα)"—as the lemma curiously puts it. (The standard Greek of Gen 12:1 is Ἐξελθε ἐκ τῆς γῆς σου καὶ ἐκ τῆς συγγενείας σου καὶ ἐκ τοῦ οἴκου τοῦ πατρός σου—i.e., "he went from his own tribe and the house of his father.") In any case I doubt that the best word for what Abraham means for the church is "typology," as Blackwell suggests. The relationship of foreshadowing is more one of a "prophecy" by which Abraham mystically becomes part of the new covenant, since the reference to "ship" alludes to Mark 1:20 (Ὁ καὶ εὐθὺς ἐκάλεσεν αὐτούς. καὶ ἀφέντες τὸν πατέρα αὐτῶν Ζεβεδαῖον ἐν τῷ πλοίῳ μετὰ τῶν μισθωτῶν ἀπῆλθον ὀπίσω αὐτοῦ), making it seem that Abraham was a disciple. Yet one cannot really call this "typology," for Irenaeus thinks that Abraham really was following Christ, not merely following someone or something in a way analogous to following Christ, which is essential for typology. Abraham's prophetic faith allows him to come across the centuries to be close to Christ. A text that Blackwell usefully adduces (in Robert Grant's translation) is the following: "Just as we were prefigured (*nos praefigurabamur*) and foretold in the first men, they again are shaped in us (*in nobis illi deformantur*), that is, in the church, and receive the wage of their labors."[3] In this rather mystical realism where the shaping and reshaping is mutual between testamental witnesses, the key thing seems to be living in the Spirit in such a way as to cut through time, as per *Haer.* 4.5.5: "Since, therefore, Abraham was a prophet and saw in the Spirit the day of the Lord's coming, and the dispensation of His suffering, through whom both he himself and all who, following the example of his faith, trust in God, should be saved, he rejoiced exceedingly."

Then there is Blackwell's observation that German scholars such as Ernst Dassmann and Rolf Noormann have had the wrong idea in claiming that Irenaeus is nothing like Paul on the matter of justification. Dassmann noted how ecclesial belonging was crucial for redemption on Irenaeus's account, but his point is perhaps

3. *Haer.* 4.22.2.

no more than any Reformer might have made: that participating in a late-medieval Catholic mass would make it almost impossible to receive justification by faith alone.[4] Belonging to the right tradition or church can make a large difference to whether one's faith is rightly directed. Irenaeus, on Dassmann's account, is tidying up a few Pauline (or Deutero-pauline?) loose ends. On inspection, Noormann, for his part ends up making Irenaeus look like Paul of the Sandersian ("old") New Perspective, since humans can be justified fully only by obedience ("staying in") with eyes on the future inheritance. Faith is opposed not to Law but only to outward ceremonial practices, including circumcision and Sabbath, in and by which Israel was constrained.[5] Law can be useful for believers now; for sons there is no bondage but the pre-Mosaic free obedience of faith (cf. *Haer.* 4.13.1), and without the practice of love there can be no salvation. Oddly, Noormann looks to Albrecht Ritschl and seems to rely on this work,[6] one that sees Irenaeus as untrue to Paul's gospel. Irenaeus certainly believes in an objective work of God into which those who have faith are incorporated, as they receive baptism and instruction. Blackwell wants to suggest that this charge of veering away from Paul is unfounded, not because Irenaeus looks like the New Perspective Paul of Sanders, but because he looks like the Paul of the Reformers, fully committed to covenants, forensic imputation, and the centrality of the faith principle. John Lawson's work[7] gets criticized for being "representative of a tired approach … how Irenaeus repeats Paul's own theology" so as to make him (Irenaeus) a true Protestant, for, as Blackwell says on the closing page, we need first to be surer what Paul's theology is before we can match Irenaeus up against him. Agreed, but we also have to do the same with Irenaeus's theology.

In line with the idea of the unity as harmony of two differing testaments Réal Tremblay has (rather too) boldly argued that for Irenaeus, the Father is he who is seen: 'Voir *Dieu*, pense encore notre auteur, c'est voir directement le Visage du propre Verbe-Fils de Dieu … la Face du Père de manière immédiate.'[8] I think Tremblay is on firmer ground when he goes on to conclude that "manifestation"

---

4. Ernst Dassmann, *Stachel im Fleisch. Paulus in der frühchristlichen Literatur bis Irenäus* (Münster: Aschendorff, 1979).

5. Rolf Noormann, *Irenäus als Paulusinterpret* (Tübingen: Mohr Siebeck, 1994), 418–19: "unter Glauben verstehen Irenäus 'die Gemüthsrichtung auf das zukünftige Erbe' und, gegen alle apostolische Denkweise und 'im Dienste einer werkthätigen Lebensrichtung,' die Erfüllung des Willens Gottes—und auf die bereits erwähnte Aussage, der Mensch werde durch die *naturalia legis* gerechtfertigt (13,1; 1f) Da Gegenüber zur Rechtfertigung aus Glauben bilden für Irenäus die Unterordnung unter Beschneidung, Sabbat und das übrige Mose-Gesetz sowie der mit diesem Gesetz verbundene äußere Gehorsame in Knechtschaft' … Der Glaube ist bei Irenäus eng mit dem Gehorsam verbunden."

6. Ritschl, *Entstehung der altkatholischen Kirche* (Bonn 1857²), 316.

7. John Lawson, *The Biblical Theology of Saint Irenaeus* (London: Epworth Press, 1948).

8. R. Tremblay, *La manifestation et la vision de Dieu selon saint Irenée de Lyon* (Collection Münsterische Beiträge zur Theologie 41; Münster: Aschendorff, 1978), 175–76.

means that God has a form, and that believers need not so much to see with their intellect as to enter into that "objective" glory, as a sphere or realm. It is a sensory-corporeal vision of the "logophanies" (to use M. Esnaola's term), because Abraham through the Spirit is effectively seeing Christ Incarnate, and that is what saves him. In *Haer* 5.1.2[9] Irenaeus explains that to see prophetically is to see what was future at the point. Also, in *Epid.* 45 it is no coincidence that the Logos at Mambre in Genesis 18 converses with human hosts, because that will happen in the incarnation. The principle coined by Tertullian of *caro-cardo*—"the flesh is the hinge (of salvation)"—that is precisely what the Gnostics deny even when they affirm an incarnation. No, corporeality belongs to the essential personhood of Jesus[10] that appeared to Abraham through the centuries. Only the manifestation in the Incarnation is "saving," although the Word apart from Incarnation "already had" a form and it is he, not the Father, who is seen directly (the Father only indirectly, *contra* Tremblay).

A major project on covenant in ante-Nicene theology was undertaken by J. L. Duncan: "It seems then that Irenaeus' fellow Christians in Lyons spoke precisely and appropriately (and perhaps with a little prescience) when they described him as 'zealous for the covenant of Christ' (Eusebius, *Ecclesiastical History*, 5.4.2)."[11] In Eusebius's text that is to say, "ζηλωτὴν ὄντα τῆς διαθήκης Χριστοῦ." But this seems to mean that the bishop of Lyons was zealous about the New Testament in book form, not the covenant of Christ as a theological theme, and since Irenaeus is the first to have four gospels and the thirteen Pauline Epistles, that would back this up. Furthermore, this is merely hearsay about what Irenaeus taught, not his *ipsissima vox*. Duncan writes, "One of the most frequently discussed and intriguing passages regarding the covenant in Irenaeus' writings is found in AH 3.11.8."[12] This reads as follows:

> For this reason were four principal (καθόλικαι) covenants given to the human race: (3) one, prior to the deluge, under Adam; the second, that after the deluge, under Noah; the third, the giving of the law, under Moses; the fourth, that which renovates man, and sums up all things in itself by means of the Gospel, raising and bearing men upon heavenly wings into the kingdom.

But Irenaeus does not expand on this matter of four covenants, because in truth he is only interested in the "fourness" corresponding to the four gospels, which

---

9. *Haer.* 5.1.2: *Praediximus autem quoniam Abraham et reliqui prophetae prophetice videbant eum, id quod futurum erat per visionem prophetantes.* (This is quite similar to Tertullian in *Marc.* 3.9.6: *in veritate quidem carnis apparuit, sed nondum natae, quia nondum moriturae, sed ediscentis iam inter homines conversari*).

10. M. Esnaola, *La amistad del verbo con Abraham según san Ireneo de Lyon* (Analecta Gregoriana 294; Rome, 2005), 53.

11. J. Ligon Duncan, "The Covenant Idea in Ante-Nicene Theology" (PhD dissertation, University of Edinburgh, 1995), 142.

12. Duncan, "The Covenant," 150 n.40.

are his real concern here; if a manifold covenant were central to his concerns, surely more would have been said. And in another passage that Duncan adduces, unfortunately "covenant" is not even mentioned.[13]

Susan Graham has attempted the more specific task of looking at the covenants in Irenaeus,[14] as the bishop himself puts it in *Haer.* 4.9.3: "successive covenants by which humanity gradually attains to salvation." The text reads,

> For the new covenant having been known and preached by the prophets, He who was to carry it out according to the good pleasure of the Father was also preached; having been revealed to men as God pleased; that they might always make progress through believing in Him, and by means of the [successive] covenants, should gradually attain to perfect salvation. For there is one salvation and one God; but the precepts which form the man are numerous, and the steps which lead man to God are not a few.

Whereas *recapitulatio* (or ἀνακεφαλαίωσις) appears only sixty times in Irenaeus's oeuvre, διαθήκη is found eighty-five times, Graham remarks. (Although in a number of places Irenaeus is talking about the "testamentum [διαθήκη]" as canonical book, not about "covenant" as a theological term.) Now, Graham admits it is clearer in *Epid.* (e.g., 5 and 11) and that a covenant there clearly is something involving "real relations" between God and humanity. Moreover at *Epid.* 12, the Word is said to have walked and talked with man in the Garden, "figuring beforehand the things that should be in the future, that He should dwell with him and talk with him and should be with men, teaching them righteousness."[15] Well, this *could* be covenantal, but if so, then it is pretty unilateral in nature. Graham comments: "In the *Epideixis* all other human encounters with the Word before his Incarnation are prophetic of visionary (*Epid.* 42b-65)—whereas the covenant ones are more than that,"[16] and these covenants provide a counterpoint to a seven-stage

---

13. *Haer.* 4.9.2: "And shall make progress, so that no longer through a glass, or by means of enigmas, but face to face, we shall enjoy the gifts of God;—so also now, receiving more than the temple, and more than Solomon, that is, the advent of the Son of God, we have not been taught another God besides the Framer and the Maker of all, who has been pointed out to us from the beginning; nor another Christ, the Son of God, besides Him who was foretold by the prophets."

14. Susan L. Graham, "Irenaeus and the Covenants: 'Immortal Diamond,'" *Studia Patristica* 40 (Leuven: Peeters, 2006), 393–98. This helps to summarize Susan L. Graham, "'Zealous for the Covenant': Irenaeus and the Covenants of Israel" (PhD dissertation, University of Notre Dame, 2001). Cf. Charles Kannengiesser, "The 'Speaking God' and Irenaeus' Interpretative Pattern: The Reception of Genesis," *Annali di storia dell'esegesi* 15 (1998), 337–52.

15. Graham, "Zealous," 394. Graham seems disappointed that large studies such as those by Fantino, Behr, and Osborn hardly notice "covenant" in Irenaeus.

16. Graham, "Zealous," 395, *pace* Denis Minns, *Irenaeus* (London: Geoffrey Chapman, 1994), 49. Minns argues (in my view quite rightly) that what was revealed was the Son,

pattern of sin and judgment. But are the covenant encounters more than that, really? If Irenaeus desired to show a progressive history of redemption in the Old Testament history, why then does *Epid.* 29–30 have only a paragraph and a half on David and the Old Testament Monarchy, out of which Jesus came? Also, despite Graham's claims that "covenant" is structuring the work, in the long section (24) on Abraham, "covenanted" is used once only and then concerning circumcision.

However, Irenaeus is not all that interested in Israel or the Law, or the covenant(s) for that matter; he is much more concerned with creation and the Creator God, who is attested as sovereignly working with his creation, developing it through promise, prophecy, and providence and leading it toward perfection in and through the Son and the Spirit on earth. This is why Genesis and the prophets dominate in his use of the Old Testament. Having said that, the whole of the Bible matters: 'scripturae dominicae ... bezeichnet die ganze Bibel.'[17]

What then about the category of covenant in Irenaeus? Well, Ben Blackwell wants us to notice just how important a covenantal theology was for Irenaeus, and perhaps it is. Abraham set up the key covenant and thus is more than just a good example of a faithful person. Admittedly so, but does this get in the way of the more typical and frequent Adam-typology, the famous doctrine of recapitulation? It might, as when Blackwell ponders on the basis of Jon Levenson. Levenson's comments about Paul could apply to Irenaeus:

> One cannot adequately grasp Paul's theology without reckoning with this simple but momentous fact: for Paul, the Gentile Christian has abandoned the Adamic identity for the Abrahamic. He has left the universal identity associated with the sin-infected human essence and been recreated as one who attains righteousness in the sight of God on the basis of his faith, just as Abraham did in the Pauline reading of Genesis 15.6.[18]

In his chapter, Blackwell states, "The children of Abraham who share in his faith in the saving, re-creative work of God in Christ, are part of a new family uniting Jews and Gentiles who will enjoy the inheritance of a renewed creation." Admittedly, a text such as the following *might* inspire that train of thought, namely *Haer.* 4.5.4:

---

and Irenaeus understood the theophanies, the revelations of God in the Old Testament, to be not so much visions of God as anticipatory, prophetic visions of God incarnate, while avoiding, even correcting Justin's notion of "two gods."

17. Norbert Brox, "Die biblische Hermeneutik des Irenaeus," *Zeitschrift für Antikes Christentum* 2 (1998), 27.

18. Jon D. Levenson, *Inheriting Abraham: The Legacy of the Patriarch in Judaism, Christianity, and Islam* (Princeton: Princeton University, 2012), 157. Cf. also Jon Levenson, *The Death and Resurrection of the Beloved Son: The Transformation of Child Sacrifice in Judaism and Christianity* (New Haven: Yale, 1993).

Righteously also the apostles, being of the race of Abraham, left the ship and their father, and followed the Word. Righteously also do we, possessing the same faith as Abraham, and taking up the cross as Isaac did the wood follow Him. For in Abraham man had learned beforehand, and had been accustomed to follow the Word of God. For Abraham, according to his faith, followed the command of the Word of God, and with a ready mind delivered up, as a sacrifice to God, his only-begotten and beloved Son, in order that God also might be pleased to offer up for all his seed His own beloved and only-begotten Son, as a sacrifice for our redemption.

So that, just as Abraham, so God; just as we have faith, so God responds. But is it really the case that Adamic identity has been "abandoned," to use Levenson's language? For Paul and a fortiori for Irenaeus the recapitulation of disobedient Adam in the obedient Second Adam does not mean dropping Adam in order to take on a new Abrahamic identity. If anything, faith presupposes God's initiative in which something first has to be done on the inside to the human condition, and faith in any case is faith in that perfect Adam, Jesus Christ. "And conquer by Adam that which by Adam had stricken us down."[19]

---

19. *Epid.* 30.

Chapter 7

TEACHING THE RULE OF FAITH IN LOVE: IRENAEUS ON 1 CORINTHIANS 8:1

Scott D. Moringiello

What does love know? And what does knowledge love? Is there anyone who can teach the difference between love and knowledge? In 1 Cor 8:1, Paul notes that knowledge (γνῶσις) puffs up (φυσιοι), but that love (ἀγαπή) builds up (οἰκοδομει). Paul warns that "if anyone supposes that he knows something, he does not yet know as he ought." These are troubling words for anyone who hopes to know something of God. Paul shifts the discussion from the human supposition of knowledge to the human desire to love God. For if "someone loves God, then he is known by him" (8:3). The immediate context for Paul's distinction between love and knowledge is the question of whether the followers of Christ in Corinth should eat meat that has been sacrificed to pagan idols. There is a related question at the beginning of the letter about who is the proper teacher and on what basis that teacher's authority rests. That authority ultimately derives from the "one God, the Father, from whom all things are and for whom we exist, and one Lord Jesus Christ through whom all things are and through whom we exist" (1 Cor 8:6). Those who love the one God and the one Lord are known by him. This love brings unity because the one community is united in love and united with the one God in love. The teacher helps bring this unity by reminding the people what God commands of them. There are times, however, when the knowledge of certain members of the community can threaten the unity of the community as a whole. For example, Paul warns his audience that "weaker" members of the community might be confused when they see more knowledgeable members of the community eating meat that has been sacrificed to idols. That weaker member might think that the idols are real gods. "Thus through your knowledge, the weak person is brought to destruction, the brother for whom Christ died" (1 Cor 8:10-11). Paul believes the Corinthians have been led astray by their teachers. These teachers have not preached the love that builds up, but they have displayed by their actions the knowledge that puffs up. Their actions have divided the community, which should be unified, and they threaten to divide it further.

These are familiar themes to a reader of *Against Heresies*. Like Paul, Irenaeus worries that his audience has been led astray by false teachers. Like Paul, Irenaeus argues that these teachers have brandished their knowledge and neglected the love that builds up the community. And like Paul, Irenaeus worries that by following knowledge rather than love, his audience compromises the unity of God. Irenaeus does not spend a great deal of time in his writings on a sustained and clear exegesis of 1 Corinthians 8. Yet I want to argue that the distinction between love and knowledge—ἀγαπή and γνῶσις—is key to understanding Irenaeus's scriptural hermeneutics. There has been a robust scholarly discussion about the rule of faith in Irenaeus and in early Christianity more generally. Apart from two important articles,[1] there has not been a sustained discussion on the relationship between love and knowledge in Irenaeus. As far as I know, there has been no discussion linking 1 Corinthians 8 with the rule of faith in Irenaeus. This chapter aims to fill that lacuna, and it will do so by showing the role of the teacher in explaining the rule of faith.

I will argue that Irenaeus uses the rule of faith to understand the economy of salvation. More specifically, he argues that human beings are *within* and not *above* that economy. And just as the Word became flesh to be part of the economy of salvation and teach God's people, so too human teachers are not somehow above the economy of salvation. True teachers teach that God's love builds up the economy, and they follow Paul in knowing that ersatz knowledge puffs up. On this account, then, the church, which is also within the economy of salvation, guards the rule of faith and acts as a place where God's love can be understood and celebrated. The church is the community where God's love is built up. While Irenaeus categorizes the teachers in the church as teaching the love that builds up, he categorizes his opponents as preaching a knowledge that puffs up. Irenaeus links Satan during the temptation of Christ with Simon Magus in Acts with Marcion and with Valentinus and all his followers. All of these teachers, on Irenaeus's account, are puffed up. They all sought knowledge outside the economy of love that is to be found in the proper reading of the scriptures. Like Paul's correspondents in Corinth, their "knowledge" has divided them from the community.[2]

Irenaeus's opponents threaten the unity of the church because they do not teach the rule of faith that the church teaches. For Irenaeus, the rule of faith enables the reader of scripture to see how the scriptures recount the economy of salvation that the one God the Creator and Father of Jesus Christ offers to human beings. One can only be a part of the economy of salvation when one recognizes one's own knowledge must be at the service of God's love. Recognizing this means recognizing that God's love builds up, and it means that one is built up by God's

---

1. D. Jeffrey Bingham, "Knowledge and Love in Irenaeus of Lyons," *StPatr* 36 (2000), 184–99; Richard A. Norris, "Irenaeus' Use of Paul in His Polemic against the Gnostics," in *Paul and the Legacies of Paul*, ed. W. S. Babcock (Dallas: Southern Methodist University Press, 1990), 79–98.

2. For a discussion of how certain "gnostic" teachers divided themselves from the Christian community in Rome, see John Behr, *Irenaeus of Lyons: Identifying Christianity* (Oxford: Oxford University Press, 2013), 21–47.

love. This, Irenaeus would stress, is Paul's message to the Corinthians. Irenaeus, like Paul, stresses that the community needs proper teachers to understand the rule of faith. Irenaeus, like Paul, links the discussion of love and knowledge in 1 Corinthians 8 with his focus on the one God and one Christ. Thus one cannot understand the rule of faith without also understanding the role of the teacher in passing on that rule of faith and understanding the proper relationship between love and knowledge. I will make my argument in three steps. First, I want to offer some brief background from ancient rhetorical theory that will set Irenaeus's argument in context. Second, I want to point to Irenaeus's exposition of the rule of faith in Book 1 of *Against Heresies* to ground our discussion. And third, I want to chart Irenaeus's discussions of and allusions to 1 Cor 8:1. I will pay particular attention to how he uses "puffed up (φυσιόω/*elatos*)." Irenaeus returns, again and again, to height metaphors in his discussion. Those who teach and follow the apostolic rule of faith and respond to God's love are *within* the economy of salvation; those who valorize their own knowledge think they are somehow *above* the economy of salvation.

First, then, some context from ancient rhetorical theory. When he discusses the rule of faith in Book 1, Irenaeus, refers to the *hypothesis* of scripture, and throughout the text he refers to the *oikonomia* of God's creation and salvation.[3] The *hypothesis* of an ancient speech would be its overall theme. The speech's *oikonomia* would be how the speech was organized. It is important to note, though, that *hypothesis* and *oikonomia* involve the audience as well as the orator. *Hypothesis*, of course, means "place before." The reader of a text or the listener of a speech must "accede" to what the author or speaker has placed before him. He has to "imagine" it in the same way the orator or poet does. *Oikonomia*, similarly, refers to the "psychological preparation of the reader" as well as to the ordering that the author or orator proposes. In a deep way, then, the intellectual milieu in which Irenaeus was educated recognized that oratory implies community. If that community were not united in some way, it would cease to be a community and the communication between orator and audience would not occur.

Irenaeus worries that certain teachers have led certain members of the Christian community astray. Their "knowledge" has torn the community apart. This is why he writes *Against Heresies* in the first place. At the beginning of the text, Irenaeus announces that he will detect and overthrow knowledge falsely so-called. Ultimately, though, Irenaeus's concern is not "gnosticism" or certain "gnostic" teachers. His concern is with the proper interpretation of scripture and more specifically with the proper principles one must keep in mind while interpreting scripture. The most important principle for Irenaeus is the love of God offered in

---

3. In this paragraph I draw on Roos Meijering, *Literary and Rhetorical Theories in Greek Scholia* (Groningen: E. Forsten, 1987), see esp. 107, 129, 134, 200. For a full discussion of Irenaeus's use of ancient rhetoric, see Scott D. Moringiello, "Irenaeus Rhetor" (PhD dissertation, University of Notre Dame, 2008). See also Robert M. Grant, *Irenaeus of Lyons* (New York: Routledge, 1997).

Christ through the economy of scripture. Other teachers, however, believe that the most important principle of scriptural interpretation is the salvific knowledge that Christ brings. Irenaeus aims to counter those who "pervert according to the persuasion of their exegesis,"[4] because "each one of their sayings damages the truth, abusing the names, transferring it into their own hypothesis."[5] In order to overthrow the rule because of its instability he must first detect it because of its persuasiveness.

The hypothesis that Irenaeus opposes persuades in part because it appeals to its audience's knowledge. Its plan of scriptures places a very specific class of human beings at the center of the economy of salvation. Valentinus and his disciples focus on the πνευματικός of 1 Corinthians 2, the spiritual human being who judges all and is judged by no one.[6] Unlike the gnostic rule, which is available only to spiritual human beings, believers in the apostolic tradition receive the rule of truth at baptism. Because of it, they know "the names from the scriptures and the laws and the parables."[7] Thanks to this rule, the teacher of the apostolic tradition hands down "each of the sayings in its own order" and through the body of truth "denudes and shows as insubstantial" "the fabrication" of the gnostics.[8] The rule of truth enables the believer to see that all gnostic persuasion is seduction. The individual believers will "be judged most accurately and for the demonstration, the foundation on which the church proclaims the truth and from this confounds lies."[9] At the heart of these lies is a profound misunderstanding of how to interpret the words of scripture.

---

4. *Haer.* 1.9.2, οὗτοι παρατρέποντες κατὰ τὸ πιθανὸν τὴν ἐξήγησιν.

5. *Haer.* 1.9.2, καὶ ἓν ἕκαστον τῶν εἰρημένων ἄραντες ἀπὸ τῆς ἀληθείας, καταχρησάμενοι τοῖς ὀνόμασιν, εἰς τὴν ἰδίαν ὑπόθεσιν μετήνεγκαν.

6. See Scott D Moringiello, "The *Pneumatikos* as Scriptural Interpreter: Irenaeus on 1 Cor 2:15," *StPatr* 65 (2013), 105–18.

7. *Haer.* 1.9.4, τὰ μὲν ἐκ τῶν γραφῶν ὀνόματα, καὶ τὰς λέξεις, καὶ τὰς παραβολὰς ἐπιγνώσετα. On the rule of truth in Book 1, see Thomas C. K. Ferguson, "The Rule of Truth and Irenaean Rhetoric in Book 1 of Against Heresies," *VC* 55 (2001), 356–75. On rhetoric in Book 1 more generally, see Pheme Perkins, "Irenaeus and the Gnostics: Rhetoric and Composition in Adversus Haereses Book One," *VC* 30.3 (1976), 193–200.

8. *Haer.* 1.9.4, ἓν ἕκαστον δὲ τῶν εἰρημένων ἀποδοὺς τῇ ἰδίᾳ τάξει, καὶ προσαρμόσας τῷ τῆς ἀληθείας σωματίῳ, γυμνώσει καὶ ἀνυπόστατον ἐπιδείξει τὸ πλάσμα αὐτῶν.

9. *Haer.* 1.9.5, Καὶ ἐκ τούτου γὰρ ἀκριβῶς συνιδεῖν ἔσται, καὶ πρὸ τῆς ἀποδείξεως, βεβαίαν τὴν ὑπὸ τῆς Ἐκκλησίας κηρυσσομένην ἀλήθειαν, καὶ τὴν ὑπὸ τούτων παραπεποιημένην ψευδηγορίαν. D. B. Reynders, "Paradosis: Le progrès et l'idée de tradition jusqu'à saint Irénée," *Recherches de théologie ancienne et médiévale* 5 (1933), 18–19, states, "L'exégèse hérètique ramène la parole divine à un systèm subjectif construit à priori. L'exégèse de S. Irénée vérifie l'harmonie de tous les aspect et de toutes les formes de la parole divine. Le 'caractère' gnostique est créé par l'individu. Le cors de verité est, par l'intermediare de l'Eglise, reçu cu de Dieu."

Irenaeus does not tell us *how* the rule of faith ought to be applied to the scriptures. Nor does he give us a general template to decode difficult scriptural passages. Instead, the rule of faith states who God is, that God has created, and that God through Christ has redeemed his creation. Here, of course, we hear echoes of Paul's words in 1 Cor 8:6. There is one God, the Father, and one Lord Jesus Christ. Because he sets it up in contrast to the gnostic teachers, one of Irenaeus's central concerns in his rehearsal of the rule of faith is unity. Just as there is one God, there is one community of God's people who are united in baptism. There are no "classes" of Christians. The rule unifies the church, it unifies the scriptures, and it most importantly unifies how the church reads the scriptures. Irenaeus points out that the church is "spread through the whole economy to the end of the earth"[10] and has one rule of faith. The church "diligently guards this preaching and this faith that she has received as if living in one house."[11] Indeed, even if the "languages of the world are different ... still the strength of the tradition is one and the same."[12]

At this point, a word of explanation is in order for the term *oikonomia*.[13] Although the manifestation of God in Christ is the central message—the true hypothesis—in Irenaeus's work, it would be fair to say that Irenaeus's most distinctive contribution is the understanding of Christ within the economy of God's salvific plan.[14] Irenaeus is not the first author to discuss *oikonomia*. Although we do not find the word in 1 Corinthians, we do find it in the letter to the Ephesians.[15] The gnostic teachings present a danger because "they repudiate the teaching of Christ and ... they argue against the entire economy of God."[16] In order for Irenaeus to prove the gnostic teaching wrong, he must persuade his audience that Jesus Christ is the fulfillment of the Hebrew prophets and the Son of the same God who created the universe.

---

10. *Haer.* 1.10.1, ὅλης τῆς οἰκουμένης ἕως περάτων τῆς γῆς διεσπαρμένη.

11. *Haer.* 1.10.2, τοῦτο τὸ κήρυγμα παρειληφυῖα καὶ ταύτην πίστιν ... ἐπιμελῶς φθλάσσει ὡς ἕνα οἶκον οἰκοῦσα, καὶ τὴν αὐτὴν ἔχοθσα καρδιαν. Cf. Acts 4:32. Irenaeus's use of οἶκος here is suggestive.

12. *Haer.* 1.10.2, καὶ γὰρ εἰ αἱ κατὰ τὸν κόσμον διάλεκτοι ἀνόμοιαι, ἀλλ' ἡ δύναμις τῆς παραδόσεως μία καὶ ἡ αὐτή.

13. On the difference between "apostolic" and "gnostic" understandings of *oikonomia*, see D. Jeffrey Bingham, *Irenaeus' Use of Matthew's Gospel in* Adversus haereses (Louvain: Peeters, 1998), 52.

14. On Irenaeus's use of *oiknonomia* generally, see A. d'Ales, "Le mot 'oikonomia' dans la langue théologique de saint Irénée," *Revue des Etudes Grecques* 32 (1919), 1–9.

15. Eph 1:10. Gerhard Richter, *Oikonomia: Der Gebrauch des Wortes Oikonomia im Neuen Testament, bei den Kirchenvätern und in der theologischen Literatur bis ins 20. Jahrhundert* (AKG 90; Berlin: De Gruyter, 2005), 94. See also Jacques Fantino, *La theologie d'Iréné. Lecture des Écritures en reponse à l'exégèse gnostique: Une approche trinitaire* (Paris: Éditions du Cerf, 1994), 108–16.

16. *Haer.* 4.1.1, *et doctrinam quidem Christi praetermittentes, et a semetipsis autem falsa divinantes, adversus universam Dei dispositionem argumentantur.*

In other words, he, like Paul, must stress that the rule of faith requires that the scriptures be read with one God and one Lord Jesus Christ in mind.

We should note too that there is a rhetorical as well as Pauline precedent for *oikonomia*. For the rhetor, *oikonomia* is the arrangement of the speech after he has decided what points he will discuss.[17] Of course, the word *oikonomia* itself means the management of a household. And it is in this sense that the economy of God can be understood as God's rule over and care for creation.[18] We can view creation and the history of salvation as God's ordered *oikonomia*, the management of God's household. And if we remember that Christ is the Word of God, we can see that all of creation is, in a real sense, God's speech that through Christ God recapitulates.[19]

By recapitulating the entire economy of salvation, God unifies. Love, Irenaeus wants to stress, unites the community of God's people. Love is the hypothesis and *oikonomia* of scripture. Love is the beginning and end of interpretation. Any teacher who teaches differently leads his students toward their own "knowledge" and away from God's love. By leading his students toward their own knowledge, such a teacher lifts them out of the economy of salvation that Christ recapitulates, the scriptures recount, and the church lives.

We are now in a position to examine Irenaeus's text more closely. First, I want to examine his most "systematic" discussion of 1 Cor 8:1, which we find in Book 2, chapters 25–28. After we examine this passage, we will be in a position to examine passages where Irenaeus alludes to 1 Cor 8:1 while discussing specific teachers. That is, we begin with a discussion of how Irenaeus understands the distinction between love and knowledge, and then we move to Irenaeus's discussion of how other teachers teach (or, in most cases, confound) that distinction. All of this, I would argue, is very much in keeping with Paul's discussion in 1 Corinthians. Irenaeus develops Paul's teaching to apply to interpreting the scriptures and the economy of salvation that they recount.

Chapters 25–28 of Book 2 follow Irenaeus's refutation of his opponents' arguments about the relationship between numerology and exegesis, or better, how his opponents applied numerology that was based on their understanding of the Pleroma to the Gospel texts.[20] Although Irenaeus does not accuse his

---

17. See George Kennedy, *The Art of Persuasion in Greece* (Princeton, NJ: Princeton University Press, 1963), 304.

18. See Richter, *Oikonomia*, 15. See also Fantino, *La théologie d'Irénée*, 117–19.

19. As John Behr writes, "The divine economy thus begins in the glory which the Word had with the Father before the creation of the world, and culminates in the glorification of the Incarnate Son by the Father, a glory in which the disciples, by beholding it, participate" (*Asceticism and Anthropology in Irenaeus and Clement* [Oxford: Oxford University Press, 2000], 37). Fantino lists four different senses of economy at work in Irenaeus (*La théologie d'Irénée*, 93).

20. Chapters 25 through 28 clearly form a unit because at the beginning of chapter 25 Irenaeus discusses names and at the end of chapter 28, he says he has talked enough about what Valentinians do to numbers and names. *Haer*. 2.25.1 and 2.28.9. Irenaeus often bookends his arguments this way. See, e.g., *Haer*. 4.33.1 and 4.33.15.

opponents of eating meat that has been sacrificed to idols, he does accuse them of using their "knowledge" to shape the scriptures to their liking.[21] The difference between building up and puffing up is the difference between harmonizing one's interpretation with the harmony already present in the scriptures and creating one's own harmony and forcing the scriptures to conform to that.[22] Any interpretative scheme should be at the service of understanding the scriptures themselves. This is why the rule of faith conforms to the *oikonomia* and uncovers the true *hypothesis* of the scriptures. The scriptures—and indeed all of creation—do not exist to valorize our interpretative schemes. Irenaeus writes, "For rule does not come from numbers, but numbers from the rule; nor does God come from what is made, but what is made comes from God. For all things originate from one and the same God."[23] Paul assumed the Corinthians knew there was only one God; Irenaeus is not so sure of his opponents. It is hard not to hear Paul's distinction between knowledge puffing up and love building up when Irenaeus admonishes his reader: "Preserve the order of your knowledge and do not try to rise above God himself."[24]

The issue for Irenaeus is not knowledge per se; the issue is falling away from God's love because of the false pretense of knowledge. This pretense puffs up and

---

21. Although my argument does not engage with them because I am specifically discussing love rather than philosophy, I should note that there has been a robust scholarly discussion of the role of Greek philosophy in Irenaeus's theological method. William R. Schoedel, "Theological Method in Irenaeus (*Adversus haereses* 2:25-28)," *JTS* 35.1 (1984), 31–49. Schoedel builds off earlier studies, especially Robert M. Grant, "Irenaeus and Hellenistic Culture," *HTR* 42.1 (1949), 41–51. In his article, Grant tried to correct earlier articles by Reynders, "Paradosis"; Morton Scott Enslin, "Irenaeus: Mostly Prolegomena," *HTR* 40.3 (1947), 137–65; and Th-André Audet, "Orientations théologiques chez Saint Irénée: le contexte mental d'une *gnōsis alēthēs*," *Traditio* 1 (1943), 15–54; these claimed Irenaeus had little formation in the Hellenistic culture of his time. Philip J. Hefner, "Theological Methodology and St Irenaeus," *JR* 44.4 (1964), 294–309, focuses on the importance of the hypothesis of scripture or the rule of faith in Irenaeus's theological method. Hefner does not address broader cultural issues in his article. See also the important article by Anthony Briggman, "Revisiting Irenaeus' Philosophical Acumen," *VC* 65.2 (2011), 115–24; and Michel Rene Barnes, "Irenaeus's Trinitarian Theology," *Nova et Vetera* 7.1 (2009), 67–106, who argues that Irenaeus borrowed from Stoicism.

22. As John Behr notes, Irenaeus sees scripture as a "'treasury' of images, words, and reports, which give flesh to the Christ proclaimed by the Apostles, who in turn reveals the work of God deployed throughout the whole economy described in Scripture." Behr, *Irenaeus of Lyons*, 128. Behr notes his own indebtedness to James L. Kugel, *The Bible as It Was* (Cambridge, MA: Belknap Press, 1997).

23. *Haer.* 2.25.1, *Non enim regula ex numeris, sed numeri ex regula, neque Deus ex factis, sed ea quae facta sunt ex Deo; omnia ex uno et eodem Deo*.

24. *Ordinem ergo serva tuae scientiae et ne ut bonorum ignarus supertranscendas ipsum Deum*.

makes Irenaeus's opponents think that they have risen above the God who created the universe and reached the God and Father of Jesus Christ. Because they have the wrong hypothesis of scripture, they miss scripture's *oikonomia*. Yet Irenaeus uses Paul to argue that such "knowledge" is not truly knowledge because it puffs one up out of the economy of salvation. If *this* is what you mean by knowledge, Irenaeus wants to say, it is better to "know" nothing. For such people, Irenaeus writes, it would be better if they knew very little and "came close to God through love (*caritas*)" than "think they had risen above their creator" (*Haer.* 2.26.1). These people should "believe God and remain in his love (*dilectione*)"[25] rather than be "puffed up by this kind of knowledge which cuts them off from the love that gives life to human beings" (*Haer.* 2.26.1). Irenaeus believes that one should not "go in search of knowledge about anything else than Jesus Christ, the Son of God, who was crucified for us, than through subtle questions and hairsplitting to fall into impiety."[26]

It should be no surprise that Christ crucified is the key to understanding God's love. This is another way of saying that Christ crucified is the key to understanding the scriptures.[27] Irenaeus claims that his opponents are more concerned with subtle questions and hairsplitting points about the scriptures than they are about understanding the scriptures as a guide to God's love. When someone looks for a literal understanding of God counting the hairs on one's head (cf. Matt 10:30) or numbering the sparrows that fall to the earth (cf. Matt 10:29), he "thinks that he himself has found more than the others, and he calls the rest unskilled and idiotic and animal-like because they do not take up such vain work." Notice that here again the pretense of knowledge leads to a separation within the community. Irenaeus uses the metaphor of lifting up to describe what such a person does. "Through the knowledge he thinks he has found, he changes God. And he throws his thought above the greatness of the Creator."[28] With his talk of knowledge

---

25. The Latin translation of Irenaeus uses two different words for love. In John's Gospel, though, from which Irenaeus must have been drawing, we find ἀγαπή used twice. See John 15:9-10.

26. *Haer.* 2.26.1, Ἄμεινον <οὖν> καὶ συμφερώτερον ἰδιώτας καὶ ὀλιγομαθεῖς ὑπάρχειν καὶ διὰ τῆς ἀγαπης πλησίον γενέσθαι τοῦ θεοῦ ἢ πολυμαθεῖς καὶ ἐμπείροθς δοκοῦντας εἶναι βλασφήμοθς εἰς τὸν ἑαυτῶν εὑρίσκεσθαι Δεσπότην. *Melius itaque est, sicut praedixi, nihil omnino scientiam quempiam, ne quidem unam causam cuiuslibet eorum quae facta sunt cur factum sit, credere Deo et perservare eos in dilectione, aut per huiusmodi scientiam inflatos excidere a delietione quae hominem vivificat, neque aliud inquirere ad scientiam nisi Iesum Christum Filium Dei qui pro nobis crufixus est (1 Cor 2.2) aut per quaestionem subtilitates et minutiloquium impietatem cadere.*

27. See Behr, *Irenaeus of Lyons*, 133.

28. *Haer.* 2.26.3, *Et quo magis praeter ceteros in huiusmodi quaestinibus occupater et plus aliis ad invenire se existimat, reliquos imperitos et idiotas et animales vocans eo quod non suscipiant eius tam vanum laborem, hoc magis insanus est et stupidus, tamquam fulmine percussus in nullo cedens Deo; sed per scientiam quam invenisse se putat ipsum mutat Deum, et iaculatur sententiam suam super magnitudinem Factoris.*

lifting up, Irenaeus surely has Paul in mind here. For Irenaeus and Paul, there is no "above" God. The God and Father of Jesus Christ is the creator of all. Anyone who attempts to use his knowledge to lift himself above the creator ends up taking himself out of the economy of God's salvation.

True knowledge recognizes that God's love is the hypothesis and the *oikonomia* of the scriptures.[29] True knowledge is grounded in love, and this love helps the reader to understand that the point of the scriptures is not to count hairs or falling sparrows but to grow in the relationship of God's saving love. For Irenaeus *this* is why the rule of faith is so important. In Irenaeus's mind, one does not simply *know* the truth, one *loves* the truth. And as Irenaeus writes, a person who "loves the truth" will seek out the things that "God gave to the power of human beings and handed over to our knowledge" (*Haer.* 2.27.1). Indeed, if one focuses on what God has granted to human knowledge, such a person will "progress in them and by daily study, make the knowledge of them easy."[30] To find the knowledge of God grounded in the scriptures, one must adhere to the rule of truth. Without it, a person would always be searching, but never finding "because he has rejected the very method of investigation."[31]

The love of God, shown forth in Christ's crucifixion and at the very heart of the scriptures, safeguards reason; it makes sure that people do not interpret the scriptures irrationally.[32] By adhering to the rule of faith in one's interpretation of

---

29. In recent articles Paul Blowers and Nathan MacDonald have disagreed about the rule of faith in Irenaeus: Paul M. Blowers, "The Regula Fidei and the Narrative Character of Early Christian Faith," *Pro Ecclesia* 6.2 (1997), 199–228; Nathan MacDonald, "Israel and the Old Testament Story in Irenaeus's Presentation of the Rule of Faith," *Journal of Theological Interpretation* 3.2 (September 1, 2009), 281–98. For Blowers, the rule of faith ought to be "understood precisely as an identification with and 'in' a narrative" ("The Regula Fidei," 202). MacDonald argues, however, that the rule "is not identical with Scripture, nor does it trace Scriptures's narrative plot. Rather the Rule of Faith provides Scripture's hypothesis" ("Israel and the Old Testament Story," 290). If my basic point here is correct, a focus on love and especially love in the context of 1 Corinthians 8 can help navigate these waters. For Irenaeus one cannot talk about the rule without simultaneously talking about both hypothesis and oikonomia. Both are two sides of the same coin of God's love.

30. *Haer.* 2.27.1, Ὁ <δὲ> ὑγιὴς νοῦς καὶ ἀκίνδυνος καὶ εὐλαβὴς καὶ φιλαλήθης, ὅσα ἐν τῇ ἡμετέρᾳ γνώσει ταῦτα προθύμως ἐκμελετήσει καὶ ἐν αὐτῆς προκόει διὰ τῆς καθημερινῆς ἀσκήσεως ῥᾳδίαν τὴν μάθησιν αὐτῶν ποιούμενος.

31. *Haer.* 2.27.2, *Itaque secundum hanc rationem homo quidem semper inquiret, numquam autem inveniet, eo quod ipsam inventionis abiecerit disciplinam.*

32. Eric Osborn has argued for the importance of reason in the rule of faith. As he notes, "The rule did not limit reason to make room for faith but used faith to make room for reason. With a credible first principle, reason was lost in an infinite regress." Eric F. Osborn, "Reason and the Rule of Faith in the Second Century AD," in *Making of Orthodoxy: Essays in Honour of Henry Chadwick*, ed. Rowan Williams (Cambridge: Cambridge University Press, 1989), 57. My point in this chapter is that love for Irenaeus, as for Paul, is that credible first principle.

the scriptures and investigating "the mystery and economy of the existing God," one can "grow in the love of the one who has done and does so much for us."[33] This, of course, is the love that builds up. With love as the criterion for interpretation, one focuses on what God has done for humanity in his economy of salvation. Any questions about the scriptures that do not focus on love are mere distractions whose aim is to lift one outside that economy.

To say that love is the beginning of interpretation and its goal is to say that scriptural interpretation is not simply or even primarily about *knowledge*. We could say instead that scriptural interpretation is about love, that is, growing in one's relationship with God in the economy of salvation. Human beings can grow in this relationship because they have learned about God's love from God himself, who is their teacher. As Irenaeus notes, "For faith in our teacher continues firm, assuring us that there is only one who is truly God and that we should really love God always, since he alone is Father." This faith leads to a hope "to receive something more and to learn from God that he is good and possesses unlimited riches, an eternal kingdom, and infinite knowledge."[34] Notice here that faith and hope and love (an obvious allusion to 1 Corinthians 13) lead to "infinite knowledge." True knowledge of God cannot come apart from these three.

By stressing that God the Father is a teacher, Irenaeus implicitly contrasts the true teaching, based in love, that comes from God himself, with the false teaching, based on falsely so-called knowledge, that comes from his opponents. The Father's teaching is also the Son's teaching, for without the revelation of the Son, the love of the Father would remain unknown. Yet like Paul, Irenaeus knows that there are some led astray by false teaching about Christ. Such people are "puffed up in an irrational manner." They believe that they know "all the ineffable mysteries of God" even though Christ himself "admitted that the Father alone knows the very day of judgement and the hour."[35] Irenaeus's choice of words here is suggestive. Those who assert these things are "puffed up" and they are puffed up irrationally. Any puffing up that occurs because the reader of scripture thinks he knows more than he does is always irrational. To try to be "above" the teaching of Christ is, simply, to try to be above the economy of love that the scriptures recount and that Christ—himself part of that economy—interprets. Indeed, Christ's revelation is part of the Father's loving pedagogy in the economy of salvation. Anyone asking why Christ said only the Father knows the hour or the day, Irenaeus writes that

---

33. *Haer.* 2.28.1, *exerceri quidem convenit per inquisitionem mysterii et dispositionis exsistentis Dei augeri autem in caritate eius qui tanta propter nos fecit et facit.*

34. *Haer.* 2.28.3, *Semper enim fides quae est ad magistrum nostrum permanet firma, adseverans nobis quoniam solus vere Deus, et ut diligamus eum semper, quoniam ipse solus Pater, et speremus subinde plus aliquid accipere et discere a Deo, quia bonus est et divitias habens indeterminabiles et regnum sine fine et disiplinam immensam.*

35. *Haer.* 2.28.6, *Irrationabiliter autem inflati, audaciter inenarrabilia Dei mysteria scire vos dicitas, quandoquidem et Dominus, ipse Filius Dei, ipsum iudicii diem et horam concessit scire solum Patrem.*

such a person "will find no more fitting, proper, or safe answer in the present life than this, namely that we might learn through the Lord who alone is the true teacher, that the Father is above all things."³⁶

Christ shares the responsibility of teaching with his followers. As Paul knew, this is one of the most important responsibilities that his followers have. That is why Paul spends so much time in his letters correcting misunderstandings of Christ and what Christ desires from his followers. As we have seen, the distinction between the love that builds up and the knowledge that puffs up comes from Paul himself. Irenaeus draws on Paul (and on 1 Corinthians) again in noting that if knowledge were central to the economy of salvation, even though Christ himself avowed complete knowledge, then Paul would not have said that we "know only in part, and we prophesy only in part" (1 Cor 13:9). Anyone who claims to have complete knowledge claims too much. This is to recognize that there are some questions that the scriptures raise that we cannot answer. "So in proportion to our partial knowledge, we ought to leave all difficulties up to him who presents grace in part."³⁷ Irenaeus concludes this key section of *Against Heresies* by noting that if someone "thinks that he has received not only partial knowledge but absolutely real knowledge of all things that exist—he is another Valentinus, or Ptolemaeus, or Basilides, or any other of those who claim they have search out the depths (cf. 1 Cor 2:10) of God."³⁸ The problem with Valentinus, Ptolemy, and Basilides is that these teachers have not followed Paul's (and therefore Christ's) teaching about the relationship between love and knowledge, and this is related to their confusion about the rule of faith and the identity of God. By focusing on knowledge, these teachers have separated themselves from the love of God found in the community of the church. They have repeated the same mistake as the meat eaters in Corinth.

The paragraphs from Book 2 provided us with Irenaeus's most "systematic" discussion of 1 Cor 8:1. But those paragraphs are not the only place where Irenaeus alludes to this passage. In Books 1 and 3, Irenaeus alludes to the passage in the context of "heretical" teachers. When one reads the scriptures filled with the love of God, he or she is built up in the economy of salvation. The reader carries on the tradition of reading handed on from the Apostles. Such ecclesial reading does not draw attention to any teacher other than Christ himself. And when a teacher does set himself apart, it is because he is puffed up by the pretense of knowledge rather than built up by the love of God. In Book 1, Irenaeus maintains that two teachers— Marcus and Tatian—are so puffed up. Irenaeus spends a great deal of time in

---

36. *Haer.* 2.28.8, *neque aptabilem magis neque decentioruem neque sine periculo alteram quam hanc inveniat in praesenti quoniam enim solus verax magister est Dominus, ut discamus per ipsum super opmnia esse Patrem.*

37. *Haer.* 2.28.7, *Sicut igitur ex parte cognosciums, sic et de universis quaestionibus concedere oportet ei qui ex parte nobis praestat gratiam.*

38. *Haer.* 2.28.9, *putet se non ex parte sed universaliter universam cepisse eorum agnitionem, Valentinus aliquis exsistens aut Ptolemaeus aut Bssilides vel aliquis eorum qui altitudines Dei exquisisse se dicunt.*

Book 1 discussing Marcus's teaching. Marcus seems to be of particular concern to Irenaeus because Marcus takes advantage of women. Irenaeus relates one episode where Marcus induced a woman to prophesy. After "certain invocations" that Marcus performs, the woman was "puffed up and elated" by his words and then she "utters some nonsense."[39] The problem here is obvious: Marcus leads the woman to a private utterance that is divorced from the economy of salvation. Love is neither the beginning nor the end of Marcus's interpretation or hers. She herself becomes "puffed up" and thinks she can somehow rise above the economy as it is presented in the scriptures. This is why her speech is nonsense. But such nonsense comes from anyone who is puffed up by false knowledge. Like Marcus and the woman, Tatian has separated himself from the Church. Tatian's case is more tragic because he had been a disciple of Justin, to whom Irenaeus often refers. Tatian separated himself because he was "excited and puffed up by the thought of being a teacher, as if he were superior to others, he composed his own peculiar type of doctrine."[40] In both cases, a person has removed himself from the economy of salvation recounted in the scriptures and found in the church. Marcus and Tatian opted for knowledge divorced from love. In so doing, they divorced themselves from the community united in God's love.

The peculiar doctrines of Marcus and Tatian are nothing, though, compared to the peculiar doctrines of Simon Magus, Marcion, and Valentinus. When we come to Irenaeus's description of Simon, Marcion, and Valentinus in Book 3, we see Irenaeus underscoring the connection between their puffed-up pride and their interpretation of scripture. It should be remembered that at the end of that eighth chapter of 1 Corinthians Paul stressed that there was one God who made all things. According to Irenaeus, Simon, Marcion, and Valentinus reject this teaching. Instead they proclaim various gods and secret teaching. Although Irenaeus focuses on apostolic teaching in Book 3, he brings up Simon, Marcion, and Valentinus to contrast their teaching with that of the Apostles. In this contrast, he distinguishes between the love that builds up the Apostles' interpretation and the knowledge that puffs up his opponents. In fact, Irenaeus goes so far as to say that his opponents "have been deserted by the Father's love and puffed up by Satan" (*Haer.* 3.12.12). They believe that they are "more sincere and wiser" than the Apostles.[41] They have been deserted by the Father's love because they have abandoned the love found in the community of the church in the name of their own "knowledge." This abandonment points to a deeper issue. Those who "are

---

39. *Haer.* 1.13.3, ἐπικλήσεις τινὰς ποιούμενος ἐκ δευτέρου εἰς κατάπληξιν τῆς ἀπατωμένης φησὶν αὐτῇ ... Ἡ δὲ χαυνωθεῖσα καὶ κεπφωθεῖσα ὑπο τῆς προσδοκίας τοῦ μέλλειν αὐτὴν προφητεύειν, τῆς καρδίας πλέον τοῦ δέοντος παλλούσης ἀποτολμᾷ καὶ λαλεῖ ληρώδη καῖ τὰ τυχόντα πάντα κενῶς καὶ πολμηρῶς.

40. *Haer.* 1.28.1, οἰήματι διδασκάλου ἐπαρθεὶς καὶ τυφωθεὶς ὡς διαφέρων τῶν λοιπῶν, ἴδιον χαρακτῆρα διδασκαλείου συνεστήσατο.

41. *Haer.* 3.12.12, *Deserti igitur cum sint a paterna dilectione et inflati a Satana ... et putaverunt semetipsos plus invenisse quam apostoli alterum Deum adinvenientes.*

puffed with a false knowledge indeed recognize the scriptures, but they pervert their interpretation."[42] Ultimately, though, they are ignorant of God's economy.

The problem, of course, is that this love is not self-evident. The line between the love that builds up and the knowledge that puffs up can be hard to detect. If it were not, there would be no need for Irenaeus to write. Valentinus and his followers conceal the line between love and knowledge particularly well. It would not be too much of a stretch to say that Irenaeus's interpretation of 1 Cor 8:1 could serve as the key text for his refutation of Valentinianism.[43] The disciples of Valentinus look to apostolic precedent—especially Paul—to justify their actions. Irenaeus says that the followers of Valentinus believe that the Apostles "teach some things secretly and other things openly."[44] Such action, Irenaeus tells us, "is the subterfuge of liars, evil seducers, and hypocrites."[45] Because the line between love and knowledge is so thin, it is easy for the followers of Valentinus to "trap the simple people and entice them" because "they imitate our way of treating a subject, so that these might listen more often."[46] But according to Irenaeus, Valentinus and his followers have crossed that line and have thus separated themselves from the church and from the economy of salvation. The Valentinians turn around and say that those who follow the interpretation of the Apostles are the ones who have separated themselves. They "complain that, since they hold beliefs similar to ours, we keep ourselves away from communication with them for no reason and though they say the same things and have the same teaching, we call them 'heretics.'"[47] Obviously, Irenaeus does not quote 1 Corinthians 8 here, but we see similar themes. Because of a claim to knowledge, one group has separated itself from the community, but that very same group uses that claim to argue that it has not separated itself at all.

---

42. *Reliqui vero omnes falso scientiae nomine inflati scripturas quidem confitentur, interpretationes vero convertunt.*

43. *Haer.* 3.12.12. As we especially see in Book 5, 1 Cor 15:50 would also be central to the discussion. Others have rightly focused on the importance of 1 Cor 15:50. Among many titles, see Ysabel de Andia, *Homo Vivens: Incorruptibilite et Divinisation de L'homme Selon Irenee de Lyons* (Paris: Etudes augustiniennes, 1986); and Mark William Olson, *Irenaeus, the Valentinian Gnostics, and the Kingdom of God (A. H. Book V): The Debate About 1 Corinthians 15: 50* (Lewiston, NY: Mellen Biblical Press, 1992). As I have noted, there has been less attention on 1 Corinthians 8.

44. *Haer.* 3.15.1, *Igitur testificatio eius vera et doctrina apostolorum manifesta et firma et nihil subtrahens* (Acts 20:27) *neque alia quidem in abscondito, alia vero in manifesto docentium.*

45. *Haer.* 3.15.2, *hoc enim fictorum et prave seducentium et hypocritarum est molimen.*

46. *Haer.* 3.15.2, *capiunt simpliciores et illiciunt eos, simulantes nostrum tractatum, uti saepius audient.*

47. *Haer.* 3.15.2, *qui etiam queruntur de nobis quod, cum similia nobiscum sentiant, sine causa abstineamus nos a communicatione eorum, et cum eadem dicant et adndem habeant doctrinam vocemus illos haereticos.*

The Valentinians have separated themselves because, like the meat eaters of Corinth, they believe they have the proper interpretation of scripture. And this proper interpretation shows that *knowledge* saves.[48] Irenaeus stresses this difference not simply to show how the Valentinians have separated themselves from the community because of their knowledge (as some of the Corinthians did), but also in the way the Valentinians understand salvation. Irenaeus argues that the apostolic interpretation of scripture shows that God's love saves. And thus the whole point of the rule of faith is to remind readers of that love. A full exploration of Valentinian soteriology is beyond the scope of this chapter,[49] but I want to show one place where Irenaeus clearly alludes to 1 Cor 8:1 as part of an argument to show what is at stake in the disagreement. When someone challenges a Valentinian teacher, this person hears that "he does not grasp the truth and does not possess the seed of the mother on high."[50] That is, this person is ignorant and his ignorance shows that he will not be redeemed. If, however, someone follows the Valentinian teaching, and "attained even their 'redemption,'" such a person is so "puffed up" that "he thinks he is neither in heaven nor on earth, but has entered the Fullness and is already in the embrace of his angel." Such a person "walks about with arrogance and pride and has the puffed up nature of a proud rooster."[51] To say that someone is neither on earth nor in heaven is to say that the person is outside the economy of salvation. In one way, we could say that Irenaeus and his Valentinian opponents agree: those who follow the apostolic rule of faith and those who follow the Valentinian rule of faith are not redeemed in the same way. But for Irenaeus these differences affect how both groups live now. The Valentinians

---

48. My argument does not depend on an exegesis of Valentinian or other "gnostic" texts. Whether or not Irenaeus properly understood his opponents is not my concern. That said, the opening lines of the *Gospel of Truth* show that text's focus on knowledge, thought, and intellect rather than on love. See Bentley Layton, *The Gnostic Scriptures: A New Translation with Annotations and Introductions* (Garden City, NY: Doubleday, 1987), 253.

49. For some of the discussion on Valentinian eschatology, see Elaine Pagels, "Conflicting Versions of Valentinian Eschatology: Irenaeus' Treatise *vs* the Excerpts from Theodotus," *HTR* 67.1 (1974), 35–53. There were responses from James F. McCue, "Conflicting Versions of Valentinianism: Irenaeus and the *Excerpta ex Theodoto*," in *Rediscovery of Gnosticism*, vol. 1, ed. Bentley Layton (Leiden: Brill, 1980), 404–16; and Roland Bergmeier, "'Königlösikeit' als nachvalentinianisches Heilsprädikat," *NovT* 24 (1982), 316–39; and Daniel L. Hoffman, "Irenaeus, Pagels, and the Christianity of the Gnostics," in *Light of Discovery: Studies in Honor of Edwin M. Yamauchi*, ed. John Wineland (Eugene, OR: Pickwick, 2007), 65–82.

50. *Haer.* 3.15.2, *hunc quasi non capientum veritatem et non habentum de superioribus a Matre sua semen adfirmantes.*

51. *Haer.* 3.15.2, *Si autem aliquis quasi parvam ovem deditum semetipsum ipsis praebeat, initiationi illorum et redemptionem illorum consecutus, est inflatus iste talis, neque in caelo neque in terra putat se esse, sed intra Pleroma introisse et complexum iam angelum suum; cum institorio et supercilio incedit, gallinacii elationem habens.*

believe that "they are already perfect," and because of this they "live irreverently and contempously."⁵² The Valentinians have separated themselves by what they believe and by how they act. Once again, we hear echoes of 1 Corinthians.

The devil fathers forth all heresies, and so we should not be surprised to see Irenaeus connect Valentinus with the original heretical teacher. Irenaeus's discussion of the devil's temptation of Christ ties together many of the topics we have been discussing and serves as a conclusion to our discussion of the role teachers play. He casts the devil's temptation of Christ in terms that are familiar to us by now. The temptation is essentially about the proper way to interpret scripture. According to Irenaeus, when Christ tells the devil that human beings do not live by bread alone, he teaches "by His commandment that we who have been set free should, when hungry, take that food which is given by God."⁵³ And once human beings receive God's gifts, they should not "be lifted up with pride, nor should we tempt God, but should feel humility in all things."⁵⁴ The devil, of course, shows no such humility. When the devil says, "All these things are delivered to me and to whomever I give them," Irenaeus argues that these words show that the devil is "puffed up with pride."⁵⁵ We have seen that this puffed up pride is common to Satan, Valentinus, Justin, and Marcus. All of them teach their students that they can somehow be above the economy of salvation that the scripture recounts because for them knowledge, not love, is the true hypothesis of scripture.

Thus far our discussion of teachers has been largely negative. We have shown how Irenaeus argues that certain teachers went astray in that they lauded knowledge over love and in the process separated themselves from the economy of salvation. Part of the problem for the Corinthians, of course, was which teacher to follow. Paul does not specifically address the question about interpreting the scriptures when he warns against partisanship with regard to teachers. We would be remiss to think that Irenaeus's remarks on teachers was only negative, that he was only concerned with explaining which teachers one should not follow. In a crucial section in Book 4⁵⁶ Irenaeus discusses the presbyter's role in the interpretation

---

52. *Haer.* 3.15.2, *Plurimi autem et contemptores facti quasi iam perfecti, sine reverentia et in contemptu viventes.*

53. *Haer.* 5.22.2, *Nos autem solutos per ipsum praeceptum docuit esurientes quidem sustinere eam quae a Deo datur escam.*

54. *Haer.* 5.22.2, *extolli neque temptare Deum, sed humilia sentire in omnibus.*

55. *Haer.* 5.22.2, *Deinde quoniam dominatur omnibus et ei ipsi et nolente Patre nostro qui est in caelis neque passer cadet in terram* (cf Matt 10:29), *illud igitur quod ait: "Hanc omnia mihi tradita sunt et cui volo do ea"* (Luke 4:6) *ut in superbiam elatus ait*. It is interesting here that just before what I quoted, Irenaeus writes, "Without the will of our Father in heaven not even a sparrow falls to the ground." Earlier we saw Irenaeus use just this verse as an example of knowledge divorced from love.

56. For a full discussion of this passage, see Charles E. Hill, *From the Lost Teaching of Polycarp: Identifying Irenaeus' Apostolic Presbyter and the Author of Ad Diognetum* (WUNT; Tübingen: Mohr Siebeck, 2006). Hill argues that Irenaeus's presbyter is none other than Polycarp.

of scripture. Christians ought to obey the presbyters "who have succession from the Apostles."[57] Only the bishops have the "charism of truth according to the good pleasure of the Father." Irenaeus contrasts such Christians with those who act as if they are knowledgeable and are "puffed up and please themselves." Such people do not follow the teaching that has come down from the Apostles. Although many follow the presbyter, there are others who "serve their own desires and do not put the fear of God into their hearts."[58] Irenaeus's shift here is subtle but important: *either* one follows the presbyter's interpretation of scripture *or* one follows one's own desires and does not fear God. We could say: either one is within the economy of salvation and the church or one is without it. Or even: either one loves or one pretends that one knows. Now Irenaeus does not say any of this explicitly, but given our analysis thus far, such a conclusion follows. He does seem to warrant such a conclusion when he quotes the presbyter saying, "We ought not be proud ... but we should fear lest after having the knowledge of Christ we do something by chance that is not pleasing to him and we no longer have remission of sins and are excluded from the kingdom."[59] Once again, knowledge by itself is not the goal of the Christian life. If it were, Paul would not have admonished the Corinthians. The goal of the Christian life is a loving relationship with God. Proud knowledge gets in the way of that relationship.

As we have seen, one cannot have this loving relationship if one is puffed up with one's own knowledge. Teachers are so important because they help their students distinguish between the love that builds up and the knowledge that puffs up. Each Christian teacher aims to have his students build up a relationship of love with the one teacher, Christ himself. Thus we should not find it surprising that Irenaeus alludes to 1 Corinthians 8 in one of his discussions of the Eucharist, where the encounter with Christ occurs. Irenaeus even argues that the Eucharist guards against human beings becoming puffed up. Human bodies receive the nourishment of the Eucharist "in order that we may never become puffed up, as if we had life from ourselves and exalted against God, our minds becoming ungrateful because they were" (*Haer.* 5.2.3). Indeed, precisely because the body has been nourished by the Eucharist it "shall rise at the appointed time, the Word of God granting them resurrection to the glory of God." The Father "freely gives to this mortal immortality and to this corruptible incorruption, because the strength of God is made perfect in weakness."[60] Above we saw how the Valentinians believed

---

57. *Haer.* 4.26.2, *Quapropter eis qui in Ecclesia sunt presbyteris obaudire oportet, his qui successionem habent ab Apostolis.*

58. *Haer.* 4.26.3, *qui vero crediti sunt quidem a multis esse presbyteri, serviunt autem suis voluptatibus et non praeponunt timorem Dei in cordibus suis, sed contemeliis agunt reliquos et principalis concessionis tumore elati sunt.*

59. *Haer.* 4.27.2, *Non debemus ergo, inquit ille senior, superbi esse neque reprehendere veteres, sed ipsi timere ne forte, post agnitionem Christi agentes aliquid quod non placeat Deo remissionem ultra non habeamus delictorum, sed exludamur a regno eius.*

60. *Haer.* 5.2.3, διαλυθέντα ἐν αὐτῇ ἀναστήσεται ἐν τῷ ἰδίῳ καιρῷ, τοῦ λόγου τοῦ θεοῦ τὴν ἔγερσιν αὐτοῖς χαριζομένου εἰς δόξαν θεοῦ καὶ Πατρὸς (cf. Phil 2:11) ὃς

their salvation was somehow above heaven and earth. For Irenaeus salvation is, in an important way, through the earth. To be nourished by the Eucharist is to be nourished by the earth in which the wheat and grapes grow and by the "one God, the Father, from whom all things are and for whom we exist" (1 Cor 8:6). A mind focused solely on knowledge easily becomes ungrateful. At issue here is how does one accept the Spirit of God and the Word of God. If one does not accept them in the right way, he cannot receive the nourishment of the Eucharist. And without this material nourishment, one becomes puffed up and takes oneself out of God's economy. The Eucharist ought to deepen one's gratitude to God, and this gratitude can only come about by recognizing God's love.

We have focused in this chapter on the distinction between puffing up and building up. Just as we misunderstand Irenaeus if we think that he eschews knowledge or devalues knowledge in relation to love, we also misunderstand him if we discount the importance of resurrection. Irenaeus ends *Against Heresies* reminding his reader that the salvation of human beings is at the center of God's economy of salvation. In the scriptures and the economy of salvation "the same God the Father is shown in all." This God "formed man and promised the inheritance of land to the Fathers." God led this inheritance "into the resurrection of the just and fulfilled the promises of the kingdom in his Son."[61] Thanks to the work of the Son, human beings can become "capable of the Word and ascend[ed] to him, going above the angels and becoming according to the image and likeness of God."[62] Unlike the Valentinians, who misinterpret Paul to say that only our minds—and thus only our knowledge—rise up, Irenaeus interprets Paul as saying that human beings rise in and as bodies. The hypothesis of scripture and the economy of salvation center on the love of God that has revealed itself as the Word made flesh. This love guides the teacher who follows the rule of faith and builds up the members of the community that embrace and live in that love.

ὄντως τῷ θνητῷ τὴν ἀθανασίαν περιποιεῖ καὶ τῷ φθαρτῷ τὴν αφθαρσίαν (1 Cor 15:53) προσχαρίζεται ὅτι ἡ δύναμις τοῦ θεοῦ ἐν ἀσθενείᾳ τελειοῦται (2 Cor 12:9) ἵνα μὴ ὡς ἐξ ἡμῶν αὐτῶν ἔχοντες τὴν ζωὴν φυσιωθῶμέν καὶ ἐπαρθῶμέν ποτε κατὰ τοῦ θεοῦ ἀχάριστον ἔννοιαν αναλαβόντες.

61. *Haer.* 5.36.3, *Et in omnibus his et per omnia idem Deus Pater ostenditur, qui plasmavit hominem et hereditatem terrae promisit patribus, qui eduxit illum in resurrectione justorum et promissiones adimplet in Filii sui regnum.* On the resurrection of the flesh, see Anders-Christian Jacobsen, "The Philosophical Argument in the Teaching of Irenaeus on the Resurrection of the Flesh," *StPatr* 36 (2001), 256–61.

62. *Haer.* 5.36.3, *ut progenies eius primogenitus Verbum descendat in facturam, hoc est in plasma, et capiatur ab eo, et factura iterum capiat Verbum et ascendat ad eum, supergrediens angelos et fiens secundum imaginem et similitudinem Dei.* The best book on image and likeness in Irenaeus is Fantino, *L'homme, image de Dieu, chez saint Irénée de Lyon* (Paris: Les Editions du Cerf, 1985).

Response
Being Known by God: A Response to Scott D. Moringiello

Carla Swafford Works

"We know that all of us possess knowledge. Knowledge puffs up, but love builds up." These words introduce Paul's advice concerning the consumption of idol food in 1 Corinthians 8. The apostle challenges any human knowledge by reminding the Corinthians that whatever knowledge one imagines to possess is incomplete (1 Cor 8:2; 13:9-13). Humans know in part. The foolishness of the cross shames even the wisest among us (1 Cor 1:18-31). What matters to Paul, and what Paul wants to matter to the church, is not a collection of knowledge, but a life of love. In the topsy-turvy reality created by the cross, the only knowledge that counts is being known by God.

Scott Moringiello's chapter considers Paul's advice in the battleground of second-century Christian polemics, where what would be deemed as "orthodoxy" begins to crystalize. At the center of Moringiello's discussion is Irenaeus's insistence that love, particularly the kind of love exhibited by Christ, is key to discerning whether the so-called knowledge of other teachers is really knowledge at all. While combatting gnostic teaching in *Against Heresies*, Irenaeus makes a critical distinction between love and knowledge. Moringiello contends that Paul's advice in 1 Corinthians 8 has influenced Irenaeus's argument not only against the scriptural interpretation of the other teachers, but also in his construction of the *regula fidei*.

This response will focus on how Irenaeus—or how Moringiello's interpretation of Irenaeus—has appropriated the Pauline text. First, I will summarize some of Moringiello's findings for Irenaeus's treatment of 1 Corinthians 8 so that it is possible to compare those findings to Paul's argument in 1 Corinthians. Then, I will raise larger questions about Irenaeus's use of scripture.

Irenaeus's Use of 1 Corinthians 8

Without a doubt Irenaeus finds 1 Corinthians 8 helpful in distinguishing between love and knowledge. He alludes to or quotes the text in multiple places. Moringiello emphasizes Book 2 chapters 25–28 because this is the "most systematic discussion" of 1 Corinthians 8 in *Against Heresies*, though as Moringiello notes, it is far from a sustained treatment of Paul's argument. Then Moringiello focuses his study on places where Irenaeus employs "puffed up" (φυσιόω or *elatos*) to describe the teachers as those who believe they are "above the economy of salvation." As his study demonstrates, this height metaphor appears often in his Irenaeus's discussion.

Whether or not we are to read 1 Corinthians 8 as the inspiration for all the height metaphors in *Against Heresies*, Irenaeus is influenced by this passage. Before his exposition of the biblical text in Book 2, Irenaeus has already alluded to 1 Corinthians 8 in *Against Heresies* 1.6.3-4 where he likens his opponents to the unscrupulous meat eaters who think they are perfect and consider the other teachers (i.e., Irenaeus) contemptible and ignorant. Later, Irenaeus quotes the first line of 1 Corinthians 8 to combat the teaching of those whose pursuit of knowledge have caused them to fall away from the love of God (*Haer.* 2.26.1). To contrast their knowledge with the transcendent knowledge of God, Irenaeus emphasizes the particulars of God's creation—such as the number of hairs on one's head or the stars in the sky (*Haer.* 2.26.2-3). Their so-called knowledge, as Moringiello has demonstrated, is linked to their interpretation of scripture, and it is this interpretation that is leading others astray.

Thus, Moringiello proposes a connection between Irenaeus's use of 1 Corinthians 8 and the rule of faith. The acknowledgment in 1 Cor 8:6 that there is only one God and one Lord coincides with the insistence that there is no other God than the Creator God, the God of Abraham, Isaac, and Jacob (*Haer.* 3.6.4-5). Furthermore, in *Against Heresies* 3.18.3, Irenaeus cites 1 Cor 8:11, Paul's reference to the death of Christ for the weak ones,[1] as an indication that there are not two distinct beings, Christ and Jesus, but rather that Jesus Christ suffered and died. Indeed, Jesus' suffering, a sign of God's knowledge and love, is critical for Irenaeus (see, e.g., *Haer.* 1.3.5; 1.9.3). In short, 1 Corinthians 8 serves Irenaeus's argument that the Redeemer God and the Creator God are one and the same and any who claim otherwise teach against the church's beliefs and create divisions in the community. Moringiello has demonstrated that the Apostle Paul's distinction between love and knowledge is particularly beneficial to Irenaeus's discussion. How does Irenaeus's use of 1 Corinthians 8, however, compare to the letter's original context?

Considering the Context of 1 Corinthians 8:1

Paul writes 1 Corinthians in response to two factors: oral reports from Chloe's people about divisions in the congregation (1:10-17) and a letter from the church (7:1) which appears to pose questions regarding issues such as whether to marry or give in marriage in light of an imminent return of Christ (7:1-40), whether

---

1. Irenaeus also cites Rom 14:15.

certain spiritual gifts should take precedence over others when the church is assembled for worship (12:1–14:40), and how to gather funds for a collection (16:1-4). 1 Corinthians 8 begins a long section of the letter devoted to the church's question about whether it is idolatrous to consume food that has been sacrificed to idols (8:1–11:1).[2]

Paul's advice acknowledges the concerns of both the idol food eaters and the abstainers. Apparently, those who eat freely are boasting of their knowledge in one God and one Lord who have created all things (8:6). Thus, idols are nothing. Paul agrees with this theological stance, but warns that their behavior is destroying the brother or sister for whom Christ died (8:11). Whether to eat or abstain is not simply a question of having knowledge (8:7). Otherwise, Paul may have advocated the establishment of the first seminary. Eating or abstaining relates to the worldview of the consumer. Those who believe that the idol food is connected to the idols cannot, in good conscience, partake. And Paul does not tell them to eat it anyway. For the weak the idol food has real power (8:7). Paul honors that worldview in 10:14-22 by noting that one cannot partake of the table of the Lord and the table of demons (10:21). There is also a parallel to 1 Cor 11:27-34, where consuming the Lord's Table in an unworthy manner has led to sickness and even death. Thus, following the example of the knowledgeable could lead to the destruction of their brothers or sisters in Christ (8:10-13). Paul's advice is anything but simple. Instead he places before the Corinthians some guiding principles.

Food is not the problem; love, or in this case a lack of love, is. The knowledgeable who consume whatever they want have the right to do as they please, but this behavior does not benefit the church (10:23-24). In fact, it is destroying the assembly (8:7-13). They cannot claim to love one God and one Lord and then destroy their neighbor. The apostle implores them to seek the advantage of the other for the sake of the gospel (10:24; 33). For the knowledgeable, Paul gives two examples to serve as models: himself, as one who has knowledge and status and willingly relinquishes it for the sake of the gospel; and their "ancestors" who flirted with idolatry and were destroyed in the wilderness (10:1-13). Glorifying God—rather than being right—is the goal (10:31). Glorifying God entails seeking what is beneficial for the assembly that God created (10:31-33). The only knowledge that matters is God's knowledge, or "being known by God" (8:3).

Paul does not specify who the knowledgeable are. Though Moringiello has identified them as teachers, no such claim is made in these chapters. Divisions around leaders are named at the beginning of the letter. Paul, however, does not discount the leaders but views them as coworkers (3:1-23). Later in 2 Corinthians, it seems that Paul is facing opposing teachers whom he will call the "super-apostles," but if the knowledgeable ones of 1 Corinthians 8 are teachers, Paul does not refer to them as such.

---

2. Though Moringiello and Irenaeus refer to meat eaters, the text is not that specific. Everything served within the temple precincts would have first been offered to the god or goddess of the temple (see 1 Cor 8:10).

The apostle is concerned, however, that others will be influenced to emulate the behavior of the "meat eaters." Gerd Theissen famously argued that social class plays a role in the divisions in the church.[3] This is perhaps most evident at the Lord's Table where Paul accuses those who have houses of humiliating those who have nothing (11:22). It is likely that these same divisions are part of the background of idol food consumption. Some are accustomed to being invited to banquets at the local temple, but not all in the church would have that privilege. The patronage system would confer a certain amount of authority to those of higher social class in the church, and their social sphere alone would grant them some leadership privileges—whether or not anyone ever appointed them as "teachers" in the community. Those with status must be willing to lay aside that status for the sake of the church's edification. To reiterate the opening line of 1 Cor 8:1: "love builds up." Thus, Paul ends the argument, "Be imitators of me, as I am of Christ" (11:1).

Whether the knowledgeable are teachers, though, as Moringiello has posited, does not discount the connections between 1 Corinthians 8 and Irenaeus's rule of faith. Moringiello has highlighted Irenaeus's link between the "meat eaters" and the opposing teachers. By their knowledge, neither those who consume idol food nor the other teachers are engaging in behavior that builds up the community. Boasting in knowledge is central to the problem. Paul does not condemn the knowledge of the idol food eaters, but their actions. They appear to be claiming that there is one God and one Lord. This knowledge of God, however, is not linked to loving their neighbor as themselves. By their knowledge, they are leading others astray, and, thus, destroying their brother or sister for whom Christ died. For Irenaeus, the teachers are leading others to doctrines outside what the church believes and, thus, outside the economy of salvation (*Haer.* 1.10.1-2). It would be better to have no knowledge at all if that knowledge leads one away from the love of God (*Haer.* 2.26.1).

Are there parallels between Irenaeus's purposes and Paul's? The short answer is yes. As noted above, there is a lot at stake for each of them. There are important differences, however, in their contexts. In 1 Corinthians Paul is attempting to correct divisive behavior that stems from the knowledge of some in the church. Paul does not accuse the knowledgeable of trying to elevate themselves "above the economy of salvation," as Irenaeus accuses the teachers. The apostle does not treat them as though they are teaching heresies. The tone of this letter is nothing like Galatians, for instance, where Paul is combatting teaching that he defines as a desertion of the gospel (Gal 1:6-9). Later in the development of the early churches when the expectation of the parousia is no longer imminent, there will be a concern to have teachers who teach sound doctrine, but that concern, which is central to the Pastoral Epistles, is not yet pressing at the time of Paul's writing of 1 Corinthians. The concern of 1 Corinthians 8 is that the weak, who might be

---

3. Gerd Theissen, *The Social Setting of Pauline Christianity: Essays on Corinth*, ed. and trans. John H. Schütz (Philadelphia: Fortress, 1982).

influenced by the knowledgeable's eating of idol food, could be "defiled" and even destroyed by participating in acts that return them to their former lives of idolatry.

In sum, both Irenaeus and Paul are concerned about the potential destruction caused by the "knowledgeable." Irenaeus's battle is with "heresies" that are forming in the church and that, from Irenaeus's perspective, are leading others astray and beyond the economy of salvation. Paul believes that the behavior of the knowledgeable is correctable. They are not opponents, but parishioners. His struggle is to teach non-Jews who have only recently converted that this God of Israel, who has revealed Godself through Jesus, is a jealous God who has formed a covenant with them (1 Cor 10:14-22; 11:23-25). To love this God entails both faithfulness to God and the love of neighbor.

"The Greatest of These Is Love": Loving God and Loving Neighbor?

Moringiello highlights the centrality of love to the rule of faith. He writes, "The most important principle for Irenaeus is the love of God offered in Christ through the economy of Scripture." Later he notes that love is "the hypothesis and oikonomia of Scripture" and "the beginning and end of interpretation." As stated above, love is also central to Paul's instructions regarding the consumption of idol food. Moringiello shows that Irenaeus uses 1 Corinthians 8 in his argument against those who are puffed up by their knowledge and who by their knowledge are leading others outside the "economy of salvation." Love is central to Paul's argument concerning idol food, and love is the proof that the rule of faith is not mere knowledge.

The prominence of love, while central to 1 Corinthians 8, is certainly not exclusive to this text. Scripture has taught Paul the importance of love, and the cross exhibits that love. According to Paul, "love is the fulfilling of the law" (Rom 13:10). Like Jesus, the apostle upholds the law by teaching the believers to love one's neighbor as oneself (Gal 5:14; Rom 13:8-10; cf. Matt 22:34-40). He likens "bearing one another's burdens" to fulfilling the "law of Christ" (Gal 6:2). Christ embodies love. The cross demonstrates God's love for us because while we were enemies of God Christ died for us (Rom 5:8, 10). In 1 Corinthians 8, Paul emphasizes that Christ died even for the "weak" brother or sister (1 Cor 8:11). Thus, at the end of the section on idol food consumption Paul's instruction to imitate Christ (1 Cor 11:1) is an exhortation to love one another with the love of Christ. It echoes the beginning of his argument that love—love that willingly relinquishes privileges and *lowers* status—actually *builds up* the community (1 Cor 8:1).[4]

Irenaeus uses 1 Corinthians 8 to create his argument, but he also has been influenced by scripture's teaching to love God and to love neighbor. In fact, in *Against Heresies* 4.12.2-5, Irenaeus argues that it is the first and greatest commandment that links both testaments together. This is a critical point in a work that is designed to wed the Creator God with the Redeemer God. He even

---

4. This is the same pattern seen in 1 Cor 9:19-23 and is modeled after the humbling of Christ in the Philippian hymn (Phil 2:5-11).

argues that if the Lord Jesus had come from a different Father, he would have never made use of the first and greatest commandment, but would have established an even greater commandment (*Haer.* 4.12.2). To illustrate the importance of showing love, Irenaeus refers to Jesus' woes against the scribes and Pharisees in the Gospel of Matthew. The problem was not that the Pharisees followed the law, according to Irenaeus, the issue was that they knew the law but were without love with respect to God and to neighbor (*Haer.* 4.12.4). To quote Jesus, "On these two commandments hang all the law and the prophets" (Matt 22:40). Irenaeus even cites Paul that love is the fulfilling of the law (*Haer.* 4.12.2).

Perhaps, the emphasis on love in Irenaeus's rule of faith stems not primarily from 1 Cor 8:1, but from the predominance of the commandments to love God with all one's heart, soul, and mind and to love one's neighbor as oneself. For Irenaeus and for Paul, Christ's sacrifice exhibits loving God and loving neighbor. What is beneficial in 1 Corinthians 8 for Irenaeus is the distinction between knowledge that puffs up and love that builds up.

Does Irenaeus Mangle Scripture?

Moringiello has argued that Irenaeus's primary concern is not "gnosticism" but the proper interpretation of scripture. The great irony of Irenaeus's argument to wed the God of Jesus Christ with the God of Abraham, Isaac, and Jacob is that while Irenaeus so beautifully argues for one God and one Lord as exhibited in the scriptures as a whole, he also, in his emphasis to link the love of the Creator God to the obedience of Christ on the cross, focuses all the scriptural witness on Jesus. Moringiello observes: "It should be no surprise that Christ crucified is the key to understanding God's love. This is another way of saying that Christ crucified is the key to understanding the Scriptures." Later he notes that Irenaeus places Christ within the economy of salvation: "Indeed, Christ's revelation is part of the Father's loving pedagogy in the economy of salvation." Whether Christ is "key" or "part of" is a tension that lies in Irenaeus's interpretation of scripture. Yet, the rule of faith, which makes Christ central, provides a framework for reading both testaments.

Irenaeus proposes a narrative structure that recounts the economy of salvation with Christ at the center of the storyline. In other words, all that comes before Christ prepares for Jesus. All that comes after Christ looks back at Jesus.[5] Thus, even the law prefigures Christ (*Haer.* 4.12.5). Kendall Soulen notes that Israel's history pre-Christ is summed up by the term "dispensations" in the rule of faith (*Haer.* 1.10.1).[6] Soulen writes, "Israel's history is portrayed as nothing more than the economy of redemption in prefigurative form. So construed, Israel's story contributes little or nothing to understanding how God's consummating and

---

5. For a discussion of the creation of this structure, see R. Kendall Soulen, *The God of Israel and Christian Theology* (Minneapolis: Fortress, 1996), 25–48.

6. Soulen, *The God of Israel and Christian Theology*, 42.

redemptive purposes engage human creation in universal and enduring ways."[7] As a result, God's covenant with Israel is overlooked by Irenaeus.[8] In Irenaeus's framework, God's acts of salvation, redemption, and blessing in Israel's history are virtually ignored, except that they prepare the reader for Jesus' story to come.

It is worth noting that, in the discussion of whether to consume idol food in 1 Corinthians, Paul finds scripture and God's relationship to Israel to be instructive. The apostle's response includes a lengthy argument from scripture, the lengthiest in the letter. In 1 Cor 10:1-22 Paul raises Israel's experiences in the wilderness as examples of how seriously God takes God's covenant with God's people. Paul cites example after example of the unfaithfulness of the "ancestors" (10:1-13). The purpose of these examples is to remind the Corinthians that they are now in a covenant relationship with God and with one another (10:16-21; cf. 11:23-25).

To be sure, Irenaeus draws from both testaments to refute the opposing teachers. Irenaeus even knows and cites the section of Paul's argument that contains allusions to Israel's wilderness wanderings, but Irenaeus focuses not on God's past dealings with Israel, but on the present situation of the church: "The cup of blessing which we bless, is it not the communion of the blood of Christ?" (citing 1 Cor 10:16 in *Haer.* 3.18.2). Notwithstanding, Irenaeus knows scripture and uses it in connection with his interpretation of 1 Corinthians 8. In *Against Heresies* 3.6.5, for instance, he draws a parallel between Moses's command not to make an image for God and Paul's words in 1 Cor 8:4: "We know that an idol is nothing, and that there is no other God but one. For though there be other gods, whether in heaven or in earth; yet to us there is but one God, the Father, of whom are all things, and we through Him; and one Lord Jesus Christ, by whom are all things, and we by Him." Nonetheless the framework created in the rule of faith, the framework that is supposed to provide a litmus test for the church's teaching, truncates God's history with Israel and the very scriptures that Paul finds so instructive.

By making the love of God as exhibited in Christ the focus of the rule of faith, is Irenaeus discounting the very scriptures that he is fighting so hard to save? Paul's advice in 1 Corinthians concerning idol food demonstrates that the Apostle, though seeing Christ as the epitome of love, also finds God's past actions to be instructive in their own right. If all scripture points to Christ, as Moringiello's reading of Irenaeus has highlighted, what do we make of the other references to this Creator God in scripture—God who blesses Abraham, Isaac, and Jacob, God who saves in the exodus, God who forms covenants, and so on. Irenaeus's rule of faith works well to combat gnostic teaching in the life of the church, but it is worth examining how this rule of faith has created a legacy of interpretation that has shaped Christianity's lenses when the church talks about the God of Israel.

---

7. Soulen, *The God of Israel and Christian Theology*, 32.
8. Soulen, *The God of Israel and Christian Theology*, 45.

What Matters Is Being Known by God

Moringiello has invited us to consider how Irenaeus appeals to Paul's letters to combat teaching that, from Irenaeus's perspective, upholds knowledge rather than love. After warning that knowledge puffs up and that human knowledge is limited, Paul writes, "If one loves God, one is known by him" (1 Cor 8:3). What matters to Paul is being known by God. For Paul and for Irenaeus God's knowledge and God's ways are mysterious. Paul refers to himself as an *oikonomos*, a "steward" of the mysteries of God (1 Cor 4:1), and as one who has been entrusted with an *oikonomia*, a commission that is nothing short of proclaiming God's good news (1 Cor 9:17). Irenaeus and Paul are battling different fronts, but each is proposing the love of God and the love of neighbor. What does that love look like? For both, Christ's actions embody that love and become instructive for the life of the church. Love is not an abstract principle but an active force in the body of Christ. It inspires those who have power and privilege to be willing to relinquish that status when their behavior might lead others astray. This kind of love is not a badge of honor in the world. It will not win one credit as a sage. But it is how God operates and how God has always operated—in God's desire to bless creation, in God's election of a people, in God's covenants, in God's law, in God's care and provision for God's people, in God's sending of Jesus Christ, and in God's desire to consummate creation.

Chapter 8

IRENAEUS AND PAUL: SEXUALITY, VIRGINITY, AND WOMEN

Helen Rhee

One of the crowning contributions of Irenaeus of Lyons to developing theology in the late second century and subsequent history is his famous doctrine of recapitulation (Greek—ἀνακεφαλαίωσις; Latin—*recapitulatio*) based on the Pauline typology of Adam and Christ. Responding to what he understood as the Valentinian understanding of Eph 1:10 ("in the economy [*oikonomia*] of the fullness [*pleroma*] of time, all things are recapitulated in Christ"), which sees *oikonomia* as "the internal process within the Pleroma, particularly the preserving of order which results in the coming of Christ,"[1] Irenaeus presents an alternative, historical reading of the verse, which interprets *oikonomia* as involving the "fullness" (*pleroma*) of historical time, in which Christ accomplished his work of redemption by recapitulating the marred creation as the second Adam (Rom 5:12-21; 1 Cor 15:20-50).[2] If at the center of his theological hermeneutics is the recapitulation through a more advanced Adam-Christ typology, Irenaeus, based on the same hermeneutical principle, develops one of the most unique parallels to the original Pauline typology with Eve and the Virgin Mary although he is not the first one to do so. In this double parallel, Irenaeus not only reinterprets Adam and creation from the standpoint of Christ and redemption, but also understands Eve and creation from the vintage point of the Virgin Mary and redemption.

---

1. J. T. Nielsen, *Adam and Christ in the Theology of Irenaeus of Lyons* (Assen, The Netherlands: Van Gorcum & Comp., 1968), 57.

2. For Irenaeus's use of Paul in his writings in general, in addition to Nielsen, *Adam and Christ in the Theology of Irenaeus of Lyons*, see D. L. Balás, "The Use and Interpretation of Paul in Irenaeus's Five Books *Adversus Haereses*," *SecCent* 9 (1992), 27–39; B. C. Blackwell, "Paul and Irenaeus," in *Paul and the Second Century*, ed. M. F. Bird and J. R. Dodson (London: T&T Clark International, 2011), 190–206; R. Norris, "Irenaeus' Use of Paul in His Polemic against the Gnostics," *Union Seminary Quarterly Review* (1980), 13–24; R. Noormann, *Irenäus als Paulusintepret: Zur Resephon und Wirkung der paulinschen und deteropaulinishcen Briefe im Werk des Irenäus von Lyon* (WUNT II/66; Tübingen: Mohr Siebeck, 1994).

The issue of sexuality, virginity, and women in Irenaeus's reading of Paul then is to be approached within this fundamental paradigm of Irenaeus's theological hermeneutics.

Sexuality, Woman, and Procreation in Creation and Economy

In Irenaeus's recapitulative framework, Paul's description of Adam as "a type of the one who was to come" (*typus futuri*; *Haer*. 3.22.3; Rom 5:14, τύπος τοῦ μέλλοντος; cf. *Epid*. 14) provides a ground for Irenaeus's theological anthropology.[3] Irenaeus advances Paul's words in Rom 5:14[4] in such a way that the Word, the Creator, has already prefigured in Adam the fullness of humanity that would manifest in the economy of the incarnation at the end (*Haer*. 3.22.3). This means that it is "not that the humanity has a form which the Word at His incarnation has to take" but that "humanity is created according to the pattern of the humanity which the Word assumes" as Iain MacKenzie notes.[5] God in the beginning designed the incarnate Word, who is preexistent to Adam, to be the pattern for Adam so that the former, the spiritual (*spiritali*) man, should save the latter, the psychical (*animalem*) man (*Haer*. 3.22.3; cf. 1 Cor 15:45-46). Thus God joins "the end to the beginning and points out that He [Christ] it is who recapitulates in Himself all the nations that had been dispersed from Adam onward … including Adam himself."[6]

This deliberate design of the first Adam after the second Adam lays several important and related grounds for exploring sexuality and virginity in God's economy. First, for Irenaeus, it guides and controls his understanding of creation of Adam after the image and likeness of God in Gen 1:26. Although it used to be said in the long past that (hu)man was made in the image of God (*imaginem Dei*), it was not actually shown (*ostendebatur*) to be so, states Irenaeus; for the Word, after whose image (hu)man was created, was still invisible, and because of this the

---

3. The standard editions for Irenaeus's *Adversus haereses* (*Haer*.) are the six volumes of A. Rousseau et al., *Irénée de Lyon: Contre les Hérésies, Live*, I–V (Sources Chrétiennes 100.1, 100.2, 152-53, 210-11, 263-64, 293-94; Paris: Cerf, 1965–82). All Latin and Greek quotations from those editions. For *Epideixis tou apostolikou kērygmatos* (*Epid*.), I have used K. Ter-Mejerttschian and S. G. Wilson, with Prince Maxe of Saxony (eds) and English trans., French trans. J. Barthoulot, Εἰς ἐπίδειξιν τοῦ ἀποστολικοῦ κηρύγματος; *The Proof of the Apostolic Preaching, with Seven Fragments* (PO 12.5; Paris, 1917; repr. Turnhout: Brepols, 1989); and J. Behr, *St. Irenaeus of Lyons: On the Apostolic Preaching* (Crestwood, NY: St Vladimir's Seminary Press, 1997). All English quotations come from Behr's translation.

4. "Yet death exercised dominion from Adam to Moses, even over those whose sins were not like the transgression of Adam, who is a type of the one who was to come" (NRSV).

5. I. M. MacKenzie, *Irenaeus's Demonstration of the Apostolic Preaching: A Theological Commentary and Translation* (Burlington, VT: Ashgate, 2002), 107.

6. *Haer*. 3.22.3 (SC 211:438): *finem coniungens initio et significans quoniam ipse est qui omnes gentes exinde ab Adam dispersas … cum ipso Adam in semetipso recapitulates est*.

(hu)man easily lost the likeness (*Haer.* 5.16.2). However, with the incarnation now it is different. When the Word of God became flesh, he confirmed two things: "he both showed forth the image truly, himself becoming that which was his image (*imago*), and he re-established the likeness (*similitudinem*) in a sure manner, by co-assimilating (συνεξομοιώσας; *consimilem*) man to the invisible Father through the Word become visible."[7] Christ, the Word incarnate, himself "the visible of the invisible Father" (*Haer.* 4.6.6), is the reality of a human as the image of God; this Christ assimilates in himself the human being to the invisible Father and therefore reestablishes the likeness which Adam lost through his disobedience. From the perspective of the Adam-Christ typology then, Adam being made after the image and likeness of God has both protological and eschatological dimensions. The image and likeness of God applied to humanity at the creation is not "a once and for all and complete endowment" according to Irenaeus.[8] Rather, God's act of creating humanity in his image and likeness encompasses the entire *oikonomia* of salvation, at whose end the Son fully assimilates humanity to the invisible Father and therefore grants immortality through the Spirit (*Haer.* 5.1.3).

Irenaeus explains this unity of the beginning and the end by drawing on a series of Pauline parallels between Adam and Christ in 1 Cor 15:45-48.[9] In the beginning Adam was formed as an animated flesh with rationality through a breath of life (*adspirato vitae*) from God (Gen 2:7); but in the end Christ rendered the human being in Adam living and perfect by the Spirit so that as we were all dead in the natural (animated) life in Adam, we may all be made alive in the spiritual life of Christ (*Haer.* 5.1.3; *Epid.* 11; cf. 1 Cor 15:45-6, 22). It was in this sense that Adam, a psychical being, animated by the breath of life, was both a type of, and one who would be saved by, Christ, the spiritual one, who was vivified by the Spirit (*Haer.* 3.22.3; 1 Cor 15:45).[10] Hence, while Adam was created in the image and likeness of God (*Haer.* 3.18.1; 3.23.1; 4.2.1; 4.10.1), he was not created perfect but only as an infant (*infans. Haer.* 4.38.1; *Epid.* 12). However, from the beginning to the end, "never at any time did Adam escape the hands of God" that guided and trained the humanity in order that Adam might become and grow after the image and the

---

7. *Haer.* 5.16.2 (SC 153:216): *et imaginem enim ostendit veram, ipse hoc fiens, quod erat imago ejus; et similitudinem firmans restituit, consimilem faciens hominem invisibili Patri per visibile Verbum.* Cf. *Epid.* 22: "For He [God] made man the image of God; and the image of God is the Son, after whose image man was made; and for this cause He appeared at the end of the times that He might show the image [to be] like unto Himself."

8. MacKenzie, *Irenaeus's Demonstration of the Apostolic Preaching*, 104.

9. "Thus it is written, 'The first man, Adam, became a living being'; the last Adam became a life-giving spirit. But it is not the spiritual that is first, but the physical, and then the spiritual. The first man was from the earth, a man of dust; the second man is from heaven. As was the man of dust, so are those who are of the dust; and as is the man of heaven, so are those who are of heaven" (NRSV).

10. J. Behr, *Asceticism and Anthropology in Irenaeus and Clement* (Oxford Early Christian Studies; Oxford: Oxford University Press, 2000), 58.

likeness of God (*Haer.* 5.1.3). God indeed intended that Adam would reach the likeness of God by the Spirit at the end of humanity's growth, development, and progress toward the perfection (*Haer.* 4.11.1).

How does Irenaeus's Christological and eschatological understanding of the creation of Adam relate to sexuality and woman? In paraphrasing the Genesis 2 account, Irenaeus understands the formation of woman as the same formation of Adam, a helper suitable, like (ἴσος), and equal (ὅμοιος) to Adam but sexually differentiated (*Epid.* 13).[11] God willed the formation of woman as a part of humanity's growth and development to perfection; therefore, Adam and Eve were able to kiss and embrace each other "in holiness as children" without any shameful desires and lust and to preserve their natural (animated) state as long as their breath of life remained in proper order and strength (*Epid.* 14). In the protological childhood and innocence in Paradise, bodily interaction and intimacy[12] in sexual differentiation had its proper place since "unity and diversity of humanity as male and female is the will and work of God."[13] However, Adam and Eve lost that condition of natural childhood innocence by losing the proper order and strength of the breath of life through their disobedience (*Haer.* 3.23.5). Then, following Gen 4:1-2, Irenaeus mentions Adam and Eve's sexual act and procreation *after* their expulsion from the Paradise (*Epid.* 17). It seems that sex and procreation did not belong to that protological innocence, but the reason for that might be different from the reasons given by the later Church Fathers such as Gregory of Nyssa and John Chrysostom who attributed marriage, sex, and procreation to the consequence of the fall and therefore mortality (*De virginitate*, 14; *De virginitate*, 14, respectively). Irenaeus does point out "concession" or "permission" with regard to marriage and sex in the present in consideration of "human infirmity" and because of "incontinence of some" by citing a series of Paul's words in 1 Corinthians 7:

> For in the New [Testament] also are the apostles found doing this very thing [granting concession], on the ground which has been mentioned, Paul plainly declaring, "But these things I say, not the Lord" (1 Cor 7.12). And again: "But this I speak by permission, not by commandment" (1 Cor 7.6). And again: "Now, as concerning virgins, I have no commandment from the Lord; yet I give my judgment, as one that has obtained mercy of the Lord to be faithful" (1 Cor 7.25). But further, in another place he says: "That Satan tempt you not for your incontinence" (1 Cor 7.5) ... Also in the Old Testament the same God permitted similar indulgences for the benefit of His people, drawing them on by means of the ordinances already mentioned, so that they might obtain the gift of salvation through them.[14]

11. Cf. Behr, *Asceticism and Anthropology*, 111.
12. Irenaeus does not explicitly mention sexual act in the Paradise.
13. MacKenzie, *Irenaeus's Demonstration of the Apostolic Preaching*, 119.
14. *Haer.* 4.15.2 (ANF trans.; SC 100:554-56): *quandoquidem et in novo Apostoli hoc idem facientes inveniuntur propter praedictam causam, statim dicente Paulo: Haec autem*

Does Irenaeus believe sex and marriage to be the post-lapsarian concession? The larger context of this quotation shows the limited educational purpose of the Mosaic law in light of freedom granted by Christ; and Irenaeus precedes Paul's concessionary statements with Christ's explanation of Moses's concession to divorce in light of the original law of God (that God from the beginning made male and female so that they might become one flesh; Matt 19:4-5) due to the hardness of the Israelites. Within this context, Irenaeus's use of Paul's words seems to highlight the educational and salvific function of these concessions (rather than these concessions as succumbing to the evil of sex) in humanity's journey toward perfection and full freedom as they are trained by a pledge of the life-giving Spirit.[15] If that is the case, for Irenaeus sex, marriage, and procreation were part of God's creative design for humanity's maturation process and not the result of the fall. This understanding is confirmed by the fact that Irenaeus understood the divine blessing, "increase and multiply" (Gen 1:28), in a sequential way: Adam and Eve "had recently been created and had no knowledge about procreating children; for they had first to grow up [to the adult age], and then multiply."[16] Due to their disobedience, Adam and Eve lost "the robe of holiness (*sanctitatis stolam*)" *before* they grew up and then multiplied (cf. *Haer*. 3.23.5); thus sex and procreation ended up being a post-lapsarian reality in spite of God's original intent in Paradise. Seen in this way, sex and the "procreation of children is part of God's economy for the human race, which would come into effect when the newly created 'children' have reached a suitable age and maturity"[17]; accordingly, procreation in holiness would be possible upon reaching maturity.[18]

Indeed, as John Behr persuasively shows,[19] Irenaeus's intriguing description of Adam's zealous but misguided attempt to show his repentance immediately after his disobedience confirms that Adam's self-imposed continence is not part of God's design and intent. Adam, while resisting the "lustful propensity of his flesh" (since he had lost "his guileless and childlike mind"),[20] covered himself (and Eve) with fig leaves to suffer the irritations on his body, appropriate to his disobedience,

---

ego dico, non Dominus. Et iterum: Hoc autem dico secundum indulgentiam, non secundum proeceptum. Et iterum: De virginibus autem proeceptum Domini non habeo; consilium autem do, tanquam miseriocordiam consecutus a Domino, ut fidelis sim. Sed et alio loco ait: Ne tentet vos Satanas propter incontinentiam vestram ... si et in veteri testament idem Deus tale aliquid voluit fieri pro utilitate populi, illiciens eos per praedictas observations, ut per eas salutem .

15. Cf. Behr, *Asceticism and Anthropology*, 126.

16. *Haer*. 3.22.4 (my trans.; SC 211: 440): *quoniam paulo ante facti non intellectum habebant filiorum generationis; oportebat enim primo illos adolescere, dehinc sic multiplicari.*

17. Behr, *Asceticism and Anthropology*, 112.

18. Cf. Behr, *Asceticism and Anthropology*, 113.

19. See Behr, *Asceticism and Anthropology*, 118–19; idem, "Irenaeus *AH* 3.23.5 and the Ascetic Ideal," *St Vladimir's Theological Quarterly* 37.4 (1993), 311–13.

20. SC 211, 458: *et retundens petulantem carnis impetum, quoniam indolem et perilem amiserat sensum.*

as he reasoned erroneously. The gnawing and prickly fig leaves represent an ascetic remedy for Adam's "lustful propensity of his flesh" as he "surrounded himself and his wife with a girdle of continence (*frenum continentiae sibi et uxiori suae circumdedit*)" out of fear of God (*Haer.* 3.23.5). However, Adam's self-imposed asceticism only perpetuates his original fall, that is, refusing to grow according to God's will in "the robe of holiness" by the Spirit. For God instead clothes them "with the garments of skin in place of the fig leaves (*tunicas pellicias pro foliis ficulneis*)" (*Haer.* 3.23.5), appropriate for "his fallen life, in which Adam can continue to live according to God's original plan of growth and increase," thereby correcting Adam's unwarranted continence.[21] For Irenaeus, a life of growth and increase (through sex and procreation) under the guidance of the Spirit provides an antidote to the "false type of temperance (*fictam hujusmodi continentiam*)" by heretics (e.g., Saturninus and Marcion) who attribute marriage and procreation to Satan (*Haer.* 1.24.2; 1.28.1; cf. 1 Tim 4:3).

Ultimately, however, marriage and procreation only belongs to this present age of God's economy; upon the completion of God's preordained number to which humanity should increase, people will "cease to beget and to be begotten, to marry and to be given in marriage" so to "preserve the harmony of the Father" (*Haer.* 2.33.5; cf. Matt 22:30). While marriage and procreation will have its end, fleshly, sexual existence will last; for the resurrected flesh in perfect sanctity and purity will exist in sexual differentiation (cf. *Haer.* 5.6.1-2).

Virginity, Woman, and Generation in Recapitulation

Irenaeus's elaboration of Pauline typology of Adam and Christ, especially his Christological and retrospective understanding of Adam's creation (in image and likeness of God), constructs another theme in relation to our topic: the parallel of Adam's creation from "virgin earth" and Christ's "virgin birth."

> Whence, then, was the substance of the first formed? From the will and wisdom of God and from virgin earth—"For God had not cause it to rain," says Scripture, before man was made, "and there was no man to till the ground" (Gen 2.5). So, from this [earth], while it was still virgin, God "took mud from the earth and fashioned man" (Gen 2.7), the beginning (ἀρχή) of [hu]mankind. Thus, the Lord, recapitulating this man, received the same arrangement (οἰκονομία) of embodiment (σάρκωσις) as this one, being born from the Virgin by the will and wisdom of God, that He might also demonstrate the likeness of embodiment (σάρκωσις) to Adam, and might become the man, written in the beginning, "according to the image and likeness of God." (*Epid.* 32)

---

21. Behr, *Asceticism and Anthropology*, 119; idem, "Irenaeus *AH* 3.23.5 and the Ascetic Ideal," 312.

In this passage Irenaeus alludes to another Pauline parallel in the series in 1 Cor 15:45-49: "The first man was from the earth, a man of dust; the second man is from heaven" (1 Cor 15:47; NRSV); and he reads Gen 2:7 through this Pauline paradigm. Irenaeus transforms this Pauline parallel as he builds a link between the first and the second Adam not as the relation of contrast as expected from the original context but that of analogy or likeness.[22] Irenaeus emphasizes that Adam's creation is "from the will and wisdom of God" as it is "from the virgin earth"; in the same way, the Lord's birth in his recapitulation of Adam is "by the will and wisdom of God" as it is "from the Virgin." Moreover, he says elsewhere that Adam's substance from the primal and thus virgin soil (*de rudi terra et de uirgine*) was formed by the Word of God (*Haer.* 3.21.10). Then, the Word of God traced his own form in his recapitulation of Adam, in his own handiwork (*plasmationem*), made from the purest, the finest, and the most delicate virgin soil, by his own will and wisdom (*Haer.* 3.18.7; cf. *Epid.* 11). Thus, the Word incarnate as the true image and likeness of God demonstrated the likeness of fleshness (embodiment) to Adam by the will and wisdom of God (*Epid.* 32). Hence, Irenaeus weaves this Pauline parallel into the likeness of fleshness between Adam and Christ so that the Pauline contrast in Rom 5:19 ("just as by one man's disobedience sin came and death through sin reigned, so by one man's obedience, justice was brought"[23]) corresponds in recapitulation. This is how Adam's "virgin birth" (fashioned from the virgin earth) prefigures and necessitates Christ's virgin birth in God's intentional "arc of economy" as the end will be like the beginning.[24]

Although this parallel of virgin earth and virgin birth is ambiguous in the meaning of virginity and rather contrived (the untilled earth on the one hand and the unpenetrated—female—body on the other), for Irenaeus, it still serves as a unique antidote to the Carpocrates, Cerinthus, and the Ebionites, who rejected Christ the Word incarnate and believed that Jesus was a mere man begotten by Joseph (*Haer.* 3.18.7; 3.19; 1.25-26; 4.33.4). Christ's virgin birth, just like Adam's creation from the virgin soil, demonstrates that the incarnation was God's work by his own will and wisdom, excluding any human will or production:

> He promised the King from the fruit of David's womb, which is proper to a pregnant virgin; and not from the fruit of his [David's] loins or from the fruit of his reins (*fructu lumborum eius nec de fructu renum eius*), which is proper to a man who begets and of a woman who conceives by the aid of a man. Scripture, therefore, in the promise excluded the generative powers of a man

---

22. Cf. B. H. Dunning, *Specters of Paul: Sexual Difference in Early Christian Thought* (Philadelphia: University of Pennsylvania Press, 2011), 112.

23. *Haer.* 3.21.10 (SC 211:426): *per inobaudientiam unius hominis introitum peccatum habuit et per peccatum mors obtinuit, sic et per obaudientiam unius hominis iustitia introducta.*

24. The phrase, "the arc of economy" is from J. Behr, *Irenaeus of Lyons: Identifying Christianity* (Oxford: Oxford University Press, 2013), 151.

(*Circumscripsit igitur genitalia uiri in promissione Scriptura*). Why, he [Joseph] is not even mentioned, since the one who was born was not of the will of man.[25]

Joseph symbolizes human (male) will and power of generation and therefore is excluded. Thus the fundamental likeness that Irenaeus establishes between Adam's formation (πλάσμα) from virgin earth and Christ's virgin birth is the sole divine authorship and craftsmanship of the creation and incarnation in the "arc of economy," excluding any intermediate generative powers or involvement as the gnostic groups and Ebionites claimed (*Haer.* 3.21.10).

It is in this context that Irenaeus puts forth Mary's virginal conception of Jesus against conception of Jesus by Joseph and Mary and constructs a typology of Eve and Virgin Mary as a necessary corollary to that of Adam and Christ.[26] Since Joseph is eliminated from Christ's human lineage and formation, where does Christ's human formation come from? The Spirit through the prophet as already foretold the Emmanuel who was to be born of the Virgin (Isa 7:14, LXX), as God promised the King from the fruit of David's womb (*Haer.* 3.21.4-5; 3.16.2; cf. *Epid.* 53); and the same Spirit, through the mouth of Elizabeth, blessed Mary for the fruit of her womb (*fructus uentris*). Thus God's promise to David and the prophecy in Isaiah was all "fulfilled in the birth-giving of the Virgin, that is, of Mary" since Mary was the descendant of David and certainly of Adam, confirmed by the Lukan genealogy and Pauline typology (*Haer.* 3.21.10; 3.22.3). Christ's flesh then comes from the flesh of Mary the Virgin and thus is the same as Adam's (*Haer.* 3.21.10). As Behr articulates well, by recapitulating the ancient formation of Adam through his virgin birth, "Christ preserves both our own substance, the mud from which we are made, and the manner in which Adam came to be."[27]

This in turn becomes an antidote to the Valentinians who asserted that Christ merely passed through Mary as water through a tube and received nothing from the Virgin (*Haer.* 1.7.2; 3.11.3; 3.16.1; 3.22.1). Since Irenaeus has already shown the impossibility of receiving Christ's humanity from Joseph, if Valentinian claims were true, Irenaeus argues, Christ was not human like us and his sufferings were meaningless. Furthermore, what one reads in the Scripture about Jesus eating, fasting, feeling hungry, tired, and sorrowful would not make sense (*Haer.* 3.22.2). Rather, Paul stated in Galatians, "God sent His Son, made of a woman" (4:4; *Haer.*

---

25. *Haer.* 3.21.5 (SC 211:414-16): *Propter hoc enim et de fructu ventris eius Regem promisit, quod erat proprium Virginis praegnantis, et non de fructu lumborum eius nec de fructu renum eius, quod est proprium viri generantis et mulieris ex viro conceptionem facientis. Circumscripsit igitur genitalia viri in promissione Scriptura, immo vero nec commemorator, quoniam non ex voluntate viri erat qui nascebatur.*

26. On the theological and social significance of Mary's person and role in recapitulation, see M. C. Steenberg, "The Role of Mary as Co-recapitulator in St Irenaeus of Lyons," *VC* 58 (2004), 117–37; T. Weinandy, "Annunciation and Nativity: Undoing Sinful Act of Eve," *International Journal of Systematic Theology* 14 (2012), 217–32.

27. Behr, *Irenaeus of Lyon*, 164.

3.22.1) and also in Romans, "concerning His Son, who was descended from David, according to the flesh and designated Son of God in power according to the Spirit of holiness by His resurrection from the dead, Jesus Christ our Lord."[28] Irenaeus associates and applies Paul's words in Galatians directly and exclusively to Christ's virginal conception and birth by Mary: "there is one Jesus Christ our Lord, who belongs to David's offspring by virtue of the generation from Mary"[29]—although most biblical scholars would note that "made of a woman" was rather a Semitic expression for "human being" and did not necessarily mean or imply "but not of a man."[30] Likewise in this context, Irenaeus takes the Romans passage as a confirmation of Christ's flesh coming from Mary, who was in the line of David, while affirming Christ's divinity according to the Spirit. If the Valentinian view reflects a radical form of the widespread contemporary notion that it is the father's seed (*sperma*), consisting of spirit (*pneuma*) and reason (*logos*), that produces a child while the mother only provides the formless soil for the child in conception and birth, Irenaeus's application of Paul's words here underscores not only Mary's genuine humanity (which is necessary for Christ's genuine humanity) but her unique agency against such prevalent notion.[31]

If Christ's virgin birth is critical to the salvation of humanity in his recapitulation of Adam, fighting against Satan in that same flesh and winning the prize of immortality by the Spirit in and for that same flesh, Mary's role in Christ's recapitulation is "a logical consequence of Christ's being the type of Adam."[32] "Consequently (*consequenter*)," reasons Irenaeus, not only Mary's virginal body is salvifically and thus inimitably significant but the Virgin Mary also has a critical moral role to play in human salvation as Irenaeus puts her "squarely into Christ's economy of recapitulation."[33] Just as Christ's obedience reversed Adam's defeat and the subsequent sinful order through the latter's disobedience, the Virgin Mary's obedience to the divine Word reversed the virgin Eve's sinful disobedience and its consequence (*Haer.* 3.22.4; 5.19.1; *Epid.* 33). Until now, the main concern of Irenaeus's recapitulation was the contrasting moral choices of Adam and Christ (disobedience-obedience) while sharing the same human flesh within God's

---

28. *Haer.* 3.16.3; cf. 1.3-4; 3.22.1 (SC 211:436): *De Filio autem, inquit, eius, qui factus est ex semine David secundum carnem, qui praedestinatus est Filius Dei in virtute secundum Spiritum sanctificationis ex resurrection mortuorum Iesu Christi Domini nostri.*

29. *Haer.* 3.16.3 (SC 211:296): *Unum autem Jesum Christum Dominum nostrum qui de semine David secundum cam generationem quae est ex Maria.*

30. Cf. J Pelikan, *Mary through the Centuries: Her Place in the History of Culture* (New Haven: CT: Yale University Press, 1996), 14–15.

31. See P. Brown, *The Body and Society: Men, Women and Sexual Renunciation in Early Christianity* (New York: Columbia University Press, 1988), 9–10, 111–12.

32. D. J. Unger and M. C. Steenberg, *St. Irenaeus of Lyons: Against the Heresies. Book 3* (ACW 64; New York: The Newman Press, 2012), 199; cf. Minns, *Irenaeus: An Introduction* (London: T&T Clark, 2010), 157.

33. Unger and Steenberg, *St. Irenaeus of Lyons*, 199.

economy; and both Adam's and Christ's sexuality as male has not been theologically significant as Adam represents all humanity and Christ both humanity and God beyond their individual personhood.[34] However, as Irenaeus retroactively introduces the Eve-Mary parallel from the standpoint of Christ's virgin birth from Mary, their virginal bodies and fertility as female (more than their symbolic human significance) as well as their contrasting moral choices become indispensible to Irenaeus's construction of recapitulation as the main connecting points between the two. Therefore, Irenaeus apparently applies the law of betrothal (Deut 22:23ff) that the woman who is espoused but still a virgin can be called a wife, not only to Mary but also to Eve although Eve was never considered just espoused to Adam and Irenaeus himself previously says that Eve "indeed had a husband" (*illa uirum quidem habens*) even in childhood innocence in Paradise (*Haer*. 3.22.4; 5.19.1). Yet, establishing this likeness between them as *espoused fertile virgins* is necessary to preserve an "otherwise precarious" parallel between Eve and Mary.[35] Based on this likeness, Irenaeus draws out a theological contrast: whereas Eve's voluntary, virginal disobedience led her fertility to produce only death for herself and the whole human race, Mary's voluntary, virginal obedience led her fertility to bring about salvation for herself and the whole human race (*Haer*. 3.22.4). Indeed,

> just as through a disobedient virgin man was struck and, falling, died, so also by means of a virgin, who obeyed the word of God, man being revivified (ἀναζωπυρέω), received life . . . He did not become any other formation (πλάσμα) but being born from her who was of the race of Adam, He maintained the likeness of the formation. For it was necessary for Adam to be recapitulated in Christ, that "mortality might be swallowed up in immortality" (cf., 1 Cor 15.54; 2 Cor 5.4); and Eve in Mary, that a virgin, become an advocate (*advocata*) for a virgin, might undo and destroy the virginal disobedience by virginal obedience. (*Epid*. 33; cf. *Haer*. 5.19.1)

Irenaeus complements the Pauline contrast of Adam-mortality and Christ-immortality with the Eve-death and Mary-life contrast; more precisely, he puts the latter parallel into the former so as to tighten up a single pattern of God's economy of salvation that encompasses sexuality, virginity, and generation.

Therefore, as Irenaeus builds this latter parallel, "absent here is any suggestion of the impact of sexuality on either Eve's sin or Mary's obedience" as pointed out by Donovan.[36] Eve did not lose her virginity because of her disobedience but disobeyed God *in* her virginal state as Mary obeyed God in the same virginal state. Despite her disobedience to God's command, Irenaeus's portrayal of Eve is distinct from most of the Church Fathers who linked together her sexuality and

---

34. Cf. Minns, *Irenaeus*, 71.
35. Dunning, *Specters of Paul*, 207.78.
36. M. A. Donovan, *One Right Reading? A Guide to Irenaeus* (Collegeville, MN: The Liturgical Press, 1997), 88.

the fall.³⁷ For Irenaeus, Eve is not the seducer but the serpent is (*Haer.* 3.23.2-3); when Eve blamed the serpent for her own eating of the fruit, she spoke truthfully (*Haer.* 3.23.5; cf. 5.23.1). Thus, while God cursed the serpent, "the chief actor in the transgression," he "had pity on the one who had been seduced" (*Haer.* 3.23.5). And out of grace, God cast Adam and Eve out of Paradise and removed them from the tree of life so as to deliver them ultimately, as they die to sin and begin to live by God through Christ's recapitulation (*Haer.* 3.23.5; cf. Gal 2:19; Rom 6:2, 10). Therefore, God "put enmity between the serpent and the woman with her offspring" (*inimicitiam posuit inter serpentem et mulierem et semen eius*; cf. Gen 3:15); it is clear in Irenaeus's mind who "the woman with her offspring" is—the Virgin Mary with Christ, "Mary's child, who was destined beforehand to trample on [the serpent's] head."³⁸ Here the battle wages on between the serpent on the one hand and "the woman with her offspring" on the other. In God's economy then, the Virgin Mary and Christ are inseparable as the winning team of the final battle. Thus, as Irenaeus moves from Eve to Mary, describing their roles and places within God's economy, Eve and her sexual identity as a woman as such do not bear theological blame or curse and any corresponding ontological inferiority (to Adam as a man). What is notably missing in Irenaeus's description of Eve and her disobedience is the oft-used Pauline passages such as 1 Cor 11:8-9, 2 Cor 11:3, or 1 Tim 2:11-14³⁹; Irenaeus does not read Eve (and thus women) through the lens of those Pauline passages, both "undisputed" and "disputed." Rather, because of the salvific role of "the woman with her offspring" in God's economy, Mary and her sexual identity as a woman are key factors in human salvation (here Mary is morally and spiritually superior to Adam), uniting Eve and Mary together in their sexuality even in their opposite actions. Eve will eventually exchange her virginity for physical fertility, that is procreation, but still within the plan of God's economy, as previously mentioned. However, Mary remains a virgin and is fertile in a different way. For Irenaeus, sexuality, marriage, and procreation per se are not the cause of the Paradise lost and mortality as they are for many of the later Church Fathers, although all human procreation before Mary's has taken place subsequent to the fall.⁴⁰ Nor does virginity per se become

---

37. E.g., Tertullian, *Cult. fem.* 1.1.1-2; Ambrose, *Parad.* 12.56; Chrysostom, *Hom. 1 Cor* 1. 26.2.

38. *Haer.* 3.23.7; cf. 5.21.1 and Gal 3:19 (SC 211:462): *semen praedestinatum calcare caput eius, quod fuit partus Mariae.*

39. 1 Cor 11:8-9: "Indeed man was not made from woman, but woman from man. Neither was man created for the sake of woman, but woman for the sake of man"; 2 Cor 11:3: "But I am afraid that as the serpent deceived Eve by its cunning, your thoughts will be led astray from a sincere and pure devotion to Christ"; 1 Tim 2:11-14: "Let a woman learn in silence with full submission. I permit no woman to teach r to have authority over a man; she is to keep silent. For Adam was formed first, then Eve; and Adam was not deceived, but the woman was deceived and became a transgressor" (all NRSV).

40. Cf. Dunning, *Specters of Paul*, 121.

the solution to regain that Paradise lost and immortality (as in the case of Eve's virginal disobedience). Mary's virginity is unique and exceptional because of the Word incarnate; and just as Christ's recapitulation of Adam is once for all and unrepeatable, so is Mary's recapitulation of Eve as her advocate. In the end, sexuality, marriage, procreation, and virginity do not hold any absolute value or stigma but are instrumental to and have proper and necessary places in the redemptive plan of God's economy.

Eve and Mary's respective fecundity has enormous soteriological consequences, however. Eve as the mother of humanity, her generation (after losing "the robe of holiness") clearly introduces and perpetuates death and corruptibility through all the generations that will come after her (union with Adam). Regarding Mary's generation, in the words of Benjamin Dunning, "the fertility of Mary's pure womb introduces ... the possibility of a regenerate fertility *still* in Adam's line and thus capable of transmitting Adam's likeness to Mary's offspring Christ without implicating him in Adam and Eve's sin."[41] Irenaeus then expands Paul's typological parallel of Rom 5:19 in such a way as to weave together implicitly the double recapitulation in order to point to a single story of creation, incarnation, and redemption: "For, just as through the disobedience of one man who was fashioned first from untilled earth many were made sinners and lost life, so it was fitting also through the obedience of one man who was born first of the Virgin, that many be made just and received salvation."[42] The starting point of his comparison is Adam "fashioned first from the untilled (virgin) earth" and Christ "born first of the Virgin." Just as Adam was first and thus the father of humanity, so was Christ first of the new creation and thus the author of salvation. Then, just as many "second-born" were made sinners through the first, Adam, so were many "second-born" made just through the first, Christ. Since all humans have the same nature as Adam, they all indirectly come from the virgin soil; and since all the righteous receive salvation from Christ, the first born of the Virgin, they are indirectly born of and receive their new life from the Virgin, the mother of all Christians.[43] This is how the Virgin Mary undoes death and vivifies humanity: "That which was generated [by Mary] is a holy thing, and is the Son of the Most High God, the

---

41. Dunning, *Specters of Paul*, 121 (emphasis original).

42. *Haer.* 3.18.7; cf. 5.19.1 (SC 211:468-70): *Quemadmodum enim per inobaudientiam unius hominis qui primus de terra rudis plasmatus est peccatores facti sunt multi et amiserunt vitam, ita oportuit et per obaudientiam unius hominis qui primus ex Virgine natus est iustificari multos et percipere salutem.*

43. Cf. *Haer.* 4.33.11 (SC 100:830): *quoniam Verbum caro erit et Filius Dei Filius hominis, purus pure puram aperiens vulvam eam quae regenerat homines in Deum, quam ipse puram fecit; et hoc factus quod et nos, Deus fortis, et inenarrabile habet genus* ("the Word would become flesh, and the Son of God the Son of Man, the pure one opening purely that pure womb which regenerates human beings unto God and which he himself made pure, having become that which we are, he is 'God Almighty' and has a generation which cannot be declared.").

Father of all and the one who effected the incarnation of His Son and showed forth a new generation, that as by the former generation we inherited death, so by this new generation we might inherit life."[44] Thus, this is how Irenaeus again "brackets together" creation and redemption through "the typological relationship of humanity as originally created and humanity as redeemed of the Virgin-born Savior."[45]

Irenaeus then explicitly links Christ's virgin birth, passion, and resurrection through the familiar Pauline passages. He weaves together Gal 4:4-5, Rom 1:1-4, and Col 1:15 and 18 in such a way to confirm Paul's affirmation of Christians' adoption through "one Jesus Christ our Lord (sent forth by God), who belongs to David's offspring by virtue of the generation from Mary; … This Jesus Christ was designated Son of God in power, according to the Spirit of holiness, by resurrection from the dead, that He might be the firstborn of the dead, just as He is the firstborn of all creation."[46] Christ became the beginning of the living for the new generation as not only the first born of the Virgin but also "the first born of the dead"—rather, precisely because he was the first born of the Virgin, he became the first born of the dead (*Haer.* 3.16.3; cf. 3.22.4; *Epid.* 38; Col 1:18). Christ's salvific death and redemption by his blood is only possible by his incarnation through the virgin birth (*Haer.* 5.2.2); Christ then destroyed death, demonstrated the resurrection of the flesh as "the first born of the dead," and "became preeminent (πρωτεύω) in all things" (*Epid.* 39; cf. Col 1:18). Consequently, for Irenaeus, Christ's resurrection is a result of the incarnation (*Haer.* 5.1.1-5.2.3), and therefore, Christ's resurrection is predicated upon his virgin birth:

> And, if one does not accept His birth from a Virgin, how can he accept His resurrection from the dead? For it is no astonishing, nor marvelous or extraordinary thing if, without being born, He neither rose from the dead; … So if He was not born, neither did He die; and if He did not die, neither was he raised from the dead; and if He was not raised from the dead, death is not conquered nor its kingdom destroyed; and if death [is] not conquered, how are we to ascend to life, having fallen under death from the beginning? (*Epid.* 38-39; cf. 53)

---

44. *Haer.* 5.1.3; cf. 5.19.1; *Epid.* 33; 37 (SC 153:24-26): *qua propter quod generatum est sanctum est et filius Altissimi Dei Patris omnium, qui operates est incarnationem ejus et novam ostendit generationem, uti, quemadmodum per priorem generationem mortem hereditavimus, sic per generationem hanc hereditaremus vitam.*

45. Unger and Steenberg, *St. Irenaeus of Lyons*, 177.48; cf. MacKenzie, *Irenaeus's Demonstration of the Apostolic Preaching*, 101–3.

46. *Haer.* 3.16.3 (SC 211:296-98): *unum autem Iesum Christum Dominum nostrum qui de semine David secundum eam generationem quae est ex Maria, hunc destiantum Filium Dei Iesum Christum in virtute secundum Spiitum santificationis ex resurrection mortuorum, ut sit primogenitus mortuorum, quemadmodum et primogenitus in omni conditione.*

Thus, inversely, those who reject the resurrection of Christ's flesh despise Christ's birth (*Epid.* 39). Since the Word incarnate sets the pattern for humanity's creation and salvation, Christ with human flesh and blood saves humanity, culminating in his fleshly resurrection. His resurrection in turn is a basis of the resurrection of our flesh, which completes the arc of God's economy. For Irenaeus, the resurrection of Christ and Christians serves as the ultimate antidote to the gnostic denial of the flesh. Against the Valentinians' faulty appropriation of Paul's words, "flesh and blood cannot inherit the Kingdom of God" (1 Cor 15:50), Irenaeus presents how flesh and blood could inherit the kingdom of God: the Holy Spirit takes up our flesh and blood and so transforms it to inherit the Kingdom as the Spirit enables and guides the regenerate to live by participation in the Spirit (*Haer.* 5.14.1-2; 5.9.3; cf. 1 Cor 6:13-14). As "the fruit of the work of the Spirit is the salvation of the flesh" (*Haer.* 5.12.4), the resurrected body by the Spirit's power is the spiritual body controlled by the Spirit (*Haer.* 5.6.2-7.2; cf. 1 Cor 15:44); and this spiritual, resurrected body will still be a sexually differentiated body but once again in an innocent, "virginal" state of sanctity and purity (*Haer.* 5.6.2; 1 Cor 6:13-14) as the end is like the beginning.

Women, Prophecy, and the Church

While the gift of the Spirit is indispensible for those regenerated and adopted into God through Christ's virgin birth and recapitulation, Irenaeus finds "others" in the church who reject this very Spirit, poured out on the human race in the last times (*Haer.* 3.11.9).[47] Out of fear of the false prophets, they reject both the Gospel of John with its promise to send the Paraclete and the apostle Paul, who in his letter to the Corinthians spoke "painstakingly about the charismatic gifts," and knows men *and* women prophesying in the church (*Haer.* 3.11.9; cf. 1 Cor 12:31, 10-29; 14:1-40). By rejecting the gifts and the apostolic witness to the Holy Spirit then, they commit the unpardonable sin, that is, the sin against the Holy Spirit (*Haer.* 3.11.9; cf. Matt 12:31-32). Irenaeus is particularly concerned about the prophecies of the Spirit and the prophetic ministry in the church as affirmed by the apostle Paul. Irenaeus is emphatic in his writings that it is the Spirit that ensures that the Old and New Testaments testify to the same One God and that Christ's virgin birth and Christians' adoption in recapitulation is God's intended economy through the fulfillment of its prophecies. The Holy Spirit spoke through the prophets of the Old Testament and also through John and Paul and continues to speak through both male *and* female prophets in the church (cf. *Haer.* 5.6.1). Whereas Irenaeus

---

47. On this topic, see further D. L. Hoffman, *The Status of Women and Gnosticism in Irenaeus and Tertullian* (Lewiston: The Edwin Mellen Press, 1995), 23–143; S. Parvis, "Irenaeus, Women, and Tradition," in *Irenaeus: Life, Scripture, Legacy*, ed. S. Parvis and P. Foster (Minneapolis, MN: Fortress Press, 2012), 159–64, 246–47, as they respond to E. Pagel, *The Gnostic Gospels* (New York: Random House, 1979).

seems to have assumed that the apostles and the bishops as their successors would be men (*Haer.* 3.3.1-2), it is significant for him to affirm and protect this prophetic ministry of men *and* women in the church (though it is unspecified).

It is with this larger view in mind that we should read Irenaeus's description of Marcus's women followers (*Haer.* 1.13). According to Irenaeus, Marcus, a Valentinian heretic, magician, and imposter, deceives many men and women with his teaching and ritual apparently in a "charismatic" assembly. He has many women followers, especially the wealthy. In what appears to be a form of Eucharist, he commands the women to give thanks over the elements in his presence and tricks them with his magic. He then commands those rich women "worthy of partaking of Charis (Grace)" to receive Charis through him in the bridal chamber and to prophesy. While, following Marcus's urge, some ended up uttering nonsense, considering themselves prophetesses, and giving him their possessions and bodies, "some of the most faithful women, who have the fear of God" rejected him in disgust, condemned him, and left his company (*Haer.* 1.13.4). It seems that Marcus and the former women must have held prophecy in a special position in their assembly (as in the "orthodox" assembly), and perhaps because of that it is significant that Irenaeus describes the latter women as the ones with spiritual discernment, knowing the genuine nature of prophetic gift—it cannot be given by Marcus the magician who forces it upon people but is only given by God from above. People with true prophetic gift and power speak not on command but where and when God wills (*Haer.* 1.13.4).

Often, it was these women who returned to the Catholic Church that confessed and exposed Marcus's deviant and licentious actions on some of them (*Haer.* 1.13.5). Reminiscent of 2 Tim 3:6,[48] Irenaeus then dwells on how Marcus's disciples "deceived many silly women and defiled them" (*Haer.* 1.13.6). This is a part of Irenaeus's attack and polemic against his targeted heretical groups—naming and labeling them with sexualized polemic; the heretical beliefs necessarily result in sexually deviant and promiscuous, or equally problematic encratic behaviors (e.g., the Valentinians in *Haer.* 1.6.3; the Simonians in 1.23.4; the Carpocratians in 1.25.4; the Nicolaitans in 1.26.3; the Encratites from Saturninus and Marcion in 1.24.2; 1.28.1). Irenaeus highlights these heretics' "carnal pleasures" in the flesh on the one hand and their forced continence on the other to show how they misunderstand and misapply their beloved Paul's words, "flesh and blood cannot inherit the Kingdom of God" (1 Cor 15:50), in contrast to the proper understanding and application of those words by the "orthodox" church (as mentioned above). In these stock portrayals of licentiousness, fornication, or false continence, the heretical aggressors are presumably men and their victims are usually (silly) women. This may raise some suspicion on a relatively positive role Irenaeus attributes to sex in human growth in God's economy and a remarkably restrained depiction of Eve and women in the earlier sections of this chapter. However, the sexualized polemic

---

48. "For among them are those who make their way into households and captivate silly women, overwhelmed by their sins and swayed by all kinds of desires" (NRSV).

in fact functions to support Irenaeus's recognition of the proper place of sex in the flesh inherited and controlled by the Spirit as he draws its boundaries for the "orthodox." Moreover, while it makes Irenaeus's understanding of women more ambiguous, the (unfortunate) sexualized polemic serves Irenaeus to preserve and protect authentic women prophets within the continuing "orthodox" prophetic tradition as opposed to the "heretical" groups or assemblies, and also to defend women's voices and roles in the "orthodox" church in contrast to what he thought of as the exploitation of the women in the "heretical" groups.

Conclusion

This chapter has examined Irenaeus's reading of Paul on sexuality, virginity, and women in a broader notion of recapitulation within Irenaeus's theological hermeneutics. Irenaeus's Christological and eschatological reading of Pauline typology of Adam and Christ establishes the arc of God's economy where the end is like the beginning. If Christ's recapitulation of Adam based on the likeness of the flesh restores the likeness of God in human growth toward perfection in God's *oikonomia*, sexuality, marriage, and procreation are part of that human progress to maturation led by the Spirit. At the eschaton, while marriage and procreation will cease, our fleshly, sexual existence in protological purity will be restored and continue in the resurrection. This protological and eschatological ideal of innocence in sexual existence for man and woman takes a different turn with Irenaeus's retroactive insertion of the Eve-Mary parallel into the Adam-Christ parallel as he constructs another parallel between Adam's creation from the virgin earth and Christ's virgin birth. For Irenaeus, the salvific necessity of Christ's virgin birth in his recapitulation demands both the likeness and contrast between Eve and Mary, just as that of Adam and Christ. Mary, as the espoused fertile virgin, like Eve, reverses Eve's disobedience and its disastrous consequence with her redemptive obedience. While maleness of Adam and Christ was (relatively) theologically insignificant, Irenaeus confers critical soteriological significance on the female virginity and virginal fertility of Eve and Mary in God's economy. Irenaeus does not make an explicit connection between theological and historical significance of Eve and Mary on the one hand, and women and their roles in the church on the other. However, he regards women (and men) as recipients and participants of the Spirit's gift and upholds their voices and prophetic ministry in the "orthodox" church as he invalidates the sham imitation of heretics and their women followers in sexualized polemic. In all of these points, Irenaeus reads and rereads Paul, "saving" him from heretical misreading and misapplication.

RESPONSE
IRENAEUS'S RECEPTION OF PAULINE TEACHING ON SEXUALITY, VIRGINITY, AND WOMEN: A RESPONSE TO HELEN RHEE

Judith Gundry

Helen Rhee casts a wide net in her chapter "Irenaeus and Paul: Sexuality, Virginity, and Women." She draws on a variety of texts in which Irenaeus discusses these topics in the course of developing his doctrine of recapitulation and polemicizing against "heretics." She notes his dependence on Paul in these contexts. But Rhee eschews a similarly broad engagement with the relevant Pauline texts on sexuality, virginity, and women. So her chapter may have been more fittingly entitled, "Irenaeus on Sexuality, Virginity, and Women: Reception of the Pauline Tradition."

Rhee's purpose is not only to describe Irenaeus's views on sexuality, virginity, and women and their relationship to Paul's views, but to assess them in the light of a modern Christian feminist perspective (although this perspective and the criteria for assessment are not made explicit). For the most part, Irenaeus passes muster in Rhee's view. He defends women's voices and roles (implicitly, their prophetic ministries) in the "orthodox" church against the "exploitation" of women in "heretical" circles. He ascribes a positive soteriological role to the Virgin Mary and to her birthgiving (in the incarnation). He avoids sexualizing Eve's disobedience at the fall and implying the ontological inferiority of woman, unlike Paul[1] and some of Irenaeus's contemporaries. Irenaeus however lapses into "sexualized" rhetoric when he describes the "silly" women who attach themselves to "heretics" and engage in sexually "deviant" behavior in pursuit of prophecy.

In this response to Rhee I will try to show, by engaging in a fuller discussion of the Pauline texts on sexuality, virginity, and women (here I am referring to the undisputed Pauline texts[2]), that there are far more and significant differences between Irenaeus and Paul on the topics of sexuality, virginity, and women than

---

1. Cf. 2 Cor 11:3; 1 Tim 2:1f.
2. My discussion here excludes the Pauline texts whose authorship is disputed in Colossians, Ephesians, and the Pastoral Epistles.

is evident from Rhee's discussion. I will also suggest that Irenaeus's recapitulative framework based on Eph 1:10—"in the economy of the fullness of time all things are recapitulated in Christ"—has the intention of crushing Christian sexual asceticism in Irenaeus's day, which is consistent with the teaching of the later Pauline epistles—but not with Pauline teaching in 1 Corinthians 7. The result, from my own Christian feminist perspective, is Irenaeus's relinquishing of some of the more amenable aspects of Pauline teaching on sexuality, virginity, and women. First, I will give a synthetic summary of Rhee's analysis of Irenaeus's views on sexuality, virginity, and women.[3] Then I will present my own arguments for how Irenaeus's views both agree and conflict with Paul's.

As Rhee argues, Irenaeus appeals to Paul in holding that marriage, sex, and procreation are present *concessions* to weak and incontinent human beings that have a *positive* purpose and ultimately contribute to salvation. Marriage, sex, and procreation are not the result of sin or derived from Satan, against a "false type of temperance" taught by Saturninus and Marcion. Marriage, sex, and procreation are rather means by which humanity, by the Spirit, presently grows into the likeness of God and attains the "full number" preordained by God. They are "part of that human progress to maturation led by the Spirit." Only when this process of growth toward perfection in the present age is completed and humanity is co-assimilated to God through Christ will marriage, sex, and procreation end. Sexual differentiation will then be untinged by lust and shameful desires, and the original sexual differentiation of Adam and Eve as innocent children will be recapitulated.[4] For "unity and diversity of humanity as male and female is the will and work of God"—but marriage, sex, and procreation are merely concessions with temporal benefits in this age. What Rhee's discussion does not make clear is that Irenaeus's doctrine of recapitulation enables him to insist on the crucial role of marriage, sex, and procreation in the church—against the "heretics" who teach sexual asceticism—while at the same time ruling out any ultimate or eschatological value to marriage, sex, and procreation (and thus lustful desire).

As Rhee also discusses, Irenaeus appeals to Paul in ascribing critical significance to Mary's childbearing of Christ: it is the proof of his humanity, against the Valentinians' claim that Jesus was not human. Further, Irenaeus holds that Mary's obedience to the divine word reverses Eve's disobedience and its consequence. In the light of Irenaeus's polemics against "heretics" who teach sexual asceticism, it is likely in my view that he considers Mary's childbearing in obedience to the divine word to provide the pattern for faithful women in the church—although Rhee does not suggest this. Conversely, Irenaeus holds that Mary's virginity is inimitable and exceptional, and thus without moral significance: it is rather the

---

3. Here I discuss Rhee's analysis of Irenaeus as presented in her chapter, and do not make any attempt to evaluate it on the basis of the primary texts or other secondary literature.

4. Rhee notes Irenaeus's view that Adam and Eve embraced and kissed as innocent children but apparently did not have sex and procreate until after being expelled from the Garden and growing up. For Adam was a mere infant at creation.

proof that the incarnation was solely by the will and work of God and not from man, against the claims of Carpocrates, Cerinthus, and the Ebionites that Jesus was a mere man.[5] Again in the light of Irenaeus's polemics against "heretics" who teach sexual asceticism, it is likely in my view that Irenaeus understands Mary's virginity as *inimitable* so as not to encourage women's sexual abstinence in the church—although this too is not suggested by Rhee.[6] She does however note Irenaeus's negative characterization of Adam's covering himself with prickly fig leaves symbolizing a "girdle of continence" and their replacement by God with garments of skins appropriate to a life of growth and increase under the Spirit's guidance. Thus Rhee might agree with my analysis of the moral implications of Irenaeus's views on Mary as the virgin childbearer.

As Rhee further indicates, Irenaeus appeals to Paul in support of charismatic gifts in the church so as to affirm the legitimate prophetic ministries of women (implicitly) in the "orthodox" church. And he condemns as illegitimate prophets those women (and men) who are led astray by "heretics" to pursue prophetic gifts through sexually deviant behavior, including sexual abstinence as well as licentiousness. Although Rhee does not suggest that Irenaeus's recapitulative framework has a bearing on his views on women's prophetic ministries, this seems likely, for he locates legitimate prophetic ministry in the "orthodox" church where marriage, sex, and procreation are beneficial "concessions" in the light of human incontinence. Thus he rejects as illegitimate those who associate prophecy with sexual asceticism and other forms of sexual "deviance."

In the following, I will point out two ways in which Irenaeus's recapitulative framework oversimplifies Paul's views on sexuality, virginity, and women as found especially in 1 Corinthians 7.[7] While Irenaeus rightly appeals to Paul for the view that marriage and sex are beneficial concessions or indulgences in the light of human weakness and incontinence in the present, Irenaeus ignores that Paul distinguishes *two* possible Christian lifestyles. First, it is "good" or "advantageous" to marry and have sex if one lacks self-control and "burns" (out of control) with the result of sexual immorality apart from marriage (1 Cor 7:9, 38a). But it is

---

5. In the worldview which Irenaeus presupposes, the human generative power belonged to the man, and the woman merely provided a receptacle for it.

6. Rhee concludes her discussion of Irenaeus's Mary-Eve typology with the comment: "In the end, sexuality, marriage, procreation, and virginity do not hold any absolute value or stigma but are instrumental to and have proper and necessary places in the redemptive plan of God's economy." Presumably, however, since Irenaeus regards marriage and procreation as part of the divine economy for the present, Rhee is not ruling out the moral significance of Mary's sexuality and childbearing.

7. For further discussion of this Pauline text, see Judith M. Gundry, "Anxiety or Care for People? The Theme of 1 Corinthians 7.32–34 and the Relation between Exegesis and Theology," in *Reconsidering the Relationship between Biblical and Systematic Theology in the New Testament*, ed. Benjamin E. Reynolds, Brian Lugioyo, and Kevin J. Vanhoozer (WUNT 2/369; Tübingen: Mohr Siebeck, 2014), 111–30.

"better" or "more advantageous" to remain a virgin or not to remarry, if one has control over the will or has a "gift from God" for such a way of life (7:8, 38b; cf. v. 40). For Paul, then, in contrast to Irenaeus, marriage, sex, and procreation are not "givens" for the present age. There is a choice to be made by the individual Christian. To opt for virginity or not remarrying is not to hinder a beneficial process of growth and increase through the Spirit. Rather, to opt for virginity or not remarrying is to be "consecrated both in body and in spirit" to the Lord's service in the dawning new creation (1 Cor 7:34). For marriage and sex are simply to avoid a "burning" that leads to "sexual immorality" for some (1 Cor 7:2, 9). Hence Paul describes sex in marriage as "what is due" to a spouse (1 Cor 7:3), of which a spouse is not to be defrauded "lest Satan tempt you on account of your lack of self-control" (1 Cor 7:5).[8] He also denies that the husband or wife "has control" in an exclusive sense "over his own body" or "over her own body" so as to withhold sex without agreement, including for the sake of devoting oneself to prayer (7:4f.). The aim of these injunctions is to ensure that the purpose of marriage and sex is achieved, which is simply to ward off sexual immorality for the one who "burns," not to contribute to a process of growth in humanity leading up to the eschaton.

Further, Paul does not even mention procreation in 1 Corinthians 7 when he permits marriage and sex on account of human weakness and incontinence. Nor when he cites Gen 2:24, "the two shall become one flesh," in 1 Cor 6:16 does he do so in order to affirm that procreation is the purpose of man and woman being joined in marriage and having sex, but simply to rule out illegitimate sexual unions (1 Cor 6:15-20). Furthermore, Paul refers to the children of the Corinthians as "consecrated [*hagia*]" to God (1 Cor 7:14), which arguably means that they belong to God by extension of the Christian parent(s)'s being *hagioi*, "consecrated" to God, and are thus potentially saved.[9] Thus Paul has no interest in procreation as part of a divine "economy" in the present consisting of growth and increase to attain to a preordained number of human beings.[10] Rather, children are significant as those who benefit from the in-breaking reign of God in the church. Only the later Pauline epistles link marriage necessarily with procreation as its implied or required purpose (cf. Col 3:19-21; Eph 6:1-4; 1 Tim 3:4, 12; 5:4, 8;

---

8. Paul's formulation in 7:32f. is more general, but may also refer euphemistically to sexual pleasing, in particular: "The married man strives after what belongs to the world, to serve/please his wife … the married woman strives after what belongs to the world, to serve/please her husband."

9. For further discussion, see Judith M. Gundry, "Children, Parents and God/Gods in Interreligious Roman Households and the Interpretation of 1 Corinthians 7:14," in *T & T Clark Handbook of Children and Childhood in the Biblical World*, ed. Sharon Betsworth and Julie Faith Parker (London: Bloomsbury T&T Clark, 2018), 311–33.

10. See John M. G. Barclay, "The Family as the Bearer of Religion in Judaism and Early Christianity," in *Constructing Early Christian Families: Family as Social Reality and Metaphor*, ed. Halvor Moxnes (New York: Routledge, 1997), 66–80. Paul characterizes his apostolic ministry metaphorically as "begetting" and "childbearing": "My children, for

2 Tim 1:5; Tit 1:6; 2:4). As far as Paul is concerned, procreation plays no necessary role in the present church age, even for those for whom marriage and sex is a useful concession.

Indeed, while Irenaeus encourages procreation as belonging to God's plan for the economy of this age, in 1 Corinthians 7 Paul appears to discourage it for those "upon whom the ends of the ages have come" (1 Cor 10:12). For he states that "the time is shortened" (1 Cor 7:29)—that is, the time before the end—and refers to "the present [or: impending] distress" (1 Cor 7:26). Then he says that "if you marry, you do not sin; and if the virgin marries, she does not sin. Nevertheless, such ones [viz., those who marry in order to have children] will have affliction in this life, and I am sparing you" (1 Cor 7:28). This statement echoes numerous early Christian and Jewish apocalyptic texts in which childbearing and nursing women (and parents in general) are the quintessential victims of the eschatological woes. For when the destruction strikes, it will be impossible for them and their children to flee in haste. They and their children will be killed or captured. Mothers will despair for having sat on the birthing stool, and fathers will grieve over lost sons and heirs. The blessing of fecundity will turn into a curse. The barren, on the other hand, will rejoice and be glad, for their fortunes will be reversed on that day.[11] I conclude that the way in which Paul "spares" the Corinthians is by saying nothing about an obligation to procreate or bear children or to have only procreative sex and to avoid nonprocreative sex, and by permitting sexual abstinence "for a suitable time," by agreement, in marriage (1 Cor 7:5). Such abstinence was thought to be an effective means of contraception and preferable to abortion in order to avoid having too many children.[12]

A further oversimplification of Paul's views by Irenaeus is the latter's overlooking of Paul's statement indicating the *bidirectional* orientation of the married man (and implicitly, the married woman): "And he [the married man] is divided" (1 Cor 7:32). Paul is probably suggesting here that the Christian husband is beholden not only to his wife but also to the Lord, whose "slave" or "freedman" he is, having been "purchased" by God (1 Cor 7:22f.). In the light of redemption in Christ therefore the married man no longer has a simple role but a complex one, which therefore

---

whom I am again in the pains of childbirth until Christ is formed in you" (Gal 4:19); "For in Christ Jesus I became your father in the gospel" (1 Cor 4:15); "We were gentle among you, like a nursing mother caring for her children" (1 Thess 2:7). It is not clear however whether Paul's spiritual "increase" is related to the "full number" preordained by God (Rom 11:25).

11. For further discussion, see Judith M. Gundry, "Affliction for Procreators in the Eschatological Crisis: Paul's Marital Counsel in 1 Corinthians 7.28 and Contraception in Greco-Roman Antiquity," *JSNT* 39 (2016), 141–61.

12. See also Judith M. Gundry, "1 Cor 7,5b in the Light of a Hellenistic-Jewish Tradition on Abstinence to 'Devote Leisure': Sufficiency in Paul and Philo," in *Paulus—Werk und Wirkung*, ed. Paul-Gerhard Klumbies and David du Toit (FS Lindemann; Tübingen: Mohr Siebeck, 2013), 21–44.

cannot be reduced to natural increase through marriage, sex, and procreation, as in Irenaeus's divine economy of the present.[13]

Paul's understanding of the Spirit's work in the church has also been oversimplified by Irenaeus in the interests of his recapitulative framework. According to Paul, the Spirit distributes diverse gifts in the church (1 Cor 12:4-11). In 1 Cor 7:7, one of those is the *charisma* of celibacy: "I wish that all were as I am [unmarried]. But each has his/her own *charisma* from God: the one [empowered to serve the Lord] in this manner, and the other [empowered to serve the Lord] in that manner" (1 Cor 7:7). Here Paul's continence is imitable by those who have the same *charism* from God, or the Spirit, whether men or women. By contrast, in Irenaeus Mary's virginity is inimitable for women. Likewise, Paul's defense of the widow who does not remarry—"she is more fortunate, in my opinion, if she remains [as she is]"—by appealing to the Spirit—"and I think that I have the Spirit of God" (1 Cor 7:40)[14]—would have stuck in the craw of Irenaeus. For he could not abide the "heretics" who falsely claimed to be prophets and were sexually "deviant," whether through sexual abstinence or license, and led astray women (as well as men) to such "deviance" out of a desire for prophetic gifts. For Irenaeus the legitimate Spirit of prophecy resided in the "orthodox" church, where male and female prophets married, had sex, and procreated.

In summary, Irenaeus's appeals to Pauline teaching on sexuality, virginity, and women are superficial and for the purpose of imposing his own recapitulative framework in the interests of a "natural" process of human growth to maturity, under the Spirit's guidance, in the church age. This framework leaves no place in the church for virginity and not remarrying and not procreating, or for a bidirectional orientation of the married man and woman, as Paul's eschatological framework allows, without sacrificing sexual differentiation.[15] Pauline teaching on virginity, sexuality, and women as I have described it here is more amenable from a Christian feminist perspective, in my view. For his teaching does not prescribe for women the roles of wife and childbearer as a matter of cooperating with what the Spirit is doing in the church in anticipation of the eschatological renewal of humanity.

---

13. The "divided" married man (or woman) perhaps alludes especially to such early Christian married gospel workers as Prisca and Aquila (Rom 16:3), or Junia and Andronicus (Rom 16:7), or the male apostles with their "sister" wives who traveled together to do gospel work (1 Cor 9:5).

14. For further discussion, see Judith M. Gundry, "Jesus-Tradition and Paul's Opinion about the Widow Remaining as a Widow (1 Cor 7.40)," in *Portraits of Jesus: Studies in Christology*, ed. Susan E. Myers (WUNT 2.321; Tübingen: Mohr Siebeck, 2012), 175–200.

15. For Paul's insistence on the retention of male and female identities by those in Christ, of which there are many examples, cf. 1 Cor 11:2-16; for further discussion, see Judith M. Gundry-Volf, "Gender and Creation in 1 Corinthians 11:2-16: A Study in Paul's Theological Method," in *Evangelium–Schriftauslegung–Kirche. Festschrift für Peter Stuhlmacher zum 65. Geburtstag*, ed. O. Hofius et al. (Göttingen: Vandenhoeck & Ruprecht, 1997), 151–71.

Chapter 9

PAUL AND THE JERUSALEM CHURCH IN IRENAEUS'S *AGAINST HERESIES*

Benjamin White

By the late-second century CE, Saul of Tarsus had become Paul, "*the* apostle," for Christians of wide-ranging theological dispositions—not just *an* apostle, as the opening of most of the Pauline epistles had claimed, but *the* apostle. Basilides, Theodotus, Ptolemy, Heracleon, Athenagoras, Clement of Alexandria, Irenaeus, Tertullian, and the authors of the *Treatise on the Resurrection* and *A Prayer of Paul, the Apostle* all employ this epithet, evidencing Paul's widespread and developing charisma as the figure par excellence of the apostolic age.[1] Irenaeus, then, was not alone when he used "the apostle" (in place of Paul's name), "Paul, the apostle," or "the apostle Paul" eighty-one times in *Against Heresies*. He was but one of many who had adopted this appellation for the once controversial Jewish, Christ-believing missionary, whose apostleship seemed to be in serious question at least at one phase of his ministry more than one hundred years earlier (cf. esp. Galatians and 2 Corinthians).[2]

---

1. Cf. Benjamin L. White, *Remembering Paul: Ancient and Modern Contests over the Image of the Apostle* (New York: Oxford University Press, 2014), 7–9, for the relevant data. The original Greek texts standing behind their Coptic translations from Nag Hammadi are notoriously difficult to date. The *Treatise on the Resurrection* and *A Prayer of Paul, the Apostle* have been included here based on their connection with certain strains of Valentinian thinking that were prominent in the late-second century CE.

2. The data from Irenaeus are enumerated in David H. Warren, "The Text of the Apostle in the Second Century: A Contribution to the History of its Reception" (ThD dissertation, Harvard University, 2001), 308. On later "Jewish Christian" opposition to Paul in the second century, cf. Joel Willitts, "Paul and Jewish Christians in the Second Century," in *Paul and the Second Century*, ed. M. F. Bird and J. R. Dodson (LNTS 412; London: T&T Clark, 2011), 140–68. Willitts tempers the argument that anti-Paulinism characterized the entirety of Jewish Christianity in the second century. Rather, it was a more localized phenomenon. Markus Bockmuehl, *The Remembered Peter: In Ancient Reception and Modern Debate* (WUNT 262; Tübingen: Mohr Siebeck, 2010), 94–113, argues similarly, calling into

Irenaeus's appeal to "the apostle" in the opening lines of the preface to Book 1, citing 1 Tim 1:4, in place of any explicit reference to "Paul" is indicative of how this moniker, in particular, had come to signify Paul by the late-second century:

> Certain people are discarding the Truth and introducing deceitful *myths and endless genealogies*, which, as the Apostle says, *promote speculations rather than the divine training that is in faith*. By specious argumentation, craftily patched together, they mislead the minds of the more ignorant and ensnare them by falsifying the Lord's words. Thus they become wicked interpreters of genuine words.[3]

Paul not only receives pride of place in *Against Heresies*, appearing as its first cited authority, but is also its most frequently invoked witness. Irenaean scholars have noted as many as 342 direct and indirect uses of Pauline letters in *Against Heresies*, coming from all of the canonical Pauline letters except for Philemon.[4] On at least one occasion Irenaeus refers to a Pauline text as γραφή (cf. the use of Gal 5:21 in *Haer.* 1.6.3), although this particular point is marginalized by the variegated ways in which Irenaeus used this term for a whole range of writings, including his own

---

question the traditional interpretation of the *Pseudo-Clementines*, which equated Simon Magus with Paul.

3. *Haer.* 1.pref.1. All English translations from Books 1, 2, and 3 of *Adversus haereses* come from Dominic J. Unger, *St. Irenaeus of Lyons: Against the Heresies*, 3 vols (ACW 55, 64, 65; New York: Paulist, 1992–2012), while translations from Books 4 and 5 come from *The Ante-Nicene Fathers*, ed. A. Roberts and J. Donaldson (Grand Rapids: Eerdmans, 1985 [1885–87]), unless noted otherwise. Emphasis here original to Unger.

4. I use "Pauline" here as marking early Christian texts that bear Paul's name as author without privileging the authenticity of any of them. W. W. Harvey, *Sancti Irenaei Episcopi Lugdunensis: Libros quinque adversus haereses* (Cambridge: Cambridge University Press, 1857), listed 324 references to Pauline letters in his index. Johannes Werner, *Der Paulinismus des Irenaeus: Eine kirchen- und dogmengeschichtliche Untersuchung über das Verhältnis des Irenaeus zu der paulinischen Briefsammlung und Theologie* (TUGAL 6.2; Leipzig: J.C. Hinrichs, 1889), 8, identified 206 Pauline citations in *Adversus haereses*, excluding 18 instances where Irenaeus relayed information about his opponents' use of Paul. J. Hoh, *Die Lehre des Hl. Irenäus über das Neue Testament* (NTAbh 7; Münster: Aschendorff, 1919), 198, put the number of direct citations at 247 and the number of indirect at 95 (although on p. 38.4 he puts the number of direct citations at 248). Relatively more recent are Bruce Metzger, *The Canon of the New Testament: Its Origin, Development, and Significance* (Oxford: Clarendon, 1987), 154, who counted 280; and Mark Olson, *Irenaeus, the Valentinian Gnostics, and the Kingdom of God: The Debate about 1 Corinthians 15:50* (Lewiston, NY: Mellen Biblical, 1995), 127–41, who lists 333 references to Pauline texts. The differences, as has been pointed out by D. H. Warren, "Text of the Apostle," 314, are related to how any individual modern interpreter distinguishes between overt citations and indirect allusions. Warren explores at length the mechanics of Irenaeus's citations of Paul (294–317).

(*Haer.* 3.6.4; 3.17.4; 5.pref.1) and his opponents' (*Haer.* 1.20.1; 3.3.3).⁵ More telling is how Paul functions in Irenaeus's argumentation.⁶ He places the testimony of "the apostle Paul" (*Haer.* 3.6.5-7.2), for example, between the "scriptures/prophets" (3.6.1-4) and "the Lord" (3.8.1-3) in his defense of the unity of God. In fact, Paul's testimony in this instance represents the totality of "the apostles" (*Haer.* 3.8.1; line 3: *apostoli*). The Spirit was the common authority leading each of these witnesses to the canon of truth (*Haer.* 3.7.2; 4.8.1).

Since Polycarp of Smyrna was an early influence on Irenaeus (*Haer.* 3.3.4; Eusebius, *Hist. eccl.* 5.20) and possibly also Irenaeus's anonymous "presbyter" (*Haer.* 4.27.1), Pauline traditions, among several others, would certainly have been part of Irenaeus's theological upbringing.⁷ The rather extraordinary and

---

5. Cf. F. R. Montgomery Hitchcock, *Irenaeus of Lugdunum: A Study of His Teaching* (Cambridge: Cambridge University Press, 1914), 226, and now Ben C. Blackwell, "Paul and Irenaeus," in *Paul and the Second Century*, 193, on this latter caveat. The Greek of *Haer.* 1.6.3 (fr. gr. 1.630-633) reads: Διὸ δὴ καὶ τὰ ἀπειρημένα πάντα ἀδεῶς οἱ τελειότατοι πράττουσιν αὐτῶν, περὶ ὧν αἱ γραφαὶ διαζεζαιοῦνται τοὺς ποιοῦντας αὐτὰ βασιλείαν Θεοῦ μὴ κληρονομήσειν. Greek and Latin citations are given throughout from the critical edition of Adelin Rousseau and Louis Doutreleau, *Irénée de Lyon: Contre les Hérésies*, 5 vols (SC; Paris: Éditions du Cerf, 1965-82). While Werner, *Paulinismus*, 33, 38, 44, insisted that Irenaeus never referred to Pauline epistles as γραφή, most have not followed him on account of *Haer.* 1.6.3: Hitchcock, *Irenaeus*, 223–24; Hoh, *Lehre des Hl. Irenäus*, 64–65, 90–91; André Benoit, *Saint Irénée: Introduction à l'étude de sa théologie* (Études d'histoire et de philosophie religieuses 52; Paris: Presses Universitaires de France, 1960), 136–41; Pierre Nautin, "Irénée et la canonicité des Épîtres pauliniennes," *RHR* 182 (1972): 113–30; Ernst Dassmann, *Der Stachel im Fleisch: Paulus in der frühchristlichen Literatur bis Irenäus* (Münster: Aschendorff, 1979), 301–5; David Rensberger, "As the Apostle Teaches: The Development of the Use of Paul's Letters in Second-Century Christianity" (PhD dissertation, Yale University, 1981), 317–18, 320; Rolf Noormann, *Irenäus als Paulusinterpret: zur Rezeption und Wirkung der paulinischen und deuteropaulinischen Briefe im Werk des Irenäus von Lyon* (WUNT 2.66; Tübingen: Mohr Siebeck, 1994), 68 n. 177, 307 n. 255; Olson, *Irenaeus*, 62–63; and Warren, "Text of the Apostle," 298–99. The Pauline Epistles may also be deemed γραφή in *Haer.* 1.8.2-3; 1.9.1; 2.35.4; 3.12.12; 4.pref.1; and 5.14.4.

6. Cf. Noormann, *Irenäus als Paulusinterpret*, 68–69.

7. On the use of Pauline traditions in Polycarp, cf., most recently, Michael W. Holmes, "Paul and Polycarp," in *Paul and the Second Century*, 57–69, and the long list of other studies in White, *Remembering Paul*, 218 n. 9. On Polycarp as Irenaeus's anonymous "presbyter," cf. Holmes, "Paul and Polycarp," 58, and the studies cited there: Frank D. Gilliard, "The Apostolicity of Gallic Churches," *HTR* 68 (1975): 29 n. 30; Pier Franco Beatrice, "Der Presbyter des Irenäus, Polycarp von Smyrna und der Brief an Diognet," in *Pléroma Salus Carnis. Homenaje a Antonio Orbe, S.J.*, ed. E. Romero-Pose (Santiago de Compostella, 1990), 179–202; and Charles E. Hill, *From the Lost Teaching of Polycarp: Identifying Irenaeus' Apostolic Presbyter and the Author of Ad Diognetum* (WUNT 186; Tübingen: Mohr Siebeck, 2006), 7–24. On the Pauline traditions that Irenaeus identifies as coming from this presbyter, cf. Adolf von Harnack, "Der Presbyter-Prediger des Irenäus (IV,27,1—IV,32,1). Bruchstücke

disproportionate role that they play in *Against Heresies*, however, is likely due to the fact that large parts of *Haer.*, including the whole of Book 5, is a defense of Paul against those who read him differently. Irenaeus concludes Book 4 in anticipation of the next volume:

> But it is necessary to subjoin to this composition, in what follows, also the doctrine of Paul after the words of the Lord, to examine the opinion of this man, and expound the apostle, and to explain whatsoever [passages] have received other interpretations from the heretics, who have altogether misunderstood what Paul has spoken, and to point out the folly of their mad opinions; and to demonstrate from that same Paul, from whose [writings] they press questions upon us, that they are indeed utterers of falsehood, but that the apostle was a preacher of the truth, and that he taught all things agreeable to the preaching of the truth.[8]

1 Corinthians 15:50, which declares that "flesh and blood cannot inherit the kingdom of God," was particularly problematic for Irenaeus. "This is the passage," he laments, "which is adduced by all the heretics in support of their folly, with an attempt to annoy us, and to point out that the handiwork of God is not saved."[9]

Beyond the need to sustain readings of Paul's anthropology, cosmology, and eschatology that made space for the divinization of the flesh in the face of what he deemed anti-material readings of the Apostle, Irenaeus also had to deal with certain champions of Paul (probably Marcion and his followers) who taught that "Paul *alone* had knowledge of the truth."[10] By the time that Irenaeus wrote *Against Heresies*, however, a broadly accepted, though not universally recognized, literary canon of four gospels (Matthew, Mark, Luke, and John), one history of the early

---

und Nachklänge der ältesten exegetisch-polemischen Homilieen," in *Philotesia: Paul Kleinert zum LXX Geburtstag* (Berlin: Trowitzsch & Sohn, 1907), 1–37; Andreas Lindemann, *Paulus im ältesten Christentum: Das Bild des Apostels und die Rezeption der paulinischen Theologie in der frühchristlichen Literatur bis Marcion* (BHT 58; Tübingen: J.C.B. Mohr (Paul Siebeck), 1979), 391–92; Rensberger, "As the Apostle Teaches," 208–13; and Noormann, *Irenäus als Paulusinterpret*, 40–41, 519 n. 17.

8. *Haer.* 4.41.4.

9. *Haer.* 5.9.1. Cf. White, *Remembering Paul*, 158–66, on Irenaeus's defense of this verse.

10. *Haer.* 3.13.1; lines 1–2: *solum Paulum vertitatem cognovisse* (emphasis mine). There is some disagreement over whom Irenaeus has in mind here. Cf. Lindemann, *Paulus im ältesten Christentum*, 97, who posits either Marcion (following Harnack) or the Valentinians (following Pagels). A number of studies have shown, however, that the Valentinians were not overly dependent on Paul's epistles in relation to other early Christian authorities. Cf. Lindemann, *Paulus im ältesten Christentum*, 300, 304–5, 341–43; Dassmann, *Stachel im Fleisch*, 176–244, esp. 199; Rensberger, "As the Apostle Teaches," 359–75; and Jacqueline Williams, *Biblical Interpretation in the Gnostic Gospel of Truth from Nag Hammadi* (SBLDS 79; Atlanta: Scholars, 1988), 186–87.

church (Acts of the Apostles) and thirteen (or fourteen) Pauline epistles had developed and were beginning to be treated as equal in authority to the Jewish scriptures.[11] Irenaeus found the attempt to wrench Paul from both the prophets and other apostolic authorities, whether Peter, James, John, or the other gospel writers, to be heterodox. Thus, *Against Heresies* is concerned not just with interpreting "the apostle" rightly, but with showing how "*the* apostle" was also "*an* apostle," who was both in concert with and *subject to* the other apostles that had preceded him in Christ. This chapter sketches the ways that Irenaeus attempts to bind Paul to his apostolic brethren in response to these unnamed Pauline champions, paying special attention to his handling of Galatians 1–2 in relation to Acts 10 and 15 (*Haer.* 3.12.14-3.13.3)—a thorny problem that has proven to be one of the central questions in Pauline studies since the mid-nineteenth century. The chapter also situates Irenaeus's view of the relationship between Paul and the other apostles within the context of other second-century evidence.

Paul, an Apostle

Ferdinand Christian Baur, the nineteenth-century father of modern Pauline studies, made the comparison between Galatians and the canonical Acts on Paul's relationship to the Jerusalem congregation a central feature of his dialectical reading of early Christian history, which posited an initial division between two theological camps: a Jewish-Christian faction under Cephas (Peter) and James and a pro-Gentile faction under Paul. The entirety of early Christian literature (at least into the late-second century) could be assigned to one of these two sides or to the later "Catholic" synthesis of the mid-second century (cf. the harmonizing tendencies of Acts).[12] Many, even in Baur's own generation (cf. Albrecht Ritschl and Adolf Hilgenfeld), were unable to accept such a rigid schematization of early Christian history and literature, dependent as it appeared to be on Hegel, whom Baur began to read in the early 1830s.[13] His emphasis, however, on conflict in the nascent church predated any known references to Hegel's work in his own and was ultimately rooted in the Pauline letters themselves, particularly 1 Corinthians

---

11. Cf. Harry Y. Gamble, "The New Testament Canon: Recent Research and the Status Quaestionis," in *The Canon Debate*, ed. L. M. McDonald and J. A. Sanders (Peabody, MA: Hendrickson, 2002), 267–94 (esp. 280, 287, 288, 291).

12. F. C. Baur, *The Church History of the First Three Centuries*, trans. A. Menzies; 3rd ed., 2 vols (London: Williams and Norgate, 1878–79 [1853–60]). On Baur's Paul, see White, *Remembering Paul*, 21–27.

13. Cf. Hans Rollmann, "From Baur to Wrede: The Quest for a Historical Method," *SR* 17 (1988): 447–50; and Heinz Liebing, "Historical-Critical Theology: In Commemoration of the One Hundredth Anniversary of the Death of Ferdinand Christian Baur, December 2, 1960," in *Distinctive Protestant and Catholic Themes Reconsidered*, ed. Ernst Käsemann et. al. (JTC Church 3; Tübingen: Mohr Siebeck, 1967), 62–64.

1-4 and Galatians.¹⁴ And even without the Hegelian superstructure, most New Testament scholars today still follow Baur in preferring these letters over Acts for the naked truth about tensions among Jesus of Nazareth's earliest followers.

Baur was not the first, by a long shot, to give primacy to Galatians in this way. Marcion had already done so in the mid-second century, finding in it not only a forceful statement of Paul's superiority to the Jerusalem church, but also a complete antithesis between Law and Gospel, and extrapolating from this an absolute antithesis between the ethnic God of the Jews (the Creator) and the universal God of Jesus and Paul (the Unknown God of Love).¹⁵ Marcion tried to relieve the burgeoning Catholic Church, according to Adolf von Harnack, of its "*complexio oppositorum*"—its attempt to hold the old and new together in harmony.¹⁶

Irenaeus was well aware of Marcion and his followers and had promised in Book 1 of *Against Heresies*, after describing Marcion's heresy, to "answer him separately and expose him by his own writings, and also from the discourses of the Lord and the apostles which he himself kept and used."¹⁷ This was a task to which he would never return, focusing rather on his primary target, the various manifestations of Valentinianism that were spreading across the empire. Yet one never gets the sense that Marcion had left Irenaeus's field of vision, as he repeatedly tries to tie Marcion to the Valentinians, beginning in Book 2 (*Haer.* 2.1.2, 4; 2.3.1; 2.28.6; 2.30.9; 2.31.1). He was trying to deliver a few fatal blows to the Pontic Wolf in the meantime.¹⁸ By the time that Irenaeus writes Book

---

14. Cf. Baur, "Die Christuspartie in der Corinthischen Gemeinde," *Zeitschrift für Theologie* 4 (1831), 61–206.

15. Cf. Adolf von Harnack, *Marcion: The Gospel of the Alien God*, trans. J. E. Steely and L. D. Bierma (Durham, NC: Labyrinth Press, 1990 [1921]), 21–24. On the hermeneutical and ordinal priority of Galatians in Marcion's *Apostolikon*, see Tertullian, *Marc.* 3.4.2 and Epiphanius, *Pan.* 42.9.4; 42.11.8.

16. Harnack, *Marcion*, 5. On Marcion and Paul in recent scholarship, see White, *Remembering Paul*, 33–36.

17. *Haer.* 1.27.4; cf. 3.12.12.

18. While gnosis, election, allegorical interpretation, and a complicated cosmogony were not primary features of Marcion's thought, other emphases, including cosmological dualism and a separation between the Jewish and Christian gods were quite consistent with classical "Gnosticism." This particular question about Marcion's relationship to "Gnosticism," of course, hinges on how broadly one wants to apply the term "Gnostic." More recent studies on "Gnosticism" by Michael Williams and Karen King have alerted us to the ethical and historical problems with this term, and its cognate, "Gnostics." Cf. Williams, *Rethinking "Gnosticism": An Argument for Dismantling a Dubious Category* (Princeton: Princeton University Press, 1996); and King, *What Is Gnosticism?* (Cambridge, MA: Harvard University Press, 2003). I do not think that Williams's "biblical demiurgical traditions" helps to clarify matters. One could easily include under this term the Gospel of John, Colossians, Philo, much of the Jewish wisdom literature, and so on. Further, there is some evidence in both Irenaeus (*Haer.* 1.25.6) and Hippolytus (*Haer.* 5.6) that suggests that several of these groups self-identified as "Gnostics." In the end, I am more drawn to

3—the opening chapters of which contain a defense of the wider apostolic tradition—Marcion seems to continue to haunt Irenaeus's vision. In the first thirteen chapters of Book 3, right up to the point where Irenaeus discusses the Jerusalem Council, Marcion is named more often than the Valentinians (13x vs. 11x, respectively).[19] One suspects, then, that Irenaeus has Marcion in mind (in *Haer.* 3.12.14-3.13.3) as he tries to mitigate differences between Paul and Peter (and the rest of the Jerusalem church and its founding apostles) through a harmonizing reading of Galatians 2 and Acts 15 in an expressed attempt to silence "those who assert that he [Paul] alone had knowledge of the truth, inasmuch as the mystery was manifested to him by revelation."[20] The "revelation" likely refers to Paul's brief and obscure account of his conversion in Marcion's favorite epistle, Gal 1:15-17 (cf. also 2 Cor 12:1-7; Eph 3:3).[21] In Book 1, Irenaeus had initially mentioned that Marcion possessed a collection of redacted Pauline letters, a common accusation by the early church Fathers, although he did not describe Paul as a particular authority for Marcion (*Haer.* 1.27.2). Later, however, in Book 3, just as he ramps up his apology for the apostolic union between Paul and Peter, Irenaeus describes the special place that Paul and the Gospel of Luke had for Marcion:

> Wherefore, Marcion, as well as his followers, have occupied themselves with cutting up the Scripture. They disown some books entirely; [then] they mutilate the Gospel of Luke and the letters of Paul and assert that these *alone*, in their shortened form, are genuine.[22]

Irenaeus also goes out of his way at places, including here, to insist that Marcion's subtractions from the fourfold gospel tradition were a particularly hubristic act. He sees this diminution of the tradition as unique in comparison with the Valentinians, who at least found other meanings in the apostolic gospels without getting rid of them (*Haer.* 1.27.2; 1.27.4; 3.11.7; 3.11.9; 3.12.12).

---

the projects of Bentley Layton, "Prolegomena to the Study of Ancient Gnosticism," in *The Social World of the First Christians: Essays in Honor of Wayne A. Meeks*, ed. L. M. White and O. L. Yarborough (Minneapolis: Fortress Press, 1995), 334–50; Birger Pearson, *Ancient Gnosticism: Traditions and Literature* (Minneapolis: Fortress Press, 2007); and David Brakke, *The Gnostics: Myth, Ritual and Diversity in Early Christianity* (Cambridge, MA: Harvard University Press, 2011); which are critical, yet constructive, and good attempts at unity in diversity.

19. On Marcion, see *Haer.* 3.2.1; 3.3.4 (2x); 3.4.3 (4x); 3.11.2; 3.11.7; 3.11.9; 3.12.5; and 3.12.12 (2x).

20. *Haer.* 3.13.1, lines 1–3: *qui dicunt solum Paulum vertitatem cognovisse, cui per revelationem manifestatum est mysterium.*

21. Cf. Unger and Steenberg, *St. Irenaeus of Lyons: Against the Heresies, Book 3*, 155 n. 1.

22. *Haer.* 3.12.12 (emphasis mine).

Irenaeus attempts, in refutation of Marcion, to bind Paul to the other apostles and thus the wider apostolic tradition.[23] The proceedings and results of the so-called Jerusalem Council in Acts 15 and Galatians 2 are particularly important for him.[24] Before examining his treatment of this meeting (Gal 2:1-10) and the closely associated "Antioch Incident" (Gal 2:11-21), we should describe the broader context of Book 3.

The book opens with an explanation of the apostolic authorship of the gospels of Matthew, Mark, Luke, and John (Chapter 1). Their four gospels captured the life and words of Jesus as delivered by his Spirit-filled apostles. The apostolic rule of truth (which Irenaeus describes most succinctly in *Haer.* 1.10.1) was embedded not only in these texts, but also in the traditions handed down through a succession of elders and then bishops at important apostolic sees, including Rome, Ephesus, and Smyrna (3.2-4). Irenaeus's argument here is directed against both Marcion and the Valentinians, the latter of whom did not dispute the apostolic authority of the proto-orthodox gospels. Thus, Irenaeus needs to assert that the Valentinians did not hold to the proper apostolic tradition for interpreting them (*Haer.* 3.2.2). Moreover, whenever Valentinus, Marcion, Cerinthus, or any other heretic (by implication) had encountered an apostle or one of the apostolic successor-bishops, they were always put to shame (*Haer.* 3.3.4). Their upstart and deviant views could not stand up to the faith handed down and protected by the church (*Haer.* 3.4.1-4).

Irenaeus then turns to the Psalms, prophets, and four gospels to show how none of them ever suggests that the God who created the world was a lesser, inferior God to some other unknowable Spirit from the Pleroma (3:5-11). In the midst of this argument he deals with thorny passages that seem contradictory to his view (cf. the discussion of 2 Cor 4:4 and Matt 6:24 in 3:7-8), and he next describes why there can only be four gospels (3.11.7-9). He then moves through sections of Acts, highlighting early sermons, including those of Paul in Lystra (Acts 14:15-17) and Athens (Acts 17:22-31), that show continuity between the old and the new, the creator God of Israel and the God of Jesus (*Haer.* 3.12.1-13).

In short, these opening chapters of Book 3 provide the first extended proto-orthodox mythology of the origins and transmission of its rule of truth. The Jerusalem Council enters Irenaeus's argument at this point for a number of reasons. First, he seems to be moving more or less chronologically through Acts' description of the early Christians. Second, the Council represents a point of

---

23. Cf. Julius Wagenmenn, *Die Stellung des Apostels Paulus neben den Zwölf in den ersten zwei Jahrhunderten* (BZNW 3; Gießen: Töpelmann, 1926), 202–17; Wilhelm Schneemelcher, "Paulus in der griechischen Kirche des zweite Jahrhunderts," *ZKG* 75 (1964): 12; and Noormann, *Irenäus als Paulusinterpret*, 39–52. Wagenmenn, *Die Stellung*, 217, is typical: "Dies zu unternehmen sah sich auch Irenäus deshalb genötigt, weil die Gegner von allen Seiten gegen die Katholizität und Apostolizität des Paulus Sturm liefen."

24. Irenaeus (*Haer.* 3.13.3) equates Gal 2:1-10 with Acts 15 and not with Paul's second trip to Jerusalem as recorded in Acts 11:13 and 12:25.

decided apostolic unity about the nature of the early Christian gospel in relation to the old dispensation. While the church, according to Irenaeus's understanding of the account in Acts, proclaims "the New Covenant of liberty to those who recently believed in God through the Holy Spirit," it in no way believes the old covenant to have come from "another god" (*Haer.* 3.12.14). The defense of Paul's Gentile converts qua Gentiles by Peter and James, even in the face of their own continued conservative practice of eating kosher (cf. Irenaeus's references to Acts 10 and Gal 2:12 in this section), factors prominently in this conclusion. The latter indicated that

> the apostles, whom the Lord made witnesses of all His acts and His doctrine—as a matter of fact, Peter and James and John were always found present with Him—acted reverently toward the economy of the Law of Moses, and thus they indicated that it was from one and the same God. This they certainly would not have done, in keeping with what we have said, if they had learned from the Lord about another Father besides the one who made the economy of the law. (*Haer.* 3.12.15)[25]

The relationship between Peter and Paul is of particular interest to Irenaeus, and on several occasions toward the beginning of Book 3 he reiterates that Peter and Paul *both* "evangelized," "founded," and "built up" the "greatest and most ancient Church" in Rome (*Haer.* 3.1.1; 3.3.2).[26] The early assertion that these two were cofounders of the Roman church provides a context of harmony within which their relationship should be read.[27]

Third, Paul's account of the Jerusalem Council and the ensuing encounter between him and Peter in Antioch could be read in ways that suggested a serious underlying tension between the apostles. That some preferred Paul's account of the meeting over the one in Acts seems all but certain when Irenaeus concludes:

---

25. Irenaeus has confused James, the brother of Jesus and leader of the Jerusalem Church, with James, son of Zebedee and brother of John. Cf. Rousseau and Doutreleau, *Irénée de Lyon: Contre les Hérésies: Livre III*, 1.304; and Unger and Steenberg, *St. Irenaeus of Lyons: Against the Heresies, Book 3*, 155 n. 9. The only other mention of a James in *Haer.*, outside of 3.12.14-15, is 2.24.4, where Peter, James, and John are described as seeing the transfiguration and the resuscitation of Jairus's daughter. Irenaeus never indicates that he knows a second James, the brother of Jesus.

26. On the debate over Peter's presence in Rome, see the skeptical Otto Zwierlein, *Petrus in Rom: die literarischen Zeugnisse* (Untersuchungen zur antiken Literatur und Geschichte 96; Berlin: Walter de Gruyter, 2009); and his numerous respondants in S. Heid, R. von Haehling, V. M. Strocka, and M. Vielberg (eds.), *Petrus und Paulus in Rom: eine interdisziplinäre Debatte* (Freiburg: Herder, 2011).

27. Irenaeus also mentions the double-apostolic founding of the Ephesian church (Paul and John), but never explores this further (*Haer.* 3.3.4).

Now if anyone diligently examines the Acts of the Apostles about the period under discussion, when he went up to Jerusalem on account of the aforementioned dispute, he will find that the years that Paul mentioned agree. Thus the preaching of Paul agrees with and is the same as the testimony of Luke [in Acts] in regard to the apostles.[28]

A unified version of these accounts, then, was necessary for Irenaeus's larger project at this point.

Paul and the Jerusalem Church

In reading Acts and Galatians together, Irenaeus notes places where the Apostle sees his own ministry as part of the larger apostolic movement (3.13.1). He heads straight for Gal 2:8: "For he [Paul] said that one and the same God who worked through Peter for the mission to the circumcised worked also through himself for the Gentiles." Irenaeus then reinforces this sentiment with support from other Pauline texts:

Even Paul says, "How beautiful are the feet of *those* who bring good news" (Rom 10:15b); and "Whether then it was I, or *they*, so *we* preach and so you believed." (1 Cor 15:11)[29]

Paul's description of his relationship with the Jerusalem church, thus, differed little from what Luke had recorded in Acts 15. Apostolic harmony abounded on all sides!

Approval from and agreement with the Jerusalem apostles, however, was not enough. Irenaeus reminds his readers, citing Gal 2:5, that from Paul's side there was a willing subjection to them: "For we *did* ... yield submission, even for a moment, that the truth of the Gospel might be preserved for you."[30] Irenaeus's text of Galatians here stands at odds with most of the rest of the manuscript tradition, including the so-called Alexandrian text—"to whom we *did not* yield in subjection for even an hour!" (οἷς οὐδὲ πρὸς ὥραν εἴξαμεν τῇ ὑποταγῇ)—the latter of which most modern commentators have followed as being original.[31] Irenaeus's

---

28. *Haer.* 3.13.3.
29. Emphases mine. Cf. Maurice Wiles, *The Divine Apostle: The Interpretation of St. Paul's Epistles in the Early Church* (Cambridge: Cambridge University Press, 1967), 18–19; and James Aageson, *Paul, the Pastoral Epistles, and the Early Church* (Library of Pauline Studies; Peabody, MA: Hendrickson, 2008), 163.
30. *Haer.* 3.13.3; 49: *ad horam cessimus subiectioni*. Cf. Wagenmann, *Die Stellung des Apostels Paulus*, 217.
31. Cf. UBS4rev.ed. for the manuscript evidence. In support of the latter reading, cf., among just about all others, Ernest D. W. Burton, *A Critical and Exegetical Commentary on the Epistle to the Galatians* (ICC; New York: Charles Scribner's Sons, 1920), 84–85; Hans

rendering, however, is not unique and is in line with other "Western" evidence.[32] His text was known and preferred by Tertullian, Marius Victorinus, Ambrosiaster, Pelagius, Augustine, and Primasius. The important bilingual Claromontanus (D^P: sixth century) and the Old Latin Codex Budapestiensis (b: ninth century) also support Irenaeus's rendering. These few surviving manuscripts must not have been alone, for Victorinus and Jerome mention that the manuscript tradition was split on this matter. The earliest evidence for the text of Gal 2:5 comes from Marcion, who supported the inclusion of οὐδὲ, and whom Tertullian (in support of Irenaeus's reading) accused of doctoring the text:

> For let us pay attention to the meaning of his [Paul's] words, and the purpose of them, and your falsification of scripture will become evident ... *they did give place* because there were people on whose account concession was advisable. For this was in keeping with faith unripe and still in doubt regarding the observance

---

Dieter Betz, *Galatians* (Hermeneia; Philadelphia: Fortress Press, 1979), 91; F. F. Bruce, *The Epistle to the Galatians: A Commentary on the Greek Text* (NIGTC; Grand Rapids: Eerdmans, 1982), 114–15; Richard N. Longenecker, *Galatians* (WBC 41; Dallas: Word Books, 1990), 52; J. L. Martyn, *Galatians* (AB 33A; New York: Doubleday, 1997), 197–98; Martinus C. de Boer, *Galatians: A Commentary* (NTL; Louisville: Westminster John Knox, 2011), 112; and Douglas J. Moo, *Galatians* (BECNT; Grand Rapids, MI: Baker Academic, 2013), 139. Theodor Zahn, *Commentar zum Neuen Testament: Der Brief des Paulus an die Galater* (1905), 93ff., and, reservedly, Benjamin W. Bacon, "The Reading of οἷς οὐδὲ in Gal. 2.5," *JBL* 42 (1923), 69–80, preferred Irenaeus's text as original. A number of witnesses that contain οὐδὲ lack the relative οἷς (Marcion, the Peshitta, Ephraem, Ambrose, and certain Greek and Latin manuscripts according to Victorinus and Ambrosiaster). The absence of οἷς likely resulted from a scribal attempt to remove the troublesome anacoluthon in the text. But this improvement had consequences for the meaning of the passage. Now Paul and Titus did or did not yield to the Jerusalem apostles rather than the "false brethren" of v. 4.

32. It is theoretically possible that the Latin translation of Irenaeus's Greek original has "Westernized" or "Latinized" Irenaeus's citations of scriptures. But a number of studies have shown the translator's general fidelity to Irenaeus's Greek, as well as Irenaeus's pervasive use of the "Western" text-type in his composition of *Haer*. On this matter, see Alexander Souter, "The New Testament Text of Irenaeus," in *Novum Testamentum sancti Irenaei episcopi Lugdunensis*, ed. W Sanday and C. H. Turner (Old-Latin Biblical Texts 7; Oxford: Clarendon, 1923); John Chapman, "Did the Translator of St Irenaeus Use a Latin N.T.?," *RBen* 36 (1924), 34–51; August Merk, "Der Text des Neuen Testaments beim hl. Irenaeus," *ZKT* 49 (1925), 302–15; Karl Schäfer, "Die Zitate in der lateinischen Irenäusübersetzung und ihr Wert für die Textgeschichte des Neuen Testamentes," in *Vom Wort des Lebens: Festschrift für Max Meinertz des 70. Lebensjahres 19. Dezember 1950*, ed. N. Adler (NTAbh 1; Münster: Aschendorff, 1951), 50–59; Unger, *St. Irenaeus of Lyons: Against the Heresies, Book 1*, 9; and Noormann, *Irenäus als Paulusinterpret*, 29–30.

of the law, when even the apostle himself suspected he might have run, or might still be running, in vain. So there was cause to discountenance those false brethren who were spying upon Christian liberty, to prevent them from leading it astray into the bondage of Judaism before Paul learned that he had not run in vain, before those who were apostles before him gave him their right hands, before with their agreement he undertook the task of preaching among the gentiles. Of necessity therefore he gave place, for a time, and so also had sound reason for circumcising Timothy [Acts 16:3], and bringing nazirites into the temple [Acts 21:26], facts narrated in the Acts, and to this extent true, that they are in character with an apostle who professes that to the Jews he became a Jew that he might gain the Jews, and one living under the law for the sake of those who were living under the law—and so even for the sake of those brought in unawares—and lastly that he had become all things to all men, that he might gain them all [1 Cor 9:20, 22].[33]

Irenaeus's and Tertullian's texts of Galatians imply that either Paul and Barnabas entertained the idea of circumcising Titus, at least for a little while, or Titus was indeed circumcised, but only willingly and not out of compulsion (cf. Gal 2:3), or, as Tertullian and later patristic commentators stated, we have here a reference to Paul's circumcision of Timothy in Acts 16:3 and to Paul's own stated philosophy of accommodation 1 Cor 9:20-23.[34] Marius Victorinus (*Comm. Gal.* 2:5) argued in line with Tertullian:

Still, seeing that in quite a few codices, both Latin and Greek, the verse runs *for an hour we submitted in subjection* (meaning that we did things their way although we had no intention of always following that path), one can in many ways prove that it ought to be read thus: *for an hour we submitted in subjection*. First, because Paul really did submit: for in fact he also circumcised Timothy *on account of the Jews*, as it says in the Acts of the Apostles [Acts 16:3]. So the apostle was under no pressure to lie ... Anyway, I've always made his policy clear: on some occasions Paul submitted, even when it came to matters of the truth. For this is the meaning of his saying *as a Jew that I might win over the Jews* [1 Cor 9:20], and so on.[35]

Similarly, Ambrosiaster (*Comm. Gal.* 2:5) asserted:

---

33. *Marc.* 5.3.3. Translation from Ernest Evans, *Tertullian: Adversus Marcionem* (Oxford: Oxford University Press, 1972), 521.

34. On the implication that, if Irenaeus's text is accepted, Titus is still in view in Gal 2:5, see Betz, *Galatians*, 91; Bruce, *The Epistle to the Galatians*, 113–14; Frank J. Matera, *Galatians* (SP 9; Collegeville, MN: Liturgical, 1992), 75; and de Boer, *Galatians*, 112 n. 165.

35. Translation from Stephen Andrew Cooper, *Marius Victorinus' Commentary on Galatians: Introduction, Translation, and Notes* (Oxford Early Christian Studies; Oxford: Oxford University Press, 2005), 270–71.

The epistle indicates that he gave in, and the history proclaims the fact. Why would he deny that he had given in for a moment, when it is known that he had circumcised Timothy because of the Jews [Acts 16:3], and had gone up to the temple after purifying himself according to the law [Acts 21:26]?[36]

Irenaeus's text of Gal 2:5, then, portrays an Apostle who is ready, when necessary, to subject his own ministry and gospel to the Jerusalem church.

Other texts that might suggest something different would have to be read in light of Gal 2:5. Paul's boast to have "worked harder than all of them [the other apostles]" in 1 Cor 15:10, for instance, would not be allowed to stand as a potential wedge between Paul and the others. Irenaeus explains this claim in light of the special difficulties Paul had in ministering to Gentiles, who lacked both the prophetic oracles about Christ in the Jewish scriptures as well as any notion of the resurrection of the dead (*Haer.* 4.24.1).[37]

In producing a representation of the Jerusalem Council that will allow Galatians to be read in concert with Acts, Irenaeus cites those portions of Galatians that are helpful for his cause, while passing over those bits that do not cohere with his program, as can be seen in Table 9.1.

Irenaeus brings attention to those places in Paul's account where he "lays his gospel before" and "yields submission" to the Jerusalem church and where he upholds that "one and the same God" authorized both his and Peter's apostleship. At the same time, he conveniently omits verses in the same account where Paul refers to the "reputed" leadership of James, Cephas, and John, where he proclaims his indifference to how they appear, where he emphasizes that they "contributed nothing" to his work, and where he mentions the work of the "false brethren" (who were likely connected, in his mind, to the Jerusalem church).

This particular tactic of remembering and forgetting particular elements of Galatians also occurs in Irenaeus's treatment of Gal 1:15-24 and Gal 2:11-14—the closely related autobiographical sections that surround Paul's description of the Jerusalem Council. On several occasions in Book 5 Irenaeus draws attention to Paul's description of his conversion in Gal 1:15-16 (*Haer.* 5.12.5; 5.15.3). Yet in doing so he leaves off the last portion of 1.16, "I did not immediately consult with flesh and blood," and then fails to deal at any point in *Against Heresies* with the key section of Gal 1:17-24 in which Paul insists that he did not visit Jerusalem in the immediate aftermath of his conversion, but rather did a number of other things, only eventually going to Jerusalem for a mere fifteen days at least three years after this point. His visit was so short and inconsequential that he saw only Cephas and James from among the apostles. Paul's point was that his apostleship was in no way dependent on those who were apostles before him. Irenaeus only offers alternative exegeses of troubling Pauline texts on a few occasions in

---

36. Ambrosiaster, *Commentaries on Galatians-Philemon*, trans. and ed. G. Bray (Ancient Christian Texts; Downer's Grove, IL: InterVarsity, 2009), 10.
37. Cf. Wiles, *The Divine Apostle*, 18–19.

Table 9.1 Portions of Gal 2:1-10 included in and excluded from *Against Heresies* (emphases mine)

	Included in *Against Heresies* (translations of *AH* from Unger)	**Excluded from *Against Heresies*** (my translations of Gal 2:1-10)
Gal 2:1-2a	Then after fourteen years I went up to Jerusalem with Barnabas, taking Titus along with me. I went up by revelation; and *I laid before them* ... the Gospel which I preached among the Gentiles. (*Haer.* 3.13.3)	
Gal 2:2b-4		but I did so privately among *those who appear to be something*, lest in some way I might be running or have run in vain. But not even Titus, who was with me, although he was Greek, was compelled to be circumcised. *And we did so on account of sneaky false brothers, who stealthily entered to spy out the freedom that we have in Christ with the intention of enslaving us.*
Gal 2:5	For we *did ... yield submission*, even for a moment, that the truth of the Gospel might be preserved for you. (*Haer.* 3.13.3)	
Gal 2:6-7		And from *those who appear to be something—what they really were matters little to me, for God shows no partiality—well, those who appear to be something contributed nothing to me*. Rather, when they saw that I had been entrusted the gospel for uncircumcised as Peter for the circumcised.
Gal 2:8	For he [Paul] said that *one and the same God who worked through Peter for the mission to the circumcised worked also through himself for the Gentiles*. (*Haer.* 3.13.1)	
Gal 2:9-10		And recognizing the grace that had been given to me, James and Cephas and John, *those who appeared to be pillars*, gave to me and to Barnabas the right hand of fellowship, in order that we might go to the Gentiles, but they to the circumcised. But only if we would remember the poor, a thing which I was eager to do.

Against Heresies—particularly when they have become the focus of his opponents' reading of Paul (cf. his exegeses of 1 Cor 15:50 and 2 Cor 4:4 in *Haer.* 5.9 and 3.7, respectively). On other occasions, like here, narrative details can be simply forgotten so as to create a biography that is more amenable to the notion of apostolic harmony.

The same can be said of his treatment of the so-called Antioch Incident. It is unclear whether Irenaeus understood the events described in Gal 2:11-14 to have happened before or after the Jerusalem Council, or whether he understood the withdrawal of Peter to have occurred at Antioch or somewhere else.[38] He narrates Acts 15 first (*Haer.* 3.12.14), then moves backward to narrate Peter's vision and encounter with Cornelius in Acts 10 (*Haer.* 3.12.15), and only then, before moving into his description of Paul's version of the Jerusalem Council (*Haer.* 3.13.1-3), does he mention Gal 2:12-13 (*Haer.* 3.12.15):

> They themselves [James and the apostles with him], however, acknowledging the same God, continued in the ancient observances, so that even Peter, though earlier he had eaten with the Gentiles because of the vision and the Spirit who rested on them, still when some persons came from James, feared lest he be blamed by them [the Jews]; so he separated himself from the Gentiles and did not eat with them. And Paul said that even Barnabas did this.[39]

He never mentions, however, the preceding statement: "But when Cephas came to Antioch, I [Paul] opposed him to his face, because he stood condemned" (Gal 2:11). Nor does he include the accusation of "hypocrisy" embedded within Gal 2:13. With these elements omitted, the passage becomes useful for Irenaeus's point, mentioned above, that the Jerusalem church saw no disassociation between Christ/Spirit and Law. The passage, in Irenaeus's hands, is more about Peter and James than about Peter and Paul.

Through a number of strategies, then, Irenaeus brings Paul and the Jerusalem church into apostolic agreement. Yet it goes beyond agreement for Irenaeus. From

---

38. Several commentators, going back to Augustine (*Exp. Gal.*), have argued that the Antioch Incident occurred before the Jerusalem Conference, including Theodor Zahn, Johannes Munck, and now Gerd Lüdemann, *Paul, Apostle to the Gentiles: Studies in Chronology* (Philadelphia: Fortress, 1984), 75–77. Cf. Bruce, *The Epistle to the Galatians*, 128, for the relevant bibliography.

39. The best Latin manuscripts of Irenaeus (C, V), in addition to several others (Q, S), have *cum tamen advenisset quidam a Iacobo* ("when someone came from James"), sharing the reading of P46 and the Old Latin tradition (d e gc r*). But Rousseau and Doutreleau go with the secondary reading found in manuscript A: *cum tamen advenissent quidam a Iacobo* ("when some came from James"). For brief descriptions of the Latin manuscripts of *Haer.*, see Unger, *St. Irenaeus of Lyons: Against the Heresies, Book 1*, 12–15. Whether one or several were sent from James to exert pressure on Peter to withdrawal matters little for Irenaeus's reading of the text.

Paul's side, there was a willing submission of his ministry and gospel to the apostolic tradition of the Jerusalem church. At least that is what his text of Galatians seemed to suggest. Marcion's version of Gal 2:5 said otherwise. The very text of Galatians at this key point and what the epistle as a whole might signify as evidence of apostolic harmony or division was a highly contested matter. One wonders, against Marcion and against the overwhelming tendency in the scholarship on Christian origins to privilege Galatians over Acts, whether or not we should fault Irenaeus for his reading of Galatians 2. How innovative was it? Was his project of bringing Peter and Paul together all that unique? What if we set the highly volatile Galatians, including its several positive references to apostolic *coordination* between Peter and Paul (Gal 1:18; 2:7-9), to the side for a moment and ask about the portrayal of the relationship between Peter and Paul in the rest of early Christian literature—from the other epistles of Paul all the way up to the period of Irenaeus? What would we find?[40]

As we have already noted, Irenaeus points to several places in Paul's letters (Rom 10:15b; 1 Cor 15:11) where the Apostle includes himself within a group of apostles who all preach the same gospel and are active in the same mission. Throughout 1 Corinthians, in particular, Paul works to establish continuity between himself and other apostolic ministers, including Cephas (1 Cor 1:12-13; 3:4-23; 9:5; 15:1-11). 1 Corinthians and Galatians, then, exhibit a certain tension with respect to Paul's view of his relationship with the other apostles. 1 Corinthians uses technical terminology for the traditioning process (cf. 15:1, 3: παραλαμβάνω and παραδίδωμι) to place Paul within the context of a larger framework of early Christian experience (15:8) and apostolic calling (15:10-11).[41] Galatians 1 then uses the exact same language to differentiate Paul's gospel from human authorities, including those in Jerusalem: "For neither did I receive it from a human source, nor was I taught it, but I received it through a revelation of Jesus Christ" (Gal 1:12: οὐδὲ γὰρ ἐγὼ παρὰ ἀνθρώπου παραραβον αὐτὸ οὔτε ἐδιδάχθην ἀλλὰ δι' ἀποκαλύψεως Ἰησοῦ Χριστοῦ).

This tension allowed the earliest layer of the Pauline tradition to be stretched in either direction, depending on which text was allowed to be the interpretive filter for the other. While Marcion would go with the fiery Galatians, most of the rest of early Christian literature upheld that the relationship was more like the one advocated in 1 Corinthians. Luke's depiction of the Jerusalem Council (Acts 15) is an endorsement of Paul's circumcision-free gospel. Writing from a

---

40. See Markus Bockmuehl, "The Icon of Peter and Paul between History and Reception," in *Seeing the Word: Refocusing New Testament Study* (Studies in Theological Interpretation; Grand Rapids, MI: Baker Academic, 2006), 121–36, for a critique of Baur's narrative of Pauline/Petrine opposition in earliest Christianity. Bockmuehl points to the overwhelmingly early picture of Pauline/Petrine cooperation/coordination (Acts, *1 Clement*, Ignatius of Antioch, 2 Peter). Cf. also his *The Remembered Peter*, 67–70.

41. Cf. Anders Eriksson, *Traditions as Rhetorical Proof: Pauline Argumentation in 1 Corinthians* (ConBNT; Stockholm: Almqvist & Wiksell International, 1998), 73–134.

pro-Gentile perspective, the author of Acts has cast the story of the earliest church as a preparatory scene for the arrival of the Pauline gospel and has turned Peter into a transitional figure, who was already pushing for Paul's circumcision-free gospel before the council ever met (Acts 10:1–11:17), but only after the narration of Paul's calling (Acts 9:1-30).[42] By the second century, whether through the influence of 1 Corinthians (the most widely cited Pauline text in the second century), the circulation of Acts, or other oral traditions about the apostles, or some combination of these, Peter and Paul were widely viewed as apostolic brothers in the proto-orthodox tradition (cf. 1 Pet 5:12-13; *1 Clement* 5.4-7; 47.1-4; Ignatius, *Rom.* 4.3; 2 Pet 3:15-16; *Epistula Apostolorum* 31–33; *Acts of Peter* 1–6, 40; Dionysius of Corinth, according to Eusebius, *Hist. eccl.* 2.25.8; and *3 Corinthians* 1:4; 2:4).[43] One could argue that Paul stood as the taller of the two, particularly in the early second century.[44]

But, as 2 Peter attests, Paul's letters quickly became contested sites of interpretation, and as the second century progressed it would be he that needed to be pulled toward Peter, the prized disciple of the earthly Jesus and father of the Roman church, not the other way around. The *Epistula Apostolorum*, originating from Asia Minor in the early- to mid-second century and clearly concerned with combating theologies that deny the salvation of the flesh (*Ep. Apos.* 12, 21, 24, 26, 39), was the first to portray emphatically Paul's *dependence* on the teaching of the other apostles.[45] In the *Epistula Apostolorum* it is the eleven apostles who heal

42. Cf. J. A. Fitzmyer, *The Acts of the Apostles: A New Translation with Introduction and Commentary* (AB 31; New York: Doubleday, 1998), 544; and Gregory E. Sterling, "From Apostle to the Gentiles to Apostle of the Church: Images of Paul at the End of the First Century," *ZNW* 99 (2008), 90–91.

43. Outside of the proto-orthodox tradition, cf., similarly, the Coptic *Apocalypse of Paul* from Nag Hammadi (V, 2), which offers its own version of Galatians 1–2. A little child (the Holy Spirit) appears to Paul and tells him to "[go up to Jerusalem] to your fellow [apostles] … Now it is to the twelve apostles that you shall go, for they are elect spirits, and they will greet you" (V 18,19–V 19, 18). Paul is then transported through the various heavenly realms and at several stages of the journey observes the twelve accompanying him until, upon reaching the Ogdoad, they greet him (in the heavenly Jerusalem). Translation from George W. MacRae and William R. Murdock, "The Apocalypse of Paul (V, 2)," in *The Nag Hammadi Library in English*, rev. ed., ed. J. M. Robinson (San Francisco: Harper Collins, 1988 [1978]), 257–58. On the dating of this *Apocalypse of Paul*, see Michael Kaler, Louis Painchaud, and Marie-Pierre Bussières, "The *Coptic Apocalypse of Paul*, Irenaeus' *Adversus haereses* 2.30.7, and the Second-Century Battle for Paul's Legacy," *JECS* 12 (2004), 182–90.

44. Cf. Andreas Lindemann, "Paul's Influence on 'Clement', and Ignatius," in *Trajectories through the New Testament and the Apostolic Fathers*, ed. A. F. Gregory and C. M. Tuckett (Oxford: Oxford University Press, 2005), 10; and Richard I. Pervo, *The Making of Paul: Constructions of the Apostle in Early Christianity* (Minneapolis: Fortress, 2010), 132.

45. Cf. Charles Hill, "The *Epistula Apostolorum*: An Asian Tract from the Time of Polycarp," *JECS* 7 (1999), 1–53; and A. Stewart-Sykes, "The Asian Context of the New Prophecy and of the *Epistula Apostolorum*," *VC* 51 (1997), 416–38.

Paul's blindness, not Ananias, as in Acts 9. Jesus, moreover, exhorts the eleven to "Teach and remind (him) what has been said in the scriptures and fulfilled concerning me, and then he will be for the salvation of the Gentiles" (31).[46] The original apostles provide the legitimizing force for and doctrinal content of Paul's ministry. The late-second-century pseudegraphon *3 Corinthians* portrays a similar scenario. It's Paul, invoking language from 1 Corinthians (11:23; 15:3), says, "For I entrusted to you in the beginning what I also received from the apostles who came before me, and who spent all their time with Jesus Christ" (*3 Cor.* 2:4).[47]

As in the *Epistula Apostolorum* and *3 Corinthians*, the relationship between Paul and the apostles in *Adversus haereses* is one of unity, but also of subordination and dependence. Paul may be "*the* apostle" for Irenaeus, but he is also just "an apostle"—one whose gospel was submitted to and found acceptable by the Jerusalem church. Paul played a unique role in "teaching righteousness to the whole world," as *1 Clement* 5:7 states, but his mission was in service of the widely attested rule of truth.

Conclusion

Irenaeus may have been the first to argue so forcefully and at such length for Paul's coordination with and dependence upon the other apostles. He was not, however, unique in his assertion that this relationship was basically harmonious. He lived within a tradition, going back to 1 Corinthians and at least portions of Galatians, that viewed Paul and Peter, in particular, as apostolic partners. I have argued elsewhere that Irenaeus participated in a broad stream of proto-orthodox tradition about the Apostle that had developed in western Asia Minor in the mid-second century in reaction to certain docetic and gnosticizing tendencies in that region.[48] It was a complex tradition that, in addition to seeing Paul as dependent upon the other apostles, increasingly incorporated the Pastoral Epistles, for instance, into its portrayal of Paul as primarily a defender of orthodoxy. From within this developing tradition, Irenaeus was no doubt one of Paul's greatest reputational entrepreneurs. Moreover, in a canon as variegated as was the earliest layer of the Pauline tradition, the Apostle's entrepreneurs could easily shift pieces of the tradition forward and backward, bringing into conscious view particular elements, eliminating others from social memory, and introducing new bits that had to cohere with those that already had currency.

Irenaeus's handling of Galatians in relation to Acts is a perfect reminder that the processes of forgetting and remembering are at the heart of constructing

---

46. English translation from J. K. Elliott, *The Apocryphal New Testament: A Collection of Apocryphal Christian Literature in an English Translation based on M.R. James* (Oxford: Clarendon, 1999 [1993]). Cf. Rensberger, "As the Apostle Teaches," 88–92, 166.

47. See White, *Remembering Paul*, 114–16, on Paul and the apostles in *3 Cor.*

48. White, *Remembering Paul*, 167–69.

portrayals of the past and that social memory is both retrieved and reconstructed. It displays strong lineages with the past, but is always shaped and formed in the context of present needs.[49] In response to Marcion, Irenaeus works in Book 3 of *Adversus haereses* to solidify a particular representation of Paul vis-à-vis the Jerusalem Church for proto-orthodox memory. He does so by bringing forward and moving backward pieces of his tradition that are helpful for the conservation of his proto-orthodox story. Manuscripts of Paul's letters were part of this received tradition. Manuscripts, their texts, and their producers were participants of a period in which Paul's legacy was a contentious matter. Thus, the manuscripts for reconstructing Paul have never been innocent. Rather, they were firmly entrenched within ancient discourses about Paul. The addition or deletion of an οὐδὲ in Gal 2:5 went a long way in distancing Paul from or drawing him near to the apostles who preceded him. Tertullian certainly argued that this was the case.

I am not interested here in evaluating whether or not Marcion or Irenaeus got the "historical" Paul "right" on this matter. Nor in what was the "original" text of Galatians. The rhetorical intentions of even just the *Hauptbriefe* already resisted systemization on the issue of Paul's relationship to the Jerusalem Church. Rather, I have been asking about Irenaeus's Paul. Which Pauline texts were employed to construct a particular image of Paul that was helpful for his rhetorical assault on Marcion's assertion that "Paul *alone* had knowledge of the truth"? How were the texts used and arranged, and what place did they have in his ideological program? Among the many sites of memory that could have been brought forward from the tradition and fixed for perpetual consideration, why these and not others? What was forgotten for the sake of rhetorical simplicity and the protection of tradition and its underlying ideologies?

All who have had a stake in remembering Paul rightly have proceeded in the manner of Irenaeus. It is in the relationship between the represented and the remainder—the displayed and the discarded—that we find the entrepreneur at work. Marcion was no different in this regard from Irenaeus. Nor are those since the nineteenth century who have followed F. C. Baur in thinking that there is an Archimedean point (the *Hauptbriefe*) from which the "real" Paul can be leveraged against the Paul of "tradition" different from Paul's second-century entrepreneurs. Baur's Paul, after all, ended up looking a lot like Baur himself—or we might say that he ended up looking like the radical form of the Protestant tradition in which Baur was situated at the time.[50] The Apostle continues to ask each of his entrepreneurs: "What do you have that you did not receive?" (1 Cor 4:7). Yet it is in the traditioning process that the latter work to find ways for the *traditum* to speak to new situations, such that the Apostle, in hands of his interpreters, both ancient and modern, can "become all things to all people" (1 Cor 9:22).

---

49. On the nature of tradition and social memory, see White, *Remembering Paul*, 70–107.
50. Cf. White, *Remembering Paul*, 20–27.

Response
Irenaeus, Jerusalem, and Remembering the Poor: A Response to Benjamin White

Bruce W. Longenecker

When reading Ben White's productive chapter on Irenaeus's attempt to smooth out the relationship between Paul and the Jerusalem church, I was intrigued by what was omitted—not omitted by White's treatment of Irenaeus, but by Irenaeus's treatment of Pauline texts. White demonstrates that Irenaeus approached the subject by "picking and choosing" his passages when seeking to demonstrate the unity of the earliest apostolic voices. But why did Irenaeus pick some passages to deal with and not others? This question goes to both sides of the issue—both (1) further passages that Irenaeus might have used to support his argument, and (2) passages that could be read to contradict Irenaeus's argument. White demonstrates that Irenaeus spent time dealing with both, but it is also clear that Irenaeus could have gone further in interpreting Pauline texts, whether to support his argument better or to engage passages that might suggest the opposite of his argument.

A simple example of the first tendency (i.e., not engaging supportive passages) can be registered here, since it will be helpful to contrast it momentarily with observations about the second tendency. As White notes, since 1 Cor. 15:10 ("I worked harder than any of them") could be read to suggest that Paul had a haughty and condescending attitude toward the Jerusalem apostles, Irenaeus chose to disarm that interpretation of this verse in a creative defense of the apostle (*Haer.* 4.24.1). In the process, however, Irenaeus failed to mention Paul's comments only one verse earlier—"I am the least of the apostles" (15:9), a comment that could easily have been spun in favor of Irenaeus's argument.

Simple examples of the second tendency (i.e., not engaging contradicting passages) are also easy to spot. For instance, despite Irenaeus's extensive interaction with the text of Galatians 2, he clearly failed to engage passages that might have been used as counterevidence to his thesis within that chapter—such as (as White notes) Gal 2:11, where Paul recounts how he "opposed" Peter "to his face because he [Peter] stood self-condemned"; or Gal 2:13, where Paul accuses Peter of "hypocrisy." This neglect of pertinent data seems to extend beyond Galatians 2 to include Gal 4:21–5:1—Paul's allegory (with deprecatory force) about "the present Jerusalem" being in bondage, in contrast to "the Jerusalem above," which Paul says "is our mother." Of course, it is not clear whether Paul's analogy was meant to attribute bondage to non-Christian Judeans or to Christian Judeans, and a case can be made either way.[1] But if Irenaeus dealt with the fairly innocuous phrase of 1 Cor 15:10 in order to hinder a reading that could possibly be used to disrupt his case, he took no initiative to place controls on the potentially much sharper polemic of Paul's Galatian allegory. Even when quoting the allegory directly (*Haer.* 5.35.2), Irenaeus made no attempt to disarm its potential to problematize his case regarding unity among the apostles.

With this most basic survey in hand, it seems that Irenaeus did not see the need (or did not want) to engage in a reading of every possible verse that might impact the subject in one way or another. Of course, this means that Irenaeus's case is exposed to the charge of being incomplete at best and unconvincing at worst. Those who would be antagonistic to his argument could easily have cited as counterevidence the passages that he leaves out of the frame. Marcion had dealt with counterevidence by cutting out vast swaths of authoritative texts, thereby ensuring that what remained of those texts could be used to authorize his own priorities without much complication. Irenaeus did not adopt that convenient strategy, but evidently at times he dealt with counterevidence simply by failing (whether intentionally or not) to recognize the existence of such counterevidence.

Curious Omissions

But even with that said, it seem to me curious that Irenaeus neglected to make any mention of one strand of evidence that might easily have provided him with significantly more fodder for his argumentative cannon. I am thinking here of Paul's collection "for the poor among the saints at Jerusalem" (as he calls it in Rom 15:26). In Romans, Paul had this to say about his pending visit "to Jerusalem in a ministry to the saints" (15:26-27):

> [Gentile Jesus-followers in] Macedonia and Achaia have been pleased … to do this [i.e., share their resources], and indeed they owe it to them [Christian Jews

---

1. For instance, the allegory depicts a scenario in which "the child who was born according to the flesh persecuted the child who was born according to the Spirit" (4.29), while Paul asks only a few verses later, "why am I still being persecuted" (5.11)—which can be read to mean, "persecuted by those who identify with the Jerusalem churches" (at least in relation to his autobiographical narrative of Galatians 1–2; see, for instance, the fear of persecution that Paul describes in 2:12). Reading these "persecution" verses together would result in identifying the child of "the flesh" (who is to be expelled from relationship with the offspring of "the Spirit"; Gal 4:30) as adherents of Jerusalem-based forms of Christianity.

in Jerusalem]; for if the Gentiles have come to share in their spiritual blessings, they ought also to be of service to them in material things.

In earlier texts, Paul had given instructions to the Corinthians about the collection for Jerusalem-based Jesus-followers: "And when I arrive, I will send any whom you approve with letters to take your gift to Jerusalem" (1 Cor 16:3). In fact, Paul exhorted the Corinthians to contribute to this financial initiative in two extensive chapters of theological arm-twisting (2 Corinthians 8–9). There the phrase "ministry to the saints" appears on two occasions (8:4; 9:1), and Paul says of those saints that "they long for you and pray for you" (9:14).

How is it that Irenaeus failed to deal with passages such as these? They would have been ideally suited to bolster his argument, including the following features:

- gifts being sent from Paul's communities to Jerusalem saints;
- material benefits being owed to those saints by Paul's gentile communities;
- Pauline communities being pleased to reach out to the needy in Jerusalem communities of Jesus-followers; and
- the longings and prayers of Jerusalem Jesus-followers for the benefit of Paul's communities.

What might explain Irenaeus's curious omission of these passages, when they could have supplied his case with rich resources? Is there method here, or simply oversight? Does this lacuna tell us anything about Irenaeus's perception of things?

Could our answer lie in the fact that, upon its delivery in Jerusalem, the collection seems to have gone badly wrong (as the narrative of Acts 21–24 could be read to suggest)? Might Irenaeus have intentionally omitted any mention of these "collection texts" (at least in his discussions about harmony among the apostles) since he foresaw that the Acts narrative could be used to argue that James and the Jerusalem community did nothing to assist Paul at the time of his arrest and his trials in their city of residence?[2]

Of course, this is a possibility, but it seems unlikely, since a person of Irenaeus's argumentative creativity could easily have dealt with such an inference about dysfunctional apostolic relations. For instance, he could have laid the blame for the collection's failed reception at the feet of non-Christian Judeans rather than Christian Judeans, drawing precisely on the distinction offered by Paul himself in Rom 15:30-31:

> I appeal to you, brothers and sisters, by our Lord Jesus Christ and by the love of the Spirit, to join me in earnest prayer to God on my behalf, that I may be rescued from

---

2. See, for instance, James D. G. Dunn, *Unity and Diversity in the New Testament: An Inquiry into the Character of Earliest Christianity* (Philadelphia: The Westminster Press, 1977), 256–57.

the unbelievers in Judea, and that my ministry to Jerusalem may be acceptable to the saints.

This text provides an interpretative lens for understanding how the situation might have gone wrong when Paul delivered his collection to "the saints at Jerusalem." If Irenaeus needed a culprit to explain the situation, this passage would easily have handed him "the unbelievers in Judea" to fit the bill. Evidently, then, Irenaeus's omission of the collection initiative was probably not motivated by potential embarrassment about its apostolic reception.

What else might explain this curious omission? The answer probably does not lie in a concern for rhetorical brevity. Irenaeus frequently engages in extensive proof-texting without thinking twice about the need for lucid brevity. Moreover, it would not have taken much for Irenaeus to point even briefly to Paul's collection, using a short sentence or two to register the supporting evidence.

Perhaps the best answer to our question lies elsewhere, and reveals something about Irenaeus's view of Paul's collection effort. In the passage where he dealt most extensively with Paul's relationship with the Jerusalem apostles (*Haer.* 3.13), Irenaeus seems to have been concerned primarily with the unity of the apostles with regard to their shared "doctrine"; with that at the forefront of his interests, Irenaeus seems not to have been interested in connecting the dots between "doctrinal" harmony and relational harmony. If this were the case, it would seem that a single-minded interest in "doctrine" has done Irenaeus a disservice, creating a blind-spot in his vision of discursive effectiveness. If this explanation has merit, it shows a disparity between Irenaeus and Paul, precisely since Paul saw his collection initiative not simply as a good moment in corporate polity and intercommunal relational management. In Paul's view, the collection testified to a rigorous theological outlook that was shared across the boundaries of geographical location and apostolic leadership (e.g., Rom 15:27, cited above).

Remember the Poor

Curiously, even in Irenaeus's omissions we might be able to discern something of interest regarding another feature of Paul's texts that Irenaeus fails to engage—that is, the phrase "remember the poor" in Gal 2:10. This phrase is sometimes thought to refer to Paul's collection efforts, along with the passages mentioned above from Romans, 1 Corinthians, and 2 Corinthians. In this interpretation, when the Jerusalem apostles shook hands with Paul and Barnabas and added that the ministry to gentiles should "remember the poor," the pillar apostles were effectively saying, "We are authenticating your mission to the gentiles, and in return, we expect you to send money to Jesus-followers here in Jerusalem."[3]

---

3. We might imagine that a few theological nuances could be added to this bald statement in order to deflect attention away from the economic bottom line inherent within

As I have illustrated elsewhere, however, this "Jerusalem-centric" reading has no foothold among the earliest interpreters of the verse until the second half of the fourth century and beyond (as illustrated by Ephrem the Syrian [306–73], Jerome [329–420], and John Chrysostom [347–407]).⁴ Prior to that time, there is no indication that the phrase was understood to be restricted in terms of an ethnic contingency (Judean) in a specific location (Jerusalem). Instead, the phrase "remember the poor" in Gal 2:10 was consistently interpreted as an instruction meant to enhance Christian generosity in general. This is evident in the way the verse was interpreted by Tertullian (160–220), Origen (185–254), Athanasius (293–373), and Aphrahat (died *ca.* 350). When interpreting "remember the poor" as a general exhortation, these interpreters never found the need to explain that the phrase was originally intended as a context-specific exhortation from a previous period of history that had now passed. Instead, they understood the phrase simply as a general exhortation, applicable in any age. The shift to a Jerusalem-centric reading (which in effect relegated the relevance of the phrase to only the first generation of Jesus-followers) was facilitated by the mistaken view that arose some time around the early fourth century. In that view, the Ebionites (i.e., "the poor ones") became identified with the early Jesus-followers in Jerusalem. With that identification improperly made, the term "the poor" in Gal 2:10 could be read as a technical term for Jerusalem-based Jesus-followers of the mid-first century—a reading that only arises in the second half of the fourth century.

The evidence against this Jerusalem-centric view is significant.⁵ But if the earliest extant readings of the phrase do not predate the time of Tertullian, does Irenaeus shed any further light on the issue?

---

this interpretation—lest Christian apostles look like tele-evangelists of the late twentieth century. But any such nuances cannot ultimately dislodge the implications of this traditional reading of things. This is exposed in Robert Orlando's glaringly substandard book *Apostle Paul: A Polite Bribe* (Eugene: Cascade, 2014), which, among its many problematic aspects (especially chronological), strips away all important nuances in order to exaggerate "the bottom line" of economic interest. This is the natural endpoint of the traditional reading of Gal 2:10 as meaning, in effect, "send us money."

4. For the earliest readings of Gal 2:10, see Bruce W. Longenecker, *Remember the Poor: Paul, Poverty, and the Greco-Roman World* (Grand Rapids: Eerdmans, 2010), 157–82. For an earlier version, see Bruce W. Longenecker, "The 'Poor' of Galatians 2:10: The Interpretative Paradigm of the First Centuries," in *Engaging Economics: New Testament Scenarios and Early Christian Reception*, ed. Bruce W. Longenecker and Kelly D. Liebengood (Grand Rapids: Eerdmans, 2009), 205–21.

5. See especially Longenecker, *Remember the Poor*, esp. 183–219. David Downs had already gone some way in this direction when he dissociated Gal 2:10 from Paul's collection efforts of the 1950s; see David J. Downs, *The Offering of the Gentiles: Paul's Collection for Jerusalem in Its Chronological, Cultural, and Cultic Contexts* (Tübingen: Mohr Siebeck, 2007), 33–36.

Our first impulse might reasonably be to think that Irenaeus offers no interpretative resources to adjudicate this issue. After all, unlike Tertullian and others, Irenaeus makes no mention of the phrase under consideration. Moreover, we have seen that Irenaeus is not concerned to deal with every possible text that impinges on the issue. And furthermore, it could easily be argued that his silence regarding Paul's collection for "the poor among the saints at Jerusalem" (as noted above) simply coincides with his silence regarding "the poor" in Gal 2:10.

But even if this first impression has some force, it is not the most compelling interpretation of the full spread of the data. This is because Irenaeus is locked in debate with interlocutors and his engagement with Galatians 2 reveals something about the position of those with whom he is in vigorous disagreement.

White's chapter demonstrates two things about the view that Irenaeus is disputing: (1) it was most likely rooted in Marcionite soils, and (2) it involved prioritizing Galatians 2 over the Acts narrative with regard to the decision of the apostolic council. Quite simply, it would make no sense to add a Jerusalem-centric interpretation of Gal 2:10 to these two aspects of the interlocutory position. One of these three things is not like the others. That is, a Marcionite position that privileged Galatians 2 over Acts 15 is unlikely to have held that "the poor" of Gal 2:10 referenced Jerusalem Christians specifically, since that would involve Paul admitting to a desire ("I was eager," Gal 2:10) to bolster the communities that were under the leadership of the Jerusalem apostles. This in turn would have complicated the interlocutors' view that "Paul alone had knowledge of the truth" (*Haer.* 3.13.1). At the very least, if Irenaeus's interlocutors had held that "the poor" of Gal 2:10 were Jerusalem-based Christians, those interlocutors would have wanted to square that aspect of the text in relation to other components of their view—and, moreover, we would expect to see Irenaeus engaging with all that in one way or another. But we see nothing like that in Irenaeus. Instead, we get silence.

In this case, silence is golden. Here, the absence of evidence is, in fact, evidence of absence. That is, Irenaeus omission of Gal 2:10 from his discussion must indicate that, in the second half of the second century, the phrase "remember the poor" was not being interpreted in a manner that identified "the poor" with Jerusalem-based Christians. In view of the fact that New Testament scholarship repeatedly imagines that the phrase does, in fact, reference Jerusalem-based Christians, it bears repeating that a Jerusalem-centric interpretation of the phrase "remember the poor" was not even on the radar of debate in Irenaeus's time; instead, the phrase must have been understood to be applicable without regard to the geographical location of "the poor"—precisely as the texts of Tertullian, Origen, Athanasius, and Aphraphat suggest.

We see, then, that Irenaeus's failure to discuss the phrase opens an important window of historical insight. In short, it moves the relevant data back half a century or so prior to the first interpreter who explicitly interpreted the phrase (i.e., Tertullian). If Irenaeus shows no cognizance of a Jerusalem-centric interpretation of "remember the poor," the same is likely to have been true of his interlocutors, with their theological roots extending back to Marcion in the mid-second century. We can conclude, then, that the evidence from the mid-second through to the mid-fourth centuries consistently undermines a Jerusalem-centric interpretation of the phrase "remember the poor" in Gal 2:10. In this instance, even Irenaeus's curious omission yields productive historical fruit.

Chapter 10

PAUL IN IRENAEUS ON THE LAST THINGS

Adela Yarbro Collins

It may be helpful to begin with a few general observations concerning Paul's views on the last things as they can be reconstructed from his letters. Paul wrote about "the day of wrath" as the day on which God will conduct a universal and final judgment.[1] Those in Christ are included among those who will undergo judgment at the end.[2] He also wrote about "sudden destruction" and "the destruction of the flesh."[3] It is not clear whether these phrases are equivalent to the final judgment or refer to the destruction of this world prior to the last judgment, as in 4 Ezra,[4] or to the destruction that sinners will experience after the judgment.[5] If Paul defined the judgment of God as the eschatological destruction of the wicked at the time of the coming of the Lord, that would explain why he never mentions Hades[6] or Gehenna. Thus those in Christ will be rescued by him from the wrath that is coming, whereas those not in Christ, including the man handed over to Satan, will suffer the consequences of that wrath. A problem with this interpretation, however, is that Paul allows for a positive outcome at the judgment for those who do what is good and avoid evil, even if they do not belong to the Jewish people or, presumably, to a community "in Christ."[7] This problem is alleviated if Paul believed that only the wicked, not all those who are not "in Christ," will be destroyed by the "sudden destruction."

Certain aspects of Paul's eschatological scenario are clear from 1 Cor 15:20-28. A proleptic event is the resurrection of Christ (vv. 20–22). The eschatological

---

1. Rom 2:3-11; cf. 1 Thess 1:10.
2. Rom 13:1-2; 1 Cor 11:29-34; Gal 5:2-4.
3. 1 Thess 5:3; 1 Cor 5:5.
4. *4 Ezra* 7:29-31; cf. Rev 20:11.
5. 2 Thess 1:9 is also ambiguous on this point.
6. Assuming that the reading of papyrus 46, Sinaiticus (uncorrected), B, et al. is the earliest recoverable form of the text of 1 Cor 15:55.
7. Rom 2:9-10, 13-16.

scenario proper begins with the return of Christ, when those who belong to Christ will rise from the dead (v. 23). The abrupt transition to "the end" (τὸ τέλος) in v. 24 suggests that Christ has already been reigning since his resurrection. This inference may be confirmed by Rom 1:4, if "son of God" is understood to be equivalent to Messiah. The human Jesus had already been appointed by God as Messiah but only began to reign as the eschatological king at the time of his resurrection. The activity of Christ during his reign apparently, in Paul's view, focuses on a process of bringing every rule and authority and power to an end (v. 24). The precise meaning of this process is not clarified significantly by the allusion to Ps 110:1 that follows (v. 25).

The last enemy to be defeated is death (v. 26). A consequence of this statement seems to be the resurrection of the rest of the dead (besides those who belong to Christ). Presumably those in Christ who rise at his coming cannot die again. This is the point at which one would expect the general judgment, but Paul does not mention it.

The next event in Paul's eschatological scenario is that all things, which have been subjected to the son, will then be subjected to God, so that God may be all in all. This terse statement is not further elaborated, except by the allusion to Ps 8:7.[8]

Paul's letters are also open to interpretation as to whether the resurrection body includes the flesh of the earthly body[9] and whether the restored creation has the same form and substance as the original one (whatever those may have been) or as the creation in which those in Christ lived before his return.[10]

Especially in formulations that include the events of the end, the notion of the "history of salvation" is relevant to a discussion of the last things. Paul took some steps toward such a conception. Elements in the Pauline letters that became important for Irenaeus as he developed his own concept of salvific history include the claim that the law "came in as a side issue,"[11] that is, came into the divine plan to achieve a secondary goal, namely, the increase in sinning (or in awareness of sin) so that grace might abound.[12] Another form of this idea occurs in Galatians, where Paul attempts to dissuade the Galatians from being circumcised. They should not do so because the law was given after the more important promise to Abraham and was in effect only until Christ came.[13] Another element important for Irenaeus is the contrast between the old and the new covenant, as can be seen in Irenaeus's view of the structure of salvation history.[14]

---

8. Ps 8:6 in English translations.
9. 1 Cor 15:35-55.
10. Rom 8:19-25.
11. Παρεισῆλθεν.
12. Rom 5:20.
13. Gal 3:19-29.
14. Gal 4:21-5.1; 2 Cor 3:7-18; cf. 1 Cor 11:25, 2 Cor 3:6.

The Structure of the History of Salvation according to Irenaeus

As Rolf Noormann has pointed out, the contexts of Paul's remarks about an old and a new covenant make clear the continuity from the first to the second, for example, in the affirmation that the eschatological people of God is made up of both Jews and Gentiles. This continuity was important for two of Irenaeus's main goals, namely, to argue that the two covenants and their respective texts belong together and that the God of each testament is one and the same. His arguments were polemical, directed against those who rejected such views, namely, the Marcionites and the Valentinians as Irenaeus knew or construed them.[15] For example, Irenaeus wrote:

> And when [anyone who imagines that what the apostles say about God should be allegorized] has rejected so great an error from his mind, and also the blasphemy against God, he will of himself come to reason and realize that both the law of Moses and the grace of the New Covenant, each in its suitable time, were bestowed by one and the same God for the benefit of the human race.[16]

This simple schema is sometimes broadened to include a period prior to that of the old covenant, namely, the pre-Mosaic time of the fathers or ancestors. According to Noormann, this three-part division is the most common one in Irenaeus's magnum opus.[17] At one point Irenaeus declares:

> Moreover, all the rest of the multitude of those righteous men who lived before Abraham, and of those patriarchs who preceded Moses, were justified independently of [circumcision and Sabbath observance], and without the law of Moses.[18]

The "righteous fathers had the meaning of the Decalogue written in their hearts and souls."[19] In this passage Irenaeus takes from Paul the idea that Abraham was

---

15. Rolf Noormann, *Irenäus als Paulusinterpret: Zur Rezeption und Wirkung der paulinischen und deuteropaulinischen Briefe im Werk des Irenäus von Lyon* (WUNT 2.66; Tübingen: Mohr Siebeck, 1994), 380–81. Brian E. Daley infers that Irenaeus wrote in Lyon against "local varieties of Gnostic Christianity"; *The Hope of the Early Church* (Cambridge: Cambridge University, 1991), 29.

16. *Haer.* 3.12.11; translation from Dominic J. Unger and Irenaeus M. C. Steenberg, *St. Irenaeus of Lyons: Against the Heresies, Book 3* (ACW 64; New York: Newman, 2012).

17. Noormann, *Irenäus als Paulusinterpret*, 388.

18. *Haer.* 4.16.2; translation from ANF, vol. 1, 481, col. 1. In addition to Abraham he mentions Lot, Noah, and Enoch. Cf. Adelin Rousseau (ed.), *Irénée de Lyon: Contre les heresies Livre IV, Tome II* (SC 100; Paris: Éditions du Cerf, 1965), 564–65.

19. *Haer.* 4.16.3; translation from ANF, vol. 1, 481, col. 2. Cf. Rousseau, *Livre IV, Tome II*, 564–65.

justified by faith (citing Gal 3:6 in section 2) and the notion of a νόμος ἄγραφος (Rom 2:14-16).[20]

In the context of this three-part schema, Irenaeus defines the period of the old covenant as the time from Moses to Christ.[21] He characterizes the Mosaic law as a yoke of slavery.[22] This yoke was laid upon Israel because they turned away and made themselves a calf and wanted to return to slavery in Egypt.[23] It is also *disciplina* (παιδεία) and *prophetia futuorum*.[24] The latter claim is supported with the citation of Exod 25:40 and 1 Cor 10:4b, 11.[25] It was probably Paul's statement that ταῦτα δὲ τυπικῶς συνέβαινεν in 1 Cor 10:11 that inspired the idea that the events related to the old covenant are sometimes "prophetic."[26]

The third phase of the schema is "the new covenant of freedom."[27] The Word of God, the Lord Jesus Christ, produced both covenants, and by establishing the new covenant restored freedom to "us" and "has multiplied that grace which is from himself."[28] The freedom in question is freedom from the Mosaic laws:

> The laws of bondage, however, were one by one promulgated to the people by Moses, suited for their instruction or for their punishment, as Moses himself declared [citation of Deut 4:14]. These things, therefore, which were given for bondage, and for a sign to them, [the Lord] cancelled by the new covenant of freedom. But He has increased and widened those laws which are natural, and noble, and common to all, granting to human beings largely and without grudging, by means of adoption to know God the Father, and to love Him with the whole heart, and to follow His word unswervingly, while they abstain not only from evil deeds, but even from the desire after them.[29]

---

20. Noormann, *Irenäus als Paulusinterpret*, 390–91.

21. *Haer.* 4.9.1.

22. *servitutis jugum*; Noormann concludes that the Greek was probably δουλείας ζυγόν (*Irenäus als Paulusinterpret*, 396).

23. *Haer.* 4.15.1; these remarks are based on Acts 7:38–43, which is cited.

24. *Haer.* 4.15.1; Noormann, *Irenäus als Paulusinterpret*, 397; Rousseau, *Livre IV, Tome II*, 548–49.

25. *Haer.* 4.14.3.

26. Noormann, *Irenäus als Paulusinterpret*, 397; citing Irenaeus's *Epideixis* (*Demonstration of the Apostolic Teaching*), 96, he suggests that Irenaeus's view of the old covenant as disciplinary for the people of Israel is based on Paul's use of the image of a παιδαγωός in Gal 3:24 (in *Haer.* 4.14.3, cited in notes 25 and 111).

27. *Haer.* 3.12.14; it belongs to "those who recently believed in God through the Holy Spirit." Translation from Unger and Steenberg, *Irenaeus, Book 3*, 70. I have changed "liberty" to "freedom."

28. *Haer.* 4.9.1; translation from ANF, vol. 1, 472. Cf. Rousseau, *Livre IV, Tome II*, 480–81.

29. *Haer.* 4.16.5; translation from ANF, vol. 1, 482. I have changed "liberty" to "freedom" and "men" to "human beings." Cf. Rousseau, *Livre IV, Tome II*, 570–73.

As Noormann points out, Irenaeus claims that the "yoke of slavery" could be abolished because it had fulfilled its function: The human being had become mature enough for freedom.[30] As he further points out, there is no empirical basis for this claim. The "fullness of the time of freedom" is fixed by the arrival of Christ; as Paul put it, ἐλθούσης δὲ τῆς πίστεως.[31]

The most important exception to the threefold division of the fathers, the old covenant, and the new covenant is the Trinitarian structure of salvation history influenced by 1 Cor 15:25-28. When he uses this schema, Irenaeus distinguishes between three fundamental epochs of history: the time from creation to incarnation, the time from the incarnation to the end of the millennium, and the time of the kingdom of the Father.[32] He connects these epochs respectively with the Spirit, the Son, and the Father.[33] For example, he argues that God was truly seen prophetically through the Spirit, is seen adoptively through the Son, and shall be seen paternally in the kingdom of heaven, the Spirit truly preparing human beings for[34] the Son of God "and the Son leading them to the Father, while the Father, too, confers [upon them] incorruption for eternal life, which comes to all from the fact of their seeing God."[35] In this passage Irenaeus emphasizes that God can only be seen because in his love and kindness he makes himself visible to those who love him.

In another passage, the transition from the Son to the Father is discussed by means of citations from 1 Cor 15:25-28. Irenaeus attributes to "the presbyters" or "the elders,"[36] the disciples of the apostles, the teaching that

> [those who are saved] advance through steps of this nature; also that they ascend through the Spirit to the Son, and through the Son to the Father, and that in due time the Son will yield up His work to the Father, even as it is said by the apostle, "For He must reign until He hath put all enemies under His feet. The last enemy that shall be destroyed is death" [1 Cor 15:25-26]. For in the times of the

---

30. *Haer.* 4.4.1.

31. Gal 3 :25; cf. Noormann, *Irenäus als Paulusinterpret*, 406-7.

32. Charles E. Hill has argued that Irenaeus "made his decisive adoption of chiliasm ... sometime in the midst of writing (probably the fourth book of) his *Against Heresies*" and that he did so because of "the increasing urgency of the confrontation with Gnosticism." *Regnum Caelorum: Patterns of Future Hope in Early Christianity* (OECS; Oxford: Clarendon, 1992), 184, 187.

33. Noormann, *Irenäus als Paulusinterpret*, 388, note 48.

34. Some read *in filium* (which is translated above), while others read *in filio* (which is translated in the ANF, vol. 1, 489, col. 1; see note 4). Rousseau has "*in Filium*" in her Latin text (*Livre IV, Tome II*, 638).

35. *Haer.* 4.20.5; translation from ANF, vol. 1, 489, col. 1. I have changed "him" to "them" and "every one" to "all." Cf. Rousseau, *Livre IV, Tome II*, 638-41.

36. Daley identifies these "elders" with those "of earlier Asiatic Christianity" (*Hope of the Early Church*, 31).

kingdom, the righteous person who is on the earth shall then forget to die. [Then 1 Cor 15:27-28 is cited as a description of the transition from the kingdom of the Son to that of the Father].[37]

The translation of Norbert Brox brings out more clearly that the elders taught that the saved make progress from the new Jerusalem on earth to Paradise and from Paradise to heaven, that is, through the Spirit to the Son, and through the Son to the Father.[38] Thus progress is made by human beings in general in the history of salvation, as well as by individuals, even after death.

Noormann points out that the explanatory remark Irenaeus inserts between the quotation of 1 Cor 15:25-26 and 15:27-28 specifies that the rule of Christ mentioned in vv. 25–26 is the millennium, which involves a kingdom on earth, in which the righteous will already have forgotten death. The introduction to the citation, however, shows that Irenaeus is particularly concerned with vv. 27–28, the giving of the rule of the Son to the rule of the Father, which is interpreted as the transition from the kingdom of the Son to the kingdom of the Father in the sense of stages in the history of salvation, in which one stage follows upon another.[39]

Citing *Haer.* 4.9.3, Noormann rightly concludes that for Irenaeus the individual stages of salvation are not so much in opposition to one another as a unified process of growth. The new covenant in relation to the old and the eschaton in relation to the new each bring an increase in the giving of God's grace. The history of salvation can thus be characterized as a single salvific work of the one God that progresses as an historical process.[40]

The Antichrist

Discussion of the Antichrist in Irenaeus's work is a theme that derives in part from 2 Thessalonians, which, in his view, was a work of Paul. The Antichrist will appear near the end of the Kingdom of the Son, will devastate everything in the world, and then reign for three years and six months, a length of time used in the book of Daniel regarding the rule of the king represented by the little horn.[41]

The Antichrist is mentioned for the first time after a discussion of the victory of Christ over the enemy of humanity, Satan (*Haer.* 5.21-24).[42] The appearance of the

---

37. *Haer.* 5.36.2; translation from ANF, vol. 1, 567. I have changed "man" to "person." Cf. Rousseau, *Livre V, Tome II*, 458–61; Noormann, *Irenäus als Paulusinterpret*, 206, note 196.

38. Norbert Brox, *Irenäus von Lyon: Adversus Haereses, gegen die Häresien* (Fontes Christiani 8.5; Freiburg: Herder, 2001), 271, 273.

39. Noormann, *Irenäus als Paulusinterpret*, 374–75. Daley makes a similar point (*Hope of the Early Church*, 29).

40. Ibid., 384.

41. *Haer.* 5.30.4; cf. Dan 7:8, 25; 12:7.

42. *Haer.* 5.25.1; Noormann, *Irenäus als Paulusinterpret*, 349.

Antichrist for Irenaeus stands in continuity with that of the serpent in Paradise and the Tempter in the wilderness, but he represents a more potent form of devilish activity. He will receive all the power of the devil, will recapitulate in himself all diabolical apostasy, and sum up in himself the error of all other idols. Thus, as earlier the devil was worshipped through many idols, now he will be worshipped through this one idol. Irenaeus found this process brought to expression in 2 Thess 2:3-4[43]:

> Unless there shall come a falling away first, and the man of sin shall be revealed, the son of perdition, who opposes and exalts himself above all that is called God, or that is worshipped; so that he sits in the temple of God, showing himself as if he were God.[44]

The interpretation of Irenaeus focuses on v. 4, taking Paul's language to refer to idols. He thus reprises an argument he had made earlier to the effect that the Antichrist is not able to exalt himself above the true God but only above those that are called gods by those who are ignorant of God, namely, above the idols. He supported his interpretation with a citation of 1 Cor 8:4b-6.[45] As noted above, by putting aside all the idols, the Antichrist presents himself as the only idol, thus summing up all idolatry in himself and recapitulating all apostasy.[46]

Also in 2 Thess 2:4, the Antichrist is depicted as seating himself in the temple of God, displaying himself as God. Irenaeus interprets the last phrase as "endeavoring to show himself as Christ."[47] He interprets the event as a whole as the abomination of desolation described in Matt 24:15, 21.[48] Then he cites Dan 7:7-8, 20-22[49] to make the point that the Antichrist is represented by the little horn in Daniel 7, a point that is summarized in *Haer.* 5.30.4. Irenaeus rightly interprets the time, times, and a half time of Daniel as three years and six months.[50]

Immediately following the identification of the Antichrist with the little horn of Daniel 7, Irenaeus returns to 2 Thessalonians 2, citing vv. 8-12 to make the point that the Antichrist will be destroyed by the Lord at his coming by the breath of his mouth.[51]

---

43. Noormann, *Irenäus als Paulusinterpret*, 360.

44. *Haer.* 5.25.1; translation from ANF, vol. 1, 553; I have updated the English. Cf. Rousseau, *Live V, Tome II*, 310–11.

45. *Haer.* 3.6.5; Unger and Steenberg, *Irenaeus, Book 3*, 40. Cf. Noormann, *Irenäus als Paulusinterpret*, 119–20.

46. Noormann, *Irenäus als Paulusinterpret*, 361.

47. *Haer.* 5.25.2; he repeats this interpretation in *Haer.* 5.25.4.

48. *Haer.* 5.25.2.

49. *Haer.* 5.25.3; he also cites Dan 7:23-25.

50. He does so both in *Haer.* 5.25.3 and 30.4. Irenaeus also discusses Dan 9:27 and comments that half a week is also equivalent to three years and six months (25:4).

51. *Haer.* 5.25.3.

In 5.26.1, Irenaeus turns to the book of Revelation and comments that the ten kings mentioned in that work are those "among whom the empire which now rules [the earth] shall be partitioned." These are the same ten kings of whom Daniel spoke. Like the Antichrist they will also be destroyed "by the coming of our Lord."

In 5.28.2, Irenaeus cites 2 Thess 2:10-12 again as at least a partial explanation of why some people shun the light and separate themselves from God. In the same section he introduces a further prophecy of the Antichrist by commenting that he will be cast into the lake of fire.[52] He elaborates this point by interpreting John's vision of the beast from the sea in Rev 13:2-10 as another description of the coming of the Antichrist and the beast from the land in 13:11-13 as his armor-bearer. At the end of the section, he interprets the number of the beast, 666, given in Rev 13:18, as "a summing up of the whole of that apostasy [recapitulated by the Antichrist] which has taken place during six thousand years."[53]

Next (*Haer.* 5.28.3), Irenaeus explains his understanding of the duration of world history. The principle by which he determines that length of time is, "For in as many days as this world was made, in so many thousand years shall it be concluded."[54] He derives this principle from Gen 2:2, which states that on the seventh day God rested from all the work that he had done. He takes this statement as describing what is past as well as a prophecy of things to come. A second hermeneutical principle is taken from 2 Pet 3:8, "with the Lord a day is like a thousand years" and vice versa.[55] So he concludes that the things that have been created will come to an end after six thousand years.[56]

Irenaeus goes on to state that, as in the saying attributed to John the Baptist (Matt 3:12//Luke 3:17), the chaff must be separated from the wheat. The former represents apostasy, the latter those who bring faith to God as fruit. This process means tribulation for those who are being saved because they must be, as it were, ground, kneaded, and baked in order to be worthy of the royal banquet.[57]

At the beginning of the next chapter (5.29) Irenaeus contrasts those who are being saved, whose free will is ripening toward immortality and who are becoming fit for eternal subjection to God, with those among the nations who have not lifted their eyes to heaven and thanked their creator. Because the latter are useless to the just, the church will suddenly be taken up,[58] and there will be "a tribulation such as has not been from the beginning of the world until now" (Matt 24:21). He goes on

---

52. Rev 19:20.

53. Irenaeus elaborates this point in 5.29.2.

54. *Haer.* 5.28.3; translation from ANF, vol. 1, 557, col. 2. Cf. Rousseau, *Livre V, Tome II*, 358–59.

55. 2 Pet 3:8 itself is an adaptation of Ps 90:4.

56. The author of the letter of *Barnabas* makes a similar argument (15:3-4).

57. *Haer.* 5.28.4.

58. The Latin phrase is *repente hinc Ecclesia assumetur*. In Fragment 24, the corresponding Greek phrase is ἀθρόως ἐντεῦθεν τῆς ἐκκλησίας ἀναλαμβανομένης; see Brox, *Irenäus von Lyon*, 218; and Rousseau, *Livre V, Tome II*, 364.

to say, "For this is the last contest of the righteous, in which, when they overcome, they are crowned with incorruption."⁵⁹

The notion that "the church will be taken up" may have been inspired by 1 Thess 4:17. This suggestion is supported by the fact that not long after that statement and in the context of a reference to οἱ χρόνοι καὶ οἱ καιροί and the Day of the Lord, Paul mentions the "sudden destruction," from which there will be no escape, that will come upon those who say, "peace and security" (1 Thess 5:3).

As noted above, at the end of 5.28.1 Irenaeus discusses the number of the beast in Rev 13:18. He returns to that topic in 5.30. The beast (from the sea, the one to which reference is made in that verse) is interpreted by Irenaeus as the Antichrist. In light of that identification, he interprets the number 666 symbolically. In it the number of the tens is equal to the number of the hundreds, and the number of the hundreds is equal to that of the units. Thus the numeral reflects the apostasy "which occurred at the beginning, during the intermediate periods, and which shall take place at the end."⁶⁰ This statement reprises the earlier discussion of the Antichrist based on 2 Thess 2:4.⁶¹

Irenaeus warns against the reading that presents the numeral as 616. This reading should be rejected for a variety of reasons. One is the danger that those "who falsely presume that they know the name of the Antichrist" will not recognize the actual Antichrist when he comes because he has another name. Thus, since they do not guard against him, they will be easily led astray.⁶²

To guard against being led astray by the Antichrist, people ought to "await, in the first place, the division of the kingdom into ten."⁶³ Then they should watch for a time when one will "come claiming the kingdom for himself, and terrify those [ten kings], having a name containing the aforesaid number [666]." This man "is truly the abomination of desolation," that is, the Antichrist. Irenaeus calls upon support from Paul for this point, citing 1 Thess 5:3, "When they shall say, Peace and safety, then sudden destruction shall come upon them." This verse is interpreted as applying to the ten kings, and the destruction is wrought by the Antichrist.⁶⁴

After discussing a few of the many names that have the number 666, Irenaeus concludes, "We will not, however, incur the risk of pronouncing positively as to the name of Antichrist; for if it were necessary that his name should be distinctly revealed in this present time, it would have been announced by him who beheld the apocalyptic vision."⁶⁵

---

59 *Haer.* 5.29.1.

60. *Haer.* 5.30.1.

61. See the discussion of *Haer.* 3.6.5, 5.25.1.

62. *Haer.* 5.30.1; translation from ANF, vol. 1, 559. Cf. Rousseau, *Livre V, Tome II*, 376–77.

63. *Haer.* 5.30.2. See the discussion above of Irenaeus's identification of the ten kings of Dan 7:7 with those of Rev 13:1.

64. For the identification of the Antichrist with the abomination of desolation, see *Haer.* 5.25.2.

65. *Haer.* 5.30.3.

The Kingdom of the Son and the Millennium

Irenaeus ends chapter 30 of Book 5 with the following summarizing statement:

> But when this Antichrist shall have devastated all things in this world, he will reign for three years and six months and sit in the temple in Jerusalem; and then the Lord will come from heaven in the clouds, in the glory of the Father, sending this man and those who follow him into the lake of fire; but bringing in for the righteous the times of the kingdom, that is, the rest, the hallowed seventh day; and restoring to Abraham the promised inheritance, in which kingdom the Lord declared, that "many coming from the east and from the west should sit down with Abraham, Isaac, and Jacob."[66]

The kingdom brought in for the righteous, defined as the rest, the hallowed day, reveals once again Irenaeus's use of Gen 2:2 and 2 Pet 3:8 as one way of structuring human history and determining its duration.[67] The "rest" signifies the seventh day of creation, on which God rested after completing all the works of creation during the previous six days. It also signifies the Millennium, which belongs to the period of the Kingdom of the Son or is perhaps identical with it.[68]

The transition from the summary quoted above to chapter 31 is abrupt. Instead of taking up some element from that summary for elaboration, Irenaeus enters into a polemical discussion of resurrection. He picks up the thread of the narrative of the last things in chapter 32. In any case, it is not clear when the Kingdom of the Son begins for Irenaeus. As noted in the introduction to this chapter, Paul probably thought of the reign of Christ as beginning with his resurrection. In the section on the structure of the history of salvation above, the incarnation was suggested as constituting that beginning.[69] Another possibility is that the Kingdom of the Son begins with "the coming of Christ" since the summary at the end of chapter 30 may be understood as implying that with that event, the earthly kingdom of the Antichrist ends and the rule of Christ begins.

It is clear, however, that the main focus of Irenaeus with regard to the Kingdom of the Son is the Millennium, "the times of the kingdom" for the righteous, which is symbolized by the seventh day of rest.[70] In his polemic against those who deny the salvation of the flesh, he states that they despise the arrangement for the advancement of the just and are ignorant of the methods of preparing (human

---

66. *Haer.* 5.30.4; translation from ANF, vol. 1, 560. Cf. Rousseau, *Livre V, Tome II*, 386–87. The text cited at the end is Matt 8:11.

67. Cf. *Haer.* 5.28.2-3; see the discussion above.

68. See the section above on "The Structure of the History of Salvation according to Irenaeus."

69. Following Noormann, *Irenäus als Paulusinterpret*, 206, note 196.

70. *Haer.* 5.30.4; ANF, vol. 1, 560. Cf. Rousseau, *Livre V, Tome II*, 386–87.

beings) for incorruptibility.[71] Human beings, Irenaeus claims, do not ascend to heaven immediately after death; rather, their souls go to an invisible place determined by God to await the bodily resurrection.[72]

Irenaeus returns to discussions of the narrative of the last things in chapter 32. The context suggests that the Kingdom of the Son, the Millennium, begins with the resurrection of the just. Their resurrection is to the kingdom in which those who are worthy gradually become accustomed to comprehending God.[73] Another purpose of the millennium is to fulfill the divine promise to the fathers of an inheritance. This inheritance is earthly but set in a creation (*conditio*) that has been renovated. The just will reign in this kingdom.[74] For Irenaeus, the creation will be restored to its original condition, and it will serve the just without restraint. He supports this conclusion by citing Rom 8:19-21.

> For the expectation of the creation[75] waits for the revelation of the sons of God. For the creation has been subjected to transitoriness, not voluntarily, but on account of him who subjected it in hope; for this very creation will be set free from the slavery of corruption to the glorious freedom of the sons of God.[76]

In the next section, Irenaeus remarks that, since Abraham did not receive the promised land during his lifetime, he will receive it, along with his seed, at the resurrection of the just. His seed is the church (*ecclesia*), which received the adoption through the Lord. Support comes from the saying of John the Baptist, "For God is able from the stones to raise up children to Abraham."[77]

He also cites Paul to make the latter point, "You, brothers, are sons of the promise, as Isaac is" (Gal 4:28). He also cites Gal 3:16, in which the singular "seed" refers to Christ. Finally, he cites the more extensive passage Gal 3:6-9, which attests to the conviction that those who are of faith will be blessed with faithful Abraham. Neither Abraham nor his seed possess the earth in the present time. They will, however, possess it at the resurrection of the just.[78]

---

71. *Haer.* 5.31.1; paraphrase based on the Latin text with consultation of the German translation in Brox, *Irenaeus von Lyon*, 232–33. Cf. Rousseau, *Livre V, Tome II*, 388–89.

72. *Haer.* 5.31.2.

73. *Haer.* 5.32.1; I follow here Brox's translation (*Irenäus von Lyon*, 237) of *capere Deum*. Rousseau's translation is similar: *saisir Dieu* (*Livre V, Tome II*, 397).

74. Denis Minns argues that the kingdom of the just will be a social and political reality, not just a physical one: *Irenaeus: An Introduction* (New York: T&T Clark, 2010), 145.

75. I follow Brox and Rousseau in translating *creatura* with "creation," rather than with "creature," as in ANF, vol. 1, 561.

76. *Haer.* 5.32.1; I translate from the Latin, consulting the translation of Brox, *Irenäus von Lyon*, 236–39. Cf. Rousseau, *Livre V, Tome II*, 398–99.

77. *Haer.* 5.32.2; Matt 3:9, Luke 3:8; translation from ANF, vol. 1, 561, col. 2.

78. *Haer.* 5.32.2; the passage closes with a citation of the beatitude, "Blessed are the meek, for they will inherit the earth" (Matt 5:5).

Chapter 33 is devoted to demonstrating that the kingdom of the just will be earthly in the sense of involving eating and drinking, which, he argues, one can do only in the flesh.[79] Strikingly section 2 ends with the remark that, since the kingdom is the true Sabbath, the just shall do no tiring work[80] but will "have a table at hand prepared for them by God, supplying them with all sorts of dishes." Section 3 offers further proofs for this argument that the kingdom of the just will be earthly. It goes further in arguing that the renovated earth will bring forth abundant fruit and every kind of food. Irenaeus cites the presbyters or elders as saying that they heard John, the disciple of the Lord, proclaim that the Lord taught about these times and said:

> Days are coming in which vines will grow, each with ten thousand branches, and on every branch ten thousand twigs, and on every twig ten thousand shoots, and on every shoot ten thousand clusters, and in every one of the clusters there will be ten thousand grapes, and every grape when pressed will give twenty-five measures of wine. And when one of the saints picks a cluster, another one will shout, I am better, take me! Bless the Lord through me![81]

According to Irenaeus, the Lord went on to say something analogous concerning wheat, fruit-bearing trees, seeds, and grass. Further, all the animals will eat the produce of the earth and therefore live harmoniously with one another. He elaborates this discussion in the next section, citing Papias and the passages from scripture that he quoted.[82]

In chapter 34 Irenaeus elaborates the joyfulness and earthly character of the renovated earth by citing his own selection of passages from scripture, both of the old and the new covenant, the former dominating. In the last section of that chapter, he cites Isaiah concerning the restoration of Jerusalem and the reign of a righteous king.[83]

After asserting that prophecies of this kind cannot be interpreted allegorically, he cites more passages from Isaiah and claims that all such statements are made with regard to the resurrection of the just, which will take place after the coming of the Antichrist and after the destruction of all the nations under his rule. Then, instead of the Antichrist, the just will reign on the earth.[84]

---

79. *Haer.* 5.33.1-2. He cites Matt 26:27-29 (with "new" modifying "covenant") and Matt 19:29 in section 1 and Luke 14:12-14 in section 2.

80. Reading ἐπίτροπον with Brox (*Irenäus von Lyon*, 244, note 111) inferred from the Armenian, rather than the Latin *terrenum*. So also Rousseau, *Livre V, Tome II*, 410–11.

81. *Haer.* 5.33.3. Translation from ANF, vol. 1, 563, modified in light of Brox's translation (*Irenäus von Lyon*, 247). Cf. Rousseau, *Livre V, Tome II*, 415.

82. *Haer.* 5.33.4.

83. *Haer.* 5.34.4.

84. *Haer.* 5.35.1.

In spite of the earthly and physical character of the setting of the resurrection of the just, they will not only rule but they will also be strengthened by the vision of the Lord (Christ) and through him become accustomed to comprehend the glory of God the Father. They will also enjoy association and community with the holy angels and union with spiritual beings in the kingdom.[85]

In spite of Irenaeus's assertion that the passages he cited cannot be understood in terms of regions above the heavens, he claims that in the Kingdom of the Son, Jerusalem will be rebuilt on the model of the Jerusalem above. In addition to Isa 49:16, he cites Gal 4:26, "The Jerusalem above, however, is free, which is our mother." The Jerusalem to which Paul refers, according to Irenaeus, is not an aeon of the typical Gnostic cosmology, but is the same one described as descending from heaven in Rev 21:2.[86]

The Kingdom of the Father

Irenaeus goes on, "For after the times of the kingdom, [John] says, 'I saw a great white throne, and Him who sat upon it, from whose face the earth fled away, and the heavens; and there was no more place for them.'"[87] The remark made in passing, "after the times of the kingdom," suggests that the transition from the Kingdom of the Son (the Millennium) begins with the last judgment carried out by the Father. When God appears as judge on his great white throne, heaven and earth flee away and are no more (Rev 20:11). This implies that the new heaven and the new earth (Rev 21:1) belong to the Kingdom of the Father. In the restored creation of the Millennium, Jerusalem was rebuilt after the pattern of the one above.[88] In the Kingdom of the Father, "Jerusalem" and "the City" refer to the new Jerusalem, which descends from heaven after the last judgment (Rev 21:2).

At the time of the appearance of God as judge, the general resurrection occurs, according to Irenaeus.[89] Neither the author of Revelation nor Irenaeus attempts to clarify the relationship between the first resurrection and the general resurrection. Irenaeus cites Rev 21:3-4 to characterize the Kingdom of the Father, emphasizing the divine presence with the people. He also cites Isaiah's prophecy of a new heaven and a new earth (Isa 65:17-18). To support the passing away of heaven and (the renewed) earth, he cites 1 Cor 7:31, "For the state (or condition: *habitus*) of this world passes away."[90] Finally, he cites the saying of the Lord, "Heaven and earth shall pass

---

85. *Haer.* 5.35.1.
86. *Haer.* 5.35.2.
87. Rev 20:11; *Haer.* 5.35.2; translation from ANF, vol. 1, 566, col. 1.
88. *Haer.* 5.35.2.
89. *Haer.* 5.35.2, following Rev 20:12-15.
90. *Haer.* 5.35.2; translation from the Latin with consultation of the German translation by Brox (*Irenaeus of Lyon*, 266–67). Rousseau translates *habitus* with "*figure*" (*Livre V, Tome II*, 449).

away."[91]

At the end of 35.2, Irenaeus emphasizes once more that these things are not allegories. God truly raises human beings, and they truly rise from the dead. As they truly rise:

> so also shall they be actually disciplined beforehand [in the Kingdom of the Son, the Millennium] for incorruption, and shall go forwards and flourish in the times of the kingdom [of the Son], in order that they may be capable of receiving the glory of the Father. Then, when all things are made new, they will truly dwell in the city of God.[92]

So for Irenaeus, those who are worthy receive the glory of the Father in the Kingdom of the Father, in which all things are made new.

Next (in 5.36.1), Irenaeus returns to the Kingdom of the Son and describes it in more detail. He also refers briefly to the transition to the Kingdom of the Father. What follows is my translation of the first part of 5.36.1.[93]

> Since it is a matter of real human beings, their transfer[94] (into the Kingdom of the Son) must also be real. They cannot go away into a (world) that does not exist, but must make progress in the one that does exist. For neither the substance (*substantia*) nor the material of the creation (*materia conditionis*) will be abolished, for true and steadfast is the one who established it; but the form of this world is passing away (another citation of 1 Cor 7:31).[95] In other words, the (conditions) in which transgression occurred (pass away), for human beings became old in them. When the temporary form (of the world) passes away and human beings are renewed and have grown so as to be ready for incorruptibility, so that they can no longer grow old, then "will there be a new heaven and a new earth" [Isa 65:17], in which the new human being will remain, conversing forever in a new way with God.

Irenaeus's account of the Kingdom of the Son involves a mixture of elements of the world in which he and his audience lived with radically new elements. For him the setting of the Kingdom is the creation, unchanged in its matter and nature.

---

91. Matt 24:35//Mark 13:31.

92. *Haer.* 5.35.2; translation from ANF, vol. 1, 566, col. 2. I have changed "he" to "they."

93. I have used the Latin text in Brox (*Irenäus von Lyon*, 268, 270) and consulted his translation (269, 271), as well as that in the ANF, vol. 1, 566–67. Cf. Rousseau, *Livre V, Tome II*, 452–55.

94. In Brox's text, *translationem* (*Irenäus von Lyon*, 268). So also the Latin text of Rousseau (*Livre V, Tome II*, 452).

95. Greek fragment 29 reads, οὐ γὰρ ἡ ὑπόστασις οὐδὲ ἡ οὐσία τῆς κτίσεως ἐξαφανίζεται (for neither the substance nor the essence of the creation is destroyed); Brox, *Irenäus von Lyon*, 268; Rousseau, *Livre V, Tome II*, 452.

The only changes are that human beings will not die, and they will have realistic interaction with God, just as Adam and Eve did in the Garden of Eden.

Irenaeus goes on to explain the differentiation among those who are saved based on degrees of worthiness. He ascribes this view to "the presbyters" or "the elders." What follows is my translation of the rest of 5.36.1 and the first part of 5.36.2.[96]

> Those who are worthy to live in heaven will go forward to that place, others will enjoy the delights of Paradise, and others will possess the beauty and splendor of the City.[97] Everywhere, however, God will be seen in whatever way the viewers are worthy to see him.[98]
>
> (The same elders say that) this is, moreover, the distinction of those who bear one hundred-fold, and those who produce sixty-fold, and those who bear thirty-fold.[99] Of these the first will be taken up into heaven, the others will dwell in Paradise, and the third will inhabit the City. It was for this reason that the Lord said, "In my Father's house there are many mansions" [John 14:2] ... The elders, the disciples of the apostles, affirm that this is the gradation and arrangement of those who are saved, and that they advance through steps of this nature. Thus they ascend through the Spirit to the Son, and then from the Son to the Father.

The notions of degrees of worthiness and progress may owe something to popular philosophy. It is clear at least that the allegorical interpretation of the degrees of bearing fruit allows Irenaeus, and apparently the elders before him, to include three different traditions concerning the salvation of the faithful.

As Noormann has pointed out, after discussing the ranks of the saved, Irenaeus turns once more to the transition from the Kingdom of the Son to the Kingdom of the Father.[100] Whereas the saved progress step by step through the Spirit to the Son and through the Son to the Father, the Son at the end will give over his work to the Father. Once again, Irenaeus cites 1 Cor 15:25-28, but here the citation is interrupted by an explanatory remark. This remark specifies that the rule of Christ mentioned in vv. 25-26 is the Millennium, which involves a kingdom on earth, in which the righteous will already have forgotten death.[101] As suggested in the

---

96. I have used the Latin text in Brox (*Irenäus von Lyon*, 270, 272) and consulted his translation (271, 273), as well as that in the ANF, vol. 1, 567. Cf. Rousseau, *Livre V, Tome II*, 452–61.

97. The City in the Kingdom of the Son is the one rebuilt (on earth) "after the pattern of the Jerusalem above" (5.35.2; translation from ANF, vol. 1, 565). The new or heavenly Jerusalem comes down from heaven in the time of the Kingdom of the Father. See the discussion above.

98. *Haer.* 5.36.1.

99. Cf. the parable of the sower (Mark 4:8, 20//Matt 13:8, 23).

100. *Haer.* 5.36.2.

101. Noormann, *Irenäus als Paulusinterpret*, 374.

introduction to this chapter, the conquering of death may instead refer to the general resurrection. According to Revelation at least, at that time the sea, Death, and Hades must give up the dead who are in them.[102]

The introduction to the citation, however, shows that Irenaeus is particularly concerned with 1 Cor 15:27-28, the giving over of the rule of the Son to the Father, which is interpreted as the transition from the Kingdom of the Son to the Kingdom of the Father in the sense of stages of the history of salvation, in which one stage follows upon the other. Although Paul does not articulate such thoughts, the reception on the part of Irenaeus of related ideas in 1 Cor 15:24-28 is unmistakable. According to Noormann, this handing over is not so much an "end" of the kingdom of the Son for Irenaeus as its completion.[103]

In the last section of his work, Irenaeus implies that the Kingdom of the Father is the time when God will bestow that which "eye has not seen, ear has not heard, and has not arisen in the human heart" (1 Cor 2:9). In it, by the wisdom of God, "his handiwork (*plasma*), confirmed and incorporated with his Son, is brought to perfection." The goal of the Kingdom of the Father, of the whole history of salvation, is that his handiwork pass "beyond the angels, and be made after the image and likeness of God."[104]

Conclusion

Neither Paul nor Irenaeus forged a consistent, systematic doctrine of the last things. Both addressed exigencies in their social settings by creating rhetorical, agonistic arguments in which they drew upon authoritative texts to support their conclusions. A number of Pauline texts plays an important role in Irenaeus's remarks on the structure of the history of salvation, the Antichrist, the coming of Christ, the Kingdom of the Son, and the Kingdom of the Father. One of these, 2 Thess 2:3-12, Irenaeus read realistically about the coming, career, and destruction of the Antichrist. He elaborated the text first of all, by giving "Paul's" "man of iniquity" the name "Antichrist." He also expands it by claiming that the same figure plays a role in Revelation, introduced as the beast from the sea in chapter 13. This association leads to the identification of the Antichrist as a king who will rule the inhabited world after defeating the ten kings who have divided the (Roman) empire among themselves.[105] He follows 2 Thess 2:8 in arguing that the Lord at his coming will destroy the Antichrist with the breath of his mouth.

Another text Irenaeus reads realistically is 1 Cor 15:23-28. He elaborates it partially. He does not indicate when Christ begins to reign but may imply that his reign begins when he defeats the Antichrist. Irenaeus associates Paul's

---

102. Rev 20:13-14.
103. Noormann, *Irenäus als Paulusinterpret*, 375.
104. *Haer.* 5.36.3; translation from ANF, vol. 1, 567.
105. The ten kings are taken from Dan 7:7 and identified with those of Rev 17:12.

"kingdom" (v. 24) with the thousand-year reign of Christ that begins after the first resurrection.[106] He also associates it with traditions current in his time about the Millennium. Neither 1 Cor 15:24-25 nor Rev 20:4 explicitly states whether the reign of Christ takes place in heaven or on the earth. It is clear from the literary context that the thousand-year reign in Revelation takes place on earth. This is also Irenaeus's position.

It is not, however, the earth as it was before the coming of Christ. Rather it must be restored to its former condition,[107] that is, to its state at the time of Adam and Eve. He goes on to say that Paul makes this manifest in his letter to the Romans:

> For the expectation of the creation looks forward to the revelation of the sons of God. For the creation has been subjected to futility, not willingly, but on account of him who subjected it in hope, because the creation itself will be freed from its slavery to corruption into the glorious freedom of the sons of God.[108]

In his introduction to the quotation, Irenaeus makes the point that the restoration of the creation to its original state means that it "should without restraint be under the dominion of the righteous." This statement may entail freedom from the wiles of the devil, but Adam and Eve were not free from those. More likely it refers to the undoing of the curse of the ground that involves difficulty for Adam and his descendants in eating the produce of the earth (Gen 3:16). This interpretation fits the miraculous fertility of the earth described in 5.33.3.[109]

For Paul, however, δουλεία τῆς φθορᾶς seems to address a different issue. It is the decay that inevitably follows, eventually, the birth of human beings and animals and the growth of plants. It is decay and death that Paul seems to name here as the problem with the creation in this age. If that is the case, then Paul expected the creation to be transformed in a way beyond what Irenaeus envisaged for the Kingdom of the Son. Paul's notion of the transformation probably involves an analogous transformation to that of the resurrection of the children of God. Whether the flesh is left behind or transformed, the result is a spiritual being. Not an incorporeal spirit, but a spiritual body. By analogy, Paul expected the creation somehow to become spirit, not immaterial but comprising spiritual matter.

On the basis of this reading of Rom 8:21, the statement in 1 Cor 7:31 may be interpreted similarly: παράγει γὰρ τὸ σχῆμα τοῦ κόσμου τούτου. Irenaeus cites this passage in his discussion of the new heaven and the new earth and the descent of the new Jerusalem from heaven.[110] In this case, Irenaeus's interpretation may

---

106. Rev 20:4; cf. 1 Cor 15:23.

107. *Haer.* 5.32.1. *reintegratam ad pristinum* (Brox, *Irenäus von Lyon*, 236, line 20; Rousseau, *Livre V, Tome II*, 398, line 18).

108. Rom 8:19–21 as cited by Irenaeus in *Haer.* 5.32.1.

109. Enrico Norelli concludes that in this first renovation of the earth it loses none of its characteristics except those brought about by human sin: "Il duplice rinnovamento del mondo nell'escatologia di San Ireneo," *Augustinianum* 18 (1978), 89–106 (here 90).

110. *Haer.* 5.35.2.

be closer to Paul's than is the case with Romans 8. In the new Jerusalem righteous human beings will have become "fit for the glory of God; then, when all things have been made new they will truly inhabit the city of God."[111]

It is somewhat confusing that Irenaeus cites Rom 8:19-21 in two different ways.[112] He cites it, as observed immediately above, to characterize the Millennium. He also cites it, however, to explain the nature of the Kingdom of the Father, which follows the Millennium.[113] When he cites it in relation to the Millennium, he departs from the probable import of Paul's remark in Rom 8:21. Irenaeus speaks there about a creation restored to its primeval state. When he cites it in relation to the Kingdom of the Father, however, he relates Rom 8:21 to the new heaven and the new earth, to the final state. In this application he interprets the text in a way closer to the likely significance of the text for Paul.

---

111. *Haer.* 5.35.2; *ut fiat capax gloriae Patris; deinde omnibus renovatis, vere in civitate habitabit Dei* (Brox, *Irenäus von Lyon*, 268, lines 7–9; Rousseau, *Livre V, Tome II*, 450, lines 115–16); my translation with consultation of the translations of Brox (269), Rousseau (451), and ANF, vol. 1, 566, col. 2.

112. Cf. the discussion of Norelli, who distinguishes the renovation of the earth (*terra*) from the renovation of the universe (*kosmos*); "Il duplice rinnovamento," 91–106.

113. *Haer.* 5.36.3.

RESPONSE
APPROPRIATING PAUL: IRENAEUS'S USE OF THE APOSTLE IN FORMING AND EXPRESSING HIS ESCHATOLOGICAL THOUGHT

Todd D. Still

Irenaeus's construal of and language for things eschatological were decisively and demonstrably shaped by the letters of the one to whom the bishop of Lyon repeatedly and reverently refers as "the apostle." This is particularly true with respect to 2 Thessalonians 2, 1 Corinthians 15, and Romans 8, as Professor Adela Yabro Collins has clearly shown in her learned chapter "Paul in Irenaeus on the Last Things."

Through her work, Collins also informs readers how the erstwhile bishop conceived of the structure of salvation history, the Antichrist, the Kingdom of the Son and the Millennium, and the Kingdom of the Father, as he sought to combat "heretics" by appealing to any number of biblical texts both within and beyond Pauline corpus, not least certain portions of Revelation.

To be sure and to be fair, Irenaeus did not intend *Against Heresies* in general and Books 3–5 of this work in particular to function as an eschatological treatise, much less a comprehensive eschatological magnum opus. That being said, in reading and rereading *Against Heresies* and Collins's treatment of Irenaeus's repeated appeals to Paul with respect to last things, this Pauline interpreter cannot help but note what is present in Irenaeus's eschatology that is absent from Paul's on the one hand and what is absent from Irenaeus's eschatology that is present in Paul's on the other. I will explore such presence and absence in my brief response chapter that follows.

While Irenaeus may be granted an interpretative pardon for confusing and/or conflating 2 Thessalonians' "man of lawlessness" with Revelation's "sea beast" (while he may have been among the first Christian interpreters to do so, he was by no means the last) and for reading the rapture of the church into 1 Thess 4:17 (again, he may have been one of the first to make this misstep, but his interpretative heirs are legion), the Millennium, which features prominently in Irenaeus's eschatology, is altogether absent from Paul—and from the whole of scripture for that matter spare Revelation 20. While this single aspect of Irenaeus's eschatological thought might be regarded as comparatively inconsequential given his overall teaching on last things, closer analysis reveals his view on the Millennium causes him, perhaps unwittingly, to omit any number of relevant Pauline passages pertaining to the end. Moreover, the priority Irenaeus gives to the Millennium in his eschatological thought appears to have kept him from appreciating the sense of suddenness that marks and even animates the apostle's thinking regarding last things.

With the possible and partial exception of 2 Thessalonians, whose authenticity continues to be debated among Pauline interpreters, it is more than less a truism in New Testament Studies that Paul thought and taught his converts to think that the *parousia* of the Lord Jesus Christ would be both soon and sudden. This, of course, is well known with respect to 1 Thessalonians, where Paul expects to be— or at least allows for his being—alive at the time of Christ's coming (4:17; cf. 5:10), which he likens to a thief in the night even as he calls upon the Thessalonians to live as children of light as they prepare for and anticipate the Day of the Lord (= the *parousia*) that will come as suddenly as birth-pangs come upon a pregnant woman (so 5:2-6; cf. 1:10; 2:19; 3:13; 5:23).

It is not only in 1 Thessalonians, however, where one encounters Pauline passages that envision that Lord's coming sooner than later. In 1 Corinthians 7, for example, a text with which Irenaeus was well acquainted, Paul instructs Corinthian Christ-followers to remain as they are in light of the present distress (7:26), an ambiguous expression that is arguably clarified by the apostle's subsequent remarks that "the time is short" (7:29) and "the form of this world is passing away" (7:31). One might also note in passing that in 1 Cor 11:26 Paul speaks of the observance of the Lord's Supper as a proclamation of the Lord's death until he comes (in the not too distant future).

Later in the letter known to us as 1 Corinthians, in a chapter to which Irenaeus frequently appeals, one does well to note that Paul proclaims this *mysterion*: "We will not all sleep (that is, die [cf. 1 Thess 4:13]), but we will all be changed" (15:51). What is more, in the verses that follow 15:51 until the end of 1 Corinthians 15, the apostle's anticipation of the soon-to-come transformation wrought by resurrection is palpable. The same may be said of the early Christian cry "Maranatha!" ("Lord, come!") that occurs near the close of the letter (16:22).

If Paul's hope in and expectation for the Lord's imminent *parousia* do not feature in the letters to which we refer as 2 Corinthians and Galatians (and understandably so given the occasions that gave rise to those pastoral communications), it is erroneous to conclude, as not a few Pauline scholars are wont to do, that the apostle's anticipation of Christ's coming waned over the miles and the years. On the contrary, we see in Philippians, for example, typically dated from the mid-50s to the early 60s AD, that he not only declares in a deliciously ambiguous expression *ho kyrios engys* ("The Lord is near" [4:5b]), but he also instructs the Philippian fellowship, "Our *politeuma* is in heaven, from where also we eagerly await a Savior, the Lord Jesus Christ" (3:20).

Turning to Romans, commonly though by no means unanimously thought to be Paul's last extant letter, one continues to discover an author who anticipates that all things will soon be culminated in and through Christ at the time of his return. So, in addition to Paul's assertion that "The God of peace will soon (*en tachei*) crush Satan under your feet [i.e., at the time of Christ's coming]," the Apostle to the Gentiles encourages Roman Christians to realize that "our salvation is nearer (*engyteron*) than when we believed" (13:11). Furthermore, he maintains, "the night is far spent, and the day is at hand" (13:12).

If Irenaeus's construal of time and his effort to harmonize Paul and Revelation kept him from perceiving and presenting aright Paul's belief in the proximity of Christ's *parousia*, it would be wrongheaded not to recognize the considerable congruity that exists between Irenaeus's and Paul's eschatological thought. Like Paul, Irenaeus embraced both continuity and discontinuity between the old and the new covenants. Additionally, although the bishop employed various schema to depict salvation history, he regarded one and the same God, a God who is mighty and merciful to save, to be at work in the world. This was no less true of Paul before him.

Irenaeus also shared Paul's conviction regarding the resurrection. If the bishop, unlike the apostle, differentiated between a first and a general resurrection, between various ranks of the saved, and between the restoration of creation during the Kingdom of the Son and the transformation of creation in conjunction with the Kingdom of the Father, he, as Paul, embraced and espoused that Christians would be raised as Christ himself was raised.

Even as Paul combatted certain Jewish-Christian agitators in Galatia (and elsewhere) regarding the nature of the covenant and various Corinthian believers with respect to the resurrection, Irenaeus sought to counter his Gnostic Christian competitors and forged his doctrine of covenant in the cauldron of conflict. In so doing, the bishop was aided in no small measure by the apostle.

Both Collins's chapter and my response have highlighted congruous and incongruous elements between Paul's and Irenaeus's eschatological thought. Decided, and even irreconcilable, differences notwithstanding, one can well imagine that these early Christian theologians could have enthusiastically declare in unison and with considerable conviction: "No eye has seen and no ear has heard and no human heart has conceived what God has prepared for those who love him" (1 Cor 2:9).

What is more, their confidence in God and commitment to Christ and his church would almost certainly cause them to concur with the hopeful assessment of Julian of Norwich, not least with respect to the resurrection of Christ and Christians, namely, "It behooved that there should be sin; but all shall be well, and all shall be well, and all manner of thing shall be well" (*Revelations of Divine Love* 13.27).

BIBLIOGRAPHY

Aageson, James. *Paul, the Pastoral Epistles, and the Early Church*. Library of Pauline Studies. Peabody, MA: Hendrickson, 2008.

Abelson, Joshua. *The Immanence of God in Rabbinical Literature*, 2nd ed. New York: Hermon, 1969.

Adams, Edward. *Constructing the World: A Study in Paul's Cosmological Language*. SNTW. Edinburgh: T&T Clark, 2000.

Adams, Edward. *The Stars Will Fall From Heaven: "Cosmic Catastrophe" in The New Testament and Its World*. LNTS 347. London: T&T Clark, 2007.

Aland, Barbara. "Marcion: Versuch einer neuen Interpretation." *ZTK* 70 (1973): 420–47.

Aland, Barbara. "Sünde und Erlösung bei Marcion und die Konsequenz für die sog. beiden GötterMarcions." Pages 147–57 in *Marcion und seine kirchengeschichtliche Wirkung/Marcion and his Impact on Church History: Vorträge der Internationalen Fachkonferenz zu Marcion, gehalten vom 15.-18. August 2001 in Mainz*. Edited by Gerhard May et al. TUGAL 150. Berlin: De Gruyter, 2002.

Allenbach, J., et al. *Biblia Patristica: Index des citations et allusions bibliques dans la littérature patristique*, vol. 1. Paris: Éditions du centre national de la recherché scientifique, 1975.

Altermath, François. *Du corps psychique au corps spiritual: Interpretation de 1 Cor 15,35-49 par les auteurs chrétiens des quatre premiers siècles*. Tübingen: Mohr Siebeck, 1977.

Andia, Ysabel de. *Homo Vivens: Incorruptibilite et Divinisation de L'homme Selon Irenee de Lyons*. Paris: Etudes augustiniennes, 1986.

Asher, Jeffrey R. *Polarity and Change in 1 Corinthians 15: A Study of Metaphysics, Rhetoric, and Resurrection*. HUT 42. Tübingen: Mohr Siebeck, 2000.

Attridge, Harold W. (ed.). *Nag Hammadi Codex I (The Jung Codex)*, 2 vols. NHS 22–23. Leiden: Brill, 1985.

Audet, Th-André. "Orientations théologiques chez Saint Irénée: le contexte mental d'une *gnōsis alēthēs*." *Traditio* 1 (1943): 15–54.

Aune, David E. *Prophecy in Early Christianity and the Ancient Mediterranean World*. Grand Rapids, MI: Eerdmans, 1983.

Ayres, Lewis. "Irenaeus vs. the Valentinians: Toward a Rethinking of Patristic Exegetical Origins." *JECS* 23.2 (2015): 153–87.Bacon, Benjamin W. "The Reading of οἷς οὐδὲ in Gal. 2.5." *JBL* 42 (1923): 69–80.

Bacq, Philippe. *De l'ancienne à la nouvelle Alliance selon S. Irénée: Unité du livre IV de l'Adversus Haereses*. Paris: Editions Lethielleux, 1978.

Balas, David L. "The Use and Interpretation of Paul in Irenaeus' Five Books *Adversus Haereses*." *Second Century* 9 (1992): 27–39.

Barclay, John M. G. "The Family as the Bearer of Religion in Judaism and Early Christianity." Pages 66–80 in *Constructing Early Christian Families: Family as Social Reality and Metaphor*. Edited by Halvor Moxnes. New York: Routledge, 1997.

Barclay, John M. G. "Stoic Physics and the Christ-Event: A Review of Troels Engberg-Pedersen Cosmology and Self in the Apostle Paul: The Material Spirit." *JSNT* 33.4 (2011): 406–14.
Barnes, Michel René. "The Beginning and End of Early Christian Pneumatology." *Augustinian Studies* 39.2 (2008): 169–86.
Barnes, Michel René. "Irenaeus's Trinitarian Theology." *NV* 7 (2009): 67–106.
Barrett, C. K. *A Critical and Exegetical Commentary on the Acts of the Apostles*, 2 vols. Edinburgh: T&T Clark, 1994–98.
Bassler, Jouette M. "A Response to Jeffrey Bingham and Susan Graham: Networks and Noah's Sons." Page 139 in *Early Patristic Readings of Romans*. Edited by Kathy L. Gaca and L. L. Welborn. New York: T&T Clark, 2005.
Bastit, Agnès. "Quelques appels à la rationalité chez Irénée de Lyon." *Revue de Théologie et de Philosophie* 149.1–2 (2017): 105–24.
Bastit, Agnès, and Joseph Verheyden. *Irénée de Lyon et les débuts de la Bible chrétienne. Actes de la Journée du 1. VII. 2014 à Lyon*. Turnhout: Brepols, 2017.
Bates, Matthew W. *The Hermeneutics of the Apostolic Proclamation: The Center of Paul's Method of Scripture Interpretation*. Waco, TX: Baylor University Press, 2012.
Bates, Matthew W. *The Birth of the Trinity: Jesus, God, and Spirit in New Testament and Early Christian Interpretation of the Old Testament*. Oxford: Oxford University Press, 2015.
Bates, Matthew W. "A Christology of Incarnation and Enthronement: Romans 1.3-4 as Unified, Nonadoptionist, and Nonconciliatory." *CBQ* 77 (2015): 107–27.
Bauckham, Richard. *Jesus and the God of Israel: God Crucified and Other Essays on the New Testament's Christology of Divine Identity*. Milton Keynes: Paternoster, 2008.
Baur, Christian. "Die Christuspartie in der Corinthischen Gemeinde." *Zeitschrift für Theologie* 4 (1831): 61–206.
Beatrice, Pier Franco. "Der Presbyter des Irenäus, Polycarp von Smyrna und der Brief an Diognet." Pages 179–202 in *Pléroma Salus Carnis. Homenaje a Antonio Orbe, S.J.* Edited by Eugenio Romero-Pose. Santiago de Compostella, 1990.
BeDuhn, Jason David. *The First New Testament: Marcion's Scriptural Canon*. Salem, OR: Polebridge Press, 2013.
Behr, John. *Irenaeus: On the Apostolic Preaching*. Crestwood, NY: St. Vladimir's Seminary Press, 1997.
Behr, John. *Asceticism and Anthropology in Irenaeus and Clement*. Oxford: Oxford University Press, 2000.
Behr, John. *Irenaeus of Lyons: Identifying Christianity (Christian Theology in Context)*. Oxford: Oxford University Press, 2013.
Behr, John. "Scripture and Gospel: Intertextuality in Irenaeus." Pages 179–94 in *Intertextuality in the Second Century*. Edited by D. Jeffrey Bingham and Clayton N. Jefford. Leiden: Brill, 2016.
Belleville, Linda L. *Reflections of Glory: Paul's Polemical Use of the Moses-Doxa Tradition in 2 Corinthians 3.1–18*. JSNTSup 52. Sheffield, UK: Sheffield Academic, 1991.
Benoit, André. *Saint Irénée: Introduction à l'étude de sa théologie*. Études d'histoire et de philosophie religieuses 52. Paris: Presses Universitaires de France, 1960.
Bergmeier, Roland. "'Königlösikeit' als nachvalentinianisches Heilsprädikat." *NT* 24 (1982): 316–39.
Best, Ernest. "The Use and Non-use of Pneuma by Josephus." *NovT* 3.3 (1959): 218–25.
Best, Ernest. *A Commentary on the First and Second Epistles to the Thessalonians*. London: Adam & Charles Black, 1977.

Betz, Hans Dieter. *Galatians*. Hermeneia. Philadelphia: Fortress Press, 1979.
Bingham, D. Jeffrey. *Irenaeus' Use of Matthew's Gospel in* Adversus haereses. Louvain: Peeters, 1998.
Bingham, D. Jeffrey. "Knowledge and Love in Irenaeus of Lyons." *Studia Patristica* 36 (2000): 184–99.
Bingham, D. Jeffrey. "Irenaeus Reads Romans 8: Resurrection and Renovation." Pages 114–32 in *Early Patristic Readings of Romans*. Edited by Kathy L. Gaca and L. L. Welborn. New York: T&T Clark, 2005.
Bingham, D. Jeffrey. "Irenaeus and Hebrews." Pages 65–80 in *Irenaeus: Life, Scripture, Legacy*. Edited by Paul Foster and Sara Parvis. Minneapolis: Fortress, 2012.
Bingham, D. Jeffery. "Senses of Scripture in the Second Century: Irenaeus, Scripture, and Noncanonical Christian Texts." *Journal of Religion* 97.1 (2017): 26–55.
Bird, Michael F., and Joseph R. Dodson (eds.). *Paul and the Second Century*. LNTS 412. London: T&T Clark, 2011.
Blackwell, Ben C. *Christosis: Pauline Soteriology in Light of Deification in Irenaeus and Cyril of Alexandria*. WUNT 2.314. Tübingen: Mohr Siebeck, 2011.
Blackwell, Ben C. "Paul and Irenaeus." Pages 190–206 in *Paul and the Second Century: The Legacy of Paul's Life, Letters, and Teaching*. Edited by Michael F. Bird and Joseph R. Dodson. London: T&T Clark, 2011.
Blackwell, Ben C. "Two Early Perspectives on Participation in Paul: Irenaeus and Clement of Alexandria." Pages 331–55 in *"In Christ" in Paul: Explorations in Paul's Theological Vision of Union and Participation*. Edited by Kevin J. Vanhoozer, Constantine R. Campbell, and Michael J. Thate. WUNT II.314. Tübingen: Mohr Siebeck, 2015.
Blackwell, Ben C. "Partakers of Adoption: Irenaeus and His Use of Paul." *Letter & Spirit* 11 (2016): 35–64.
Blackwell, Ben C. "Second Century Perspectives on the Apocalyptic Paul: Reading the *Apocalypse of Paul* and the *Acts of Paul*." Pages 177–97 in *Paul and the Apocalyptic Imagination*. Edited by Ben C. Blackwell, John K. Goodrich, and Jason Maston. Minneapolis: Fortress Press, 2016.
Blowers, Paul M. "The Regula Fidei and the Narrative Character of Early Christian Faith." *Pro Ecclesia* 6.2 (1997): 199–228.
Bockmuehl, Markus. "The Icon of Peter and Paul between History and Reception." Pages 121–36 in *Seeing the Word: Refocusing New Testament Study. Studies in Theological Interpretation*. Grand Rapids, MI: Baker Academic, 2006.
Bockmuehl, Markus. *The Remembered Peter in Ancient Reception and Modern Debate*. WUNT 262. Tübingen: Mohr Siebeck, 2010.
de Boer, Martinus C. *Galatians: A Commentary*. NTL. Louisville: Westminster John Knox, 2011.
de Boer, Martinus C. "Apocalyptic as God's Eschatological Activity in Paul's Theology." Pages 45–63 in *Paul and the Apocalyptic Imagination*. Edited by Ben C. Blackwell, John K. Goodrich, and Jason Maston. Minneapolis: Fortress Press, 2016.
Bouteneff, Peter. *Beginnings: Ancient Christian Readings of the Biblical Creation Narratives*. Grand Rapids, MI: Baker Academic, 2008.
Brakke, David. *The Gnostics: Myth, Ritual, and Diversity in Early Christianity*. Cambridge, MA: Harvard University Press, 2010.
Briggman, Anthony. "Revisiting Irenaeus' Philosophical Acumen." *VC* 65.2 (2011): 115–24.
Briggman, Anthony. *Irenaeus of Lyons and the Theology of the Holy Spirit*. Oxford: Oxford University Press, 2012.

Briggman, Anthony. "Irenaeus' Christology of Mixture." *JTS* 64.2 (2013): 516–55.
Briggman, Anthony. "Irenaeus on Natural Knowledge." *CH* 95.2 (2015): 133–54.
Briggman, Anthony. "Literary and Rhetorical Theory in Irenaeus, Part 1." *VC* 69.5 (2015): 500–27.
Briggman, Anthony. "Literary and Rhetorical Theory in Irenaeus, Part 2." *VC* 70.1 (2016): 31–50.
Briggman, Anthony. "Theological Speculation in Irenaeus: Perils and Possibilities." *VC* 71.2 (2017): 175–98.
Brown, Peter. *The Body and Society: Men, Women and Sexual Renunciation in Early Christianity*. New York: Columbia University Press, 1988.
Brown, Raymond E. *The Gospel According to John*. 2 vols. Garden City, NY: Doubleday, 1966–70.
Brox, Norbert. "Die biblische Hermeneutik des Irenaeus." *Zeitschrift für Antikes Christentum* 2 (1998): 26–48.
Brox, Norbert. *Irenäus von Lyon: Adversus Haereses, gegen die Häresien, Fontes Christiani* 8.5. Freiburg: Herder, 2001.
Brox, Norbert. "Irenaeus and the Bible." Pages 483–506 in *Handbook of Patristic Exegesis: The Bible in Ancient Christianity*. Edited by Charles Kannengiesser. Leiden: Brill, 2006.
Bruce, F. F. *Paul: Apostle of the Heart Set Free*. Grand Rapids, MI: Eerdmans, 1977.
Bruce, F. F. *The Epistle to the Galatians: A Commentary on the Greek Text*. NIGTC. Grand Rapids, MI: Eerdmans, 1982.
Brunner, Emil. *The Mediator*. London: Lutterworth, 1934.
Büchsel, D. Friedrich. *Der Geist Gottes im Neuen Testament*. Gütersloh: Bertelsmann, 1926.
Bultmann, Rudolf. *Theology of the New Testament*. Translated by Kendrick Grobel. London: SCM, 1965.
Burnett, David A. "'So Shall Your Seed Be': Paul's Use of Genesis 15:5 in Romans 4:18 in Light of Early Jewish Deification Traditions." *JSPL* 5 (2015): 211–36.
Burton, Ernest D. W. *A Critical and Exegetical Commentary on the Epistle to the Galatians*. ICC. New York: Charles Scribner's Sons, 1920.
Campbell, Douglas A. "The Story of Jesus in Romans and Galatians." Pages 97–124 in *Narrative Dynamics in Paul: A Critical Assessment*. Edited by Bruce W. Longenecker. Louisville: Westminster John Knox, 2002.
Canlis, Julie. *Calvin's Ladder: A Spiritual Theology of Ascent and Ascension*. Grand Rapids, MI: Eerdmans, 2010.
Caputo, John D. *Radical Hermeneutics: Repetition, Deconstruction, and the Hermeneutic Project*. Bloomington: Indiana University Press, 1987.
Caputo, John D. *The Prayers and Tears of Jacques Derrida: Religion without Religion*. Bloomington: Indiana University Press, 1997.
Caputo, John D. *More Radical Hermeneutics: On Not Knowing Who We Are*. Bloomington: Indiana University Press, 2000.
Caputo, John D. *On Religion*. London: Routledge, 2001.
Caputo, John D. *The Weakness of God: A Theology of the Event*. Bloomington: Indiana University Press, 2006.
Cartwright, Sophie. "The Image of God in Irenaeus, Marcellus, and Eustathius." Pages 173–82 in *Irenaeus: Life, Scripture, Legacy*. Edited by Sara Parvis and Paul Foster. Minneapolis: Fortress, 2012.
Casey, Robert Pierce. *The Excerpta ex Theodoto of Clement of Alexandria*. London: Christophers, 1934.

Chapman, John. "Did the Translator of St Irenaeus Use a Latin N.T.?" *RBen* 36 (1924): 34–51.
Chevallier, Max-Alain. *Ancien Testament, hellénisme et judaïsme, la tradition synoptique, l'oeuvre de Luc.* vol. 1 of *Souffle de Dieu: Le Saint-Esprit dans le Nouveau Testament.* Point théologique 26. Paris: Beauchesne, 1978.
Chiapparini, Giuliano. *Valentino gnostico e platonico: Il Valentinianiesimo della 'Grande Notizia' di Ireneo di Lione: fra esegesi gnostica e filosofia medioplatonica.* Milan: Vita e Pensiero, 2012.
Chiapparini, Giuliano. "Irenaeus and the Gnostic Valentinus: Orthodoxy and Heresy in the Church of Rome around the Middle of the Second Century." *Zeitschrift für antikes Christentum* 18.1 (2013): 95–119.
Collins, Adela Yarbro, and John J. Collins. *King and Messiah as Son of God: Divine, Human, and Angelic Messianic Figures in Biblical and Related Literature.* Grand Rapids, MI: Eerdmans, 2008.
Conzelmann, Hans. *An Outline of the Theology of the New Testament.* New York: Harper & Row, 1969.
Coolidge, John S. "The Pauline Basis of the Concept of Scriptural Form in Irenaeus Scriptural Form." Pages 1–16 in *Protocol of the Colloquy of the Center for Hermeneutical Studies in Hellenistic and Modern Culture.* Edited by Wilhelm Whellner. Berkley, CA: Center for Hermeneutical Studies, 1975.
Cooper, John M. "Posidonius on Emotions." Pages 71–111 in *The Emotions in Hellenistic Philosophy.* Edited by Juha Sihvola and Troels Engberg-Pedersen. TSHP 46. Dordrecht: Kluwer Academic, 1998.
Cooper, Stephen Andrew. *Marius Victorinus' Commentary on Galatians: Introduction, Translation, and Notes.* Oxford Early Christian Studies. Oxford: Oxford University Press, 2005.
Coppens, J. "Le don de l'Esprit d'après les textes de Qumrân et le quatrième évangile." Pages 209–23 in *L'Évangile de Jean: Études et problems.* RechBib 3. Leuven: Desclée de Brouwer, 1958.
Dahl, Nils A. "The Arrogant Archon and the Lewd Sophia." Pages 689–712 in *The Rediscovery of Gnosticism: Proceedings of the International Conference on Gnosticism at Yale, New Haven, Connecticut, March 28–31, 1978.* Vol. 2 of *Sethian Gnosticism.* Edited by Bentley Layton. SHR 41. Leiden: Brill, 1981.
d'Alès, Adhémar. "Le mot οἰκονομία dans la langue théologique de Saint Irénée." *Revue des Études Grecques* 32 (1919): 1–9.
Daley, Brian E. *Hope of the Early Church.* Grand Rapids, MI: Baker Academic, 2003.
Daley, Brian E. "Christ, the Church, and the Shape of Scripture: What We Can Learn from Patristic Exegesis." Pages 267–88 in *From Judaism to Christianity: Tradition and Transition.* Edited by Patricia Walters. Leiden: Brill, 2010.
Daniélou, Jean. *From Shadows to Reality: Studies in the Biblical Typology of the Fathers.* London: Burns & Oates, 1960.
Dassmann, Ernst. *Der Stachel im Fleisch: Paulus in der frühchristlichen Literatur bis Irenäus.* Münster: Aschendorff, 1979.
Derrida, Jacques. "Différance." Pages 1–28 in *Margins of Philosophy.* Translated by Alan Bass. Chicago: University of Chicago, 1986.
Desjardins, Michel R. *Sin in Valentinianism.* Atlanta, GA: Scholars, 1990.
Dillon, John M. *The Middle Platonists: 80 B.C. to A.D. 220.* Ithaca, NY: Cornell University Press, 1977.

Dodson, Joseph R. "Introduction." Pages 1–18 in *Paul and the Second Century*. Edited by Michael F. Bird and Joseph R. Dodson. LNTS 412. London: T&T Clark, 2011.

Donovan, Mary Ann. *One Right Reading? A Guide to Irenaeus*. Collegeville, MN: Liturgical, 1997.

Downs, David J. *The Offering of the Gentiles: Paul's Collection for Jerusalem in Its Chronological, Cultural, and Cultic Contexts*. Tübingen: Mohr Siebeck, 2007.

Duncan, J. Ligon. "The Covenant Idea in Ante-Nicene Theology." PhD dissertation, University of Edinburgh, 1995.

Duncan, J. Ligon. "The Covenant Idea in Irenaeus of Lyons: An Introduction and Survey." Pages 31–55 in *Confessing our Hope: Essays in Honor of Morton Howison Smith on His Eightieth Birthday*. Edited by J. A. Pipa, Jr. and C. N. Willborn. Taylors: Southern Presbyterian, 2004.

Dunderberg, Ismo. "The School of Valentinus." Pages 64–99 in *A Companion to Second-Century "Heretics."* Edited by Antti Marjanen and Petri Luomanen. VCSup 76. Leiden: Brill, 2005.

Dunderberg, Ismo. *Beyond Gnosticism: Myth, Lifestyle, and Society in the School of Valentinus*. New York: Columbia University Press, 2008.

Dunn, James, D. G. *Unity and Diversity in the New Testament: An Inquiry into the Character of Earliest Christianity*. Philadelphia: The Westminster Press, 1977.

Dunn, James D. G. *Romans 1–8*. Word Biblical Commentary 38A. Dallas: Word, 1998.

Dunn, James D. G. *The Theology of Paul the Apostle*. Grand Rapids, MI: Eerdmans, 1998.

Dunning, B. H. *Specters of Paul: Sexual Difference in Early Christian Thought*. Philadelphia: University of Pennsylvania Press, 2011.

Dupont, Jacques. *The Salvation of the Gentiles: Essays on the Acts of the Apostles*. Translated by John R. Keating. New York: Paulist, 1979.

Elliott, J. K. *The Apocryphal New Testament: A Collection of Apocryphal Christian Literature in an English Translation Based on M.R. James*. Oxford: Clarendon, 1999.

Engberg-Pedersen, Troels. "The Material Spirit: Cosmology and Ethics in Paul." *NTS* 55.2 (2009): 179–97.

Engberg-Pedersen, Troels. *Cosmology and Self in the Apostle Paul: The Material Spirit*. Oxford: Oxford University Press, 2010.

Enslin, Morton Scott. "Irenaeus: Mostly Prolegomena." *HTR* 40.3 (1947): 137–65.

Eriksson, Anders. *Traditions as Rhetorical Proof: Pauline Argumentation in 1 Corinthians*. ConBNT. Stockholm: Almqvist & Wiksell International, 1998.

Esnaola, Manuel Aróztegui. *La Amistad del Verbo con Abraham según San Ireneo de Lyon*. Rome: Editrice Pontificia Università Gregoriana, 2005.

Evans, Ernest. *Tertullian: Adversus Marcionem*. Oxford: Oxford University Press, 1972.

Fantino, Jacques. *L'homme image de Dieu, chez saint Irénée de Lyon*. Paris: Les Editions du Cerf, 1985.

Fantino, Jacques. *La théologie d'Irénée: Lecture des Ecritures en réponse à l'exégèse gnostique: une approche trinitaire*. Cogitatio fidei 180. Paris: Editions du Cerf, 1994.

Fee, Gordon D. *God's Empowering Presence: The Holy Spirit in the Letters of Paul*. Peabody, MA: Hendrickson, 1994.

Ferguson, Everett. "The Covenant Idea in the Second Century." Pages 135–62 in *Texts and Testaments: Critical Essays on the Bible and Early Church Fathers*. Edited by W. Eugene March. San Antonio: Trinity University Press, 1980.

Ferguson, Thomas C. K. "The Rule of Truth and Irenaean Rhetoric in Book 1 of Against Heresies." *VC* 55 (2001): 356–75.

Filioramo, Giovanni. *A History of Gnosticism*. Cambridge, MA: Blackwell, 1992.

Fitzmyer, J. A. *The Acts of the Apostles: A New Translation with Introduction and Commentary.* AB 31. New York: Doubleday, 1998.
Flowers, Harold J. "*En pneumati hagiō kai puri.*" *ExpT* 64.5 (1953): 155–56.
Flusser, David. "Jewish Messianism Reflected in the Early Church." Pages 258–88 in *Judaism of the Second Temple Period*, 2 vols. Translated by Azzan Yadin. Grand Rapids, MI: Eerdmans, 2007–2009.
Förster, Niclas. *Marcus Magus: Kult, Lehre und Gemeindeleben einer valentinianischen Gnostikergruppe.* Sammlung der Quellen und Kommentar. WUNT 114. Tübingen: Mohr Siebeck, 1999.
Fredriksen, Paula. *Paul: The Pagans' Apostle.* New Haven, CT: Yale University Press, 2017.
Gamble, Harry Y. "The New Testament Canon: Recent Research and the *Status Quaestionis.*" Pages 267–94 in *The Canon Debate*. Edited by L. M. McDonald and J. A. Sanders. Peabody, MA: Hendrickson, 2002.
Gill, Christopher. "Galen and the Stoics: Mortal Enemies or Blood Brothers?" *Phronesis* 52.1 (2007): 88–120.
Gilliard, Frank D. "The Apostolicity of Gallic Churches." *HTR* 68 (1975): 17–33.
Ginsburg, Christian D. *The Essenes: Their History and Doctrines; The Kabbalah: Its Doctrines, Development, and Literature.* London: Routledge & Kegan Paul, 1955.
Graham, Susan L. "'Zealous for the Covenant': Irenaeus and the Covenants of Israel." PhD dissertation, University of Notre Dame, 2001.
Graham, Susan L. "Irenaeus and the Covenants: 'Immortal Diamond.'" *Studia Patristica* 40 (2006): 393–98.
Grant, Robert M. "Irenaeus and Hellenistic Culture." *HTR* 42.1 (1949): 41–51.
Grant, Robert M. *Gnosticism and Early Christianity*, 2nd ed. New York: Columbia University Press, 1966.
Grant, Robert M. *Jesus after the Gospels: The Christ of the Second Century.* Louisville: Westminster John Knox, 1990.
Grassi, Joseph A. "Ezekiel xxxvii.1–14 and the New Testament." *NTS* 11.2 (1965): 162–64.
Grillmeier, Aloys. *Christ in Christian Tradition: From the Apostolic Age to Chalcedon.* Translated by John Bowden. Atlanta: John Knox, 1964.
Gundry, Judith M. "Jesus-Tradition and Paul's Opinion about the Widow Remaining as a Widow (1 Cor 7.40)." Pages 175–200 in *Portraits of Jesus: Studies in Christology*. Edited by Susan E. Myers. WUNT 2.321. Tübingen: Mohr Siebeck, 2012.
Gundry, Judith M. "1 Cor 7,5b in the Light of a Hellenistic-Jewish Tradition on Abstinence to 'Devote Leisure': Sufficiency in Paul and Philo." Pages 21–44 in *Paulus—Werk und Wirkung*. Edited by Paul-Gerhard Klumbies and David du Toit. FS Lindemann. Tübingen: Mohr Siebeck, 2013.
Gundry, Judith M. "Anxiety or Care for People? The Theme of 1 Corinthians 7.32–34 and the Relation between Exegesis and Theology." Pages 111–30 in *Reconsidering the Relationship between Biblical and Systematic Theology in the New Testament*. Edited by Benjamin E. Reynolds, Brian Lugioyo, and Kevin J. Vanhoozer. WUNT 2/369. Tübingen: Mohr Siebeck, 2014.
Gundry, Judith M. "Affliction for Procreators in the Eschatological Crisis: Paul's Marital Counsel in 1 Corinthians 7.28 and Contraception in Greco-Roman Antiquity." *JSNT* 39 (2016): 141–61.
Gundry, Judith M. "Children, Parents and God/gods in Interreligious Roman Households and the Interpretation of 1 Corinthians 7:14." Pages 311–33 in *T&T Clark Handbook of Children and Childhood in the Biblical World*. Edited by Sharon Betsworth and Julie Faith Parker. London: Bloomsbury/T&T Clark, 2018.

Gundry-Volf, Judith M. "Gender and Creation in 1 Corinthians 11:2–16: A Study in Paul's Theological Method." Pages 151–71 in *Evangelium–Schriftauslegung–Kirche. Festschrift für Peter Stuhlmacher zum 65. Geburtstag*. Edited by O. Hofius et al. Göttingen: Vandenhoeck & Ruprecht, 1997.

Harnack, Adolf von. "Der Presbyter-Prediger des Irenäus (IV,27,1-32,1): Bruchstücke und Nachklänge der ältesten exegetisch-polemischen Homilieen." In *Philotesia: Paul Kleinert zum LXX Geburtstag*. Berlin: Trowitzsch & Sohn, 1907.

Harnack, Adolf von. *Marcion: Das Evangelium vom fremden Gott.* TUGAL 45. Leipzig: Hinrichs, 1924.

Harnack, Adolf von. *Marcion: The Gospel of the Alien God*. Translated by John E. Steely and Lyle D. Bierma. Durham, NC: Labyrinth Press, 1990.

Harvey, W. W. *Sancti Irenaei Episcopi Lugdunensis: Libros quinque adversus haereses*. Cambridge: Cambridge University Press, 1857.

Hays, Richard B. *Echoes of Scripture in the Letters of Paul*. New Haven: Yale University Press, 1989.

Hays, Richard B. "Christ Prays the Psalms: Paul's Use of an Early Christian Convention." Pages 122–36 in *The Future of Christology: Essays in Honor of Leander E. Keck*. Edited by Abraham Malherbe and Wayne A. Meeks. Minneapolis: Fortress, 1993.

Hefner, Philip J. "Theological Methodology and St Irenaeus." *JR* 44.4 (1964): 294–309.

Heid, S., R. von Haehling, V. M. Strocka, and M. Vielberg (eds.). *Petrus und Paulus in Rom: eine interdisziplinäre Debatte*. Freiburg: Herder, 2011.

Henry, W. Benjamin. "Introduction." Pages xiii–xxxiv in *Philodemus: On Death*. SBLWGRW 29. Atlanta: Society of Biblical Literature, 2009.

Hill, Charles E. *Regnum Caelorum: Patterns of Future Hope in Early Christianity*. OECS. Oxford: Clarendon, 1992.

Hill, Charles E. "The Epistula Apostolorum: An Asian Tract from the Time of Polycarp." *JECS* 7 (1999): 1–53.

Hill, Charles E. *From the Lost Teaching of Polycarp: Identifying Irenaeus' Apostolic Presbyter and the Author of Ad Diognetum*. WUNT. Tübingen: Mohr Siebeck, 2006.

Hitchcock, F. R. Montgomery. *Irenaeus of Lugdunum: A Study of His Teaching*. Cambridge: Cambridge University Press, 1914.

Hoffman, Daniel L. *The Status of Women and Gnosticism in Irenaeus and Tertullian*. Lewiston: The Edwin Mellen Press, 1995.

Hoffman, Daniel L. "Irenaeus, Pagels, and the Christianity of the Gnostics." Pages 65–82 in *Light of Discovery: Studies in Honor of Edwin M. Yamauchi*. Edited by John Wineland. Eugene, OR: Pickwick, 2007.

Hoh, Paul. J. *Die Lehre des Hl. Irenäus über das Neue Testament*. NTAbh 7. Münster: Aschendorff, 1919.

Holmes, Michael W. "Paul and Polycarp." Pages 57–69 in *Paul and the Second Century*. Edited by Michael F. Bird and Joseph R. Dodson. London: Bloomsbury/T&T Clark, 2011.

Holsinger-Friesen, Thomas. *Irenaeus and Genesis: A Study of Competition in Early Christian Hermeneutics*. Winona Lake, IN: Eisenbrauns, 2009.

Horbury, William. *Jewish Messianism and the Cult of Christ*. London: SCM Press, 1998.

Horrell, David G., Cherryl Hunt, and Christopher Southgate. *Greening Paul: Rereading the Apostle in a Time of Ecological Crisis*. Waco, TX: Baylor University Press, 2010.

Housiau, A. "Le baptême selon Irénée de Lyon." *Ephemerides theologicae lovanienses* 60.1 (1984): 45–59.

Hull, J. H. E. *The Holy Spirit in the Acts of the Apostles*. London: Lutterworth, 1967.

Hur, Ju. *A Dynamic Reading of the Holy Spirit in Luke-Acts.* JSNTSup 211. Sheffield: Sheffield Academic, 2001.

Hurtado, Larry W. *Lord Jesus Christ: Devotion to Jesus in Earliest Christianity.* Grand Rapids, MI: Eerdmans, 2003.

Isaacs, Marie E. *The Concept of Spirit: A Study of Pneuma in Hellenistic Judaism and Its Bearing on the New Testament.* Heythrop Monographs 1. London: Heythrop College Press, 1976.

Jacobsen, Anders-Christian. "The Philosophical Argument in the Teaching of Irenaeus on the Resurrection of the Flesh." *Studia Patristica* 36 (2001): 256–61.

Jaschke, Hans-Jochen. *Der Heilige Geist im Bekenntnis der Kirche: eine Studie zu Pneumatologie des Irenäus von Lyon im Ausgang vom altchristliche Glaubensbekenntnis.* Münster: Aschedorff, 1976.

Jipp, Joshua W. "Ancient, Modern, and Future Interpretations of Romans 1.3-4: Reception History and Biblical Interpretation." *JTI* 3 (2009): 241–59.

Jipp, Joshua W. *Christ Is King: Paul's Royal Ideology.* Minneapolis: Fortress Press, 2015.

Kaler, Michael, Louis Painchaud, and Marie-Pierre Bussières. "The Coptic Apocalypse of Paul, Irenaeus' Adversus haereses 2.30.7, and the Second-Century Battle for Paul's Legacy." *JECS* 12 (2004): 182–90.

Kalvesmaki, Joel. "Formation of the Early Christian Theology of Arithmetic: Number Symbolism in the Late Second and Early Third Century." PhD dissertation, The Catholic University of America, 2006.

Käsemann, Ernst. "On the Subject of Primitive Christian Apocalpytic." Pages 108–37 in *New Testament Questions of Today.* Translation by W. J. Montague. London: SCM Press, 1969.

Keener, Craig S. *The Spirit in the Gospels and Acts: Divine Purity and Power.* Peabody, MA: Hendrickson, 1997.

Keener, Craig S. *The Gospel of John: A Commentary,* 2 vols. Grand Rapids, MI: Baker Academic, 2003.

Keener, Craig S. "Spirit, Holy Spirit, Advocate, Breath, Wind." Pages 484–96 in *The Westminster Theological Wordbook of the Bible.* Edited by Donald E. Gowan. Louisville: Westminster John Knox, 2003.

Keener, Craig S. *1 and 2 Corinthians.* New Cambridge Bible Commentary. Cambridge: Cambridge University Press, 2005.

Keener, Craig S. *Acts: An Exegetical Commentary,* 4 vols. Grand Rapids, MI: Baker Academic, 2012–15.

Keener, Craig S. *The Mind of the Spirit: Paul's Approach to Transformed Thinking.* Grand Rapids, MI: Baker Academic, 2016.

Keener, Craig S. *Galatians.* Cambridge New Testament Commentary. Cambridge: Cambridge University Press, 2018.

Kelly, J. N. D. *Early Christian Doctrines.* New York: Harper San Francisco, 1978.

Kennedy, George. *The Art of Persuasion in Greece.* Princeton, NJ: Princeton University Press, 1963.

King, Karen. *What Is Gnosticism?* Cambridge, MA: Belknap Press of Harvard University, 2003.

Klauck, Hans-Josef. *The Religious Context of Early Christianity: A Guide to Graeco-Roman Religions.* Translated by Brian McNeil. Minneapolis: Fortress, 2003.

Koch, Hugo. "Zur Lehre vom Urstand und von der Erlösung bei Irenaeus." *Theologische Studien und Kritiken* 96–97 (1925): 183–214.

Konstan, David. "Of Two Minds: Philo on Cultivation." *Studia Philonica Annual* 22 (2010): 131–38.
van Kooten, George H. *Paul's Anthropology in Context: The Image of God, Assimilation to God, and Tripartite Man in Ancient Judaism, Ancient Philosophy, and Early Christianity*. WUNT 232. Tübingen: Mohr Siebeck, 2008.
Koschorke, Klaus. "Paulus in den Nag-Hammadi-Texten: Ein Beitrag zur Geschichte der Paulusrezeption in frühen Christentum." *ZTK* 78 (1981): 177–205.
Lake, Kirsopp. "The Holy Spirit." Pages 96–111 in volume 5 of *The Beginnings of Christianity: The Acts of the Apostles*. Edited by F. J. Foakes-Jackson and Kirsopp Lake. London: Macmillan, 1926.
Lanne, Emmanuel. "La 'xeniteia' d'Abraham dans l'œuvre d'Irénée: Aux origines du thème monastique de la 'peregrinatio.'" *Irénikon* 47 (1974): 163–87.
Lashier, Jackson. *Irenaeus on the Trinity*. VCSup 127. Leiden-Boston: Brill, 2014.
Lawson, John. *The Biblical Theology of Saint Irenaeus*. London: Epworth Press, 1948.
Layton, Bentley. *The Gnostic Scriptures: A New Translation with Annotations and Introductions*. Garden City, NY: Doubleday, 1987.
Layton, Bentley (ed.). *Nag Hammadi Codex II,2–7*, 2 vols. NHS 20–21. Leiden: Brill, 1989.
Layton, Bentley. "Prolegomena to the Study of Ancient Gnosticism." Pages 334–50 in *The Social World of the First Christians: Essays in Honor of Wayne A. Meeks*. Edited by L. M. White and O. L. Yarborough. Minneapolis: Fortress Press, 1995.
Leahy, Brendan. "'Hiding Behind the Works': The Holy Spirit in the Trinitarian Rhythm of Human Fulfillment in the Theology of Irenaeus." Pages 11–31 in *The Holy Spirit in the Fathers of the Church: The Proceedings of the Seventh International Patristic Conference, Maynooth, 2008*. Edited by D. Vincent Twomey and Janet E. Rutherford. Dublin: Four Courts, 2010.
Leese, J. J. Johnson. *Christ, Creation and the Cosmic Goal of Redemption: A Study of Pauline Creation Theology as Read by Irenaeus and Applied to Ecotheology*. LNTS 580. London: Bloomsbury T&T Clark, 2018.
Leisegang, Hans. *Pneuma hagion: Der Ursprung des Geistbegriffs der synoptischen Evangelienaus der griechischen Mystik*. Leipzig: J. C. Hinrichs, 1922.
Leonhardt J. *Jewish Worship in Philo of Alexandria*. TSAJ 84. Tübingen: Mohr Siebeck, 2001.
Levenson, Jon D. *The Death and Resurrection of the Beloved Son: The Transformation of Child Sacrifice in Judaism and Christianity*. New Haven: Yale, 1993.
Levenson, Jon D. *Inheriting Abraham: The Legacy of the Patriarch in Judaism, Christianity, and Islam*. Princeton: Princeton University Press, 2012.
Levison, John R. "Paul in the Stoa Poecile: A Response to Troels Engberg-Pedersen, Cosmology and Self in the Apostle Paul: The Material Spirit." *JSNT* 33.4 (2011): 415–32.
Lewis, Nicola Denzey. *Introduction to "Gnosticism": Ancient Voices, Christian Worlds*. Oxford: Oxford University Press, 2013.
Liebing, Heinz. "Historical-Critical Theology: In Commemoration of the One Hundredth Anniversary of the Death of Ferdinand Christian Baur, December 2, 1960." Pages 62–64 in *Distinctive Protestant and Catholic Themes Reconsidered*. Edited by Ernst Käsemann et al. JTC Church 3. Tübingen: Mohr Siebeck, 1967.
Lillge, Otto. "Das patristische Wort οἰκονομία, seine Geschichte und seine Bedeutung bis auf Origines." PhD dissertation, Friedrich-Alexander Universität Erlangen, 1955.

Lindemann, Andreas. *Paulus in ältesten Christentum: Das Bild des Apostels und die Rezeption der paulinischen Theologie in der frühchristlichen Literatur bis Marcion.* BHT 58. Tübingen: Mohr Siebeck, 1979.

Long, A. A. *Hellenistic Philosophy: Stoics, Epicureans, Sceptics.* New York: Scribner's, 1974.

Long, A. A. "Soul and Body in Stoicism." *Center for Hermeneutical Studies Protocol* 36 (1980): 1–17.

Longenecker, Bruce W. "The 'Poor' of Galatians 2:10: The Interpretative Paradigm of the First Centuries." Pages 205–21 in *Engaging Economics: New Testament Scenarios and Early Christian Reception.* Edited by Bruce W. Longenecker and Kelly D. Liebengood. Grand Rapids, MI: Eerdmans, 2009.

Longenecker, Bruce W. *Remember the Poor: Paul, Poverty, and the Greco-Roman World.* Grand Rapids, MI: Eerdmans, 2010.

Longenecker, Richard N. *Galatians.* WBC 41. Dallas: Word Books, 1990.

Lüdemann, Gerd. *Paul, Apostle to the Gentiles: Studies in Chronology.* Philadelphia: Fortress,1984.

Ma, Wonsuk. *Until the Spirit Comes: The Spirit of God in the Book of Isaiah.* JSOTSup 271. Sheffield:. Sheffield Academic, 1999.

MacDonald, John. *The Theology of the Samaritans.* Philadelphia: Westminster, 1964.

MacDonald, Nathan. "Israel and the Old Testament Story in Irenaeus's Presentation of the Rule of Faith." *JTI* 3 (2009): 281–98.

MacDonald, Paul S. *History of the Concept of Mind: Speculations about Soul, Mind and Spirit from Homer to Hume.* Aldershot: Ashgate, 2003.

MacKenzie, I. M. *Irenaeus's Demonstration of the Apostolic Preaching: A Theological Commentary and Translation.* Burlington, VT: Ashgate, 2002.

Marjanen, Antti (ed.). *Was There a Gnostic Religion?* Göttingen: Vandenhoeck & Ruprecht, 2005.

Marjanen, Antti. "Montanism: Egalitarian Ecstatic 'New Prophecy.'" Pages 185–212 in *A Companion to Second-Century Christian "Heretics."* Edited by Antti Majanen and Petri Luomanen. Leiden: Brill, 2008.

Markschies, Christoph. *Gnosis: An Introduction.* Translation by John Bowden. London: T&T Clark, 2003.

Marmorstein, Arthur. *Essays in Anthropomorphism.* London: Oxford University Press, 1937.

Marshall, Bruce D. "The Deep Things of God: Trinitarian Pneumatology." In *The Oxford Handbook of the Trinity.* Edited by Gilles Emery and Matthew Levering. Oxford: Oxford University Press, 2011.

Martin, Dale B. *The Corinthian Body.* New Haven: Yale University Press, 1999.

Martyn, J. L. *Galatians.* AB 33A. New York: Doubleday, 1997.

Matera, Frank J. *Galatians.* SP 9. Collegeville, MN: Liturgical, 1992.

Matera, Frank J. *II Corinthians: A Commentary.* NTL. Louisville: Westminster John Knox, 2003.

May, Gerhard. "Marcion in Contemporary Views: Results and Open Questions." *Second Century* 6 (1987–88): 129–51.

McCue, James F. "Conflicting Versions of Valentinianism: Irenaeus and the *Excerpta ex Theodoto*." Pages 404–16 in *Rediscovery of Gnosticism*, vol. 1. Edited by Bentley Layton. Leiden: Brill, 1980.

McDonnell, K. "*Questio disputata*: Irenaeus on the Baptism of Jesus." *TS* 59 (1998): 317–19.

McGowan, Andrew. "Marcion's Love of Creation." *JECS* 9 (2001): 295–311.

McHugh, J. "A Reconsideration of Ephesians 1,10b in Light of Irenaeus." Pages 302–9 in *Paul and Paulinism: Essays in Honour of C.K. Barrett*. Edited by M. D. Hooker and S. G. Wilson. London: S.P.C.K., 1982.

Meijering, Roos. *Literary and Rhetorical Theories in Greek Scholia*. Groningen: E. Forsten, 1987.

Menzies, Robert P. *The Development of Early Christian Pneumatology with Special Reference to Luke-Acts*. JSNTSup 54. Sheffield: Sheffield Academic, 1991.

Menzies, Robert P. *Empowered for Witness: The Spirit in Luke-Acts*. London: T&T Clark, 2004.

Merk, August. "Der Text des Neuen Testaments beim hl. Irenaeus." *ZKT* 49 (1925): 302–15.

Merlan, Philip. *From Platonism to Neoplatonism*. The Hague: Martinus Nijhoff, 1953.

Metzger, Bruce. *The Canon of the New Testament: Its Origin, Development, and Significance*. Oxford: Clarendon, 1987.

Meyer, Marvin W. *The Gnostic Discoveries: The Impact of the Nag Hammadi Library*. San Francisco: HarperSanFrancisco, 2005.

Meyer, Marvin, and James M. Robinson (eds.). *The Nag Hammadi Scriptures: The Revised and Updated Translation of Sacred Gnostic Texts*. New York: HarperOne, 2008.

Minns, Denis. *Irenaeus: An Introduction*. London: T&T Clark, 2010.

Minns, Denis. "The Parable of the Two Sons (Matt. 21:28–32) in Irenaeus and Codex Bezae." Pages 55–63 in *Irenaeus: Life, Scripture, Legacy*. Edited by Sara Parvis and Paul Foster. Minneapolis: Fortress, 2012.

Miola, Maria del Fiat. "Mary as Un-tier and Tier of Knots: Irenaeus Reinterpreted." *JECS* 24.3 (2016): 337–61.

Moll, Sebastian. *The Arch-heretic Marcion*. WUNT 250. Tübingen: Mohr Siebeck, 2010.

Moo, Douglas J. *Galatians*. BECNT. Grand Rapids, MI: Baker Academic, 2013.

Morenz, Ludwig D. "Ka." Pages 1–2 in volume 7 of *Brill's New Pauly*. Edited by Hubert Cancik et al. Leiden: Brill, 2006.

Moringiello, Scott D. "Irenaeus Rhetor." PhD dissertation, University of Notre Dame, 2008.

Moringiello, Scott D. "The *Pneumatikos* as Scriptural Interpreter: Irenaeus on 1 Cor 2:15." *Studia Patristica* 65 (2013): 105–18.

Mutschler, Bernhard. *Irenäeus als johanneischer Theologe: Studien zur Schriftauslegung bei Irenäeus von Lyon*. Studien und Texte zu Antike und Christentum 21. Tübingen: Mohr Siebeck, 2004.

Nautin, Pierre. "Irénée et la canonicité des Epîtres pauliniennes." *RHR* 182 (1972): 113–30.

Nielsen, Jan Tjeerd. *Adam and Christ in the Theology of Irenaeus of Lyons: An Examinations of the Function of the Adam-Christ Typology in the Adversus haereses of Irenaeus, against the Background of the Gnosticism of His Time*. Assen: Van Gorcum, 1968.

Nock, Arthur Darby. *Early Gentile Christianity and Its Hellenistic Background*. New York: Harper & Row, 1964.

Nolan, Daniel. "Stoic Gunk." *Phronesis* 51.2 (2006): 162–83.

Noormann, Rolf. *Irenäus als Paulusinterpret: Zur Rezeption und Wirkung der paulinischen und deuteropaulinischen Briefe im Werk des Irenäus von Lyon*. WUNT 2.66. Tübingen: Mohr Siebeck, 1994.

Norelli, Enrico. "Il duplice rinnovamento del mondo nell'escatologia di San Ireneo." *Augustinianum* 18 (1978): 89–106.

Norris, Richard A. "Who Is the Demiurge? Irenaeus' Picture of God in *Adversus haereses* 2." Pages 9–36 in *God in Early Christian Thought: Essays in Memory of Lloyd G. Patterson*. Edited by Andrew B. McGowan et al. VCSup 94. Leiden: Brill, 2009.
Norris Jr., Richard A. *The Christological Controversy*. Philadelphia: Fortress, 1980.
Norris, Jr., Richard A. "Irenaeus' Use of Paul in his Polemic Against the Gnostics." Pages 78–98 in *Paul and the Legacies of Paul*. Edited by William S. Babcock. Dallas: Southern Methodist University Press, 1990.
Novenson, Matthew V. *Christ among the Messiahs: Christ Language in Paul and Messiah Language in Ancient Judaism*. Oxford: Oxford University Press, 2012.
Novenson, Matthew V. *The Grammar of Messianism: An Ancient Jewish Political Idiom and Its Users*. Oxford: Oxford University Press, 2017.
O'Hagan, Angelo P. "The First Christian Pentecost (Acts 2.1–13)." *SBFLA* 23 (1973): 50–66.
O'Keefe, John J., and R. R. Reno. *Sanctified Vision: An Introduction to Early Christian Interpretation of the Bible*. Baltimore: Johns Hopkins University Press, 2005.
Olson, Mark William. *Irenaeus, the Valentinian Gnostics, and the Kingdom of God (A. H. Book V): The Debate About 1 Corinthians 15: 50*. Lewiston, NY: Mellen Biblical Press, 1992.
Orbe, Antonio. "San Ireneo y la creacion de la materia." *Gregorianum* 59 (1978): 103–8.
O'Regan, Cyril. *Gnostic Return in Modernity*. Albany: State University of New York Press, 2001.
Orlando, Robert. *Apostle Paul: A Polite Bribe*. Eugene: Cascade, 2014.
Osborn, Eric F. "Reason and the Rule of Faith in the Second Century AD." Pages 40–61 in *Making of Orthodoxy: Essays in Honour of Henry Chadwick*. Edited by Rowan Williams. Cambridge: Cambridge University Press, 1989.
Osborn, Eric F. *Irenaeus of Lyons*. Cambridge: Cambridge University Press, 2005.
Pagels, Elaine. "Conflicting Versions of Valentinian Eschatology: Irenaeus' Treatise vs. The Excerpts of Theodotus." *HTR* 67 (1974): 35–53.
Pagels, Elaine. *The Gnostic Paul: Gnostic Exegesis of the Pauline Letters*. Philadelphia: Trinity Press International, 1975.
Pagels, Elaine. *The Gnostic Gospels*. New York: Random House, 1979.
Pagels, Elaine. "Exegesis and Exposition of the Genesis Creation Accounts in Selected Texts from Nag Hammadi." Pages 257–85 in *Nag Hammadi, Gnosticism, and Early Christianity*. Edited by Charles W. Hedrick and Robert Hodgson, Jr. Peabody, MA: Hendrickson, 1986.
Parke, H. W. *A History of the Delphic Oracle*. Oxford: Blackwell, 1939.
Parvis, Sara. "Irenaeus, Women, and Tradition." Pages 159–64 in *Irenaeus: Life, Scripture, Legacy*. Edited by Sara Parvis and Paul Foster. Minneapolis, MN: Fortress Press, 2012.
Pearson, Birger A. *Ancient Gnosticism: Traditions and Literature*. Minneapolis: Fortress Press, 2007.
Pelikan, Jaroslav. *Mary through the Centuries: Her Place in the History of Culture*. New Haven, CT: Yale University Press, 1996.
Perkins, Pheme. "Irenaeus and the Gnostics: Rhetoric and Composition in *Adversus haereses* Book One." *VC* 30 (1976): 193–200.
Perrin, Nicholas. "Paul and Valentinian Interpretation." Pages 126–39 in *Paul and the Second Century*. Edited by Michael F. Bird and Joseph R. Dodson. LNTS 412. London: T&T Clark, 2011.
Philonenko, Marc. "De Qoumrân à Doura-Europos: La vision des ossements desséchés (Ézéchiel 37,1–4)." *RHPR* 74.1 (1994): 1–12.

Presley, Stephen O. *The Intertextual Reception of Genesis 1–3 in Irenaeus of Lyons.* Leiden: Brill, 2015.
Presley, Stephen O. "The Demonstration of Intertextuality in Irenaeus of Lyons." Pages 195–214 in *Intertextuality in the Second Century.* Edited by D. Jeffrey Bingham and Clayton N. Jefford. Leiden: Brill, 2016.
Puech, Émile. "L'Esprit saint à Qumrân." *SBFLA* 49 (1999): 283–97.
Räisänen, Heikki. "Marcion." Pages 100–24 in *A Companion to Second-Century "Heretics."* Edited by Antti Marjanen and Petri Luomanen. VCSup 76. Leiden: Brill, 2005.
Ramelli, Ilaria. *Hierocles the Stoic: Elements of Ethics, Fragments, and Excerpts.* Translated by David Konstan. SBLWGRW 28. Atlanta: SBL, 2009.
Rasimus, Tuomas. *Paradise Reconsidered in Gnostic Mythmaking: Rethinking Sethianism in Light of the Ophite Evidence.* NHMS 68. Leiden: Brill, 2009.
Rensberger, David K. "As the Apostle Teaches: The Development of the Use of Paul's Letters in Second Century Christianity." PhD dissertation, Yale University, 1981.
Reumann, John. "Oikonomia = 'Covenant'; Terms for Heilsgeschichte in Early Christian Usage." *NovT* 3 (1959): 282–92.
Reumann, John Henry Paul. "The Use of Oikonomia and Related Terms in Greek Sources to about A.D. 100, as a Background for Patristic Applications." PhD dissertation, University of Pennsylvania, 1957.
Reynders, D. B. "Paradosis: Le progrès et l'idée de tradition jusqu'à saint Irénée." *Recherches de Théologie ancienne et médiévale* 5 (1933): 155–91.
Richter, Gerhard. *Oikonomia: Der Gebrauch des Wortes Oikonomia im Neuen Testament, bei den Kirchenvätern und in der theologischen Literatur bis ins 20. Jahrhundert.* AKG 90. Berlin: De Gruyter, 2005.
Roldanus J. "L'héritage d'Abraham d'après Irénée." Pages 212–24 in *Text and Testimony: Essays on New Testament and Apocryphal Literature in Honour of A.F.J. Klijn.* Edited by T. Baarda et al. Kampen: J.H. Kok, 1988.
Rollmann, Hans. "From Baur to Wrede: The Quest for a Historical Method." *SR* 17 (1988): 447–50.
Roukema, Riemer. *Gnosis and Faith in Early Christianity.* London: SCM, 1999.
Rousseau, Adelin, et al. (eds.). *Irénée de Lyon: Contre les hérésies.* SC 100.1, 100.2, 152, 153, 210, 211, 263, 264, 293, 294; Paris: Éditions du Cerf, 1952–82.
Sáez, Andrés. "La Tradition d'Irénée et l'Évangile de Paul: La naissance de la conscience canonique néotestamentaire et quelques conséquences sur la nature de la Révélation chrétienne." *Revue des sciences religieuses* 90.3 (2016): 357–83.
Sagnard, François M.-M. *La gnose valentinienne et le témoignage de Saint Irénée.* Études de philosophie médiévale 36. Paris: Libraire philosophique J. Vrin, 1947.
Sanday, William, Alexander Souter, and Cuthbert H. Turner. *Novum Testamentum Sancti Irenaei episcopi Lugdunensis: being the New Testament quotations in the Old-Latin version of the Elenchos kai paratrope pseudonymou gnoseos.* Oxford: Clarendon Press, 1923.
Schäfer, Karl. "Die Zitate in der lateinischen Irenäusübersetzung und ihr Wert für die Textgeschichte des Neuen Testamentes." Pages 50–59 in *Vom Wort des Lebens: Festschrift für Max Meinertz des 70. Lebensjahres 19. Dezember 1950.* Edited by N. Adler. NTAbh 1. Münster: Aschendorff, 1951.
Schneemelcher, Wilhelm. "Paulus in der griechischen Kirche des zweite Jahrhunderts." *ZKG* 75 (1964): 1–20.
Schoedel, William R. "Philosophy and Rhetoric in the *Adversus haereses* of Irenaeus." *VC* 13.1 (1959): 22–32.

Schoedel, William R. "'Topological' Theology and Some Monistic Tendencies in Gnosticism." Pages 88–108 in *Essays on the Nag Hammadi Texts in Honour of Alexander Böhlig*. Edited by Martin Krause. Leiden: Brill, 1972.

Schoedel, William R. "Theological method in Irenaeus (*Adversus haereses* 2:25–28)." *JTS* 35.1 (1984): 31–49.

Schweizer, Eduard. *The Holy Spirit*. Translated by Reginald H. Fuller and Ilse Fuller. Philadelphia: Fortress, 1980.

Scott, Ernest F. *The Spirit in the New Testament*. London: Hodder & Stoughton, 1923.

Secord, Jared. "The Cultural Geography of a Greek Christian: Irenaeus from Smyrna to Lyons." Pages 25–33 in *Irenaeus: Life, Scripture, Legacy*. Edited by Sara Parvis and Paul Foster. Minneapolis: Fortress, 2012.

Simonetti, Manlio. *Biblical Interpretation in the Early Church: A Historical Introduction to Patristic Exegesis*. Edinburgh: T&T Clark, 1994.

Slusser, Michael. "The Heart of Irenaeus's Theology." Pages 133–39 in *Irenaeus: Life, Scripture, Legacy*. Edited by Sara Parvis and Paul Foster. Minneapolis: Fortress, 2012.

Smith, Christopher R. "Chiliasm and Recapitulation in the Theology of Irenaeus." *VC* 48 (1994): 323–24.

Smith, D. A. "Irenaeus and the Baptism of Jesus." *TS* 58 (1997): 618–42.

Smith, Geoffrey S. *Guilt by Association: Heresy Catalogues in Early Christianity*. Oxford: Oxford University Press, 2014.

Sorabji, Richard. *Emotion and Peace of Mind: From Stoic Agitation to Christian Temptation*. New York: Oxford University Press, 2000.

Soulen, R. Kendall. *The God of Israel and Christian Theology*. Minneapolis: Fortress, 1996.

Souter, Alexander. "The New Testament Text of Irenaeus." Pages cxii–clxx in *Novum Testamentum sancti Irenaei episcopi Lugdunensis*. Edited by W. Sanday and C. H. Turner. Old-Latin Biblical Texts 7. Oxford: Clarendon, 1923.

Stählin, Otto., Ludwig Früchtel, and Ursula Treu. (eds.). *Clemens Alexanadrinus*, 2nd ed. GCS 17. Berlin: Akademie-Verlag, 1970.

Steenberg, Matthew C. "The Role of Mary as Co-Recapitulator in St Irenaeus of Lyons." *VC* 58 (2004): 117–37.

Steenberg, Matthew C. *Irenaeus on Creation: The Cosmic Christ and the Saga of Redemption*. VCSup. Leiden: Brill, 2008.

Steenberg, Matthew C. *Of God and Man: Theology as Anthropology from Irenaeus to Athanasius*. London: T&T Clark, 2009.

Steenberg, Matthew C., and Dominic J. Unger. *St. Irenaeus of Lyons: Against the Heresies (Book 3)*. Ancient Christian Writers 64. New York: Paulist Press, 2012.

Sterling, Gregory E. "From Apostle to the Gentiles to Apostle of the Church: Images of Paul at the End of the First Century." *ZNW* 99 (2008): 74–98.

Stevens, George B. *The Johannine Theology: A Study of the Doctrinal Contents of the Gospel and Epistles of the Apostle John*. New York: Scribner's, 1894.

Stewart, Alistair. "'The Rule of Truth ... which He Received through Baptism' (*Haer*. I.9.4): Catechesis, Ritual, and Exegesis in Irenaeus's Gaul." Pages 151–58 in *Irenaeus: Life, Scripture, Legacy*. Edited by Sara Parvis and Paul Foster. Minneapolis: Fortress, 2012.

Stewart-Sykes, Alistair. "The Asian Context of the New Prophecy and of the *Epistula Apostolorum*." *VC* 51 (1997): 416–38.

Still, Todd D. "Shadow and Light: Marcion's (Mis)Construal of the Apostle Paul." Pages 91–107 in *Paul and the Second Century*. Edited by Michael F. Bird and Joseph R. Dodson. LNTS 412. London: T&T Clark, 2011.

Still, Todd D., and David E. Wilhite (eds.). *Tertullian and Paul*. London: T&T Clark, 2013.
Still, Todd D., and David E. Wilhite (eds.). *The Apostolic Fathers and Paul*. London: Bloomsbury/T&T Clark, 2017.
Stoike, Donald A. "*De genio Socratis* (*Moralia* 575A-598F)." Pages 236–85 in *Plutarch's Theological Writings and Early Christian Literature*. Edited by Hans Dieter Betz. SCHNT 3. Leiden: E. J. Brill, 1975.
Stowers, Stanley K. "Paul and Self-Mastery." Pages 524–50 in *Paul in the Greco-Roman World: A Handbook*. Edited by J. Paul Sampley. Harrisburg, PA: Trinity Press International, 2003.
Stuckenbruck, Loren T. "Posturing 'Apocalyptic' in Pauline Theology: How Much Contrast to Jewish Tradition?" Pages 240–56 in *The Myth of Rebellious Angels: Studies in Second Temple Judaism and New Testament Texts*. WUNT 335. Tübingen: Mohr Siebeck, 2014.
Stuckenbruck, Loren T. "Some Reflections on Apocalyptic Thought and Time in Literature from the Second Temple Period." Pages 137–55 in *Paul and the Apocalyptic Imagination*. Edited by Ben C. Blackwell, John K. Goodrich, and Jason Maston. Minneapolis: Fortress Press, 2016.
Tabbernee, William. *Fake Prophecy and Polluted Sacraments: Ecclesiastical and Imperial Reactions to Montanism*. Leiden: Brill, 2007.
Taylor, Charles. *A Secular Age*. Cambridge: Belknap, 2007.
Theissen, Gerd. *The Social Setting of Pauline Christianity: Essays on Corinth*. Edited and translated by John H. Schütz. Philadelphia: Fortress, 1982.
Thiselton, Anthony. *The First Epistle to the Corinthians: A Commentary on the Greek Text*. NIGTC. Grand Rapids, MI: Eerdmans, 2000.
Thomassen, Einar. "The Platonic and Gnostic 'Demiurge.'" Pages 226–43 in *Apocryphon Severini: Studies in Ancient Manichaeism and Gnosticism Presented to Soren Giversen*. Edited by P. Bilde et al. Aarhus: Aarhus University Press, 1993.
Thomassen, Einar. "Notes pour la délimination d'un corpus valentinnien à Nag Hammadi." Pages 243–59 in *Les textes de Nag Hammadi et le problème de leur classification: Actes du colloque tenu à Québec du 15 au 19 septembre 1993*. Edited by Louis Painchaud and Anne Pasquier. BCNH: E 3. Québec: Les presses de l'Université Laval and Éditions Peeters, 1995.
Thomassen, Einar. *The Spiritual Seed: The Church of the "Valentinians."* NHMS 60. Leiden: Brill, 2006.
Thomassen, Einar, and Louis Painchaud (eds.). *Le traité tripartite*. NH I, 5. BCNH: T 19. Québec: Les presses de l'Université Laval, 1989.
Thrall, Margaret E. *A Critical and Exegetical Commentary on the Second Epistle to the Corinthians*, 2 vols. Edinburgh: T&T Clark, 1994–2000.
Tremblay, Real. *Irénée de Lyon: L'empreinte des doigts de Dieu*. Rome: Editions Academiae Alfonsianae, 1979.
Tronier, Henrik. "The Corinthian Correspondence between Philosophical Idealism and Apocalypticism." Pages 165–96 in *Paul Beyond the Judaism/Hellenism Divide*. Edited by Troels Engberg-Pedersen. Louisville, KY: Westminster John Knox, 2001.
Turner, John D. *Sethian Gnosticism and the Platonic Tradition*. BCNH:E 6. Québec: Les presses de l'Université Laval, 2001.
Turner, Max. *Power from on High: The Spirit in Israel's Restoration and Witness in Luke-Acts*. Sheffield, UK: Sheffield Academic, 1996.
Turner, Max. *The Holy Spirit and Spiritual Gifts in the New Testament Church and Today*, rev. ed. Peabody, MA: Hendrickson, 1998.

Unger, Dominic J. *St. Irenaeus of Lyons: Against the Heresies (Book 2)*. Ancient Christian Writers 65. New York: The Newman Press, 2012.
Unger, Dominic J., and J. J. Dillon. *St. Irenaeus of Lyons: Against the Heresies (Book 1)*. Ancient Christian Writers 55. New York: Paulist Press, 1992.
Van der Horst, Pieter W. "Hellenistic Parallels to the Acts of the Apostles." *JSNT* 8.25 (1985): 49–60.
Van der Waerdt, Paul A. "Peripatetic Soul-Division, Posidonius, and Middle Platonic Moral Psychology." *Greek, Roman & Byzantine Studies* 26.4 (1985): 373–94.
VanMaaren, John. "The Adam-Christ Typology in Paul and its Development in the Early Church Fathers." *Tyndale Bulletin* 64.2 (2013): 275–97.
de Vaux, Roland. *The Bible and the Ancient Near East*. Translated by Damian McHugh. London: Darton, Longman & Todd, 1971.
Vogt, Katja Maria. "Sons of the Earth: Are the Stoics Metaphysical Brutes?" *Phronesis* 54.2 (2009): 136–54.
Wagenmenn, Julius. *Die Stellung des Apostels Paulus neben den Zwölf in den ersten zwei Jahrhunderten*. BZNW 3. Gießen: Töpelmann, 1926.
Waldstein, Michael, and Frederik Wisse (eds.). *The Apocryphon of John: Synopsis of Nag Hammadi Codices II,1; III,1; and IV,1 with BG 8502,2*. NHS 33. Leiden: Brill, 1995.
Walton, John H. *Ancient Near Eastern Thought and the Old Testament: Introducing the Conceptual World of the Hebrew Bible*. Grand Rapids, MI: Baker Academic, 2006.
Warren, David H. "The Text of the Apostle in the Second Century: A Contribution to the History of its Reception." ThD dissertation, Harvard University, 2001.
Watson, Francis. "The Triune Divine Identity: Reflections on Pauline God-Language, in Disagreement with J.D.G. Dunn." *JSNT* 23.80 (2001): 99–124.
Weinandy, Thomas. "Annunciation and Nativity: Undoing Sinful Act of Eve." *International Journal of Systematic Theology* 14 (2012): 217–32.
Werner, Johannes. *Der Paulinismus des Irenaeus*. TU 6.2. Leipzig: J.C. Hinrichs, 1889.
White, Benjamin L. *Remembering Paul: Ancient and Modern Contests over the Image of the Apostle*. Oxford: Oxford University Press, 2014.
Widmann, Martin. "Der Begriff οἰκονομία im Werk des Irenäus und seine Vorgeschichte." PhD dissertation, University of Tübingen, 1956.
Wiles, Maurice. *The Divine Apostle: The Interpretation of St. Paul's Epistles in the Early Church*. Cambridge: Cambridge University Press, 1967.
Wilhite, David E. *The Gospel According to Heretics: Discovering Orthodoxy through Early Christological Conflicts*. Grand Rapids, MI: Baker Academic, 2015.
Wilken, Robert L. *Judaism and the Early Christian Mind: A Study of Cyril of Alexandria's Exegesis and Theology*. Eugene: Wipf & Stock, 2004 (reprint of 1971 original).
Williams, Jacqueline. *Biblical Interpretation in the Gnostic Gospel of Truth from Nag Hammadi*. SBLDS 79. Atlanta: Scholars, 1988.
Williams, Michael A. *The Immovable Race: A Gnostic Designation and the Theme of Stability in Late Antiquity*. NHS 29. Leiden: Brill, 1985.
Williams, Michael A. *Rethinking "Gnosticism": An Argument for Dismantling a Dubious Category*. Princeton, NJ: Princeton University Press, 1996.
Williams, Michael A. "Negative Theologies and Demiurgical Myths in Late Antiquity." Pages 277–302 in *Gnosticism and Later Platonism*. Edited by John D. Turner and Ruth Majercik. SBLSymS 12. Atlanta: Society of Biblical Literature, 2000.
Williams, Michael A. "Life and Happiness in the 'Platonic Underworld.'" Pages 497–523 in *Gnosticism, Platonism and the Late Ancient World: Essays in Honour of John D. Turner*. Edited by Kevin Corrigan et al. NHMS 82. Leiden: Brill, 2013.

Williams, Michael A. "A Life Full of Meaning and Purpose: Demiurgical Myths and Social Implications." Pages 19–59 in *Beyond the Gnostic Gospels: Studies Building on the Work of Elaine Pagels*. Edited by Eduard Iricinschi et al. STAC 82. Tübingen: Mohr Siebeck, 2014.
Williamson, Clark M. "The '*Adversus Judaeos*' Tradition in Christian Theology." *Encounter* 39 (1978): 273–96.
Willitts, Joel. "Paul and Jewish Christians in the Second Century." Pages 140–68 in *Paul and the Second Century*. Edited by M. F. Bird and J. R. Dodson. LNTS 412. London: T&T Clark, 2011.
Wilson, R. McL. "The Spirit in Gnostic Literature." Pages 345–55 in *Christ and Spirit in the New Testament: Studies in Honour of C.F.D. Moule*. Edited by Barnabas Lindars and Stephen S. Smalley. Cambridge: Cambridge University Press, 1973.
Wingren, Gustaf. *Man and the Incarnation: A Study in the Biblical Theology of Irenaeus*. Translation by Ross MacKenzie. London: Oliver and Boyd, 1959.
Wingren, Gustaf. *Man and the Incarnation: A Study of the Biblical Theology of Irenaeus*. Translated by Ross Mackenzie. Eugene, OR: Wipf & Stock, 2004 (reprint of 1947 original).
Wolfson, Harry Austryn. *Philo: Foundations of Religious Philosophy in Judaism, Christianity, and Islam*, 4th ed., 2 vols. Cambridge, MA: Harvard University Press, 1968.
Worthington, Jonathan D. *Creation in Paul and Philo: The Beginning and Before*. WUNT 2.317. Tübingen: Mohr Siebeck, 2011.Wright, Christopher J. H. *Knowing the Holy Spirit through the Old Testament*. Downers Grove, IL: IVP Academic, 2006.
Wright, N. T. *Romans*. NIB 10. Nashville: Abingdon, 2002.
Wright, N. T. *Justification: God's Plan and Paul's Vision*. Downers Grove, IL: InterVarsity, 2009.
Wright, N. T. *Paul and the Faithfulness of God*, 2 vols. London: SPCK, 2013, 2:1059.
Wright, N. T. "Paul and the Patriarch: The Role of Abraham in Romans 4." *JSNT* 35 (2013): 207–41.
Zahn, Theodor. *Commentar zum Neuen Testament: Der Brief des Paulus an die Galater*. Kommentar zum Neuen Testament 9. Leipzig: Deichert, 1905.
Zevit, Ziony. *What Really Happened in the Garden of Eden*. New Haven: Yale University Press, 2013.
Zwierlein, Otto. *Petrus in Rom: die literarischen Zeugnisse*. Untersuchungen zur antiken Literatur und Geschichte 96. Berlin: Walter de Gruyter, 2009.

INDEX OF ANCIENT SOURCES

APOCRYPHA
Wisdom of Solomon 30
9:15   120

Baruch
3:12   115

4 Maccabees
6:2   117

OLD TESTAMENT PSEUDEPIGRAPHA
1 Enoch   30
48:1   115
49:1   115
62:2, 91   116
91:1   119

2 Baruch
59:7   115

4 Ezra
3:19   116
3:26   117
7:29-31   253
8:4   115
13:27   116
14:22   119
14:40   116
14:47   115

Jubilees
1:3   116
25:14   119
31·12   119

Life of Adam and Eve
25.3   116

Psalms of Solomon
16:2   116

Sibylline Oracles
1:33-34   115

Testament of Judah
14.8   119
20.1, 5   119

Testament of Simeon
3.1   119

Dead Sea Scrolls
                       116, 117, 119

MISHNA, TALMUD, TARGUMS, AND RABBINIC WORKS
Exodus Rabbah
48:4   117

Genesis Rabbah
14:8   117
96:5   117

Megillah
14b   117

Mekilta Pisha
1.150ff   119
2.15   119
4.14   119

Mekilta Shirata
7.17-18   119

Shemini Mekhilta deMiluim
94.5.12   119

Shequalim
3:3   117

Sipra Behuqotai
6.267.2.1   119

Sipre Deuteronomy
22.1.2	119
48.2.7	115
306.19.1	115
306.22–25	115
306.28.3	117
355.17.1-3	119
356.4.1	119

Sipra Vayyiqra Dibura Denedabah
1.1.3.3	119
5.10.1.1	119

Targum Neofiti
(on) Gen 2:7	116

Targum Pseudo-Jonathan
(on) Gen 2:7	116

APOSTOLIC FATHERS
1 Clement
5.4-7	241
5.7	242
30.3	118
47.1-4	241
47.3	119

Barnabas
9	119
9.2	119
14.2	119
15.3-4	260

Epistle to Diognetus
6.1-7	122

Ignatius
To the Ephesians
20.2	93

To the Romans
4.3	241

Polycarp
To the Philippians
1.2	118

NEW TESTAMENT APOCRYPHA AND PSEUDEPIGRAPHA
Acts of Peter
1–6	241
40	241

Apocryphon of John 29, 34

3 Corinthians
1:4	241
2:4	241
2:4	242

Epistle to the Apostles
12	241
21	241
24	241
26	241
31–33	241
39	241

NAG HAMMADI
I 3 Gospel of Truth
10-35	16
25	16

I 5 Tripartite Tractate
1	27
3	42
4	42
5-12	27
5-23	43
5-77	27
6-11	28
7	42
8	42, 43
8.21	42
8.25	42
9	42
10-11	42
10	42, 43
10.17	42
11	42
12	43
14	42
15	42
18	27
19	42
19-21	27
19-108	43

22-23	42	*II 5 On the Origin of the World*	
23-28	27	5-10	31
24-27	28	24-28	43
28-29	27	113	31
29	42	117	43
30-33	27	123.28–31	50
31-32	28		
32-35	27	*III 3 Eugnostos the Blessed*	
32	42	1	42
34-35	28	3-71	42
35-105	27	20	43
35	42	70	42
36	27	70	43
58	27	74.12–19	50
76	27, 28		
77	28, 42	*III 4 Wisdom of Jesus Christ*	
88	42	2	43
89	42	3-9	42
91	42	4-6	42
94	42	7-93	42
95	42	8	42
96	42	91	42
99	42	92	42
100	42, 27, 28	93	43
101	42	98.13–19	50
104	27		
105	27	*V 1 Eugnostos the Blessed*	
107	43	1	42
108	42, 43, 27	3-24	42
109	43		
115	42	*V 2 Revelation of Paul*	
116	42	2	241
118	42, 27	18	241
122	42	19	241
127	42		
132	27	*XI 2 A Valentinian Exposition*	
133	42	10-15	26
		10-36	26
II 1 Secret Book of John		12-17	26
8-9	35	15-17	26
11-31	43	31	26
13	35	35	26
25	43	36	26
30	43	38	26
II 4 The Hypostasis of the Archons		Berlin Gnostic Codex	
86,20-27	33	*BG 3 Wisdom of Jesus Christ*	
87.8–11	50	1-3	42
96,11-13	34	2-11	42

4-81	42	3.3.5	122
9	43	3.10.22	122
17	42	4.13.28	122
78	42	4.4.9	121
80	42		
81	43	\multicolumn{2}{l}{Clement of Alexandria}
90.4–12	43		

OTHER CLASSICAL AND ANCIENT WRITINGS

Ambrose
De paradiso
12.56   213

Ambrosiaster
Commentarii in Galatas
2:5   236

Anaxagoras in Arist
Soul
1.2   120
405a   120

Aristotle
Ethica nicomachea
1.12.6, 1102a   122

Arius Didymus
Epitome of Stoic Ethics
2.7.5a   114
2.7.7b   122

Augustine
Expositio in epistulam ad Galatas   239

Cicero
De divinatione
1.36.79   118
2.57.117   118

De finibus
3.22.75   122

De Officiis
1.28.101   121

Tusculanae disputationes
2.21.47   121

Clement of Alexandria
Excerpta ex Theodoto
33.3   38
43.2-65.2   25
43:2-3   25
43.3   25
46.2-47.1   26
58.1-2   39

Stromateis
2.52.6   16
6.141.3-4   41

Diodorus Siculus
1.11.6   122

Diogenes Laertius
3.63   122
3.67   121
7.1.110   120
7.156   122
8.1.30   121
90   121
157   120

Dio Chrysostom
De habitu
72.12   118

Eusebius,
Historia ecclesiastica
2.25.8   241
5.1.4   107
5.1.9   107
5.1.10   107
5.1.19   107
5.1.23   107
5.1.34   107
5.2.3   107
5.3.8   2
5.4.2   173
5.13.2-7   35
5.20   227
5.3.8   1

5.20.1-8	1-2	Homer	
5.24.1-18	2	*Ilias*	
5.26.1.	2	19.159	117

Epictetus
Diatribai
1.12.26   122

Epiphanius
Panarion
42.9.4   230
42.11.8   230

Heracleon
1   26
22   27

Hermas
Shepherd of Hermas
4   118
5.6   111
10   118
20.2   118
22.8   118
26.2   118
27.4   118
34.8   118
39.7   118
42.1   118
43.4   118
43.9   119
44.1   118
45.4   118
61.2   118
65.3   118
75.1   118
90.2   118

Hierocles
Elements of Ethics
1.14-15.   114
4.4-6   122
4.11-14   122
44–46   122

Pseudo-Hippolytus of Rome
Refutatio omnium haeresium
5.16.9   36

Iamblichus
De anima
1.3, §363   122
1.2, §363   122
1.9, §366   122
2.10, §367   122
2.11, §369   121
2.12, §369   120

Irenaeus
Adversus haereses
1.Preface.1   15, 91, 125, 226
1.Preface.3   1
1.1   108
1.1.3   94
1.1.7   108
1.2.3-4   94
1.2.5   94
1.2.6   25
1.3.1   24, 27
1.3-4   211
1.3.4   24, 126
1.3.5   196
1.4.1-2   94
1.4.2-3   50
1.4.5-1.7.1   25
1.4.5   25, 26, 94
1.5.1-1.6.1   37
1.5.1   25, 94
1.5.2   38, 124
1.5.4   90, 94, 107
1.6.1   39, 97
1.6.2   97, 120
1.6.3-4   196
1.6.3   49, 97, 127, 217, 227, 236
1.7.2   39, 102, 210
1.7.4   104, 118
1.7.5   94
1.8.1   68, 103, 127, 130
1.8.2   102
1.8.2-3   227
1.8.3   94, 130
1.9.1   227
1.9.2   180

1.9.3	196	1.30.6-9	31
1.9.4	108, 180	1.30.6	35
1.9.5	91, 180	1.30.10	151, 154
1.10.1-2	198	1.30.11-12	32
1.10.1	92, 181, 200	1.30.13	32, 62
1.10.1-2	20	1.31.4	123
1.10.2	181	1.83.3	40
1.11.1	94	2.Preface	125
1.13.1-1.21.5	40	2.Preface.1	130
1.13.3	49, 92, 133, 188	2.1.2	230
1.13.4	105	2.1.4	35
1.13.6	133	2.2.1	47
1.13.7	40	2.2.6	21
1.14.6	41	2.3.1	94, 230
1.15.3	39, 40	2.7.5-6	50
1.15.5	22, 133	2.8.1	50
1.16.3	91, 139, 144	2.9.1	47
1.17.1	50	2.9.2	128
1.18.3	40	2.10.2	127
1.20.3	32	2.10.3	47, 50
1.21.1	110, 129	2.10.4	96
1.21.4	97	2.11.1	126, 127, 131, 136
1.22.1	22, 118, 165, 227	2.12.7	94
1.23.4	139, 217	2.13.3	96
1.23.1	118	2.14.7	125, 139
1.23.4	125	2.17.2	94
1.24.4	41	2.17.3	94
1.24.2	49, 217, 208	2.17.9	22, 94
1.25.4	217	2.18.1	94
1.24.5	49	2.18.5-6	96
1.25-26	209	2.18.5	95
1.25.6	230	2.19.2	94
1.26.1	102	2.19.3-4	97
1.26.3	217	2.19.7	129, 139
1.27.2	16, 34	2.19.9	94
1.27.2-3	52	2.20.3	124, 144, 137, 139
1.27.2	231	2.21.2	95
1.27.3	152	2.22.4	137
1.27.4	230, 231	2.22.6	148
1.28.1	52, 129, 188, 208, 217	2.24.4	233
1.28.2	49	2.25-28	182, 183, 196
1.29	34	2.25.1-2	131
1.29.4	35	2.25.1	182, 183
1.29-30	29	2.25.2	47
1.30	31, 33, 34, 50	2.26.1	128, 136, 140, 143, 196, 198, 184
1.30.1-2	30		
1.30.3	30, 31	2.26.2-3	196
1.30.4-13	97	2.26.3	47, 184
1.30.5	31, 94	2.27.1	185

2.27.2	185	3.6.4	104, 227
2.28.1-2	47	3.6.5	21, 105, 131, 139, 143, 261
2.28.1	186		
2.28.2	106	3.6.5-7.2	227
2.28.3	104, 186	3.7.1	35, 57
2.28.4	22, 95, 96	3.7.2	105, 227
2.28.5	95	3.8.1-3	227
2.28.6	94, 186, 230	3.8.2	92
2.28.7	94, 95, 110, 113, 128, 139, 187	3.8.3	21
		3.9-12	153
2.28.8	187	3.9.1	152, 153, 158, 162
2.28.9	95, 182	3.9.2	85, 87
2.29.2	47	3.9.3	83, 85, 102, 103, 161
2.30.1	93	3.10.1-3	87
2.30.2	47	5.10.1-2	100
2.30.2-3	46	3.10.1	103
2.30.7	129, 140, 144	3.10.2	103, 104, 118, 131, 154
2.30.8	110	3.10.3	110
2.30.9	21, 165, 230	3.10.4	39
2.31.1	132, 230	3.10.5	85
2.31.2	133	3.10.6	103
2.31.3	91, 107	3.11.2	231
2.32.4	105	3.11.3	39, 210
2.32.5	104	3.11.5	47, 133
2.33.3	103	3.11.6	103
2.33.5	97, 208	3.11.7	231
2.34.3	103, 110, 118, 133, 140	3.11.8	92, 130, 153, 161, 169, 173
2.35.4	227		
3.Preface.107	47	3.11.9	107, 105, 118, 216, 231
3	81		
3.1.1	5, 109, 130, 139, 233	3.11.7-9	232
3.2.1	231	3.11.8-9	5, 104
3.2-4	232	3.12	153
3.2.2	232	3.12.1-13	232
3.2.3	23	3.12.1	105
3.3.1-2	217	3.12.2	188
3.3.2	233	3.12.3	154, 161, 164
3.3.3	227	3.12.5	103, 104, 231
3.3.4	1, 125, 231, 232, 227, 233	3.12.7	103
		3.12.9	68, 69, 74, 80
3.4.1-4	227, 232	3.12.11	255
3.4.2	109	3.12.12	127, 128, 189, 227, 230, 231
3.4.1	137		
3.4.3	231	3.12.14	106, 239, 256
3.5.2	124	3.12.14-3.13.3	229, 231
3.5.3	132, 139	3.12.14-15	233
3.6.1	83, 85, 87	3.12.15	106, 239
3.6.3-4	165	3.13	248
3.6.4-5	196	3.13.1-3	239

Reference	Pages
3.13.1	46, 131, 228, 234, 238, 250
3.13.3	232, 234, 238
3.14	140
3.14.1-4	130, 145
3.15.1	189
3.15.2	22, 85. 97, 129, 189, 190, 191, 210
3.16	4
3.16.1	107, 130, 136, 210
3.16.3	75, 76, 85, 87, 92, 93, 103, 104, 139, 196, 211, 215
3.16.6	39, 102, 126, 131
3.16.7	131
3.16.8	23, 106
3.16.9	70, 107
3.16.12	161
3.17.1-2	92
3.17.1	39, 103
3.17.2	105, 106
3.17.4	227
3.17.12	133
3.18.1-7	66
3.18.1	205
3.18.2	201
3.18.6-7	70
3.18.7	70, 71, 104, 132, 136. 209. 214
3.18.7–3.19.1	136, 139
3.18-23	70, 75
3.19	209
3.19.1-3	66
3.19.1	87, 129, 137, 139
3.19.2	103
3.20.2	94, 140, 133
3.21.1-10	71
3.21.3	127, 130
3.21.4	106
3.21.4-5	210
3.21.8	107
3.21.10	70, 71, 106, 209, 210
3.22.1	70, 87, 99, 100, 210, 211
3.22.2	73, 210
3.21.9	106
3.22.3-4	70
3.22.3	35, 73, 74, 102, 106, 131, 204, 20, 210
3.22.4	76, 207, 211, 212, 215
3.23.2-3	213
3.23.5	24, 93, 100, 125, 206, 207, 208, 213
3.23.7-8	75
3.23.7	70, 213
3.23.8	128
3.24.1	24, 107, 111, 130, 137, 139, 144
3.24.2	24, 126
3.25.3	35
3.26.3	144
4	230
4.Preface.1	227
4.Preface.2	23
4.Preface.3-4	132
4.Preface.3	23, 107, 126, 129
4.Preface.4-4	108
4.Preface.4	22, 99, 109
4.1-36	154
4.1.1	109, 181
4.2.1-3	130
4.2.1	205
4.2.3	152
4.2.4	103, 159
4.3	47
4.4.1	70, 87, 257
4.4.3	105
4.5.2-5	154
4.5.3-5	163
4.5.3-5	154
4.5.1	154
4.5.2	165
4.5.3	162
4.5.4	163, 171, 175
4.5.5	39, 103, 155, 162, 171
4.6	155
4.6.2	20
4.6.6	47
4.6.7	47, 107
4.7.1-4.8.1	155
4.7.1-2	163
4.7.1	103, 118, 155, 161, 163
4.7.2	152, 155, 170
4.7.4	21, 118, 152
4.8.1	104, 152, 161, 163, 165, 227
4.9.2	105, 174
4.9.1	156, 158, 256

4.10.1	152, 205	4.25.1	152, 155, 161
4.11-13	156	4.26.1	40
4.11.1-2	3	4.26.2	192
4.11.1	106, 206	4.26.3	192
4.11.2	133	4.27-32	20
4.11.4	127, 133	4.27.1	47, 106, 227
4.12.2-5	199	4.27.2-3	128, 139
4.12.2	126, 133, 139, 143, 200	4.27.2	128, 130, 140, 192
4.12.4	200	4.27.3-28.1	20
4.12.5	200	4.27.3	104
4.13.1	156, 172	4.27.4	129
4.13.4	163	4.28.2	133
4.14.2	103, 106	4.29.1	36, 126, 139
4.14.3	256	4.30.1	49
4.15.1	21, 256	4.30.2	49
4.15.2	206	4.31.1	40
4.16	162	4.31.2	104
4.16.1-5	20	4.32.1	21, 133, 140, 143
4.16.1-3	156	4.33.1	182
4.16.1	163	4.33.2	35
4.16.2	255	4.33.3	21
4.16.3	157, 255	4.33.4	209
4.16.5	256	4.33.7	21, 109, 129
4.17.1	99, 157	4.33.9	105
4.17.5	47, 133, 135	4.33.10	40, 105
4.18.4-5	47, 133	4.33.11	214
4.18.1	47	4.33.14	92
4.18.4	127, 133, 140, 142	4.33.15	106, 136, 182
4.18.5	92	4.34.4	130, 159
4.19.1	92	4.36.2	107, 118
4.20-35	157	4.36.4	133
4.20.1-4	21	4.36.6	92, 93, 117, 132
4.20.9	104	4.36.8	103, 118, 161, 165
4.20.1	22, 95, 126, 135	4.37-39	133
4.20.2	5, 21	4.37.1	134, 140
4.20.3	95, 118	4.37.4	133, 139, 141
4.20.4	103	4.38.1-2	93
4.20.5	97, 257	4.38.1	143, 205
4.20.6	97, 118	4.38.2	137, 140, 143
4.20.7	133, 135	4.38.4	133
4.20.8	97	4.39.1	126, 136
4.20.10	92	4.39.3	152
4.20.12	111, 118, 157	4.41.4	69, 80, 228
4.21-25	162	5.Preface.1	227
4.21.1-3	157	5.1-15	141
4.21.1	106, 158, 162, 170, 171	5.1.1-5.2.3	215
4.21.3	40, 152	5.1.1-3.	66
4.22.2	158, 171	5.1.1	102, 132, 140
4.24.1	137, 237, 245	5.1.2	173

5.1.3	22, 75, 102, 132, 140, 205, 206, 215	5.14.4	130, 135, 136, 141, 142, 227, 102, 141, 102
5.2.2-3	47	5.15.1	92
5.2.2	126, 140, 215	5.15.3	237
5.2.3-5.3.2	127	5.15.4	135
5.2.3	102, 141, 192	5.16-36	159
5.3-7	120	5.16.1	135
5.3.1	129, 140, 141	5.16.2	205
5.5.1	97, 141	5.17.4	21, 39
5.6	230	5.18.2	21, 118
5.6.1-2	208	5.18.3	22
5.6.1	22, 99, 111, 120, 141, 216	5.18.12	96
5.6.2-7.2	216	5.19.1	211, 212, 214, 215
5.6.2	100, 141	5.19.2	126
5.7-13	61	5.20.1	107, 131
5.7.1	99, 100, 141	5.20.2	96, 97, 103, 125, 126, 132, 136, 137, 139, 144
5.7.2	100		
5.8.1	141		
5.8.4	135, 136, 139	5.21.1	137, 139
5.9-13	32, 49, 62	5.21-24	258
5.9	239	5.22.2	128, 139, 191
5.9.1-4	162	5.23.1	213
5.9.1	32, 62, 100, 101, 120, 137, 228	5.23.2	41
		5.25.3	105, 126, 136. 140
5.9.2	99, 101	5.25.1	258, 259, 261
5.9.3	100, 216	5.25.3	259
5.9.4	100	5.25.4	22, 92, 259
5.10.1	100, 132, 135, 140, 141, 142	5.26.1	260
		5.26.2	92, 131, 171
5.10.2	135, 139, 144	5.27.2	136
5.11.1	100, 132, 141	5.28.1	133, 261
5.12.1	136	5.28.2	92, 260
5.12.2	101, 137	5.28.2-3	262
5.12.3-44	140	5.28.3	260
5.12.3-4	135, 141	5.28.4	22, 99, 260
5.12.5	141, 237	5.29.1	37, 135, 261
5.12.3	75, 79, 101	5.30.1-3	261
5.12.4	216	5.30.4	258, 259, 261
5.12.6	22	5.31.1	126, 263
5.13.1	141	5.31.2	263
5.13.2-5	142	5.32	159
5.13.2	129, 140	5.32.1	159, 263, 269
5.13.3	102, 141	5.32.2	147, 152, 159, 161, 162, 170, 263
5.13.5	132		
5.14.1-2	216	5.33.1-4	263
5.14.1	75, 159	5.34.1	152, 160, 170
5.14.2	132, 140, 144	5.34.3	106
		5.34.4	263

5.35	171	90	104
5.35.1	264, 265	93	103
5.35.2	246, 265, 266, 267, 269, 270	96	92
		97	95
5.36.1	266, 267	99	100
5.36.2	97, 267	100	91
5.36.3	97, 133, 193. 268, 270		

Epideixis tou apostolikou kērygmatos

Jerome
Commentariorum in Isaiam libri XVIII
17.34   2

2	104
5	174
5-6	96
6-7	97
8	103, 165
10	95
11	174, 205, 209
12	174, 205
13	108, 206
14	206
17	92, 206
21	165
22	205
24-25	165
24	99, 154, 162, 163
29-30	175
30	85, 103, 176
31	71
32	208, 209
33	22, 211, 212
35	149, 162, 163
36-37	87
36	85
38-39	215
40-4	103
42	105
42-65	174
44	163, 171
45	173
47	83, 93
51	103
53	103, 210
56	104
57	85, 92
59-60	85
59	103
67	103
71	103, 110
73	104
89	92

John Chrysostom
Homiliae in epistulam i ad Corinthios.
26.2   213

Josephus
Against Apion
1.37   119

Jewish Antiquities
1.34   120
6.166   119
17.353   120

Jewish War
1.650   120
3.372   120

Justin Martyr
Apologia i
1.6   118
13   118
26   128
32.5-11   92
46   95
33.6   111

Dialogus cum Tryphone
25   119
87-88   103

Lucian
De saltatione
70   121

Lucretius
De rerum natura
3.370-95   122
3.417-977   122

Marcus Aurelius
7.13   122
3.16   121
12.3   121

Marius Victorinus
Commentarii in epistulas Pauli ad Galatas
2.5   236

Maximus of Tyre
33.7–8   122
4.8   117

Musonius Rufus
6   122

Origen
Commentarii in evangelium Joannis
2.14   26
4.23   27

Contra Celsum
6.38   31

Philo
De confusione linguarum
21   121

De decalogo
175   116, 119

Quod deterius potiori insidari soleat
117   121
135   116

De ebrietate
112   115

De fuga et invention
186   119

De gigantibus
23   116

Quis rerum divinarum heres sit
225   121
265   119

Legum allegoriae
1.70   121

2.86-87   115
2.91   121
3.115   121
4.49   119
72   121

De sacrificiis Abelis et Caini
95   115
138   115

De specialibus legibus
4.140   115

De vita Mosis
1.175   119
1.277   119
2.265   119

De virtutibus
79   115
217   116, 117

Philodemus of Gadara
De morte
7.6-20   122

Pseudo-Philo
Liber antiquitatum biblicarum
11.5   116
23.10   116
27.9-10   117
28.6   119
32.7   116

Plato
Leges
4.715e   24

Respublica
6.504   121
9.580D   121

Phaedrus
250C   122

Timaeus
29e   24
30–38   122
86B   124
89E   121

Plutarch
Against Pleasure
14   122

Moralia
500B-502A   122
592B   121
672F-673A   121
1002B   121
1096E   121

Marcellus
9.154–58   122
13.234–35   121
26.412   121

Quaestionum convivialum libri IX
5.intro   122

Quaestiones platonicae
3.1   122

Plotinus
Enneades
1.1   121

Sextus Empiricus
Pyrrhoniae hypotyposes
1.79   122

Tertullian
De cultu feminarum
1.1.1-2   213

Adversus Marcionem
1.11.9   35
2.26.1   35
3.4.2   230
3.9.6   173
5.3.3   236
5.11.9-12   35
5.17.1   46
5.17.7-9   35
5.18.1   46
5.21   16

Tatian
Oratio ad Graecos
12   120

Theodoret of Cyrus
Commentarium in 2 Corinthi
305–6   115

Theophilus
Ad Autolycum
2.18   22

SCRIPTURE INDEX

The Old Testament
Genesis
1-3	16, 125, 148	3:21-22	49
1:1	53	19:16,18,19	116
1:2	30, 31, 100	25:40	256
1:3	57	31:3	116
1:11	95	35:31	116
1:26	77–80, 204	40:34-38	116
1:28	207		
2:1	71, 80	Numbers	
2:2	260, 262	11:25-26	119
2:5	72–3, 80	24:17	85
2:6-7	71		
2:7	56, 77–80, 101, 116–17, 132, 205, 209	Deuteronomy	
		4:11	116
		4:14	256
		6:4	56
2:8	141	10:16	156
3:15	213	22:23ff	212
3:16	269	34:9	116
3:19	79–80		
3:20	30	Joshua	
4:1-2	206	2:1	118
12:1	171		
12:2	161	Judges	
13:14-15	159	6:34 LXX	118
14:22	155		
15:5	154, 161–2	1 Samuel	
15:6	147, 150–1, 163, 166, 175	1:15	116
		2:10, 35	82
		10:6, 10	119
15:18	159	19:20, 23	119
17:9-14	151	24:7-11	82
18:1-3	171	26:9-16	82
19:33-35	40		
22:17	162	2 Samuel	
26:4	162	1:14, 16	82
49:8-12	85	5:24	116
49:10-11	92	7:12-14	85–6
		19:22	82
Exodus			
3:2	116	2 Kings	
3:14	104	2:11	116

Scripture Index

1 Chronicles
12:18 LXX — 118

2 Chronicles
7:1-3 — 116
24:20 LXX — 118

Job
10:8 — 72
38:1 — 116

Psalms
1:1 — 104
2 — 84
2:6-8 — 86
2:7 — 85
3:6 — 104
8 — 61, 84
8:6-7 — 254
22:31 LXX — 141
24:1 — 54
29:3-10 — 116
32 — 21
32:6 — 21, 96, 110
32:9 — 21
42:5 [LXX 41:5; ET 42:4] — 116
45:6 — 83
44 — 45:17 76–7, 80
50:12 — 54
68:10 LXX — 84
68:27 69:26 — 73
71:17 — 85
82 — 87
88:27-28 LXX — 86
89:11 — 54
90:4 — 260
97:2-5 — 116
104:3 — 116
109:3 LXX — 85
110:1 — 85–6, 254
132:11 — 85
148:5 — 21
148:5-6 — 110

Proverbs
9:1 LXX — 25
16:22 — 115
18:4 — 115

Isaiah
4:4 — 117
6:4 — 116
7:14 — 71–2, 80, 210
11:1-4 — 82–3, 85, 103
30:27-28 — 116
32:15 — 116
42:1-4 — 103
42:5 — 101
44:3 — 116
45:5-6 — 35
49:16 — 265
52:1 — 117
61:1 — 83–4
61:1-2 — 103
65:17 — 266
65:17-18 — 265
66:15 — 116

Jeremiah
18:1-10 — 56
22:28-31 — 106

Lamentations
2:11 — 116
4:20 — 82, 110

Ezekiel
1:4 — 116
36:25-27 — 116
36:26 — 117
37 — 116
37:9-10 — 117
39:29 — 116

Daniel
7:7 — 261, 268
7:7-8 — 259
7:8 — 258
7:20-22 — 259
7:25 — 258
12:7 — 258

Joel
2 — 105
3:1-2 [ET 2:28-29] — 116, 119

Micah
3:8 — 116

Zechariah
3:3-4	117
12:10	116

Malachi
3:2	117

The New Testament

Matthew
1:1	161
1:23-25	72–3, 80
1:31-32	107
3:9	150, 152, 155, 160–1, 170, 263
3:11	116
3:11-12	117
3:12	260
4:2	73
5:5	141, 263
5:14	162
6:24	232
7:19	141
8:11	155, 262
10:29, 30	184
11:27	25, 32
12:18-21	103
12:31-32	216
13:8, 23	267
13:44	40
18:11	79
19:4-5	207
19:29	264
19:30	76–7, 80
20:16	76–7
21:28-32	106
22:11-13	117
22:29-32	154
22:30	208
22:34-40	199
22:40	200
24:15	259
24:21	259–60
24:35	266
26:27-29	264
26:38	73
26:41	99, 141
28:19	118

Mark
1:1-3	103
1:8	116
1:20	171
4:8, 20	167
4:28	142
12:36	119
13:11	119
13:31	266
14:36	86

Luke
1:9, 17	103
1:27-34	72
1:31-35	87
1:35	77–8, 80
1:46	104, 155
1:67	119
1:68-69	87
2:8, 22	155
2:1-11	87
3:8	161, 263
3:16	116
3:16-17	105, 117
3:17	260
3:23-38	73–4, 76–7, 80
4:18	84
4:18-19	83
6:43-49	134, 139, 142
7:12	141
10:16	105
10:22	25, 32
13:29	155
14:12-14	264
15:4-6	79–80
18:27	97
22:44	73

John
1:3	26, 72–3, 80
1:6-7	103
1:14	22, 70–1, 80
1:33	116
2:19-21	141
3:6	115
4:6	73
4:23	26
4:24	115

5:28	141	Romans	
6:63	115	1:1-3	84
7:37-39	116	1:1-4	126, 144, 215
8:33-58	150	1:19-20	50
8:56	155, 169	1:19-25	136
8:56-57	154	1:21	134
9:30	141	1:25	16, 27, 56, 128
11:35	73	1:28	126, 139
14:2	267	2:3-11, 9-10	253
14:16, 26	115	2:4, 5, 7	134
14:17	107	2:5	136
15:9-10	184	2:14-16	256
15:26	115	2:25-29	151
16:13	107	3:23	128, 130
16:13-15	113	3:30	131, 158
19:34	73	4	150
20:22	116	4:1-12	162
20:23	141	4:1-21	163
		4:3	104, 147, 150, 154
Acts		4:10-12	156
1:5	116	4:11-12	150, 159
1:8	105	4:12, 28	155
1:16	119	4:15	196
2:1–13	116	4:16-17	150
2:2-3	116	4:17	55, 96
2:17-18	119	5:19	136
4:25	119	5	36, 106
5:30	22	5:8, 10	199
7:38-43	256	5:12-14	27, 43
8:5-25	128	5:12-19	70-76, 80
9	242	5:12-21	70, 81, 203
9:1-30	241	5:14	22, 102, 204
10	233	5:19	139, 214
10:1-11:17	241	5:20	254
10:28-29	106	6:2, 10	213
10:38	103	6:9	27
10:44-48	119	6:12	127, 134, 141, 144
11:15-18	119	6:12, 23	136
11:16	116	6:23	139
12:25	232	7:6	104
14:15-17	232	8	61, 271
15:29	106	8:2, 10, 11	57
16:3	236–7	8:3, 14-16, 19, 21, 23, 29-30	86
16:16-18	92	8:6	98
17:22-31	232	8:8	135, 144
17:28	96	8:8-10, 13	139
19:6	119	8:9-10, 13	141
21:11	119	8:9-11, 15	100
21:26	236–7	8:9, 15	141
28:25	119	8:9-17, 26-30	97

8:10-11, 23-24	60	2:6	141
8:11	141	2:9	268, 273
8:14-16	87	2:10	95, 128, 139, 187
8:14-17, 23	159	2:10-11	110
8:15	96, 109, 113	2:10-16	113
8:15-16	119	2:11-12	115
8:19-21	159, 263, 269–70	2:14	135, 139, 142
8:19-22	55	3:1-23	197
8:19-23	59	3:2	93
8:19-25	254	3:2-3	137, 143
8:20-23	61	3:16	111, 122
8:29	58	3:16-17	100, 141
8:32	163	4:1	202
8:34-38	84	4:7	243
9:5	126, 139, 144	4:15	223
9:19-22	56	5:4	141
10:15b	234, 240	5:5	253
11:17	132, 135, 141	6:9-10	20
11:17, 24	100	6:9-11	141
11:17-24	143	6:11-12	142
11:21	139	6:13-14	216
11:21, 17	128	6:14	141
11:25	223	6:15-20	222
11:32	94, 134, 140	6:20	141
11:33-36	56	7:1-40	222
11:36	24	7:5-32	223
12:3	97, 125, 139	7:7, 40	224
12:16	128, 139	7:26, 29, 31	272
13:8-10	199	7:31	55, 58–9, 265–6, 269
13:10	133, 139, 143		
13:11, 12	273	7:32-34	221
13:12, 14	117	8:1	140, 182, 189, 198, 200
14:6	134		
14:17	119	8:1, 3, 6, 10-11	177
15:1-3	84	8:1, 11	199
15:3	84	8:4	201
15:9-12	84	8:4-6	21, 56, 62, 131
15:12	84	8:4b-6	259
15:26-27	246	9:20-23	236
15:27	248	9:24-27	142
15:30-31	247	10:1	128, 139
16:3; 7	224	10:1-12	20, 104
		10:1-22	201
1 Corinthians		10:1-11:17	241
1:4	134	10:4b, 11	256
1:10-17	196	10:11	59
1:12-13	240	10:12	223
1:18-31	195	10:14-22	199
1:26, 28	129	10:16	140
2	180	10:26	54

11:1, 22	198	15:23-28	268
11:1, 23-25	199	15:24-28	97
11:2-16	224	15:25-28	257–8, 267
11:23	242	15:27-28	133
11:23-25	201	15:42, 36	141
11:25	254	15:43-44	141
11:26	272	15:44	77-79
11:27-34	197	15:44, 50	216
11:29-34	253	15:45	56
12:1-14:40	197	15:45-46	204
12:2	128, 140, 161	15:45-48	205
12:2-3, 10	119	15:45-49	209
12:2, 7-10	144	15:45, 50	79
12:3	104	15:45-46, 50	101
12:3-6	97	15:46	73-74
12:3, 10	119	15:47	41
12:4	139	15:48	130
12:4-6	95, 118	15:48-49	141
12:4-11	224	15:50	32, 49, 62, 127, 135, 141–2, 189, 217, 228, 239
12:7-10	129		
12:13	116		
12:28	107, 111, 130, 139, 144	15:50, 53	139
		15:51	272
12:31, 10-29	216	15:52	141
13:2	126	15:53	141, 144, 193
13:2-10	260	15:54	212
13:2, 13	133, 139, 143	15:57	134, 140
13:9	95, 128, 139, 187	16:1-4	197
13:9-10	105	16:3	247
13:9-13	195	16:22	272
14:1	119		
14:1-40	216	2 Corinthians	
14:2, 14-15	120	1:21-22	83
15:1-11	240	3:3	102, 141
15:3	242	3:6	57
15:3-4, 12	75	3:6, 7-18	254
15:8-9	129, 139	3:17	115
15:9, 10	245	4:4	35–6, 62, 126, 232, 239
15:11	234		
15:13	141	4:4-6	57
15:20	237, 246	4:10	141
15:20, 23	58	5:1-10	60
15:20-28	84	5:4	93, 100, 132, 141, 212
15:20-50	203		
15:20-22, 50, 53	132	5:4-5	102
15:20-28, 55	253	8–9	247
15:20-28, 35-55	254	11:3	213, 219
15:21-22	70, 75–81	12:1-7	231
15:22	76-77, 102, 140	12:4	97, 141
15:23, 24-25	269	12:7-9	141

12:9	193	4:28	160, 263
13:13	118	5:1	21
		5:2-4	253
Galatians		5:14	199
1–2	229, 246	5:19	141
1:4	55, 59	5:16	106
1:6-9	198	5:19-20	100
1:12, 18	240	5:21	98, 127, 226
1:15	141	6:2	199
1:15-17	231	6:15	59
1:15-24	237		
2	231	Ephesians	
2:5, 7-9	240	1:8-10	43
2:5, 11-14	237	1:9-10	46
2:1-10	238	1:10	21–2, 24, 72–4, 80,
2:1-21	232		126, 131, 137, 139,
2:3, 5	236		181, 203, 220
2:5	235, 243	1:13	141
2:5, 8	234	1:13-14	97, 100
2:8	130	1:20-23	84
2:10	12, 248–51	1:21	35
2:11, 13	245	1:22-23	27
2:11-14	239	1:23	96
2:12	233	2:10	56
2:19	213	2:17	132, 139
3	150	3:1-4, 9	43, 45
3-4	150, 162	3:3	46, 231
3:2, 5, 14	119	3:8-9	46
3:5-9	106, 157	3:9	21, 161
3:6	104, 147, 150, 154	3:21	24, 27
3:6-9, 16	160, 263	4:4-5	96
3:6-11	151	4:4-6	118
3:6-18	161, 163	4:5, 6, 16	133
3:7, 29	150	4:5-6	143
3:15-4:7	137, 139	4:6	21, 56, 96, 126
3:17-18	150	4:8	124, 137, 144
3:19-29	254	4:8, 25, 29	139
3:25	257	4:15-16	142
3:27	117	4:19	98
3:28	27	4:24	117
4:4	100, 106	4:25, 29	134, 142
4:4-5	126, 139, 144, 215	5:20	134
4:4-6	86–7	5:30	102
4:4-7	97	6:1-4	223
4:6	96, 113, 118	6:11	117
4:6, 8-9	105	6:12	33, 94, 107
4:8-9	21, 131, 139, 143	6:13	129, 142
4:19	119, 223		
4:21-5:1	246, 254	Philippians	
4:26	265	1:22	79, 102, 141

2:5-11	199	2 Thessalonians	
2:7-8	70	1:3	134
2:10	26	1:9	20, 253
2:11	192	2	271
3:3	115	2:3-4, 8-12	259
3:11	141	2:3-12	268
3:13-14	129, 142	2:4	21, 131, 139, 143, 261
3:20	272		
3:20-21	60, 84	2:8	136, 140
4:5b	272	2:8-9	105
4:18	142	2:10	126, 133
		2:10-12	260
Colossians		2:12	126
1:13	33		
1:14-15	126	1 Timothy	
1:15-20	57	1:2	109
1:15, 18	215	1:3, 4	91
1:16	16, 35	1:4	2, 15, 125, 226
1:18	27, 58, 76–7, 80	2:1f	219
1:21	132, 144	2:4	109
1:25-27	43, 45	2:5	109
2:9	24, 127	2:11-14	213
2:11	156	3:4, 12	223
2:19	133	3:15	130, 139
3:1-4	84	3:16-4:1	109
3:5	101	5:4, 8	223
3:5, 9-10	79, 135, 141	5:20	2
3:10	16	6:20	16, 91, 125, 139
3:10, 12-14	117		
3:11	24, 27	2 Timothy	
3:17	134	1:5	223
3:19-21	223	1:14	107
		2:5	142
1 Thessalonians		2:5, 23	129
1:2	134	2:20-21	16
1:10	253, 272	3:6	128, 217
2:7	223	3:7	125
2:13	134	3:16	119
2:19	272		
3:13	272	Titus	
4:13	60	1:6	223
4:13, 17	272	2:4	223
4:17	261, 271	3:5	134
5:2-6	272	3:10	125, 129, 144
5:3	253, 261		
5:8	117	Hebrews	
5:10	272	3:7	119
5:18	134	4:12	120
5:23	99, 120, 141, 272	8:8-12	104

11	163	1 John	
11:10	16	4:1-3	106
		4:1-6	119
James		5:6	107
2:21-26	156, 163		
2:23	154, 156	Revelation	
3:15	98	1:4-6	118
		1:15	106
1 Peter		2:7	119
1:8	141	13:1, 18	261
2:16	141	13:2-10, 11-13, 18	260
5:12-13	241	17:12	268
		19:10	119
2 Peter		19:20	260
1:21	119	20	271
3:8	260, 262	20:4	269
3:15-16	241	20:11	253
3:16	169	20:11, 12-15	265
		20:13-14	268
		21:1-4	265

SUBJECT INDEX

Abraham 11, 39–40, 62, 69, 74, 84–5, 104, 106, 147–66, 169–71, 173, 175–6, 196, 200–1, 254–5, 262–3
Adam 10–11, 18, 20–2, 27–8, 30–2, 36, 41, 44–5, 51, 55, 58–60, 65–8, 70–81, 88, 93, 100, 102, 107, 116, 120, 125, 128, 132, 136–7, 140, 141, 144, 148, 151, 153–4, 164–5, 169, 173, 175–6, 203–14, 218, 220–1, 267, 269
adoption 4, 82, 86, 87, 88, 109, 152, 160, 162, 215, 216, 256, 257, 263
aeon, aeons 3, 4, 24–7, 32, 40, 44, 45, 46, 50, 54, 94, 95, 102, 110, 124, 265
allegory 230, 246, 255, 264, 266, 267
Ambrosiaster 235–7
angel, angels 27, 41, 42, 47, 58, 85, 93, 190, 193, 265, 268
anthropology 11, 54, 57, 58, 60, 66, 78, 79, 90, 94, 98, 99, 100, 120, 127, 130, 135, 182, 204–8, 228
antichrist 12, 104, 258–62, 264, 268, 271
Apollinaris of Laodicea 88
apostle, apostolic 91, 95, 97, 100, 104–5, 107–8, 111, 114–17, 125, 128–30, 133–5, 145, 148–9, 154, 157, 171–2, 176, 179–81, 183, 187–92, 195–9, 201, 204–6, 215, 222, 224–37, 239–43, 245–50, 254, 255–7, 259–61, 267, 271–3
Aquila 224
Aquinas, Thomas 145
Athanasius 88, 99, 249–50
Athenagoras 225
athlete, athletic 129, 140, 142
Augustine 123, 136, 145, 235, 239

Basilides 41, 187, 225
beast 12, 54, 123, 260–1, 268, 271
bishop 1–2, 4, 10–1, 70, 80, 111, 128, 173–4, 192, 217, 232, 271, 273
breath 21, 77–9, 92, 101–2, 105, 107, 110, 116–17, 137, 205–6, 259, 268

cain 115, 152
canon, canonical 3, 5, 8–9, 11, 16, 20, 91, 96, 108–10, 147, 153, 169, 174, 226–9, 242
Carpocrates 209, 221
Cerinthus 102, 209, 221
Chalcedon 4, 65
Christology, Christological 3–4, 7, 21, 30, 56–57, 60–1, 65–71, 73–5, 77–85, 87–8, 90, 98, 111, 126, 163, 166, 206, 208, 218, 224
Claromontanus 235
Clement of Alexandria 16, 25, 39, 41, 92, 99, 167, 182, 205, 225
continuity, discontinuity 4, 10, 13, 59–62, 66, 67, 71–5, 79–80, 147–9, 151–2, 156–7, 159–61, 165–6, 169, 232, 240, 255, 259, 273
cosmogony 4, 9, 18, 90, 94, 98, 230
cosmology 18, 35–6, 50, 55, 57–8, 61, 114–15, 122, 128, 144, 228, 230, 265
covenant 11, 17, 20, 37, 104, 128, 130, 147, 149–57, 159–61, 163–7, 169, 171–5, 199, 201–2, 233, 254–8, 264, 273
creation 4, 6, 9–12, 15–37, 39–41, 43, 45–7, 49–53, 55–63, 65, 68, 73, 75, 78, 80–1, 94–6, 98–9, 101–2, 110, 128, 131–4, 136, 140, 147–8, 150, 155, 159–60, 165–6, 170–1, 175, 179, 181–3, 196, 200–10, 213–16, 218, 220–4, 254, 257, 262–3, 265–6, 269–70, 273
creator 3, 4, 9, 15–5, 27–31, 33–7, 39, 41 3, 45–9, 51, 53, 55–57, 59, 61–3, 91, 93, 96, 109–10, 126–8, 131–2, 134, 142, 151, 163, 175, 178, 184–5, 196, 199–201, 204, 223, 230, 232, 260
creature 3–4, 29, 37, 128, 134, 263
Cyril of Alexandria 87–8, 100, 123, 149

David, Davidic 83–7, 100, 104, 106, 161, 175, 209–11, 215

Demiurge 4, 19, 25–8, 37–9, 45–6, 50, 53, 93, 104, 108, 110, 126, 140, 143, 151
Derrida, Jacques 10, 89–90, 95, 103
destruction 58–9, 177, 197, 199, 223, 253, 261, 264, 268
Dionysius of Corinth 241
diversity 1, 6, 18, 23, 95, 130, 166, 206, 220, 231, 247

Ebionites 16, 77, 151, 209, 210, 221, 249
economy, economic 123–4, 126, 129, 131–3, 135–7, 149, 151, 154–6, 158–61, 164–6, 178–93, 196, 198–200, 203–4, 207–14, 216–18, 220–4, 233, 248–9
Ephrem the Syrian 249
Epicureanism 114, 122
eschatology 6, 12, 16, 25, 36, 54–5, 58–60, 62, 75, 107, 119, 134, 144, 155, 159, 169–70, 190, 205–6, 218, 220, 223–4, 228, 253–5, 271–3
Eucharist 24, 47, 92, 134, 140, 143, 192–3, 217

feminist, feminism 12, 219–20, 224
flesh 135, 193

Gehenna 253
Gentiles 22, 106, 117, 132, 150–3, 157–8, 160–1, 164, 166, 169, 175, 233–4, 236–9, 241–2, 247–9, 255, 273
gnostics, gnosticism 3–5, 7–9, 16, 18, 26–35, 38–9, 41, 43–5, 48–50, 65–7, 70–1, 73, 75, 79, 91, 93–6, 108, 120, 123–5, 127, 135–6, 143–4, 147–8, 151, 165, 173, 178–81, 189–90, 195, 200–1, 203, 210, 216, 226, 228, 230–1, 242, 255, 257, 265, 273
gospel 3, 5, 8–9, 15–16, 20, 34, 57, 65, 72, 73–4, 76, 83, 86–7, 113, 115–16, 124, 130, 139, 142, 152–7, 159, 161, 164–6, 172–3, 181–2, 184, 190, 197–8, 200, 216, 223–4, 228–34, 237–8, 240–2

Hades 43, 152, 253, 268
Hegel 90, 103, 229–30
hellenism, hellenistic 21, 67, 93, 114, 116–18, 120–1, 183, 223
Heracleon 26–7, 151, 225

heresy, heretic, heretics 1, 3, 7, 11, 17, 22, 23, 34, 47, 91, 95, 97, 100, 107, 109, 125, 127–9, 150, 187, 189, 191, 208, 217–21, 224, 228, 230, 232, 271
hermeneutics, hermeneutical 5, 7–8, 18, 33, 66–9, 84, 90, 122, 126–7, 130, 145, 148, 175, 178, 203–4, 218, 230, 260

Ialdabaoth 30–2, 34–5, 151
idol, idolatry, idol meat 22, 49, 135, 141, 143, 170, 177, 183, 195, 197–9, 201, 259
Ignatius of Antioch 88, 93, 240–1
incarnation 4–5, 39, 65, 67, 70–81, 85–7, 91, 102, 104, 107–8, 110–11, 131–2, 136–7, 140, 144, 148, 158–9, 164, 173–5, 182, 204–5, 209–10, 214–16, 219, 221, 257, 262
intertextuality 3, 8, 16, 34, 69, 77, 86, 148
Israel 45, 49, 56, 62, 82, 84–8, 117, 119, 143, 149, 162, 172, 174–5, 185, 199–201, 207, 232, 256

James 12, 156, 163, 229, 233, 237–9, 247
Jerome 2, 235, 249
Jerusalem 12, 106, 171, 225, 227, 229–35, 237–43, 245–51, 258, 262, 264–5, 267, 269–70
Jerusalem Council 106, 231–3, 237–9
Jew, Jews, Jewish 1, 9–10, 20–1, 24, 26, 30–1, 33–5, 40–1, 43, 45, 51, 56–59, 81–2, 85, 88, 99, 104, 114–17, 119, 121, 125, 132, 144–5, 148, 150–4, 158, 161–6, 175, 199, 223, 225, 229–30, 236–7, 239, 246, 253, 255, 273
John 5, 12, 65, 70, 109, 115, 184, 216, 229, 233, 237–8, 260, 264, 265
John Chrysostom 88, 117, 206, 213, 249
John the Baptist 117, 152, 161, 170, 260, 263
judgment 12, 24, 30, 103, 126, 135–6, 140, 163, 175, 206, 253, 265
Junia 224

kerygma 68, 82
Kierkegaard 90
kingdom 25, 32, 52, 58, 60, 79, 83, 97, 101, 106, 127, 132, 135, 156, 158–9, 161, 170, 173, 186, 189, 192–3, 215–17, 226, 228, 257–8, 261–71, 273

knowledge 7, 10–11, 15–16, 24, 28, 91, 95, 97, 109, 124–6, 128, 131, 133–6, 140, 143–4, 149, 153, 177–80, 183–93, 195–200, 202, 228, 231, 243, 250

last things, last times 22, 69, 253–5, 257, 259, 261–3, 265, 267, 269, 271–3
love 11, 27–8, 47, 51–52, 83–4, 123, 126, 128, 133–4, 136, 143, 154, 156, 163, 172, 176–9, 183–93, 195–202, 217, 230, 247, 256–7, 273
Luke 73–4, 76–7, 87, 116–17, 119, 130, 228, 231–2, 234, 240

Man of Lawlessness 271
Manichaean 4, 26, 145
Marcion, Marcionite 16, 18, 20, 23–4, 33–6, 45–6, 51–2, 54, 108, 131, 151–3, 155–6, 165, 178, 188, 208, 217, 220, 228, 230–2, 235, 240, 243, 246, 250–1, 255
Marcus Aurelius 120–2
Marcus, Marcosian, Marcosians 39–41, 49, 92, 105, 125, 127, 131, 133, 187–8, 191, 217
Marius Victorinus 235–6
Mark 109, 228
marriage 12, 52, 196, 206–8, 213–14, 218, 220–4
Matthew 74, 109, 161, 228, 232
Messiah, Messianism, Messianic 81–8, 254
millennium, millennial 12, 52, 257–8, 262–3, 265–7, 269–72
Monarchy 175
monotheism 9, 18, 21–2, 53, 56, 62

Nag Hammadi 17, 19, 26–7, 29, 32–5, 37–9, 42, 93, 95, 127, 225, 228, 241
Nestorius, Nestorianism 5
New Perspective on Paul 11, 164, 172,

Ogdoad 40, 241
Oikonomia 10, 37, 39, 43, 149–50, 179, 181–5, 199, 202–3, 205, 218
Ophite 29–34, 50, 98
Origen 26–7, 31, 88–9, 249–50
orthodox, orthodoxy 3–4, 7, 185, 195, 217–19, 221, 224, 232, 241–3

Papias 8, 264
Parousia 13, 198, 272–3
Pastoral Epistles 5, 15–16, 198, 219, 234, 242
Pelagius 145, 235
person, personal 7, 10, 15, 22, 40, 43, 48–9, 56, 65, 68, 72, 74–81, 85, 89–91, 93, 95–97, 99, 101–3, 105, 107–9, 111, 114–15, 117–21, 124, 136, 140, 156, 170, 173, 175, 177, 184–5, 187–8, 190, 210, 212, 239, 247, 258
Peter 5, 12, 130, 225, 229, 231, 233–4, 237–42, 245
philosophy, philosophical 7–10, 18, 24, 26, 30, 35, 42–3, 56, 89, 93, 96, 99, 108, 114, 120–2, 124, 144, 183, 193, 227, 236, 267
Platonic, Platonism 4, 7, 24, 26, 28–9, 31, 43, 48, 52, 93, 120–2, 124
Pleroma 3, 24–5, 38, 40, 44, 94–5, 110, 182, 190, 203, 227, 232
polytheism, polytheistic 21–2, 24, 53
poor 12, 46, 83–4, 238, 245–6, 248–51
presbyter 1, 20, 125, 191–2, 227, 257, 264, 267
pride 123, 127–9, 188, 190–1, 226
Primasius 235
Prisca 224
Priscillianist 4
procreation 12, 52, 204, 206–8, 213–14, 218, 220–4
prophecy 1, 10, 40, 89–93, 95, 97, 99–101, 103–9, 111, 115–19, 121, 157, 171, 175, 210, 216–17, 219, 221, 224, 241, 260, 265
Providence 9, 26, 31, 42–4, 175
Pseudo-Clementines 226
Ptolemy 127, 187, 225

recapitulation 7, 10–12, 21, 23, 41, 45, 65, 72–4, 76–7, 106, 126, 130–1, 137, 159, 164, 174–6, 182, 203–4, 208–14, 216, 218–24, 259–60
resurrection, resurrected 10, 12, 32, 37, 42, 48, 55, 57–62, 65, 75–8, 80–1, 84–6, 98, 100–2, 126, 141, 147, 154, 159–60, 162, 165, 169–71, 175, 192–3, 208, 211, 215–16, 218, 225, 237, 253–4, 262–5, 268–9, 272–3

revelation 17, 24, 42, 45, 136, 140, 152, 157, 175, 186, 200, 231, 238, 240, 263, 269
rule of faith 3, 5, 17, 85, 108, 177–9, 181–3, 185, 187, 189–91, 193, 196–201

Sabbath 41, 156, 172, 255, 264
sacraments 1, 4, 92
salvation 7, 11, 18, 36–8, 43–5, 51–2, 62, 69–78, 81–3, 85–7, 100–1, 109, 117, 124–6, 129, 132, 137, 140, 142, 144, 147–9, 152, 115, 165, 172–4, 178–80, 182, 185–93, 196, 198–1, 205–6, 211–14, 216, 220, 241–2, 254–5, 257–8, 262, 267–8, 271, 273
salvation history, salvation–historical 45, 65–6, 70, 75, 77–8, 80–1, 147–9, 153, 160, 164–6, 169, 182, 254–5, 257–8, 262, 268, 271
Satan 105, 128, 136, 140–1, 178, 188, 191, 206–8, 211, 220, 222, 253, 258, 272
schism, schismatic 107, 129, 132
separation 11, 52, 107, 124, 129, 132–3, 135, 141, 184, 187–91, 260
Sethian Gnosticism 29–31, 35
sex, sexual, sexuality 11–12, 40, 49, 52, 114, 133, 203–9, 211–24
Simon Magus 128, 178, 188, 226
sin 10–1, 70–2, 77–8, 101, 107, 123–5, 127, 129–41, 143–5, 165, 175, 209, 212–14, 216, 220, 223, 254, 259, 269, 273
spirit, spirits, pneumatology 3–4, 10, 17, 21–2, 24–5, 27, 30–1, 32, 33–4, 38–9, 53, 57, 60–2, 73–4, 78–9, 82–7, 89–11, 113–30, 132, 134–5, 137, 141, 143–4, 152, 156–7, 162–3, 171, 173, 175, 180, 193, 197, 204–8, 210–11, 213, 215–18, 220–4, 227, 232–3, 239, 241, 246–7, 256–8, 265, 267, 269

stoic, stoics, stoicism 24, 43, 114–15, 118, 120–2, 183
substance, substantial 10, 33, 50, 60–1, 68–9, 72–9, 87, 89–111, 114–19, 121–2, 124, 131, 140, 144, 153, 156, 180, 208–10, 249, 254, 266
systematic theology 3, 210, 221, 268

Tatian 52, 120, 187–8
Tertullian 16, 35, 46, 88, 173, 213, 216, 225, 230, 235–6, 243, 249–50
tradition 2, 8, 9, 15, 18, 20–1, 23–5, 28–34, 40–2, 44, 58, 65, 82, 85, 106, 108, 109, 114–17, 123–4, 129, 136, 138, 145, 150, 152, 158, 162–3, 172, 180–1, 187, 216, 218–19, 223–4, 226–7, 230–2, 234–5, 239–43, 249, 267, 269
training 125, 129, 205, 207, 226
typology 10, 30, 65–8, 70–8, 80–1, 88, 157–8, 165, 170–1, 175, 203, 205, 208, 210, 214–15, 218, 221

Valentinus, Valentinians 6–8, 16–19, 22–8, 33–5, 38–46, 49–51, 53, 75, 91, 108, 120, 124, 126–8, 130–3, 135–7, 144, 165, 178, 180, 182, 187–93, 203, 210–11, 216–17, 220, 225–6, 228, 230–2, 255
virgin birth 77, 208–12, 215–16, 218
virginity 12, 32, 71–3, 77, 85, 100, 106, 203–24

wisdom, Wisdom Christology 21–2, 24–7, 30–2, 42–4, 46–7, 50–1, 53, 56, 95, 115, 124–5, 143–4, 208–9, 230, 268
women 12, 49, 128, 133, 188, 203–5, 207, 209, 211, 213, 215–21, 223–4
Word of God 5, 22, 49, 71–3, 83, 87, 94, 97, 100, 129, 131, 133, 143, 176, 182, 192–3, 205, 209, 212, 256

www.ingramcontent.com/pod-product-compliance
Lightning Source LLC
Chambersburg PA
CBHW070014010526
44117CB00011B/1570